Lecture Notes in Computer Science 8111

Commenced Publication in 1973
Founding and Former Series Editors:
Gerhard Goos, Juris Hartmanis, and Jan van Leeuwen

Roberto Moreno-Díaz Franz Pichler
Alexis Quesada-Arencibia (Eds.)

Computer Aided Systems Theory – EUROCAST 2013

14th International Conference
Las Palmas de Gran Canaria, Spain, February 10-15, 2013
Revised Selected Papers, Part I

 Springer

Volume Editors

Roberto Moreno-Díaz
Universidad de Las Palmas de Gran Canaria
Instituto Universitario de Ciencias y Tecnologías Cibernéticas
Campus de Tafira, 35017 Las Palmas de Gran Canaria, Spain
E-mail: rmoreno@ciber.ulpgc.es

Franz Pichler
Johannes Kepler Universität
Altenbergerstrasse 69, 4040 Linz, Austria
E-mail: pichler@cast.uni-linz.ac.at

Alexis Quesada-Arencibia
Universidad de Las Palmas de Gran Canaria
Instituto Universitario de Ciencias y Tecnologías Cibernéticas
Campus de Tafira, 35017 Las Palmas de Gran Canaria, Spain
E-mail: aquesada@dis.ulpgc.es

ISSN 0302-9743   e-ISSN 1611-3349
ISBN 978-3-642-53855-1   e-ISBN 978-3-642-53856-8
DOI 10.1007/978-3-642-53856-8
Springer Heidelberg New York Dordrecht London

Library of Congress Control Number: 2013956452

CR Subject Classification (1998): H.1.1, J.1, I.4, I.5.4, I.5, J.2, C.2.1, J.6

LNCS Sublibrary: SL 1 – Theoretical Computer Science and General Issues

Typesetting: Camera-ready by author, data conversion by Scientific Publishing Services, Chennai, India

Printed on acid-free paper

Springer is part of Springer Science+Business Media (www.springer.com)

Preface

The University of Linz, organized the first CAST workshop in April 1988, promoted and chaired by Franz R. Pichler, dealing with computer theoretical and practical tools for problems in system science. This meeting demonstrated the acceptance of the concepts by the scientific and technical community. Next, Roberto Moreno-Díaz, of the University of Las Palmas de Gran Canaria joined Franz Pichler, motivated and encouraged by Werner Schimanovich of the University of Vienna (present Honorary Chairman of Eurocast), and they organized the first international meeting on CAST, (Las Palmas February 1989), under the name EUROCAST 1989, which again proved to be a very successful gathering of systems theorists, computer scientists and engineers from most of European countries, North America and Japan. It was agreed that EUROCAST international conferences would be organized every two years, alternating between Las Palmas de Gran Canaria and a continental Europe location, later being decided to host them in Las Palmas. Thus, successive EUROCAST meetings took place in Krems (1991), Las Palmas (1993), Innsbruck (1995), Las Palmas (1997), Vienna (1999), Las Palmas (2001), Las Palmas (2003) Las Palmas (2005), Las Palmas (2007), Las Palmas (2011), in addition to an extra-European CAST Conference in Ottawa in 1994. Selected papers from these meetings were published in Springer's *Lecture Notes in Computer Science* series as volume nos. 410, 585. 763, 1030, 1333, 1798, 2178, 2809, 3643, 4739, 5717, 6927, 6928, and in several special issues of *Cybernetics and Systems: An International Journal.* EUROCAST and CAST meetings are definitely consolidated, as shown by the number and quality of the contributions over the years.

EUROCAST 2013 took place in the Elder Museum of Science and Technology of Las Palmas, during February 6–11. It continued the approach tested in the last conferences as an international computer-related conference with a true interdisciplinary character, in accordance to the nature of modern systems science. There were different specialized workshops devoted to:

1. Modeling Biological Systems, chaired by Nobile and Di Crescenzo (Salerno)
2. Mobile and Autonomous Transportation Systems, chaired by De Pedro (Madrid)
3. Systems Theory and Applications, chaired by Pichler (Linz) and Moreno-Díaz (Las Palmas)
4. Intelligent Information Processing, chaired by Freire (A Coruña)
5. Computer Vision, Sensing and Image Processing, chaired by F. Llorca (Madrid)
6. Computer-Based Methods and Virtual Reality for Clinical and Academic Medicine, chaired by Rozenblit (Tucson) and Klempous (Wroclaw)

7. Computer-Aided System Optimization, chaired by Lunglmayr (Klagenfurt) and Jungwirth (Wels)
8. Modelling and Control of Mechatronics Systems, chaired by Schlacher and Scheild (Linz)
9. Theory and Applications of Metaheuristic Algorithms, chaired by Affenzeller and Jacak (Hagenberg) and Raidl (Vienna)
10. Model-Based System Design, Verification and Simulation, chaired by Ceska (Brno)
11. Computerized Medical Imaging and Visualization, chaired by Ortega, Barreiro, Penedo (A Coruña), Mosquera (Compostela)
12. Digital Signal Processing Methods and Applications chaired by Astola (Tampere), Moraga (Dortmund) and Stankovic (Nis)
13. Modeling and Control of Robots, chaired by Bremer and Gattringer (Linz)
14. Process Modeling and Simulation, chaired by Grossmann and Rinderle Ma (Vienna)
15. Mobile Computing Platforms and Technologies, chaired by Rene Mayrhofer, Clemens Holzmann (Austria)
16. Traffic Behavior, Modeling and Optimization, chaired by Avineri (Bristol), Galán-Moreno, Rubio-Royo and Sánchez-Medina (Las Palmas)
17. Marine Robotics and Applications, chaired by Pascoal (Lisbon), Rajan (California) and
18. Systems Applications

The first two workshops of this edition were dedicated to the memory of two very distinguished scientists and important collaborators and contributors to Eurocast for many years, who unfortunately passed away after the last Eurocast. The first, to the memory of Prof. Luigi Ricciardi, of the University of Naples, a leading world scientist in biomathematics, who had been a continuous collaborator together with his group in Eurocast since 1993. He established, promoted and was Chairman of the Workshop on Modelling Biological Systems, which is now chaired by his advanced disciples.

The second workshop was devoted to the memory of Prof. Ricardo García Rosa, of the CSIC, Madrid, eminent authority in automation and control, leader in autonomous vehicles. His group presented an impacting successful demonstration in Eurocast 2007. He, his wife, Teresa de Pedro, and his group had been participants and collaborators of Eurocast since Krems (1991). The couple Ricardo Teresa established and chaired the important Workshop on Mobile and Autonomous Transportations, which is now firmly continued by Teresa.

In this conference, as in prior ones, most of the credit from success is due to the chairs of the workshops. They and the sessions chairs, with the counseling of the International Advisory Committee, selected from 201 initially presented papers, after oral presentations and subsequent corrections, the 131 revised papers included in these volumes.

In addition to the chairs of the workshops, the organizers must express their gratitude to all contributors and participants. In particular, to the invited speakers: Prof. Rudolf Kalman, presently at Zurich (Switzerland), well-known world reference in systems and signals theory, who delivered a master lecture on "A New Direction in Systems Theory: Results on Identification from Invariant Theory"; second, to Prof. Kurt Schlacher from Linz University (Austria), one of the European leaders of IFAC, an authority in mechatronics, who presented the lecture "Control Theory and Practice in Mechatronics." And third, to Prof. Antonio di Crescenzo, presently at the University of Salerno (Italy), outstanding disciple of the late Prof. Ricciardi and enjoying international recognition in biocomputing, who presented the lecture in the memory of his master, entitled "Randomness and Dynamic Systems."

Also, we would like to acknowledge the essential collaboration of the general administrator of the Elder Museum of Science and Technology, D. José Miranda, and to the staff of the museum. Special thanks are due to the staff of Springer in Heidelberg for their valuable support in the publication of these volumes.

A group of Eurocast 2013 attendants visiting Casa de Colón Museum

From left, Prof. and Mrs. Kalman, Prof. and Mrs. Píchler, and Prof. Moreno-Díaz at the Casa de Colón Museum, Eurocast 2013

October 2013

Roberto Moreno-Díaz
Franz Pichler
Alexis Quesada-Arencibia

Organization

Organized by

Instituto Universitario de Ciencias y Tecnologías Cibernéticas,
Universidad de Las Palmas de Gran Canaria, Spain

Johannes Kepler University Linz, Austria

Museo Elder de la Ciencia y la Tecnología,
Las Palmas de Gran Canaria, Spain

Conference Chair

Roberto Moreno-Díaz, Las Palmas

Program Chair

Franz Pichler, Linz

Honorary Chair

Werner Schimanovich   Austrian Society for Automation and Robotics,
Austria

Organizing Committee Chair

Alexis Quesada Arencibia   Universidad de Las Palmas de Gran Canaria,
Spain

Table of Contents – Part I

Modelling Biological Systems

Systems Theory and Applications

Intelligent Information Processing

Theory and Applications of Metaheuristic Algorithms

Model-Based System Design, Verification and Simulation

Process Modeling, Simulation and System Optimization

Table of Contents – Part II

Mobile, Autonomous Transportation and Traffic Control Systems

Computer Vision, Sensing, Image Processing and Medical Applications

Computer-Based Methods and Virtual Reality for Clinical and Academic Medicine

Digital Signal Processing Methods and Applications

Mechatronic Systems, Robotics and Marine Robots

Mobile Computing Platforms and Technologies

Systems Applications

A Note on Some Past and Present Advances in Neuroscience: A Personal Perspective

Dedicated to the Memory of Luigi Ricciardi

K.N. Leibovic

Department of Biophysical Sciences,
University of Buffalo,
The State University of New York
bphknl@buffalo.edu

1 Introduction

I met Luigi Ricciardi in 1972 when I spent part of my sabbatical at the Instituto di Cibernetica in Arco Felice, directed by Eduardo Caianiello, the most prominent Italian cyberneticist of his generation. Luigi was a member of the Institute and we had many talks about stochastic processes underlying neuron firing. Later we exchanged visits in Italy and in Buffalo, where Luigi gave us a seminar at the Center for Theoretical Biology "On the First Passage Time Problem in a Model Neuron". We came from somewhat different backgrounds but we were both interested in quantitative neuroscience. Luigi was more mathematically inclined while my interests turned increasingly towards biology. But Luigi had wide interests as witnessed by his numerous publications and his leadership in organizing conferences and workshops in a variety of fields on quantitative medicine and biology, including the meetings of Eurocast.

Early in his career Luigi was influenced by Norbert Wiener whom he met during Wiener's visit to Naples in the 1960's. Wiener was on the faculty of MIT and an important member of the group which included McCulloch, Lettvin and their co-workers. In 1948 Wiener published his book "Cybernetics" which resonated strongly with the post World War II (WWII) "Zeitgeist". For, WWII was a time when there was an extraordinary collaboration of scientists and engineers from different disciplines. They had been recruited to work on problems ranging from gunnery to radar to guided missiles, atomic power and intelligence. The spirit of interdisciplinary cooperation carried over to the post war years. Wiener had made important contributions during the war, especially on automatic control, and his book reflected his belief that quantitative methods which had so successfully been used in physics and engineering could also be applied to biological systems.

In that spirit McCulloch and Pitts wrote their paper "A Logical Calculus Immanent in Nervous Activity" (1943). Later, Lettvin, Maturana, McCulloch and Pitts published "What the Frog's Eye Tells the Frog's Brain" (1959). And so were launched the fields of cybernetics, artificial intelligence (AI), and more quantitative approaches to neuroscience, where advances in AI and biology have had fruitful interactions. It is

R. Moreno-Díaz et al. (Eds.): EUROCAST 2013, Part I, LNCS 8111, pp. 1–11, 2013.
© Springer-Verlag Berlin Heidelberg 2013

interesting to note that these interactions go back to the dawn of modern computation, where the pioneers such as Turing and von Neumann also had a strong interest in how the brain works.

2   Quantitative Neuroscience

While quantitative methods are, of course, used by experimentalist as well as theoreticians, the problems they address are usually different. The questions an experimental biologist asks depend on what is technically feasible: e.g. if there is a response gradient along the outer segment of a retinal rod photoreceptor is this accompanied by an ionic gradient inside the cell (Leibovic and Bandarchi, 1997)? It is different to ask what may be the functional significance of such a gradient or of the different outer segment lengths in different species. The first concerns mechanism, the second design (e.g. Leibovic and Moreno-Diaz Jr., 1992). Or consider the overlapping of receptive fields in the retina: an experimentalist may look for a description in terms trigger features, size or density; theoretically, however it concerns the nature of information processing and has implications for representation, such as the problem of "grandmother cells" (Leibovic, 2003), or "Jenifer Aniston cells".

There have been enormous advances in the last 50 years or so in the range of technologies available to experimentalists. So the kinds of question we can ask have become more sophisticated and have encouraged a convergence between experimental and theoretical approaches.

Ultimately we should like to know how the brain works from the cellular (or molecular) to the behavioral levels. In what follows I should like to illustrate this, much from our own work.

3   How the Brain Works

3.1   The Cellular Level

The information flowing through the brain is carried by changes in neuronal membrane polarization and synaptic transmission. It is now well established that in addition to the constant amplitude nerve impulse and the decaying electrotonic potential in dendrites there is an active dendritic pulse of varying amplitude. Interactions between neurons take place at numerous synaptic sites and include dendro-dendritic as well as axo-dendritic synapses and they may occur in local circuits or over long distances. Some neurons such as the cerebellar Purkinje cells have very large dendritic trees where distal electrotonic, decaying signals can have no direct effect on the cell soma.

As far as I know we were the first to point to the theoretical possibility of active, graded pulses in nerve membranes. Our analysis was based on the Hodgkin-Huxley model of the nerve impulse (Leibovic and Sabah 1969). By varying the membrane parameters, such as the time constants of the ionic conductances, the ionic permeabilities or the density of ion channels one could get active, graded pulses (g-pulses, as we called them) which would either increase or decrease in amplitude as they propagated along a nerve fiber, depending on the initial stimulus and the membrane parameters (Figs. 1 and 2).

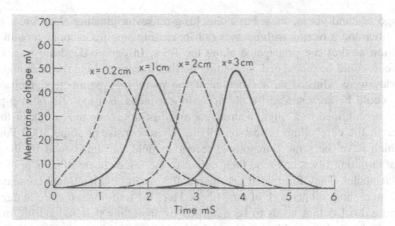

Fig. 1. Propagation of a graded pulse along a H-H cable. Membrane conductances reduced to a quarter of normal values. Stimulus 6μA and I ms duration. Conduction speed 11.4 m/s. Hyperpolarizations omitted. (From Leibovic and Sabah, Fig. 7, ch. 14 in "Information Processing in the Nervous System". K.N.Leibovic Ed., Springer Verlag, New York NY, 1969.)

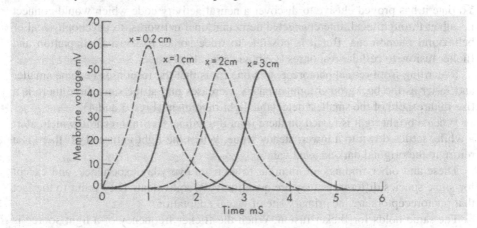

Fig. 2. As in Figure 1 with a stimulus of 4μA. Conduction speed 10.8 m/s. (From Fig. 8, as for Figure 1).

At the time there were few data on such signals. Decaying pulses had been discovered in Purkinje cell dendrites, although the generating mechanism was apparently calcium and not sodium and potassium dependent as in the H-H model. Since then dendrites with active membrane properties based on sodium and potassium have been found in various brain areas, including the hippocampus.

The existence of active, graded pulses has some interesting implications. For example, signals in dendrites can be propagated over long distances without dying out; due to their slower time course and smaller amplitude, g-pulses should be less refractory than the action potential and summate in a manner more similar to electrotonic signals. They should be more flexible than the all-or-none action potential and more reliable than an electrotonic signal. Also in large dendritic trees g-pulse can support a rich range of local interactions. For example, g-pulses originating at different points along a fiber and traveling with decaying or increasing amplitude could contain place information as they are propagated along the fiber. In dendro-dendritic interactions their effects could be modulated, depending on their location along the fiber and if the amplitudes were adjusted as a function of the membrane parameters, their signal strength could be orchestrated locally according to need. But the effects of g-pulses need not be confined to a single neuron. As an illustration one may think of the microzones in the cerebellum (Oscarson 1979). These consist of some 1000 Purkinje cells which have the same somatotopic receptive field, are innervated by the same subset of climbing fibers and send their output to the same cluster of cells in the deep cerebellar nuclei. They form what one may call a small computational compartment with an interconnected network of long fibers. Here the traditional picture of dendritic input and axonal output needs to be modified by including dendrodendritic interactions in which g-pulses could play a crucial role as described here.

3.2   The Connection between Psychophysics and Neural Activity

To date it has proved elusive to discover a neural activity code which would connect it, albeit through local, interconnected computational networks, to psychophysical or behavioral phenomena. But it is possible to trace some, like visual adaptation and flicker fusion, to cellular responses (Leibovic et al. 1987).

Recording from retinal photoreceptors one finds that the responses become smaller and faster as the background light intensity increases and at the same time there is a rise in threshold of the smallest detectable light increment (Figs. 3 and 4).

When a bright light is turned on there is an immediate rise in threshold which, after a while, settles down to a lower, steady value. When the light is turned off there is a return to the original dark adapted value.

These and other findings are familiar to us from everyday experience, and except for some species differences they are quantitatively equivalent. They point to the fact that photoreceptors are the primary site of visual adaptation.

The same holds for flicker fusion. When the flicker frequency of a light source is increased there comes a point when we can no longer perceive the flickering. The light appears to be continuous. Again one can show that the phenomenological aspects of flicker are mirrored in the properties of retinal photoreceptors (Leibovic, 1990).

The connection between psychophysical data and cellular responses has been demonstrated not only for vision but also for other sensory modalities.

Psychophysics can open an important window on how the brain works. Take the example of binocular space perception under reduced cue conditions, in particular the experiments on fronto-parallel lines (FPLs). In these a subject is placed in a dark room and is asked to position a set of dim lights along a line perpendicular to his line of sight on a horizontal plane at different distances from him and passing through the convergence point at that distance. It is found that at near distances the subject sets up the lights along a curve that is concave towards him, while at far distances the curve becomes convex towards him.

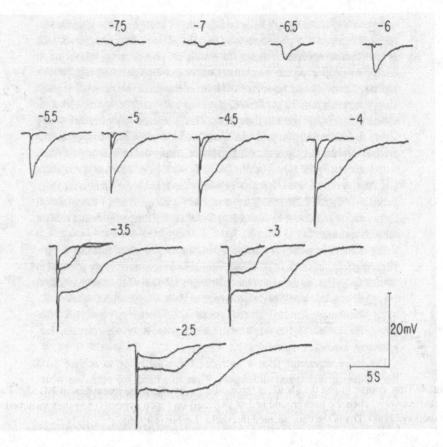

Fig. 3. Each of the superimposed responses were obtained at the 100 ms flash intensities of neutral density (ND) shown above each of the records. The weakest flash was at ND -7.5, the strongest at ND -2.5. The largest responses were for the dark adapted cell, the middle responses for a background light of ND -5.5 and the smallest responses for a background of ND -4.5. As the background intensity increases the response amplitudes and durations decrease (Leibovic 1983).

The major cue in this situation is the disparity of the two images in each retina. Other cues, like accommodation or the angle of convergence of the eyes play, at most, a minor part. The lights project their images onto each retina. Therefore, knowing what these images are, it is possible to predict what the experimentally derived FPL should look like at any distance from just one such curve at a given distance. For, if the percept FPL has an invariant representation, it should arise from the same retinal images and the only variable in the experiment is then the distance from the observer.

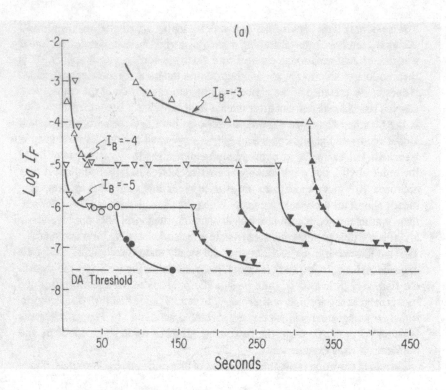

Fig. 4. Time course of rod thresholds at three different background intensities of ND -5, -4 and -3 respectively, when the background is first switched on (open symbols) and then switched off (closed symbols). DA is the dark adapted threshold (Leibovic 1986).

It turns out that the curves thus derived differ significantly from the experimental curves (Leibovic et al 1971 and Figure 5). It follows that the perceived FPL's at different distances produce different images on the retinae, and since each retina projects point by point onto the primary visual cortex V1, they also activate different cells in V1. The same percept is represented by the activities of different cells in cortex. So, unless there is a special area or areas which contain "representation neurons" or "grandmother cells", percepts are not encoded in fixed cells or fixed cell assemblies.

It is interesting to note a related finding, that visual perceived space is context dependent (Foley 1969) and cannot be described by even the most general Riemannian geometry (Balslev and Leibovic 1971).

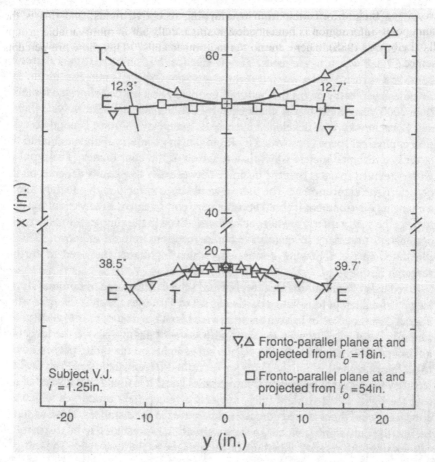

Fig. 5. Experimental (E) and theoretical (T) FPLs at 18 in. and 54 in. from the subject. The theoretical points at 18 in. (resp. 54 in.) are projected from the experimental points at 54 in. (resp. 18 in.), (Leibovic 1990).

3.3 Neural Organization and the Problem of Representation

Each neuron in the nervous system receives inputs from many other neurons which may be called its receptive field and it sends its output to many other neurons which may be called its responsive field. Groups of neurons performing similar functions are arranged in layers or zones or nuclei and there is considerable convergence and divergence of information flowing from one layer or zone to another. This results in extensive overlapping of receptive and responsive fields. At the same time each neuron is multivariable and "broadly tuned" (see e.g. Leibovic 1990). This raises the question how it is possible for accurate information to be transmitted between the different groups of neurons. The answer is illustrated in Figure 6. Mathematically it is equivalent to a set of simultaneous equations where, under appropriate conditions, all the information is preserved. However, it is contained not in a single cell but in subsets of cells receiving their information from overlapping receptive fields; and this is the important point: information is not encoded in single cells but in multivariable groups of cells (Leibovic, 1988). There are no "grandmother cells". Then how are percepts represented?

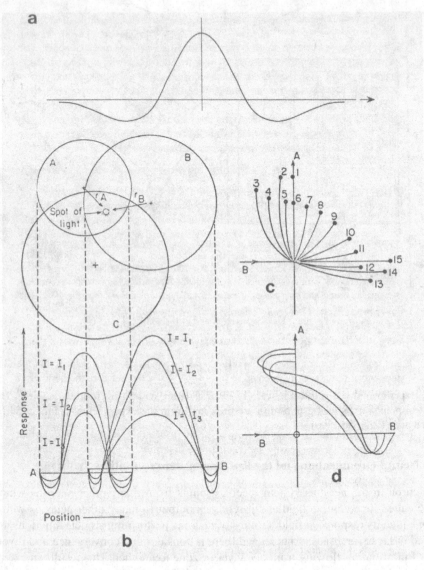

Fig. 6. (a): Idealized response profile of a neuron to a spot of light in different positions of its receptive field. (b): Thre overlapping receptive fields A, B and C on top and the reposes of A and B to three different spot light intensities I_1, I_2 and I_3. at the bottom. (c): Responses of A vs. B; each numbered curve plots the responses for a fixed position and varying intensity of the spot of light. (d): Similarly as in (c) for a fixed position and varying intensity on each curve (from Leibovic 1990).

We must remember that information enters the brain through many channels: the visual, auditory and other sensory channels, as well as the internal milieu, each with their sub-channels, like those for movement and form in vision. Similarly motor output is projected through many channels from the nervous system. Corresponding to this segregation in input and output, the central nervous system itself is comprised of many subsystems dealing with different modalities. For example, in cortex there are different areas for vision, movement etc. At the same time all areas of the brain are richly interconnected, so that ultimately every neuron is connected to every other neuron, either directly or indirectly. Keeping these facts in mind there are some interesting experimental data which lead to insights into the problem of representation. Here it will be sufficient to quote just two examples (see also Leibovic 2013).

First, there is now an extensive literature on mirror neurons from single cell recordings (Rizzolatti et al., 1984). When observing an action, such as moving an arm to grasp an object, some of the same neurons become active as when one is executing the action oneself. It implies that thought and action use overlapping neural representations.

The second example comes from imaging studies in which subjects were walked through a route in a city and then had to imagine walking the same route (Kosslyn and Ochsner 1994). It was found that some of the same cortical areas were active in both situations and V1, the first cortical area receiving the visual input, was involved in the action (walking the route) as well as in the mental task (imagining walking the route). This is interesting because V1 is usually associated with the initial cortical analysis of the component parts rather than the neural product underlying the final percept.

My proposal is that areas of the brain which are involved in information processing, whether sensory or motor, input or output, are also active in thought processes involving the same objects of perception or the same motor performance. We know that any observation, sensation or action involves many distributed areas of the brain. If we remember that corresponding areas participate in these tasks it also implies that representations are encoded in a distributed manner over the same areas. A well formed percept has a neural representation corresponding to the neural activity arising from the external or internal stimulus giving rise to the percept. We could say that the same "computing " modules and the same "sub-routines" are involved in the distributed "programs" representing sensation, thought and action.

4 Higher Mental Processes

The development of powerful new technologies, especially X-ray tomography, PET-scans and MRI have made it possible to see the brain in action and have revived scientific interest in topics such as feelings, consciousness and free will. For example, it has been possible to identify cortical areas which are activated in response to a variety of feelings: feeling disgust when experiencing a noxious odor (Wicker et al. 2003) or feelings of anger and fear and their modulation (Hariri et al. 2000). But it has not been possible to pinpoint a seat of consciousness.

There seems to be no clear, universally accepted definition of consciousness. Some equate it with awareness, some with the waking state, others with a quality of mind or all of the above. Here I should like to make a distinction between consciousness and awareness. I equate the conscious state with the physical condition that differs from brain death or coma and is under the control of the reticular activating system (RAS) in the brain stem. The RAS receives inputs from the internal milieu, from sensory modalities and feedback from motor output and many parts of the CNS and sends its output to virtually all parts of the CNS. There is a continuum of states from zero to full consciousness in which the brain is primed so that it can access those willful and intentional faculties of which it is capable. This excludes autonomic functions and subconscious operations, although the transitions between the latter and full consciousness are necessarily graded. Awareness then is a process of zeroing in to a selected subset of the active, conscious brain which is highlighted and made explicit.

If we agree to this framework then consciousness is enabled by the brain stem and its expression in awareness and intentional, mental activity is a function of evolutionarily more recent brain structures. Then consciousness may well be a primitive characteristic of living things and what makes us human is not so much consciousness as the functional capabilities of our brain.

5   Conclusion

Many of the advances of the last half century have their origin in the foundations laid down after WWII, through the interdisciplinary co-operation which was established during that time. Computers have been an integral component and have aided in cross- fertilizing the work in the physical and biological sciences. Norbert Wiener captured the spirit of the times in his book "Cybernetics", and the question how the brain works has been of keen interest to the early pioneers like McCulloch, von Neumann and Turing. Since then new advances in instrumentation have made it possible to obtain new insights, including images of the brain in action. We now have a much better understanding of cellular phenomena and how they form the basis of psychophysical and behavioral expression. Many have contributed to this progress, including Luigi Ricciardi with his work on neuronal firing, population biology and his organizational contributions to interdisciplinary collaboration.

References

1. Balslev, E., Leibovic, K.N.: Theoretical analysis of binocular space perception. J. Theoret. Biol. 31, 77–100 (1971)
2. Foley, J.M.: Distance in stereoscopic vision: the three point problem. Vision Res. 9, 1505–1521 (1969)
3. Hariri, A.R., Bookheimer, S.Y., Mazziotta, J.C.: Modulating emotional responses: effects of a neocortical network on the limbic system. Neuroreport 11(1), 43–48 (2000)
4. Kosslyn, S.M., Ochsner, K.N.: In search of occipital activation during visual mental imagery. TINS 17(7), 290–291 (1994)

5. Leibovic, K.N.: Phototransduction in vertebrate rods: an example of the interaction of theory and experiment in neuroscience. IEEE Transactions on Systems, Man and Cybernetics. SM 13(5), 732–741 (1983)
6. Leibovic, K.N.: Adaptation, brightness perception and their correlation with photoreceptor responses. In: Proc. 8th Annual Conference of the Cognitive Science Society. Erlbaum Associates, Amherst (1986)
7. Leibovic, K.N.: Parallel processing in nervous systems with converging and diverging transmission. In: Ricciardi, L.M. (ed.) Biomathematics and Related Computational Problems, pp. 65–72. Kluwer Academic Publishers (1988)
8. Leibovic, K.N.: Vertebrate photoreceptors. In: Leibovic, K.N. (ed.) Science of Vision. Springer, New York (1990)
9. Leibovic, K.N.: Visual information: structure and function. In: Leibovic, K.N. (ed.) Science of Vision. Springer, New York (1990)
10. Leibovic, K.N.: Design and operation of brains. Scientiae Mathematicae Japonicae 58(2), 237–244 (2003)
11. Leibovic, K.N., Bandarchi, J.: Phototransduction and calcium exchange along the length of the retinal rod outer segment. Neuroreport 8(5), 1295–1300 (1997)
12. Leibovic, K.N., Moreno-Diaz Jr., R.: Rod outer segments are designed for optimum photon detection. Biol. Cybern. 66, 301–306 (1992)
13. Leibovic, K.N., Sabah, N.H.: On synaptic transmission, neural signals and psychophysiological phenomena. In: Leibovic, K.N. (ed.) Information Processing in the Nervous System, ch. 14, pp. 273–292. Springer, New York (1969)
14. Leibovic, K.N., Dowling, J.E., Kim, Y.Y.: Background and bleaching equivalence in steady state adaptation of vertebrate rods. J. Neurosc. 7(4), 1056–1063 (1983)
15. Lettvin, J., Maturana, M., McCulloch, W.S., Pitts, W.H.: What the frog's eye tells the frog's brain. Proc. IRE 43(3), 1940–1951 (1959)
16. McCulloch, W.S., Pitts, W.H.: A logical calculus of the ideas immanent in nervous activity. Bull. Math. Biophys. 5, 115–133 (1943)
17. Oscarsson, O.: Functional units of the cerebellum-sagittal zones and microzones. Trends Neurosci. 2, 143–145 (1979)
18. Rizzolatti, G., Fadiga, L., Fogassi, L., Gallese, V.: Premotor cortex and the recognition of moter actions. Cogn. Brain Res. 3(2), 131–141 (1984)
19. Wicker, B., Keysers, C., Plailly, J., Royet, J.-P., Gallese, V., Rizzolatti, G.: Both of us disgusted in my insula: the common neural basis of seeing and feeling disgust. Neuron 40, 655–664 (2003)
20. Wiener, N.: Cybernetics. MIT Press, Cambridge (1948)

Solving Towers of Hanoi and Related Puzzles

Paul Cull, Leanne Merrill, Tony Van, Celeste Burkhardt, and Tommy Pitts

Oregon State University
Corvallis, OR 97331
pc@cs.orst.edu

Abstract. Starting with the well-known Towers of Hanoi, we create a
new sequence of puzzles which can essentially be solved in the same way.
Since graphs and puzzles are intimately connected, we define a sequence
of graphs, the *iterated complete graphs*, for our puzzles. To create puzzles
for all these graphs, we need to generalize another puzzle, Spin-Out, and
cross the generalized Towers puzzles with the the generalized Spin-Out
puzzles. We show how to solve these combined puzzles. We also show how
to compute distances between puzzle configurations. We show that our
graphs have Hamiltonian paths and perfect one-error-correcting codes.
(Properties that are $\mathcal{NP}$-complete for general graphs.) We also discuss
computational complexity and show that many properties of our graphs
and puzzles can be calculated by finite state machines.

Keywords: Puzzles, Graphs, Towers of Hanoi, Spin-Out, Algorithms,
Hamiltonian Paths, Error-correcting Codes.

1 Introduction

The well known Towers of Hanoi puzzle can be solved using a simple recursive
algorithm. While this algorithm is time optimal, it is not space optimal. We
[2] showed some years ago that a counting algorithm was both time and space
optimal. Spin-Out, a slightly less familiar puzzle, can also be solved by recursive
algorithms and counting algorithms. [4,13] Each of these puzzles has an associated graph whose vertices are the configurations of the puzzle and whose edges
specify the allowed moves in the puzzle.

Here, we generalize these graphs to the iterated complete graphs K_d^n which are
formed by starting with the complete graph K_d on d vertices and building a new
graph by replacing each vertex with a copy of K_d. Iterating this construction
$n - 1$ times produces K_d^n. In general, between corner vertices of the graphs
$2^n - 1$ moves are necessary and sufficient. Because in Spin-Out the "start" and
"end" vertices are not corner vertices of the graph only $\lceil \frac{2}{3}(2^n - 1) \rceil$ moves are
needed. Given two arbitrary configurations, how many moves are required to
take one configuration to the other? While actually computing the sequence of
moves takes exponential time, the number of moves can be computed in time
linear in n.

In our puzzles only one piece can be moved at a time, so the labels will have
the Gray property, that is the labels of adjacent vertices differ in exactly one

R. Moreno-Díaz et al. (Eds.): EUROCAST 2013, Part I, LNCS 8111, pp. 12–19, 2013.

position.[14,7] Any Hamitonian path through our labeled K_d^n will produce a Gray sequence in base d. We show that such Hamitonian paths exist.[16]

Our K_d^n graphs also support perfect one-error-correcting codes. [6,5,11,10,12] We show that there are Hamiltonian paths which respect these codes in the sense that every $(d+1)^{\text{st}}$ vertex is a codevertex. Further we argue that these paths are finite state computable in the sense that given an index in the path the machine can return the label, and given the label the machine can produce the index of the vertex with that label. [1].

2   Puzzles

The well-known Towers of Hanoi puzzle is shown to the left. The puzzle requires moving n disks from one tower to another with the restrictions that:
1) only one disk may be moved at a time
2) no larger disk can be placed on top of a smaller disk.
The results on this puzzle are well-known and are summarized in the following theorem.

Theorem 1. *The n disk Towers of Hanoi puzzles requires $2^n - 1$ moves and these can be computed by Recursive, Iterative, and Counting algorithms. [2]*

Spin-Out is another popular, but somewhat lesser-known puzzle. The physically embodied puzzle **Spin-Out** was invented by William Keister in 1970. Copies of this embodied puzzle may be purchased for around \$12.[15] (See Figure 1.) Another embodiment **The Brain** was produced by Mag-Nif but no longer seems to be available.[9] The **Chinese Rings** are also a realization of this puzzle.

The following locking system describes the Spin-Out puzzle.[4]

1. Lock 1 may be changed from locked to unlocked or from unlocked to locked, at any time.
2. For $j > 1$, lock j may be changed from locked to unlocked (or vice versa), only if locks 1 through $j - 2$, are unlocked and lock $j - 1$ is locked.

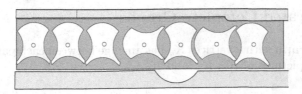

Fig. 1. Spin-Out in the configuration 1110101

2.1   Binary Reflected Gray Code

Definition 1. *A labeling of a graph G has the* Gray code *property if every pair of adjacent vertices has labels that differ in exactly one position.*

Theorem 2. *The state space for Spin-Out with n spinners is the binary reflected Gray code with n bits.*

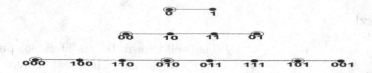

Fig. 2. The labeled graphs for Spin-Out with 1, 2, and 3 spinners

Well-known properties of the Gray code [7,14] can be used to solve this puzzle. Pruhs [13] gave a recursive algorithm and we [3] have given other algorithms. The following Count algorithm solves Spin-Out and also solves generalized Spin-Out in which each piece consists of a stack of m spinners with each spinner having 2 states, giving 2^m states for each piece.

```
            Count Algorithm for Generalized Spin-Out (Dimension 2^m)

PROCEDURE
GrayLabel := All 1s (n bits)
BCount := ⌈2/3(2^n − 1)⌉ (n bits)

WHILE rightmost 0 is in position b in BCount DO
      BCount:= BCount − 1
      Switch position b in GrayLabel from 0 to d−1 or d−1 to 0
      IF GrayLabel = all 0s THEN return
ENDWHILE
```

Theorem 3. *Spin-Out requires $\lceil \frac{2}{3}(2^n - 1) \rceil$ and these moves can be computed by Recursive, Iterative and, Count algorithms.*

3   The Iterated Complete Graphs

A **complete graph** with d vertices K_d has an edge between each pair of vertices. Below we give pictures of K_3, K_5, and K_8.

An **iterated complete graph** K_d^n is constructed by starting with K_d as K_d^1, and replacing each vertex of K_d^{n-1} by a copy of K_d.

Each vertex has degree d or $d-1$. The vertices with degree $d-1$ are called **corners.** We show the graphs K_5^1, K_5^2, and K_5^3. These graphs correspond to Generalized Towers of Hanoi with 5 towers, and 1, 2, and 3 disks respectively. For a vertex labeled $t_1 t_2$ the 2nd disk can move to the vertex with label $t_1(2t_1 - t_2)$.

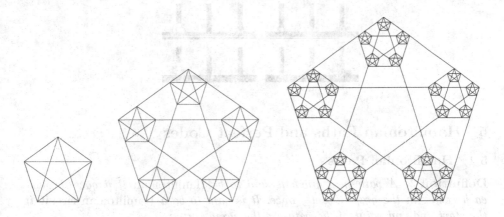

4 The Combination Puzzle

The Combination Puzzle uses the rules of both generalized Towers of Hanoi and generalized Spin-Out to create a new puzzle that may have any dimension.

- The smallest piece may always move to any total orientation.   (This rule is the same in both puzzles)
- Another piece may move if:
  - all of the smaller pieces are together on the same tower,
    (This rule is from the Towers of Hanoi)
  - and, all of the smaller pieces have orientation 0 *except possibly* the next smallest piece   (This rule is from Spin-Out)

Total orientation change function: The tower t_j of a piece j changes to $(2t_{j-1} - t_j) \mod q$ and its spin changes to $r_{j-1} \oplus r_j$.

4.1   How to Solve It

This 6-Dimension puzzle puzzle has $q = 3$ towers and $2^1 = 2$ orientations for each spinner. The following is the sequence of configurations for solving this puzzle for $n = 3$ pieces. The configuration is given by $2t + s$ for each piece where t is the tower and s is the spin. The starting configuration is 111 and the final configuration is 444. Notice that in every move one piece changes tower, but this piece's spin does not change in every move. The **black** dots indicate spin **1** and the **white** dots indicate spin **0**.

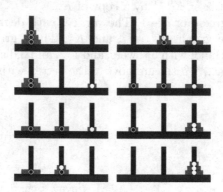

5   Hamiltonian Paths and Perfect Codes

5.1   Hamiltonian Paths

Definition 2. *A path in a graph is said to be* Hamiltonian *if it goes through each vertex in the graph exactly once. It is said to be a* Hamiltonian circuit *if the start and end point of the path are the same vertex.*

Theorem 4. *Every complete iterated graph K_d^n contains a Hamiltonian path, and if $d > 2$, a Hamiltonian circuit.*

Theorem 5. *There is a unique Hamiltonian path between any two corner vertices in K_3^n.*

This Hamiltonian path follows the ternary reflected Gray code.

Let t be some ternary number. Denote the k-th digit in t by t_k. To find the k-th digit in the corresponding Gray code,

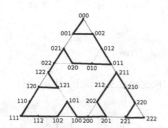

If $\displaystyle\sum_{i=k+1}^{n} t_i = 0 \mod 2$ then $g_k = t_k$

If $\displaystyle\sum_{i=k+1}^{n} t_i = 1 \mod 2$ then $g_k = 2 - t_k$

5.2 Perfect 1-Error-Correcting Codes

Definition 3. *A Perfect 1-Error-Correcting Code on a graph, G, is a subset C of G's vertices, so that*

1. *no two vertices in C are adjacent*
2. *any vertex not in C is adjacent to **exactly one** vertex in C.*

Theorem 6. *Every complete iterated graph K_d^n contains an* essentially *unique Perfect 1-Error-Correcting Code.*

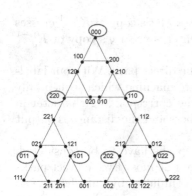

We'd like to know if these Hamiltonian circuits have any special properties related to the graph labels. For Spin-Out every 3rd vertex is a **code-vertex** and for Towers of Hanoi every 4th vertex is a **code-vertex**. The example to the left shows K_3^3.

There is a unique Hamiltonian path between any two corner vertices in K_3^n The Hamiltonian path from 000 to 222 visits the vertices so that every 4th vertex is a **code-vertex**. Every circled vertex is a *code-vertex*.

Theorem 7. *For every complete iterated graph K_d^n there is a Hamiltonian path which visits the vertices so that every $(d+1)^{st}$ vertex is a* **code-vertex.**

We have recently proved the following. The proof is constructive but it is too long to include here. It consists of an induction with 8 parts. We believe that the proof badly overestimates the number of states needed, because for $d = 2$ there is a two state machine while the proof constructs an equivalent but highly redundant 12 state machine.

Theorem 8. *[1] For every complete iterated graph K_d^n there is a Hamiltonian path which visits the vertices so that every $(d+1)^{st}$ vertex is a* **code-vertex.** *AND there is a finite state machine with $O(d^3)$ states which computes the configuration label (in base d) from the sequence index (also in base d) along this Hamiltonian path.*

6 Distances between Configurations

6.1 Distance Upper Bound

The distance between two vertices is the same as the number of moves needed to change one configuration of a puzzle to another. The following result is based on the structure of the iterated complete graphs and it is proved by essentially the same argument as used for the traditional Towers of Hanoi.

Theorem 9. *For every complete iterated graph K_d^n, the maximum distance between vertices is $2^n - 1$, and this bound is tight because the distance between any two* **corner** *vertices is $2^n - 1$.*
(Notice that this distance depends only on n. This bound is *independent* of d.)

6.2 Distance between Two Vertices

To compute the distance between two vertices x and y, one has to consider several paths as possible shortest paths. The "direct" path from x to y goes from x to a corner vertex of x's copy of K_d^{n-1} then crosses to y's copy of K_d^{n-1} and then proceeds to y.

An "indirect" path goes from x to a corner vertex of x's copy of K_d^{n-1} crosses to another copy of K_d^{n-1} traverses this copy, then crosses to y's copy of K_d^{n-1} and then proceeds to y.

If x or y is a corner, then the shortest path is the direct path. With our labeling, this distance can be computed by a finite state machine which sequentially compares the characters in the label of x with the corresponding character in the label of y. The labels are input as base d numbers and the distance is output in binary (base 2).

For general x and y, both direct and indirect paths have to be considered. With a little "look-ahead" only the direct path and at most two indirect paths need to be considered. So, the distance can be computed by calculating two "distances" and outputting the shorter, but this process cannot be carried out by a single finite state machine. These results are summarized in the following.

Theorem 10. *The distance between any two vertices in an iterated complete graph K_d^n can be computed in time $O(n)$ but cannot be computed by a finite state machine.*
The distance from a **corner** *vertex to an arbitrary vertex can be computed by a finite state machine.*

7 Computational Complexity

The sequence of moves to solve our puzzles can be computed by various algorithms. The essential idea is that this sequence will have length $2^n - 1$, which gives the lower bound on time, and any algorithm has to be able to count up to $2^n - 1$, otherwise the algorithm would find itself in a repeated state and be unable to terminate correctly. The space lower bound follows because at least n bits are need to count up to $2^n - 1$.

Theorem 11. *Any algorithm which outputs the moves to solve*
Towers of Hanoi or Spin-Out or the Combination Puzzle
must use at least $\Theta(2^n)$ time and at least $n + O(1)$ bits of memory.
The COUNT algorithms are **time** *and* **space** *optimal.*
(The Recursive and Iterative algorithms are time optimal but not space optimal.)

8   Conclusions

The Gray codes appear in our puzzles because of the stipulation that only one piece is moved at a time, but there is also another appearance of the binary Gray code. As Martin Gardner [8] has mentioned, the bit which is flipped in the binary Gray code tells us which disk to move in the Towers of Hanoi. In fact, this property holds for ALL our puzzles, but our interpretation is different. In our counting algorithms,the position of the rightmost 0 in a counter which is counting from 0 to $2^n - 1$, tells us which piece to move. This rightmost 0 rule applies to all our puzzles. Since it also applies to Spin-Out whose state space is the binary Gray sequence, the Gray code flip rule follows from the rightmost 0 rule.

References

1. Burkhardt, C., Pitts, T.: Hamiltonian paths and perfect one-error-correcting codes on iterated complete graphs. Oregon State REU Proceedings (2012)
2. Cull, P., Ecklund Jr., E.F.: Towers of Hanoi and Analysis of Algorithms. American Mathematical Monthly 92(6), 407–420 (1985)
3. Cull, P., Merrill, L., Van, T.: A Tale of Two Puzzles: Towers of Hanoi and Spin-Out. Journal of Information Processing 21(3), 378–392 (2013)
4. Cull, P., Flahive, M., Robson, R.: Difference Equations. Springer, New York (2005)
5. Cull, P., Nelson, I.: Error-correcting codes on the Towers of Hanoi graphs. Discrete Math. 208(209), 157–175 (1999)
6. Cull, P., Nelson, I.: Perfect Codes, NP-Completeness, and Towers of Hanoi Graphs. Bull. Inst. Combin. Appl. 26, 13–38 (1999)
7. Doran, R.W.: The Gray code. Journal of Universal Computer Science 13(11), 1573–1597 (2007)
8. Gardner, M.: Curious properties of the Gray code and how it can be used to solve puzzles. Scientific American 227(2), 106–109 (1972)
9. Jaap. Jaap's puzzle page, http://www.jaapsch.net/puzzles/spinout.htm
10. Klažar, S., Milutinović, U., Petr, C.: 1-perfect codes in Sierpinski graphs. Bull. Austral. Math. Soc. 66, 369–384 (2002)
11. Kleven, S.: Perfect Codes on Odd Dimension Serpinski Graphs. Oregon State REU Proceedings (2003)
12. Li, C.-K., Nelson, I.: Perfect codes on the Towers of Hanoi graph. Bull. Austral. Math. Soc. 57, 367–376 (1998)
13. Pruhs, K.: The SPIN-OUT puzzle. ACM SIGCSE Bulletin 25, 36–38 (1993)
14. Savage, C.: A survey of combinatorial Gray codes. SIAM Review 39, 605–629 (1996)
15. Spin-Out. Amazon, http://www.amazon.com/Think-Fun-5401-Thinkfun-Spinout/dp/B000EGI4IA
16. Weaver, E.: Gray codes and puzzles on iterated complete graphs. Oregon State REU Proceedings (2005)

Some Remarks on the First-Crossing Area
of a Diffusion Process with Jumps
over a Constant Barrier

Marco Abundo and Mario Abundo

Tor Vergata University, Rome, Italy
marco.abundo@gmail.com, abundo@mat.uniroma2.it

Abstract. For a given barrier $S > 0$ and a one-dimensional jump-diffusion process $X(t)$, starting from $x < S$, we study the probability distribution of the integral $A_S(x) = \int_0^{\tau_S(x)} X(t) \, dt$ determined by $X(t)$ till its first-crossing time $\tau_S(x)$ over S.

Keywords: First-crossing time, first-crossing area, jump-diffusion.

1 Introduction

This paper deals with the first-crossing area (FCA), $A_S(x) = \int_0^{\tau_S(x)} X(t) \, dt$, determined by a jump-diffusion process $X(t)$ starting from x, till its first-crossing time (FCT), $\tau_S(x)$, over a threshold $S > x$, and it extends the results of previous papers by the authors (see [1], [2]), concerning the area swept out by $X(t)$ till its first-passage below zero. Note that $A_S(x) = \overline{X}_{[0,\tau_S(x)]} \cdot \tau_S(x)$, where $\overline{X}_{[0,\tau_S(x)]}$ denotes the time average of $X(t)$ over the interval $[0, \tau_S(x)]$. We improperly call $A_S(x)$ "the FCA of $X(t)$ over S". Indeed, the area of the plane region determined by the trajectory of $X(t)$ and the t-axis in the first-crossing period $[0, \tau_S(x)]$ is $\int_0^{\tau_S(x)} |X(t)| \, dt$, which coincides with $A_S(x)$ only if $X(t)$ is non-negative in the entire interval $[0, \tau_S(x)]$.

The FCA has interesting applications in Biology, e.g. in diffusion models for neural activity, if one identifies $X(t)$ with the neuron voltage at time t, and τ_S with the instant at which the neuron fires, i.e. $X(t)$ exceeds the potential threshold value S; then, A_S/τ_S represents the time average of the neural voltage till the FCT over S. Another application can be found in Queueing Theory, if $X(t)$ represents the length of a queue at time t, and one identifies the FCT τ_S over the threshold S with the congestion time, that is the instant at which the queue system first collapses; then, the FCA represents the cumulative waiting time experienced by all the "customers" till the congestion time.

2 Notations, Formulation of the Problem and Main Results

Let $X(t) \in I := (0, a)$, $0 < a \le +\infty$, be a time-homogeneous, one-dimensional jump-diffusion process which satisfies the stochastic differential equation (SDE):

R. Moreno-Díaz et al. (Eds.): EUROCAST 2013, Part I, LNCS 8111, pp. 20–27, 2013.
© Springer-Verlag Berlin Heidelberg 2013

$$dX(t) = b(X(t))dt + \sigma(X(t))dB_t + \int_{-\infty}^{+\infty} \gamma(X(t), u)\nu(dt, du) \tag{1}$$

with assigned initial condition $X(0) = x$, where B_t is a standard Brownian motion (BM), b, σ, γ are regular enough functions and ν is a Poisson random measure on $(0, \infty) \times \mathbb{R}$ (see [4]), which is homogeneous with respect to time translation, that is, its intensity measure $E[\nu(dt, du)]$ is of the form $E[\nu(dt, du)] = dt\pi(du)$, for some positive measure π defined on the Borel σ−field of subsets of $\mathbb{R}$, and we suppose that the jump intensity $\Theta = \int_{-\infty}^{+\infty} \pi(du) \geq 0$ is finite. Moreover, we suppose that the coefficients satisfy conditions for the existence of a unique non-explosive solution of (1) (see [4]). Notice that, if $\gamma \equiv 0$, or $\nu \equiv 0$, then the SDE (1) becomes the usual Itô's SDE for a simple-diffusion (i.e. without jumps). In the special case when the measure π is concentrated e.g. over the set $\{u_1, u_2\} = \{-1, 1\}$ with $\pi(u_i) = \theta_i$ and $\gamma(u_i) = \epsilon_i$, the SDE (1) writes $dX(t) = b(X(t))dt + \sigma(X(t))dB_t + \epsilon_2 dN_2(t) + \epsilon_1 dN_1(t)$, where $\epsilon_1 < 0$, $\epsilon_2 > 0$ and $N_i(t), t \geq 0$ are independent homogeneous Poisson processes of amplitude 1 and rates θ_1 and θ_2, respectively governing downward (N_1) and upward (N_2) jumps. The differential operator associated to the process $X(t)$ which is the solution of (1), is defined for any sufficiently regular function f by:

$$Lf(x) = L_d f(x) + L_j f(x) \tag{2}$$

where the "diffusion part" is $L_d f(x) = \frac{1}{2}\sigma^2(x)\frac{d^2 f}{dx^2}(x) + b(x)\frac{df}{dx}(x)$, and the "jump part" is $L_j f(x) = \int_{-\infty}^{+\infty}[f(x + \gamma(x, u)) - f(x)]\pi(du)$. For $S > 0$ and $0 \leq x < S$, let us define:

$$\tau_S(x) = \inf\{t > 0 : X(t) \geq S | X(0) = x\} \tag{3}$$

that is the FCT of $X(t)$ over S, with the condition that $X(t)$ has started from x, and suppose that $\tau_S(x)$ is finite with probability one. Really, it is possible to show (see [6]) that the probability $p_0(x)$ that $X(t)$ ever leaves the interval $(-\infty, S)$ satisfies the partial differential-difference equation (PDDE) $Lp_0 = 0$, with outer condition $p_0(x) = 1$ if $x \geq S$. The equality $p_0(x) = 1$ is equivalent to say that $\tau_S(x)$ is finite with probability one.

Let U be a functional of the process X; assume that $\tau_S(x)$ is finite with probability one, and for $\lambda > 0$ denote by

$$M_{U,\lambda}(x) = E\left[e^{-\lambda \int_0^{\tau_S(x)} U(X(s))ds}\right] \tag{4}$$

the Laplace transform of the integral $\int_0^{\tau_S(x)} U(X(s))ds$. Then, the following theorem holds (it is analogous to Theorem 1 in [1]).

Theorem 1. Let $X(t)$ be the solution of the SDE (1), starting from $X(0) = x < S$; then, under the above assumptions, $M_{U,\lambda}(x)$ is the solution of the problem:

$$LM_{U,\lambda}(x) = \lambda U(x)M_{U,\lambda}(x) \ , x \in [0, S) \tag{5}$$

with outer conditions:

$$M_{U,\lambda}(y) = 1, \text{ for } y \geq S \ ; lim_{x \to -\infty} M_{U,\lambda}(x) = 0,$$

where L is the generator of X, which is defined by (2). $\square$

We recall that the n-th order moment of $\int_0^{\tau_S(x)} U(X(s))ds$, if it exists finite, is given by $T_n(x) = E\left[\left(\int_0^{\tau_S(x)} U(X(s))ds\right)^n\right] = (-1)^n \left[\frac{\partial^n}{\partial \lambda^n} M_{U,\lambda}(x)\right]_{\lambda=0}$. Then, taking the n-th derivative with respect to λ in both members of the equation (5), and calculating it for $\lambda = 0$, one easily obtains that $T_n(x)$, whenever it exists finite, is the solution of the PDDE:

$$LT_n(x) = -nU(x)T_{n-1}(x), \ \ 0 < x < S \tag{6}$$

which satisfies $T_n(x) = 0$, for $x \geq S$, and an appropriate additional condition. Note that for a diffusion without jumps ($\gamma \equiv 0$) and for $U(x) \equiv 1$, (6) is nothing but the celebrated Darling and Siegert's equation ([3]) for the moments of the FCT, and the outer condition $T_n(x) = 0$, for $x \geq S$, becomes simply the boundary condition $T_n(S) = 0$.

Remark 1. The FCT and the FCA of $X(t)$ over S can be expressed in terms of the FCT and the FCA of a suitable process below zero. For instance, if $X(t)$ is BM with positive drift, i.e. $X(t) = x + B_t + \mu t$, with $\mu > 0$, then $\tau_S(x) = \inf\{t > 0 : X(t) \geq S\}$ has the same distribution as $\inf\{t > 0 : S - x + B_t - \mu t \leq 0\} \equiv \tilde{\tau}(S-x)$, where $\tilde{\tau}(y)$ denotes the FCT of the process $Y(t) = y + B_t - \mu t$ below zero. Moreover, it is easy to see that $A_S(x) = \int_0^{\tau_S(x)} X(t)dt = S \cdot \tilde{\tau}(S-x) - \tilde{A}(S-x)$, where $\tilde{A}(y)$ denotes the area swept out by $Y(t)$ till its first-passage below zero. Thus, the Laplace transform $E(\exp(-\lambda \tau_S(x)))$ and the moments of $\tau_S(x)$ and $A_S(x)$ can be obtained by those of $\tilde{\tau}(S - x)$ and $\tilde{A}(S - x)$.

3   A Few Examples

3.1   Simple Diffusions (i.e. with No Jump)

Let $X(t)$ be the solution of (1), with $\gamma \equiv 0$, that is:

$$dX(t) = b(X(t))dt + \sigma(X(t))dB_t, \ X(0) = x. \tag{7}$$

In this case $\tau_S(x) \equiv \inf\{t > 0 : X(t) = S | X(0) = x\}$, that is the first-passage time of $X(t)$ through S. Since the generator L coincides with its diffusion part L_d, by Theorem 1 we obtain that, for $x < S$, $M_{U,\lambda}(x) = E\left[e^{-\lambda \int_0^{\tau_S(x)} U(X(s))ds}\right]$

is the solution of the problem (M' and M'' denote first and second derivative with respect to x) :

$$\frac{1}{2}\sigma^2(x)M''_{U,\lambda}(x) + b(x)M'_{U,\lambda}(x) = \lambda U(x)M_{U,\lambda}(x), \qquad (8)$$

with boundary conditions:

$$M_{U,\lambda}(S) = 1, \quad \lim_{x \to -\infty} M_{U,\lambda}(x) = 0.$$

Moreover, by (6) the n-th order moments $T_n(x)$ of $\int_0^{\tau(x)} U(X(s))ds$, if they exist, satisfy the recursive ODEs:

$$\frac{1}{2}\sigma^2(x)T''_n(x) + b(x)T'_n(x) = -nU(x)T_{n-1}(x), \quad \text{for } 0 < x < S \qquad (9)$$

with the condition $T_n(S) = 0$, plus an appropriate additional condition.

Example 1 (BM with drift)
Let be $X(t) = x + \mu t + B_t$, with $\mu > 0$ and $x < S$. Note that, since the drift is positive, $\tau_S(x) = \tau_S^\mu(x) = \inf\{t > 0 | X(t) = S\}$ is finite with probability one, for any $x < S$. Taking $b(x) = \mu$, $\sigma(x) = 1$, the equation in (8) for $M_{U,\lambda}(x) = E(e^{-\lambda \int_0^{\tau_S^\mu(x)} U(X(s)ds)})$ becomes

$$\frac{1}{2}M''_{U,\lambda}(x) + \mu M'_{U,\lambda}(x) - \lambda U(x)M_{U,\lambda}(x) = 0. \qquad (10)$$

(i) The moment generating function of $\tau_S^\mu(x)$
By solving (10) with $U(x) = 1$, and taking into account the boundary conditions, we explicitly obtain:

$$M_{U,\lambda}(x) = E(\exp(-\lambda\tau_S^\mu(x))) = \exp[(\mu - \sqrt{\mu^2 + 2\lambda})(S - x)]. \qquad (11)$$

By inverting this Laplace transform, we obtain the (inverse-Gaussian) density of $\tau_S^\mu(x)$:

$$f_{\tau_S^\mu(x)}(t) = \frac{S - x}{\sqrt{2\pi}t^{3/2}}e^{-(S-x-\mu t)^2/2t}. \qquad (12)$$

For $\mu > 0$ the moments $T_n(x) = E(\tau_S^\mu(x))^n$ of any order n, are finite and they can be easily obtained by calculating $(-1)^n[\partial^n M_{U,\lambda}(x)/\partial\lambda^n]_{\lambda=0}$. We obtain, for instance, $E(\tau_S^\mu(x)) = \frac{S-x}{\mu}$ and $E((\tau_S^\mu(x))^2) = \frac{S-x}{\mu^3} + \frac{(S-x)^2}{\mu^2}$.

(ii) The moments of $A_S^\mu(x) = \int_0^{\tau_S^\mu(x)}(x + \mu t + B_t)dt$
For $U(x) = x$ the equation (10) becomes $\frac{1}{2}M''_{U,\lambda} + \mu M'_{U,\lambda} = \lambda x M_{U,\lambda}$, where now $M_{U,\lambda}(x) = E(e^{-\lambda A_S^\mu(x)})$. Its explicit solution can be written in terms of the Airy function (see [5]) though it is impossible to invert the Laplace transform $M_{U,\lambda}$

to obtain the probability density of $A_S^\mu(x)$. In the special case $\mu = 0$, it can be shown ([5]) that the solution of the above equation is:

$$M_{U,\lambda}(x) = 3^{2/3} \Gamma\left(\frac{2}{3}\right) \text{Ai}(2^{1/3}\lambda^{1/3}x),$$ (13)

where $\text{Ai}(x)$ denotes the Airy function; then, by inverting this Laplace transform one finds that the FCA density is ([5]):

$$f_{A_S^0(x)}(a) = \frac{2^{1/3}}{3^{2/3}\Gamma(\frac{1}{3})} \frac{x}{a^{4/3}} e^{-2x^3/9a}.$$ (14)

Thus, the distribution of $A_S^0(x)$ has an algebraic tail of order $\frac{4}{3}$ and so the moments of all orders are infinite.

Now, for $\mu > 0$, we find closed form expression for the first two moments of $A_S^\mu(x)$, by solving (9) with $U(x) = x$. For $n = 1$, we get that $T_1(x) = E(A_S^\mu(x))$ must satisfy the equation $\frac{1}{2}T_1''(x) + \mu T_1'(x) = -x$. By imposing $T_1(S) = 0$ and that, for any $x \le 0$, $T_1(x) \to 0$, as $\mu \to +\infty$, we find that the explicit expression of the mean first-crossing area is:

$$E(A_S^\mu(x)) = \frac{S-x}{2\mu}\left[S + x - \frac{1}{\mu}\right].$$ (15)

As far as the second moment of $A_S^\mu(x)$ is concerned, we have to solve (9) with $U(x) = x$ and $n = 2$, obtaining for $T_2(x) = E[(A_S^\mu(x))^2]$ the equation $\frac{1}{2}T_2''(x) + \mu T_2'(x) = -x(S - x)(S + x - 1/\mu)$. By imposing $T_2(S) = 0$ and that, for any $x \le 0$, $T_2(x) \to 0$, as $\mu \to +\infty$, we obtain that the second order moment of the FCA is of the form:

$$E[(A_S^\mu(x))^2] = A(x^4 - S^4) + B(x^3 - S^3) + C(x^2 - S^2) + D(x - S),$$ (16)

where the constants A, B, C, D can be determined. For $\mu > 0$, a closed form expression for the density of the FCA $A_S^\mu(x)$ cannot be found, so it must be obtained numerically. As in the case of the first-passage area below zero (see [2]), we have estimated it by simulating a large number of trajectories of BM with drift $\mu > 0$, starting from the initial state $x > 0$. The first and second order moments of the FCT τ_S and of the FCA A_S^μ thus obtained, well agree with the exact values. For $S = 2$, $x = 1$ and several values of $\mu > 0$, we report in the Figure 1 the estimated density of the FCA, for $X(t) = x + \mu t + B_t$. For some values of parameters we have compared the estimated density of the FCA with a suitable Gamma density; in the Figure 2, we report for $S = 2$, $x = 1$ and $\mu = 1.5$, the comparison of the Laplace transform $M_\lambda(x) = E(e^{-\lambda A_S^\mu(x)})$ of the FCA density and the Laplace transform of the Gamma density with the same mean and variance. Although the two curves agree very well for small values of $\lambda > 0$ (this implying a good agreement between the moments), for large values of λ the graph of the Laplace transform of $A_S^\mu(x)$ lyes below the other one, which is compatible with an algebraic tail for the distribution of $A_S^\mu(x)$.

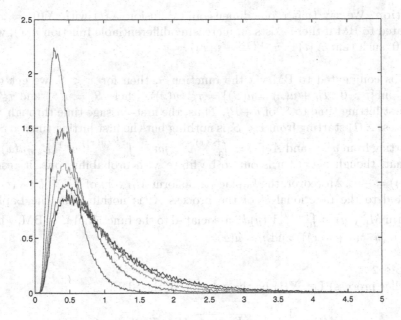

Fig. 1. Estimated density of the FCA $A_S^\mu(x)$ of $X(t) = x + \mu t + B_t$ over S, for $S = 2$, $x = 1$ and several values of μ. From top to bottom, with respect to the peak of the curve: $\mu = 3$; $\mu = 2$; $\mu = 1.5$; $\mu = 1.2$; $\mu = 1$.

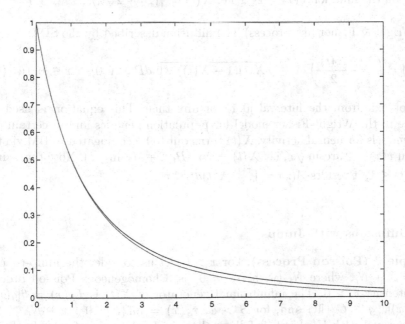

Fig. 2. Comparison of the Laplace transform $M_\lambda(x) = E(e^{-\lambda A_S^\mu(x)})$ of the FCA $A_S^\mu(x)$ (*lower curve*) and the Laplace transform of the Gamma density with the same mean and variance (*upper curve*), as functions of λ, for $S = 2$, $x = 1$ and $\mu = 1.5$.

Definition. We say that a one-dimensional diffusion $X(t)$ with $X(0) = x$, is conjugated to BM if there exists an increasing differentiable function $u(x)$, with $u(0) = 0$, such that $X(t) = u^{-1}(B_t + u(x))$.

If $X(t)$ is conjugated to BM via the function u, then for $x < S$, we get that $\tau_S(x) = \inf\{t > 0 : B_t + u(x) = u(S)\} = \tau_{S'}^B(u(x))$, where $S' = u(S)$ and $\tau_{S'}^B(y)$ is the first hitting time to S' of $y + B_t$. Thus, the first-passage time through S of the process $X(t)$ starting from $x < S$, is nothing but the first hitting time to S' of BM starting from $u(x)$, and $A_S(x) = \int_0^{\tau_S(x)} X(t)dt = \int_0^{\tau_{S'}^B(u(x))} u^{-1}(B_t + u(x))dt$. Note that, though $\tau_S(x)$ turns out to be finite with probability one, it results $E(\tau_S(x)) = +\infty$. Moreover, the Laplace transform $M_{U,\lambda}(x)$ of $\int_0^{\tau_S(x)} U(X(t))dt$, associated to the functional U of the process X, is nothing but the Laplace transform $M_{V,\lambda}^S(y)$ of $\int_0^{\tau_{S'}^B(y)} V(y)dt$, associated to the functional V of BM, where $V(s) = U(u^{-1}(s + u(x)))$ and $y = u(x)$.

Example 2
(i) (Feller process) Let $X(t)$ be the solution of the SDE:

$$dX(t) = \frac{1}{4}dt + \sqrt{X(t) \vee 0}\ dB_t\ , X(0) = x \geq 0. \tag{17}$$

The process $X(t)$ is non-negative for all $t \geq 0$ and it turns out to be conjugate to BM via the function $v(x) = 2\sqrt{x}$ i.e. $X(t) = \frac{1}{4}(B_t + 2\sqrt{x})^2$.

(ii) (Wright & Fisher-like process) The diffusion described by the SDE:

$$dX(t) = \left(\frac{1}{4} - \frac{X(t)}{2}\right)dt + \sqrt{X(t)(1 - X(t)) \vee 0}\ dB_t,\ X(0) = x \in [0,1], \tag{18}$$

does not exit from the interval $[0,1]$ for any time. This equation is used for instance in the Wright-Fisher model for population genetics and in certain diffusion models for neural activity. $X(t)$ turns out to be conjugated to BM via the function $v(x) = 2\arcsin\sqrt{x}$, i.e. $X(t) = \sin^2(B_t/2 + \arcsin\sqrt{x})$. Note that, since $0 \leq X(t) \leq 1$, it results $A(x) = \int_0^{\tau(x)} X(t)dt \leq \tau(x)$.

3.2   Diffusions with Jumps

Example 3 (Poisson Process). For $x > 0$, let us consider the jump-process $X(t) = x + N_t$, where N_t (with $N_0 = 0$) is a homogeneous Poisson process with intensity $\theta > 0$. The infinitesimal generator of $X(t)$ is $Lg(x) = \theta[g(x + 1) - g(x)]$, $g \in C^0(\mathbb{R})$ and, for $S > x$, $\tau_S(x) = \inf\{t > 0 : x + N_t \geq S\}$. By Theorem 1 with $U(x) = 1$, it follows that the Laplace transform $M_{U,\lambda}(x)$ of $\tau_S(x)$ is the solution of the equation $LM_{U,\lambda}(x) = \lambda M_{U,\lambda}(x)$, with outer condition $M_{U,\lambda}(y) = 1$ for $y \geq S$. By solving this equation, we get $M_{U,\lambda}(x) = \left(\frac{\theta}{\theta + \lambda}\right)^{S-x}$, if $S-x \in \mathbb{N}$, otherwise it is equal to $\left(\frac{\theta}{\theta+\lambda}\right)^{[S-x]+1}$, where $[a]$ denotes the integer part of a. Note that the condition $M_{U,\lambda}(-\infty) = 0$ also holds. Thus, recalling the expression of the Laplace transform of the Gamma density, we find that $\tau_S(x)$ has Gamma distribution with parameters $(S-x, \theta)$ if $S-x$ is a positive integer, while it has Gamma distribution with parameters $([S-x]+1, \theta)$ if $S-x$ is not an integer. The moments $T_n(x) = E\left[\tau_S^n(x)\right]$ are soon obtained by taking the derivatives at $\lambda = 0$, so we obtain that $E(\tau_S(x)) = \frac{S-x}{\theta}$, if $S-x \in \mathbb{N}$, otherwise it is equal to $\frac{[S-x]+1}{\theta}$; moreover $E(\tau_S^2(x)) = \frac{(S-x)^2}{\theta^2} + \frac{S-x}{\theta^2}$, if $S-x \in \mathbb{N}$, otherwise it is equal to $\frac{([S-x]+1)^2}{\theta^2} + \frac{[S-x]+1}{\theta^2}$.

By Theorem 1 with $U(x) = x$, we get the Laplace transform $M_{U,\lambda}(x)$ of $A_S(x)$ as the solution of the equation $LM_{U,\lambda}(x) = \lambda x M_{U,\lambda}(x)$, with outer condition $M_{U,\lambda}(y) = 1$ for $y \geq S$. By solving this equation, we get:

$$M_{U,\lambda}(x) = \theta^{S-x}\{(\theta+\lambda x)(\theta+\lambda(x+1))\cdots(\theta+\lambda(x+(S-x)-1))\}^{-1}, \text{ if } S-x \in \mathbb{N}$$

$$M_{U,\lambda}(x) = \theta^{[S-x]+1}\{(\theta+\lambda x)(\theta+\lambda(x+1))\cdots(\theta+\lambda(x+[S-x]))\}^{-1}, \text{ if } S-x \notin \mathbb{N}$$

Note that the condition $M_{U,\lambda}(-\infty) = 0$ is fulfilled.

We observe that $M_{U,\lambda}(x)$ turns out to be the Laplace transform of a linear combination of $S-x$ independent exponential random variables with parameter θ, with coefficients $x, x+1, \ldots, S-1$, if $S-x$ is an integer, while it is the Laplace transform of a linear combination of $[S-x]+1$ independent exponential random variables with parameter θ, with coefficients $x, x+1, \ldots, x+[S-x]$, if $S-x$ is not an integer.

By calculating the first and second derivative at $\lambda = 0$, we obtain $E(A_S(x)) = \frac{S-x}{2\theta}(x+S-1)$, if $S-x \in \mathbb{N}$, otherwise it is equal to $\frac{[S-x]+1}{2\theta}(2x + [S-x])$. Moreover, $E(A_S^2(x)) = \frac{k}{12\theta^2}\{12x^2(k+1) + 12x(k^2-1) + 3k^3 - 2k^2 - 3k + 2\}$, if $S-x = k \in \mathbb{N}$, otherwise it is equal to $\frac{[S-x]+1}{12\theta^2}\{12x^2([S-x]+1) + 12x([S-x]^2+1) + 36[S-x]x + 3[S-x]^3 + 7[S-x]^2 + 2[S-x]\}$.

References

1. Abundo, M.: On the first-passage area of one-dimensional jump-diffusion process. Methodol. Comput. Appl. Probab. 15, 85–103 (2013)
2. Abundo, M., Abundo, M.: On the first-passage area of an emptying Brownian queue. Intern. J. Appl. Math (IJAM) 24(2), 259–266 (2011)
3. Darling, D.A., Siegert, A.J.F.: The first passage problem for a continuous Markov process. Ann. Math. Stat. 24, 624–639 (1953)
4. Gihman, I.I., Skorohod, A.V.: Stochastic differential equations. Springer, Berlin (1972)
5. Kearney, M.J., Majumdar, S.N.: On the area under a continuous time Brownian motion till its first-passage time. J. Phys. A: Math. Gen. 38, 4097–4104 (2005)
6. Tuckwell, H.C.: On the first exit time problem for temporally homogeneous Markov processes. Ann. Appl. Probab. 13, 39–48 (1976)

On a Bilateral Linear Birth and Death Process in the Presence of Catastrophes

Virginia Giorno and Amelia G. Nobile

Dipartimento di Studi e Ricerche Aziendali (Management & Information Technology)
Università di Salerno, Via Giovanni Paolo II, n. 132, 84084 Fisciano (SA), Italy
{giorno,nobile}@unisa.it

Abstract. A bilateral linear birth-death process with disasters in zero is considered. The Laplace transforms of the transition probabilities are determined and the steady-state distribution is analyzed. The first-visit time to zero state is also studied.

1 Introduction and Background

Birth and death processes have been extensively used as models for populations growth, in epidemiology, in queueing systems and in many other areas of both theoretical and applied interest (cf., for instance, [1], [5], [7], [10], [11], [13], [14], [17]). In a variety of applications, some bilateral birth and death processes are taken in account to analyze the behavior of dynamic systems (cf. [2], [4], [6], [8], [9], [12], [15], [16]). In particular, in [2] a continuous-time random walk on $\mathbb{Z}$ governed by two independent Poisson streams with intensities α and β ($\alpha > 0, \beta > 0$) for motion to the right and left, respectively, is considered. Furthermore, in [8] a random walk on $\mathbb{Z}$, subject to catastrophes occurring at constant rate, and followed by exponentially-distributed repair times is analyzed. Instead, in [6] and [12] a special bilateral birth-death process characterized by nonlinear birth and death rates λ_n and μ_n such that $\lambda_n + \mu_n = \alpha + \beta$ and $\lambda_{n-1}\mu_n = \alpha\beta$ ($\alpha > 0, \beta > 0, n \in \mathbb{Z}$) is studied.

In this paper we consider a bilateral linear birth and death process in the presence of catastrophes $\{N(t), t \geq 0\}$, with state-space $\mathbb{Z}$, such that

$$\lambda_n = \begin{cases} n\lambda + \alpha, & n = 0, 1, \dots \\ |n|\mu, & n = -1, -2, \dots \end{cases} \qquad \mu_n = \begin{cases} n\mu, & n = 1, 2, \dots \\ |n|\lambda + \alpha, & n = 0, -1, -2, \dots, \end{cases} \tag{1}$$

where λ, μ, α are positive constants. We assume that the catastrophes occur according to a Poisson process with intensity ξ; the effect of each catastrophe is the transition to the zero state (cf. Fig. 1). When $\lambda \downarrow 0$, the process $N(t)$ identifies with the bilateral $M/M/\infty$ queueing systems with catastrophes. Let

$$p_{0,n}(t) = P\{N(t) = n | N(0) = 0\} \qquad (n \in \mathbb{Z}) \tag{2}$$

be the transition probabilities for the bilateral linear birth and death process. Since $N(t)$ is a symmetric process, for $t \geq 0$ one has $p_{0,n}(t) = p_{0,-n}(t)$ ($n \in \mathbb{N}$)

R. Moreno-Díaz et al. (Eds.): EUROCAST 2013, Part I, LNCS 8111, pp. 28–35, 2013.

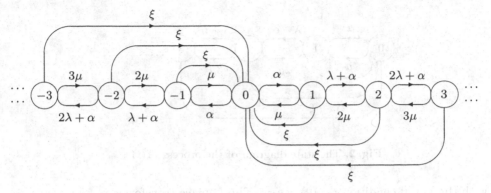

Fig. 1. The state diagram of the process $N(t)$

and $p_{0,0}(t) + 2 \sum_{k=1}^{+\infty} p_{0,k}(t) = 1$. Furthermore, (2) are solution of the Chapman-Kolmogorov forward equations:

$$\frac{dp_{0,0}(t)}{dt} = -(2\alpha + \xi)\,p_{0,0}(t) + 2\,\mu\,p_{0,1}(t) + \xi$$

$$\frac{dp_{0,n}(t)}{dt} = -[(\lambda + \mu)\,n + \alpha + \xi]\,p_{0,n}(t) + (n+1)\,\mu\,p_{0,n+1}(t) \qquad (3)$$
$$+[(n-1)\lambda + \alpha]\,p_{0,n-1}(t) \qquad (n = 1, 2, \ldots),$$

with the initial condition $p_{0,n}(0) = \delta_{0,n}$.

In Section 2 the immigration-birth-death process with catastrophes, with state-space $\mathbb{N}_0$, is considered. Explicit expressions for the Laplace transforms of transition probabilities are determined and the first-visit time (FVT) to 0 is analyzed. The results obtained in Section 2 are then used in Section 3 to study some properties of the bilateral linear birth-death process with catastrophes.

2   Immigration-Birth-Death Process with Catastrophes

We consider a birth-death process $\{M(t), t \geq 0\}$ in the presence of catastrophes, with state-space $\mathbb{N}_0$, such that

$$\lambda_n = n\lambda + \alpha \quad (n = 0, 1, \ldots), \qquad \mu_n = n\mu \quad (n = 1, 2, \ldots), \qquad (4)$$

where λ, μ, α are positive constants (cf. Fig. 2). The transition probabilities

$$r_{0,n}(t) = P\{M(t) = n | M(0) = 0\} \qquad (n = 0, 1, 2, \ldots) \qquad (5)$$

are solution of the system:

$$\frac{dr_{0,0}(t)}{dt} = -(\alpha + \xi)\,r_{0,0}(t) + \mu\,r_{0,1}(t) + \xi$$

$$\frac{dr_{0,n}(t)}{dt} = -[(\lambda + \mu)\,n + \alpha + \xi]\,r_{0,n}(t) + (n+1)\,\mu\,r_{0,n+1}(t) \qquad (6)$$
$$+[(n-1)\lambda + \alpha]\,r_{0,n-1}(t) \qquad (n = 1, 2, \ldots),$$

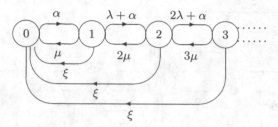

Fig. 2. The state diagram of the process $M(t)$

with the initial condition $r_{0,n}(0) = \delta_{0,n}$. The Laplace transforms

$$\Omega_{0,n}(s) = \int_0^{+\infty} e^{-st} r_{0,n}(t)\, dt \qquad (n \in \mathbb{N}_0;\ s > 0) \tag{7}$$

satisfy the system

$$
\begin{aligned}
(s + \alpha + \xi)\, \Omega_{0,0}(s) &= \mu\, \Omega_{0,1}(s) + (s + \xi)/s \\
[s + \alpha + (\lambda + \mu)\, n + \xi]\, \Omega_{0,n}(s) &= [\alpha + \lambda\, (n-1)]\, \Omega_{0,n-1}(s) \\
&\quad + \mu\, (n+1)\, \Omega_{0,n+1}(s) \qquad (n = 1, 2, \ldots),
\end{aligned}
\tag{8}
$$

with the condition $\sum_{n=0}^{+\infty} \Omega_{0,n}(s) = 1/s$.

Let $\{\widetilde{M}(t),\ t \geq 0\}$ be the birth-death process obtained from $M(t)$ as $\xi \downarrow 0$ and let $\widetilde{r}_{0,n}(t) = \lim_{\xi\downarrow 0} r_{0,n}(t)$ ($n \in \mathbb{N}_0, t \geq 0$). The process $\widetilde{M}(t)$ identifies with the queueing system $M/M/\infty$ as $\lambda \downarrow 0$; furthermore, when $\lambda = \alpha$, $\widetilde{M}(t)$ describes an adaptive queueing system (Model D) with panic-buying and compensatory reaction of service (cf., for instance, [3]). As well known, one has (cf. [17]):

$$
\widetilde{r}_{0,n}(t) =
\begin{cases}
\dfrac{(\alpha/\lambda)_n}{n!} \left(\dfrac{1}{1+\lambda t}\right)^{\alpha/\lambda} \left(\dfrac{\lambda t}{1+\lambda t}\right)^n, & \lambda = \mu \\[3ex]
\dfrac{(\alpha/\lambda)_n}{n!} \left[\dfrac{\lambda - \mu}{\lambda\, e^{(\lambda-\mu)t} - \mu}\right]^{\alpha/\lambda} \left[\dfrac{\lambda\big(e^{(\lambda-\mu)t} - 1\big)}{\lambda\, e^{(\lambda-\mu)t} - \mu}\right]^n, & \lambda \neq \mu,
\end{cases}
\tag{9}
$$

for $n \in \mathbb{N}_0$, where $(\gamma)_n$ denotes the Pochhammer symbol, which is defined as $(\gamma)_0 = 1$ and $(\gamma)_n = \gamma(\gamma+1)\ldots(\gamma+n-1)$ if $n = 1, 2, \ldots$. We note that $\widetilde{M}(t)$ admits a steady-state distribution if and only if $\lambda < \mu$ and from (9) one has:

$$\widetilde{\omega}_n = \lim_{t\to\infty} \widetilde{r}_{0,n}(t) = \frac{(\alpha/\lambda)_n}{n!} \left(1 - \frac{\lambda}{\mu}\right)^{\alpha/\lambda} \left(\frac{\lambda}{\mu}\right)^n \qquad (n \in \mathbb{N}_0). \tag{10}$$

For $\lambda < \mu$, the following monotonicity properties hold:

- when $\alpha < \mu$, then $\widetilde{\omega}_{n+1} < \widetilde{\omega}_n$ for $n \in \mathbb{N}_0$;
- when $\alpha = \mu$, then $\widetilde{\omega}_0 = \widetilde{\omega}_1$ and $\widetilde{\omega}_{n+1} < \widetilde{\omega}_n$ for $n \in \mathbb{N}$;

- when $\alpha > \mu$, by setting $m = (\alpha - \mu)/(\mu - \lambda)$, one has:
  - if $m \in \mathbb{N}$, then $\widetilde{\omega}_n < \widetilde{\omega}_{n+1}$ $(n = 0, 1, \ldots, m-1)$, $\widetilde{\omega}_m = \widetilde{\omega}_{m+1}$, $\widetilde{\omega}_n > \widetilde{\omega}_{n+1}$ $(n = m+1, m+2, \ldots)$;
  - if $m \notin \mathbb{N}$, then $\widetilde{\omega}_n < \widetilde{\omega}_{n+1}$ $(n = 0, 1, \ldots, \lceil m \rceil - 1)$, $\widetilde{\omega}_n > \widetilde{\omega}_{n+1}$ $(n = \lceil m \rceil, \lceil m \rceil + 1, \ldots)$, where $\lceil m \rceil$ is the smallest integer not less than m.

Let $\widetilde{\Omega}_{0,n}(s)$ be the Laplace transform of $\widetilde{r}_{0,n}(t)$. Recalling (9), one obtains:

$$\widetilde{\Omega}_{0,n}(s) = \begin{cases} \dfrac{\left(\frac{\alpha}{\lambda}\right)_n \left(\frac{\lambda}{\mu}\right)^n \left(1 - \frac{\lambda}{\mu}\right)^{\frac{\alpha}{\lambda}}}{s \left(\frac{s}{\mu-\lambda} + 1\right)_n} F\left(\frac{\alpha}{\lambda} + n, \frac{s}{\mu-\lambda}; \frac{s}{\mu-\lambda} + n + 1; \frac{\lambda}{\mu}\right), & \lambda < \mu \\[4mm] \dfrac{\left(\frac{\alpha}{\lambda}\right)_n \left(\frac{s}{\lambda-\mu} + \frac{\alpha}{\lambda}\right)^{-1}}{\lambda \left(\frac{s}{\lambda-\mu} + \frac{\alpha}{\lambda} + 1\right)_n} F\left(\frac{s}{\lambda-\mu} + 1, n + 1; \frac{s}{\lambda-\mu} + \frac{\alpha}{\lambda} + n + 1; \frac{\mu}{\lambda}\right), & \\[2mm] & \lambda > \mu \\[4mm] \dfrac{1}{s}\left(\frac{\alpha}{\lambda}\right)_n \left(\frac{s}{\lambda}\right)^{\alpha/\lambda} \psi\left(\frac{\alpha}{\lambda} + n, \frac{\alpha}{\lambda}; \frac{s}{\lambda}\right), & \lambda = \mu, \end{cases}$$
$$\tag{11}$$

where

$$\Phi(a, c; x) = \sum_{n=0}^{+\infty} \frac{(a)_n}{(c)_n} \frac{x^n}{n!}, \qquad F(a, b; c; x) = \sum_{n=0}^{+\infty} \frac{(a)_n (b)_n}{(c)_n} \frac{x^n}{n!},$$

$$\Psi(a, c; x) = \frac{\Gamma(1-c)}{\Gamma(a-c+1)} \Phi(a, c; x) + \frac{\Gamma(c-1)}{\Gamma(a)} x^{1-c} \Phi(a-c+1, 2-c; x)$$

denote the Kummer function, the Gauss hypergeometric function and the Tricomi confluent hypergeometric function, respectively. The probabilities $r_{0,n}(t)$ can be expressed in terms of $\widetilde{r}_{0,n}(t)$ as follows:

$$r_{0,n}(t) = e^{-\xi t} \widetilde{r}_{0,n}(t) + \xi \int_0^t e^{-\xi \tau} \widetilde{r}_{0,n}(\tau) \, d\tau \qquad (n \in \mathbb{N}_0, t > 0), \tag{12}$$

from which

$$\Omega_{0,n}(s) = \frac{s + \xi}{s} \widetilde{\Omega}_{0,n}(s + \xi) \qquad (n = 0, 1, \ldots, \; s > 0). \tag{13}$$

The steady-state probabilities of $M(t)$ can be obtained from (12) and (13):

$$\omega_n = \lim_{t \to \infty} r_{0,n}(t) = \lim_{s \to 0} s \, \Omega_{0,n}(s) = \xi \, \widetilde{\Omega}_{0,n}(\xi) \qquad (n = 0, 1, \ldots), \tag{14}$$

with $\widetilde{\Omega}_{0,n}(\xi)$ given in (11). Note that the probability ω_0 is in agreement with the results given in [11]; furthermore, the probabilities ω_n $(n = 1, 2, \ldots)$ can be also numerically computed by using the recursive formula:

$$\omega_n = \frac{1}{\mu n}\left\{[\alpha + \lambda(n-1)]\,\omega_{n-1} + \xi \sum_{k=0}^{n-1} \omega_k - \xi\right\} \qquad (n = 1, 2, \ldots).$$

Let

$$T_j = \inf\{t \geq 0 : M(t) = 0\}, \qquad M(0) = j > 0$$

be the first-visit time (FVT) of $M(t)$ to 0 starting from the initial state j and let $g_j(t) = dP(T_j \leq t)/dt$ be its probability density function (pdf). For $t > 0$ one has:

$$g_j(t) = e^{-\xi t}\, \widetilde{g}_j(t) + \xi\, e^{-\xi t} \left[1 - \int_0^t \widetilde{g}_j(\tau)\, d\tau\right] \qquad (j = 1, 2, \ldots), \qquad (15)$$

where $\widetilde{g}_j(t)$ is the pdf of the random variable $\widetilde{T}_j$, describing the first-passage time (FPT) from j to 0 for $\widetilde{M}(t)$. The density $\widetilde{g}_j(t)$ is solution of the integral equation:

$$\widetilde{r}_{j,0}(t) = \int_0^t \widetilde{g}_j(\tau)\, \widetilde{r}_{0,0}(t - \tau)\, d\tau \qquad (j = 1, 2, \ldots), \qquad (16)$$

with

$$\widetilde{r}_{j,0}(t) = P\{\widetilde{M}(t) = 0 \mid \widetilde{M}(0) = j\} = \left[\frac{1}{j!}\left(\frac{\alpha}{\lambda}\right)_j \left(\frac{\lambda}{\mu}\right)^j\right]^{-1} \widetilde{r}_{0,j}(t) \quad (j = 1, 2, \ldots). \quad (17)$$

Denoting by $\widetilde{\chi}_j(s)$ and by $\chi_j(s)$ the Laplace transforms of $\widetilde{g}_j(t)$ and $g_j(t)$, respectively, and making use of (15), (16) and (17), for $j = 1, 2, \ldots$ one obtains:

$$\chi_j(s) = \frac{\xi}{s + \xi} + \frac{s}{s + \xi}\widetilde{\chi}_j(s + \xi) = \frac{\xi}{s + \xi} + \frac{s}{s + \xi}\left[\frac{1}{j!}\left(\frac{\alpha}{\lambda}\right)_j \left(\frac{\lambda}{\mu}\right)^j\right]^{-1} \frac{\widetilde{\Omega}_{0,j}(s + \xi)}{\widetilde{\Omega}_{0,0}(s + \xi)},$$
$$(18)$$

with $\widetilde{\Omega}_{0,j}(s)$ given in (11). We note that $P(T_j < +\infty) = 1$, i.e. the first-visit time of $M(t)$ to zero state occurs with probability 1, whereas for $\widetilde{M}(t)$ such an event has probability equal to 1 only if $\lambda < \mu$.

3 Bilateral Birth-Death Process with Catastrophes

We consider the bilateral linear birth-death process defined in Section 1. For the process $N(t)$, let

$$\Pi_{0,n}(s) = \int_0^{+\infty} e^{-st} p_{0,n}(t)\, dt \qquad (n \in \mathbb{Z};\ s > 0) \qquad (19)$$

be the Laplace transforms of $p_{0,n}(t)$. For the symmetry of the process, one has $\Pi_{0,n}(s) = \Pi_{0,-n}(s)$ and $\Pi_{0,0}(s) + 2\sum_{n=1}^{+\infty}\Pi_{0,n}(s) = 1/s$. Moreover, from (3) it follows:

$$(s + 2\alpha + \xi)\, \Pi_{0,0}(s) = 2\mu\, \Pi_{0,1}(s) + (s + \xi)/s$$
$$[s + \alpha + (\lambda + \mu)n + \xi]\, \Pi_{0,n}(s) = [\alpha + \lambda(n - 1)]\, \Pi_{0,n-1}(s) \qquad (20)$$
$$+ \mu(n + 1)\, \Pi_{0,n+1}(s) \qquad (n = 1, 2, \ldots).$$

Comparing (8) and (20), and recalling (13), for $n \in \mathbb{N}_0$ it follows:

$$\Pi_{0,n}(s) = \Pi_{0,-n}(s) = \frac{\Omega_{0,n}(s)}{2 - s\,\Omega_{0,0}(s)} = \frac{s+\xi}{s} \frac{\widetilde{\Omega}_{0,n}(s+\xi)}{2-(s+\xi)\,\widetilde{\Omega}_{0,0}(s+\xi)}. \tag{21}$$

The steady-state probabilities can be obtained from (21); indeed, by virtue of (11) and (14), one obtains:

$$q_n = q_{-n} = \lim_{t\to+\infty} p_{0,n}(t) = \lim_{s\to 0} s\,\Pi_{0,n}(s) = \lim_{s\to 0} \frac{s\,\Omega_{0,n}(s)}{2 - s\,\Omega_{0,0}(s)} = \frac{\omega_n}{2 - \omega_0}$$

$$= \begin{cases} \dfrac{\left(\frac{\alpha}{\lambda}\right)_n \left(\frac{\lambda}{\mu}\right)^n \left(1-\frac{\lambda}{\mu}\right)^{\frac{\alpha}{\lambda}} F\left(\frac{\alpha}{\lambda}+n, \frac{\xi}{\mu-\lambda}; \frac{\xi}{\mu-\lambda}+n+1; \frac{\lambda}{\mu}\right)}{\left(\frac{\xi}{\mu-\lambda}+1\right)_n \left[2 - \left(1-\frac{\lambda}{\mu}\right)^{\frac{\alpha}{\lambda}} F\left(\frac{\alpha}{\lambda}, \frac{\xi}{\mu-\lambda}; \frac{\xi}{\mu-\lambda}+1; \frac{\lambda}{\mu}\right)\right]}, & \lambda < \mu \\[3em] \dfrac{\frac{\xi}{\lambda}\left(\frac{\alpha}{\lambda}\right)_n \left(\frac{\xi}{\lambda-\mu}+\frac{\alpha}{\lambda}\right)^{-1} F\left(\frac{\xi}{\lambda-\mu}+1, n+1; \frac{\xi}{\lambda-\mu}+\frac{\alpha}{\lambda}+n+1; \frac{\mu}{\lambda}\right)}{\left(\frac{\xi}{\lambda-\mu}+\frac{\alpha}{\lambda}+1\right)_n \left[2 - \frac{\xi}{\lambda}\left(\frac{\xi}{\lambda-\mu}+\frac{\alpha}{\lambda}\right)^{-1} F\left(\frac{\xi}{\lambda-\mu}+1, 1; \frac{\xi}{\lambda-\mu}+\frac{\alpha}{\lambda}+1; \frac{\mu}{\lambda}\right)\right]}, & \\ & \lambda > \mu \\[2em] \dfrac{\left(\frac{\alpha}{\lambda}\right)_n \left(\frac{\xi}{\lambda}\right)^{\alpha/\lambda} \psi\left(\frac{\alpha}{\lambda}+n, \frac{\alpha}{\lambda}; \frac{\xi}{\lambda}\right)}{2 - \left(\frac{\xi}{\lambda}\right)^{\alpha/\lambda} \psi\left(\frac{\alpha}{\lambda}, \frac{\alpha}{\lambda}; \frac{\xi}{\lambda}\right)}, & \lambda = \mu. \end{cases}$$

$$\tag{22}$$

Alternatively, after determining q_0 via (22), the probabilities $q_n = q_{-n}$ ($n = 1, 2, \ldots$) can be computated recursively as follows:

$$q_1 = \frac{(\xi + 2\alpha)\,q_0 - \xi}{2\mu}, \qquad q_n = \frac{1}{\mu n}\left\{[\alpha + \lambda(n-1)]\,q_{n-1} + \xi \sum_{k=1}^{n-1} q_k + \xi\,\frac{q_0 - 1}{2}\right\}.$$

We note that the probabilities $q_n = q_{-n}$ of $N(t)$ remain unchanged when the parameters $\lambda, \mu, \alpha, \xi$ are multiplied by the same factor $\gamma > 0$. The steady-state distribution is a symmetric function, such that the following monotonicity properties hold:

• when $\lambda < \mu$ and $\alpha < \mu\,[1 + \xi/(\mu - \lambda)]$, then $q_{n+1} < q_n$ for $n \in \mathbb{N}_0$;
• when $\lambda > \mu$ and $\alpha < \lambda$, then $q_{n+1} < q_n$ for $n \in \mathbb{N}_0$;
• when $\lambda = \mu$, then $q_{n+1} < q_n$ for $n \in \mathbb{N}_0$.

In the remaining cases, the steady-state distribution may possess one or more maxima, as shown in Fig. 3.

The steady-state probabilities for the bilateral $M/M/\infty$ queueing system with catastrophes (cf. Fig. 4) can be evaluated taking $\lambda \downarrow 0$ in (22):

$$q_n = q_{-n} = \frac{(\alpha/\mu)^n}{(1+\xi/\mu)_n} \frac{e^{-\alpha/\mu}\,\Phi\left(\frac{\xi}{\mu}, \frac{\xi}{\mu}+n+1; \frac{\alpha}{\mu}\right)}{2 - e^{-\alpha/\mu}\,\Phi\left(\frac{\xi}{\mu}, \frac{\xi}{\mu}+1; \frac{\alpha}{\mu}\right)} \qquad (n \in \mathbb{N}). \tag{23}$$

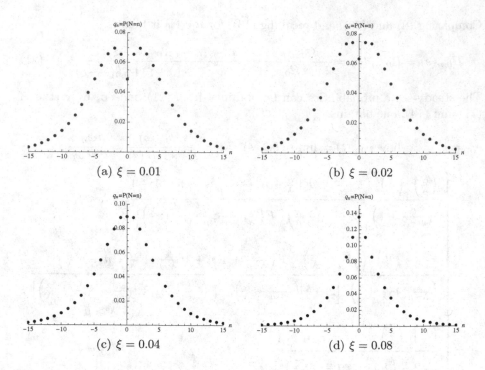

Fig. 3. The probabilities q_n given in (22) are plotted for $\lambda = 0.2$, $\mu = 0.3$ and $\alpha = 0.5$

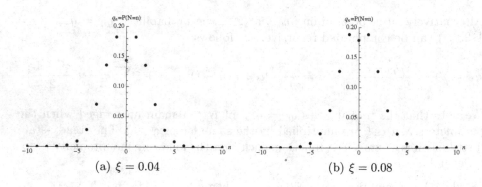

Fig. 4. For the bilateral $M/M/\infty$ queue with catastrophes the probabilities q_n are plotted for $\mu = 0.3$ and $\alpha = 0.5$

Let

$$\mathcal{T}_j^* = \inf\{t \geq 0 : N(t) = 0\}, \qquad N(0) = j \neq 0$$

be the FVT of $N(t)$ to 0 starting from the initial state j. The random variables $\mathcal{T}_j^*$ and $\mathcal{T}_{-j}^*$ are identically distributed as $\mathcal{T}_j$ ($j \in \mathbb{N}$, so that from (18) the FVT mean to zero can be easily derived:

$$E(\mathcal{T}_j^*) = E(\mathcal{T}_{-j}^*) = -\frac{d\chi_j(s)}{ds}\bigg|_{s=0} = \frac{1}{\xi}\left\{1 - \left[\frac{1}{j!}\left(\frac{\alpha}{\lambda}\right)_j\left(\frac{\lambda}{\mu}\right)^j\right]^{-1}\frac{\widetilde{\Omega}_{0,j}(\xi)}{\widetilde{\Omega}_{0,0}(\xi)}\right\} \quad (j \in \mathbb{N}),$$

with $\widetilde{\Omega}_{0,j}(s)$ given in (11).

More general bilateral birth-death processes with catastrophes, and their continuous approximations, will be the object of future works.

References

1. Buonocore, A., Di Crescenzo, A., Giorno, V., Nobile, A.G., Ricciardi, L.M.: A Markov chain-based model for actomyosin dynamics. Sci. Math. Jpn. 70, 159–174 (2009)
2. Conolly, B.: On Randomized Random Walks. SIAM Review 13(1), 81–99 (1971)
3. Conolly, B.: Lecture Notes on Queueing Systems. Ellis Horwood Ltd., Halsted (John Wiley & Sons), Chichester, New York (1975)
4. Di Crescenzo, A., Nastro, A.: On first-passage-time densities for certain symmetric Markov chains. Sci. Math. Jpn. 60(2), 381–390 (2004)
5. Di Crescenzo, A., Giorno, V., Nobile, A.G., Ricciardi, L.M.: A note on birth-death processes with catastrophes. Statistics and Probability Letters 78, 2248–2257 (2008)
6. Di Crescenzo, A., Martinucci, B.: On a symmetric, nonlinear birth-death process with bimodal transition probabilities. Symmetry 1, 201–214 (2009)
7. Di Crescenzo, A., Giorno, V., Nobile, A.G., Ricciardi, L.M.: On time non-homogeneous stochastic processes with catastrophes. In: Trappl, R. (ed.) Cybernetics and Systems 2010, pp. 169–174. Austrian Society for Cybernetics Studies, Vienna (2010)
8. Di Crescenzo, A., Giorno, V., Krishna Kumar, B., Nobile, A.G.: A double-ended queue with catastrophes and repairs, and a jump-diffusion approximation. Method. Comput. Appl. Probab. 14, 937–954 (2012)
9. Di Crescenzo, A., Iuliano, A., Martinucci, B.: On a bilateral birth-death process with alternating rates. Ricerche di Matematica 61(1), 157–169 (2012)
10. Dimou, S., Economou, A.: The single server queue with catastrophes and geometric reneging. Method. Comput. Appl. Probab. (2011), doi:10.1007/s11009-011-9271-6
11. Economou, A., Fakinos, D.: A continuous-time Markov chain under the influence of a regulating point process and applications in stochastic models with catastrophes. European J. Oper. Res. (Stochastics and Statistics) 149, 625–640 (2003)
12. Hongler, M.-O., Parthasarathy, P.R.: On a super-diffusive, non linear birth and death process. Physics Letters A 372, 3360–3362 (2008)
13. Karlin, S., McGregor, J.: Linear growth, birth and death processes. Journal of Mathematics and Mechanics 7(4), 643–662 (1958)
14. Medhi, J.: Stochastic Models in Queueing Theory. Academic Press, Amsterdam (2003)
15. Pollett, P.K.: Similar Markov chain. J. Appl. Probab. 38A, 53–65 (2001)
16. Pruitt, W.E.: Bilateral birth and death processes. Trans. Amer. Math. Soc. 107, 508–525 (1963)
17. Ricciardi, L.M.: Stochastic population theory: birth and death processes. In: Hallam, T.G., Levin, S.A. (eds.) Mathematical Ecology, Biomathematics, vol. 17, pp. 155–190. Springer, Heidelberg (1986)

On the Dynamics of a Couple of Mutually Interacting Neurons*

A. Buonocore[1], L. Caputo[1], M.F. Carfora[2], and E. Pirozzi[1]

[1] Dipartimento di Matematica e Applicazioni, Università di Napoli Federico II,
Via Cintia, 80126 Napoli, Italy
{aniello.buonocore,luigia.caputo,enrica.pirozzi}@unina.it
[2] Istituto per le Applicazioni del Calcolo "Mauro Picone",
Consiglio Nazionale delle Ricerche,
Via Pietro Castellino, 111 80131 Napoli, Italy
f.carfora@na.iac.cnr.it

Abstract. A model for describing the dynamics of two mutually interacting neurons is considered. In such a context, maintaining statements of the Leaky Integrate-and-Fire framework, we include a random component in the synaptic current, whose role is to modify the equilibrium point of the membrane potential of one of the two neurons when a spike of the other one occurs. We give an approximation for the interspike time interval probability density function of both neurons within any parametric configurations driving the evolution of the membrane potentials in the so-called subthreshold regimen.

1 Introduction

In the present paper we consider the model proposed in [4] of two interacting neurons each one subject to the stochastic Leaky Integrated-and-Fire (LIF) dynamics (see, for instance, [5] and [6] for a detailed review of stochastic LIF models) modified in such a way that an additional stochastic synaptic current realizes the connection between the two neuronal units. Specifically, indicated by $\{V_i(t) : t \geq 0\}$ the membrane potential of Neuron i $(i = 1, 2)$,[1] we refer to the two following stochastic differential equations:

$$dV_i(t) = \left[-\frac{V_i(t)}{\theta_i} + \frac{\rho_i + \mu_i \theta_i}{\theta_i} + C_{i,3-i}(t) \right] dt + \sqrt{\sigma_i^2} dW_i(t). \qquad (1)$$

In this context a spike (or firing) of the Neuron i occurs when its membrane potential achieves a constant firing threshold S_i; then, the dynamics restarts

---

* This work has been performed under partial support by F.A.R.O Project (Finanziamenti per l'Avvio di Ricerche Originali, III tornata) "Controllo e stabilità di processi diffusivi nell'ambiente", Polo delle Scienze e Tecnologie, Università degli Studi di Napoli Federico II.

[1] In the sequel we omit such a specification.

R. Moreno-Díaz et al. (Eds.): EUROCAST 2013, Part I, LNCS 8111, pp. 36–44, 2013.
© Springer-Verlag Berlin Heidelberg 2013

from its reset potential $v_{0,i} < S_i$. In the sequel, we denote by $\{T_{i,n}\}_{n \in \mathbb{N}}$ $(T_{i,0} = 0)$ the sequence of the firing times of Neuron i.

In Eqs. (1), $W_1 = \{W_1(t) : t \geq 0\}$ and $W_2 = \{W_2(t) : t \geq 0\}$ are two independent standard Brownian motions. The parameters $\theta_i > 0$, ρ_i and μ_i are the membrane decay time constants, the membrane resting potentials and the constant currents, respectively. Finally, during the time interval between two successive spike instants $(T_{i,n-1}, T_{i,n})$ $(n \in \mathbb{N})$, the additional synaptic currents $C_{i,3-i} = \{C_{i,3-i}(t) : t \geq 0\}$ are such that (cf. [11], [12])

$$C_{i,3-i}(t) = c_{0,i}\, e^{-(t-T_{i,n-1})/\alpha_i} + k_i \left[1 - e^{-(t-T_{i,n-1})/\alpha_i}\right] H_{3-i}(t). \qquad (2)$$

The process $H_{3-i} = \{H_{3-i}(t) : t \geq 0\}$ is zero until a spike time T_{3-i,m_n} occurs in $(T_{i,n-1}, T_{i,n})$, after which it assumes the value 1. Specifically, if an integer $m_n \geq 1$ exists such that

$$m_n := \min\{r \in \mathbb{N} : T_{3-i,r} \in (T_{i,n-1}, T_{i,n})\}, \qquad (3)$$

one has:

$$H_{3-i}(t) := \begin{cases} 0, & \text{for } T_{i,n-1} \leq t < T_{3-i,m_n}, \\[2mm] 1, & \text{for } T_{3-i,m_n} \leq t < T_{i,n}. \end{cases}$$

Whenever such an m_n does not exist, then $H_{3-i}(t)$ is zero in the overall considered interval. In Eqs. (2), by means of k_1 and k_2 we modulate the intensities of the interactions: if their sign is positive (negative) an excitatory (inhibitory) current is injected after T_{3-i,m_n}. The parameters α_i represent the decay time constants of the synaptic currents and $c_{0,i}$ are the reset values for the currents, i.e. $C_{i,3-i}(T_{i,n}) = c_{0,i}$.

In this setting, the interspike interval (ISI), i.e. the time elapsed between two successive spikes of each neuron, cannot be identified with the first passage time (FPT) of the stochastic process $\{V_i(s) : s \geq T_{i,n}\}$, starting at $v_{0,i}$ at time $T_{i,n}$, through the threshold $S_i > v_{0,i}$: the reset of the Neuron i occurs (every time) after a different time spent from the last firing time of the Neuron $3 - i$.

Staying in the so called subthreshold regimen, i.e. the firing threshold is much larger than the mean of the membrane potential, (see, for instance, [9] and references therein) the aim of the present paper is to obtain a better approximation for the ISI's probability density function (pdf) of both neurons with respect to that proposed in [4]. For this purpose, with reference to the aforementioned paper, we will proceed along a different, but substantially equivalent, line by making use of some theoretical results and computational methods for Gauss-Diffusion processes and for their FPT through a constant threshold. As it can be seen from the figures provided at the end of this paper, the approximations above are quite satisfactory even in situations that do not fit properly the subthreshold regimen.

2   First Passage Time for Gauss-Diffusion Processes

Results and methods reported in this section related to FPT for Gauss-Diffusion processes can be found in [3] and [7]. In the following we denote by $\mathbb{P}$ the probability measure and by $\mathbb{E}$ and $\mathbb{C}$ the mean and the autocovariance function of the considered process, respectively. For a Gauss-Diffusion process $X = \{X(t) : t \geq t_0\}$ it is known that its autocovariance function factorizes as the product of two functions, that we denote by $u_\mathrm{x}(t)$ and $v_\mathrm{x}(t)$.

We shall now focus on the first passage time problem for a Gauss-Diffusion process: $m_\mathrm{x}(t) := \mathbb{E}[X(t)]$, $u_\mathrm{x}(t)$ and $v_\mathrm{x}(t)$ are $C^1([t_0, +\infty[)$ functions. Henceforth we shall assume that $X(t_0) = m_\mathrm{x}(t_0) \equiv x_0$, almost surely. Hereafter, without loss of generality, we shall assume that $u_\mathrm{x}(t)$ and $v_\mathrm{x}(t)$ are both positive in $(t_0, +\infty)$. Let now $S(t)$ be a continuous function in $[t_0, +\infty[$, in the sequel denoted as "threshold", and let $x_0 < S(t_0)$. The FPT of the considered process through $S(t)$ is the random variable

$$T \equiv T_{\mathrm{x},\mathrm{s}}(x_0, t_0) := \inf\{t > t_0 : X(t) \geq S(t)\}.$$

Since the sample paths of X are continuous in $[t_0, +\infty[$, T is absolutely continuous and we indicate by

$$g_\mathrm{x}[S(t), t] \equiv g_\mathrm{x}[S(t), t | x_0, t_0] := \frac{d}{dt}\mathbb{P}(T \leq t)$$

its probability density function.

Let $m_\mathrm{x}(t)$, $u_\mathrm{x}(t)$, $v_\mathrm{x}(t)$ and $S(t)$ in $C^2_-([t_0, +\infty[),^2$ $f_\mathrm{x}[x, t | y, \tau]$ the transition pdf and let

$$\psi_\mathrm{x}[S(t), t | y, \tau] := \left\{ \dot{S}_\mathrm{x}(t) - \dot{m}_\mathrm{x}(t) - [S(t) - m_\mathrm{x}(t)] \frac{\dot{u}_\mathrm{x}(t)v_\mathrm{x}(\tau) - \dot{v}_\mathrm{x}(t)u_\mathrm{x}(\tau)}{u_\mathrm{x}(t)v_\mathrm{x}(\tau) - v_\mathrm{x}(t)u_\mathrm{x}(\tau)} \right.$$
$$\left. - [y - m_\mathrm{x}(\tau)] \frac{\dot{v}_\mathrm{x}(t)u_\mathrm{x}(t) - v_\mathrm{x}(t)\dot{u}_\mathrm{x}(t)}{u_\mathrm{x}(t)v_\mathrm{x}(\tau) - v_\mathrm{x}(t)u_\mathrm{x}(\tau)} \right\} f_\mathrm{x}[S(t), t | y, \tau],$$

the so-called singularity removed probability current. Then, the pdf of T is the solution of the non-singular integral equation:

$$g_\mathrm{x}[S(t), t] = -\psi_\mathrm{x}[S(t), t | x_0, t_0] + \int_{t_0}^{t} \psi_\mathrm{x}[S(t), t | S(\tau), \tau] g_\mathrm{x}[S(\tau), \tau]\, d\tau. \qquad (4)$$

A closed form solution of Eq. (4) can be obtained only in few particular cases: in general, a numerical approximation of both FPT pdf and distribution function is given by composite quadrature rules (see, for instance, [2] and [7]).

The main drawback, due the $O(n^2)$ computational complexity of considered procedures, is related to the determination of the tail of $g_\mathrm{x}[S(t), t]$ when, for all $t > t_0$, one has $S(t) \gg m_\mathrm{x}(t)$. In such a case the following result, adapted by [8], can be useful.

---

[2] Here, $C^2_-([t_0, +\infty[)$ represents the class of functions with left–continuous second derivative in $(t_0, +\infty)$.

Theorem 1. *Suppose that, with characteristic time constant β, the following limit holds:* $\lim\limits_{t \to +\infty} -\psi_x[S(t), t|y, \tau] = h_x > 0$. *If*

$$\inf_{t \geq t_0} [S(t) - m_x(t)] > \sup_{t \geq t_0} \sqrt{2u_x(t)v_x(t)},$$

for $t - t_0 \gg \beta$ one has:

$$g_x[S(t), t|x_0, t_0] \approx h_x \, e^{-h_x \cdot (t-t_0)}.$$

3 ISI's Distribution

For the theoretical results used in this section related to Gauss-Markov processes, one can take as a reference, for example, [1].

Let $\{\mathcal{F}_t := \sigma(\{V_1(s), V_2(s) : 0 \leq s \leq t\})\}_{t \geq 0}$ the natural filtration of V_1 and V_2 and let $t_i \equiv t_{i,n-1}$ a realization of $T_{i,n-1}$. For $s, t \in (t_i, T_{i,n})$, one has:

$$\mathbb{C}[V_i(s), V_i(t)] = \frac{\sigma_i \theta_i}{2} \left[e^{(s-t_i)/\theta_i} - e^{-(s-t_i)/\theta_i} \right] \sigma_i e^{-(t-t_i)/\theta_i} =: u_{V_i}(s) v_{V_i}(t).$$

Now, with m_n defined in (3) and denoting by $t^*_{3-i,i} \equiv t^*_{3-i,i}(t_i)$ a realization of $T_{3-i,m_n-1},$[3] we consider the following function:

$$\tilde{P}_{3-i,i}(s|t^*_{3-i,i}, t_i) := \mathbb{E}\left[H_{3-i}(s)|\mathcal{F}_{t_i}\right] = \mathbb{P}\left(T_{3-i,m_n} \leq s\right). \tag{5}$$

For $t \in (t_i, T_{i,n})$, the mean of the membrane potential of Neuron i is:

$$\mathbb{E}[V_i(t)] = \mathbb{E}\{\mathbb{E}[V_i(t)|\mathcal{F}_{t_i}]\} = \overline{m}_i(t|t_i) + m_i(t|t_i) + m_{i,3-i}(t|t^*_{3-i,i}, t_i) \tag{6}$$

where,

$$\overline{m}_i(t|t_i) = v_{0,i} e^{-(t-t_i)/\theta_i} + (\rho_i + \mu_i\theta_i)\left[1 - e^{-(t-t_i)/\theta_i}\right],$$

$$m_i(t|t_i) = c_{0,i}\left[\frac{e^{-(t-t_i)/\alpha_i} - e^{-(t-t_i)/\theta_i}}{1/\theta_i - 1/\alpha_i}\right],$$

$$m_{i,3-i}(t|t^*_{3-i,i}, t_i) = k_i e^{-(t-t_i)/\theta_i} \tag{7}$$

$$\times \int_{t_i}^{t} \left[1 - e^{-(s-t_i)/\alpha_i}\right] e^{(s-t_i)/\theta_i} \tilde{P}_{3-i,i}(s|t^*_{3-i,i}, t_i)\, ds.$$

We now consider the random variable

$$T_{V_{3-i}, S_{3-i}}(v_{0,3-i}, t^*_{3-i,i}) := \inf\{t \geq t^*_{3-i,i} : V_{3-i}(t) \geq S_{3-i}\}$$

representing the FPT of Neuron $3 - i$ membrane potential through its firing threshold S_{3-i} conditioned by $V_{3-i}(t^*_{3-i,i}) = v_{0,3-i}$, and we denote by

$$G_{3-i,i}(t) \equiv G_{V_{3-i}}(S_{3-i}, t|v_{0,3-i}, t^*_{3-i,i}) := \mathbb{P}(T_{V_{3-i}, S_{3-i}}(v_{0,3-i}, t^*_{3-i,i}) \leq t)$$

---

[3] We underline that $t^*_{3-i,i}$ is the firing time of Neuron $3 - i$ just before t_i. Note that $t^*_{3-i,i} \leq t_i$.

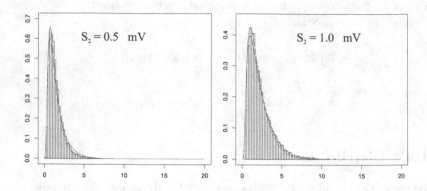

Fig. 1. Plots of the FPT pdf for V_2 (red lines) and corresponding histograms for the indicated S_2 values. The blue lines refer to the approximation given in Section 4. Other parameters are: $\rho_1 = \rho_2 = 0$, $\mu_1 = \mu_2 = 0$, $\theta_1 = \theta_2 = 1$ ms, $\alpha_1 = \alpha_2 = 1$ ms, $c_{0,1} = c_{0,2} = 1$ mV·ms^{-1}, $k_1 = 0$, $k_2 = 1$ mV·ms^{-1}, $\sigma_1^2 = \sigma_2^2 = 2$ mV^2·ms^{-1}. On the horizontal axis the time is in θ_2 units; the vertical axis unit is ms^{-1}.

its distribution function. Recalling the definition of m_n in (3) and the meaning of the times $t^*_{3-i,i}$ and t_i, it is quite easy to realize that for the function defined in (5) one has

$$P_{3-i,i}(s|t^*_{3-i,i}, t_i) = \mathbb{P}\left(T_{V_{3-i},S_{3-i}}(v_{0,3-i}, t^*_{3-i,i}) \le s | T_{V_{3-i},S_{3-i}}(v_{0,3-i}, t^*_{3-i,i}) \ge t_i\right)$$
$$= \frac{G_{3-i,i}(s) - G_{3-i,i}(t_i)}{1 - G_{3-i,i}(t_i)}.$$

$$(8)$$

Now, it is possible to proceed numerically using the system of two coupled integral equations (4) written for V_1 and V_2, respectively. In the case of one–way interaction, for example $k_1 = 0$ and $k_2 \neq 0$, this can be quite easily accomplished. However, we stress that the distribution of $T_{i,n} - t_i$ is not the distribution of ISIs $T_{i,n} - T_{i,n-1}$, but it only represents the distribution of the FPT of V_i through its firing threshold S_i conditioned by $V_i(t_i) = v_{0,i}$. Red lines in Figures 1 and 2 show the approximated FPT pdf we obtained for V_2 superimposed to an histogram of the corresponding FPT as simulated by discretizing the related stochastic differential equation. It can be noted that the agreement is quite satisfactory for all the considered firing thresholds.

In the next Section, we will see that, under not very restrictive assumptions regarding the parametric configuration of the model, it is possible to determine an approximation for the ISI's pdf of both neurons.

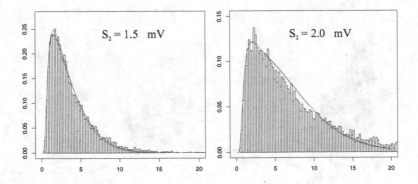

Fig. 2. Plots of the FPT pdf for V_2 (red lines) and corresponding histograms for the indicated S_2 values. The blue lines refer to the approximation given in Section 4. Other parameters as in Fig. 1.

4 ISI's Distribution in an Asymptotic Regimen

By substituting $P_{3-i,i}(s|t^*_{3-i,i}, t_i)$ and $\left[1 - e^{-(s-t_i)/\alpha_i}\right]$ with 1 in Eq. (7), one has

$$m_{i,3-i}(t|t^*_{3-i,i}, t_i) \leq k_i \theta_i \left[1 - e^{-(t-t_i)/\theta_i}\right].$$

This fact ensures that if

$$S_i - \sup_{t \geq t_i} \left\{ \overline{m}_i(t|t_i) + m_i(t|t_i) + k_i \theta_i \left[1 - e^{-(t-t_i)/\theta_i}\right]\right\} > \sqrt{\sigma_i^2 \theta_i} \qquad (9)$$

the process V_i is in the asymptotic regimen depicted in the Theorem 1.

In this Section we suppose that (9) holds for $i = 1, 2$. Therefore, setting $l_i = \lim\limits_{t \to +\infty} m_{i,3-i}(t|t^*_{3-i,i}, t_i)/k_i$, and recalling that

$$h_{V_i} = \lim_{t \to +\infty} -\psi_{V_i}(S_i, t|y, \tau)$$

$$= \frac{S_i - k_i(2l_i - \theta_i) - (\rho_i + \mu_i \theta_i)}{\theta_i \sqrt{\pi \sigma_i^2 \theta_i}} \, e^{-\dfrac{[S_i - k_i l_i - (\rho_i + \mu_i \theta_i)]^2}{\sigma_i^2 \theta_i}}, \qquad (10)$$

by applying Theorem 1, for $t - t_i \gg \max\{\alpha_i, \theta_i\}$, one has

$$g_{V_i}(S_i, t|v_{0,i}, t_i) \approx h_{V_i} \, e^{-h_{V_i} \cdot (t-t_i)}. \qquad (11)$$

Without loss of generality we focus our attention on the Neuron 2 and let t_2 be one of its firing times. Let $t_1 = t^*_{1,2}(t_2)$, i.e. the firing time of the Neuron 1 just before t_2 and $\bar{t}_2 = t^*_{2,1}(t_1)$, the firing time of the Neuron 2 just before t_1. For $s \geq t_2$, from (8) and (11) written with $i = 1$, we have

$$P_{1,2}(s|t_1, t_2) \approx P_{1,2}(s|t_2) = 1 - e^{-h_{V_1} \cdot (s-t_2)}. \qquad (12)$$

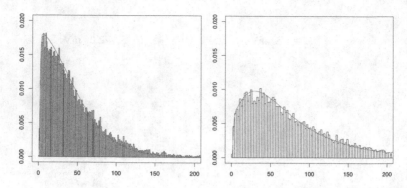

Fig. 3. The case of the mutual excitation: $k_1 = k_2 = 0.25$ mV·ms^{-1}. The red line is the plot of the our approximation of the FPT pdf for the processes $V_1(t)$ (on left) and $V_2(t)$ (on right). The histograms refer to the corresponding ISI pdf by simulations: Neuron 1 on left, Neuron 2 on right. Other parameter values are: $\rho_1 = \rho_2 = 0$, $\mu_1 = \mu_2 = 0$, $c_{0,1} = c_{0,2} = 0.25$ mV·ms^{-1}, $\theta_1 = \theta_2 = 1$ ms, $\alpha_1 = \alpha_2 = 1$ ms, $v_{0,1} = v_{0,2} = -2$ mV, $\sigma_1^2 = 1, \sigma_2^2 = 0.75$ mV^2·ms^{-1} and $S_1 = S_2 = 2$ mV.

By using (12) in (7), an approximation $\widetilde{m}_{2,1}(t|t_2)$ to $m_{2,1}(t|t_1, t_2)$, not depending on t_1 is now achievable:

$$
\begin{aligned}
\widetilde{m}_{2,1}(t|t_2) = {} & k_2\theta_2\left[1 - e^{-(t-t_2)/\theta_2}\right] - k_2\frac{e^{-(t-t_2)/\alpha_2} - e^{-(t-t_2)/\theta_2}}{1/\theta_2 - 1/\alpha_2} \\
& + k_2\frac{e^{-h_{V_1}(t-t_2)/\theta_2} - e^{-(t-t_2)/\theta_2}}{h_{V_1} - 1/\theta_2} \\
& - k_2\frac{e^{-(h_{V_1}+1/\alpha_2)(t-t_2)} - e^{-(t-t_2)/\theta_2}}{h_{V_1} + 1/\alpha_2 - 1/\theta_2}.
\end{aligned}
\tag{13}
$$

However, we outline that the value h_{V_1} remains dependent on l_1. We proceed in analogous way for Neuron 1, obtaining also $\widetilde{m}_{1,2}(t|t_1)$ that is the same of (13) substituting the index 1 with 2 and vice versa. Now, in order to make actually usable the procedure described so far, we make use of the relation $l_1 = \lim_{t\to+\infty} m_{1,2}(t|\bar{t}_2, t_1)/k_1 \approx \lim_{t\to+\infty} \widetilde{m}_{1,2}(t|t_1)/k_1 = \theta_1$.

Therefore, substituting $m_{2,1}(t|t_1, t_2)$ with $\widetilde{m}_{2,1}(t|t_2)$ in Eq. (6) and l_1 with θ_1 in Eq. (10), a numerical approximation for the FPT pdf of V_2 can be obtained by means of (4): since in it the dependency on t_1 has vanished, we can argue that it also approximate the ISI's pdf of Neuron 2. The same can be said for the Neuron 1. In Figs. 3, 4 and 5 ISI's pdf approximations are shown obtained by means of proposed method with reference to a couple of neurons characterized by different noises ($\sigma_1^2 = 1, \sigma_2^2 = 0.75$) in the three different situations: the mutual balanced excitation ($k_1 = k_2 = 0.25$), the inhibition-excitation ($k_1 = -0.1, k_2 = 0.25$) and the excitation-inhibition ($k_1 = 0.25, k_2 = -0.1$). In such figures they are compared with the ISI histograms obtained by simulating the trajectories of the processes V_1 and V_2. Comparing the plots for the Neuron 1 (on left of

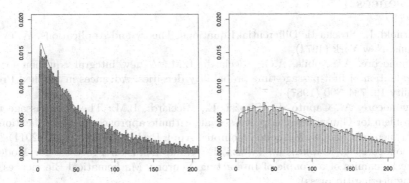

Fig. 4. The case of the inhibition-excitation. Other parameters as in Fig.3 with $k_1 = -0.1, k_2 = 0.25$ mV·ms^{-1}.

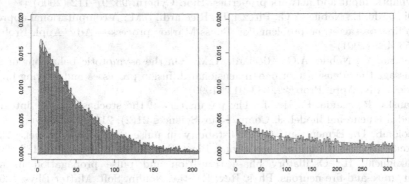

Fig. 5. The case of the excitation-inhibition. Other parameters as in Fig.3 with $k_1 = 0.25, k_2 = -0.1$ mV·ms^{-1}.

Fig. 3 and Fig. 4), we note how the effect of the inhibition provided by the Neuron 2 changes the profile of the densities: the probability mass becomes less concentrated in correspondence of smaller values of the time and stretches over time. Such an effect, but less evident, can be observed also for the Neuron 2 (on right of Fig. 3 and Fig. 4). In the Fig. 4 and Fig. 5, the plots for the Neuron 1 (on left) are not too much different: indeed, in Fig. 5, the Neuron 1 is again subject to the inhibition not in direct way but as a feedback effect by means the inhibition action that itself applies to the Neuron 2. Obviously, the choice of $k_2 = -0.1$ provides a direct inhibitory effect on the dynamics of Neuron 2 that makes flatter the ISI density (compare the right sides of Fig. 4 and Fig. 5). Finally, from all figures of this section, we note that as larger is the noise as more visible is the effect of the additional applied currents by interaction on each neuron, in both cases of the exciting and the inhibitory currents.

References

1. Arnold, L.: Stochastic Differential Equations: Theory and Applications. Wiley and Sons, New York (1974)
2. Buonocore, A., Nobile, A.G., Ricciardi, L.M.: A new integral equation for the evaluation of first-passage-time probability densities. Advances in Applied Probability 19, 784–800 (1987)
3. Buonocore, A., Caputo, L., Pirozzi, E., Ricciardi, L.M.: The first passage time problem for Gauss-diffusion processes: algorithmic approaches and applications to LIF neuronal model. Methodol. Comput. Appl. Probab. 13(1), 29–57 (2011)
4. Buonocore, A., Caputo, L., Pirozzi, E.: Gauss-Diffusion Processes for Modeling the Dynamics of a Couple of Interacting Neurons. Mathematical Biosciences and Engineering (in press)
5. Burkitt, A.N.: A review of the integrate-and-fire neuron model: I. Homogeneous synaptic input. Biol. Cybern. 95, 1–19 (2006)
6. Burkitt, A.N.: A review of the integrate-and-fire neuron model: II. Inhomogeneous synaptic input and network properties. Biol. Cybern. 95, 97–112 (2006)
7. Di Nardo, E., Nobile, A.G., Pirozzi, E., Ricciardi, L.M.: A computational approach to first-passage-time problems for Gauss-Markov processes. Adv. Appl. Prob. 33, 453–482 (2001)
8. Giorno, V., Nobile, A.G., Ricciardi, L.M.: On the asymptotic behaviour of first-passage-time densities for one-dimensional diffusion processes and varying boundaries. Adv. Appl. Prob. 22, 883–914 (1990)
9. Lansky, P., Sanda, P., He, J.: The parameters of the stochastic leaky integrate-and-fire neuronal model. J. Comp. NeuroSciences 21(2), 211–223 (2006)
10. Golomb, D., Ermentrout, G.B.: Bistability in pulse propagation in networks of excitatory and inhibitory populations. Phys. Rev. Lett. 86(18), 4179–4182 (2001)
11. Sakaguchi, H.: Oscillatory phase transition and pulse propagation in noisy integrate-and-fire neurons. Phys. Rev. E. Stat. Nonlin. Soft. Matter Phys. (2004)
12. Sakaguchi, H., Tobiishi, S.: Synchronization and spindle oscillation in noisy integrate-and-fire-or-burst neurons with inhibitory coupling. Progress of Theoretical Physics 114(3), 1–18 (2005)

Soft Control of Self-organized Locally Interacting Brownian Planar Agents

Guillaume Sartoretti* and Max-Olivier Hongler

Polytechnic Federal School of Lausanne (EPFL)
CH-1015 Lausanne, Switzerland
{guillaume.sartoretti,max.hongler}@epfl.ch
http://www.epfl.ch

Abstract. This contribution is addressed to the dynamics of heterogeneous interacting agents evolving on the plane. Heterogeneity is due to the presence of an unfiltered externally controllable fellow, a *shill*, which via mutual interactions ultimately drives (i.e. *soft controls*) the whole society towards a given goal. We are able to calculate relevant dynamic characteristics of this controllable agent. This opens the possibility to optimize the soft controlling of a whole society by infiltrating it with a properly designed shill. Numerical results fully corroborate our theoretical findings.

Keywords: homogeneous and heterogeneous Brownian agents, limited-range mutual interactions, soft control, mixed canonical-dissipative dynamics, mean-field description, analytical results.

1   Introduction

The *Soft Control* of a swarm of interacting agents consists in introducing an externally controllable agent into an homogeneous swarm of autonomous agents. By suitably choosing the externally controllable fellow, one ultimately can (softly) control the whole swarm. While her dynamics differs, the controllable infiltrated agent, often refered to as the *Shill* (SH), is detected by the other fellows as being an ordinary member of the society. The SH's influence can be used to stimulate specific positive features to the whole group (optimal driving to targets, enhancement of flocking capability, extra energy scavenging, etc. [1–3]). Alternatively the SH's presence may destroy the overall swarm's coherence [1]. Soft control is also commonly used in ethology, by introducing robotic shills in societies of animals, see for instance [4–6].

In the sequel, we consider an homogeneous swarm of Brownian agents following a planar mixed canonical-dissipative dynamics as introduced in [7]. After showing how the agents asymptotically converge to (and circulate on) a self-selected closed annular orbits on $\mathbb{R}^2$, we then introduce a SH agent into the swarm. We then use the SH's presence to soft control the angular speed of the whole society.

---

* Supported by the Swiss National Funds for Scientific Research.

R. Moreno-Díaz et al. (Eds.): EUROCAST 2013, Part I, LNCS 8111, pp. 45–52, 2013.

2 Interacting Diffusion Processes on $\mathbb{R}^2$

For $\overline{\mathbf{X}}(t) = (\mathbf{X}_1(t), \mathbf{X}_2(t), \cdots, \mathbf{X}_N(t)) \in \mathbb{R}^{2N}$ with $\mathbf{X}_k(t) = (x_{1,k}(t), x_{2,k}(t)) \in \mathbb{R}^2$, our class of dynamics is given by a collection of N mutually interacting planar Brownian agents evolving according to a set of Stochastic Differential Equations (SDE) on $\mathbb{R}^{2N}$:

$$
\begin{cases}
d\mathbf{X}_k(t) = dt\, [\mathcal{A}_k(t) - \Lambda\,(\mathcal{L}_{k,\rho}(t) - \mathcal{H}(\mathbf{X}_k))] \bigtriangledown \mathcal{H}(\mathbf{X}_k) + \sigma\, d\mathbf{W}_k(t), \\
\mathbf{X}_k(0) = \mathbf{X}_{0,k},
\end{cases}
\tag{1}
$$

where $\sigma, \Lambda \in \mathbb{R}^+$ are control parameters, and the definitions of the dynamical inputs are:

i) **the Hamiltonian function** $\mathcal{H}(x_1, x_2) : \mathbb{R}^2 \mapsto \mathbb{R}^+$ are used to define a family of closed, non-intersecting, planar curves with equations given by $[\mathcal{H}(x_1, x_2) - R] = 0, \forall\, R > 0$. We note $\bigtriangledown \mathcal{H}(\mathbf{X}_k) = \begin{pmatrix} \frac{\partial}{\partial x_1}\mathcal{H}(x_1, x_2) \\ \frac{\partial}{\partial x_2}\mathcal{H}(x_1, x_2) \end{pmatrix}\bigg|_{\mathbf{X}_k}$

ii) **The Tangent Dynamical Map at the Origin.** In absence of noise source ($\sigma \equiv 0$), the origin is a singular point of Eq.(1) and its associated linear map $\mathcal{A}_k(t)$:

$$
\mathcal{A}_k(t) = \begin{pmatrix} \frac{N_{k,\rho}(t)}{N} - \frac{1}{M} & \frac{N_{k,\rho}(t)}{N} \\ -\frac{N_{k,\rho}(t)}{N} & \frac{N_{k,\rho}(t)}{N} - \frac{1}{M} \end{pmatrix}
\tag{2}
$$

where $M \in [1, N] \subseteq \mathbb{R}^+$ is a control parameter and $(N_{k,\rho}(t)/N)$ is the fraction of the total swarm detected by agent a_k in the neighborhood $\mathcal{D}_{k,\rho}(t)$ defined as:

$$
\mathcal{D}_{k,\rho}(t) = \left\{ \mathbf{X} \in \mathbb{R}^2 \mid \|\mathbf{X} - \mathbf{X}_k(t)\|_2 \leq \rho \right\}
\tag{3}
$$

iii) **The Self-Adaptive Hamiltonian Level**. The scalar quantity:

$$
\mathcal{L}_{k,\rho}(t) := \frac{1}{N_{k,\rho}(t)} \sum_{i \in V_{k,\rho}(t)} \mathcal{H}(\mathbf{X}_i)
$$

where $N_{k,\rho}(t)$ has been defined in ii). The summation extends over the agents' set $V_{k,\rho}(t) := \{i \mid \mathbf{X}_i \in \mathcal{D}_{k,\rho}(t)\}$

iv) **The Noise Sources.** $d\mathbf{W}_k(t) = (dW_{1,k}(t), dW_{2,k}(t))$ are $2N$ independent standard White Gaussian Noise (WGN) processes

Proposition 1. *For $t \to \infty$, the dissipative dynamics Eq.(1) reaches a stationary regime characterized by the time-invariant probability product measure:*

$$
P_s(\overline{\mathbf{x}})\, d\mathbf{x} = [P_s(\mathbf{x})\, d\mathbf{x}]^N \quad \text{with} \quad P_s(\mathbf{x})\, d\mathbf{x} = \mathcal{Z}^{-1} \exp\left\{ -\frac{\Lambda}{\sigma^2}\, [\mathcal{L}_{s,\rho} - \mathcal{H}(\mathbf{x})]^2 \right\} d\mathbf{x}.
\tag{4}
$$

where $\mathcal{Z}$ is the normalization factor, and $\mathcal{L}_{s,\rho}$ is the stationary Hamiltonian level curve statistically reached by the agents.

Proof of Proposition 1

We first write the Fokker-Planck equation (FPE) associated with the diffusion process of Eq.(1):

$$\partial_t P(\overline{\mathbf{x}}, t | \overline{\mathbf{x}}_0) = -\nabla \cdot \left\{ [\mathcal{A}(t) \nabla \mathcal{H}(\mathbf{x}) - \nabla V_\rho(\overline{\mathbf{x}}, t)] \cdot P(\overline{\mathbf{x}}, t | \overline{\mathbf{x}}_0) + \frac{\sigma^2}{2} \nabla P(\overline{\mathbf{x}}, t | \overline{\mathbf{x}}_0) \right\}, \tag{5}$$

with $\mathcal{A}(t)$ the $(2N \times 2N)$ block-simplectic matrix

$$\mathcal{A}(t) := \begin{pmatrix} A_1(t) & & 0 \\ & \ddots & \\ 0 & & A_N(t) \end{pmatrix}, \quad \text{with } A_k(t) = \begin{pmatrix} 0 & \frac{N_{k,\rho}(t)}{N} \\ -\frac{N_{k,\rho}(t)}{N} & 0 \end{pmatrix}$$

The dissipative component of the drift is derived from the time-dependent generalized potential $V_\rho(\overline{\mathbf{x}}, t)$, which reads as:

$$V_\rho(\overline{\mathbf{x}}, t) = \sum_{k=1}^{N} \left\{ \overbrace{\left[\frac{N_{k,\rho}(t)}{N} - \frac{1}{M} \right]}^{:= \mathcal{R}_{k,\rho}(t)} + \frac{\Lambda}{2} [\mathcal{L}_{k,\rho}(t) - \mathcal{H}(\mathbf{X}_k)]^2 \right\} \nabla \mathcal{H}(\mathbf{x}). \tag{6}$$

The parameters $\mathcal{R}_{k,\rho}(t)$ and $\mathcal{L}_{k,\rho}(t)$ in Eq.(6) implicitly depend on the agents' configurations, implying that Eq.(5) is effectively a nonlinear FPE. The potential $V_\rho(\overline{\mathbf{x}}, t)$ is globally attractive on $\mathbb{R}^{2N}$ (i.e $V_\rho(\overline{\mathbf{x}}, t) \to \infty$ for $\|\overline{\mathbf{x}}\| \to \infty$). Global attraction on $\mathbb{R}^{2N}$ in Eq.(1) together with the WGN driving forces imply that the diffusive dynamics is **ergodic**. Hence, it exists a unique invariant measure $P_s(\overline{\mathbf{x}})$ implying that both $\mathcal{R}_{k,\rho}(t)$ and $\mathcal{L}_{k,\rho}(t)$ asymptotically converge towards stationary (time-independent) values $\mathcal{R}_{k,s,\rho}$ and $\mathcal{L}_{k,s,\rho}$. Moreover, as Eqs.(5) and (6) are invariant under permutations of the agents labeling, we shall have $\mathcal{R}_{k,s,\rho} =: \mathcal{R}_{s,\rho}$ and $\mathcal{L}_{k,s,\rho} =: \mathcal{L}_{s,\rho}$ ($\forall k$). Dissipation drives the system to its minimal energy configuration, leading to the specific values $\mathcal{R}_{s,\rho} \equiv 0$ and to $\lim_{t\to\infty} \mathcal{A}(t) = \mathcal{A}_s$ with:

$$\mathcal{A}_s := \begin{pmatrix} A_s & & 0 \\ & \ddots & \\ 0 & & A_s \end{pmatrix}, \quad A_s = \begin{pmatrix} 0 & \frac{1}{M} \\ -\frac{1}{M} & 0 \end{pmatrix}.$$

Observe that the gradient $\nabla V_\rho(\overline{\mathbf{x}}, t)$ is systematically orthogonal to the antisymmetric component $\mathcal{A}(t) \nabla \mathcal{H}(\mathbf{x})$. This remains true in the stationary regime $\mathcal{A}_s$, allowing us to write the stationary solution of the FPE Eq.(5) in the *product-form* $P_s(\overline{\mathbf{x}})$:

$$P_s(\overline{\mathbf{x}}) = [P_s(\mathbf{x})]^N = \left[\mathcal{N}^{-1} e^{\{V_{s,\rho}(\mathbf{x})\}} \right]^N, \tag{7}$$
$$V_{s,\rho}(\mathbf{x}) = +\frac{\gamma}{2} [\mathcal{L}_{s,\rho} - \mathcal{H}(\mathbf{x})]^2$$

with $\overline{\mathbf{x}} = (\mathbf{x}_1, \mathbf{x}_2, \cdots, \mathbf{x}_N) \in \mathbb{R}^{2N}$, $\mathbf{x}_k \in \mathbb{R}^2$. In Eq.(7), $\mathbf{x} \in \mathbb{R}^2$ stands for one representative agent in the swarm. The product form of $P_s(\overline{\mathbf{x}})$ explicitly shows that our dynamics propagates chaos, validating the use of a Mean Field (MF) approach, where the behaviour of a single agent of the swarm effectively reflects the global dynamics.

Here the stationary regime of the single representative agent $\mathbf{X}(t) = (x_1(t), x_2(t))$ is characterized by the invariant probability density $P_s(\mathbf{x})$:

$$0 = -\nabla \left\{ [\mathcal{A}_s \nabla \mathcal{H}(\mathbf{x}) - \nabla V_{s,\rho}(\mathbf{x})] \cdot P_s(\mathbf{x}) \right\} + \frac{\sigma^2}{2} \Delta P_s(\mathbf{x}), \tag{8}$$

Autoconsistency of the nonlinear FPE here implies:

$$\frac{N_{s,\rho}}{N} = \int_{\mathbf{x} \in D_{s,\rho}} P_s(\mathbf{x})\, dx_1\, dx_2 \left(= \frac{1}{M} \right) \tag{9}$$

where here $D_{s,\rho}$ is the stationary representative agent's neighborhood.

□

Corollary 1. *For the harmonic oscillator's Hamiltonian function*
$$\mathcal{H}(x_1, x_2) = 1/2\, (x_1^2 + x_2^2), \tag{10}$$

and with $\Lambda \to \infty$, the stationary probability measure converges to a uniform distribution of the agents on the limit cycle. Following the argument in the caption of Figure 1, the radius of the limit cycle can be in this case explicitly written as

$$\mathcal{L}_{s,\rho} = \frac{\rho}{\sqrt{2 - 2\cos(\frac{\pi}{M})}}. \tag{11}$$

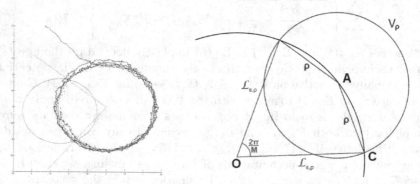

Fig. 1. Left: An example run with $N = 100$ agents, and a range $\rho = 1$. In black, the theoretic limit cycle, and in blue the positions through time of one agent.
Right: Geometric explanation of the computation of $\mathcal{L}_{s,\rho}$: In the stationary regime, each agent has in average $\frac{N}{M}$ agent in her neighborhood. As the agents are uniformly distributed on the limit cycle, the number of neighbors is directly correlated with the arc length contained within the neighborhood of each agent. Thus each agent's range exactly encompasses an arc of $\frac{2\pi}{M}$, and the rule of cosine in the triangle OAC leads to the result of Eq.(11).

3   Swarm Soft Controlling - Harmonic Oscillator Hamiltonian

Now we focus on cylindrically symmetric configurations involving the Hamiltonian Eq.(10), and for thiese cases we generalize Eq.(1) by allowing the agents to self-adapt their circulation velocities. This can be achieved by replacing the nominal matrix $\mathcal{A}_k(t)$ in Eq.(2) by $\mathbb{A}_k$:

$$\mathbb{A}_k = \begin{pmatrix} \frac{N_{k,\rho}(t)}{N} - \frac{1}{M} & \omega_k(t)\frac{N_{k,\rho}(t)}{N} \\ -\omega_k(t)\frac{N_{k,\rho}(t)}{N} & \frac{N_{k,\rho}(t)}{N} - \frac{1}{M} \end{pmatrix}, \tag{12}$$

where the now adaptive angular velocity $\omega_k(t)$ of agent a_k obeys to the relaxation dynamics:

$$\begin{cases} \dot{\omega}_k(t) = \gamma_1 \cdot [\langle\omega\rangle_{k,\rho}(t) - \omega_k(t)] + \gamma_2 \cdot [\Omega - \omega_k(t)], & \omega_k(0) = \omega_{0,k}, \\ \langle\omega\rangle_{k,\rho}(t) := \frac{1}{N_{k,\rho}(t)} \sum_{j \in V_{k,\rho}(t)} \omega_j(t), \end{cases}$$

(13)

with $\gamma_i > 0$ $(i = 1, 2)$.

Remark. The set of ODE's in Eq.(13) describes an autonomous, systematically dissipative linear dynamical system. Accordingly, the unique resulting attractor is here given by $\lim_{t \to \infty} \omega_k(t) = \Omega$, $\forall k$.

3.1 Inhomogeneous Swarm - Shill Soft Controlling Mode

Let us now introduce an externally controllable agent, to be called the *shill* (SH) agent, into the swarm. Agent SH is, without loss of generality, taken as a_1 and we assume that we can fix $\omega_1(t) \equiv \omega_s$. Regarding the radial dynamics, we assume that SH behaves as an ordinary agent. In presence of SH, the swarm is heterogeneous, thus precluding analytical approaches for general parameter ranges. Nevertheless, for limiting regimes, we will now see that our dynamics still lend itself to an approximate analytical treatment.

We assume in Eq.(1) that the signal to noise ratio (SNR) $(\Lambda/\sigma^2) \ll 1$. In absence of SH, the stationary regime of the homogeneous swarm uniformly distributes the agents along the arcs of a narrow annular ring with radius $\mathcal{L}_{s,\rho}$. The agents circulate with a common angular velocity $\omega_k \equiv \Omega$. Let us now introduce SH into the swarm.

We shall consider the cases where $\omega_s > \Omega$ (the other possibilities can be discussed along the same lines). Taking into account the presence of SH in the swarm, our goal is to first show that for $\langle\omega\rangle_{k,\rho}(t)$ in Eq.(13), we can approximately write:

$$\langle\omega\rangle_{k,\rho}(t) \simeq \begin{cases} \frac{\omega_s + (\frac{N}{M} - 1)\omega_k(t)}{N/M} & \text{when} \quad SH \in V_{k,\rho}(t), \\ \omega_k(t) & \text{otherwise.} \end{cases}$$

(14)

To heuristically derive Eq.(14), we assume that at initial time $t = -\infty$, we have an homogeneous population involving N agents. At time $t = 0^-$, this homogeneous swarm has reached its stationary regime, i.e. the agents are confined in a ring close to the cycle $\mathcal{L}_{s,\rho}$ and their stationary circulation has the common angular velocity $\omega_k \equiv \Omega$. For times $t \geq 0^+$, we switch on SH's action by imposing $\omega_1(t) \equiv \omega_s > \Omega$. Via mutual interactions, SH is able to enhance the a_k's angular velocities for $k = 2, \ldots, N$. Therefore, besides the intrinsic dissipation mechanism given in Eqs.(1) together with Eqs.(12) and (13), the a_k's $(k = 2, \ldots, N)$ do effectively scavenge rotational energy from SH and ultimately an energy balance will be reached.

For large populations N, we assume SH's influence to be **quasi-adiabatic**. That is to say, we assume that the a_k's distribution on the limit cycle $\mathcal{L}_{s,\rho}$

remains essentially unaltered. Since we choose SH's angular speed $\omega_s \equiv \omega_1 > \Omega$ and because SH itself circulates with high probability inside the thin annulus $\mathcal{L}_{s,\rho}$, SH periodically crosses the $V_{k,\rho}(t)$ for $k = 2, 3, \ldots, N$. During the SH's transit time inside $V_{k,\rho}(t)$, interaction with SH enhances ω_k. Conversely, when SH lies outside $V_{k,\rho}(t)$, then ω_k freely relaxes towards Ω. To be consistent with the adiabatic energy exchange assumption, the SH's influence on ω_k during one $V_{k,\rho}(t)$ over-crossing has to remain small. At a given time t, and for a tagged a_k ($k = 2, 3, \ldots, N$), two configurations are alternatively realized depending on whether SH belongs to $V_{k,\rho}(t)$ or not:

i) SH $\notin V_{k,\rho}(t)$: only regular neighbors surround a_k. Their individual speed very slightly differs from $\omega_k(t)$. These differences are due to SH leaving the neighbouring a_k's $V_{k,\rho}(t)$ at different successive times. Some of the neighbors of a_k will have an angular velocity slightly higher than $\omega_k(t)$ (the rapids), while others will have a slightly lower angular velocities (i.e. the slows). SH's constant rotation, always leaves a wake of agents with a slight angular velocity enhancement in SH's trail. Constant rotation implies that the rapids and slows are approximatively spatially distributed symmetrically with respect to a_k and close to the cycle $\mathcal{L}_{s,\rho}$. As the a_k's neighbors present in $V_{k,\rho}(t)$ are approximately uniformly distributed on the cycle $\mathcal{L}_{s,\rho}$, on average the numbers of rapids and slows are identical. Hence, the average speed of the agents in $V_{k,\rho}(t)$ is approximately $\omega_k(t)$ (i.e. the rapids approximately compensate for the slows).

ii) SH $\in V_{k,\rho}(t)$: here we invoke the fact that a_k has in average $\frac{N}{M}$ neighbors. Using i) for the $\frac{N}{M} - 1$ regular neighbors of a_k and taking into account SH's presence, the weighted average of the angular velocities leads to the first line in Eq.(14).

Using Eq.(14) into Eq.(13) enables to write:

$$
\dot{\omega}_k(t) = \begin{cases} (\gamma_1 \frac{M}{N} + \gamma_2) \cdot \left[\overbrace{\frac{\gamma_1 \frac{M}{N}\omega_s + \gamma_2 \Omega}{\gamma_1 \frac{M}{N} + \gamma_2}}^{\nu_1} - \omega_k(t) \right], \\[2ex] \gamma_2 \cdot \left[\underbrace{\Omega}_{\nu_2} - \omega_k(t) \right]. \end{cases} \tag{15}
$$

For an ultra-fast relaxation regime $\gamma_k \to \infty$ ($k = 1, 2$), Eq.(15) implies:

$$
\omega_k(t) \simeq \begin{cases} \nu_1 & \text{when SH in } V_{k,\rho}(t), \\ \nu_2 & \text{otherwise.} \end{cases} \tag{16}
$$

Now, we can calculate the time spend into the alternative states of Eq.(16). To this aim consider Figure 2, where we sketch the approximative resulting behavior for an arbitrary agent k together with SH.

In view of Figure 2, we now can write:

$$
\begin{cases} \frac{2\pi}{M} + T_1 \cdot \nu_1 = T_1 \cdot \omega_s & \Rightarrow \quad T_1 = \frac{2\pi}{M(\omega_s - \nu_1)}, \\[1ex] \frac{pi}{M} + T_2 \cdot \omega_s = T_2 \cdot \nu_2 + \frac{2M-1}{M}\pi & \Rightarrow \quad T_2 = \frac{(2M-2)\pi}{M(\omega_s - \nu_2)}. \end{cases} \tag{17}
$$

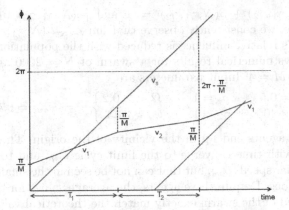

Fig. 2. Computation of the time intervals T_1 and T_2 spent by the agents in each of the states of Eq.(16). The state 1 starts when SH enters the agent's range (that is when their phase differs by $\frac{\pi}{M}$ in one direction), and lasts until they differ by $\frac{\pi}{M}$ in the other direction. Then, the time interval T_2 lasts until SH re-enters the agent's range, that is when their phases differ of $\frac{2M-1}{M}\pi$.

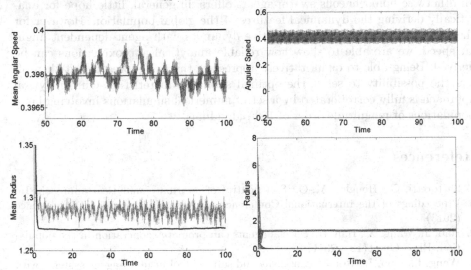

Fig. 3. Top left: In blue, the average angular speed of the regular agents, with in red its average over the period $t \in [50; 100]$. In black, the expected value $\omega_{ave} = 0.4$. right: Individual angular speeds of each agent as a function of time. Bottom left: In blue the average radius of the regular agents, and in red the radius of SH. In black, the expected value $\mathcal{L}_{s,\rho} =\simeq 1.31$. right: Individual radii of each agent as a function of time.

Hence, on a single time period $T = T_1 + T_2$, the resulting weighted average angular velocity yields:

$$\omega_{ave} = \frac{T_1 \cdot \nu_1 + T_2 \cdot \nu_2}{T_1 + T_2} = \underbrace{\frac{\gamma_2 N}{\gamma_1 + \gamma_2 N}}_{\alpha(N,\gamma_1,\gamma_2)} \cdot \Omega + \underbrace{\frac{\gamma_1}{\gamma_1 + \gamma_2 N}}_{\beta(N,\gamma_1,\gamma_2)} \cdot \omega_s.$$

Note that $\alpha(N, \gamma_1, \gamma_2) + \beta(N, \gamma_1, \gamma_2) = 1$ and $[\alpha(N, \gamma_1, \gamma_2)/\beta(N, \gamma_1, \gamma_2)] = N(\gamma_2/\gamma_1)$. Hence, we consistently observe that $\lim_{N\to\infty} \alpha(N, \gamma_1, \gamma_2) = 1$, showing that the SH's relative influence is reduced with the population size N.

Figure 3 shows numerical results for a swarm of $N = 2000$ agents for time $t \in [0; 100]$ with $M = 4$. Input parameters are

$$\left.\begin{array}{lll} \sigma = 0.5 & \rho = 1 & \Omega = -0.2 \\ \gamma_1 = 40 & \gamma_2 = 1 & \omega_s = 31.4 \end{array}\right\} \Rightarrow \omega_{ave} = 0.4.$$

Note that some agents end up in the vicinity of the origin. These agents will asymptotically with time converge to the limit cycle $\mathcal{L}_{s\rho}$, and to the theoretic consensual angular speed ω_{ave}, but that can not be seen in the small time window of these simulations. Despite these agents, the average values for the radius and the angular speed of the swarm exactly match the theoretical values.

4   Conclusion

The intrinsic swarm's heterogeneity due to the presence of a shill fellow into an otherwise homogeneous swarm agents offers, in general, little hope for analytically deriving the dynamical features of the global population. However for the present mixed canonical-dissipative dynamics with agent-dependent angular speed, we are able to show how reliable analytical approximations can be derived. Being able to quantitatively appreciate the shill's presence, it then offers the possibility to select the optimal shill's characteristics. Our analytical approach is fully corroborated by a set of numerical simulations involving large populations of magnitude order of 10^3 individuals.

References

1. Sartoretti, G., Hongler, M.-O.: Soft control of swarms - analytical approach. In: Proceedings of the International Conference on Agents and Artificial Intelligence (2013)
2. Han, J., Wang, X., Han, H.: Special agents can promote cooperation in the population. PLoS One 6(12) (2011)
3. Wang, L., Guo, L.: Robust consensus and soft control of multi-agent systems with noises. Journal of Systems Science and Complexity 21(3), 406–415 (2008)
4. Deneubourg, J.L., Bleuler, H., Gribovskiy, A., Halloy, J., Mondada, F.: Towards mixed societies of chickens and robots. In: IEEE/RSJ 2010 International Conference on Intelligent Robots and Systems, Conference Proceedings, pp. 4722–4728 (2010)
5. Caprari, G., Rivaullt, C., Asadpour, M., Ame, J.M., Detrain, C., Correl, N., Martinoli, A., Halloy, J., Sempo, G., Mondada, F.: Social integration of robots into groups of cockroaches to control self-organized choices. Science 318, 1155 (2007)
6. Dyer, J.R.G., Faria, J.J., Krause, J.: A novel method for investigating the collective behaviour of fish: Introducing 'robofish'. Behavioral Ecology and Sociobiology 64(8), 1211–1218 (2010)
7. Sartoretti, G., Hongler, M.-O.: Self-organized mixed canonical-dissipative dynamics for brownian planar agents. Cybernetics and Physics (in press)

Some Results on Brownian Motion Perturbed by Alternating Jumps in Biological Modeling

Antonio Di Crescenzo[1], Antonella Iuliano[2], and Barbara Martinucci[1]

[1] Dipartimento di Matematica, Università di Salerno
I-84084 Fisciano (SA), Italy
{adicrescenzo,bmartinucci}@unisa.it
[2] CNR, Istituto per le Applicazioni del Calcolo (IAC), Naples, Italy
a.iuliano@na.iac.cnr.it

Abstract. We consider the model of random evolution on the real line consisting in a Brownian motion perturbed by alternating jumps. We give the probability density of the process and pinpoint a connection with the limit density of a telegraph process subject to alternating jumps. We study the first-crossing-time probability in two special cases, in the presence of a constant upper boundary.

Keywords: Brownian motion, alternating jumps, first-crossing time.

1 Introduction

In certain biological contexts some phenomena can be viewed as subject to streams of perturbations of various nature and at different scales. We consider systems which evolve according to the Brownian motion and are subject to perturbations driven by suitable stochastic processes. Usually such perturbations produce abrupt changes on the state of the process and can be described by jumps. These phenomena can be often modeled as the superposition of Brownian motion and a pure jump process.

Numerous examples of random motions perturbed by jumps arise in the biological literature. For instance Berg and Brown [1] described the motion of microorganisms performed as gradual or abrupt changes in direction. Moreover, a general framework for the dispersal of cell or organisms is provided in Othmer *et al.* [10], where a position jump process is proposed to describe a motion consisting of sequence of alternative pauses and jumps. See also the general mechanistic movement-model framework employed for biological populations by Lutscher *et al.* [8]. Furthermore we recall the paper by Garcia *et al.* [7], where Brownian-type hopping motions of various *Daphnia* species are studied in detail.

In neuronal modeling framework the Brownian motion process describes the dynamics of the membrane potential in an integrate-and-fire model. This is characterized by the superposition of downward and upward jumps that correspond respectively to the effect of excitatory and inhibitory pulses in a neuronal network (see, for instance, Sacerdote and Sirovich [12] and [13], and references therein).

R. Moreno-Díaz et al. (Eds.): EUROCAST 2013, Part I, LNCS 8111, pp. 53–60, 2013.

A further model is provided by the description of mechanisms of acto-myosin interaction, that is responsible for the force generation during muscle contraction. In this context the rising phase dynamics can be viewed as the superposition of a Brownian motion and a jump process (see, e.g. Buonocore *et al.* [3] and [4]).

Stimulated by the need to give formal and analytical tools to describe biological phenomena perturbed by dichotomous streams, in this paper we study some features of a Brownian motion perturbed by jumps driven by an alternating renewal process. In Section 2 we provide the probability law, mean and variance of such stochastic process, and notice a connection with the jump-telegraph process. Section 3 is devoted to the first-crossing-time problem through a constant boundary. We study the probability that the first-crossing time occurs before or at the occurrence of the first jump.

2   Brownian Motion Perturbed by Alternating Jumps

Let $\{W(t), t > 0\}$ be a Wiener process with drift $\mu \in \mathbb{R}$ and infinitesimal variance σ^2, with $\sigma > 0$. We consider a particle moving on the real line according to $W(t)$, and perturbed by alternating jumps driven by a Poisson process $\{N(t), t > 0\}$ with parameter $\lambda > 0$. Assume that $N(t)$ is independent of $W(t)$. The jumps have constant size $\alpha > 0$, and are directed forward and backward alternately. Moreover, the sequence of jumps is regulated by a Bernoulli random variable B, such as at the k-th event of $N(t)$ the particle performs a displacement $(-1)^{k+B}\alpha$, for $k = 1, 2, 3, \ldots$, with B independent of processes $W(t)$ and $N(t)$. Hence, if $B = 1$ (with probability p) then the first jump is forward and thus the sequence of jumps is $\alpha, -\alpha, \alpha, -\alpha, \ldots$, whereas if $B = 0$ (with probability $1 - p$) the sequence of jumps is $-\alpha, \alpha, -\alpha, \alpha, \ldots$.

Let us consider the stochastic process $\{X(t), t > 0\}$, where

$$X(t) = W(t) + \alpha \sum_{k=1}^{N(t)} (-1)^{k+B}, \qquad t > 0. \tag{1}$$

According to the above assumptions, $X(t)$ gives the position of the particle at time t. A sample-path of $X(t)$ is shown in Figure 1, where the first jump is upward. For $x \in \mathbb{R}$ and $t > 0$ let the probability density of $X(t)$ be denoted as

$$f_X(x, t) = \frac{\partial}{\partial x} P\{X(t) \leq x\}. \tag{2}$$

Hereafter we express the density (2) as a time-varying mixture of three Gaussian densities. It involves the following probabilities, for $t > 0$:

$$\pi_{\mathrm{o}}(t) = P\{N(t)\,\mathrm{odd}\} = \sum_{n=0}^{+\infty} \frac{e^{-\lambda t}(\lambda t)^{2n+1}}{(2n+1)!} = e^{-\lambda t}\sinh(\lambda t) = \frac{1 - e^{-2\lambda t}}{2},$$

$$\pi_{\mathrm{e}}(t) = P\{N(t)\,\mathrm{even}\} = \sum_{n=0}^{+\infty} \frac{e^{-\lambda t}(\lambda t)^{2n}}{(2n)!} = e^{-\lambda t}\cosh(\lambda t) = \frac{1 + e^{-2\lambda t}}{2}, \tag{3}$$

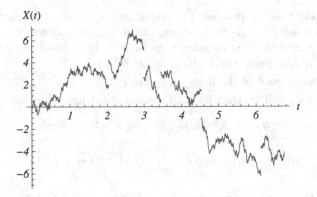

Fig. 1. A simulated sample-path of $X(t)$, for $\mu = 0$, $\sigma = 2$, $\alpha = 2.5$ and $\lambda = 1$

and the Gaussian probability density of process $W(t)$, given by

$$f_W(x,t) := \frac{1}{\sqrt{2\pi\sigma^2 t}} \exp\left\{ -\frac{(x - \mu t)^2}{2\sigma^2 t} \right\}, \quad x \in \mathbb{R},\ t > 0. \tag{4}$$

Proposition 1. *For $x \in \mathbb{R}$, $t > 0$, the probability density of $X(t)$ is:*

$$f_X(x,t) = \pi_e(t)\, f_W(x,t) + \pi_o(t)\left[p\, f_W(x - \alpha, t) + (1 - p) f_W(x + \alpha, t) \right]. \tag{5}$$

Moreover, mean and variance of process (1) are, for $t > 0$,

$$E[X(t)] = \mu t + \pi_o(t)(2p - 1)\alpha, \qquad Var[X(t)] = \sigma^2 t. \tag{6}$$

Remark 1. It is worthwhile noting that when $p = 1/2$, $\mu = 0$ and in the limit as $\lambda \to +\infty$, the density (5) tends to the function $g_1(x,t)$ given in Proposition 4.3 of Di Crescenzo and Martinucci [5], which is the limit density of a telegraph process subject to deterministic jumps occurring at velocity reversals. This confirms that under suitable scaling assumptions the density of the Wiener process with alternating jumps is the limit of the density of a telegraph process subject to the same kind of jumps, this being in agreement to analogous results holding in the absence of jumps (see Orsingher [9]).

3 First-Crossing-Time Problem

In this section we consider the first-crossing-time problem of process $X(t)$ through a constant boundary. We aim to determine the first-crossing-time probability in two different cases, i.e. when the first passage of $X(t)$ through the boundary occurs (i) before the first jump, or (ii) at the occurrence of first jump.

Let J_k be the random time in which the moving particle performs the k-th jump, with $k = 1, 2, \ldots$. We denote by

$$T_\beta^X = \inf\{t > 0 : X(t) > \beta\}, \qquad X(0) = 0 \text{ a.s.}, \tag{7}$$

the first-crossing time of process $X(t)$ through the upper boundary $\beta > 0$, so that the first crossing occurs from below. In the following, we aim to investigate the probability that the first-crossing time of $X(t)$ through β occurs

(i) before the first jump takes place, i.e. $P[T_\beta^X < J_1]$,

(ii) at the occurrence of the first jump, i.e. $P[T_\beta^X = J_1]$.

The case $T_\beta^X > J_1$ will be the object of a subsequent investigation.

Proposition 2. *For $\beta > 0$, $\lambda > 0$, $\mu \in \mathbb{R}$ and $\sigma > 0$ we have*

$$P[T_\beta^X < J_1] = \exp\left\{ -\frac{\beta}{\sigma^2}\left[\sqrt{\mu^2 + 2\lambda\sigma^2} - \mu\right]\right\}. \tag{8}$$

Proof. Under the given assumptions, since J_1 has exponential distribution with parameter λ, we get

$$P[T_\beta^X < J_1] = E[P[T_\beta^X < J_1 | T_\beta^X]] = E[e^{-\lambda T_\beta^X}].$$

Hence, recalling that the probability density of (7) is given by (cf. Eq. 2.0.2, p. 223, of Borodin and Salminen [2])

$$f_{T_\beta^X}(t) = \frac{\beta}{\sqrt{2\pi\sigma^2 t^3}} \exp\left\{-\frac{(\beta - \mu t)^2}{2\sigma^2 t}\right\}, \qquad t > 0,$$

rearranging the terms we have

$$P[T_\beta^X < J_1] = \int_0^{+\infty} e^{-\lambda t} f_{T_\beta^X}(t)\, dt$$

$$= e^{\beta\mu/\sigma^2} \int_0^{+\infty} e^{-\left(\lambda + \frac{\mu^2}{2\sigma^2}\right)t} \frac{\beta}{\sqrt{2\pi\sigma^2 t^3}} e^{-\beta^2/(2\sigma^2 t)}\, dt.$$

Recalling Eq. (28) of § 4.5 of Erdélyi *et al.* [6] we thus obtain

$$P[T_\beta^X < J_1] = e^{\beta\mu/\sigma^2} e^{-\sqrt{\frac{2\beta^2}{\sigma^2}\left(\lambda + \frac{\mu^2}{2\sigma^2}\right)}},$$

so that Eq. (8) immediately follows.

From Eq. (8) we note that $P[T_\beta^X < J_1]$ is increasing in μ and σ, whereas it is decreasing in β and λ. Figure 2 shows some plots of such probability.

Proposition 3. *For $\beta > 0$, $0 < p < 1$, $\lambda > 0$, $\mu \in \mathbb{R}$ and $\sigma > 0$ we have*

$$P[T_\beta^X = J_1] = \begin{cases} p\, e^{\frac{\beta(\mu-\gamma)}{\sigma^2}} \left\{ e^{-\frac{\alpha\mu}{\sigma^2}}\left[\cosh\left(\frac{\alpha\gamma}{\sigma^2}\right) + \frac{\mu}{\gamma}\sinh\left(\frac{\alpha\gamma}{\sigma^2}\right)\right] - 1\right\}, & 0 < \alpha \leq \beta, \\[2ex] p\left\{ 1 - e^{\frac{\beta(\mu-\gamma)}{\sigma^2}} - \left(1 - \frac{\mu}{\gamma}\right) e^{-\frac{\alpha(\gamma+\mu)}{\sigma^2}} e^{\frac{\beta\mu}{\sigma^2}} \sinh\left(\frac{\beta\gamma}{\sigma^2}\right)\right\}, & \alpha \geq \beta, \end{cases} \tag{9}$$

where we have set $\gamma = \sqrt{\mu^2 + 2\lambda\sigma^2}$.

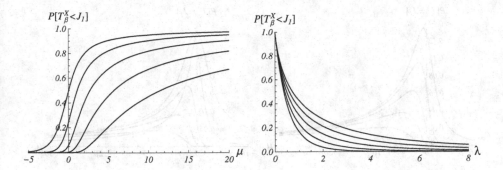

Fig. 2. Probability (8) for $-5 \le \mu \le 20$, when $\lambda = 1$, $\sigma = 1$ and $\beta = 0.5, 1, 2, 4, 8$ (from top to bottom, left plot) and for $0 \le \lambda \le 8$, when $\beta = 2$, $\mu = 1$ and $\sigma = 0.5, 1, 1.5, 2, 2.5$ (from bottom to top, right plot)

Proof. By conditioning on the instant of the first jump and exploiting the properties of the first-crossing times we have

$$
\begin{aligned}
P[T_\beta^X = J_1] &= E[P[T_\beta^X = J_1 | J_1]] \\
&= E[P[\beta - \alpha \le W(J_1^-) < \beta, T_\beta^W > J_1^-, B = 1 | J_1]].
\end{aligned}
\tag{10}
$$

Let us consider the β-avoiding density of process $W(t)$:

$$
\begin{aligned}
f_W^{\langle\beta\rangle}(x,t) &:= \frac{\partial}{\partial x} P[W(t) \le x, T_\beta^W > t] \\
&= f_W(x,t) - \exp\left\{ -\frac{2\mu(\beta - x)}{\sigma^2} \right\} f_W(2\beta - x, t),
\end{aligned}
\tag{11}
$$

where f_W is the density of $W(t)$, given in (4), and where the last equality follows from a suitable symmetry property of $W(t)$ (see, for instance, Example 5.4 of Ricciardi *et al.* [11]). Due to (10) we thus have

$$
P[T_\beta^X = J_1] = p \int_0^{+\infty} \lambda e^{-\lambda t} \int_{\beta-\alpha}^\beta f_W^{\langle\beta\rangle}(x,t) \, dx \, dt.
$$

Making use of Eq. (11) after some calculations we get, for $\gamma = \sqrt{\mu^2 + 2\lambda\sigma^2}$,

$$
\begin{aligned}
P[T_\beta^X = J_1] = \frac{\lambda p}{\sqrt{\mu^2 + 2\lambda\sigma^2}} \int_{\beta-\alpha}^\beta \bigg[&\exp\left\{ \frac{\mu x - |x|\gamma}{\sigma^2} \right\} \\
&- \exp\left\{ -\frac{2\mu}{\sigma^2}(\beta - x) \right\} \exp\left\{ \frac{\mu x - |x - 2\beta|\gamma}{\sigma^2} \right\} \bigg] \, dx.
\end{aligned}
\tag{12}
$$

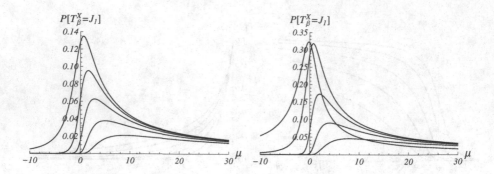

Fig. 3. Probability (9) for $-10 \leq \mu \leq 30$, when $p = 1$, $\lambda = 1$, $\sigma = 1$ and $\beta = 0.5, 1, 2, 4, 8$ (from top to bottom near the origin), for $\alpha = 0.5$ (left plot) and $\alpha = 1$ (right plot)

Noting that

$$\int_{\beta-\alpha}^{\beta} \exp\left\{\frac{\mu x - |x|\gamma}{\sigma^2}\right\} dx$$

$$= \begin{cases} \frac{(\gamma+\mu)}{2\lambda}\left[\exp\left\{\frac{(\beta-\alpha)(\mu-\gamma)}{\sigma^2}\right\} - \exp\left\{\frac{\beta(\mu-\gamma)}{\sigma^2}\right\}\right], & 0 < \alpha \leq \beta, \\ \frac{\gamma}{\lambda} - \frac{1}{2\lambda}\left[(\gamma-\mu)\exp\left\{\frac{(\beta-\alpha)(\gamma+\mu)}{\sigma^2}\right\} + (\gamma+\mu)\exp\left\{\frac{\beta(\mu-\gamma)}{\sigma^2}\right\}\right], & \alpha \geq \beta, \end{cases}$$

and

$$\int_{\beta-\alpha}^{\beta} \exp\left\{-\frac{2\mu}{\sigma^2}(\beta - x)\right\}\exp\left\{\frac{\mu x - |x - 2\beta|\gamma}{\sigma^2}\right\} dx$$

$$= \frac{\gamma-\mu}{2\lambda}\exp\left\{\frac{\beta(\mu-\gamma)}{\sigma^2}\right\}\left[1 - \exp\left\{-\frac{\alpha(\mu+\gamma)}{\sigma^2}\right\}\right],$$

Eq. (9) thus finally follows from Eq. (12).

Remark 2. From Eq. (9) we have:

$$\lim_{\lambda\to+\infty} P[T_\beta^X = J_1] = \begin{cases} 0, & \alpha < \beta, \\ p/2, & \alpha = \beta, \\ p, & \alpha > \beta, \end{cases} \qquad \lim_{\alpha\to+\infty} P[T_\beta^X = J_1] = p\left\{1 - e^{\frac{\beta(\mu-\gamma)}{\sigma^2}}\right\},$$

$$\lim_{\beta\to+\infty} P[T_\beta^X = J_1] = \lim_{\mu\to+\infty} P[T_\beta^X = J_1] = \lim_{\sigma\to+\infty} P[T_\beta^X = J_1] = 0.$$

Moreover,

$$\lim_{\sigma\to0} P[T_\beta^X = J_1] = P(\beta-\alpha < \mu J_1 < \beta) = \begin{cases} p\,e^{-\beta\lambda/\mu}\left(e^{\alpha\lambda/\mu} - 1\right), & \mu \geq 0,\, \alpha \leq \beta, \\ 0, & \mu \leq 0,\, \alpha \leq \beta, \\ p\left(1 - e^{-\beta\lambda/\mu}\right), & \mu \geq 0,\, \alpha \geq \beta, \\ p\left(1 - e^{-(\beta-\alpha)\lambda/\mu}\right), & \mu \leq 0,\, \alpha \geq \beta. \end{cases}$$

$$(13)$$

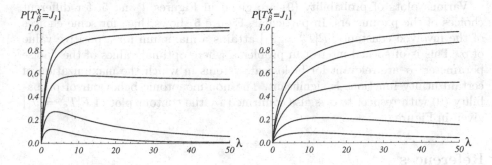

Fig. 4. Probability (9) for $0 \leq \lambda \leq 50$, when $p = 1$, $\mu = 1$, $\beta = 1$ and $\alpha = 0.5, 0.75, 1, 1.25, 1.5$ (from bottom to top), for $\sigma = 1$ (left plot) and $\sigma = 2$ (right plot)

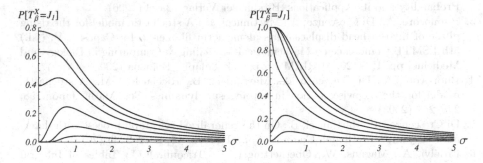

Fig. 5. Probability (9) for $0 \leq \sigma \leq 5$, with $p = 1$, $\beta = 1$, $\lambda = 1$ and $\alpha = 0.5, 0.75, 1, 1.25, 1.5, 1.75$ (from bottom to top), for $\mu = -0.5$ (left plot) and $\mu = 0.1$ (right plot)

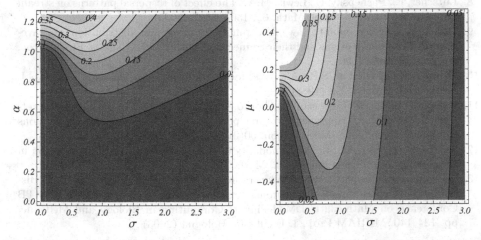

Fig. 6. Contour plot of (9) for $0 \leq \sigma \leq 3$, $p = 1$, $\beta = 1$, $\lambda = 1$, with $0 \leq \alpha \leq 1.25$, $\mu = -0.5$ (left plot), and $-0.5 \leq \mu \leq 0.5$, $\alpha = 0.8$ (right plot)

Various plots of probability (9) are given in Figures 4 and 5, for different choices of the parameters. In particular, Figure 5 shows that, for some choices of the involved constants, $P[T_\beta^X = J_1]$ attains a maximum for a positive value of σ. This is of special interest in problems where optimal values of the "noise parameter" σ are relevant for biological systems in which the maximization of certain utility functions is significant. The non-monotonic behaviour of probability (9) with respect to σ is also confirmed by the contour plot of $P[T_\beta^X = J_1]$ given in Figure 6.

References

1. Berg, H.C., Brown, D.A.: Chemotaxis in Escherichia coli analysed by three-dimensional tracking. Nature 239, 500–504 (1972)
2. Borodin, A.N., Salminen, P.: Handbook of Brownian motion – facts and formulae. Probability and its Applications. Birkhäuser Verlag, Basel (1996)
3. Buonocore, A., Di Crescenzo, A., Martinucci, B.: A stochastic model for the rising phase of myosin head displacements along actin filaments. In: Capasso, V. (ed.) 5th ESMTB Conference on Mathematical Modelling & Computing in Biology and Medicine, pp. 121–126. MIRIAM Proj., 1, Esculapio, Bologna (2003)
4. Buonocore, A., Di Crescenzo, A., Martinucci, B., Ricciardi, L.M.: A stochastic model for the stepwise motion in actomyosin dynamics. Sci. Math. Japon. 58, 245–254 (2003)
5. Di Crescenzo, A., Martinucci, B.: On the generalized telegraph process with deterministic jumps. Methodol. Comput. Appl. Probab. 15, 2012–2235 (2013)
6. Erdélyi, A., Magnus, W., Oberhettinger, F., Tricomi, F.G.: Tables of Integral Transforms, vol. I. McGraw-Hill Publisher, New York (1954)
7. Garcia, R., Moss, F., Nihongi, A., Strickler, J.R., Göller, S., Erdmann, U., Schimansky-Geier, L., Sokolov, I.M.: Optimal foraging by zooplankton within patches: the case of Daphnia. Math. Biosci. 207, 165–188 (2007)
8. Lutscher, F., Pachepsky, E., Lewis, M.A.: The effect of dispersal patterns on stream populations. SIAM J. Appl. Math. 65, 1305–1327 (2005)
9. Orsingher, E.: Probability law, flow function, maximum distribution of wave-governed random motions and their connections with Kirchoff's laws. Stoch. Proc. Appl. 34, 49–66 (1990)
10. Othmer, H.G., Dunbar, S.R., Alt, W.: Models of dispersal in biological systems. J. Math. Biol. 26, 263–298 (1988)
11. Ricciardi, L.M., Di Crescenzo, A., Giorno, V., Nobile, A.G.: An outline of theoretical and algorithmic approaches to first passage time problems with applications to biological modeling. Math. Japon. 50(2), 247–322 (1999)
12. Sacerdote, L., Sirovich, R.: Multimodality of the interspike interval distribution in a simple jump-diffusion model. Sci. Math. Japon. 58, 307–322 (2003)
13. Sacerdote, L., Sirovich, R.: A Wiener process with inverse Gaussian time distributed jumps as a model for neuronal activity. In: Capasso, V. (ed.) 5th ESMTB Conference on Mathematical Modelling & Computing in Biology and Medicine, pp. 134–140. MIRIAM Proj., 1, Esculapio, Bologna (2003)

A Stochastic Gompertz Model with Jumps for an Intermittent Treatment in Cancer Growth

Virginia Giorno[1] and Serena Spina[2]

[1] Dipartimento di Studi e Ricerche Aziendali
(Management & Information Technology)
Università di Salerno, Via Ponte don Melillo, Fisciano (SA), Italy
[2] Dipartimento di Matematica
Università di Salerno, Via Ponte don Melillo, Fisciano (SA), Italy
{giorno,sspina}@unisa.it

Abstract. To analyze the effect of a therapeutic program that provides intermittent suppression of cancer cells, we suppose that the Gompertz stochastic diffusion process is influenced by jumps that occur according to a probability distribution, producing instantaneous changes of the system state. In this context a jump represents an application of the therapy that leads the cancer mass to a return state randomly chosen. In particular, constant and exponential intermittence distribution are considered for different choices of the return state. We perform several numerical analyses to understand the behavior of the process for different choices of intermittence and return point distributions.

1 Introduction

Growing attention is devoted to the analysis of growth models because they play an important role in many fields such as economy, biology, medicine, ecology. These models are described generally via a deterministic differential equation in which it introduces the effect of random oscillations for modeling environmental fluctuations that are not captured by deterministic models. The curves that best describe the phenomenon of growth are of exponential type characterized by the presence of a carring capacity that represents the limit of the size of the population. Among all the exponential growths, the Gompertz curve plays an important role because in several contexts it seems to fit experimental data in a reasonable precise way ([5], [8]). In particular, various stochastic models based on this curve have been proposed recently to analyze the evolution of a tumor mass subject to anti-proliferative or pro-apoptotic therapies that alter the growth rates of cells ([1], [4]).

In this paper, we consider a diffusion process $\{X(t), t > 0\}$ based on the Gompertz model to construct the corresponding process with jumps $X_J(t)$ in order to analyze the effect of a therapeutic program that provides intermittent suppression of cancer cells. The process $X_J(t)$ consists of recurring cycles whose

R. Moreno-Díaz et al. (Eds.): EUROCAST 2013, Part I, LNCS 8111, pp. 61–68, 2013.

duration is described by a random variable, interjump interval, that represents the time elapsing between successive jumps or applications of the therapy.

The paper is organized as follows. In Section 2 we introduce the model. To analyze the evolution of $X_J(t)$ we study its transition probability density function (pdf), the average state of the system, representing the mean size of the tumor, and the number of therapy applications to be carried out in time intervals of fixed amplitude. In Section 3, we focus our attention on two probability distributions for the interjump intervals and for each of these we consider three distributions for the random variable describing the return point, because we want to take into account that the therapy would not be precise. Finally, in Section 4, various simulations are performed in order to understand the behavior of the process for different choices of intermittence and return point distributions.

2   The Model

Let $\{X(t),\, t > 0\}$ be the Gompertz stochastic process, it is described by the following stochastic differential equation

$$dX(t) = X(t)\left[\alpha - \beta \ln X(t)\right] dt + \sigma X(t)\, dW(t)$$

where $\alpha, \beta \geq 0$ denote growth and decay rates respectively, $\sigma > 0$ is the amplitude of the random fluctuations and $W(t)$ is a standard Wiener process. The time homogeneous process $X(t)$ is defined in $I = (0, \infty)$ and it is characterized by a lognormal pdf:

$$f(x,t|y) = \frac{1}{x\,\sqrt{2\,\pi\,V^2(t)}}\, \exp\left\{\frac{[\ln x - M(t|\ln y)]^2}{2\,V^2(t)}\right\}, \qquad (1)$$

where

$$M(t|y) = e^{-\beta(t)}\log y + \frac{\sigma^2/2 - \alpha}{\beta}\left(1 - e^{-\beta t}\right), \qquad V^2(t) = \frac{\sigma^2}{2\beta}\left(1 - e^{-2\beta t}\right).$$

Morever, the moments of $X(t)$ are

$$\mu^{(n)}(t|y) = \exp\left\{n\,M(t|\ln y)] + \frac{n^2}{2}\,V^2(t)\right\}. \qquad (2)$$

In order to analyze the effect of a therapeutic program that provides intermittent suppression of cancer cells, (cf. [3], [7]), we suppose that $X(t)$ is influenced by jumps that occur according to a probability distribution, producing instantaneous changes of the system state. More precisely, we define the resulting process with jumps $X_J(t)$ as follows (cf. [6]). Starting from $X_J(0) = X(0) = x_0$, $X_J(t)$ evolves as $X(t)$ as long as a jump occurs leading the process in a state $\rho > 0$ randomly chosen according to the probability density $\phi(x)$; from here, after a variable time interval, coinciding with the duration of the therapeutic application, $X_J(t)$ evolves with the same dynamics of $X(t)$ as long as another jump occurs, representing a new application of the therapy, which leads $X_J(t)$ in ρ, and so on. The process $X_J(t)$ consists of recurring cycles $\mathcal{I}_1, \mathcal{I}_2 \ldots$ whose durations are described by the independent and identically distributed random variables $I_1, I_2, \ldots$ with pdf $\psi(\cdot)$. Moreover, we denote by $\Theta_1, \Theta_2, \ldots$ the times in which the jumps occur. The variables I_k and Θ_k are related, indeed it results: $\Theta_1 = I_1$ and for $k > 1$ one has $\Theta_k = I_1 + I_2 + \ldots I_k$. Furthermore, for $0 < \tau < t$, $\xi_t(\tau)d\tau \sim P(\tau < \Theta_i < \tau + d\tau)$ represents the probability that a jump occurs in the infinitesimal interval $(\tau, \tau + d\tau)$. The transition density of $X_J(t)$ can be expressed in terms of the transition pdf of $X(t)$ via the following relations:

$$f_J(x, t|y) = R_t(0)\, f(x, t|y) + \int_0^t \xi_t(\tau)\, R_t(\tau) \left(\int_0^\infty \phi(z)\, f(x, t - \tau|z)\, dz \right) d\tau, \tag{3}$$

where $R_t(\tau) = 1 - P(\tau < I_k < t) = 1 - \int_\tau^t \psi(s)\, ds$ and $f(x, t|y)$ is given in (1). The first term represents the case in which there aren't jumps between 0 and t. The second term analyses the case in which at the time $0 < \tau < t$ the last jump occurs and then the process starts at ρ and evolves according to $X(t)$ to reach the state x in the time interval of width $t - \tau$.

The moments of $X_J(t)$, $\mu_J^{(n)}(t|y, \tau)$, follow from (3):

$$\mu_J^{(n)}(t|y) = R_t(0)\mu^{(n)}(t|y) + \int_0^t \xi_t(\tau)\, R_t(\tau) \left(\int_0^\infty \phi(z)\, \mu^{(n)}(t - \tau|z)\, dz \right) d\tau \tag{4}$$

with $\mu^{(n)}(t|y)$ given in (2). Moreover, we consider the stochastic process $N(t)$ representing the number of therapeutic treatments to be applied until a fixed time t.

In the following we analyze some therapeutic protocols assuming that different pdf's characterize the interjump intervals I_k.

3 Analysis of Some Intermittent Therapeutic Treatments

In the present section we consider two kinds of intermittent therapeutic treatments defined in terms of the pdf's characterizing the random variables I_k. In particular, we assume that the function ψ is a degenerate pdf (constant intermittence) and an exponential pdf (exponential intermittence). Furthermore, for the specified ψ we assume three pdf's for the random variable ρ: degenerate, uniform and bounded bi-exponential. In the first case we suppose that the therapy is so precise that the process jumps exactly in the chosen point; otherwise the therapy would lead the cancer mass in a its neighborhood of a certain amplitude without any preferences, in the first case; with the other choice the situation is similar, but ρ is the favorite point.

3.1 Constant Intermittence Therapeutic Treatment

We assume that intermittent therapeutic treatments are at fixed time intervals of duration $1/\zeta$, $(\zeta > 0)$ so that I_k can be described by a degenerate pdf

$\psi(t) = \delta\left(t - \frac{1}{\zeta}\right)$, where $\delta(\cdot)$ is the Dirac delta-function. In this case the time instant $\Theta_k = k/\zeta$, almost surely (a.s.). Let N_t the number of treatments to be applied until the time t, one has that

$$N_t = \sum_{k=1}^{\infty} H\left(t - \frac{k}{\zeta}\right),$$

where $H(x) = \int_{-\infty}^{x} \delta(u)\, du$ denotes the Heaviside unit step function. Note that in this case $\xi_t(\tau) = \delta\left(\tau - \frac{N_t}{\zeta}\right)$ and $R_t(\tau) = H\left(1/\zeta - t\right) + H\left(\tau - 1/\zeta\right)$ so that

$$\mu_J^{(n)}(t|y) = \begin{cases} \mu^{(n)}(t|y), & t < 1/\zeta \\ \int_0^{\infty} \phi(z) \mu^{(n)}\left(t - \frac{N_t}{\zeta}|z\right) dz, & t > 1/\zeta. \end{cases} \tag{5}$$

Hence, $\mu_J^{(n)}(t|y) \equiv \mu^{(n)}(t|y)$ for $t < 1/\zeta$.

Case a): Degenerate ρ. We suppose that $\phi(z) = \delta(z - \rho)$, is a degenerate distribution in ρ. In this case from (5) one has:

$$\mu_J^{(n)}(t|y) = \mu^{(n)}\left(t - \frac{N_t}{\zeta}|\rho\right), \qquad t > 1/\zeta.$$

Case b): Uniform ρ. We consider $\phi(z) = \frac{1}{2l}$ for $z \in [\rho - l, \rho + l]$. In this case (5) becomes:

$$\mu_J^{(n)}(t|y) = \frac{1}{2l} \int_{\rho-l}^{\rho+l} \mu^{(n)}\left(t - \frac{N_t}{\zeta}|z\right) dz, \qquad t > 1/\zeta.$$

In particular one has:

$$\mu_J^{(n)}(t|y) = \frac{1}{2l} \exp\left\{ \frac{n^2}{2}\sigma^2(1 - e^{-2\beta(t-k/\zeta)}) - n\frac{\sigma^2/2 - \alpha}{\beta}(1 - e^{-\beta(t-k/\zeta)}) \right\}$$
$$\times \frac{1}{n(e^{-\beta(t-k/\zeta)} + 1)}\left[(\rho + l)^{ne^{-\beta(t-k/\zeta)}+1} - (\rho - l)^{ne^{-\beta(t-k/\zeta)}+1}\right], \quad t > 1/\zeta$$

where

$$c_{1,2} = \frac{1}{\sqrt{2V^2(t - k/\zeta)}}\left\{ e^{-\beta(t-k/\zeta)}\ln(\rho \mp l) - \left[\ln x + \frac{\sigma^2/2 - \alpha}{\beta}(1 - e^{-\beta(t-k/\zeta)})\right] \right.$$
$$\left. - \sigma^2\left(e^{\beta(t-k/\zeta)} - e^{-\beta(t-k/\zeta)}\right) \right\}$$

and $Erf(x) = \frac{2}{\sqrt{\pi}} \int_0^x e^{-s^2}\, ds$ is the error function.

Case c): Bounded bi-exponential ρ. We assume that $\phi(z) = \frac{1}{2(1-e^{\lambda l})}e^{-\lambda|z-\rho|}$ for $z \in (\rho - l, \rho + l)$ so that from (5) it results:

$$\mu_J^{(n)}(t|y) = \frac{1}{2(1 - e^{\lambda l})} \int_{\rho-l}^{\rho+l} e^{-\lambda|z-\rho|}\mu^{(n)}\left(t - \frac{N(t)}{\zeta}|z\right) dz, \qquad t > 1/\zeta.$$

3.2   Exponential Intermittence Therapeutic Treatment

In this subsection we assume that I_k is described by an exponential pdf with mean $1/\zeta$, i.e. $\phi(x) = \zeta e^{-\zeta x}$ for $x > 0$. In this case $R_t(\tau) = e^{-\zeta(t-\tau)}$, $\xi_t(\tau) = \zeta$, consequently, from (3) and (4) one has:

$$f_J(x,t|y) = e^{-\zeta t}f(x,t|y) + \zeta \int_0^t d\tau e^{-\zeta(t-\tau)} \int_0^\infty f(x,t-\tau|z)\phi(z)dz \qquad (6)$$

and

$$\mu_J^{(n)}(t|y) = e^{-\zeta t}\mu^{(n)}(t|y) + \zeta \int_0^t d\tau e^{-\zeta(t-\tau)} \int_0^\infty \mu^{(n)}(t-\tau|z)\phi(z)dz. \qquad (7)$$

The number of treatments to be applied until the time t is a Poisson process of parameter ζ.

Case a): Degenerate ρ. If $\phi(z) = \delta(z - \rho)$ from (7) the moments of $X_J(t)$ follow:

$$\mu_J^{(n)}(t|y) = e^{-\zeta t}\mu^{(n)}(t|y) + \zeta \int_0^t e^{-\zeta(t-\tau)}\mu^{(n)}(t-\tau|\rho)d\tau.$$

If $\rho = 1$, $\alpha = \sigma^2/2$, from (6) and (7) we have the following closed forms:

$$f_J(x,t|y) = e^{-\zeta t}f(x,t|y) + \frac{\zeta}{2x}\left[C_1(\log x) - C_2(\log x, t)\right],$$

and

$$\mu_J^{(n)}(t|y) = e^{-\zeta t}\mu^{(n)}(t|y)$$

$$-\frac{\zeta}{2\beta}\left(\frac{4\beta}{n^2\sigma^2}\right)^{\frac{\zeta}{2\beta}} e^{\frac{n^2\sigma^2}{4\beta}}\left[\Gamma\left(\frac{\zeta}{2\beta}, \frac{n^2\sigma^2}{4\beta}\right) - \Gamma\left(\frac{\zeta}{2\beta}, \frac{n^2\sigma^2}{4\beta}e^{-2\beta t}\right)\right]$$

with

$$C_1(w) = \frac{2^{1+\zeta/(2\beta)}}{\sigma\zeta}\sqrt{\frac{\beta}{\pi}}\Gamma\left(\frac{\zeta}{2\beta} + 1\right)\exp\left\{-\frac{\beta w^2}{2\sigma^2}\right\}D_{-\zeta/\beta}\left(\frac{w\sqrt{2\beta}}{\sigma}\right),$$

$$C_2(w,t) = \frac{1}{\sigma\sqrt{\beta\pi}}\sum_{k=0}^{+\infty}(-1)^k\binom{-\frac{\zeta}{2\beta}-1}{k}\left[\exp\left\{-\frac{\beta w^2}{\sigma^2}\right\}\Psi\left(1, \frac{1}{2} - k; \frac{\beta w^2}{\sigma^2}\right)\right.$$

$$\left. - \left(1 - e^{-2\beta t}\right)^{k+1/2}\exp\left\{-\frac{\beta w^2}{\sigma^2(1 - e^{-2\beta t})}\right\}\Psi\left(1, \frac{1}{2} - k; -\frac{\beta w^2}{\sigma^2(1 - e^{-2\beta t})}\right)\right],$$

where $\Gamma(\nu)$ is the Gamma function, $\Gamma(a,\nu)$ is the Incomplete Gamma function, $D_{-\nu}(x)$ is the Parabolic Cylinder function (cf. [2], p. 1028, n. 9.240) and $\Psi(a,b;x)$ is the Kummer's function of the second kind (cf. [2], p. 1023, n. 9.210.2).

Case b): Uniform ρ. For $\phi(z) = \frac{1}{2l}$ for $z \in [\rho - l, \rho + l]$ (7) one has:

$$\mu_J^{(n)}(t|y) = e^{-\zeta t}\mu^{(n)}(t|y) + \frac{\zeta}{2l}\int_0^t d\tau e^{-\zeta(t-\tau)}\int_{\rho-l}^{\rho+l}\mu^{(n)}(t-\tau|z)\phi(z)dz.$$

Case c): Bounded bi-exponential ρ. When $\phi(z) = \frac{1}{2(1-e^{\lambda l})}e^{-\lambda|z-\rho|}$ for $z \in (\rho - l, \rho + l)$ making use of (7) we obtain:

$$\mu_J^{(n)}(t|y) = e^{-\zeta t}\mu^{(n)}(t|y) + \frac{\lambda\zeta}{2(1-e^{\lambda l})}\int_0^t d\tau e^{-\zeta(t-\tau)}\int_{\rho-l}^{\rho+l} e^{-\lambda|z-\rho|}\mu^{(n)}(t-\tau|z)\phi(z)dz.$$

4   Numerical Results

The aim of this section is to analyze the effects of the proposed intermittent treatments by comparing the means of the process $X_J(t)$ in the corresponding of the two therapeutic protocols for the three different return distributions. We assume that the growth rates of $X(t)$ are $\alpha = 1$, $\beta = 0.5$, furthermore $\sigma = 1$, $y = 0.1$, $\rho = 0.5$ and $\zeta = 0.1$.

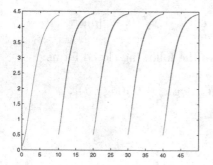 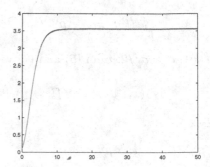

Fig. 1. The means of $X_J(t)$ are shown with $\alpha = 1$, $\beta = 0.5$, $\sigma = 1$, $y = 0.1$ and $\rho = 0.5$, $\zeta = 0.1$ for constant (on the left) and exponential (on the right) intermittences and for different return pdf: degenerate (blue curve), uniform (red curve) and bi-exponential (magenta curve) for $l = 0.4$ and $\lambda = 1$.

In Fig. 1 the means of $X_J(t)$ are shown when a constant treatment (on the left) and exponential protocol (on the right) is applied. For both therapeutic treatments the three different return distributions are compared: degenerate pdf (blue curve), uniform pdf (red curve) with $l = 0.4$ and bi-exponential pdf (magenta curve) for $l = 0.4$ and $\lambda = 1$. Note that, although the red and magenta curves are below the blue curve, they are comparable, so we can study the only degenerate case without loss of generality.

Figures 2 and 3 show the mean of $X_J(t)$ for the constant (blue full curve) and exponential (dashed curve) intermittences in the corresponding of degenerate distribution of the return point. In particular, in Fig. 2 we choose $1/\zeta = 10$ (on the left) and $1/\zeta = 5$ (on the right), whereas in Fig. 3 $1/\zeta = 4$ (on the left) and $1/\zeta = 3$ (on the right). The green line represents the carrying capacity of the deterministic Gompertz growth: $k = \exp\{\alpha/\beta\}$, the magenta line is $k/2$

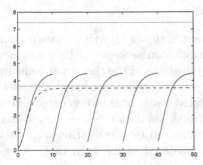 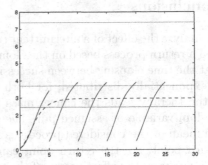

Fig. 2. The means of $X_J(t)$ are shown with $\alpha = 1$, $\beta = 0.5$, $\sigma = 1$, $y = 0.1$ and $\rho = 0.5$ for a constant (blue full curve) and exponential (dashed curve) intermittences with $1/\zeta = 10$ (on the left) and $1/\zeta = 5$ (on the right) for degenerate return point. The green, magenta and red lines are $k, k/2$ and $k/3$, respectively.

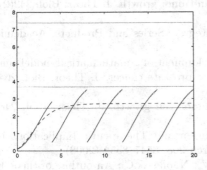 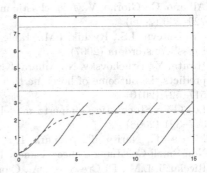

Fig. 3. As in Fig. 2 with $1/\zeta = 4$ (on the left) and $1/\zeta = 3$ (on the right). The green, magenta and red lines are $k, k/2$ and $k/3$, respectively.

and the red one is $k/3$. In all cases we note that the mean of the process for the exponential distribution is less than the mean for the constant case. In particular, for $1/\zeta = 10$ (on the left of Fig. 2), only for the exponential treatment the mean size is kept under the level $k/2$. Its understandable because in the exponential case the probability of occurrence of more than one jump before of the time 10 is non-zero, while in the constant case it is equal to zero. The mean of the jump process decreases by reducing the mean of the interjump intervals, however the better results are obtained for the exponential intermittences (dashed curves). In particular for $1/\zeta = 3$ (on the right of Fig. 3) the exponential treatment reduces the mean of the tumor size below $k/3$.

Conclusions

To analyze the effect of a intermittent treatment in tumor growth we have considered a return process based on the Gompertz diffusion process. We have assumed that the time elapsing between successive applications of the therapy is constant or exponentially distributed; for both cases we have considered that the effect of the therapy leads the cancer mass to a fixed value or, more generally, to a random variable of assigned pdf. The performed simulations have showed that the mean of the considered process is not influenced by the distribution of the return point. So, the return point can be considered as fixed. In this case we have analyzed the effectiveness of the two treatments by comparing the mean of the jump process for different mean durations of interjump intervals. Based on the considered model and on the chosen parameters, we can conclude that the exponential protocol produces better effects than the constant one.

References

1. Albano, G., Giorno, V.: A stochastic model in tumor growth. J. Theor. Biol. 242(2), 229–236 (2006)
2. Gradshteyn, I.S., Ryzhik, I.M.: Table of Integrals Series and Products. Academic Press, Amsterdam (2007)
3. Hirata, Y., Bruchovsky, N., Aihara, K.: Development of a mathematical model that predicts the outcome of hormone therapy for prostate cancer. J. Theor. Biol. 264, 517–527 (2010)
4. Lo, C.F.: Stochastic Gompertz model of tumor cell growth. J. Theor. Biol. 248, 317–321 (2008)
5. Migita, T., Narita, T., Nomura, K.: Activation and Therapeutic Implications in Non-Small Cell Lung Cancer. Cancer Research 268, 8547–8554 (2008)
6. Ricciardi, L.M., Di Crescenzo, A., Giorno, V., Nobile, A.G.: An outline of theoretical and algorithmic approches to first passage time problems with applications to biological modeling. Math. Japonica 50, 247–322 (1999)
7. Tanaka, G., Hirata, Y., Goldenberg, S.L., Bruchovsky, N., Aihara, K.: Mathematical modelling of prostate cancer growth and its application to hormone therapy. Phil. Trans. R. Soc. A 368, 5029–5044 (2010)
8. Wang, J., Tucker, L.A., Stavropoulos, J.: Correlation of tumor growth suppression and methionine aminopetidase-2 activity blockade using an orally active inhibitor. In: Matthews, B.W. (ed.) Global pharmaceutical Research and Development, Abbott Laboratories, University of Oregon, Eugene, OR (2007)

A New Diffusion Process to Epidemic Data

Desire Romero, Nuria Rico, and Maribel G-Arenas

Universidad de Granada, Spain
{deromero,nrico}@ugr.es, mgarenas@atc.ugr.es

Abstract. In this paper, a new non-homogeneous diffusion process is introduced, which is a combination between a Gompertz-type and a log-normal diffusion process, so that the mean function is a mixture between Gompertz and exponential curves. The main innovation of the process is that the trend, after reaches a bound, changes to be increasing or decreasing to zero, a situation that is not provided by the previous models. After building the model, a comprehensive study of its main characteristics is presented. Our goal is to use the process with preditive purpose, so how to get the estimations of the parameters of the process and theirs characteristics functions is presented in this paper. Finally, the potential of the new process to model epidemic data are illustrated by means of an application to simulated data.

Keywords: Growth curve, Gompertz curve, exponential curve.

1 Introduction

Growth is an important characteristic to study in many application fields, as in economy, biology and ecology, for instance. Many attempts have been made to build mathematical models to describe its behavior. Many and diverse representations of growth have been proposed, with a wide variety of curves associated. Increasing growth curves are usually classified into bounded and unbounded curves. In the first group, the S-shaped or sigmoidal curves are very common. They are monotonous and present an inflection point where the curve changes from concave to convex. One of these is the Gompertz-type curve

$$f(t) = x_0 \exp \left\{ -\frac{m}{\beta} \left(e^{-\beta t} - e^{-\beta t_0} \right) \right\}, \ t \geqslant t_0, \ m > \beta > 0 . \tag{1}$$

The most representative of the second group is the exponential curve,

$$f(t) = x_0 \exp \left\{ c(t - t_0) \right\}, \ t \geqslant t_0, \ c \in \mathbb{R}^+ , \tag{2}$$

which is monotonous, concave, and is referred to as a J-curve.

By other way, there exits data that show an initial increasing trend but, after reach the bound, the trend changes decreasing to zero, for instance in epidemic data.

There exit various stochastic models related to some of the growth curves being considered that are available to model data showing this kind of behavior.

R. Moreno-Díaz et al. (Eds.): EUROCAST 2013, Part I, LNCS 8111, pp. 69–76, 2013.

One of them is the lognormal diffusion process [1] that might be suitable to describe situations governed by time-continuous variables and an exponential trend (2). If the studied variables have a bounded sigmoidal behavior, whose bound dependent of the initial value, the Gompertz-type diffusion processes [2] associated with the Gompertz curve (1) can be used to model the data. However, no one of these models is appropriate if the trend changes after to reach the bound either to grow indefinitely or decrease to zero. This fact justifies the interest on obtaining a stochastic model to deal with this situation that can appear, for example, when we treat with epidemic data witch decrease to zero after reach a bound.

In this paper it is proposed a generalization of both curves in a single one, that will be called Gompertz-exponential curve, in order to find a single model depicting the mixed growth pattern. A growth curve which combines both before is given by

$$f(t) = x_0 \exp \left\{ -\frac{m}{\beta} \left(e^{-\beta t} - e^{-\beta t_0} \right) + c(t - t_0) \right\}, \, t \geqslant t_0, \, m > \beta > 0, \, c \in \mathbb{R} \, .$$

(3)

The growth of this curve depends on the values considered of parameters c, m and β. The Gompertz-exponential curve (3) is always increasing and unbounded when $c > 0$, it is a Gompertz curve when $c = 0$, and shows an exponential increasing growth at the beginning that changes after reach the bound to decrease until zero when $c < 0$.

The most interesting case is when $c < 0$, because the curve shows at most two changes in curvature. Other characteristics on this case can be studied, like the bound time and the inflexion times. In addition, there is a symmetry between these times. All these properties are commons in the sample paths of epidemic data so they are present into the real world every day.

So, the main aim of this work is to introduce and to study a diffusion process that allows to describe, and to model, phenomena associated with the Gompertz-exponential curve (3). To do this, the method proposed by Capocelli and Ricciardi have been applied, that is, to look for a process whose solution of the Fokker-Planck equation, without noise, be such curve. Moreover, after this procedure is realized, the obtained process have to verify the condition that the mean function (conditioned to the initial value), coincides with the Gompertz-exponential curve. This property is specially useful for forecasting aims.

The new process will be called Gompertz-lognormal diffusion process because of its origins and allows to describe situations where: The studied phenomenon can be modeled by a stochastic process in continuous time, the dynamic variable under consideration shows a trend following a Gompert-exponential curve, and finally the main aim is to make inference about the trend of the process.

2   The New Process

Firstly, according to the method developed by Capocelli and Ricciardi in [3], and having into account that the solution of this first order equation

$$\frac{\partial f}{\partial t} = -\frac{\partial}{\partial x}\left[(me^{-\beta t} + c)xf\right] ,$$

with this initial condition $\lim_{t \to t_0} f(x,t|x_0,t_0) = \delta(x - x_0)$, is the Gompertz-exponential curve (3), the Fokker-Planck equation for the homogeneous lognormal diffusion process with infinitesimal moments $A_1(x) = mx$ and $A_2(x) = \sigma^2 x^2$ ($m > 0$ and $\sigma > 0$) is considered,

$$\frac{\partial f}{\partial t} = -\frac{\partial}{\partial x}[mxf] + \frac{\sigma^2}{2}\frac{\partial^2}{\partial x^2}[x^2 f] ,$$

and modified its infinitesimal mean by multiplying it by $e^{-\beta t} + \frac{c}{m}$, resulting the Fokker-Planck equation

$$\frac{\partial f}{\partial t} = -\frac{\partial}{\partial x}\left[(me^{-\beta t} + c)\, xf\right] + \frac{\sigma^2}{2}\frac{\partial^2}{\partial x^2}[x^2 f], 0 < x < \infty, c \in \mathbb{R}^+, m > \beta > 0 ,$$

of a non homogeneous process, which infinitesimal moments are $A_1(x,t) = (me^{-\beta t} + c)x$ and $A_2(x,t) = \sigma^2 x^2$.

On the other hand, considering this Langevin equation

$$\frac{dX(t)}{dt} = (me^{-\beta t} + c)X(t) + X(t)\Lambda(t) ,$$

where $\Lambda(t)$ is a white noise with variance σ^2, and rewriting this equation in the usual form of stochastic differential equations,

$$dX(t) = (me^{-\beta t} + c)X(t)dt + \sigma X(t)dW(t) ,$$

that is where $W(t)$ denotes the standard Wiener process, it is obtained that its solution is a non-homogeneous diffusion process taking values on $\mathbb{R}^+$ and with these infinitesimal moments,

$$A_1(x,t) = h(t)x; \quad A_2(x,t) = \sigma^2 x^2; \quad h(t) = \begin{cases} me^{-\beta t} + c \\ me^{-\beta t} + c + \dfrac{\sigma^2}{2} \end{cases} ,$$

where $h(t)$ is different according to if the Itô or Stratonovich integral has been used to solve it, respectively. In addition, the infinitesimal moments of the previous diffusion process are the same considering the Ito's solution. In this case, it is not difficult to prove that the mean function, conditioned to the initial value coincides with the Gompertz-exponential curve (3),

$$E\left[X(t)|X(t_0) = x_0\right] = x_0 \exp\left\{-\frac{m}{\beta}\left(e^{-\beta t} - e^{-\beta t_0}\right) + c(t - t_0)\right\} .$$

Thus, and taking into account the aims previously stated, the new lognormal-Gompertz diffusion process associated with the curve (3) is defined like a diffusion process $\{X(t); t \geqslant t_0\}$ with values in $\mathbb{R}^+$ and infinitesimal moments

$$A_1(x,t) = \left(me^{-\beta t} + c\right)x$$
$$A_2(x,t) = \sigma^2 x^2 \,, \tag{4}$$

where $m > \beta > 0$, $c \in \mathbb{R}$ and $\sigma > 0$.

In addition, t his process is obtained using other procedures: One of them is the consideration of a discrete random growth pattern and the deduction of the diffusion equations through iterative division of the time and state spaces. This idea is more thoroughly described for the non homogeneous case in [4]. On the other hand, the process can be obtained starting from discrete population growth patterns, through the randomization and limit passage of growth models that generalize the Malthusian model. A similar development, though applied to a non homogeneous process can be found in [5].

2.1   The Distribution

The transition probability density function of the process is obtained by looking for a transformation that changes its Kolmogorov (or backward) equation into the Wiener process equation. Infinitesimal moments (4) verify the conditions of Ricciardi's first theorem [6] and so it is known that such transformation exists. The transformation changes the state space $\mathbb{R}^+$ in $\mathbb{R}$ and allows to find the transition density function of the process which is associated with a lognormal distribution. Thus, for $t > s$:

$$X(t)|X(s) = y \sim \Lambda_1 \left[\ln y - \frac{m}{\beta}\left(e^{-\beta t} - e^{-\beta s}\right) + \left(c - \frac{\sigma^2}{2}\right)(t-s); (t-s)\sigma^2 \right].$$

To obtain the finite-dimensional distributions of the process, having into account that it is Markovian, is only necessary to know the initial and the transition distributions, but the last have been obtained before. If it is consider a degenerate initial distribution, $P[X(t_0) = x_0] = 1$, or a lognormal initial distribution, $X(t) \sim \Lambda(\mu_0; \sigma_0^2)$, the finite-dimensional distributions are lognormal.

2.2   The Characteristics

The characteristics most employed in practice, especially with forecasting aims, are the mean, mode and quantile functions which expressions can be formulated jointly for the two initial distributions considered

$$m(t) = E[X(t_0)]\exp\left\{-\frac{m}{\beta}\left(e^{-\beta t} - e^{-\beta t_0}\right) + c(t-t_0)\right\},$$

$$Mo(t) = Mo[X(t_0)]\exp\left\{-\frac{m}{\beta}\left(e^{-\beta t} - e^{-\beta t_0}\right) + \left(c - \frac{3\sigma^2}{2}\right)(t-t_0)\right\},$$

$$C_\alpha(t) = \alpha - quantile[X(t_0)]\exp\left\{-\frac{m}{\beta}\left(e^{-\beta t} - e^{-\beta t_0}\right) + \left(c - \frac{\sigma^2}{2}\right)(t-t_0)\right\} \times$$
$$\times \exp\left\{z_{1-\alpha}\left(\sqrt{\sigma^2(t-t_0) + Var[\ln(X(t_0))]} - \sqrt{Var[\ln(X(t_0))]}\right)\right\}.$$

Here $z_{1-\alpha}$ is the alpha quantile of a standard normal distribution. In addition the conditional versions of these functions can be also calculated. Note that the mean function is a Gompertz-exponential function, showing its possibilities, for example, in forecasting. All these functions depend on the parameters of the model, which are unknown. For this reason it is necessary to study how to obtain estimations of them.

2.3   Inferential Study

This section presents the maximum likelihood estimation (MLE) for the parameters of the model, from which the parameters of the previously introduced parametric functions can be found.

Let us consider a discrete sampling of the process, done over d paths, in which the observation of each path has been made for n_i instants, t_{ij} ($i = 1, ..., d$, $j = 1, ..., n_i$). These instants are different for each sampling, although $t_{i1} = t_1$, $i = 1, ..., d$. This implies that, after setting time parameters, variables $X(t_{ij})$ are observed, and their values are the base sample of the inferential study. Be $\{x_{ij}\}$, $i = 1, ..., d$ and $j = 1, ..., n_d$ the observed values.

The likelihood function depends on the choice of the initial distribution. If $X(t_1) \sim \Lambda(\mu_1; \sigma_1^2)$ the likelihood contains two additional parameters which must be included in the estimation process. Nevertheless, the estimations of μ_1 and σ_1^2 only depend on the initial time instant and do not have an effect on the estimation of other parameters, and the MLE of m, β, c and σ^2 are the same in both cases. Therefore, from now on the case for the lognormal initial distribution is considered.

Noting $a = \frac{m}{\beta}$, $b = e^{-\beta}$ and $k = \sum_{i=1}^{d} n_i$, and deriving the logarithm for the likelihood function associated with the sample with respect to a, σ^2, b and c, considering $t_{ij} - t_{ij-1} = h$ (the usual case when time intervals between observations are equally spaced), and setting to zero the derivative functions, the maximum likelihood estimators for a, b, σ^2 and c verify the system of equations, from which an explicit solution can not be found. Nevertheless, from that system it can be obtained functions that relate the estimations of the parameters a, σ^2, and c with the estimation of the parameter b:

$$\sigma_b^2 = \frac{1}{h(k-d)} \frac{A_{4,b}A_{1,b}^*A_{2,b} - A_{4,b}A_{1,b}A_{2,b}^* + A_{1,b}A_{3,b}^*A_{3,b}}{A_{1,b}^*A_{2,b} - A_{1,b}A_{2,b}^*} +$$

$$+ \frac{-A_{1,b}^*A_{3,b}^2 + A_{3,b}A_{2,b}^*A_{5,b} - A_{3,b}^*A_{2,b}A_{5,b}}{A_{1,b}^*A_{2,b} - A_{1,b}A_{2,b}^*},$$

$$a_b = \frac{A_{1,b}A_{3,b}^* - A_{1,b}^*A_{3,b}}{(b^h - 1)[A_{1,b}^*A_{2,b} - A_{1,b}A_{2,b}^*]} \qquad c_b = \frac{\sigma_b^2}{2} - \frac{1}{h}\frac{A_{3,b}A_{2,b}^* - A_{3,b}^*A_{2,b}}{A_{1,b}^*A_{2,b} - A_{1,b}A_{2,b}^*},$$

where

$$A_{1,b}=\sum_{i=1}^{d}\sum_{j=2}^{n_i}b^{t_{ij}-1} , \qquad A_{2,b}=\sum_{i=1}^{d}\sum_{j=2}^{n_i}b^{2t_{ij}-1} , \qquad A_{3,b}=\sum_{i=1}^{d}\sum_{j=2}^{n_i}b^{t_{ij}-1}\ln\frac{x_{ij}}{x_{ij-1}} ,$$

$$A_{1,b}^{*}=\sum_{i=1}^{d}\sum_{j=2}^{n_i}t_{ij-1}b^{t_{ij}-1} , \quad A_{2,b}^{*}=\sum_{i=1}^{d}\sum_{j=2}^{n_i}t_{ij-1}b^{2t_{ij}-1} , \quad A_{3,b}^{*}=\sum_{i=1}^{d}\sum_{j=2}^{n_i}t_{ij-1}b^{t_{ij}-1}\ln\frac{x_{ij}}{x_{ij-1}} ,$$

$$A_{4,b}=\sum_{i=1}^{d}\sum_{j=2}^{n_i}\ln^{2}\frac{x_{ij}}{x_{ij-1}} , \quad A_{5,b}=\sum_{i=1}^{d}\sum_{j=2}^{n_i}\ln\frac{x_{ij}}{x_{ij-1}} .$$

Moreover, this equation is obtained but it can not be explicitly solved and must be treated by numerical methods

$$A_{5,b} + a_b(b^h - 1)A_{1,b} + \left(\frac{\sigma_b^2}{2} - c_b\right)h(k - d) = 0 .$$

Once $\widehat{b}$ has been calculated, it can be deduced that $\widehat{a} = a_{\widehat{b}}$, $\widehat{\sigma^2} = \sigma_{\widehat{b}}^2$ and $\widehat{c} = c_{\widehat{b}}$.

Thus, once the MLE for parameters a, b, c and σ^2 have been found, those for the original parameters of the model, m and β, are $\widehat{\beta} = -\ln\widehat{b}$ and $\widehat{m} = \widehat{a} \times \widehat{\beta}$.

Finally, the ML estimation of the mean, mode and cuantile functions can be calculated by applying Zehna's theorem.

3   Application to Simulated Data

Based on the algorithms derived from the numerical solution of stochastic differential equations (Kloeden et al. [7], Rao et al. [8]) a simulation algorithm for the Gompertz-lognormal diffusion process can be obtained. This simulation algorithm allows to find paths that ilustrate the proposed model and its potential for modeling data. To this end, several different paths have been generated. Since this algorithm is recursive, an initial value is required for x_0. Said value is determined by the initial distribution being considered either degenerate or lognormal. For the generation of sample paths (see figure 1), it has been considerated a lognormal $\Lambda_1(1.5;0.5)$ as initial distribution and parameters to obtain paths that show a pattern similar to influenza epidemic data.

Thus has been got five sample paths which can represent the total number of influenza viruses detected in several years. The obtained diffusion process lets to model multiple sample paths, using all the information that data provide.

To test the obtained estimated process with forecasting aims, it has not been considerated one of the sample paths in the estimation of the parameters of the process getting the following maximum likelihood estimations of the parameters:

$$\widehat{m} = 1.06357, \ \widehat{\beta} = 0.108626, \ \widehat{c} = -0.142717, \ \widehat{\sigma}^2 = 0.00134802$$

Figure 2 shows each sample path with black points, its estimated conditional mean function, its estimated conditional mode function and a band obtained with the estimated conditional quantile functions.

In figure 3, it has been used the model to estimate the data of the sample path that was removed before.

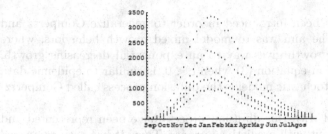

Fig. 1. Simulated paths for a Gompertz-lognormal process (4) with parameters $m = 1$, $\beta = 0.1$, $c = -0.15$ and $\sigma^2 = 0.001$

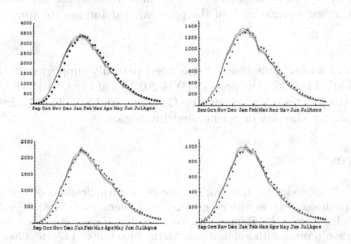

Fig. 2. Estimated mean, mode and quantile conditional functions

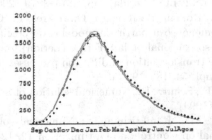

Fig. 3. Estimated mean, mode and quantile conditional functions

4   Conclusions

A diffusion process has been introduced in order to generalize Gompertz and lognormal processes. The aim was to model mixed growth behaviors, where a temporary bounded growth gives way to an exponential decreasing growth. Such growth, described in equation (3) when $c < 0$, is similar to epidemic data growth. Its associated stochastic model is the diffusion process called Gompertz-lognormal.

The paths associated with this diffusion process have been represented and they have been carried out with predictive purpose. Then, it has been compared the maximum likelihood estimation from the simulated paths with the real value, as well as the simulated paths with the estimated mean, mode and quantile conditional functions. The results point out that the process is appropriate to model this kind of data which shows the typical pattern of epidemic data, even when a big noise can be appreciate in the data. Indeed, the estimated model have adjust a new sample path of the process, that implies its applicability in forecasting.

Acknowledgments. This research has been partially supported by MICINN (Spain) MTM2011-28962, the proyect PYR-2012-14 of the CEI BioTIC GENIL (CEB09-0010) program, Universidad de Granada, and by TIN2011-28627-C04-02 of the Spanish Ministry of Science and Innovation.

References

1. Gutiérrez, R., Román, P., Romero, D., Torres, F.: Applications of the univariate lognormal diffusion process with exogenous fact. Cybern. Syst. 34(8), 709–724 (2003)
2. Gutiérrez, R., Román, P., Romero, D., Serrano, J.J., Torres, F.: A new Gompertz-type diffusion process with applications. Math. Biosci. 208, 147–165 (2007)
3. Capocelli, R.M., Ricciardi, L.M.: Growth with regulation in random enviroment. Kybernetik 15, 147–157 (1974)
4. Gutiérrez, R., Rico, N., Román, P., Romero, D., Torres, F.: Obtención de procesos de difusión no homogéneos a partir de esquemas discretos. In: Actas del Decimoséptimo Congreso Nacional de la S.E.I.O. (Lérida), pp. 4274–4279 (2003)
5. Gutiérrez, R., Rico, N., Román, P., Romero, D., Torres, F.: Obtención de un proceso de difusión no homogéneo a partir de modelos de crecimiento. In: Actas del Decimoséptimo Congreso Nacional de la S.E.I.O. (Lérida), pp. 4280–4287 (2003)
6. Ricciardi, L.M.: On the transformation of diffusion processes into the Wienner Process. J. Math. Anal. Appl. 54, 185–199 (1976)
7. Kloeden, P.E., Platen, E., Schurz, H.: Numerical solution of SDE through computer experiments. Springer (1994)
8. Rao, N.J., Borwankar, J.D., Ramkrishna, D.: Numerical solution of Ito integral equations. SIAM Journal on Control and Optimization 12, 124–139 (1974)

Physical Activity Classification Using Resilient Backpropagation (RPROP) with Multiple Outputs

Mustapha Maarouf and Blas J. Galván-González

Instituto de Sistemas Inteligentes y Aplicaciones Numéricas en Ingeniería (IUSIANI),
División de Computacín Evolutiva y Aplicaciones (CEANI),
Universidad de Las Palmas de Gran Canaria, Islas Canarias, Spain
http://www.ceani.siani.es

Abstract. Considerable research has been conducted into the classification of Physical activity monitoring, an important field in computing research. Using artificial neural networks model, this paper explains novel architecture of neural network that can classify physical activity monitoring, recorded from 9 subjects. This work also presents a continuation of benchmarking on various defined tasks, with a high number of activities and personalization, trying to provide better solutions when it comes to face common classification problems. A brief review of the algorithm employed to train the neural network is presented in the first section. We also present and discuss some preliminary results which illustrate the performance and the usefulness of the proposed approach. The last sections are dedicated to present results of many architectures networks. In particular, the experimental section shows that multiple-output approaches represent a competitive choice for classification tasks both for biological purposes, industrial etc.

Keywords: Resilient Backpropagation, Classification, Physical Activity Monitoring, Activity Recognition.

1 Introduction

Recently, data sets from different fields of activity and recognition have become publicly. Monitoring objectives are to estimate physical activity intensity and recognize activities. The approach and challenges in this field are the different conditions, monitoring and the difficulty of common classification problems. This area of research suffers from many problems; there is a deficient of standard dataset, due to differing physical conditions of individuals, and also established benchmarking problems. However, only a few limited datasets are publicly available in this field of research [1]. Hence, there is a need for datasets specifically created for physical activity monitoring, and benchmarked on tasks defined in this field. However, only a few, limited datasets are publicly available in this research field.

R. Moreno-Díaz et al. (Eds.): EUROCAST 2013, Part I, LNCS 8111, pp. 77–83, 2013.

Physical activity has been identified as one of three key health behaviors impacting the major chronic diseases of aging that are increasingly responsible for a substantial proportion of global mortality, the goals of physical activity monitoring are to estimate the intensity and to recognize activities like sitting, walking, running or cycling, etc.

Physical activity has been identified as one of three key health behaviors impacting the major chronic diseases of aging that are increasingly responsible for a substantial proportion of global mortality.

2   Problem Description and Review of Existing Approaches

It's important to note that the detection of relevant actions in real life is necessary in many areas. the works of [1],[3],[4],[5] have presented several works, for the classification of physical activities, using various techniques of classification and recognition of activities.

However, usually tests and algorithms are performed in their own databases using particular specifications related to research groups. For this reason, its difficult to compare and conclude which methodology or technique is better. Therefore there is a need for databases that allow the comparison of different learning algorithms under the same conditions. This would allow replication of the procedures using different approaches, and should be flexible allowing different experimental setups.

In [9] illustrates the use of the dataset addressing the recognition of gestures and modes of locomotion using body-worn sensors for comparing different techniques by presenting a benchmarking study of four classification techniques (K-nearest neighbors, Nearest Centroid Classier, Linear and Quadratic Discriminant Analysis). In [1] have used five different classifiers selected from the Weka toolkit for creating the benchmark: Decision tree (C4.5), Boosted C4.5 decision tree, Bagging C4.5 decision tree, Nave Bayes and KNN. It has achieved good (90% and more) performance using the KNN and the boosted decision tree classifiers, but when comparing classification performance individually for the 9 subjects, a high variance can be observed: the individual performance varies on the all task between 74.02% and 100%. Therefore, personalization approaches (subject dependent training) could significantly improve on the results of the benchmark, and are highly encouraged.

The intensity estimation and activity recognition tasks can be regarded as classification problems.

In our experiment, we will try to achieve better results considering classification with all task at the same time.

3   Artificial Neural Nestworks Algorithms

3.1   Introduction

The power and utility of artificial neural networks (ANNs) have been shown in several applications including speech synthesis, diagnostic problems, medicine, business and finance, control, robotics, signal processing, computer vision and many other problems that are included in the category of pattern recognition. In some application areas, neural models are promising to achieve human-like performance through artificial intelligence techniques more traditional.

Nowadays significant progress has been made in the field of neural networks, enough to attract a lot of attention and research funding. Research in the field is advancing on many fronts. New neural concepts are emerging and applications to complex problems developing. Clearly, today is a period of transition for neural network technology.

A neural network is a powerful data modeling tool that is able to capture and represent complex relationships between inputs and outputs. The motivation for the development of neural network technology stemmed from the desire to develop an artificial system that could perform "intelligent" tasks similar to those performed by the human brain. The models of ANNs are being applied successfully for solving a variety of complex problems in various fields of research.

The Backpropagation algorithm is a learning algorithm used to train networks with multiple layers by minimizing propagation error by gradient descent method that iteratively adjusts the parameters of the neural network (weights) to minimize the sum of errors The choice of the learning rate, which scales the derivative, has a significant effect on the time required to achieve the convergence. If set too small, too many steps are necessary to reach an acceptable solution, instead a possibly large learning rate will lead to oscillations, preventing the error falls below a certain value. To overcome these inherent disadvantages, many algorithms have been proposed to deal with the problem, doing some kind of adaptation of parameters during learning (e.g. global and local adaptive algorithms) [6].

3.2   Reslient Backpropagation

The resilient Backpropagation (RPROP) algorithm proposed by Riedmiller and Braun is one of the best performing learning methods for neural networks. RPROP is an effective new learning that performs a direct adaptation of the weight scale information based on the local gradient. A fundamental difference with adaptive techniques previously developed, the adaptation effort does not tarnish the gradient behavior whatsoever [6]. In [7] Present description of RPROP algorithm and implementation details. We propose a novel neural using resilient Backpropagation to train, with different architectures, is performed on classification problem. Our dataset for physical activity monitoring, recorded from 9 subjects, performing 18 different activities [1]-[2], are publicly available, and can be downloaded from [8].

In the algorithm 1 we describe the Rprop algorithm as proposed in [6]. The basic principal of RPROP is the direct adaptation of the weight update values Δ_{ij}, in contrast to learning rate employed with gradient descent. With the gradient descent learning, the size of the derivative decreases exponentially, but the size of the weight step is only dependent on the sequence of signs and not on the magnitude of the derivative using RPROP.

Algorithm 1. The Rprop algorithm as introduced in [6]

1: Algorithm describes Rprop+.
2: **for** each w_{ij} **do**
3:     **if** $\frac{\partial E(t-1)}{\partial w_{ij}} \cdot \frac{\partial E(t)}{\partial w_{ij}} > 0$ **then**
4:         $\Delta_{ij}^{(t)} := \min\left(\Delta_{ij}^{(t-1)} . \eta^+, \Delta_{\max}\right);$
5:         $\Delta_{ij}^{(t)} := -sign\left(\frac{\partial E(t)}{\partial w_{ij}}\right) . \Delta_{ij}^{(t)}$
6:         $w_{ij}^{(t+1)} := w_{ij}^{(t)} + \Delta w_{ij}^{(t)}$
7:     **end if**
8:     **if** $\frac{\partial E(t-1)}{\partial w_{ij}} \cdot \frac{\partial E(t)}{\partial w_{ij}} < 0$ **then**
9:         $\Delta_{ij}^{(t)} := \max\left(\Delta_{ij}^{(t-1)} . \eta^-, \Delta_{\min}\right);$
10:         $w_{ij}^{(t+1)} := w_{ij}^{(t)} - \Delta w_{ij}^{(t)};$
11:         $\frac{\partial E(t)}{\partial w_{ij}} := 0;$
12:     **end if**
13:     **if** $\frac{\partial E(t-1)}{\partial w_{ij}} \cdot \frac{\partial E(t)}{\partial w_{ij}} = 0$ **then**
14:         $\Delta_{ij}^{(t)} := -sign\left(\frac{\partial E(t)}{\partial w_{ij}}\right) . \Delta_{ij}^{(t)}$
15:         $w_{ij}^{(t+1)} := w_{ij}^{(t)} + \Delta w_{ij}^{(t)}$
16:     **end if**
17: **end for**

3.3   Neural Network Implementation

There is a wide variety of literature available in the field of artificial intelligence. Usually one of the main concerns is to identify network settings for our application. The important points to consider for this are:

- Identification of the input variables.
- Network type and transfer / activation function.
- Number of training patterns.
- Network structure (number of layers, the number of neurons, the number of neurons in each layer).
- Training.
- Validation of the network.

As we need to define a good set of training data to the neural network, we have been made data mining process that we can explain briefly in the following steps:

- Data Preparation: general cleaning (removing bad data measured, and complementing the missing data with the basic methods of similarity, and statistics, if necessary, the potential impact they can have missing data on the representativeness of the data analyzed).
- Selecting the data set: the target variables (those that we want to classify)
- Extract the significant periods of the output variables.

Once we have defined the training data, we have adopted various architectures to define how many hidden neurons and hidden layers should have our neural network.

4   Simulation and Results

We have addressed the problem of classifying the 18 different physical activities (such as walking, cycling, playing soccer, etc.), performed by 9 subjects wearing 3 inertial measurement units and a heart rate monitor [8], without having to reduce the input variables, or discarding some activity. This has not been carried out in previous work due to the difficulties of the classification by increasing number of activities and the size of data to be used during the training and the evaluation of our method. The power of RPROP is assuring the convergence in a few time steps.

The best neural network architecture, having varied the number of hidden layers, is just with only three layers (the first layer for input, one hidden layer, and the last is for output neurons). Activation function which has been used to modify the weights is the hyperbolic tangent.

We performed two types of neural architectures using RPROP as a training method.

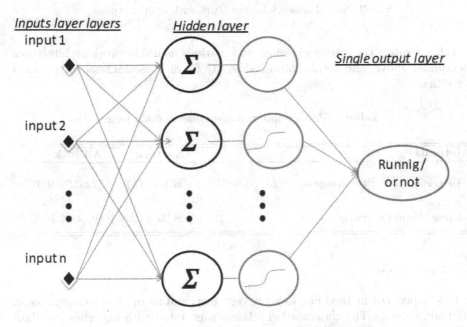

Fig. 1. Neural network architecture with single-outputs

The first is to classify only if it is a specific activity or not. In Fig.1, we can see an example of a neural network to classify if the individual is running or not. The same architecture has been used to the others activities.

And the second architecture aims to classify over all the activities which is of them are the objective (see Fig.2).

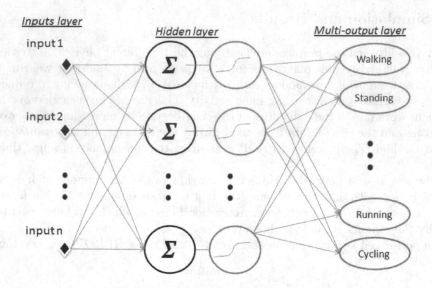

Fig. 2. Neural network architecture with multi-outputs

Table 1 shows the results obtained with various neural network architectures mentioned above, and results obtained in [1] for the classification of physical activities.

Table 1. Performance measures classification task

Methods	One task	All task
[1]Decision tree, Bootstrapping, SVM, Nave Bayes	(93%-100%)	(74,02%-100%)
Rprop Neural networks	(98,26%-100%)	(91,48%-100%)

5   Conclusion

In this paper, the method employed is very fast, and assure the convergence in the training step. The classification scheme was tested with experimental data collected in [1]-[2]. The classification was successfully realized and the performance varies between $98,26\%$ and 100% to classify one activity and between $91,48\%$ and 100% to classify all the activity, is an improvement of the results obtained in [1]. Nevertheless, more algorithms and techniques should be investigated in future work, combining different features.

Another point to be noted is to enlarge the dataset, and to look if there is a way to create a universal dataset for comparing and test with another results and techniques.

Acknowledgements. The authors would like to thank the project PAMAP for the intention of offering a open database, to learn and share knowledge.

References

1. Reiss, A., Stricker, D.: Creating and Benchmarking a New Dataset for Physical Activity Monitoring. In: PETRA 2012, Crete Island, Greece, June 6-8 (2012)
2. Reiss, A., Stricker, D.: Towards Global Aerobic Activity Monitoring. In: 4th International Conference on Pervasive Technologies Related to Assistive Environments "PETRA" (2011)
3. Bao, L., Intille, S.: Activity recognition from user-annotated acceleration data. In: Proc. 2nd Int. Conf. Pervasive Comput., pp. 1–17 (2004)
4. Reiss, A., Weber, M., Stricker, D.: Exploring and Extending the Boundaries of Physical Activity Recognition. In: IEEE SMC Workshop on Robust Machine Learning Techniques for Human Activity Recognition, pp. 46–50 (2011)
5. Xue, Y., Jin, L.: A Naturalistic 3D Acceleration-Based Activity Dataset & Benchmark Evaluations. In: International Conference on Systems, Man and Cybernetics (SMC), pp. 4081–4085 (2010)
6. Riedmiller, M., Braun, H.: A Direct Adaptive Method for Faster Backpropagation Learning: The RPROP Algorithm. In: IEEE International Conference on Neural Networks, vol. 1, pp. 586–591 (1993)
7. Riedmiller, M.: Rprop - Description and Implementation Details. Technical Report (January 1994)
8. PAMAP project's website, http://www.pamap.org/demo.html
9. Sagha, H., Digumarti, S.T., del R. Milln, J., Chavarriaga R., Calatroni A., Roggen D., Trster, G.: Benchmarking classification techniques using the Opportunity human activity dataset. In: IEEE International Conference on Systems, Man, and Cybernetics (2011)

On the Relevance of Discrepancy Norm for Similarity-Based Clustering of Delta-Event Sequences

B. Moser[1], F. Eibensteiner[2], J. Kogler[3], and Gernot Stübl[1]

[1] Software Competence Center Hagenberg (SCCH), Austria
{bernhard.moser,gernot.stuebl}@scch.at
[2] Upper Austria University of Applied Sciences, Hagenberg, Austria
florian.eibensteiner@fh-hagenberg.at
[3] Austrian Institute of Technolog (AIT), Vienna, Austria
juergen.kogler@ait.ac.at

Abstract. In contrast to sampling a signal at equidistant points in time the on-delta-send sampling principle relies on discretizing the signal due to equidistant points in the range. On-delta-send sampling is encountered in asynchronous event-based data acquisition of wireless sensor networks in order to reduce the amount of data transfer, in event-based imaging in order to realize high-dynamic range image acquisition or, via the integrate-and-fire principle, in biology in terms of neuronal spike trains. It turns out that the set of event sequences that result from a bounded set of signals by applying on-delta-send sampling can be characterized by means of the ball with respect to the so-called discrepancy norm as metric. This metric relies on a maximal principle that evaluates intervals of maximal partial sums. It is discussed how this property can be used to construct novel matching algorithms for such sequences. Simulations based on test signals show its pontential above all regarding robustness.

1 Introduction

The way in which biological neurons respond on stimuli follows a threshold-based sampling scheme. Rather than sampling equidistant in time, as classical sampling is designed, this sampling is triggered by the event whether the intensity of a signal surpasses a threshold or not. Inspired from biology this sampling principle has also been studied and used for technical applications. In the signal processing context this sampling principle is known as on-delta-send, Lebesgue, level or event based sampling [18,17]. Reasons for studying and introducing level-based sampling are a) the reduction of the amount of data transfer e.g. in wireless sensor networks [7] and b) the realization of high-dynamic ranges for bio-inspired sensory systems like Silicon Retina [6,5] or Silicon Choclea [3].

First of all the geometric structure of the space of event sequences resulting from on-delta-send sampling is studied. It is shown that a recently published result from discrete geometry [9] can be applied in order to characterize its geometry which turns out to be closely related to the so-called discrepancy measure.

R. Moreno-Díaz et al. (Eds.): EUROCAST 2013, Part I, LNCS 8111, pp. 84–91, 2013.
© Springer-Verlag Berlin Heidelberg 2013

The discrepancy measure goes back to Hermann Weyl [16] and was proposed in the context of measuring irregularities of probability distributions. It turns out that this measure satisfies the axioms of a norm which distinguishes by a monotonicity and a Lipschitz property of its auto-misalignment function [8,10]. Applications of the discrepancy measure can be found in the field of numerical integration, especially for Monte Carlo methods in high dimensions [11] or in computational geometry [4] and image processing [1,12]. In this paper we study the discrepancy norm from the point of view of clustering event sequences and, thereby, show up a new field of applications for this metric.

2   On-Delta-Send Sampling

In this section we study on-delta-send sampling under mathematically idealized conditions. We assume that the sampling event can take place at any point in time. Consider a continuous signal $f : [t_0, \infty) \to \mathbb{R}$, $t_0 \in \mathbb{R}$ then the integrale on-delta-send sampling, synonymously integrate-and-fire, can be defined recursively by

$$t_{n+1} := \inf\{t > t_n : |\int_t^{t_n} f\, dt| \geq \Delta\} \tag{1}$$

which yields the resulting event function $\eta^{(\Delta)} : [t_0, \infty) \to \{-\Delta, 0, \Delta\}$ defined by

$$\eta^{(\Delta)}(t_n) := \int_{t_n}^{t_{n+1}} f\, dt \tag{2}$$

for $n \geq 1$ and $\eta^{(\Delta)}(t) = 0$ else with threshold $\Delta > 0$. Alternatively we represent the event function $\eta^{(\Delta)}$ by a sequence of binary entries, i.e., $\eta^{(\Delta)} = \Delta \eta$, where $\eta : [t_0, \infty) \to \{-1, 0, 1\}$.

Each non-zero entry in the information sequence indicates whether the sample was generated by the analogue signal crossing the upper or the lower threshold represented by $+\Delta$ and $-\Delta$, respectively. We expect from such a quantization procedure that given an event at time t there is a well defined next event in both directions in time. Therefore, by generalizing (2) we call the function $\eta^{(\Delta)} : [t_0, \infty) \to \{-\Delta, 0, \Delta\}$ a (binary) event function if there are no accummulation points in the set $\{t \in [t_0, \infty) | |\eta^{(\Delta)}(t)| = \Delta\}$. The pair $(t, \eta^{(\Delta)}(t))$, $t \in [t_0, \infty)$ and $|\eta^{(\Delta)}(t)| = \Delta$, can be interpreted as event at time t with impluse $\eta^{(\Delta)}(t)$.

The following proposition characterizes the space of event functions induced by bounded measureable functions. In this context the expression

$$\|\eta\|_D = \sup_{I \in \mathcal{I}}\{|\int_I \eta\, d\mu|\}, \tag{3}$$

shows up, where $\mathcal{I}$ denotes the set of finite intervals of $\mathbb{R}$ and μ the counting measure.

Proposition 1. *Let* $\eta^{(\Delta)} : [t_0, \infty) \to \{-\Delta, 0, \Delta\}$ *be an event function and* $\Delta > 0$ *induced by (2). The event function* $\eta^{(\Delta)} = \eta(f; \Delta)$ *is induced by some bounded and integrable signal* $f : [t_0, \infty) \to \mathbb{R}$ *with* $\Phi = \sup_t \int_{t_0}^t f d\mu - \inf_t \int_{t_0}^t f d\mu$ *if and only if* $\eta^{(\Delta)}$ *satisfies the inequality*

$$\|\eta^{(\Delta)}\|_D \leq \Phi. \tag{4}$$

Proof. Let f be bounded and integrable, and consider the finite interval $I = [t, s] \subseteq [t_0, \infty)$. Assume that η is an event function unduced by f. Due to the integrababilty assumption of f there are finitely many points $t \in I$ such that $|\eta^{(\Delta)}(t)| = \Delta$. Let denote this set of events by $\{(t_k, \eta^{(\Delta)}(t_k)), \ldots, (t_K, \eta^{(\Delta)}(t_K))\}$, $|\eta^{(\Delta)}(t_i)| = \Delta$ for $i \in \{k, \ldots, K\}$. Now, assume that $k \geq 1$, and denote $g(t) = \int_{t_0}^t f d\mu$. According to (1) and (2) we obtain $|\int_I \eta^{(\Delta)} d\mu| = |\sum_{j=k}^K \eta^{(\Delta)}(t_j)| = |\sum_{j=k}^K (g(t_j) - g(t_{j-1}))| \leq |g(t_K) - g(t_{k-1})| \leq \Phi$. If $k = 0$ the right-hand sum of this equations expands to $|\eta(t_0) + f(t_1) - f(t_0) + \cdots + f(t_K) - f(t_{K-1})|$. Due to Defintion (2) we have $\eta(t_0) = 0$, hence inequality (4) does also hold for intervals I with $t_0 \in I$.

Now, let us consider an event function $\eta^{(\Delta)} : [t_0, \infty) \to \{-\Delta, 0, \Delta\}$, $\Delta > 0$ which satisfies (4). Let denote $\{(t_n, \eta^{(\Delta)}(t_n))_n\}$ the sequence of events of η. Define a piecewise linear function $f : [t_0, \infty) \to \mathbb{R}$ at $(t_n)_n$ by $f(t) := f(t_i) + \kappa_i(t - t_i)$, on $t \in [t_i, t_{i+1}]$ where $\kappa_i = 2(\Delta - (t_{i+1} - t_i)f(t_i))/(t_{i+1} - t_i)^2$. The resulting function f is continuous, due to (4) bounded, and satisfies $|\int_{t_n}^{t_{n+1}} f d\mu| = \Delta$ for $n \geq 1$, hence η turns out to be induced by f. $\square$

It turns out that (3) is a norm. For details on the discrepancy norm (3) see [8,10,9].

3   Test Signals

For this let us consider the example of test signals illustrated in Figure 1.

The question is whether by measuring the dissimilarity between the sequences η_i the correct dissimilarity between the orinal signals f_i can be discovered.

In Table 1 we apply various methods to assess the (dis-)similarity between η_1, η_2 and η_2, η_3: While *Euclidean* refers to the Euclidean metric, $\|\eta\|_2$, *Euclidean on sum* applies $\|.\|_2$ on the integral $\int_{t_0}^t \eta d\mu$, *normalized correlation (NC)* means the centered and normalized correlation, *NC on sum* analogously NC applied on $\int_{t_0}^t \eta d\mu$. The method *van Rossum* refers to a convolution with a causal exponantial with time parameter $\tau > 0$, see [13]. *Victor Purpura* refers to an edited cost-based metric, that transforms one event sequence to another one by deleting, inserting and shifting of events. For each operation a cost value c is defined. For deletion and insertion the cost is set $c = 1$, while for a shift its cost is proportional to the shift distance Δt with proportionality constant $s \geq 0$. For details see e.g. [15,14]. *Hamming* is the distance that counts the number of events that are not in common. *Hausdorff* is a distance from set theory that determines the maximum distance of a set to the nearest point in the other set. In this context

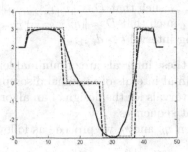 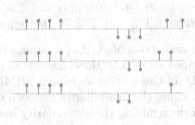

Fig. 1. Test signals, left, and resulting event squences, right, after applying integrate-and-fire sampling with respect to $\Delta = 0.8$. The signal f_2 with black dashed line, left, refers to the second sequence η_2, right. Its neighboring signal f_1 with black dotted line, left, is mapped to the sequence η_1 on top, right. The third signal f_3, more smooth, with solid line refers to the sequence η_3 in the bottom, right.

Table 1. Computation of (dis-)smilarites between η_1 and η_2, as well as η_2 and η_3 of the example of Figure 1. The evaluation 'ok ?' indicates whether the classification is correct or not.

$\Delta = 0.8$	η_1, η_2	η_2, η_3	ok?
Euclidean	2.0577	1.8384	not ok
Euclidean on sum	5.9837	2.8277	not ok
normalized correlation (NC)	0.7011	0.7447	not ok
NC on sum	0.8411	0.9484	not ok
van Rossum, $\tau = 0.1$	2.8327	2.4053	not ok
van Rossum, $\tau = 1.0$	2.0189	1.7610	not ok
Victor Purpura, $s = 0$	1	2	ok
Victor Purpura, $s = 0.16$	2.160	2.160	not clear
Victor Purpura, $s = 1.0$	4	3	not ok
Hamming	5	4	not ok
Hausdorff	6	6	not clear

we apply the Hausdorff metric on the set of positive and negative events, respectively, and add the resulting distances. Table 1 shows that for the test signals of Figure 1 only Victor Purpura leads to an unambiguously correct decision that η_1 is more similar to η_2 than η_2 compared to η_3.

4   Application to Delta Event Sequence Matching

It is interesting to observe that (3) is defined by means of a maximum. The intervals of maximal discrepancy $[d_i, d_{i+1})_i$ on which such maximal partial sums are assumed can be determined in linear time in the following way:

D1 First of all determine the discrepancy norm $D = |\eta|_D$ by means of $\|\eta\|_D = \max_t \int_{t_0}^t \eta d\mu - \min_t \int_{t_0}^t \eta d\mu$, see [8].

D2 For $i > 0$ determine minimal $d_{i+1} > d_{i-1}$ such that $D = \|\eta|_{[d_{i-1}, d_{i+1}]}\|_D$.
D3 For $i > 0$ determine maximal $d_i < d_{i+1}$ such that $D = \|\eta|_{[d_i, d_{i+1}]}\|_D$.
D4 Repeat [D2] and [D3] for the remaining interval $t > d_{i+1}$.

The construction of $[d_i, d_{i+1})_i$ implies that these intervals are of minimal length. Therefore we refer to these interals as minimal interals of maximal discrepancy, MIMD. In this section we exploit MIMD intervals for the design of an algorithm for checking the dissimilarity between event sequences.

For determining the dissimilarity between η_k and η_l we procede as follows

P1 Compute the corresponding MIMD intervals $(d_i^{(j)}, d_{i+1})_i^{(j)})_i$, $j \in \{l, k\}$.
P2 Compute step functions $\tau_k(t) = \sum_I 1_I(t)\alpha_I$ based on the MIMD intervals I where the values α_I are chosen such that $\sum_{t_i \in I} \eta_k(t_i) = |I|\alpha_I$.
P3 Compute the error functional

$$\Gamma(\eta_k, \eta_l) = \|\tau_k - \tau_l \circ T\|_2^2 + \lambda \int (T' - 1)^2 dt \qquad (5)$$

where $\|.\|_2$ denotes the Euclidean metric and T denotes a strictly monotonic transformation function that respects the MIMD intervals in the sense that T never maps an MIMD interval I such that a border point $d_j^{(l)}$ of an MIMD intveral is element of the interior of $T(I)$. The parameter $\lambda \geq 0$ controls the weight of the deformation error. T is chosen to mimize (5) which algorithmically can be realized by means of dynamic programming, see e.g. [2].

The experiments of the Figures 2, 3, 4 and 5 show the classification results with respect to Victor Purpura and with respect to the discrepancy norm induced method outlined in [P1]-[P3]. These experiments are made without and with

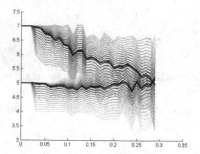 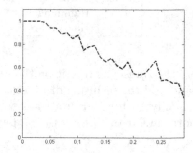

Fig. 2. Dissimilarity between η_1 and η_2, below, versus dissimilarity between η_2 and η_3, above, based on Victor Pupura metric with cost parameter $s = 0$ at different levels σ of additive white Gaussian noise on the original signals. The event sequences η_i are result from applying integrate-and-fire on f_i of Figure 1 with $\Delta = 0.8$. The graph left shows the dissimilarities for 400 trials. The graph right shows the percentage of correct decisions versus the total number of trials at various noise levels.

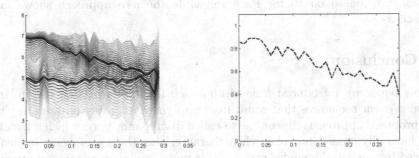

Fig. 3. Same as in Figure 2 but with additional spike noise that randomly switches the sign of an event or erases an event with probability $p = 0.01$

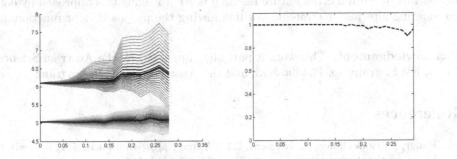

Fig. 4. Same as in Figure 2 but now based on the error functional (5) with $\lambda = 1$

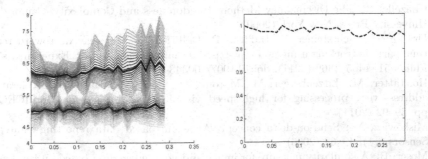

Fig. 5. Same as in Figure 4 but with additional spike noise that randomly switches the sign of an event or erases an event with probability $p = 0.01$

spike noise. It is interesting to observe that spike noise seriously affects the classification based on Victor Purpura, while the new approach shows more robustness.

5   Conclusion

In this paper we introduced a novel approach for measuring the dissimilarity between event sequences that result from applying integrate-and-fire sampling. The proposed approach relies on the so-called discrepancy norm which is a metric that naturally comes into play when characterizing the set of event sequences induced from a set of bounded signals. This metric relies on a maximal principle which yields minimal intervals of maximal partial sums. These intervals can be looked at as spike clusters which are exploited for registering two event sequences by taking deformations in the time domain into account. Based on test signals computer simulations demonstrate the improved robustness of this approach compared to state-of-the-art methods like the Victor-Purpura cost-based metric or the van Rossum metric. Future research is left to refine this approach by e.g. considering alternative strategies for minimizing the proposed error functional.

Acknowledgement. This work is partially supported by the Austrian Science Fund, FWF, grant no. P21496 N23, and the Austrian COMET program.

References

1. Bauer, P., Bodenhofer, U., Klement, E.P.: A fuzzy algorithm for pixel classification based on the discrepancy norm. In: Proc. 5th IEEE Int. Conf. on Fuzzy Systems, New Orleans, LA, vol. III, pp. 2007–2012 (September 1996)
2. Bellman, R.E.: Dynamic Programming. Dover Publications, Incorporated (2003)
3. Chan, V., Liu, S.-C., van Schaik, A.: AER EAR: A matched silicon cochlea pair with address event representation interface. IEEE Transactions on Circuits and Systems I 54(1), 48–59 (2007)
4. Chazelle, B.: The Discrepancy Method: Randomness and Complexity. Cambridge University Press, New York (2000)
5. Drazen, D., Lichtsteiner, P., Häfliger, P., Delbrück, T., Jensen, A.: Toward real-time particle tracking using an event-based dynamic vision sensor. Experiments in Fluids 51, 1465–1469 (2011), doi:10.1007/s00348-011-1207-y
6. Hofstätter, M., Litzenberger, M., Matolin, D., Posch, C.: Hardware-accelerated address-event processing for high-speed visual object recognition. In: ICECS, pp. 89–92 (2011)
7. Miskowicz, M.: Send-on-delta concept: An event-based data reporting strategy. Sensors 6(1), 49–63 (2006)
8. Moser, B.: A similarity measure for image and volumetric data based on Hermann Weyl's discrepancy. IEEE Trans. Pattern Analysis and Machine Intelligence 33(11), 2321–2329 (2011)
9. Moser, B.: Geometric characterization of Weyl's discrepancy norm in terms of its n-dimensional unit balls. Discrete and Computational Geometry, 1–14 (2012)

10. Moser, B., Stübl, G., Bouchot, J.-L.: On a non-monotonicity effect of similarity measures. In: Pelillo, M., Hancock, E.R. (eds.) SIMBAD 2011. LNCS, vol. 7005, pp. 46–60. Springer, Heidelberg (2011)
11. Niederreiter, H.: Random Number Generation and Quasi-Monte Carlo Methods. Society for Industrial and Applied Mathematics, Philadelphia (1992)
12. Stübl, G., Bouchot, J.-L., Haslinger, P., Moser, B.: Discrepancy norm as fitness function for defect detection on regularly textured surfaces. In: Pinz, A., Pock, T., Bischof, H., Leberl, F. (eds.) DAGM/OAGM 2012. LNCS, vol. 7476, pp. 428–437. Springer, Heidelberg (2012)
13. van Rossum, M.C.W.: A novel spike distance. Neural Computation 13(4), 751–763 (2001)
14. Victor, J.D.: Spike train metrics. Current Opinion in Neurobiology 15(5), 585–592 (2005)
15. Victor, J.D., Purpura, K.P.: Nature and precision of temporal coding in visual cortex: a metric-space analysis. Journal of Neurophysiology 76(2), 1310–1326 (1996)
16. Weyl, H.: Über die Gleichverteilung von Zahlen mod. Eins. Mathematische Annalen 77, 313–352 (1916)
17. Yilmaz, Y., Moustakides, G.V., Wang, X.: Channel-aware decentralized detection via level-triggered sampling. CoRR, abs/1205.5906 (2012)
18. Zhao, Y.-B., Liu, G.-P., Rees, D.: Using deadband in packet-based networked control systems. In: Proceedings of the 2009 IEEE International Conference on Systems, Man and Cybernetics, SMC 2009, pp. 2818–2823. IEEE Press, Piscataway (2009)

Escaping the Linearity Trap:
Better Simulation Models for Management Support

Markus Schwaninger[1] and Stefan N. Groesser[2]

[1] University of St. Gallen, Switzerland
Dufourstrasse 40a, 9000 St. Gallen, Switzerland
markus.schwaninger@unisg.ch
[2] University of Applied Science, Berne, Switzerland

Abstract. This contribution aims to show a way towards better models for management support. We compare linear and nonlinear models in terms of their performance. Based on a case study, the respective benefits and shortcomings are fleshed out. A linear spreadsheet model and a nonlinear System Dynamics model are used to deal with one and the same issue: capacity planning in a large telecommunications company. Our analysis refers to both the qualities of the models and the process of model building in that firm. The necessity of nonlinear models, when dealing with complex dynamic issues, is substantiated, and strategies for the implementation of such models in organizations are outlined.

Keywords: Linearity, Nonlinearity, Modeling and Simulation, Model-building, Capacity Planning.

1   Purpose

The difference between linear and nonlinear models has important implications for the way we manage organizations and other social systems. Linear models can be misleading as they often do not adequately represent the reality of socio-technical systems. If one is misguided by a model, it is difficult to know that one is. The purpose of this paper is to explore that discrepancy and show a way out of that linearity trap.

Getting caught in linear modeling is common in firms, but nevertheless ineffective in the context of complex situations[1], as will be demonstrated. It is essentially due to flawed or superficial mental models of dynamic systems. In this contribution, we address the limitations of the linear simplicity which abounds in modeling practice, and the benefits of adopting a nonlinear view of dynamic complexity. We will use the methodology of System Dynamics[2], which hinges on the modeling of systems essentially as webs of feedback loops and delays (Forrester 1961, Sterman 2000).

---

[1]   The prevalence of linear thinking which negates the nature of complex systems with their interrelationships and feedbacks has been observed by prominent authors, in particular Vester (2007), who criticizes the dysfunctionality of that approach.

[2]   System Dynamics is a discipline of modeling, simulation and steering. It stems from Prof. Jay Forrester at the Massachusetts Institute of Technology (MIT).

R. Moreno-Díaz et al. (Eds.): EUROCAST 2013, Part I, LNCS 8111, pp. 92–101, 2013.
© Springer-Verlag Berlin Heidelberg 2013

This contribution shows practitioners new ways of thinking in managerial contexts. Even so, management scientists also may find our paper useful, as it can open new avenues of dealing with complex dynamic issues.

We study the following research questions, always with reference to organization and management:

1. What are the weaknesses/shortcomings of linear models?
2. What are the strengths/benefits of nonlinear models?

To give a full picture, we also analyze the benefits of linear models and the shortcomings of nonlinear models. Given the limited space, this is only done in an abridged form.

Our research strategy reverts to the methodology of modeling and simulation which is embedded in a single case study. Single case studies are indicated, among other criteria, if the case at hand is revelatory (Yin 2009). This applies here, as will be shown. We will start with an introduction to the case study. In the following two sections, two planning models used in the firm under study will be described, first linear, then nonlinear. On that basis, we compare the effectiveness of these models in supporting decision-making. We embed these more technical aspects in a reflection of the process which leads to the persistency of linear thinking. Finally, conclusions are drawn about how to overcome the linearity trap to provide more accurate simulation models for management support.

2   Introduction to the Case Study and Problem Description

The case comes from a large European telecommunications enterprise. One of the businesses of that company is attending to the needs of customers who outsource their computer capacities. The leading person from the strategy staff of that unit ascertained large discrepancies between the planned volumes of capacity and those actually needed. Either there were redundancies or bottlenecks of available capacity, but rarely a demand and supply in equilibrium. The use of capacity showed an oscillatory behavior which resulted in great inefficiencies. That is, the bottlenecks were a problem, as customers were quick to switch to other suppliers. There existed only one factor mitigating that tendency, a small barrier to such "disloyalty": Customers showed some tendency to adhere to a supplier that already was one's partner, in particular when his service level was high.

The strategist considered the planning method used, and found that it had to be improved. He pondered that a good model had to take into account the feedback effects of high-use levels of existing capacity on the likelihood of acquiring and satisfying additional customers. In search of a better solution, which in his view had to be a nonlinear approach, he contacted the authors. A task force was formed to develop such a model. Under the leadership of the strategist, the capacity planners and operations specialists of the business unit and the authors convened several times. Model development took place on and off the company facilities. The main lines of the model were developed in the plenary on site, while detailed model building was delegated to the authors and accomplished outside.

3   Linearity – The Planning Model-in-Use

The current method consisted of a sequential calculus of steps along a chain of standard events. Capacity of supply was planned on the basis of a linear algebraic model of demand (Equation 1).

Demand   = *demand for connectivity + demand for direct services*
          = *f(market volume, market share, production lines, capacity utilization)*

(Equation 1)

with f being a function of the attributes mentioned.

The initial analysis of the model-in-use indicated two main deficits (Figure 1):

1. The demand for capacity was calculated as a function of market share, which was treated as an exogenous parameter which changed over time according to the input of human decision makers.
2. The supply of capacity was taken as a function of the demand, without any consideration of the delays inherent in changes in capacity.

Both of these features of the current model were grossly unrealistic.

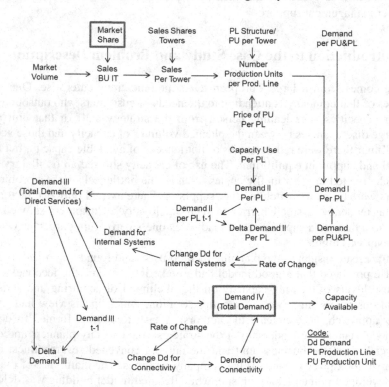

Fig. 1. The linear model (model-in-use)

The shortcomings of linear models are in that they neglect the characteristics of complex systems, such as interrelationships and nonlinearities. This makes them incongruent with reality. The advantage of linear over nonlinear models is the relatively lower conceptual modeling knowledge which is necessary to elaborate them.

4   Nonlinearity – The New Planning Model

In an attempt to remedy these deficiencies, a suitable methodology was identified for meeting that purpose: A System-Dynamics-Model was constructed, which especially addressed the shortcomings of the linear model:

1. Market share was endogenized (Equation 2). It was determined by the delivery capability, the core attribute of service quality, and a function of the level of capacity utilization (Equation 3). This entails a logically closed structure as shown in the Causal-Loop-Diagram (CLD) in Figure 2.

   Market Share = revenue of telecommunications company/revenue of total market;
   *Revenue of telecommunications company = average revenue for a contract * number of contracts*

   (Equation 2)

   and
   *Delivery capability = normal delivery capability * effect of capacity utilization on delivery capability;*
   effect of capacity utilization on delivery capability = f(capacity utilization)

   (Equation 3)

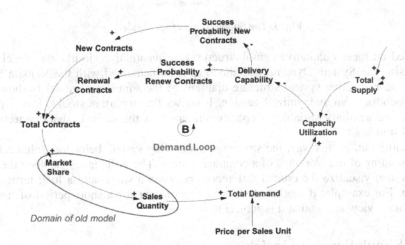

Fig. 2. The Demand Loop (new model)

2. The capacity of supply was calculated as a function of both demand and the process of building that capacity (Equation 4).

Total Capacity = internal capacity + temporary capacity

$$= \int_{s=0}^{T}(finishing\ rate\ internal\ capacity - depreciation)ds +$$
$$\int_{s=0}^{T}(acquisition\ of\ temp.\ capacity - cutback\ on\ temp.\ capacity)ds$$

(Equation 4)

where ds is the variable of integration in the interval from 0 to T which is the final time of the simulation.

The CLD in Figure 3 shows the feedback loops which describe the processes that build internal supply and temporary supply (capacity hired from outside).

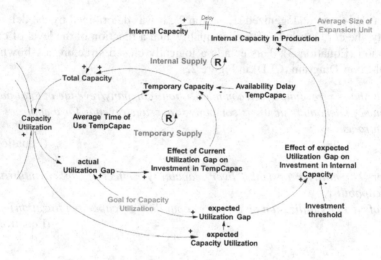

Fig. 3. The Supply Loops (new model)

Based on these qualitative causal structures, a quantitative simulation model was built using the System Dynamics Methodology, implemented with the Vensim Software. The respective system structure diagram of the simulation model is shown in the Appendix in an anonymized version. It shows the important stocks, flows, parameters, and auxiliary variables. Capacity utilization is the variable that connects the two sub-models.

Fleshing out, in this way, the structures underlying system behavior, enhances the understanding of the workings of a complex system. The differences between the two models also visualize the crucial differences between a short- and a long term perspective. For example, if market share may be constant for a short period of time, a longer-term view shows that it is subject to change.

5   Simulations and Insights

The nonlinear model proved to be superior in that the development of demand and supply could be modeled more accurately: the model now accounts for the impact of high utilization rates on the probability to renew or close a contract (demand loop) and for relevant delays in acquisition of the capacity (supply loop). In the following, the results of the nonlinear simulations are compared to the results stemming from the linear model. Figure 4 shows the output of three simulation runs, above for market share, below for capacity utilization (both in percent). The blue line is the result of the linear model; the red line is the result for the nonlinear model with only the demand loop active (Figure 2); the green line is the result for the nonlinear model which includes both demand and supply feedback dynamics (Figures 2 and 3).

The linear model assumes a constant market share of 8% over the relevant time horizon. Since the overall market volume grows at a slow rate of 2%, the capacity utilization increases slightly over time and reaches a value of 97%. Internal objectives for capacity utilization are about 0.86%. The result of the model is unrealistic.

Next, we use the nonlinear model with demand dynamics (partial nonlinear model). Initially, as Figure 4 shows, the market share increases slightly. This is because the relatively low levels of utilization of capacity favor the likelihood to close or renew contracts. However, after more and more contracts have been closed, available capacity is strongly utilized, which reduces the likelihood to have successful closures of contracts. The relevant customers accept contracts only when utilization rates are below a threshold of around 85%. This leads to the curve in Figure 4 which shows the outcome of the non-linear model (only demand side switched on), converging to the value of 85%. Since the total market still increases in size, the market share plunges. This run accounts for demand-side dynamics, but has still the same limitations on the supply-side as the linear model. This simplifying assumption is relaxed next.

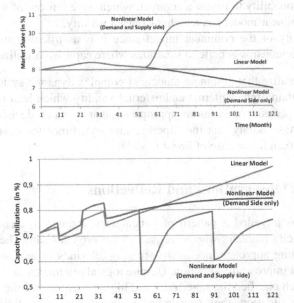

Fig. 4. Simulation runs

The oscillatory lines in Figure 4 show the results of the simulation with both demand and supply dynamics. The market share increases in waves until 12% by the end of the simulation. This is possible since waves of investments in internal capacity are triggered due to increasing utilization rates. Based on the gap for capacity utilization, capital-widening investments are triggered when the gap becomes small. After each delay for the production of capacity, strong reductions in the capacity utilization occur, as soon as the additional capacity comes online (at t=51 and t=91).

We have calculated the monetary benefit which the model is able to generate. We have used the accumulated revenues, i.e., number of contracts with an average size of a contract of 75.000 CHF, over the planning time to compare the three models. A rough calculation shows that the linear model results in a value, for total demand, of 493 Mio CHF, the partial nonlinear model including only demand dynamics results in 446 Mio CHF, and the full nonlinear model including demand and supply dynamics results in 544 Mio CHF. In summary, by representing the business dynamics more accurately, the company is likely to gain 51 Mio CHF in additional revenues over a 10-year horizon.

Strengths of the nonlinear model:

1. The model incorporates the feedback relationships characteristic of complex systems. These are not meaningful at a detailed level. In case a model accounts for many operational details, it can hardly be used for strategic planning purposes: It is neither desirable nor feasible to trace the long-term development of the multitude of details. A higher level of aggregation is required, which facilitates the representation of feedback dynamics, thereby raising internal model validity.
2. The model accounts for important relationships and effects between capacity utilization and probability to renew a contract, which were left out of the linear model. Thus, the nonlinear model has a higher external validity.
3. High generality of the nonlinear model since it is a structural model which accounts for mechanisms generic to situations where capacity is utilized.

One can generalize that nonlinear models of complex dynamic systems, if properly validated, can attain higher internal and external validity which lead to more realistic estimations and considerably more appropriate management decisions. They also have shortcomings, mainly that the expertise and sometimes the cost of elaborating them are higher than in the case of linear models.

6   Process Observations and Reflections

Our observations unveiled a pattern of vehement resistance to change, among the company's capacity planners who were part of the project team. They defended the traditional planning approach incessantly, finding all kinds of excuses why the new model would not improve the situation. Despite logical arguments of the strategist and the authors, which clarified the superiority and higher adequacy of the nonlinear model for the given situation, they succumbed to the illusion of validity (Kahnemann 2011). Repeatedly the following behavior pattern emerged: Up to a certain point these team members showed agreement with our propositions, but then invariably fell back into their defensive routines (Argyris 1990). Even though they accepted the arguments intellectually, they could not get rid of their original prejudice, which for them stayed the valid position.

After some time – the new model had already been built – we became aware of the major trigger of that behavior: The capacity planners were concerned with the details of the operations they were part of. These were pictured – in their view adequately – in the old model. They showed little interest in a larger picture. Their mentality was short-termist. Long-term considerations such as the gradual changes inherent in a system which is subject to endogenously driven dynamics, was outside their horizon. For example, the feedback-generated dynamics of market share or the building up of capacities were blinded out from their observations. In sum, this problem was essentially in the dominance of an operative orientation paired with a lack of strategic thinking.

In the time we worked on the project with the company (about six months) we have not seen much change of that situation. At least, the new model has triggered debate about the best way of carrying out capacity planning. Obviously, this company is still in a learning process. At the end of our project it was uncertain if the nonlinear model would de facto win out.

7   Conclusions and Outlook

Even though mathematics in general and dynamic simulation in particular are not much used in the management of companies (Behnam et al. 2003), there are plenty of areas where they can be used beneficially.

The analysis in the case under study showed a clear advantage of the nonlinear dynamic simulation model over the linear model. At the same time we discerned tensions in the organizational discourse between the champions of the new model and the defenders of the old one. We assume that both of these observations hold for many other organizations as well. To corroborate that claim, other cases should be studied, to extend external validity of our the empirical results gathered here.

A set of propositions that show a path towards a more effective management support by simulation models can be derived from our study. These propositions do not make up a theory, and they are not cast in stone. They are rather of an indicative type:

1. **State of modeling:** In companies, linear management models are currently prevalent. Linear thinking negates the dynamic properties of complex systems and is therefore grossly unrealistic.
2. **Current Paradigm:** Practitioners often have difficulties to accept nonlinear models. They adhere to an outdated paradigm (in the sense of a broadly accepted way of thinking or worldview).
3. **Benefits of nonlinear models:** Companies could gain very much from the advantages of nonlinear models. These provide more realistic images of system behaviors, enable more realistic scenario analysis, and hence result in better managerial decisions.

4. **Short- versus long term:** Often the resistance toward nonlinear models is in the divergence of short- and long term orientation. The awareness that the control variables at these two levels are distinct from each other is not widespread yet.
5. **Understanding of systems:** The understanding of the workings of complex systems is crucial. It can be enhanced by making the underlying structures of system behavior transparent. Therefore, building conceptual and methodological knowledge with model users is an imperative.
6. **Overcoming short-termism:** The curse of short-termism can be overcome. Clarifying system structures, and in particular, the differences between distinct time horizons is necessary to make the benefits of nonlinear models tangible.
7. **Paradigm change:** The adoption of nonlinear models requires a change of mindset. In complex, dynamics settings, the assumptions about the structure of the system must be revised. This is requisite for coping with that dynamic complexity effectively, and it relates to a new paradigm.

The discussion of the adequacy of linear and nonlinear models ultimately becomes one of mastering change management.

A discourse is crucial, in which the mental models of the existing planning team are discussed. Also, the planning team must be enabled to adopt a different planning paradigm. This begs for training in conceptual thinking and methodological skills. Do not assume that the planning team will understand and implement. The time investment of the team in the existing model(s) and method(s) is immense. According to the sunk-cost fallacy they are, most likely, not willing to write off these investments.

A nonlinear model, since it is more conceptually challenging than existing linear models, can only have a chance of implementation, when its benefits are accepted by the planning team. It is not enough if the external consulting team perceives the benefits. The barrier to change can in certain cases be prohibitive, so that including different agents in the modeling venture may be indicated.

Nonlinear systems have been discussed in science extensively, but they are only gradually finding their way into managerial practice. As the general landscape of systems changes toward more uncertainty and turbulence, a perspective, which embraces nonlinearity as an ubiquitous phenomenon, will necessarily take over: The new paradigm of nonlinear systems is under way.

References

1. Argyris, C.: Overcoming Organizational Defenses. Facilitating Organizational Learning. Allyn and Bacon, Boston (1990)
2. Behnam, M., Gilbert, D.U., et al.: Konzepte von gestern? In der Strategieentwicklung nutzen nur wenige Unternehmen das Potential erfolgssteigernder Ansätze. Absatzwirtschaft - Sonderausgabe zum Deutschen Marketing-Tag, 128–131 (2003)
3. Forrester, J.W.: Industrial Dynamics. MIT Press, Cambridge (1961)
4. Kahnemann, D.: Thinking, Fast and Slow, Farrar, Straus & Giroux (2011)
5. Sterman, J.D.: Business Dynamics. Systems Thinking and Modeling for a Complex World. Irwin/McGraw-Hill, Boston (2000)
6. Vester, F.: The Art of Interconnected Thinking: Tools and Concepts for a New Approach to Tackling Complexity. MCB-Verlag, Munich (2007)
7. Yin, R.K.: Case Study Research: Design and Methods, 4th edn. Sage Publications, Thousand Oaks (2009)

Appendix

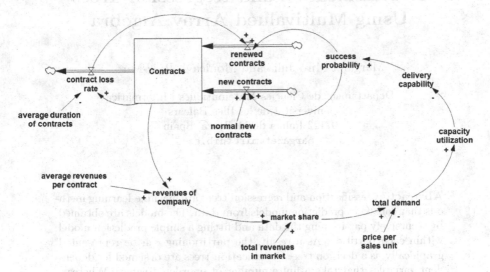

Fig. 5. Demand-Side Model

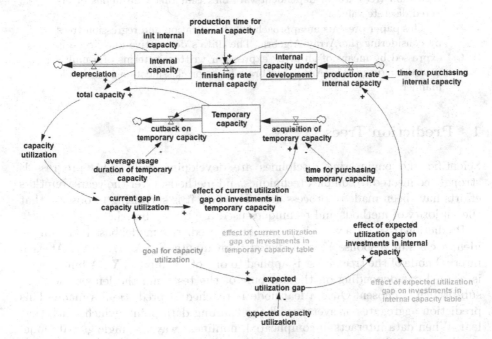

Fig. 6. Supply-Side Model

A Contribution to the Study of Classification and Regression Trees Using Multivalued Array Algebra

Margaret Miró-Julià and Monica J. Ruiz-Miró

Departament de Ciències Matemàtiques i Informàtica
Universitat de les Illes Balears
07122 Palma de Mallorca, Spain
margaret.miro@uib.es

Abstract. Classification and regression trees are machine-learning methods that construct prediction models from data. The models are obtained by recursively partitioning the data and fitting a simple prediction model within each partition. As a result, the partitioning can be represented graphically as a decision tree. Classification trees are designed for dependent variables that take a finite number of unordered values. Whereas, regression trees are for dependent variables that take continuous or ordered discrete values.

This paper presents an approach for classification and regression trees by considering the Array Algebra. The data's descriptive knowledge is expressed by means of an array expression written in terms of a multivalued language. The Array Algebra allows for classification in a simple manner.

1 Prediction Trees

Scientific and engineering disciplines are developing daily. This progress is strongly connected to complex techniques and methods. Over the years countless efforts have been made to process data. However it is surprising to observe that the majority of methods and techniques used are binary based.

Prediction trees are a very simple nonlinear predictive model based on a simple idea, a class or response Y is predicted from inputs X_1, X_2, ..., X_p. At each internal node of the tree, a test is applied to one of the inputs, X_i. A binary split is carried out depending on the outcome of the test, and the left or the right sub-branch is chosen. Once a leaf node is reached, a prediction is made. This prediction aggregates or averages all the training data points which reach that leaf. When data interacts in complicated, nonlinear ways, a single global model can be very difficult to obtain and hard to interpret. An alternative approach consists in sub-dividing, or partitioning the space into smaller regions, where interactions are more manageable and simple models can be fitted. Thus, the global model has two parts: the recursive partition, and a simple model for each block of the partition.

R. Moreno-Díaz et al. (Eds.): EUROCAST 2013, Part I, LNCS 8111, pp. 102–109, 2013.
© Springer-Verlag Berlin Heidelberg 2013

Classification and regression trees are machine-learning methods that construct prediction models by partitioning the data and fitting a simple prediction model within each partition [1]. Classification trees are designed for dependent variables that take a finite number of unordered values. Whereas, regression trees are for dependent variables that take continuous or ordered discrete values.

In a classification problem, a training set of n observations on a class variable Y that takes values $1, 2, \ldots, k$, and p attributes, $X_1, X_2, \ldots, X_p$ is considered. The goal is to find a model that will predict values of Y for a new observation $X = (X_1, X_2, \ldots, X_p)$. In theory, the solution is simply a partition of the X space into k disjoint sets, $A_1, A_2, \ldots, A_k$, such that the predicted value of Y is j if X belongs to A_j, for $j = 1, 2, \ldots, k$. If the X variables take ordered values, two classical solutions are linear discriminant analysis and nearest neighbor classification. A regression tree is similar to a classification tree, except that the Y variable takes ordered values and a regression model is fitted to each node to give the predicted values of Y.

In spite of its simplicity, the exhaustive search approach has an undesirable property. An ordered variable with m distinct values has $(m-1)$ binary splits of the form $X \leq c$, and an unordered variable with m distinct unordered values has $(2^{m-1} - 1)$ binary splits of the form $X \in S$. Different methods use different tests to split each node and selection of the split affects the integrity of inferences drawn from the tree structure.

In order to improve prediction results, some multiway splits have been considered. In [2], given the number of intervals in which data is to be divided, an optimal multiway split for a numeric attribute is considered in order to obtain small, accurate trees. Existing algorithms for multiway splits are inadequate in some ways, most algorithms have selection bias if the attributes are independent of the class variable. When a variable appears in a split, it is hard to know if the variable is indeed the most important, or if the selection is due to bias. Unbiased multiway splits are studied in [3].

There is very little discussion in the literature on the advantages of multiway versus binary splits. A tree with multiway splits can always be redrawn as a binary tree. Generally, a binary tree will have a larger depth and more effort is needed to understand a binary tree than a tree with multiway splits. Also, if k (number of classes) is large the predictions for some classes are spread over two or more terminal nodes, due to the interaction between binary splits and pruning.

This paper presents an approach for classification and regression trees by considering the Array Algebra [4]. The data's descriptive knowledge is expressed by means of an array expression written in terms of a multivalued language. The Multivalued Array Algebra allows for the construction of trees in a simple manner.

2 Knowledge Discovery

The starting point of the Knowledge Discovery in Databases (KDD) process is the data. This data has to be prepared, this step includes the selection,

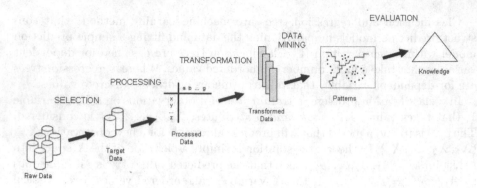

Fig. 1. The Knowledge Discovery in Databases process

subsampling, processing and transformation of the data. At this time, useful features with which to represent the data must be found. Once the data is transformed, data mining techniques are used and new models are found. These mined patterns are then interpreted and evaluated and converted into useful knowledge [5]. The processing of the data includes basic operations, such as removing noise or outliers (if appropriate), deciding on strategies for handling missing data fields, as well as deciding data types, schema, and mapping of missing and unknown values. An important step in the processing of data is the combination and integration of data from different sources. The steps involved in the Knowledge Discovery in Databases process are summarized in Figure 1.

3   Fundamental Concepts

In order to discover knowledge, the data must be selected, processed and transformed. Data's descriptive knowledge can be expressed in declarative form by means of the Multivalued Array Algebra.

Given a set of objects $D = \{d_1, d_2, \ldots, d_m\}$ and a set of attributes $R = \{r_g, \ldots, r_c, \ldots, r_a\}$, the set of values of attribute c is represented by $C = \{[c_{n_c}], \ldots, [c_j], \ldots, [c_1]\}$. A Multivalued Object Attribute Table (OAT) is a table whose rows represent the objects, and whose columns represent the attributes of these objects. Each element $[c_i]$ represents the value of attribute r_c that corresponds to object d_i.

3.1   Multivalued Language

In order to handle the multivalued OAT, where attributes take more than one value from a given set, a new multivalued algebra is used. It uses a multivalued language that describes all possible subsets. It is well known that the set of all subsets of a given set C constitutes a Boolean algebra $< \rho(C), \cup, \cap, \hat{}, \emptyset, C >$. If a symbolic representation or a description of subsets is considered, there is a Boolean algebra $< \mathcal{S}_c, +, \cdot, \hat{}, \vee_c, \wedge_c >$ defined on the set $\mathcal{S}_c$ of all possible symbols representing subsets of C. The zero of this algebra is $\vee_c$ (the symbol representing the empty set). The identity is $\wedge_c$ (the symbol representing set C).

Regular set operations can be represented symbolically as follows:

- Complement respect to C, $\hat{}$: $\widehat{c_h} \looparrowright \hat{C}_h$ where $\hat{}$ is the symbolic representation of the complement of the subset represented in symbolic notation.
- $+$ sum: $c_h \cup c_k \looparrowright C_h + C_k$ where $+$ is the symbolic representation of the union of subsets represented in symbolic notation.
- $\cdot$ product: $c_h \cap c_k \looparrowright C_h \cdot C_k$ where $\cdot$ is the symbolic representation of the intersection of the subsets written in symbolic notation.

All the concepts and operations introduced above make reference to only one set, that is, only one attribute. A multivalued OAT has more than one attribute. Let $R = \{r_g, \ldots, r_b, r_a\}$ be a set of g attributes whose attribute values are $G = \{[g_{n_g}], \ldots, [g_2], [g_1]\}, \ldots, B = \{[b_{n_b}], \ldots, [b_2], [b_1]\}$ and $A = \{[a_{n_a}], \ldots, [a_2], [a_1]\}$. An instance of a training set can be written as, $[g_k, \ldots, b_j, a_i]$, a chain ordered description of g specifications, one from set $G, \ldots$, one from set B and one from set A. Each instance represents itself and all possible permutations. Hence, $[c_k, b_j, a_i] = [c_k, a_i, b_j] = [b_j, c_k, a_i] = [b_j, a_i, c_k] = [a_i, c_k, b_j] = [a_i, b_j, c_k]$.

Definition 1. *The cross product $G \otimes \cdots \otimes B \otimes A$ is the set of all possible instances formed by one element of G, ..., one element of B and one element of A.*

$$G \otimes \cdots \otimes B \otimes A = \{[g_x, \ldots, b_j, a_i] \mid [g_x] \in G, \ldots, [b_j] \in B, [a_i] \in A\}$$

3.2 Multivalued Algebra

In all definitions that follow, $R = \{r_g, \ldots, r_b, r_a\}$ is the set of g attributes whose attribute values are given by non-empty sets $G, \ldots, B, A$ respectively.

Definition 2. *Let $G_i \subseteq G$, ..., $B_i \subseteq B$, $A_i \subseteq A$, an array $|t_i| = |g_i, \ldots, b_i, a_i|$ is the symbolic representation of the cross product $G_i \otimes \ldots \otimes B_i \otimes A_i$ where $g_i \looparrowright G_i$, ..., $b_i \looparrowright B_i$, and $a_i \looparrowright A_i$. $G_i \otimes \cdots \otimes B_i \otimes A_i = \{[g_x, \ldots, b_j, a_i] \mid [g_x] \in G_i, \ldots, [b_j] \in B_i, [a_i] \in A_i\}$, and $|t_i| = |g_i, \ldots, b_i, a_i| \looparrowright G_i \otimes \cdots \otimes B_i \otimes A_i$.*

Data can be described by algebraic expressions of arrays. An expression is a description of part of the data. In general, an expression represents a partial reality included in an OAT, the subuniverse.

The arrays describe subsets) of data, therefore regular set operations may be performed with them. Let $|t_i = |g_i, \ldots, b_i, a_i| \looparrowright G_i \otimes \cdots \otimes B_i \otimes A_i$ and $|t_j| = |g_j, \ldots, b_j, a_j| \looparrowright G_j \otimes \cdots \otimes B_j \otimes A_j$,

- $\sim$ complement of an array respect to the universe (set of all instances): $\sim |t_i| \looparrowright \sim (G_i \otimes \cdots \otimes B_i \otimes A_i)$, where $\sim$ is the symbolic representation of the complement respect to the universe.
- $\ddagger$ sum of arrays: $|t_i| \ddagger |t_j| \looparrowright (G_i \otimes \cdots \otimes B_i \otimes A_i) \cup (G_j \otimes \cdots \otimes B_j \otimes A_j)$, that is, $|t_i| \ddagger |t_j| = |g_i, \ldots, b_i, a_i| \ddagger |g_j, \ldots, b_j, a_j|$ where the $\ddagger$ sum is the symbolic representation of the union of subuniverses.

– ∘ product of arrays: $|t_i| \circ |t_j| \looparrowright (G_i \otimes \cdots \otimes B_i \otimes A_i) \cap (G_j \otimes \cdots \otimes B_j \otimes A_j)$, that is, $|t_i| \circ |t_j| = |g_i, \ldots, b_i, a_i| \circ |g_j, \ldots, b_j, a_j|$, where the ∘ product is the symbolic representation of the intersection of subuniverses. Furthermore, the ∘ product is a closed operation in the set of all arrays.

All the results obtained by use of operations $\sim$, $\ddagger$ and ∘ on arrays are symbolic representations of subuniverses.

Definition 3. *Every combination of arrays using operations* $\sim$, $\ddagger$ *and* ∘ *(well formed formula) is called an expression* E_i.

$$E_i = \sim |t_i| \ddagger |t_j| \circ |t_k| \ldots$$

In particular, an expression E_i is called an array expression if it is written as a $\ddagger$ sum of arrays: $E_i = |t_z| \ddagger \cdots \ddagger |t_y| \ddagger |t_x|$.

An array expression is called elementary if each of the arrays in the $\ddagger$ sum is an elementary array: $E_i^E = |t_z^E| \ddagger \cdots \ddagger |t_y^E| \ddagger |t_x^E|$. An elementary array is a minimal array in the sense that it cannot be expressed as a $\ddagger$ sum of other arrays. Therefore an elementary array expression is an expression made up of minimal arrays.

3.3 Zero Array and Projection Arrays

There are two arrays that deserve special consideration. First, the identity array $\bigwedge$ that describes the universe: $U \rightsquigarrow \bigwedge = |\wedge_g, \ldots, \wedge_b, \wedge_a|$. Secondly, the zero array $\bigvee$ that the describes the empty subuniverse: $\emptyset \rightsquigarrow \bigvee = |\vee_g, \ldots, \vee_b, \vee_a|$.

In the developement of the array theory the following theorem was proven in [6]:

Theorem 1. *An array with a* $\vee$ *component is equal to* $\bigvee$

$$\forall b \quad |g_i, \ldots, \vee_b, a_i| = \bigvee$$

where:

$$|g_i, \ldots, \vee_b, a_i| \looparrowright G_i \otimes \cdots \otimes \emptyset_B \otimes A_i$$

Recall that $\vee_b$ is the zero of the Boolean algebra defined on the set $\mathcal{S}_b$ of symbols describing subsets of B. This theorem gives rise to some interesting questions. Even though the cross product is not the cartesian product it inherits an undesirable property: the cartesian product of a set by the empty set is the empty set. If an OAT is considered, just because there is a missing piece of information can we say that we have no information at all?

Furthermore, if arrays with one $\vee$ component are equal to $\bigvee$ then:

$$|g_i, \ldots, b_i, \vee_a| = |g_i, \ldots, \vee_b, a_i| = |\vee_g, \ldots, b_i, a_i| = \bigvee$$

In two dimensions an array $|b_i, a_i|$ can be graphically represented by a rectangle $b_i \times a_i$, see Fig. 2. When one of the sides becomes zero, then the rectangle has zero area. In this sense $|b_i, \vee_a| = |\vee_b, a_i|$. But even though one of the sides is zero, the other is not. The array $|b_i, \vee_a|$ becomes a line of size b_i, whereas the array $|\vee_b, a_i|$ becomes a line of size a_i. Therefore there is a difference. These lines are the array projections. The projection arrays are related to Wille's formal concepts [7].

Definition 4. *Given a cartesian array* $|t_i| = |g_i, \ldots, b_i, a_i|$, *a first order array projection,* $|P^1|$, *is an array with one* $\vee$ *component and* $(g-1)$ *non-zero components, a second order projection array,* $|P^2|$, *is an array with two* $\vee$ *components and* $(g-2)$ *non-zero components, a nth order projection array* $(n < g)$, $|P^n|$, *is an array with n* $\vee$ *components and* $(g-n)$ *non-zero components.*

The first order projection arrays of array $|t_i| = |b_i, a_i|$ are: $|P_a^1| = |b_i, \vee_a|$ and $|P_b^1| = |\vee_b, a_i|$, shown on Fig. 2.

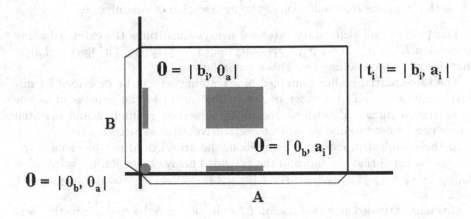

Fig. 2. Two dimensional projection arrays

A simple way to obtain a projection arrays is by means of the $\circ$ product of arrays. Let $|t_i| = |g_i, \ldots, b_i, a_i| \hookrightarrow G_i \otimes \cdots \otimes B_i \otimes A_i$ and $|t_j| = |g_j, \ldots, b_j, a_j| \hookrightarrow G_j \otimes \cdots \otimes B_j \otimes A_j$, where $a_i \cdot a_j = \vee_a \hookrightarrow A_i \cap A_j = \emptyset_A$,

$$|t_i| \circ |t_j| = |g_i \cdot g_j, \ldots, b_i \cdot b_j, a_i \cdot a_j| = |\vee_g, \ldots, b_i \cdot b_j, a_i \cdot a_j|$$

4   Classification Using Arrays

The above mentioned Array Algebra can be used to describe the knowledge contained in a data set. In a classification problem, a training set of n observations or instances on a class variable Y that takes values $y_1, y_2, \ldots, y_k$, and g attributes, $X_g, \ldots, X_b, X_a$ are considered. Each instance is characterized by a tuple $(\mathbf{X}, y)$, where $\mathbf{X} = (X_g, \ldots, X_b, X_a)$ is a vector that represents the values of the g attributes and y is an discrete attribute known as the class label. The set of values of attribute X_g is represented by G, $\ldots$, of attribute X_b by B, and of attribute X_a by A. Classification is a supervised learning method that provides a function, $y = f(\mathbf{X})$, that can predict the class label y of a given tuple $\mathbf{X}$.

Each tuple of the training set can be easily represented by an extended array $|t_i^*| = |t_i^E||y_i|$ $\forall 1 = 1, 2, \ldots, n$, where $|t_i^E| = |g_i, \ldots, b_i, a_i|$ is the elementary array determined by the attribute values of vector $X = (X_g, \ldots, X_b, X_a)$ and y_i is the class value. The extended elementary array describes the class value y_i as a function of the knowledge contained in the elementary array $|t_i^E|$.

Let $|t_i^*| = |t_i||y_i|$, where $|t_i| = |g_i, \ldots, b_i, a_i| \leftrightsquigarrow (G_i \otimes \cdots \otimes B_i \otimes A_i)$ and $|t_j^*| = |t_j||y_j|$ where $|t_j| = |g_j, \ldots, b_j, a_j| \leftrightsquigarrow (G_j \otimes \cdots \otimes B_j \otimes A_j)$, the following operations on extended arrays can be defined.

- ‡ sum of extended arrays: $|t_i^*| \ddagger |t_j^*| = |t_i \ddagger t_j||y_i \ddagger y_j|$ where the ‡ sum is the symbolic representation of the union of subuniverses.
- ∘ product of extended arrays: $|t_i^*| \circ |t_j^*| = |t_i \circ t_j||y_i \circ y_j|$ where the ∘ product is the symbolic representation of the intersection of subuniverses.

The ‡ sum of all elementary extended arrays constitutes the extended array expression $E^* = |t_n^*| \ddagger \cdots \ddagger |t_2^*| \ddagger |t_1^*| = |t_n^E||y_n| \ddagger \cdots \ddagger |t_2^E||y_2| \ddagger |t_1^E||y_1| = |t_q||y_q|$ that describes the training set. This expression can be

The same partial reality contained in a training set can be described by different expressions. The number of arrays appearing in the expression is not necessarily minimal. Algorithmic techniques based on redundant and essential arrays can be used to find equivalent declarative extended expressions.

In these equivalent extended expression, the arrays need not be elementary. It must be noted that the terms in the extended array expression $E_i^* = |t_i||y_i| = |t_q||y_q| \ddagger \cdots \ddagger |t_r||y_r| \ddagger |t_s||y_s|$, satisfy $|t_i| = |t_q| \ddagger \cdots \ddagger |t_r| \ddagger |t_s|$ and $|y_i| = |y_q| \ddagger \cdots \ddagger |y_r| \ddagger |y_s|$.

Given an extended array expression $E_i^* = |t_i||y_i|$, in order to describe the class value y_j, $j = 1, 2, \ldots, k$ as a function of the knowledge contained in the array $|t_i|$ class value projection arrays of the extended array expression are defined.

Definition 5. *Given an extended array expression $E_i^* = |t_q||y_q| \ddagger \cdots \ddagger |t_r||y_r| \ddagger |t_s||y_s|$ the y_j, $j = 1, 2, \ldots, k$ class value projection array are those extended arrays in E_i^* with $y_i = y_j$, $j = 1, 2, \ldots, k$.*

The y_j class value projection array of the extended expression E_i^*, $|P_j(E_i^*)|$, $j = 1, 2, \ldots, k$ can be found using the ∘ product,

$$|P_j(E_i^*)| = E_i^* \circ |\bigwedge, y_j|$$

The y_j, $j = 1, 2, \ldots, k$ class value projection arrays of the extended expression E_i^* form a lattice, that can be used to construct prediction trees.

5   Conclusions and Future Work

This paper proposes and addresses the use of the Multivalued Array Algebra for the construction of prediction trees. This algebra handles declarative descriptions of the multivalued data and allows a multivalued description of the knowledge contained in a training set by means of array expressions. Furthermore, the Multivalued Array Algebra provides the methods and techniques necessary to the find the y_j, $j = 1, 2, \ldots, k$ class value projection arrays and provides the basis to construct the lattice of knowledge associated with each class value.

The introduction of the array algebra improves time efficiency when comparing two sources of information. Furthermore, the technique developed here is independent of the number of attributes and the number of values of each attribute. Multivalued and binary information systems are treated similarly.

Finally, it should be mentioned that data tables can also be ambiguous. Some attributes are non-distinguishing, that is, all attribute values apply ($g_i + g_j = \wedge_G$). These non-distinguishing attribute are non-relevant for classification purposes. The projection co-arrays and their implication in determining non-relevant attributes and tree simplification should be further studied.

Acknowledgements. This work has been partially supported by the Spanish Dirección General de Investigación del Ministerio de Educación, Ciencia y Tecnología through the TIN2007-67993 project.

References

1. Breiman, L., Friedman, J.H., Olshen, R.A., Stone, C.J.: Classification and regression trees. CRC Press, New York (1998)
2. Eibe Frank, E., Ian, H., Witten, I.H.: Selecting multiway splits in decision trees. Technical Report 96/31, Department of Computer Science, University of Waikato (1996)
3. Kim, H., Loh, W.Y.: Classification trees with unbiased multiway splits. Journal American Statistics Association 96, 589–604 (2001)
4. Miró-Julià, M.: A Framework for Combining Multivalued Data: A Practical Approach. In: Moreno-Díaz, R., Pichler, F., Quesada-Arencibia, A. (eds.) EUROCAST 2011, Part I. LNCS, vol. 6927, pp. 1–8. Springer, Heidelberg (2012)
5. Cios, K.J., Pedrycz, W., Swiniarski, R.W., Kurgan, L.A.: Data Mining. A Knowledge Discovery Approach. Springer, New York (2007)
6. Miró-Julià, M.: A Contribution to Multivalued Systems. Ph.D. thesis. Universitat de les Illes Balears (2000)
7. Wille, R.: Restructuring Lattice Theory: an Approach based on Hierarchies of Concepts. Ordered Sets, pp. 445–470. Reidel Publishing Company (1982)

Modelling of Collective Animal Behavior Using Relations and Set Theory

Jan Nikodem

The Institute of Computer Engineering, Control and Robotics
Wrocław University of Technology
11/17 Janiszewskiego Street, 50-372 Wrocław, Poland
jan.nikodem@pwr.wroc.pl

Abstract. In this paper we focus on developing the formal methods and techniques necessary to model and classify a collective animal behaviour. The benefits of using set theory are the possibility of a formal examination of the local problems and to organize individuals as elements of the considered classes, defined globally. In order to describe collective activity of animals, we proposed concepts of actions, behaviour and structures. To govern collective behaviour of animals we propose three key relations and mappings determined taxonomic order on them.

Keywords: collective animal bahaviour, relations.

1 Introduction

Group behaviour is a term coined in sociology, referring to the human activity, and thus an intelligent individuals living in groups. The observation of such behaviour, its description and modelling, cause many difficulties mainly due to the numerous and complex interactions between both, members of the group and its environment. Due to interaction the behaviour of the members of the group must be treated as a system of behaviours rather than the behaviour of separate and unrelated individuals.

At first we model a collective animal behaviour because such situations are much simpler than in humans.

There are a lot of authors who believe that many aspects of collective behaviour could be modelled mathematically and using mathematical abstractions drawn interesting and useful comparisons between diverse systems. An interesting and complete overview of the work in this area can be found in [13]. While examining group behaviour, we have to deal with a set of elements which are, for example, shoal of fish or a flock of birds. Hence, using the formal abstractions which provides a set theory seems most appropriate approach. In the literature on this subject [2, 7, 8, 10, 13] we often find a formulation of the relationships both between members of the group and its environment. It seems to be obvious that to describe them we should use the relations, but the literature on this subject there are the wide road of using functions [7–11, 15] , and does not find even narrow trail of relations and set theory. Deployment of relationships and

R. Moreno-Díaz et al. (Eds.): EUROCAST 2013, Part I, LNCS 8111, pp. 110–117, 2013.

use the set theory allows for standardization approach to modelling the collective behaviour in varied distributed systems. The benefits of using set theory are the possibility of a formal examination of the local problems and to organize individuals as elements of the considered classes, defined globally.

2 Basic Concepts and Notation

Let's consider a flock of birds in the air or a fish school in the water. Birds or fish form a set of elements, which we denote as X. Any element $x \in X$ has individual size but together they form different shapes and sizes which often far exceed the size and range of relationship of individual element. Let us to define a neighbourhood abstraction for set X, wherein an individual can identify a subset of other individuals around it by a variety of relationships and share state with them. Let N denotes neighbourhood, then

$$N \in Map(X, SubX) \tag{1}$$

where $SubX$ means a family of subsets of X.

Furthermore, if $N(x)$ indicates the neighbourhood of x then, using the neighbourhood relation (here denoted as η) we can define a collection of individuals which are neighbours of the given x as

$$N(x) = \{y \mid y \in X \wedge x \eta y\}, \tag{2}$$

and we can denote the set of neighbours of all nodes that belong to the set S as:

$$N(S) = \{y \mid y \in X \wedge (\exists x \in S \mid x \eta y)\}. \tag{3}$$

The neighbourhood relation is symmetric

$$(\forall x, y \in X)(x \eta y \Rightarrow y \eta x). \tag{4}$$

which implies, that if an individual x remains in a neighbourhood relation with y (i.e. x is in interaction with y) then the individual y is also in interaction with x. This results in neighbourhood integrity.

Watching the starlings' flock we can observe how complex configurations arise from repeated actions/interactions between the individual birds. Several authors [8, 10, 12, 13] proposed a models in which individual's activity follow a few simply rules (realize a simply actions) which change its state. As a result, we observe mesmerizing collective behaviour of flock.

In order to describe collective activity of animals, we proposed concepts of actions, behaviour and structures. Action is considered as the property of each individual in group. The behaviour, on the other hand, is an external attribute, which can be considered either as an outcome of actions performed by the whole group or its subset. Action is a ternary relation which can be defined ($\times$ means Cartesian product) as follows:

$$Act : X \times State \rightarrow State. \tag{5}$$

Fig. 1. Different formation of migrating birds: **(a)** line, **(b)** wedge and **(c)** delta

Let $Act(X)$ be a set of possible actions of elements of set X and $\mathcal{R}$ be an equivalence relation on X. We define behaviour *beh* as a set of actions which are equivalent in sense to realize a common goal *rel*

$$beh : [rel] = \{act \in Act \mid act\,\mathcal{R}\,rel\}. \tag{6}$$

Next, behaviours *beh* form a quotient set

$$Beh : Act(X)/\mathcal{R} = \{[rel] \subset Act(X) \mid act\,\mathcal{R}\,rel\}, \tag{7}$$

which consists of equivalent classes (6).

Similar approach has been applied to modelling the structure as a result of collective activity. Let $Stat(X)$ be a set of possible states of elements of set X and $\mathcal{S}$ be an equivalence relation on X. We define structure *struc* as a set of states of individuals which are equivalent in sense of collective activity *col*

$$struc : [col] = \{stat \in State \mid stat\,\mathcal{S}\,col\}. \tag{8}$$

Next, structures *struc* form a quotient set

$$Struc : State(X)/\mathcal{S} = \{[col] \subset State(X) \mid stat\,\mathcal{S}\,col\}, \tag{9}$$

which consists of equivalent classes (8).

As an examples of action *act* we can mention a change of direction of individual's movement as a result of repulsion, alignment or attraction for fish schools or bird flocks, and leaving a pheromone in the case of an ant reinforced its trail. Flocking starlings is one of the most spectacular examples of behaviour in all of nature. Predator - prey interactions like flash expansions of schooling fish forming vacuoles, bait balls cruising parabolas or vortices [8], and ant bridges building [9] are another good examples of patterns of behaviour *beh*. The canonical examples of structure *struct* are migrating birds formation in the sky [10]. Delta (skein) of ducks or V-shaped formation of geese [12] and finally line of oystercatchers flock as shown on Fig.1.

3   Relations, Mappings and Orders

The contribution of this paper is to introduce a novel, based on set theory, relational way of thinking about the modelling of collective animal behaviour. In the previous chapter we consider sets, now it's time to define the relations on it, which determine how simple behavioural rules of individuals can result in complex behavioural patterns reinforced by a number of set/group members (cardinality of set).

Our approach is solidified in three key relations called subordination (π), tolerance (ϑ) and collision ($\varkappa$). These relations allow us to think about collective group activity directly in terms of relationships between individuals and their group vicinity. Three relations mentioned above are defined as follows:

$$Subordination \qquad \pi = \{< x,y >; x,y \in Act \mid x\,\pi\,y\} \qquad (10)$$

The expression $x\,\pi\,y$ - means that action x is subordinated to the action y, in other words action y dominate over action x.

$$Tolerance \qquad \vartheta = \{< x,y >; x,y \in Act \mid x\,\vartheta\,y\} \qquad (11)$$

The expression $x\,\vartheta\,y$ - states that actions x and y tolerate each other,

$$Collision \qquad \varkappa = \{< x,y >; x,y \in Act \mid x\,\varkappa\,y\} \qquad (12)$$

The expression $x\,\varkappa\,y$- means that actions x and y are in collision one to another.

In [4] we can find detailed study on properties of mentioned above relations. Here, we formulate them succinctly as:

$$\pi \cup \vartheta \cup \varkappa \subset Act \times Act \neq \emptyset \qquad (13)$$

$$\iota \cup (\pi \cdot \pi) \subset \pi \qquad (14)$$

where $\iota \subset Act \times Act$ is the identity on the set $Action$. Moreover,

$$\pi \cup \vartheta^{-1} \cup (\vartheta \cdot \pi) \subset \vartheta \qquad (15)$$

where ϑ^{-1} is the converse of ϑ so,

$$\vartheta^{-1} = \{< x,y > \in X \times Y \mid y\,\vartheta\,x\} \qquad (16)$$

Collision holds

$$\varkappa^{-1} \cup \{\pi \cdot \varkappa\} \subset \varkappa \subset \vartheta\text{'} \qquad (17)$$

where $\vartheta\text{'}$ is the complement of ϑ so,

$$\vartheta\text{'} = \{< x,y > \in X \times Y \mid < x,y > \notin \vartheta\}. \qquad (18)$$

The axiom (13) indicates that all these three relations are binary on nonempty set Act. The axiom (14) describes fundamental properties of subordination relation which is reflexive and transitive. Therefore it is also ordering relation on the set

Act. The axiom (8) states that subordination implies the tolerance. Hence we can obtain:

$$\{\forall x, y \in Act \mid x \pi y \Rightarrow x \vartheta y\} \tag{19}$$

and subordinated actions must tolerate all actions tolerated by dominants

$$\{\forall x, y, z \in Act \mid \{x \pi y \wedge y \vartheta z\} \Rightarrow x \vartheta z\}. \tag{20}$$

There are evident coincidences between relations (10)-(12) and proposed in [10, 13, 14] three rules which determine the individual animal movement:

a) adopt the same direction as your neighbours,
b) remain close to your neighbours,
c) avoid collisions with your neighbours.

Subordination (π) is an extension of alignment rules - a). Tolerance (ϑ) is an extension of cohesion (birds)/attraction (fish) rules - b). Finally, collision ($\varkappa$) is an extension of dispersion (birds)/ repulsion (fish) rules - c).

What is the advantage of employing relations to model animal collective behaviour? At the top of the list is topology. The most common mathematical models of animal collective behaviour employ metric distance model while using relation allows us to see distance as a property of topological space. A second factor is model plasticity. In traditional attempt we should determine the constant values of three radii and weighting factors of alignment, dispersion and repulsion forces. Relational attempt provides more sophisticated and powerful tools as: cardinality of each relation $\pi, \vartheta, \varkappa$ which can vary widely within different neighbourhoods; intensity quotients for each relation bounded with the way things are going in the group. This is the part of the story, but not all of it.

Relations also emphasize the importance of local decisions when we attempt to express the essence of distributed, large group of animal, behaviour patterns. Relational framework enables to firmly determine a relationship between sizes of neighbourhood and float border between local and global perceiving perspectives. To really crack the problem of collective animal behaviour, we need to figure out, how individuals faced with decisions and instructed by three simple rules of thumb, retain association between distinct sets of structure and behaviour patterns. The answer is - enforcement of order, as a result of countless conspecific and environmental factors.

Concerning the group of individuals (flock, herd, school), we define its subsets (2)-(3) and (10)-(12) (it's worth to remind here, that relation can be considered as a set). Since only subordination (10) is a transitive (see (14)), it is appropriate to employ the theory of set ordering [5].

Let X be a set of action

$$D_\pi \in Map(X, SubX) \tag{21}$$

where Map is used to mean a mapping of a set X into a $SubX$ (family of subsets of X). The (21) allows us to define four additional mappings of any elements $x \in X$:

$$A_\pi(x) = \{y \in X \mid x \in D_\pi(y)\}, \tag{22}$$

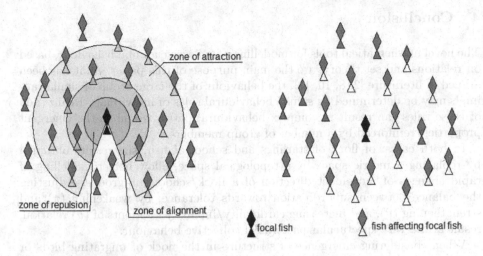

Fig. 2. Metric vs. topological distance in reference to fish school

$$M_\pi(x) = D_\pi(x) \cap A_\pi(x), \tag{23}$$

$$N_\pi(x) = D_\pi(x) \cup A_\pi(x), \tag{24}$$

$$C_\pi(x) = X \setminus N_\pi(x). \tag{25}$$

In fact, follows from (13)-(14), the mapping $D_\pi(x)$ (descendants) possess the following properties:

$$\cup D_\pi^\vdash(D_\pi(x)) \subset D_\pi(x), \qquad transivity, \tag{26}$$

$$M_\pi(x) \subset \{x\}, \qquad antisymmetry, \tag{27}$$

$$M_\pi(x) \neq \emptyset, \qquad weak\ reflexivity, \tag{28}$$

$$N_\pi(x) = \emptyset, \qquad connectness, \tag{29}$$

wehere, $D_\pi^\vdash \in Map\,(Sub(X), Sub\,(Sub(X)))$ indicates an extension of D_π. We conclude this section with the remark, that set of action (5) is weakly-ordered by any mapping $D_*(x)$ iff the conditions (26), (28) are fulfilled. Further, if (27) holds, then set Act is partially ordered since:

$$M_*(x) = \{x\}, \tag{30}$$

Finally, the set of actions Act is ordered totally when all four (26)-(29) conditions are fulfilled.

4   Conclusion

The novel mathematical tools for modelling of collective animal behaviour, based on relations and set theory, are the main purpose of this paper. As it has been argued in literature [2, 8, 10, 13], the behaviour of the large group of similar animals may be determined by simple behavioural rules of individuals. Realization of these rules can result in complex behavioural patterns and in the emergent properties, reinforced by a number of group members.

In both cases: of flock of starlings and school of fish, the results obtained by replacing a metric space by a topological space, allow better modelling of rapid changes of movement direction of a flock/school sub-groups. Adjusting the balance between subordination towards tolerance, by weakening (π) and strengthening (ϑ), and increasing cardinality/intensity quotients of (ϑ) relation, result in the very spectacular patterns of collective behaviour.

When considering emergence of structure in the flock of migrating birds or structure of shoaling fish, these phenomena are associated with mappings, which ordered subordination relation, since only this (π) relation is transitive. The V structure is the result of well-ordered and strength subordination (π). While we also strengthening tolerance (ϑ), the V structure becomes to be a delta. Going in opposite direction, i.e. completely eliminating (ϑ) but totally ordered subordination (π), we obtain a line of oystercatchers flock (see fig.1).

The existence of mapping (21) is the necessary, but not sufficient, condition for emergence of the structure. In case of flock of birds, the mapping results from aerodynamic rules and tends toward minimization of the energy consumption [1, 12]. A fish structure, commonly known as a bait ball, is a result of predators' activity and tends toward minimization of the surfaces exposed to attack. It is worth to notice, that mapping (21) works globally, since it is determined on X, and it is opposed to local (and individual) activity.

There is a plenty of empirical evidence that the proposed relational model approximates well many collective behaviours of animal group. But we also know that this model is not perfect and can fail catastrophically for some animal groups. There are two hopes for avoiding such situation: understanding better phenomena of group behaviour and improvement of methods and tools used for modelling of these processes. And the latter will still be the focus of our future work.

References

1. Alexander, R.M.: Hitching a lift hydrodynamically - in swimming, flying and cycling. J. Biol. 3(2), article7; BioMed Central Ltd. (2004)
2. Blondel, V., Hendrickx, J.M., Olshevsky, A., Tsitsiklis, J.N.: Convergence in multi-agent coordination, consensus, and flocking. In: Proc. of 44th IEEE Conf. Decision and Control and 2005 Eur. Control Conf (CDC-ECC 2005), pp. 2996–3000 (2005)
3. Girvan, M., Newman, M.E.J.: Community structure in social and biological networks. Proceedings of National Academy of Sciences 99(12), 7821–7826 (2002)

4. Jaron, J.: Systemic Prolegomena to Theoretical Cybernetics: Scientific Papers of Institute of Technical Cybernetics, no. 45, Wroclaw University of Technology (1978)
5. Kuratowski, K., Mostowski, M.: Set Theory, with introduction to descriptive set theory; Studies in Logic and the Foundations of Mathematics, vol. 86. PWN-Warsaw, North-Holland, Amsterdam, New York (1976)
6. Nikodem, J., Chaczko, Z., Nikodem, M., Klempous, R.: Smart and Cooperative Neighbourhood for Spatial Routing in Wireless Sensor Networks. In: Madarász, L., Živčák, J. (eds.) Aspects of Computational Intelligence. TIEI, vol. 2, pp. 167–184. Springer, Heidelberg (2013)
7. Olfati-Saber, R., Fax, J.A., Murray, R.M.: Consensus and Cooperation in Networked Multi-Agent Systems. Proceedings of the IEEE 95(1) (2007)
8. Parrish, J.K., Viscido, S.V., Grunbaum, D.: Selforganized fish schools: An examination of emergent properties. Biol. Bull. 202, 296–305 (2002)
9. Pratt, S.C., Mallon, E.B., Sumpter, D.J.T., Franks, N.R.: Quorum sensing, recruitment, and collective decision-making during colony emigration by the ant Leptothorax albipennis. Behav. Ecol. Sociobiol. 52, 117–127 (2002), doi:10.1007/s00265-002-0487-x.
10. Reynolds, C.W.: Flocks, Herds, and Schools: A Distributed Behavioral Model. In: SIGGRAPH 1987 Conference Proceedings, Computer Graphics, vol. 21(4), pp. 25–34 (1987)
11. Savkin, A.V.: Coordinated collective motion of groups of autonomous mobile robots, Analysis of Vicsek's model. IEEE Trans. Autom. Control 49(6), 981–982 (2004)
12. Speakman, J.R., Banks, D.: The function of flight formations in Greylag Geese Anser anser; energy saving or orientation? IBIS 140(2), 280–287 (1998), doi:10.1111/j.1474-919X.1998.tb04390.x
13. Sumpter, D.J.T.: The principles of collective animal behaviour. Phil. Trans. R. Soc. B 361, 5–22 (2006), doi:10.1098/rstb.2005.1733.
14. Vicsek, T., Czirók, A., Ben-Jacob, E., Cohen, I., Shochet, O.: Novel Type of Phase Transition in a System of Self-Driven Particles. Phys. Rev. Lett. 75(6), 1226–1229 (1995)
15. Wolpert, D., Tumer, K.: An overview of collective intelligence. In: Bradshaw, J.M. (ed.) Handbook of Agent Technology. AAAI Press/MIT Press, Cambridge (1999)

Design of Decimation-Based Sequence Generators over Extended Fields

A. Fúster-Sabater[1] and O. Delgado-Mohatar[2]

[1] Information Security Institute (CSIC), Serrano 144, 28006 Madrid, Spain
amparo@iec.csic.es
[2] Universidad Internacional de Castilla y León, Calzadas 5, 09004 Burgos, Spain
oscar.delgado@unicyl.es

Abstract. Linear Feedback Shift Registers are currently used as generators of pseudorandom sequences with application in many and different areas. In this work, analysis and software implementation of LFSRs defined over extended fields $GF(2^n)$ (where n is related to the size of the registers in the underlying processor) instead of over the binary field $GF(2)$ have been considered. Once the migration from $GF(2)$ into $GF(2^n)$ has been accomplished, a study of decimation-based sequence generators has been proposed. Definition of new decimation criteria as well as their software implementation and corresponding analysis complete the work.

Keywords: Extended LFSR, software implementation, decimation criterium, stream cipher.

1 Introduction

Pseudorandom binary sequences are widely used in many and different areas: communication systems (digital TV broadcasting, global positioning systems, error correcting codes) as well as cryptography (building blocks in stream ciphers, mobile phones communication GSM, S-boxes in block ciphers, etc.).

Inside cryptographic technologies, stream ciphers are nowadays the fastest among the encryption procedures so they are implemented in distinct technological applications e.g. RC4 for encrypting Internet traffic [1] or the encryption function E0 in Bluetooth technology [2]. Stream ciphers imitate the mythic one-time pad cipher or Vernam cipher [3] and are designed to generate a long sequence (the *keystream sequence*) of seemingly random bits. Some of the most recent designs in stream ciphers can be found in [4] as well as References [5–8] provide a solid introduction to the study of stream ciphers.

Most keystream generators are based on maximal-length Linear Feedback Shift Registers (LFSRs) [9] whose output sequences, the m-sequences, are combined in a nonlinear way to produce pseudorandom sequences of cryptographic application. Traditionally, LFSRs have been designed to operate over the binary Galois field $GF(2)$ and, in fact, all the underlying mathematics are defined over

R. Moreno-Díaz et al. (Eds.): EUROCAST 2013, Part I, LNCS 8111, pp. 118–125, 2013.

this finite field, see [9]. This approach is appropriate for hardware implementations, but its software efficiency is low because of two important drawbacks:

- In order to update the state of a LFSR, the processor has to spend many clock cycles to perform the output generation operations (e.g. the multiplication) and such operations can be specially time-consuming.
- Binary LFSRs provide only one output bit per clock pulse, which makes the software implementations very inefficient and involves a clear waste of modern processor capabilities.

Thus, the use of greater finite fields seems to be a better alternative to modern processors. Indeed, the natural choice is the Galois extended field with 2^n elements, denoted by $GF(2^n)$, where n is related to the size of the registers in the underlying processor (currently words of 8, 16 or 32 bits). In this sense, the field elements fit perfectly well the storage unit and can be efficiently handled. At the same time, the total throughput of these extended generators is increased by a factor 8, 16 or 32, respectively.

On the other hand, irregularly decimated generators are just some of the most popular keystream sequence generators for cryptographic purposes. Inside this family of generators we can enumerate: the *shrinking generator* proposed by Coppersmith *et al.* [10] that includes two LFSRs, the *self-shrinking generator* designed by Meier and Staffelbach [11] with only one LFSR or the generalization of the latter generator called the *generalized self-shrinking generator* [12, 13] that generates a whole family of keystream sequences. Since the habitual decimation rules over $GF(2)$ are based on bit-decision, they cannot be applied over $GF(2^n)$. Thus, new decimation criteria must be defined for extended LFSRs. Therefore, the aim of this work is twofold:

1. The analysis of LFSRs defined over extended fields $GF(2^n)$ and their generation operations.
2. The definition of new decimation criteria adapted to extended LFSRs for irregularly decimated generators.

The paper is organized as follows. Specific notation and basic concepts on LFSRs over extended fields are introduced in Section 2. Different algebraic operations for these LFSRs and their performances are given in Sections 3 while the definition of new decimation criteria appear in Section 4. Finally, conclusions in Section 5 end the paper.

2   Sequence Generators over Extended Fields

Extended LFSRs are defined in the same way as the traditional ones. Some basic concepts are now introduced.

Definition 1. An extended LFSR of length L is a finite state machine acting over a finite field $\mathcal{F}_q$ of characteristic p, where $q = p^e$ with $e > 1$. In this case, $q = 2^n$ thus $\mathcal{F}_q = GF(2^n)$. A LFSR is made out of L memory cells $r_{L-1}, \ldots, r_1, r_0$, where each of them stores, s_{t+i} $(0 \leq i \leq L-1)$, an element of $GF(2^n)$. At time

t, the LFSR state is denoted by $S_t = (s_{t+L-1}, s_{t+L-2}, \ldots, s_t)$. At each time unit, the register updates its state. In fact, the state S_{t+1} is derived from the state S_t such as follows:

1. The content of the cell r_{L-1} is the corresponding element of the output sequence.
2. The content of the cell r_i is shifted into the cell r_{i+1} for all i, $0 \leq i \leq L-2$.
3. The new content of the cell r_0 is the feedback element computed according to the following feedback function:

$$s_{t+L} = \sum_{i=0}^{L-1} c_i \otimes s_{t+i}, \ c_i \in GF(2^n), \tag{1}$$

where the coefficients $c_0, c_1, \ldots, c_{L-1}$ are called *feedback coefficients* and the symbol $\otimes$ denotes the multiplication in $GF(2^n)$.

These coefficients define the LFSR *characteristic polynomial*:

$$p(x) = x^L + c_{L-1} x^{L-1} + \ldots + c_1 x + c_0. \tag{2}$$

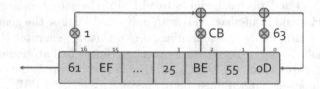

Fig. 1. Extended LFSR of 17 stages defined over $GF(2^8)$

Figure 1 shows an example of extended LFSR with 17 stages defined over $GF(2^8)$. In this new structure, the cell contents, s_{t+i} $0 \leq i \leq L-1$, as well as the feedback coefficients (all of them expressed in hexadecimal notation) are elements of $GF(2^8)$. This fact will affect the two arithmetic operations to be performed: addition and multiplication.

2.1 Arithmetic Operations in $GF(2^n)$

The elements of $GF(2^n)$ are represented by means of binary polynomials of degree less than n. For instance, the element a in $GF(2^4)$, notated $a = 0111$, can be represented by means of $a(x) = x^2 + x + 1$. Under this polynomial representation, the arithmetic operations are carried out in terms of an irreducible n-degree polynomial $R(x)$ defined as follows:

$$R(x) = x^n + d_{n-1} x^{n-1} + \ldots + d_1 x + 1, \ d_i \in GF(2). \tag{3}$$

The addition operation for such elements is simply the bit-wise XOR operation among n-dimensional vectors. The multiplication operation for such elements is the polynomial multiplication with the resulting polynomial being reduced mod $R(x)$.

In order to study the extended LFSRs, a set of polynomials $P_8(x)$, $P_{16}(x)$ and $P_{32}(x)$, defined over the fields $GF(2^8)$, $GF(2^{16})$ and $GF(2^{32})$, respectively, has been chosen. In a generic way, the feedback polynomials have the form:

$$P(x) = x^{17} + x^{15} + \alpha x^2 + \beta, \tag{4}$$

with $\alpha, \beta \in GF(2^n)$ and $\alpha, \beta \neq 0$. The corresponding feedback functions are:

$$s_{t+17} = s_{t+15} \oplus (\alpha \otimes s_{t+2}) \oplus (\beta \otimes s_t), \tag{5}$$

where $\oplus$ and $\otimes$ are addition and multiplication over $GF(2^n)$, respectively. The specific values of α, β for each polynomial and feedback function are shown in Table 1.

Table 1. Feedback function parameters used throughout the work

Polynomial	α	β
$P_8(x)$	$C6$	67
$P_{16}(x)$	$19B7$	$013C$
$P_{32}(x)$	$F21DA317$	$E28C895D$

The arithmetic multiplication deserves a specific study and will be considered in next Section.

3   The Multiplication in $GF(2^n)$

Multiplication operations in extension Galois fields are by far the most consuming time operations in extended LFSRs. For this reason, final performance greatly depends on the specific multiplication method used as experimental results seem to confirm. In next subsections, several methods for performing multiplication over the different extended Galois fields are analyzed.

3.1   MulTABLE Method

When the size of n in $GF(2^n)$ is small, the fastest procedure for multiplication is the use of look-up tables of pre-computed results. In general, the table size is $2^{(2n+2)}$ bytes, so that the method is adequate for small values of n. In Table 2, the table size increment for different values of n is depicted. It can be noticed that in practice only the value $n = 8$ is adequate as the table size equals 256 KB. For $n = 16$, the table size would be 16 GB, and for $n = 32$ the table would achieve the astronomic size of 64 EB (1 EB = 10^{18} bytes).

Table 2. Sizes for a table of pre-computed results

n	Resulting table size	Size in bytes
8	256 KB	2^{18}
10	4096 KB	2^{22}
12	64 MB	2^{26}
16	16 GB	$2^{34} \approx 10^{10}$
...	...	...
32	64 EB	$2^{66} \approx 10^{18}$

3.2   LogTABLE Method

When multiplication tables cannot be employed, the next fastest way to perform multiplication is to use log and inverse log tables, as described in [14]. Making use of these tables and somewhat of basic arithmetic, two elements can be multiplied by adding their corresponding logs and then taking their corresponding inverse log. In fact,

$$a \cdot b = invlogTable[(logTable[a] + logTable[b])]. \tag{6}$$

In this way, the multiplication is reduced to three looking-up in tables plus one addition operation. The first table, $logTable$ is defined for indices ranging from 1 up to $2^n - 1$ and stores for each field element its corresponding log. On the other hand, the second table $invlogTable$ is defined for indices ranging from 0 up to $2^n - 1$ establishing a map between these values and their inverse log. Clearly, $logTable[invlogTable[i]] = i$, and $invlogTable[logTable[i]] = i$. The size of these tables is $2^{(n+2)}$ bytes for each one of them instead of the $2^{(2n+2)}$ bytes of the previous method. Therefore, for $n = 8$ and $n = 16$ the size is 2 KB and 0.5 MB, respectively. Nevertheless for $n = 32$ the approximate size is 32 GB what is out of the capabilities of most modern processors.

3.3   SHIFT Method

When even log tables are unusable, general-purpose multiplication $a \cdot b$ can be implemented as a product of an $n \times n$ matrix and the bit-vector a, where the matrix is a function of operand b and the irreducible polynomial $R(x)$ that defines the field. Although it is significantly slower than the table methods, it is a general-purpose technique that requires no pre-allocation of memory.

3.4   SPLITW8 Method

Finally, for the special case of $n = 32$, a particular method is used that creates seven tables, each of them of 256 KB size. Such tables are employed to multiply 32-bit field elements by breaking them into four eight-bit parts, and then performing sixteen multiplications and XORs operations to calculate the product. With this optimization, the algorithm performs 7 times faster than when using the previous SHIFT method.

4   New Decimation Criteria for LFSRs over Extended Fields

Irregularly decimated generators are based on the decimation of the m-sequence produced by LFSR R_1 according to the bits of the m-sequence produced by LFSR R_2. The decimation result is the output sequence that will be used as keystream sequence.

Let $a_i, b_i, c_i \in GF(2^n)$ be the terms of the sequences generated by the registers R_1 and R_2 and the output sequence of the decimated generator, respectively. Different decimation criteria can be now stated:

4.1   Half Criterium

It can be considered as the translation from the traditional decimation criterium of the shrinking generator into extended LFSRs. It is a *simple* criterium as only the output sequence of LFSR R_1 is taken into account. In addition, half criterium is an efficient criterium as it works at the byte level and just two instructions "comparison and jump" (*cmpl, jg*) in assembly language are needed in its software implementation. The criterium is defined as:

$$\text{If } a_i < 2^{n-1} \text{ then } c_i = b_i$$
$$\text{If } a_i \geq 2^{n-1} \text{ then } b_i \text{ is discarded.}$$

4.2   Lesser Criterium

It is a *composite* criterium as output sequences from LFSR R_1 and LFSR R_2 are both taken into account. Its software implementation is less efficient than that of the previous criterium as three instructions in assembly language (*mov, cmp, jge*) are needed. The criterium is defined as:

$$\text{If } a_i < b_i \text{ then } c_i = b_i$$
$$\text{If } a_i \geq b_i \text{ then } b_i \text{ is discarded.}$$

4.3   Even Criterium

It makes use of the fact that half the terms of the sequence from LFSR R_1 are even while other half are odd. Its software implementation is much less efficient than those of the previous criteria as the parity check is based on the handling of bits. It implies the use of a mask and operations at the bit level. Several instructions in assembly language (*mov, and, test, jne*) are needed. The criterium is defined as:

$$\text{If } a_i \text{ is even then } c_i = b_i$$
$$\text{If } a_i \text{ is odd then } b_i \text{ is discarded.}$$

4.4 Nonlinear Criterium

Unlike all the previous criteria this one exhibits a nonlinear behavior. Consequently, it does not satisfy the balancedness requirement. In fact, about the 75% of the input values are discarded.

Due to its nonlinear nature, its software implementation is much slower than those of all the previous criteria here introduced. The criterium is defined as:

If $(a_i * b_i) \bmod 2^n$ is odd then $c_i = b_i$
If $(a_i * b_i) \bmod 2^n$ is even then b_i is discarded.

Finally, the experimental results obtained for each one of the decimation criteria appear in Table 3.

Table 3. Experimental results for different decimation criteria

Criterium	Type	Balancedness %	Time/decision
Half	Simple	(49.85%)	0.406 μs
Lesser	Composite	(49.66%)	0.437 μs
Even	Simple	(50.02%)	0.487 μs
Nonlinear	Composite	(74.96%)	0.571 μs

5 Conclusions

LFSRs defined over extended fields have been analyzed and implemented. Emphasis is on arithmetic operations particularly the multiplication involved in the generation mechanism of these structures. At the same time, irregularly decimated sequence generators over extended fields are considered and new decimation criteria are defined. Software implementation of such criteria have been simulated and executed. Characteristics of stability, balancedness in the number of elements discarded and efficiency in the implementation have been analyzed too. According to the practical results, Half Criterium seems to offer the better performances in what simplicity, computational cost and functionality are concerned.

Finally, the general ideas here proposed on decimated generators can be extended to any LFSR-based sequence generator operating over $GF(2^n)$.

Acknowledgments. This work has been supported by CDTI (Spain) in the frame of Project Cenit-HESPERIA as well as by Spanish MINECO and European FEDER Fund under Project TIN2011-25452.

References

1. Paul, G., Maitra, S.: RC4 Stream Cipher and Its Variants. Discrete Mathematics and Its Applications. CRC Press, Taylor & Francis Group, Boca Raton (2012)
2. Bluetooth, Specifications of the Bluetooth system, Version 1.1,
   http://www.bluetooth.com/

3. Nagaraj, N.: One-Time Pad as a nonlinear dynamical system. Communications in Nonlinear Science and Numerical Simulation 17, 4029–4036 (2012)
4. Robshaw, M., Billet, O. (eds.): New Stream Cipher Designs: The eSTREAM Finalist. LNCS, vol. 4986. Springer, Heidelberg (2008)
5. Menezes, A.: Handbook of Applied Cryptography. CRC Press (1997)
6. Paar, C., Pelzl, J.: Understanding Cryptography. Springer, Heidelberg (2010)
7. Rueppel, R.A.: Analysis and Design of Stream Ciphers. Springer, New York (1986)
8. Peinado, A., Fúster-Sabater, A.: Generation of pseudorandom binary sequences by means of linear feedback shift registers (LFSRs) with dynamic feedback. Mathematical and Computer Modelling 57, 2596–2604 (2013)
9. Golomb, S.W.: Shift Register-Sequences. Aegean Park Press, Laguna Hill (1982)
10. Coppersmith, D., Krawczyk, H., Mansour, Y.: The Shrinking Generator. In: Stinson, D.R. (ed.) CRYPTO 1993. LNCS, vol. 773, pp. 22–39. Springer, Heidelberg (1994)
11. Meier, W., Staffelbach, O.: The Self-Shrinking Generator. In: De Santis, A. (ed.) EUROCRYPT 1994. LNCS, vol. 950, pp. 205–214. Springer, Heidelberg (1995)
12. Hu, Y., Xiao, G.: Generalized Self-Shrinking Generator. IEEE Transaction on Information Theory 50, 714–719 (2004)
13. Fúster-Sabater, A., Caballero-Gil, P.: Chaotic modelling of the generalized self-shrinking generator. Appl. Soft Comput. 11, 1876–1880 (2011)
14. Greenan, K., Miller, E., Schwarz, T.: Optimizing Galois field arithmetic for diverse processor architectures and applications. In: Miller, E., Williamson, C. (eds.) Proc. of MASCOTS, pp. 257–266. IEEE Press, New York (2008)

Control and Command Systems Concepts from Early Work on a Mars Rover

Gabriel de Blasio[1], Arminda Moreno-Díaz[2], and Roberto Moreno-Díaz[1]

[1] Instituto Universitario de Ciencias y Tecnologías Cibernéticas
Universidad de Las Palmas de Gran Canaria
gdeblasio@dis.ulpgc.es,
rmoreno@ciber.ulpgc.es
[2] School of Computer Science. Madrid Technical University
amoreno@fi.upm.es

Abstract. We recover and develop some robotic systems concepts (on the light of present systems tools) that were originated for an intended Mars Rover in the sixties of the last century at the Instrumentation Laboratory of MIT, where one of the authors was involved.

The basic concepts came from the specifications for a type of generalized robot inspired in the structure of the vertebrate nervous systems, where the decision system was based in the structure and function of the Reticular Formation (RF).

The vertebrate RF is supposed to commit the whole organism to one among various modes of behavior, so taking the decisions about the present overall task. That is, it is a kind of control and command system.

In this concepts updating, the basic idea is that the RF comprises a set of computing units such that each computing module receives information only from a reduced part of the overall, little processed sensory inputs. Each computing unit is capable of both general diagnostics about overall input situations and of specialized diagnostics according to the values of a concrete subset of the input lines.

Slave systems to this command and control computer, there are the sensors, the representations of external environment, structures for modeling and planning and finally, the effectors acting in the external world.

1 Introduction and a General Structure

A research and development program being carried out at the Instrumentation Laboratory of MIT in the sixties, under the leadership of Louis Sutro [1–3], aimed at the communication of pictorial data from remote locations and to develop methods of making fast and appropriate decisions there. Both general aims were to be obtained by the use of biology as a source of ideas. Warren McCulloch, then a member of the group [4, 5], had concluded from his life-long study of the human nervous system that the essential properties of human computation must serve as the basis of the corresponding artificial systems. Although he was aware of the dangers involved in embodying mental functions in physical

R. Moreno-Díaz et al. (Eds.): EUROCAST 2013, Part I, LNCS 8111, pp. 126–133, 2013.

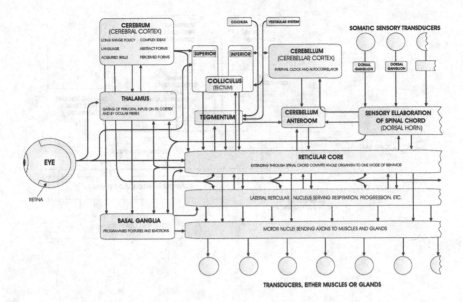

Fig. 1. Block diagram of generalized vertebrate nervous system

devices, he developed a simplified model of the vertebrate brain. His intention was merely to suggest an organizational hierarchy necessary for robot performance. Figure 1 is an outline of the model, where five principal computational areas and their connections are identified: the retina, the cerebrum, the reticular core, basal ganglia and cerebellum.

A diagram of a possible engineering equivalent, proposed by Louis Sutro, is shown in figure 2, where the equivalent substitutions beside the sensors are as follows: decision computer for reticular core; associative computer for cerebral cortex; timing, coordinating and autocorrelating computer for cerebellum; computer of effector sequences for basal ganglia and computer of specialized controls for lateral reticular nuclei. The memory is distributed and it should be associative.

These general diagrams are still nowadays very much inspiring. For the sake of simplification, we shall reduce it to a diagram showing the specific counterparts in robotic and artificial intelligent tools that each one of the large components may have. This is shown in figure 3.

In this proposal, the overall system presents a set of "modes of behavior" that mimic the accepted model of behavior of the vertebrates [6, 7]. The selection of a particular mode is performed by the command and control system, based mostly in present sensorial information (S.D.) and the status of the system. An external input (EI) is allowed from the external world (in practice, it should came from operator's console) to modulate the selection of a mode.

Information concerning the selected mode (M) is sent to the sensors, which are to be tuned to optimize the data acquisition pertinent to the mode of action. It is also sent to the component labeled Files of World Representations, in which the appropriate model of the environment and of the system in the

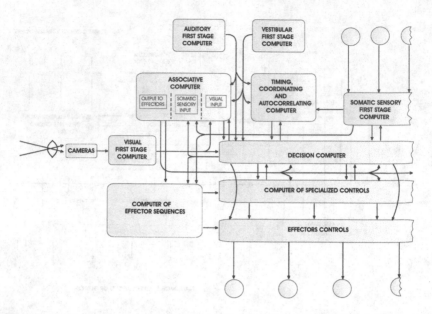

Fig. 2. Block diagram employing functional engineering nomenclature

environment is selected to be sent to the component labeled Planning in Present World Representation. Finally, the selected mode commands and controls the process of establishing goals according to the mode, the process of planning and the execution of the plan, by taking into account continuous highly processed sensory data (S). Updated world representations are sent back through W.R. lines when the mode changes. There are also direct connections between sensors and actuators (line R) which are equivalent to reflex paths. Line E provides for high level instructions to the effectors according to the plan of action, which are to be decoded into concrete motor-effector actions.

An appropriate computer architecture to embody such a system is shown in Figure 4. There are two types of specialized processors concerning the sensory data and concerning the effectors, which hung on the corresponding buses.

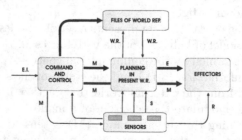

Fig. 3. A diagram showing the specific counterparts in robotic and artificial intelligent tools

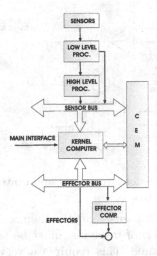

Fig. 4. Computer architecture for an integrated system

Command and control, as well as planning is performed by the Kernel, while computations corresponding to models of the environment are performed in the unit labeled C.M.E. (Computer Models of the Environment).

2   Command and Control

The basic function of a command and control system is to commit the whole system to one overall mode of behavior belonging to a not very large set. This is what enables it to behave as a well-integrated unit instead of a loose connection of separate sensors, effectors and processors. In this sense, a command and control computer is a close paradigm to the operation of the reticular formation in vertebrates [8]. Any mode of behavior is incompatible with any other. Some general properties can be established for such a computer. First, it receives relatively unprocessed information from all of the sensors situated in sensory and effector sub-systems. Second, it gives signals, which control, tune and set the filters of all external inputs. In McCulloch words [4], "this is the structure that decides what to look and having looked, what to heed". It also controls all the information flow from and to higher level computers. This is similar to the problem of decision and attention [9, 10].

From a structural point of view, the command computer must have a modular architecture, or, at least, it must simulate it. The basic idea is that a set of computing units (C.U.) is such that each computing module receives information only from a reduced part of the overall, little processed sensory inputs (see figure 5).

Each computing unit is capable of both general diagnostics about overall input situations and of specialized diagnostics according to the values of a concrete subset of the input lines.

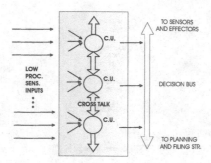

Fig. 5. Structure for a command and control computer

A crucial point is that a consensus of the diagnostics, which corresponds to the selection of a single mode of behavior, must be reached by the computing units in a relatively short time. This requires a very strong crosstalk among the computing units, which is a peculiar feature of the so-called cooperative processors [4]. There are two basic properties of the computing modules that can be stated easily by means of the terminology common in expert system.

In fact, we can look at the computing units as if they were simplified experts systems working on their own databases and with their own inference engines on their specialized domain of sensory inputs [11, 12]. But they are capable also of giving up before the evidence in diagnostics by other units, which show to have more relevant information for the case. This "giving up" must be understood in the sense of a recruiting of the rest of the modules by those having more confidence about their diagnostic. As it was stated by McCulloch [6], modules having the information pertinent to the case "cry louder", and doing so, they recruit the rest. The result of this strong crosstalk is that the system converges into one mode, in the sense that practically all the units decide the same mode of behavior, though with perhaps different degree of confidence.

Modularity and division of expertise, with overlapping among the computers units, are the two basic features of a cooperative processing system. Also, appropriate crosstalk rules are the necessary addendum to achieve convergence. This architecture is supposed to provide for two main goals: first, to speed up the decision process by which a mode of behavior is selected; second, the system is supposed to present high reliability, in such a way that it will arrive into an appropriate consented mode, even when some of the expert units are destroyed.

This second aspect, that is, the reliability intrinsic to distributed expertise, precludes any decision based upon a single majority organ, because its malfunction will imply total inoperability. That is, the conclusion that a consensus has been reached cannot be the output of any special testing unit receiving its inputs from the expert units. Instead, the decided modes must be appropriately labeled according to their origin to prevent mixing, and be present in a non-computing structure, that is, a set of wires, or axons, or in other words, in a kind of decision bus. From this, it becomes clear that reaching a rapid consensus in the mode of behavior at the command and control computer is absolutely necessary for the

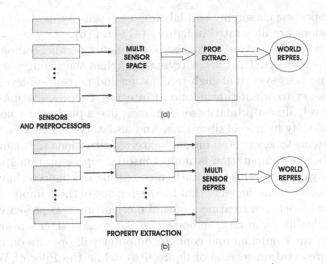

Fig. 6. Illustration of two mechanisms for representing multi-sensorial data

rest of the system to operate coherently, because, otherwise, the various higher and lower subsystems to be controlled, will have a high probability of picking up operation instructions from the decision bus, which belong to different exclusive modes of behavior, such that a kind of neurotic situation will be created.

In sum, the role of the command and control computer is to sense crude sensorial data, and to decide modes of behavior sending them to the decision bus, through a strong crosstalk among units to converge into a single mode, so that coherent behavior is secured.

3   Multi-sensorial Environment Representation

There are two basic ways to structure multi-sensorial information which, in turn, admit different levels of representation, from geometric to highly symbolic. These two ways correlate with the finality of the representation which may tend to be optimal for discriminating among environment patterns or to be a representation to optimize the acquisition of clues for actions. These correspond to:

a) Integrated representation, both at low levels of acquisition and a high level of the processing of sensory data.
b) Step by step representation, in which integration only occurs at high level, that is in symbolic structures.

In other words, and putting aside for the moment all natural systems, we may either represent the sensed environment by means of a multidimensional space where all sensory modalities are present with their own resolution at low level, while all high level processing is performed directly in this space [13]. Or we can construct a high level inter-sensorial representation space by previously extracting properties; classifying and labeling each sensory modality separately. These two options are illustrated in figure 6(a) and 6(b).

These two possibilities seem to coexist in the highly parallel computing structures of natural systems. Thus, when trying to explain the strong discriminating power of the nervous system at high recognition and perception levels, it seems logically necessary to admit that a kind of integrated representation is present, because low level, almost primarily sensed clues, like a pitch or a color, are definite clues to identify high level situations. And also, there are very fast responses of natural systems to key overall internal-external situations that cannot be explained if elaborate computation in multi-sensorial representation spaces where required. In any case, it seems that the two coexisting mechanisms have a type of principle of constancy, in the sense that increasing one of them implies decreasing the other. A more detailed treatment of said mechanisms was presented in [14].

The above duality is, in fact, embodied in the general structure proposed in figure 1. Thus, the command and control computer will operate on data which follow the representation scheme of figure 6(b), while the Files of World Representations, and, subsequently, the Planning Systems [15], operate according the scheme of figure 6(a). This implies that, when setting the mode of operation, different sensory modalities are taking separately the task of extracting medium level descriptors, which are necessary for the operation of the command and control computer. But, once the mode is decided upon, representation and planning structures shall take again the sensory data without much processing to "navigate" in a multi sensorial space where to perform processes, from low levels to high levels.

This interpretation helps to understand how the nervous system is capable of sharing high level computing structures after depression or destruction of primary sensory channels [16]. That is, the so called inter-sensorial transformations can only occur in an integrated representation space as is shown in figure 6(b). Therefore, the command and control computer in natural systems has not the ability to use directly the expertise of computing units acting upon sensory data which are depressed, while in the planning and representation spaces, this is a possibility. In other words, there seem to be two different mechanisms for attaining reliability and speeding up a decision and/or recognition process. That is, the command and control system operates with expert units which receive very restricted data, while the planning and higher structures have general purpose units which may work on almost row data form different sources.

The above systems concepts are presently developed to obtain specific artificial intelligence symbolic models and neural nets representations.

References

1. Sutro, L.L., Warren, R.E., Moulton, D., Whitman, C., Zeise, F.: 1963 Advanced Sensor Investigations R-470. Instrumentation Laboratory. MIT, Cambridge (1964)
2. Sutro, L.L., Kilmer, W., McCulloch, W.S., Catchpole, R., Tweed, D., Blum, J., Peterson, D., Moreno-Díaz, R.: Sensory, Decision and Control Systems. R-548. Instrumentation Laboratory. MIT, Cambridge (1966)

3. Sutro, L.L., Kilmer, W.: Assembly of Computers to Command and Control a Robot. R-582. Instrumentation Laboratory. MIT, Cambridge (1969)
4. McCulloch, W.S.: Logic and Closed Loops for a Computer Junket to Mars. In: Caianiello, E. (ed.), pp. 65–91. Springer (1968)
5. McCulloch, W.S., Papert, S., Blum, M., Simoes da Fonseca, J.L., Moreno-Díaz, R.: After-Dinner Address: The Fun of Failures. Ann. New York Acad. Sciences 156(2), 963–968 (1969)
6. Kilmer, W., McCulloch, W.S.: The Reticular Formation Command and Control System. In: Leibovic, K.N. (ed.) Information Processing in the Nervous System, pp. 297–308. Springer, Heidelberg (1969)
7. Kilmer, W.: A Global Imhibitory Model for Deciding Modes of Attention. In: Moreno-Díaz, R., Mira-Mira, J. (eds.) Brain Processes, Theories and Models, pp. 125–133. The MIT Press, Cambridge (1996)
8. Delgado, A.E., Mira, J., Moreno-Díaz, R.: A Neurocybernetic Model of Modal Cooperative Decisions in the Kilmer-McCulloch Space. Kybernetes 18(3), 48–57 (1989)
9. Gottlieb, J., Balan, P.F.: Attention as a decision in information space. Trends in Cognitive Sciences 14(6), 240–248 (2010)
10. Gorea, A., Sagi, D.: On decision and attention. In: Itti, Rees, Tsotso (eds.) Neurobiology of Attention. Academic Press, Elsevier (2004)
11. Nilsson, N.J.: Principles of Artificial Intelligence. Tioga, Palo Alto (1980)
12. Russell, S.J., Norvig, P.: Artificial Intelligence: A Modern Approach, 3rd edn. Prentice Hall (2009)
13. Mira, J.: Reverse Neurophysiology: The Embodiments of Mind Revisited. In: Brain Processes, Theories and Models, pp. 37–49. The MIT Press, Mass (1995)
14. Moreno-Díaz, R., Mira, J.: Conceptos para una teoría de la integración multisensorial. In: Proc. II Simpos. Nac. IFAC, pp. 227–232. Universidad, Zaragoza (1984)
15. Brooks, R., Lozano-Perez, T.: A Subdivision Algorithm Configuration Space for Findpath with Rotation. In: de Bondy, A. (ed.) Proc. Eight IJCAI, pp. 799–806. W. Kauffam, Los altos (1983)
16. Mira, J., Delgado, A.E., Manjaros, A., Ros, S., Alvarez, J.R.: Cooperative Processes at the Symbolic level in Cerebral Dynamics: Reliability and Fault Tolerance. In: Moreno-Diaz, R., Mira-Mira, J. (eds.) Brain Processes, Theories and Models, pp. 244–255. The MIT Press, Cambridge (1996)

Transaction-Level Modeling and Refinement Using State Charts

Rainer Findenig[1,2], Thomas Leitner[2], and Wolfgang Ecker[3]

[1] Upper Austrian University o. A. S., Hagenberg, Austria
`rainer.findenig@fh-hagenberg.at`
[2] DMCE GmbH & Co KG, Linz, Austria
[3] Infineon Technologies AG, Neubiberg, Germany

Abstract. Since State Charts have been introduced, they have proven to be of great use in the design of complex reactive systems. Previous work has shown that, in hardware design, they can be successfully used for transaction-level modeling as well as for cycle-callable systems. This paper presents a structure-preserving refinement approach for State Charts that allows modeling hardware on different abstraction levels, from completely untimed high-level models to cycle callable, in a single model. This single-source approach, on the one hand, eases the agility of the development since changes in any abstraction level are more easily applied in the other levels, and, on the other hand, provides a simple means for checking the consistency of the different abstraction levels.

1 Introduction

Many hardware development projects use a design flow based on transaction-level (TL) models, in which an abstract system model is, step by step, refined into a register-transfer-level model for synthesis. The most common abstraction levels in use are defined in [1], in which, in order of increasing accuracy, the terms "untimed", "loosely timed", "approximately timed" for both communication and calculation, and, for the most accurate abstractions, "register transfer logic" for calculation and "pin and cycle accurate" for communication are introduced. To simplify the terminology, we will call any model using register transfer logic as well as pin and cycle accurate communication a "cycle-callable" model and use the term "transaction-level" model to denote a model on any of those abstraction levels—usually, but not necessarily, more abstract than cycle callable.

Though much work has been done in the field of high-level synthesis, the process of refining a high-level model to a lower abstraction level is still often manual: several different models must be developed, verified against each other, and kept in sync when bugs are fixed or the specification changes. With the introduction of OSCI TLM [2], handling different abstraction levels with regard to communication was greatly simplified; the abstraction of computation is not directly handled, however. The presented approach aims to provide an extension to State Charts (SCs) that, based on "refinements", supports multiple abstraction

R. Moreno-Díaz et al. (Eds.): EUROCAST 2013, Part I, LNCS 8111, pp. 134–141, 2013.
© Springer-Verlag Berlin Heidelberg 2013

levels with regard to both communication and computation in a single model, which, using a code generator, can automatically be translated to SystemC code.

Note that, due to the limited space available, we cannot provide an introduction to SCs in this paper; a basic introduction is given in e.g. [3], [4] presents the semantics we followed in this approach.

2   Related Work

Our work extends transaction-level SCs as presented in [5] with a refinement relation, for which a graphical representation was suggested in [6]: we allow the designer to describe different abstraction levels of a SC in a single model and provide means in the code generator to seamlessly switch between those levels.

Previous work on SC refinement includes [7–9] and mostly differs in two aspects: the supported SC dialect and whether or not the structure is preserved during the refinement. For example, the refinement calculus presented in [7] allows modifications of the SC's structure, such as adding or removing transitions or states. More importantly, it guarantees that the refinement is correct by construction. However, this guarantee uses the fact that μ-Charts are based on synchronous Mealy automata with internal variables, which are less expressive with regard to high-level transaction-level models than the SC variant used in our approach, where, for all abstraction levels other than cycle callable, the behavior can consist of arbitrary action code. Other approaches, such as [8] and [9], use a similarly restricted variation of SCs, leading to the same limitations.

Compared to the approach for refinement checking in finite state machines presented in [10], we allow parallelism, hierarchy, and behavior to be specified in arbitrary C code. Moreover, their approach uses a mapping function that has to be supplied separately by the designer, that, in our approach, is implicitly part of the model since all refinements are entered in a single model.

Bombieri et al. presented an approach for equivalence checking between different abstraction levels [11]. They use a happens-before relation and filtering functions that allow comparing behavior between the two abstraction levels. Based on this, they define the black-box consistenty as producing the same outputs for the same inputs. This allows comparing arbitrary models, resulting in a higher degree of flexibility during the refinement but lower localizability of errors compared to the structure-preserving refinement approach we present. Still, the synchronization borders we define use the same idea as their happens-before relation in combination with filtering functions: they provide points during the execution in which both the abstract and the refined SC should have executed the same computation—in their approach, those points in time are based on the input/output behavior while in ours, they are based on internal state transitions.

3   State Chart Syntax

To describe SCs, we use a syntax similar to the one presented in [12]. Since our work is targeted at UML SCs [3], however, we use UML's notion of *(composite)* *states* and *regions* instead of the traditional SC notion of *OR states* and *AND states*. Furthermode, we split the set of behavior ($\mathcal{A}$), as defined in [12], into blocking and nonblocking actions, denoted $\mathcal{A}_B$ and $\mathcal{A}_N$, respectively[1]. Blocking actions can, in contrast to nonblocking actions, consume simulated time. In addition to $en, ex \in \mathcal{A}_N^*$, as defined in [12] to describe the entry and exit actions of a state, we use $do \in (\mathcal{A}_N \cup \mathcal{A}_B)^*$ to denote a state's do activity and define the terms accordingly. Also, we use $ef \in \mathcal{A}_N^*$ to denote a transition's effect. Note that we allow blocking behavior only in do activities to support zero-time evaluation [5]. Also, we do not use the source restriction and the target determinator since our approach does not support interlevel transitions. Our approach does not support history, so we do not use HT. Finally, we extend the syntax with a set $\mathcal{V}$ of variables as well as the sets $\mathcal{I}$ of input signals and $\mathcal{O}$ of output signals. For the definition, let Π denote the sets of events and G be the set of guards which are boolean expressions, possibly over elements of $\mathcal{V}$ and $\mathcal{I}$. Then, regions and states are recursively defined as follows:

Region. A term $r = [S, s_0, S_f, T]$ represents a region ("is a region term") if all $s \in S$ are state terms (i.e., $S \subset \mathcal{S}$ which will be defined later), $s_0 \in S$, $S_f \subset S$, and $T \subseteq S \times 2^\Pi \times G \times \mathcal{A}_N^* \times S$. We will denote the set of all region terms with $\mathcal{R}$.

   $s_i \in S$ are the region's mutually exclusive substates where s_0 is the initial state, S_f is the (possibly empty) set of final states, and T is the set of the region's transitions. We write transitions as $t = (s_s, e, g, ef, s_t)$ where s_s, e, g, ef, and s_t are the source state, the event to trigger the transition, the guard, the effect, and the target state, respectively. A transition with $e = \emptyset$ is called a completion transition and is executed when the transition's source state is finished executing. The guard may be given as $\top$ which always evaluates to true; this corresponds to no guard being given in the diagram.

State. A term $s = [R, (en, do, ex), V]$ is a state term if all $r \in R$ are region terms (i.e., $R \subset \mathcal{R}$), $en \in \mathcal{A}_N^*$, $do \in (\mathcal{A}_N \cup \mathcal{A}_B)^*$, and $ex \in \mathcal{A}_N^*$. We will denote the set of all state terms with $\mathcal{S}$.

   R is the (possibly empty) set of concurrently active regions contained in the state. If $|R| = 0$, the state is called a leaf state, otherwise it is called composite. $V \subseteq \mathcal{V}$ is the set of variables defined in the state s.

Finally, a SC is $SC = [r_0, V, \mathcal{I}, \mathcal{O}]$ if r_0 is a region term and $V \subseteq \mathcal{V}$. We call r_0 the State Chart's top-level region, V the set of globally available variables, and $\mathcal{I}$ and $\mathcal{O}$ the State Chart's sets of input and output signals, respectively.

Variables are subject to a scoping mechanism similar to that of most programming languages; to simplify the definition, we do not allow a variable to shadow another, however. We say that the set of visible variables and outputs ($visible(x) \subseteq \mathcal{V} \cup \mathcal{O}$) in a state or transition x is the set of variables that are defined one of x's containing states or, additionally, if x is a state, in x itself.

Support for Refinements. In the following, we will use "State Chart" or "SC" to denote a concrete abstraction level and the term "model" to denote the UML

---

[1] Note that we use $\mathcal{A}^*$ to denote the Kleene closure over $\mathcal{A}$.

model entered by the designer which may contain an arbitrary amount of different SCs on different abstraction levels: each model contains exactly one "original" SC, which is the one the model describes without applying any refinements, and zero or more refinements that can, in different combinations, be used to derive concrete SCs on other abstraction levels.

To support refinements, the presented approach introduces the set K of refinement keys defined in the model. Then, a refinement relation Ψ, similarly to the mapping function described in [10], is: $\Psi \subset (\mathcal{S} \times K \times \mathcal{S}) \cup (\mathcal{T} \times K \times \mathcal{T})$. If $(x, k, y) \in \Psi$, we write $\Psi(x, k) = y$ and say that x is refined by y under the refinement key k. Note that x can be both a state or a transition, and y must be the same type as x.

For convenience, if $K' \subseteq K$ is a set of refinements that should be applied, let $\Psi(x, K') = y \iff \exists! k \in K' : (x, k, y) \in \Psi$. If there is more than exactly one $k \in K'$ that allows a refinement of x, the set of refinements K' is illegal. Also, we will use $SC^\emptyset$ to denote the original SC, and $SC^{K'}$ a SC derived from $SC^\emptyset$ by applying the set of refinements K'. Applying a refinement k means that for every state or transition x of the model, if for some y, $(x, k, y) \in \Psi$, then the element x is replaced by the element y, leaving the rest of the SC unchanged.

4 Refinement Consistency

Our approach places a strong focus on the consistency of the refinement. To define consistency between two elements, we use the Liskov Substitution Principle (LSP) [13]. It is usually applied to class inheritance in object oriented programming, but can just as well be applied to behavioral consistency for SCs [14]. Simply put, the LSP demands that any instance of a subtype exhibits the same behavior as an instance of the original type [13]. Since the LSP is undecidable in general, it is impossible to prove whether two arbitrary SCs are equivalent. To facilitate the design of refinements, we therefore introduce a "cosimulation"-based approach, in which both models are fed the same input during a simulation. For two given sets of refinements, $K_h \subset K$ and $K_l \subset K$, where $K_h \subsetneq K_l$ and K_h may be $\emptyset$, the SC SC^{K_h} will be called "high-level" and SC^{K_l} "low-level".

Consistency under State Refinement. For behavioral inheritance [14], for each state x of SC^{K_h} that was replaced with a state y of SC^{K_l}, y must be, in the sense of the LSP, substitutable for x:

R1 For a SC SC^{K_h} and its refinement SC^{K_l} to be consistent, for every refinement key $k \in K_l \setminus K_h$, for every tuple $(x, k, y) \in \Psi$ where $x, y \in \mathcal{S}$ and x is a state in SC^{K_h}, the state y must be substitutable for x.

  A state y is substitutable for another state x iff it adheres to the LSP with regard to x, or, in other words, iff it manipulates all variables and output signals in the same way as x does.

To check the consistency of y with regard to x, we use *synchronization borders*: the low-level SC SC^{K_l} can be obtained from the high-level SC SC^{K_h} by applying the refinements $K_l \setminus K_h$. During this step, we mark every state x of SC^{K_h} that is replaced by another state as a synchronization border, and generate a corresponding scoreboard (SB) (denoted "state SB") that records $visible(x)$ whenever x is entered/left in the high-level SC or y is entered/left in the low-level SC. Note that only variables and outputs visible to x are checked: y has to modify all variables in the same way x does, but can read/write arbitrary additional variables that are only present in the low-level model.

In addition to the simulation, static code analysis can be used to detect errors early in the design phase. Specifically, we use a code-analysis based approach to check whether the set of variables and ports written in x the same as the one of y, again without considering variables only available in y.

Note that the above requirement does not consider the states' timings. The high-level SC can be approximately timed or even untimed to improve its simulation performance and reduce the implementation effort, whereas the low-level SC can incorporate a more elaborated or even the final, cycle-accurate timing to allow a more detailed evaluation. In this sense, our approach uses a white-box based check of the two abstraction levels' happens-before relations of state/variable modifications, in contrast to the happens-before relation defined over input/output behavior of [11].

Consistency under Transition Refinement. As long as transitions cannot be altered, checking the LSP for each substituted state is sufficient. When allowing transition refinement, however, one needs to ensure that the state trajectories of both SCs are stutter equivalent[2], too. Therefore, for consistency under transition refinement, a definition of substitutability for transitions needs to include both calculation (of the transition's effect) and stutter equivalence.

Recall that we defined transitions as $t = (s_s, e, g, ef, s_t)$, $t \in S \times 2^\Pi \times G \times \mathcal{A}_N^* \times S$. Consider the components:

- s_s, s_t: To preserve the SC's structure, neither the source nor the target state of a transition can be changed using transition refinement.
- e, g: Intuitively, every event that triggers the high-level transition x must also trigger the low-level transition y. Since the way an event is described may depend on the abstraction level[3], the events need to be consistent.
- $ef \in \mathcal{A}_N^*$: A transition's effect allows adding behavior to a SC, which, obviously, needs to be consistent when refined. Analogously to the substitutability for states, the LSP is sufficient to check this.

Therefore, the following two requirements were derived: for a SC SC^{K_h} and its refinement SC^{K_l} to be consistent, for every refinement key $k \in K_l \setminus K_h$, for every tuple $(x, k, y) \in \Psi$, where $x, y \in \mathcal{T}$ and x is a transition in SC^{K_h},

---

[2] Since the refinement can substitute a leaf state with a composite state that uses several substates to achieve the same computation, the refinement can stutter compared to the original model.

[3] For example, an abstract transition might be triggered on an event signifying the end of a transaction, while its refinement uses the clock event and, as its guard, an additional flag to check for the operation's end.

R2 the combination of the event and the guard of the transition y must be consistent with the combination of the event and the guard of the transition x, and

R3 the effect of the transition y must adhere to the LSP with regard to the effect of the transition x,

in which *R2* ensures the stutter equivalence, and *R3* ensures the LSP between the transitions' effects. Note that, obviously, *R2* is only sufficient to ensure the stutter equivalence iff *R1* and *R3* hold. Otherwise, internally calculated guards might differ between different abstraction levels, and, therefore, influence the state trajectories.

Checking *R3* is done analogously to the method for *R1*: the visible variables are recorded/compared in an SB (denoted "transition SB") before and after every execution of both the high-level and the low-level transition.

Let $x = (s_s, e, g, ef, s_t)$ be the high-level transition and $y = (s_s, e', g', ef', s_t)$ its refinement. For checking *R2*, consider the transitions' types, i. e. if they are normal or completion transitions. We do not allow refining a completion transition with an event-triggered transition or vice versa: a completion transition is triggered on its source state's completion event, and the low-level transition y has the same source state as x, or at least one that is substitutable. Since the completion event is internal to the SC, it is not possible for an external event to be consistent with the completion event. Changing the transition's type would therefore break the stutter equivalence.

Therefore, refinements of a transition can only use the same type. If both are normal transitions, since the trigger and the guard of the transitions can be arbitrarily changed during the refinement, the stutter equivalence of the state trajectory is not correct by construction anymore: the combination of e and g must be consistent with the combination of e' and g'. If this is not the case, one transition might be executed when the other one is not, or a different transition might be executed. Therefore, in this case, an additional SB, denoted "region SB", is generated to compare the state transitions of the two regions containing the high-level and the low-level transitions, respectively, and thereby ensuring stutter equivalence. Note that a single SB is sufficient per region, regardless of the amount of refined transitions inside the region. If both transitions are completion transitions, this is in fact a special case of the one above; inconsistencies in the state trajectory are only possible if the guards g and g' are not consistent. This can be also caught by a SB as described above.

5   Results

Our approach has, up till now, been tested on two examples: a cryptography core supporting 256 bit AES ECB encryption (as presented in [6]) and a reimplementation of the control unit of the open-source Plasma CPU[4]. Please refer to the respective sources for a complete description of the examples; due to the limited space, we can only include a high-level overview.

---

[4] http://opencores.org/project,plasma

Table 1. Scoreboards for the AES ECB core

		A1			A2			A3			A4			A5		
		S	T	R	Σ	S	T	R	Σ	S	T	R	Σ	S	T	R	Σ	S	T	R	Σ

(Original SC header spanning all columns; Refined SC label on left.)

Refined SC		A1 S	T	R	Σ	A2 S	T	R	Σ	A3 S	T	R	Σ	A4 S	T	R	Σ	A5 S	T	R	Σ
	A2	1	0	0	*1*	-	-	-	-	-	-	-	-	-	-	-	-	-	-	-	-
	A3	1	0	0	*1*	-	-	-	-	-	-	-	-	-	-	-	-	-	-	-	-
	A4	1	0	0	*1*	-	-	-	-	1	0	0	*1*	-	-	-	-	-	-	-	-
	A5	1	2	1	*4*	-	-	-	-	1	2	1	*4*	3	3	2	*8*	-	-	-	-
	A6	1	2	1	*4*	-	-	-	-	1	2	1	*4*	3	3	2	*8*	1	0	0	*1*

Table 2. Scoreboards for the Plasma control unit

(Original SC header spanning all columns; Refined SC label on left.)

Refined SC		A1 S	T	R	Σ	A2 S	T	R	Σ	A3 S	T	R	Σ
	A2	1	0	0	*1*	-	-	-	-	-	-	-	-
	A3	1	0	0	*1*	0	4	1	*5*	-	-	-	-
	A4	1	0	0	*1*	0	4	1	*5*	0	4	1	*5*

The model of the AES core includes six abstraction levels, comprising of an abstract implementation using a third-party library (A1, which corresponds to $SC^{\emptyset}$) which is refined in four increasingly detailed abstraction levels (A3 to A6, where Ai corresponds to $SC^{\{\alpha_3,...,\alpha_i\}}$ and A6 is at the RTL level) and an additional variant of A1, denoted A2 ($SC^{\{\alpha_2\}}$). Table 1 presents the amount of the amount of state (S), transition (T), region (R), and total (Σ) SBs generated for verifying the consistency of two abstraction levels. Since $K_h \subsetneq K_l$, there are illegal combinations, which are marked with "-".

A1 uses a single state for calculation, which is refined under α_2 by a state modeling timing in A2: since this is the only change, a single state SB is required for checking the consistency. A3 is again based on A1 and, under α_3, refines its calculation state with a custom implementation, again resulting in a single state SB. Note that no abstraction level is based on A2, which is why no other abstraction level can be verified against it. We'll present two further interesting cases: first, A5 refines three states and three transitions from A4, requiring three state SBs, three transition SBs, and two region SBs (since two refined transitions are in the same region). Second, if A3 is used as a reference for verifying A5, since A3 provides less detail, fewer SBs will be used: one transition refined from A4 to A5 is not available in A3 and therefore will not be checked, reducing the transition SBs to two and the region SBs to one. Furthermore, the three states refined in A5 are not available in A3, which is why their superstate, which is refined by A4 compared to A3, will be used for checking consistency, resulting in only a single state SB. Therefore, verifying A5 against A3 requires less overhead, but also reduces the localizability of bugs.

The results obtained for the Plasma control unit are presented in Table 2. It uses a simpler refinement structure in which each refinement is based on the former one. A1 uses an single, highly abstract state, for all behavior, which is refined by A2, and therefore all abstraction levels, when verified against A1, will use a single SB for that state. A3 only refines four transitions, all of which are in a single region, of A2, resulting in four transition SBs and one region SB.

6   Conclusion

We presented a SC-based approach for defining several abstraction levels of a hardware model in a single source. This provides several advantages during the design: changes in unrelated parts of the high-level model are implicitly reflected in all abstraction levels, minimizing the need to keep several models in sync. To ensure consistency between abstraction levels, we presented a cosimulation approach that, based on the structural similarities of the different abstraction levels, can be used to verify the refinements specified in the model. It should be noted that the quality of the verification achieved using cosimulation is, of course, dependent on the test vectors. Therefore, to improve the confidence in the approach, future research will include the generation of both additional code for collecting functional coverage and test vectors from the model.

References

1. Black, D.C., Donovan, J.: SystemC: from the ground up. Springer Science+Business Media, LLC (2010)
2. Aynsley, J.: OSCI TLM-2.0 Language Reference Manual (2009)
3. Object Management Group: OMG Unified Modeling Language (OMG UML), Superstructure (2011)
4. Findenig, R., Leitner, T., Esen, V., Ecker, W.: Consistent SystemC and VHDL Code Generation from State Charts for Virtual Prototyping and RTL Synthesis. In: Proceedings of DVCon 2011, San Jose, CA, USA (2011)
5. Findenig, R., Leitner, T., Velten, M., Ecker, W.: Transaction-Level State Charts in UML and SystemC with Zero-Time Evaluation. In: Proceedings of DVCon 2010, San Jose, CA, USA (2010)
6. Findenig, R., Leitner, T., Ecker, W.: Single-Source Hardware Modeling of Different Abstraction Levels with State Charts. In: Proceedings of HLDVT 2012, Huntington Beach, CA, USA (2012)
7. Scholz, P.: Incremental design of statechart specifications. Science of Computer Programming 40(1), 119–145 (2001)
8. Meng, S., Naixiao, Z., Barbosa, L.S.: On semantics and refinement of UML statecharts: a coalgebraic view. In: Proceedings of SEFM 2004, pp. 164–173 (2004)
9. Said, M.Y., Butler, M., Snook, C.: Language and Tool Support for Class and State Machine Refinement in UML-B. In: Cavalcanti, A., Dams, D.R. (eds.) FM 2009. LNCS, vol. 5850, pp. 579–595. Springer, Heidelberg (2009)
10. Hendricx, S., Claesen, L.: Verification of Finite-State-Machine Refinements Using a Symbolic Methodology. In: Pierre, L., Kropf, T. (eds.) CHARME 1999. LNCS, vol. 1703, pp. 326–330. Springer, Heidelberg (1999)
11. Bombieri, N., Fummi, F., Pravadelli, G., Silva, J.M.: Towards Equivalence Checking Between TLM and RTL Models, pp. 113–122. IEEE Computer Society Press (2007)
12. von der Beeck, M.: A structured operational semantics for UML-statecharts. Software and Systems Modeling 1(2), 130–141 (2002)
13. Liskov, B.: Data Abstraction and Hierarchy
14. Samek, M.: Practical UML Statecharts in C/C++, 2nd edn. Event-Driven Programming for Embedded Systems. Newnes (2008)

Analysis of the New Standard Hash Function*

F. Martín-Fernández and P. Caballero-Gil

Department of Statistics, Operations Research and Computing
University of La Laguna. Spain
francisco.martin.07@ull.edu.es, pcaballe@ull.es

Abstract In October 2012 the U.S. National Institute of Standards and Technology announced the new Secure Hash Algorithm SHA-3, which will be adopted as standard from now on. After a five-year process of public selection, the winner among a total of 73 candidates was Keccak.

This paper is focused on the analysis both from the points of view of security and implementation of the Keccak function, which is the base of the new SHA-3 standard. In particular, an implementation in the Android mobile platform is presented here, providing the first known external library in this operating system so that any Android developer can now use the new standard hashing. Finally, some SHA-3 applications in the Internet of Things are mentioned.

1   Introduction

A major computing paradigm is the handling of large volumes of data because the runtime of algorithms is greatly affected by the size of managed information. Thus, a reduction in the size of the data usually increases the speed of calculations and communications. A useful technique to address this problem is the hash function, which is an algorithm that maps large data sets of variable length to smaller data sets of a fixed length.

Many applications of hash functions are related to the field of cryptography (encryptions, digital signatures, authentication protocols...). Hash functions useful in cryptography are characterized by a series of properties that allow utilities that make them resistant against several types of attacks because any accidental or intentional change to the data, with very high probability, also changes the hash value. Hash functions that satisfy these properties are called cryptographic hash functions. The input of the cryptographic hash function is often called the message while its output is usually the digest. One of the best-known families of cryptographic hash functions is the one called Secure Hash Algorithm (SHA).

SHA denotes a family of cryptographic hash functions published by the National Institute of Standards and Technology (NIST) as a U.S. Federal Information Processing Standard. In 1993 the first member of this family was

* Research supported by the MINECO of Spain and the FEDER Fund under Project TIN2011-25452 and IPT-2012-0585-370000, and the FPI scholarship BES-2012-051817.

R. Moreno-Díaz et al. (Eds.): EUROCAST 2013, Part I, LNCS 8111, pp. 142–149, 2013.

published under the name of SHA but it was withdrawn shortly after its publication due to an undisclosed 'significant flaw' and replaced, in 1995, by the slightly revised version SHA-1. SHA-1 is a 160-bit hash function that resembles the earlier MD5 algorithm and that was designed by the National Security Agency to be part of the Digital Signature Algorithm. Some cryptographic weaknesses were discovered in SHA-1, and a new standard was published in 2001 as SHA-2, which is a family of two similar hash functions with different block sizes, SHA-256 and SHA-512. Although SHA-2 is still safe so far, in 2007 NIST published the terms of a public contest to choose the future successor of SHA-2 and on 2nd October 2012 it announced the new hash algorithm that will be adopted as standard from now on. Among a total of 73 candidates, the winner was Keccak, designed by a group of cryptographers from Belgium and Italy [3]. The public selection of the new standard SHA-3 took five years.

This work is focused on the analysis both from the points of view of security and implementation of the Keccak function. In particular, an implementation in the Android mobile platform is presented here, providing the first known external library in this mobile operating system so that any developer could use this new standard hash function.

This paper is organized as follows. In Section 2 the new cryptographic hash function is explained and a brief analysis of its security and performance is commented in Section 3. Section 4 provides some details of our software implementation while in Section 5 some applications in the Internet of Things are mentioned. Finally conclusions and future work close this paper.

2   Keccak

As aforementioned, the new SHA family member, known as SHA-3, is called Keccak. Keccak is a cryptographic hash function that uses a sponge construction [2], which in a cryptographic context is an operating mode on the base of a fixed length transformation and a padding rule. Particularly, it may be seen as a generalization of both a hash function, which has a fixed output length, and a stream cipher, which has a fixed input length.

The sponge construction can be used to implement cryptographic utilities like hash, pseudo-random number generation, encryption, key generation, Hash-based Message Authentication Code (HMAC) and authenticated encryption. As shown in Figure 1, it operates on a $b - bit$ state, where $b = r + c$, being r the number of blocks in which the input array of bits is split after padded with a reversible padding rule. The b bits of the state are initialized to 0, and the sponge function proceeds in two stages. The first phase is called *absorbing* and consists of applying the hash function as many times as r blocks result from the M input. The hash function receives as input of each iteration the XOR operation of the corresponding $r - bit$ block and state. Thus, each iteration of the hash function changes the state. The second stage, called *squeezing*, starts when the *absorbing*

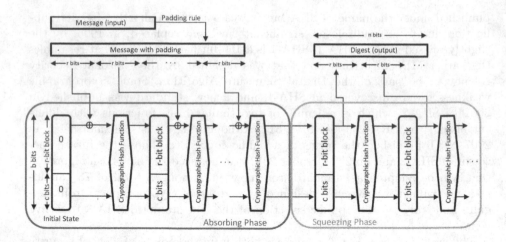

Fig. 1. Sponge Construction

phase is over, and has the object of getting the $n - bit$ output hash. At this stage, the first r bits of the state resulting from the application of the first stage are already output bits. If more bits are needed to complete the $n - bit$ output, the hash function is applied on the state as many times as necessary.

In the SHA-3 version of Keccak, a state represented by a 5×5 matrix of 64-bit lanes is used (see Figure 2). The length n of the output can have four different values: $224, 256, 386, 512$, what determines the other parameters. At the beginning of the *absorbing* stage, in order to make sure that the message can be split into $r - bit$ blocks, it is first padded with a minimum $10 * 1$ pattern that consists of a 1 bit, zero or more 0 bits (maximum $r - 1$) and a final 1 bit. In SHA-3, Keccak function is iterated 24 times, which is the maximum possible number of iterations. The basic transformation of Keccak involves 5 steps:

- Theta (θ), which is the XOR operation of each bit in the state with the XOR operation of one column that is in the same slice but in adjacent column, and again the XOR operation of another adjacent column that is not in the same slice but in an adjacent sheet.
- Rho (ρ), in which the bits are shifted in their lane by a given number of fixed transformation bits.
- Pi (π), which is a row permutation of columns.
- Chi (χ), which is the only non-linear operation as it involves the XOR operation of a particular column with the AND operation of the negation of the adjacent column and the column next to it.
- Iota (ι), which is the XOR operation of a round constant and the lane $[0,0]$ of the state.

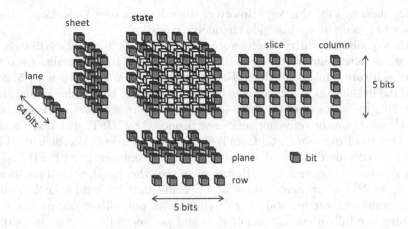

Fig. 2. State of Keccak

3   Security and Performance

One of the major requirements of any cryptographic hash function is a high security level. The analysis of Keccak [5] led to proofs of security related to the hash function structure, and the conclusion is that Keccak has indifferentiability [1], what means that the hash function behaves like a random oracle, which is a perfectly random function that can be evaluated quickly. Such indifferentiability proofs guarantee that the hash function resists generic attacks up to at least the complexity of a brute-force collision attack. Thus, assuming that the underlying permutation primitive is ideal, the hash function resists a brute-force attack consisting of finding two arbitrary inputs that produce the same hash. Also, Keccak is proven to have near-optimal security regarding the core properties of collision, preimage, and second-preimage resistance. The preimage resistance means that it is hard to find a pre-image from its known hash while the second-preimage resistance means that, given an input, it should be difficult to find another input such that the hash digests of both inputs coincide.

Another test that Keccak resisted was that of cryptanalysis on the components related directly to the core security properties of a hash function. The cryptanalysis results clarified that an attack on six rounds of a ten-round hash function would give a 40% Security Margin, which is the fraction of the hash function that has not been successfully attacked. Keccak has 79% of its hash function still unbroken, so the test results were very positive.

Another test was related to side channel analysis, which is any attack based on information gained from the physical implementation. It can be used to reveal some secret processed by a hash function, such as the key in an HMAC computation. Keccak does not have any non-invertible steps, so an attacker who learns the entire intermediate state for any HMAC-Keccak computation can use this to determine the original key used for the HMAC computation, and can forge arbitrary messages for this key. However, since Keccak uses logical operations, it is easy to protect it against side channel attacks.

All these positive security results were an important factor in the NIST choice of Keccak as new standard for SHA-3. However, one of its disadvantages is the speed of software implementations. For example, if SHA-3 is used with 512-bit output, the hashing speed at software level is quite slow. Under these conditions and for long messages (greater than 4096 bytes) the runtime would take about 22.4 cycles/byte on the reference processor proposed by NIST, which is a Sandy Bridge Desktop Processor (Intel Core i7-2600k) with Current Vector Unit. That may not be considered a good performance if we compare it with SHA2-512, which takes about 14 cycles/byte. However, on the other hand, SHA-3 resists any attack up to 2^{512} operations. Taking into account that it would take 4.2×10^{128} years to evaluate the permutation 2^{512} times with one billion computers, each performing one billion evaluations of Keccak-f per second, and that is 3×10^{118} times the estimated age of the universe, the results are decisive. Furthermore, note that just counting from 1 to 2^{512} with an irreversible computer working at $2.735°K$ would take at least 3.5×10^{131} joules, which is the total energy output of the Sun during 2.9×10^{97} years.

Due to the nature of Keccak, in software it is conveniently implemented as 64-bit logic operations, rotations, loads and stores. However, general-purpose computers cannot exploit most of the parallelism latent in the algorithm through a software implementation. On the other hand, a full hardware implementation of Keccak is naturally highly parallelizable, resulting in a very good throughput/area ratio, typically about twice or more of the throughput/area ratio of a full-round SHA-2 implementation. Thus, the conclusion is clear. Hardware implementation of Keccak is better than software [6].

4   Our Software Implementation

This work is based on the development of an Application Programming Interface (API) in the Java programming language, specifically in version 6. This API is fully developed and functional, with full support for the Android mobile platform. The API design is intended for didactic use and has both hexadecimal input and output. To the best of our knowledge, this is the first published Java code of SHA-3 for Android. As a guide for implementation, we used the official development optimized in C language and the official pseudocode. Our implementation has the same structure as the official one, but it does not use the same data types.

The API consists of several different classes, but basically the most important ones are three. The class named SHA-3 calls the other two classes that are: the one that represents the sponge function and another class representing Keccak function. The sponge function class has both the absorbing function and the squeezing function. The following code segment shows the absorbing function that calls the cryptographic hash function as many times as $r - bit$ blocks are split from the message input.

```
public static void absorbing(State state,
                            byte[] mess, Constants const){
    byte[] padKeccak = Padding.apply(mess, const.r), [] r = null;
    int iPadKeccak=0;
    while (paddingKeccak.length > iPadKeccak){
        r=Utilities.getRInArrayByte(padKeccak,iPadKeccak,const.r);
        BitsOperations.rStateXORrMess(state, r);
        Keccak.hashFunction(state, const);
        iPadKeccak+=const.r;
    }
}
```

The following code segment shows the squeezing function of the sponge function class, which takes as input the output of the last iteration of the absorbing phase.

```
public static String squeezing(State state, Constants const){
    String ret = "", laneHex;
    int outputLength=const.n, outputCounter=0;
    for(int y=0; y<State.Y; y++){
        for(int x=0; x<State.X; x++){
            laneHex=Utilities.laneToInverseHex(state.getLane(x,y));
            for (int i=0; i<laneHex.length(); i++){
                ret+=laneHex.charAt(i);
                outputCounter+=4;
                if (outputCounter == outputLength)
                    return ret;
            }
        }
    }
    return ret;
}
```

The cryptographic hash function iterates 24 times the five steps (Theta, Rho, Pi, Chi and Iota) described above. In our implementation we joined Rho and Pi steps as indicated in the original pseudocode of Keccak. Below we can see the corresponding code.

```
public static void hashFunction(State state, Constants const){
    for (int i=0; i<Const.iterationNumbers; i++){
        theta(state); // Step 1
        rhoYPi(state); // Step 2 and 3
        ji(state); // Step 4
        iota(state, i); // Step 5
    }
}
```

Once the API was designed, in order to test its performance we created a very simple Android application that generates SHA-3 hash. The application was uploaded from October 2012 on Google Play named SHA-3 Generator (see Figure 3). People started to use the application and to provide feedback on it. This feedback will be used to improve future versions and to answer to the requirements proposed by users. However, our immediate interest is in developing new applications for the SHA-3 implementation, which are briefly commented in the next Section.

Fig. 3. Android Application in Google Play

5   Applications in the Internet of Things

An area of particular interest for applications of SHA-3 is the so-called Internet of Things (IoT). Its objective is to merge the real world with the virtual world through the interconnection of everyday objects.

In this sense, SHA-3 might be used to generate:

- The digest of passwords or files to be verified.
- Challenges and/or responses in a challenge-response authentication protocol [4].
- The digest of messages to be signed with a digital signature scheme based on public keys.
- An HMAC based on secret keys.

Related to this latter possible application, note that unlike SHA-1 and SHA-2, SHA-3 does not have the length-extension weakness in which an attacker, given only $H(M)$ for some unknown message M, can append additional own blocks. Hence, SHA-3 does not need the HMAC nested construction where the key is used twice in order to use the hash to build a MAC. Instead, MAC computation can be performed by simply prepending the message with the key.

Thus, as a good hash function, the conclusion is that SHA-3 might be very useful to protect security of communications between objects of the Internet of Things, and so, different security applications for IoT based on SHA-3 may be developed.

6   Conclusions and Future Works

In this paper, we have analyzed the new recently announced standard hashing of Secure Hash Algorithm SHA-3. After an official competition that began in 2007, the winner was Keccak, a cryptographic hash function that uses the so-called sponge construction. According to several analysis and proofs, SHA-3 may be considered secure. On the other hand, due to SHA-3 design, hardware implementation is better than a pure software approach. Consequently, in order to improve the performance of software implementations, the codes must be optimized. In this work we have provided a Java API, which is fully functional on Android. In particular, for didactic purposes we have developed in this platform an application that generates a SHA-3 digest. This application is currently the only one in the Google Play that makes use of the new standard hashing.

In addition, this paper leaves several open issues for future work. First, the implementation of SHA-3 will be improved either by optimizing the code written in Java language or by rewriting the code using C language for Android. Also, the documentation level must be enhanced by adding more details. Any possible future weakness of SHA-3 will have to be taken into account in our implementation. Last but not least, the development of specific applications of SHA-3 in the Internet of Things is part of work in progress.

References

1. Andreeva, E., Mennink, B., Preneel, B.: Security reductions of the second round SHA-3 candidates. In: Burmester, M., Tsudik, G., Magliveras, S., Ilić, I. (eds.) ISC 2010. LNCS, vol. 6531, pp. 39–53. Springer, Heidelberg (2011)
2. Bertoni, G., Daemen, J., Peeters, M., Van Assche, G.: Keccak sponge function family main document (2009), http://keccak.noekeon.org/Keccak-main-2.1.pdf
3. Bertoni, G., Daemen, J., Peeters, M., Van Assche, G.: The Keccak SHA-3 submission, http://keccak.noekeon.org/Keccak-submission-3.pdf
4. Caballero-Gil, P., Hernandez-Goya, C.: Zero-knowledge hierarchical authentication in MANETs. IEICE Transactions on Information and Systems E89D(3), 1288–1289 (2006)
5. Chang, S., Perlner, R., Burr, W., Turan, M., Kelsey, J., Paul, S., Bassham, L.: Third-Round Report of the SHA-3 Cryptographic Hash Algorithm Competition, NIST (2012), http://nvlpubs.nist.gov/nistpubs/ir/2012/NIST.IR.7896.pdf
6. Homsirikamol, E., Rogawski, M., Gaj, K.: Comparing Hardware Performance of Fourteen Round two SHA-3 Candidates using FPGAs, Cryptology ePrint Archive, Report 2010/445, 210 (January 15, 2011), http://eprint.iacr.org/2010/445

Simulating Energy Efficiency
of Routing and Link-Layer Protocols
in Wireless Sensor Networks

Mariusz Słabicki and Bartosz Wojciechowski

Institute of Computer Engineering, Control and Robotics,
Wrocław University of Technology
Wybrzeże Wyspiańskiego 27, 50-370 Wrocław, Poland
mariusz.slabicki@pwr.wroc.pl

Abstract. One of the most important characteristics of Wireless Sensor Networks is energy efficiency. Exhausted batteries cannot be easily replaced and cause connectivity problems and reduced network life. Therefore it is crucial to develop methods to reduce energy usage in those networks. In this work some methods in the MAC layer and network layer were tested in simulations for energy efficiency. The best combinations of methods were used in real implementation for confirmation.

Keywords: Wireless Sensor Networks, lifetime, protocols, simulations, MAC, T-MAC, SEER, BEAR, HEED.

1   Introduction

Energy efficiency is a hot topic in wireless sensor network research since battery power is often the most crucial resource. Battery capacity is limited, recharging is difficult and often impractical while renewable energy sources are still too expensive, or too large [1]. Increasing the total amount of power available for node is hard to achieve, therefore, there is a constant strive for algorithms and methods that improve energy efficiency and extend network operation. A number of papers focus on radio communication as this is the most expensive operation (in terms of energy).

Energy efficiency can be achieved through technology improvements and improved network organisation. Technology improvements include development of more efficient radio transceivers (e.g. better power amplifiers, low noise amplifiers) or hybrid transceivers, where simple and low power radio is used just to wake-up and power-up standard transceiver capable to transmit data packets [2]. Organization methods include efficient MAC protocols, network structure and management [3], data aggregation or duty-cycling [4]. All methods aim to reduce the time nodes spend with radio transceiver enabled waiting for incoming communication (idle-listening) and reduce the number of transmissions. Time synchronisation between nodes simplifies implementation and allows to awake nodes periodically and simultaneously thus evading the need for long idle-listening.

R. Moreno-Díaz et al. (Eds.): EUROCAST 2013, Part I, LNCS 8111, pp. 150–157, 2013.

Although a number of solutions has been proposed, there is no comprehensive analysis of how different methods fit together and influence the energy efficiency of WSNs. This paper analyses 3 different MAC protocols and 5 routing protocols to verify which of them allows for the best improvement. [4–8].

This paper presents results of experiments conducted in WSN simulator OM-NeT++ and real WSN network setups deployed in our laboratory. The aim of the experiments was to analyse energy efficiency and quantitatively compare different MAC protocols and routing algorithms. Quantitative comparison is based on two parameters: network lifetime and distribution of residual power among network nodes, when network operation ends.

Many definitions of network lifetime are used across different papers on WSNs. We assume that network lifetime is a time from network initialisation until the first node in the network depletes its battery. This definition is very restrictive but simultaneously it is topology- and routing-agnostic, easy to verify and can be seen as the worst case scenario for the network. Consequently, it allows to compare various MAC and routing algorithms and provide information on how they allow to improve minimal operation time of the WSN network.

Analysing residual power and its distribution among network nodes also provides interesting information about energy efficiency and algorithms used. It shows that maximising network lifetime is not about limiting power consumed by every node but limiting the power consumed by the node with the smallest amount of remaining power. Ideally, nodes having little power should be relieved and their tasks should be taken over by other nodes. Network lifetime can be therefore extended if power consumption is evenly distributed among all the nodes [9].

Simultaneous analysis of both MAC and routing methods is crucial as neither of them itself can improve both lifetime and energy distribution. MAC protocols deal only with peer-to-peer communication and are network agnostic, consequently cannot optimise network-wide parameters (even energy distribution). Routing algorithms can support even distribution of load (power costs) among the network nodes, but power costs incurred on transmission and reception are mostly defined by the MAC layer. Additionally, proper routing facilitates data aggregation and reduces the number of transmissions.

Our simulation results were compared with real case deployment in research greenhouse owned by Wrocław University of Environmental and Life Sciences.

2   MAC and Routing Algorithms

2.1   MAC Algorithms

A typical approach for MAC algorithms in radio networks with multiple access is to use channel sense multiple access protocols with additional collision avoidance – CSMA/CA. In this technique each radio transmitter listens to the radio channel before it starts its own transmission. When channel is busy the node backs-off for a random time and retries. CSMA/CA is a technique defined in IEEE 802.15.4 standard and is used by all compatible radio transceivers.

One of the most popular MAC algorithms running on WSN nodes is Berkeley MAC protocol – B-MAC [4]. Detection of pending transmissions uses clear channel assessment that periodically samples the radio channel and measures the signal strength. Samples are stored in FIFO queue and used to calculate moving average that is then used to decide if the channel is busy or not. Simplicity and no need for time synchronisation are the biggest advantages of the B-MAC protocol, but collisions and jamming are still possible as only transmitter assesses the channel status (e.g. hidden terminal problem). The lack of time synchronisation also implies asynchronous communication. This means that all the nodes in the network need to stay in idle-listening mode burning power even if there are no transmissions. To minimise this drawback B-MAC puts nodes asleep and wakes them periodically. While asleep, radio transceiver is disabled thus saving the energy. However, due to lack of synchronisation, transmission starts with preamble that lasts longer than sleep time. This ensures that all nodes will wake up before the actual transmission starts – nodes keep the radio on when preamble is detected.

T-MAC protocol presented by Dam et al. [5] avoids collision by using time synchronisation between nodes and flow control signals (request to send – RTS, and clear to send – CTS). Time synchronisation limits channel capacity and requires additional management, but synchronised nodes do not waste time on idle-listening nor need to have long preambles before the actual transmission. In contrast to B-MAC, time of activity is not fixed. Instead, nodes are put asleep if there is no transmission for a predefined period of time.

2.2 Routing Algorithms

The most straightforward routing algorithm uses fixed routes that constitute a tree structure with base station in its root and nodes in branches and leaves. Consequently, each node has a single neighbouring node to which it transmits all the messages. Fixed routing is easy to establish but is more likely to cause uneven power consumption among network nodes.

A bit more complex algorithm (random routing) extends the fixed routing by establishing several routing trees. Each node in the network stores information about several neighbours that are closer to the base station. Upon message transmission node randomly selects a neighbour that it will send the message to. Random routing improves even power consumption among network nodes as network traffic is distributed among a number of routing paths and nodes.

Routing complexity is extended in Simple Energy Efficient Routing (SEER) algorithm [6]. In this protocol each node stores information about all neighbouring nodes together with their distances to the base station and remaining power. When routing path is selected a node selects its neighbour that is closer to the base station and has the largest remaining energy. If there is no such neighbour, then nodes that are at the same distance are analysed. SEER also implements a very simple method to minimise probability of routing loops but this does not ensure there are no loops in transmission. Information about residual power in nodes is updated periodically by broadcast messages or during periodic network reinitialisation.

Balanced Energy Aware Routing (BEAR) [7] extends previous routing by taking into account distance to the base station, residual power of each neighbour node and additionally, information about the neighbour's neighbours. This way the transmitting node can forecast two successive transmissions and select the node that is more likely to improve the resulting energy efficiency. Additionally, BEAR assumes that each node constantly sniffs the radio channel and overhears neighbouring communication. In this way nodes get information about residual power of neighbouring nodes that is piggybacked in data packets. This reduces the overhead of network management.

Aforementioned routing protocols are often classified as flat network organisation protocols in contrast to hierarchical protocols. In hierarchical protocols nodes are organised in groups with one node selected to act as a group leader. Leader is responsible for collecting the messages from its group members and routing between neighbouring group leaders. This approach aims to limit long range communication (nodes within a group communicate over a short range), reduce interferences in radio communication channel, facilitate data aggregation and simplify routing (as only group leaders take part in routing messages from nodes to the base station). Hybrid Energy Efficient Distributed [8] clustering (grouping) protocol is one of the most popular methods to establish hierarchical structure of the WSN network. Clustering in HEED is set up locally by neighbouring nodes that decide on group leader (cluster head) based on residual energy in each node. HEED is a randomised protocol meaning that it is more likely that nodes with larger residual power will become leaders.

3   Simulations

In our research we used OMNeT++ as the main simulation engine [10]. To add wireless communication we used MiXiM [11] framework. Simulations were repeated multiple times in order to achieve valuable results. Each time we saved and used exactly the same node layouts for comparison between different protocol sets. We assumed a network simulation containing 100 nodes placed in random positions with uniform distribution. Size of the network area was 300×300 m. Communication range of each node was set to reflect those of real devices operating in 2.4 GHz band, which is usually smaller than 100 m. Each simulated node was running the same application. Each node was sending a message every randomly picked time from a given range. Base station was set in one corner of the area. These assumptions were chosen to resemble a real-life deployment scenarios.

Unfortunately the available energy model implemented in the simulator was insufficient. Therefore we improved the existing model of battery usage to reflect the energy consumption of real devices during idle periods, reception and communication with different available transmission power levels. Values used in energy model were taken from our earlier research [12].

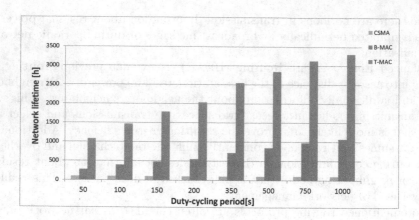

Fig. 1. Lifetime achieved for different MAC algorithms

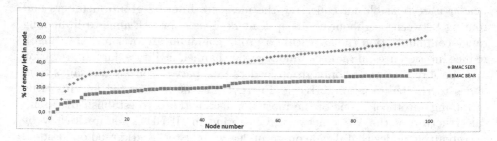

Fig. 2. Residual energy in batteries of nodes

4   Results

4.1   Simulation Results

Our results show that duty-cycling has the biggest impact on lifetime. This is consistent with our previous work showing that the most of node's energy is used by radio module (both for transmission and receiving). Because in most implementations radio service is provided by the MAC layer, the choice of MAC layer is crucial for network lifetime. Fig. 1 shows that when length of sleep time is changing, lifetime changes almost linearly. On the other hand frequency of packet transmission has negligible impact on lifetime when no duty-cycling is used.

If we assume that clocks in all nodes are well synchronized and nodes are able to wake up and fall asleep at the same time, it is possible to arbitrarily increase length of duty cycle. However, due to clock drift, duty cycles in individual nodes may desynchronize. When it happens, some messages may get lost. This increases the Packet Error Rate. Reducing this rate is possible only by retransmission. Unfortunately retransmissions increase energy usage. This is a trade-off between synchronization and length of duty cycle.

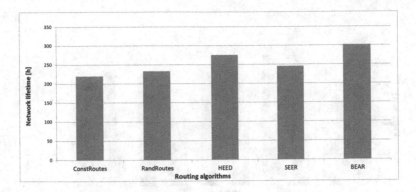

Fig. 3. Lifetime achieved for different routing algorithms

Routing algorithms also have influence on network lifetime. If we assume that network dies when first node looses all energy in battery it means that if we want to increase network lifetime we need to balance load in the network. Optimal situation occurs when the pace of battery usage is the same in all nodes. It may be impossible to achieve, but it can be the goal of the routing algorithms. Fig. 2 shows that routing algorithms should be also optimized to better balance energy usage. In our case network with SEER algorithm left more free residual energy when it finished its operation than with BEAR. On the other hand network lifetime differences shown in Fig. 3 are smaller than differences with different MAC protocols. Lifetime for T-MAC can be as much as 3 times longer than for B-MAC (Fig. 1).

Placement of nodes within the network considerably changes the behaviour of routing algorithms, which influences the network lifetime. Behaviour of routing algorithms highly depends on routing tree set in their beginning phase. Fig. 4 shows that locations of nodes have significant impact on lifetime when duty cycling is used. The main cause of this fact is the number of packets which must be sent through the routing tree. However, when duty cycling is turned off (like in CSMA/CA) all nodes run down battery in approximately the same time. In this case the number of routed messages does not matter.

4.2   Hardware Results

To verify simulation results we deployed a test network in our laboratory and have tested a subset of algorithms that we have already simulated. For data collection and testing setup we used WSN-TCP gateway architecture described in [13]. Test results matched the simulation results. Fig. 5 shows results from deployment with mixture of nodes with and without duty cycling. When battery level fell below permissible level in nodes 19, 20, and 21, node 22 still had high energy level. Results from the greenhouse show high correlation with our simulation results. Network lifetime achieved by our network was about 4 days when duty cycling was not used. However, when duty cycling was implemented in application, the lifetime reached over 18 days.

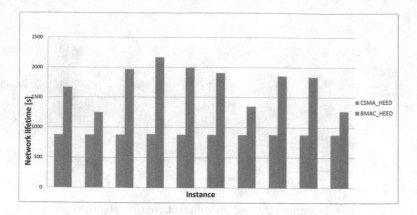

Fig. 4. Network lifetime in different deployment instances

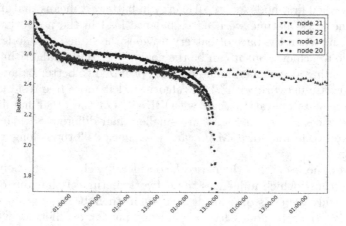

Fig. 5. Draining of battery power with TinyOS Low Power Listening switched on (node 22) and off (nodes 19, 20, 21)

5   Conclusions

In our simulations we have analysed 3 MAC protocols and 5 routing methods that are representative to various types of solutions presented in literature so far. These methods were also tested in deployed network. Both the simulations and real-case tests show that to extend the network lifetime, the most important choice is the proper MAC algorithm. Recent hardware is optimized for small energy usage in low power modes. However, the amount of energy used during transmission is still considerable. To avoid energy waste, nodes should work in duty cycle, with long sleep time and short time for transmission and sensing. The results show that the routing algorithms have smaller impact on lifetime than MAC algorithms. Though there still exists a design space for better algorithms which should improve the balance of energy usage. Tested networks ended their lifetime with high variation of residual energy in batteries. Theoretically, this is the energy which might be used to extend network lifetime.

Acknowledgment. This work was supported by grant no. N 516 483740 from the Polish National Science Centre.

References

1. Anastasi, G., Conti, M., Francesco, M.D., Passarella, A.: Energy conservation in wireless sensor networks: A survey. Ad Hoc Networks 7(3), 537–568 (2009)
2. Ansari, J., Pankin, D., Mähönen, P.: Radio-triggered wake-ups with addressing capabilities for extremely low power sensor network applications. International Journal of Wireless Information Networks 16(3), 118–130 (2009)
3. Nikodem, J., Klempous, R., Nikodem, M., Chaczko, Z.: Multi-hop and directed routing based on neighborhood cooperation in WSN. In: Proceedings of the 15th International Conference on Intelligent Engineering Systems, INES 2011, pp. 221–227 (2011)
4. Polastre, J., Hill, J., Culler, D.: Versatile low power media access for wireless sensor networks. In: Proceedings of the 2nd International Conference on Embedded Networked Sensor Systems, SenSys 2004, pp. 95–107. ACM (2004)
5. van Dam, T., Langendoen, K.: An adaptive energy-efficient mac protocol for wireless sensor networks. In: Proceedings of the 1st International Conference on Embedded Networked Sensor Systems, SenSys 2003, pp. 171–180. ACM (2003)
6. Hancke, G.P., Leuschner, C.J.: SEER: a simple energy efficient routing protocol for wireless sensor networks. South African Computer Journal (39), 17–24 (2007)
7. Ahvar, E., Fathy, M.: BEAR: A Balanced Energy-Aware Routing Protocol for Wireless Sensor Networks. Wireless Sensor Network 2(10), 793–800 (2010)
8. Younis, O., Fahmy, S.: HEED: a hybrid, energy-efficient, distributed clustering approach for ad hoc sensor networks. IEEE Transactions on Mobile Computing, 366–379 (2004)
9. Wu, X., Chen, G., Das, S.K.: On the energy hole problem of nonuniform node distribution in wireless sensor networks. In: 2006 IEEE International Conference on Mobile Adhoc and Sensor Systems (MASS), pp. 180–187. IEEE (2006)
10. Varga, A., et al.: The OMNeT++ discrete event simulation system. In: Proceedings of the European Simulation Multiconference (ESM 2001), vol. 9 (2001)
11. Köpke, A., Swigulski, M., Wessel, K., Willkomm, D., Haneveld, P., Parker, T., Visser, O., Lichte, H., Valentin, S.: Simulating wireless and mobile networks in OMNeT++ the MiXiM vision. In: 1st International Conference on Simulation Tools and Techniques for Communications, Networks and Systems & Workshops (2008)
12. Słabicki, M., Wojciechowski, B., Surmacz, T.: Realistic model of radio communication in wireless sensor networks. In: Kwiecień, A., Gaj, P., Stera, P. (eds.) CN 2012. CCIS, vol. 291, pp. 334–343. Springer, Heidelberg (2012)
13. Surmacz, T., Pieronek, T.: Implementing wireshark plugins for rapid protocol development in wireless sensor networks. In: 14th International Conference on Computer Aided Systems Theory, pp. 318–319 (2013)

Business Operation Improvement through Integrated Infrastructure Management*

Alberto Casanova, Laura M. Castro, and Antonio Blanco-Ferro

Department of Computer Science
University of A Coruña, Spain
{alberto.casanova,lcastro,blanco}@udc.es

Abstract. The constant emergence of new technologies that improve existing ones in one way or another, creates a permanent need to incorporate innovative tools and components into the existing business ecosystem of legacy components, which cannot be discarded and need to be maintained.

This paper presents an integration effort between heterogeneous architectures that goes beyond the traditional on-demand integration and creates an infrastructure management framework to give support to present and future integrations. This effort has allowed the interaction between legacy infrastructure, namely IBM Mainframes, and state-of-the-art applications, platforms, and configuration management technologies, also allowing a better management of the available resources.

The integration project, called S.G.I.I. (*Sistema de Gestión Integrada de Infraestructura*, Integrated Infrastructure Management System) is a solution developed for a real business environment: the Spanish bank NCG Banco. The framework is based on two complementary modules: a *front-end*, designed over a Microsoft Internet Information Server that provides a means of communication between external applications and the IBM Mainframe; and a *back-end*, developed over the IBM Mainframe to allow the management of its own resources.

Keywords: integration, infrastructure management, legacy, COTS.

1 Introduction

Through the history of computing, multiple heterogeneous technologies have been developed for common and for different purposes, to a point in which the thought of a single-technology system is an unimaginable idea. Thus, the difficulties in using a broad set of these technologies within a single technological business world are very common. Companies frequently use multiple platforms, multiple applications that are to interact with each other to carry out their tasks. In fact, it is usually the case that, over time, the responsibility of a given task is spread over a network of heterogeneous components, involving the use of several applications and technologies.

---

* Partially supported by TIN2010-20959.

R. Moreno-Díaz et al. (Eds.): EUROCAST 2013, Part I, LNCS 8111, pp. 158–165, 2013.
© Springer-Verlag Berlin Heidelberg 2013

Another common situation is that in which modern platforms or components need to interact with older, legacy ones. In either of these scenarios, a robust integration methodology is needed, in order to avoid repeatedly reinventing the wheel.

This article presents an integration methodology proposal for heterogeneous architectures, which specifically addresses the common need for a management platform that allows consistent management of resources, including legacy. The integration strategy is not bounded to the business operation environment from which the need for the integration arose, rather it is applicable to any enterprise environment with similar requirements.

The integration project, called S.G.I.I. (*Sistema de Gestión Integrada de Infraestructura*, Integrated Management System Infrastructure) for which the methodology was first designed, implemented, deployed and tested, has been developed for a Spanish bank, NCG Banco. The bank infrastructure included a legacy platform, namely an IBM Mainframe, and other cross-platform applications designed and implemented in modern, state-of-the-art technologies. We developed a system with two main parts: a *front-end*, based on Microsoft Internet Information Server, and a *back-end*, developed on the IBM mainframe itself. The development of this project allowed to efficiently communicate those existing components using various technologies.

2   Integration Scenario

Big companies, research centres, and banks (as is the case of NCG Banco), are frequent users of powerful data processing units which have large capabilities of data processing, in addition to high performance and high availability features (namely, providing 24/7 availability up-times). IBM Mainframes [1, 3] are a family of servers specifically designed and built to process large data sets, either via batch processes or online processing.

While the use of these mainframe servers has a number of important advantages, they also present concerning drawbacks. Even when there has been a number of updates and upgrades in the series, IBM mainframes production and commercialisation started more than 50 years, so they can be understood as a legacy platform. Completely oblivious and decoupled from modern platforms and technologies, the vast majority of the software that runs on these mainframes was developed years ago and it is difficult and expensive to maintain. The interfaces to these servers are difficult to handle, and their administration usually requires high technical profile, especially for an efficient management and maintenance of their resources. The learning curve for this kind of architectures has proven slower than more modern replacements [10]. In practise, this means that companies need to either hire a technical team capable of handling these interfaces, and managing all elements and resources of these servers, or else, when in-house administration is not possible, pay for manufacturer support or a regular basis.

Resources managed by these kind of servers (transactions, programs) must be configured and processed by system administrators on an individual basis. This is done with the assistance of *ad-hoc* tools provided by the server manufacturer, which are hence out of reach for in-house developers. Only a few administrators can manage them properly, and although over the years these tools have been updated to accommodate new needs, they remain based on old paradigms and obsolete philosophies, imposing a steep learning curve and lacking proper integration with external, more modern tools that facilitate maintenance of resources. This makes it almost impossible for developers to increase their control of their data processing programs.

These data processing programs or applications, usually referred to as *host* programs, may be either batch or online processing applications. They are usually designed to process certain data that, in the case of online programs, is grouped under what is called a *transaction*, which runs in the *host* server under a CICS application server [6–9]. Both transactions and programs are managed uniformly as a *host* type of resource.

As mentioned earlier, within the technological universe we have just described in which the IBM mainframe is a key element, there are many other elements that conform an organisation computing environment: distributed server farms, backup services, domain controllers, application servers... which have to not only coexist, but more importantly, communicate and work together with the *host* resources.

Before the integration project we will be describing in this paper started, the NCG Banco developers needed to perform several activities in order to manage the available resources: they were using the existing, in-house developed configuration management platform, to configure actions on a given resource, such as transactions or programs. Once the action was requested, the request reached the system operators via email. System operators, in turn, had to use a different management platform to attend, prioritise and schedule the different requests. Then, depending on the outcomes of each request, they will either respond to the initial developer request with the corresponding result, or else indicating whether any problem had aroused with regard to their petition. However, it could also be the case that the system operator was unable to manage the request for technical reasons (especially if the request involved use of legacy resources), so they would have to contact the administrators for additional support and assistance. In short, a request for a resource management could require the interaction of several actors, through several communication channels, and with multiple points in which a request could be stalled or delayed (such as email, phone...). This, together with the fact that requests had to be manually authorised and set for execution individually, made the overall process extremely inefficient and expensive, with an important number of points of failure to consider (cf. Fig. 1).

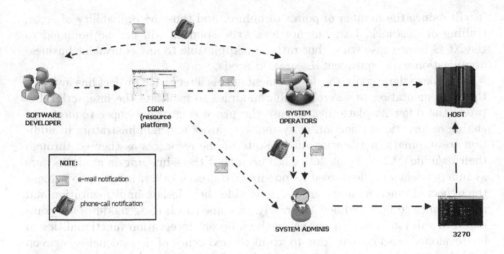

Fig. 1. Original scenario, prior to development and deployment of integration solution

3   Integration Objectives

The integration project for which the integration methodology and solution that we describe in this paper was designed and developed aims, thus, at the integration of resources and tools based on the *host*/legacy architecture described in the previous section, with any other distributed applications or platforms. The main goal is to be able to organise, facilitate and speed up management and communication between the involved parties, allowing developers to have more control over the *host* resource they need access to at a given time, but also maintaining the ultimate supervision of system operators and administrators. As a very positive side effect, we expect to impose as well significant improvement in the learning curve of in-house application development within this ecosystem, thereby saving new developers the need for a deep understanding of legacy architectures.

Once the integration project is completed we expect to see a situation in which developers objectives are met, the number of actors involved to achieve the same goals as before is considerably reduced, hence reducing the response times to resource requests. In that situation, a developer will make a request, upon reception of requests, operators and/or administrators will be notified by the system if their intervention is required, intervene on the action request as suitable, and forward the operation for execution. Finally, once the request is granted and completed, we want the results to be automatically delivered to the developer who requested them in the first place.

As mentioned before, this change in the resource request and management work-flow will significantly reduce response times and even allow management of multiple heterogeneous resources simultaneously and uniformly. In addition to reducing the number of elements involved in the configuration management, it will reduce the number of points of failure, and thus the probability of error, stalling or deadlock. Last but not least, the solution will not be bounded to the NCG Banco case study, but rather be applicable to any equivalent business organisation with equivalent integration needs.

To achieve these goals, the development of this integration project has involved the implementation of several specific modules to facilitate the interaction between the different platforms, to ease the processing of developer requests, to enable automatic notification of system operators and administrators in addition to automatic notification of the state of the resources as they go through their own life cycle. The objective has been that these integration modules were as independent and decoupled as possible from each other, in order to achieve the expected functionalities but also to enable their design, implementation and maintenance to be scheduled separately. In some cases, these modules are composed of sub-modules that specialise the different integration functionalities to be developed, also contributing to avoid the existence of dependencies between modules. The development of decoupled modules makes the integration infrastructure easily scalable, robust to changes, and ready to incorporate support of future functionalities, technologies and/or platforms.

Besides, in order for the solution to be applicable to other systems apart from our case study, we have put special attention to the use of standard and well-known integration technologies and solutions, as we will explain in the next section.

4   Integrated Management Solution

In the original scenario (cf. Fig 1) users –i.e. developers– needed to perform several steps to create a new or manage an existing resource. As already mentioned, they would use a resource management platform, to specify the desired action on a given resource (such as a transaction or program). Once requested, the action request was sent by email to the system operators, who in turn would have to configure the action using the corresponding resource-dependent application. Depending on the action result, they would answer the original user stating whether any sort of trouble arose in the process. It could also be the case that the system operator could not resolve the request for various reasons, and would need to contact the system administrator for assistance. In short, a single request for a resource management required the interaction of several actors via several communication channels (email, phone. . .). This work-flow, to be repeated on an individual basis, made the daily routine of the stakeholders slow, expensive and very error prone at a number of different points.

Given the situation from which we start and the goals to be achieved, the implementation of a software solution takes shape in the form of a bridge, as an adaptable and extensible means to create the necessary links between different and heterogeneous architectures for easy and fast interactions between actors and resources. The architecture of this integration bridge is designed to be split in two main components: a *front-end*, and a *back-end*. The *front-end* is responsible for supporting the interaction between developers, system operators, administrators, and the different management platforms in the business network. The *front-end* presents two interfaces:

- A web portal, oriented to the graphical interaction with the end user (i.e. the developers).
- A set of web services, focused on supporting the interaction of different platforms and/or systems with the *host*.

The front-end is designed to isolate the host from any other management platforms available (now or in the future), forcing these to access the host via the front-end. The technologies used to implement the front-end were C-Sharp [5] and the .NET [4] framework.

We chose SOAP [2] as the supporting technology for the web services. The use of web services for the integration of system management platforms, allows us to communicate with a great variability of platforms regardless of the technology used by them. Within the web services world, SOAP is a widely-known technology that allows us to plug different resources into the system, resources which can then be modified without further implications in the rest of the system, provided they continue to respect their SOAP API.

The second main component of the integrated software solution is the *back-end*. Hosted on the IBM mainframe, the *back-end* is designed to receive and process all the information coming from the front-end. We must keep in mind that resource management is done on the basis of requests made by users, hence these requests must have a life cycle that allows tracking.

In the new scenario, then (cf. Fig. 2), a user makes a request using either the old management platform, or the new web portal provided by the front-end. The old management platform is kept for reasons of backwards compatibility, but it now communicates with the front-end, same as the web portal. The front-end automatically forwards the request to be performed as the corresponding kind of action over the designated resource. Once received by an operator, they will dispatch and delegate the action in the back-end, which will ultimately process the action and, when finished, automatically notify the result. By reducing the number of involved agents, this new work-flow reduces response times significantly, reduces the number of points of failure (and thus, the error ratio), and even allows the simultaneous management of multiple resources.

In the development of this integration project, several specific modules have been introduced to facilitate the interaction between platforms while giving support to the processing demands of developers and administrators, also reporting on the state of their requests according to their own life cycle. During the project, the development of loosely coupled modules for each functionality has prevailed, in order to be able to implement and deploy them independently. In some cases, those modules are in turn composed by a series of sub-modules for each functionality, avoiding unnecessary dependencies between them. This decoupled architecture makes this integration project highly scalable, since the addition of new features does not imply modifications of already existing modules.

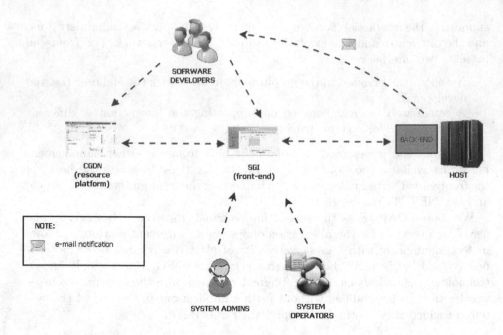

Fig. 2. Business scenario after implementing the proposed solution

5   Conclusions

We have presented an integration project of a legacy server architecture with new distributed platforms developed and deployed at the NCG Banco organisation. This integration project has facilitated and expedited communication between stakeholders, allowing developers to have more control over the management of their tasks and resources, maintaining the ultimate supervision of system administrators. Following the work explained here, NCG Banco has migrated to a new scenario, in which established goals have been achieved: the number of elements involved in resource management routines has been considerably reduced, hence reducing requests response time. Furthermore, the integrated management has enabled the improvement of the learning curve of the in-house application development environment in NCG Banco, by preventing the developers to require a deeper understanding of the legacy architecture.

In view of the work we have done, we can conclude that the objectives have been successfully met. We have developed an integrated management platform to act as a bridge for heterogeneous resource management, which allows the integration of heterogeneous platforms, and includes a substantial improvement in the management tools available nowadays. The project has helped to streamline administrative tasks that were tedious and slow, and required the manual intervention of several actors, dramatically reducing response times. Environmental understanding of all actors (developers, system operators, administrators) has also been improved, reducing training times in the application development environment. Last but not least, the proposed architecture, its components, and its benefits, are straightforward applicable to any organisation with similar integration demands.

The use of certain technologies for the development of this project has helped us to achieve our initial goals: for instance, the use of C-Sharp as a programming language, and the .NET framework for the development of the front-end, together with the use of design patterns, means that the front-end can be exported to any platform that can run a Microsoft Internet Information Server. The use of SOAP-based web services as a means of communication between the different elements of the system is also responsible for its main interoperability, adaptability and extensibility properties.

References

1. IBM Mainframes, http://www-03.ibm.com/ibm/history/exhibits/mainframe/mainframe_intro.html
2. Box, D.: A brief history of SOAP (2001), http://www.xml.com/pub/a/ws/2001/04/04/soap.html
3. Ebbers, M., O'Brien, W., Ogden, B.: Introduction to the new Mainframe: Z/OS Basics. IBM RedBooks (2006)
4. Foundation, A.: Loggin services for microsoft .net framework, http://logging.apache.org/log4net/
5. Hejlsberg, A., Wiltamuth, S., Golde, P.: The C Sharp Programming Language. Microsoft .NET Development Series. Addison Wesley Professional (2006)
6. IBM: CICS transaction server for z/os v3.1, what is cicsplex (2005), http://www-01.ibm.com/software/htp/cics/tserver/v31/wicplex/
7. IBM: CICS clients: Telnet 3270 (2006), http://publib.boulder.ibm.com/infocenter/ieduasst/v1r1m0/topic/com.ibm.iea.txseries/txseries/6.1/Administration/TXSeriesV6_Telnet3270.pdf
8. IBM: CICS transaction server for z/os, version 4.1 (2010), http://pic.dhe.ibm.com/infocenter/cicsts/v4r1/index.jsp
9. Williams, N., Lopez, L.A., Herman, R., Ebbers, M.: Implementing CICS web services (2007)
10. Tuya, J., Roman, I.R., Cosín, J.D.: Técnicas cuantitativas para la gestión de la ingeniería del software (2007)

Implementation of an IT-Services Practical Standard in Hotel and Tourism Industries

Abraham Rodríguez-Rodríguez, Silvia Tejera-Correa, Samuel Jiménez-Jiménez,
and Roberto Moreno-Díaz jr.

Instituto Universitario de Ciencias y Tecnologías Cibernéticas
Universidad de Las Palmas de Gran Canaria, Canary Islands, Spain
{arodriguez,rmorenoj}@dis.ulpgc.es,
{silvia.tejeracorrea,samuel.jimenez.jimenez}@gmail.com

Abstract. Tourism, one of the strongest growing sectors in world's economy, is not at all oblivious to information and telecommunications technologies advances, not only in their daily internal management. Travellers and visitors from all main sending European countries have a very high degree of technological use and needs [1], and expect those needs to be almost universally fulfilled in their vacation destinations. This fact has changed the client views of offered services and often makes a difference in the client's choice. Some known statistics of this behavior are that 38 percent of travellers said Wi-Fi access included in hotel room rates was a must while only 25% said breakfast was essential [2]. On the other hand, 23 percent of guests surveyed said their favourite modern in-room amenity was the use of iPads, and 85% of leisure travellers use their smartphone while abroad [3].

The "5@ Standard Project" comprises the attempt to develop a practical standard classification targeted at the categorization of the touristic facilities considering the technological services they provide. All the information about the introduction level of the Technological Services, including their technical features, will be accessible by potential guests. This standard will include a set of specifications and procedures which will ensure that the products, infrastructures, and Technological Services offered by hotels or other accommodation facilities or touristic-oriented businesses could be reliably translated into a qualitative and a quantitative evaluation system which will result in a number between 1 and 5 in our @s classification.

Keywords: standard, information technology, tourism, ontologies.

1   Goals: Standards in Touristic Industry

In a previous publication [4], the authors have stated the main Goals of the "5@ Standard Project" as follows:

- To recognize the large effort invested by the Tourism industry in IT services, thus contributing to consolidate the image of an agile, modern, and advanced tourism sector.

R. Moreno-Díaz et al. (Eds.): EUROCAST 2013, Part I, LNCS 8111, pp. 166–173, 2013.
© Springer-Verlag Berlin Heidelberg 2013

- To create *added value* advantages for the accommodation infrastructure and additional services; guests will be attracted by this new information, so they can make an informed decision on which is adapted to their real needs.
- To facilitate Hotels the decision-making process when considering the investment in technological infrastructures and services. The 5@ Standard can be used as an orientation guideline for strategic plans in the short and medium terms.
- To provide new indicators for official Administrations agencies about the real implementation of Technological Services in the industry. This can be used in the definition of policies for the investment on technological infrastructures.
- To promote competition among technological providers. This must adjust their products and services to the requirements of a structured and informed demand.

Basically, a standard is an agreed regulation or a group of requirements that have to be followed in order to enable the common use of several components (with different nature or origin.) Usually, it is a formal document that establishes technical criteria, methods, processes and practices designed for being used consciously as a rule, guide or definition. Standards increase the reliability and effectiveness of assets, services and process.

Regarding the Tourism sector, there are several quality systems which, while not being standards, are broadly used to certify the quality of the tourist facilities, such as Stars grading, the most common quality system in the sector, is worldwide renowned.

Many countries, especially those in which Tourism represents a significant contribution to their GDP, have a combined system including national or local quality systems [see e.g. 5, 6]. For instance in Spain, the quality "Q" of tourism introduced and defined by the Spanish Institute for the tourism quality. This official distinction meets a series of strictly specified features that give prestige, differentiation, reliability and accuracy to the certified tourist accommodations and can be extended to a number and variety of businesses orbiting around the tourism industry.

But, strictly speaking about standards, the International Organization for Standardization has stated the Tourism Services standard (as it is the case, ISO 18513:2003), about Hotels and other types of tourist accommodation, which is controlled by every country through its own certification organism. Moreover, certification organisms assume other norms, at least at European level, for the provision of services (UNE 182001:2008/1M:2010) or environmental management in the tourist facilities (UNE 150101:2001).

On the other hand, Hotel Technology Next Generation (HTNG) [7] is an Agency or global trade association dedicated to enhancing the deployment of technology in hotels and it carries out a certification program of technological products for hotels. It designs specifications for management software, Reservation Systems, etc. HTNG certifies specific products, having the tourism businesses as product consumers as opposed to our proposed standard. Thus, following a different perspective from that of HTNG, we pretend to certificate the hotels depending on the technologies that they actually offer, where the consumers are the hotel's clients.

Some other approaches can be identified regarding tourism standardization such as the published by Jentzsch [8] or sets of directives and procedures like Standards

Australia [9]. However, none of the aforementioned systems specifically include and measure the quality and/or variety of IT services offered by touristic facilities to the final client.

2   Technological Foundations of the 5@ Standard: Tools and Implementation

The main information processing technologies used behind our Standard definition are basically two: Semantic Web and Linked Open Data.

Determining these @s qualifications is necessary to semantically define a Categorization of Technological Services and Infrastructures in Hotels. In this sense, there are several ontologies that represent the tourism sector, e.g. Harmonise, the IFFIT Reference Model of an Electronic Tourism Market, the CIDOC conceptual reference model, OnTour or Mondeca. In this list, the two first aim for mapping data models, and the other ones for descriptions of cultural heritage or tourism activities, but none of them is about the technology offered in this field.

Using Resource Description Framework (RDF) Schema metadata makes possible an open distribution, consultation, and spreading of the standard and its results. It has been done in accordance with the W3C "Linking Open Data" project.

Linked Data is about using the WWW web to connect related data that was not previously linked. More specifically, Wikipedia defines Linked Data as "a term used to describe a recommended best practice for exposing, sharing, and connecting pieces of data, information, and knowledge on the Semantic Web using URIs and RDF". In our 5@ standard implementation, linked open data will be used for sharing the categorization of every @ got by the candidates to be graded. In this way, other systems like hotels, search engines, booking managers, etc, could use the classification by accessing directly to our publicly available data. And, in the same way, we could feed our system with public information about hotels interested in using the standard and other open data sources.

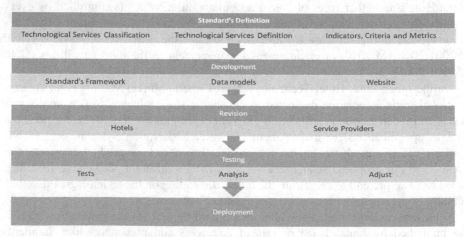

Fig. 1. Phases in the implementation of the 5@ standard

The project implementation is being carried out in several phases [Figure 1]:

1. Standard's Definition Phase
   (a) Technological Services Classification.
   (b) Definition of each Technological Services and their features.
   (c) As well as indicators and metrics determination.
2. Development Phase.
   (a) Standard's Framework, data models and Website Deployment.
3. Revision Phase. Where Stakeholders and Service Providers revision will be done.
4. Testing Phase. The Standard running in several establishments will be tested and the results will be analyzed. This may involve fine tuning of the Standard's definition.
5. And finally, Deployment Phase at the hotel industry.

The overall three-step feed-forward information basic architecture for the standard can be seen in Figure 2. This scheme is inspired in the assessment model first introduced by the CommonKADS methodology for the development of knowledge-based systems [10].

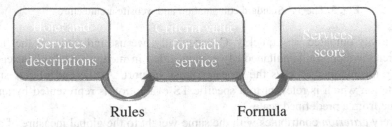

Rules   Formula

Fig. 2. Information collecting scheme to feed the 5@ standard calculations

At the first step hotel companies or touristic businesses are modeled, each of which offer its clients several kinds of technology services (TS), like Wi-Fi, tablets and laptops to rent, on-line booking, VoIP services, etc. Thus, it yields an exhaustive description of each company from the point of view of its technology services and their features. Those indicators will be used to measure each TS from several points of view, such as availability, coverage, business model, security, ease of access, client's support etc. All these *criteria* will be later combined into a generic formula, resulting on a quantitative value for each TS.

The CommonKADS approach anticipates the use of business rules to model the relationships between the technological services and the criteria. Thus, the coverage (*criterion*) for the wifi service can be measured considering some factors for the common areas and others for the in-room service (i.e. the percentage of rooms that actually has the service). Several boards of experts are currently discussing the inclusion of specific indicators and how they must be combined. We are following a client-centered approach to model these services, thus avoiding the use of parameters that

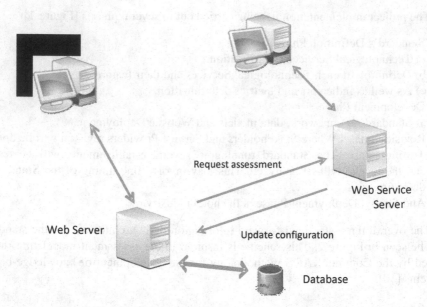

Request assessment

Web Service
Server

Web Server

Update configuration

Database

Fig. 3. The 5@ Standard computation and website architecture

could be easily outdated very quickly. Consequently, we use indicators as the 'number of clients which can simultaneously stream video in medium quality' instead of specifying the number of kB/s the repeater must support. At the end of this stage, every criterion which is relevant to a specific TS evaluation is represented by an ordinal value from a predefined scale.

Not every *criterion* contributes with the same weight to the global measure of a TS evaluation, so a nearest-neighbor formula is used for each technological service. The overall result is later obtained from the weighted combination of all the technological services. Each category in the @ scale also imposes a number of requirements on the score of services the hotel must provide. Therefore, while the wifi service with a global score of 'good' can be considered for obtaining a single @, a higher result may be needed for obtaining additional @s.

$$TS_j(t) = \sqrt{\sum_i W_i(t)C_{ij}^2(t)}$$

Where:
    TSj: is the numeric answer for the technological service j.
    Wi: is the weight for the ith-criteria.
    Cij: is the deduced value for the ith-criteria in the context of the considered
TSj.

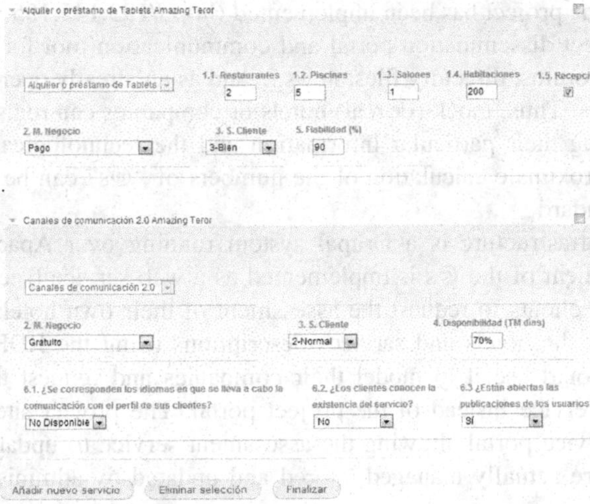

Fig. 4. Hotel's technological services description

In this expression, the dependence on time (t) reflects the idea of an evolving and adaptable TS calculation, thus avoiding obsolesce in using it and taking into account the quick evolution of IT technologies and their popular spreading and demand. The formal, mathematical properties of every function (weights and Cij values particularly) are still to be described and presumably depend not only on the business model of each touristic company but also on factors related to IT companies product release, user acceptance etc. On the other hand, we believe that once these functions are derived, an interesting feedback can be obtained from them, since the model can be used by companies to reach a desired value of TS in a certain moment of (future) time by combining the increase and/or decrease of Wi and Cij as it suits company strategies. This opens new possibilities on planning the implementation of IT deployments in touristic businesses.

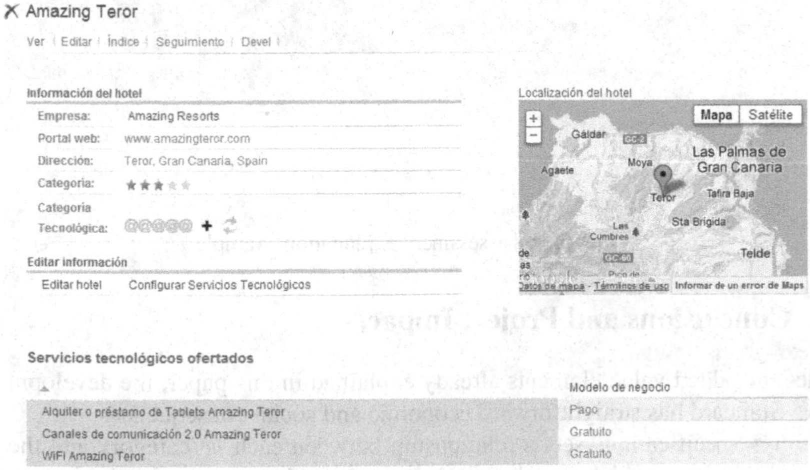

Fig. 5. Hotel's teaser view

A website for the project has been implemented (http://193.145.155.85), both functioning as a Project dissemination portal and communication tool for the teamwork through different forums, directory files, news..., and as an already operative tool with which making tests. Thus, mock-(or real) hotels or companies can register in our system and, by adding their particular information and the technological services that they offer, an approximate calculation of the numbers of "@s" can be calculated according to our standard.

The website infrastructure is a Drupal system running over Apache server, although the assessment of the @s is implemented as a web service (see Figure 3), allowing third party clients to request the assessment of their own hotels. We are currently normalizing the hotels and services descriptions using the RDF language, so potential clients could use it to model their companies and request the assessment through the web service instead of the project portal. The project site also exposes itself as a web service portal allowing the assessment service to update weights and measures which are actually managed (stored and updated by administrators) in the project website.

Regarding this website interface, privileged users can register new hotels and feed the system with detailed information about their facilities and services. For example, see Figure 4 for a snapshot of technological services interface. Once created, any user can view the hotel's teaser view in which only the essential information is shown (Figure 5). From this view, the user can click on the '+' symbol to get an explanation of how the score was obtained (Figure 6), or, if the user has the right privileges, he can even request the re-assessment of the @'s.

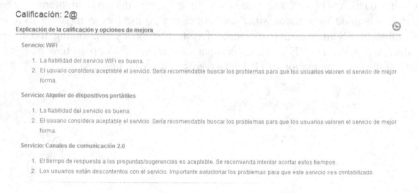

Fig. 6. @'s assessment explanation example

3   Conclusions and Project Impact

Besides the added value elements already explained in this paper, the development of the 5@ Standard has straightforward economic and social consequences.

The 5@ specifications sets a relationship between each @ category and the technological services, which can be used as a valuable source of information when planning IT investments in the hotel and tourism sectors.

Public administrations (local, regional or federal) may also benefit on having new and reliable indicators on IT services and technological implantation in the touristic sector that yield valuable information for planning incentive decisions in technology investments.

Technology providers and telecommunications operators, besides being directly benefited from the touristic sector investments in technology, can also adapt their services and products lines more efficiently to a more structured and sophisticated demand, favoring competitiveness and the surge of new businesses in this sector. The offer of products that comply with a standard gains reliability vs. an offer of products that the customers cannot evaluate.

Finally, the @s hotels clients will be better informed on the availability and functioning of IT services in their infrastructures, and the hotels investments in technology will be returned via a new offer, which has been adapted to their customer`s real needs.

Technically, the proposed 5@ Standard`s architecture is based on the Open Data categorization of the technological services, the definition of a metric for their evaluation and the use of a transparent, global and adaptable formula for the computation of the final number of @s.

Acknowledgments. This work was supported in part by a grant from the Instituto Universitario de Ciencias y Tecnologías Cibernéticas at the University of Las Palmas de Gran Canaria.

References

1. See Eurostat updated statistics at: http://epp.eurostat.ec.europa.eu/portal/page/portal/information_society/introduction
2. Hotels.com; 2012 Amenities Survey (2012)
3. Smartphone Usage Statistics (2012), http://ansonalex.com/infographics/smartphone-usage-statistics-2012-infographic/
4. Rodríguez-Rodríguez, A., Tejera-Correa, S., Moreno-Díaz Jr., R.: 5@: A Standard Specification for the Technological Services Provided at Touristic Facilities. In: Computer Aided Systems Theory; Universidad de Las Palmas de Gran Canaria, vol. 9, pp. 83–84 (February 2013) ISBN-13: 978-84-695-6971-9
5. Turismo de Portugal, Sistemas de Qualidade no Turismo, http://www.turismodeportugal.pt
6. Quality Tourism Service (QTS) Scheme - Hong Kong, http://www.discoverhongkong.com
7. Hotel Technology Next Generation, http://htng.org/certification
8. Jentsch, A.: Tourism Standards. Technical Report XML Clearinghouse Report (2005)
9. Standards Australia, http://www.standards.org.au/Pages/default.aspx
10. Schreiber, G., Col: Knowledge Engineering and Management, The CommonKADS methodology. MIT Press, London (2000)

On the Relevance of Graphical Causal Models for Failure Detection for Industrial Machinery

A.H. Kosorus[1], M. Zhariy[2], T. Natschläger[2], B. Freudenthaler[2], and Josef Küng[1]

[1] Institute of Application Oriented Knowledge Processing
Johannes-Kepler University, Linz, Austria
{hkosorus,jkueng}@faw.jku.at
[2] Software Competence Center Hagenberg, Austria
{mariya.zhariy,thomas.natschlaeger,bernhard.freudenthaler}@scch.at

Abstract. Assessing the reliability of industrial machinery is an important aspect within maintenance processes in order to maximize productivity and efficiency. In this paper we propose to use graphical models for fault detection in industrial machinery within a condition-based maintenance setting. The contribution of this work is based on the hypothesis that during fault free operation the causal relationships between the observed measurement channels are not changing. Therefore, major changes in a graphical model might imply faulty changes within the machine's functionality or its properties. We compare and evaluate four methods for the identification of potential causal relationships on a real world inspired use case. The results indicate that sparse models (using L_1 regularization) perform better than traditional full models.

Keywords: fault detection and diagnosis, graphical models, causality, condition-based maintenance.

1 Introduction

Condition-based maintenance (CBM) techniques become more and more popular to maximize productivity and efficiency of industrial machinery. This technique tries to avoid unnecessary maintenance and only take actions when indicated by the (faulty) condition or state of the machinery under supervision. *Fault detection and diagnosis* is one of the important components of a CBM technique and it deals with mapping information in the measurement space to faults in the fault space. In the past decade, within diagnostics, many data driven modeling methods have been developed [2,8]. The main challenge is to identify the proper structure of the model for the machinery under supervision: the better the model captures the physical and causal relationships the better the model is suited for effective and robust fault detection and diagnosis [10].

In this paper we propose to use *graphical models* for fault detection in industrial machinery to tackle this issue. Mining of model structures within multivariate time series, i.e. collected condition monitoring data from an industrial machinery in our setting, has received a lot of attention in the past years [3,10]

R. Moreno-Díaz et al. (Eds.): EUROCAST 2013, Part I, LNCS 8111, pp. 174–181, 2013.
© Springer-Verlag Berlin Heidelberg 2013

and is still considered to be a major challenge, especially when dealing with complex and noisy data.

Prominent recent approaches within this field are based on graphical lasso methods [5]. The idea behind the graphical lasso methods is to estimate a sparse graphical model by optimizing a L_1 regularized log-likelihood for a Gaussian graphical model. Hence, these methods based on such first principles generalize heuristic approaches like the one presented in [10]. Studies have shown that such graphical methods are well suited to reveal the true model structure, can add extra predictive accuracy and may also help to improve the interpretability of obtained models by arriving at more succinct models [1].

The contribution of this work is based on the hypothesis that during fault free operation the causal relationships between the observed measurement channels are not changing. Hence, to discover abnormal behavior in the observed data one can continuously construct graphical models among the observed measurement channels. Major changes in the graphical model might imply faulty changes within the machine's functionality or its properties. The use of *sparse* graphical models is advantageous for such applications: the sparsity of the model decreases the sensitivity of distance measures between models with respect to noise and increases the interpretability of the model and its changes. Using simulated data for a specific industrial machinery with and without defined faults we compare the proposed method with simpler non-sparse graphical model learning methods.

For these case studies we compared four different types of methods: sparse graphical [5] (graphical lasso), non-sparse graphical (simple inverse covariance), sparse linear regression (lasso regression) and standard linear regression. These methods were applied on synthetically generated data for a particular industrial machine. Results show that the lasso based sparse methods perform better than non-sparse ones.

The rest of this paper is structured as follows: section 2 gives an overview of the used methods for the evaluation of our approach; section 3 presents our adopted approach to identify potential causal relationships between observed measurement channels; section 4 introduces the example case study, presents evaluation results and discusses the efficiency of the applied methods; and, finally, section 5 summarizes the content of this paper, draws some important conclusions and presents future research issues.

2   Problem Statement and Approach

Consider the situation where to build a model of a physical system with several measurement nodes $X_1, X_2, \ldots, X_p$ (e.g. pressure, velocity, electrical power, ...) built of instances of components (e.g. pump, valve, resistor, capacitor, ...) from a class $\mathcal{C} = C^{(1)}, \ldots, C^k$. That means that each pair (i, j) of measurement nodes is connected by an instance $C_{i,j}$ of one of the possible component from $\mathcal{C}$.

The goal is to determine which component, if any at all, is located between each of the $\frac{p(p-1)}{2}$ pairs of measurement nodes. See Figure 1 for the

Table 1. Methods used to estimate the relationships between system components

	Sparse	Non-sparse
Graphical	The graphical lasso (`glasso`)	Inverse of covariance matrix (`inv(S)`)
Regression	Lasso regression (`glmnet`)	Standard linear regression (`glm`)

graphical representation of the physical system considered in the next section. In the following we refer to this graph as the causality graph.

To do this, we apply different methods (see below) to a data matrix $X \in \mathbb{R}^{n \times d}$ with n observations where the d columns represent the measurement nodes, and additional variables computed using mathematical models of the possible connecting components from the class $\mathcal{C}$. For each of the models the result are component coefficients $w_{i,j}^{(k)}$ which determine the strength of the connectivity / influence of a component of type $C^{(k)}$ between the measurement nodes (i, j). A component coefficient $w_{i,j}^{(k)} = 0$ indicates the absence of a component.

In particular we investigate the standard linear regression, the inverse of the empirical covariance matrix and the lasso regression and the graphical lasso (see Table 1 and next section). The latter two are sparse methods and produce sparse dependencies, i.e. many component coefficients $w_{i,j}^{(k)}$ will be zero, and we argue that these methods are more efficient to identify the main causality relationships in the measurement data.

3   Methods

In this section we give an overview of the used methods for the evaluation of our approach which are summarized in Table 1.

3.1   The Graphical Lasso

The graphical lasso method estimates a sparse inverse covariance matrix using a lasso (L_1) penalty[5,13], which is used to identify the structure of the undirected dependency graph from the data. Meinshausen and Bühlman[9] adopt a simple approach to solve this problem, namely, instead of estimating the full inverse covariance matrix, they only estimate the nonzero components using iterative lasso regressions.

Consider some data matrix $X \in \mathbb{R}^{n \times d}$ where each column represents one measurement variable. The idea of the graphical lasso method is to maximize the L_1-penalized log-likelihood

$$\log det(\Phi) - tr(S\Phi) - \lambda |\Phi|_1, \tag{1}$$

where $\Phi = \Sigma^{-1}$ is the inverse of the model covariance matrix Σ and $S = X^T X / n$ is the empirical covariance matrix, with n being the number of observations, and λ is the regularization parameter that controls the sparseness of the obtained inverse covariance matrix. The higher the regularization parameter λ, the sparser result will be. $|\Phi|_1$ is the L_1 norm of Φ; i.e. the sum of the absolute values of the elements of $\Phi = \Sigma^{-1}$.

3.2   Lasso Regression

The lasso linear regression fits a linear model via penalized maximum likelihood[6]. It can deal with all types of data, including very large sparse data matrices. The method approximates the regression function by a linear model $y_i = \beta_0 + x_i^T \beta$, where $y \in \mathbb{R}$ is a response variable and $x_i \in \mathbb{R}^d$ is a predictor vector. The goal of this approach is therefore

$$\min_{(\beta_0, \beta) \in \mathbb{R}^{p+1}} \left[\frac{1}{2n} \sum_{i=1}^{n} (y_i - \beta_0 - x_i^T \beta) + \lambda |\beta|_1 \right], \tag{2}$$

where n is the number of observations, $(\beta_0, \beta) \in \mathbb{R}^{p+1}$ are the parameters of the linear regression that need to be estimated and $\lambda |\beta|_1$ is the lasso penalty with $|\beta|_1 = \sum_j |\beta_j|$.

4   Case Study and Evaluation Environment

To evaluate our approach, we considered a case study where the mathematical model and the non-linear mathematical functions of the components are rather well known. We applied the four methods on a synthetic data set gathered from a detailed simulation of the physical system and compared their efficiency.

The system consists of $p = 5$ measurement nodes $X_1, \ldots, X_5$. and can contain a component instance C_{ij} from only one class of components; i.e. $\mathcal{C} = C^{(1)}$, between any measurement nodes X_i and X_j, $i, j \in \{1, \ldots, 5\}, i < j$. We therefore have a total number $\frac{p(p-1)}{2} = 10$ of possible component instances.

In the fault free case the following set of equations describe adequately the considered system:

$$\begin{bmatrix} \dot{X}_1 \\ \dot{X}_2 \\ \dot{X}_3 \\ \dot{X}_4 \\ \dot{X}_5 \end{bmatrix} = \begin{bmatrix} C_{1,3}^\theta(X) + C_{1,4}^\theta(X) + C_{1,5}^\theta(X) \\ C_{2,5}^\theta(X) \\ C_{1,3}^\theta(X) + C_{3,5}^\theta(X) \\ C_{1,4}^\theta(X) + C_{4,5}^\theta(X) \\ C_{1,5}^\theta(X) + C_{2,5}^\theta(X) + C_{3,5}^\theta(X) + C_{4,5}^\theta(X) \end{bmatrix}, \tag{3}$$

where $C_{i,j}^\theta$ denote parameterized components, which are non-linear functions of measurement data:

$$C_{i,j} = \text{sign}(X_i - X_j)\sqrt{|X_i - X_j|} \tag{4}$$

This machine operates under two different modes (see Figure 1), switching alternatively from mode A to mode B, and then from mode B back to mode A. We study the causality graphs for both of these modes.

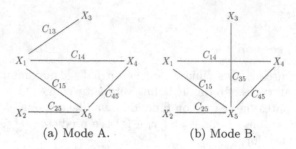

(a) Mode A.   (b) Mode B.

Fig. 1. Causality graphs in different modes of the case study system

To evaluate our approach, we constructed a synthetic data set for different scenarios: fault-free (for both modes) and four faulty states. The faulty states are:

- C_{13} does not turn on in mode A
- C_{13} does not turn off in mode B
- C_{35} does not turn on in mode B
- C_{35} does not turn off in mode A

We used the **R** software environment for statistical computing[1] to apply the four methods presented in section 2 (`glasso`, `glmnet`, `glm`, `solve`).

5 Results

For our evaluation purposes, we generated a synthetic data set according to the example system given by equation (3), to which white noise was added. Then, we applied the four methods (see Table 1) on the obtained data.

Figures (2) and (3) show the dependency matrices of the four methods in the fault-free mode A and the first faulty case ($C_{1,3}$ does not turn on in mode A), respectively. The rows in the dependency matrix are represented by the derivatives of the measurement nodes, while the columns are given by the possible 10 components (see equation (3)). While darker regions signify high dependencies, the brighter and white ones reflect weak or no dependency, correspondingly.

Results show that, overall, the lasso regularized methods are more efficient in obtaining the actual causal dependencies between measurement points, in the sense that they produce sparse models that enable a less ambiguous identification of correct component dependencies.

---

[1] The R Project of Statistical Computing, http://www.r-project.org/

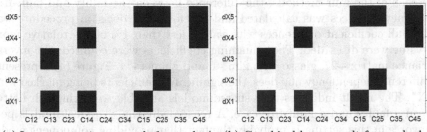

(a) Inverse covariance result for mode A. (b) Graphical lasso result for mode A.

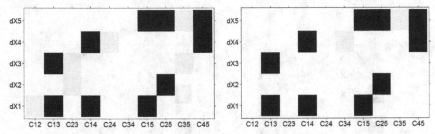

(c) Linear regression result for mode A. (d) Lasso regression result for mode A.

Fig. 2. Results for the mode A fault-free case

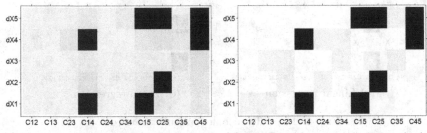

(a) Inverse covariance result for mode A. (b) Graphical lasso result for mode A.

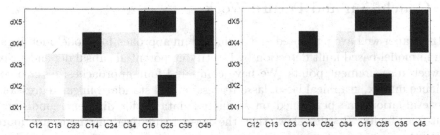

(c) Linear regression result for mode A. (d) Lasso regression result for mode A.

Fig. 3. Results for the mode A faulty case

To show how distinguishable the faulty case is from the normal, fault-free case using each of the four methods, the difference between the faulty and fault-free dependency matrices was calculated and the following decision procedure was applied: all coefficient differences with values less than 1% of the relative maximal value were discarded. The remaining coefficients were counted: the inverse covariance matrix - 27, glasso - 10, glm - 6 and glmnet - 4. Figure (4) represents the difference dependency matrices, the significant coefficients being marked with an "X". The result indicates that sparse models are able to distinguish better between a faulty and a fault-free case. A reason why the graphical models perform worse in this setting is probably the fact that providing component model partly "solves" the task of finding the causal structure.

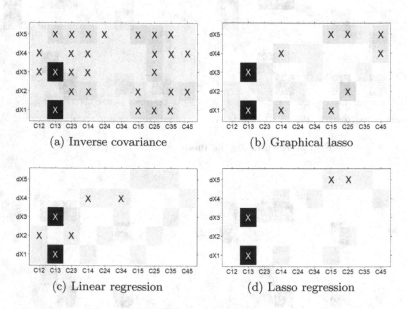

(a) Inverse covariance   (b) Graphical lasso

(c) Linear regression   (d) Lasso regression

Fig. 4. The difference dependency matrices

6   Conclusion and Future Work

In this paper we have presented and evaluated an approach for model identification in model-based fault detection by identifying potential causal dependencies between measurement points. We have compared four approaches: inverse covariance matrix, graphical lasso, lasso regression and standard linear regression. The evaluation was performed on simulated data under different conditions: fault-free, faulty. Results show that the lasso regularized methods are more efficient.

As future work, we propose to evaluate our approach on real data, test with other faulty cases (e.g. malfunction of component), investigate difference between glasso and glmnet and study the case of non-linear mathematical models.

More principled implementations based on the idea of grouped lasso regression [11] will be investigated in the future. Furthermore, challenges which are not "automagically" solved by the proposed approach are the detection of abnormalities (erroneously interpreted as faults) originating by unobservable events (e.g. user interaction with the machine when changing input parameters) and the inference of a human interpretable reason which triggered the detection of a structural model change. However, we believe that our proposed approach allows for more principled inclusion of background knowledge into fault diagnoses which will be a future research topic on its own.

References

1. Arnold, A., Liu, Y., Abe, N.: Temporal causal modeling with graphical Granger methods. In: Proceedings of the 13th ACM SIGKDD International Conference on Knowledge Discovery and Data Mining (KDD 2007). ACM, New York (2007)
2. Ding, S.X.: Model-based fault diagnosis techniques. Design schemes, algorithms and tools, 2nd edn. Advances in Industrial Control. Springer (2013)
3. Eichler, M.: Graphical modeling of dynamic relationships in multivariate time series. Open Access publications from Maastricht University (2006)
4. Eichler, M.: Causal inference from time series: What can be learned from Granger causality? Open Access publications from Maastricht University (2007)
5. Friedman, J., Hastie, T., Tibshirani, R.: Sparse inverse covariance estimation with the graphical lasso. Biostatistics 9(3), 432–441 (2008)
6. Friedman, J., Hastie, T., Tibshirani, R.: Regularization paths for generalized linear models via coordinate descent. Journal of Statistical Software 33(1), 1–22 (2010)
7. Granger, C.W.J.: Investigating causal relations by econometric models and cross-spectral methods. Econometrica 37, 424–438 (1969)
8. Jardine, A.K.S., Lin, D., Banjevic, D.: A review on machinery diagnostics and prognostics implementing condition-based maintenance. Mechanical Systems and Signal Processing 20(7), 1483–1510 (2006)
9. Meinshausen, N., Bühlmann, P.: High dimensional graphs and variable selection with the Lasso. The Annals of Statistics 34(3) (2006)
10. Schrems, A., Efendic, H., Pichler, K.: Selection of physically interpretable data driven model structures to analyze industrial processes. In: Proceedings of the 11th WSEAS International Conference on Automatic Control, Modeling and Simulation (2009)
11. Simon, N., Friedman, J., Hastie, T., Tibshirani, R.: A sparse group lasso. Journal of Computational and Graphical Statistics (2012)
12. Spirtes, P., Glymour, C., Scheines, R.: Causation, prediction, and search, 2nd edn. MIT Press, New York (2001)
13. Witten, D., Friedman, J., Simon, N.: New insights and faster computations for the graphical lasso. Journal of Computational and Graphical Statistics 20(4) (2011)

A Hybrid Cloud Computing Approach for Intelligent Processing and Storage of Scientific Data

David Horat[1,2], Eduardo Quevedo[1,3], and Alexis Quesada-Arencibia[4]

[1] Plataforma Oceánica de Canarias
Las Palmas, E35214, Spain
{david.horat,eduardo.quevedo}@plocan.eu
[2] Instituto Universitario de Sistemas Inteligentes y Aplicaciones Numéricas en Ingeniería
Universidad de Las Palmas de Gran Canaria
Las Palmas, E35017, Spain
david.horat@siani.es
[3] Instituto Universitario de Microelectrónica Aplicada
Universidad de Las Palmas de Gran Canaria
Las Palmas, E35017, Spain
equevedo@iuma.ulpgc.es
[4] Instituto Universitario de Ciencias y Tecnologías Cibernéticas
Universidad de Las Palmas de Gran Canaria
Las Palmas, E35017, Spain
aquesada@dis.ulpgc.es

Abstract. This paper covers a new approach on Cloud Computing for Scientific Data Storage and Processing using a hybrid system with both on-site and on-the-cloud systems. The system analyzes use cases which are not resolved by either one of the single systems themselves.

Keywords: Cloud Computing, Hybrid Systems, Scientific Data, Intelligent Processing.

1   Introduction

Cloud Computing provides a revolutionary model for the deployment of enterprise applications and Web services [1]. The term Cloud Computing is currently being used with several concepts behind it. One of the most accurate definitions is the one provided by The National Institute of Standards and Technology of the United States Department of Commerce [2]:

> "*A model for enabling ubiquitous, convenient, on-demand network access to a shared pool of configurable computing resources (e.g., networks, servers, storage, applications, and services) that can be rapidly provisioned and released with minimal management effort or service provider interaction.*"

R. Moreno-Díaz et al. (Eds.): EUROCAST 2013, Part I, LNCS 8111, pp. 182–188, 2013.

Most of the Cloud Computing infrastructures known nowadays are based on the concept of public clouds, where commercial providers sell part of this infrastructure in a service model. One of these examples is Amazon Web Services, where Elastic Compute Cloud (EC2) instances are sold for as low as $0,080 [3]. Unfortunately, this kind of clouds are not yet fit for all use cases, especially when dealing with security issues or cost-effectiveness in high data transmission environments. As a consequence, the concept of private clouds raises.

The primary aim of these private cloud deployments is not to sell capacity over the Internet through publicly-accessible interfaces, but to provide local users with a flexible and agile private infrastructure to run service workloads within their administrative domain [4]. Moreover, private clouds have also several constraints regarding flexibility, scalability and robustness compared to most available public clouds. For this matter, we will use a mixed approach, called Hybrid Cloud, where we will combine both public and private clouds to solve specific use cases required to process and store scientific data.

2   Use Cases

In this section we will study several typical use cases which appear in the domain of scientific data management and which will be the base for the specific architecture selection.

2.1   Big Data

Information has gone from scarce to superabundant. This brings huge new benefits, but also big headaches [5]. The precise definition of "Big Data" is hazy, but one of the most interesting ones is the one stated by Edd Dumbill [6]:

> *"Big Data is data that exceeds the processing capacity of*
> *conventional database systems. The data is too big, moves*
> *too fast, or doesn't fit the strictures of your database architectures.*
> *To gain value from this data, you must choose an*
> *alternative way to process it."*

The amount of data that comes from sensors in scientific laboratories has grown exponentially over the last years. This means that real-time transportation of this data into the internet using standard bandwidth, especially in heavy-usage time frames such as standard working hours, becomes a bottleneck in scientific organizations. As such, the most common way to store this information is using in-house data centers connected through Ethernet, fast wireless connections or fiber optics to the sensors network.

2.2   Low Latency

Big Data can be defined by reviewing its basic characteristics, sometimes referred to as the 3 Vs: Volume, Velocity and Variety. In this sense, velocity represents the increasing frequency with which data is delivered [7]. Velocity states the importance of using low latency networks to consume the information at the needed speed, so buffers don´t overflow. The most common way to transmit the information is using low latency in-house networks, such as Ethernet and fiber optics.

2.3   High Availability

High availability is an increasingly important requirement for enterprise systems, often valued more than performance. Systems designed for high availability typically use redundant hardware for error detection and continued uptime in the event of a failure [8]. However, just as large ISPs (Internet Service Providers) use multiple network providers so that failure by a single company will not take them off the air, we believe that the one of the most appropriate solutions to achieve very high availability is multiple cloud computing providers [9].

2.4   Scalability

Nowadays, scalability is a major issue. When scientific data becomes public and has an impact, the number of requests to access that data grows exponentially. Therefore, there is a need to marshal resources in such a way that a program continues running smoothly even though the number of users grows is in high demand. It's not just that servers must respond to hundreds or thousands of requests per second; the system must also coordinate information coming from multiple sources, not all of which are under the control of the same organization [10].

2.5   Disaster Recovery

There is no question that scientific data must be preserved overtime [11]. To accomplish this task, we must assure that the data is copied and that the storage of this copy is duplicated in different geographical locations so if any natural, human or mechanical disaster happens, data can be saved.

Disaster recovery is not the same as high availability. Though both concepts are related to business continuity, high availability is about providing undisrupted continuity of operations, whereas disaster recovery involves some amount of downtime, typically measured in days [12].

3   Architecture Proposal

From the analysis of the uses cases, it is clear that there is no single system which could cover them all. Therefore, we need a mixture of different systems integrated together and seen as a System of Systems. For this purpose, and due to the rise and fitness of Cloud Computing technologies, we will use a combination of public cloud computing and private cloud computing technologies, also known as a *hybrid cloud*.

From an engineering perspective, Cloud Computing is a distributed computing paradigm that focuses on providing a wide range of users with distributed access to virtualized hardware and/or software infrastructure over the internet. From a business perspective, it is the availability of computing resources that are scalable and billed on a usage basis. While scalability is the primary principle of cloud computing, a host of other advantages are advertised as being inherently obtained through cloud computing [13].

3.1   Public Cloud

There are many Public Cloud Computing providers in the current landscape of internet services. In this case, we will focus on the ones which cover Infrastructure as a Service. The most well-known and well-established services as of nowadays are: Amazon Web Services ©, Microsoft Azure ©, Google Compute Engine © and Rackspace Cloud ©.

In our case, we selected Amazon Web Services © for several reasons:

1. It provides the widest range of IaaS (Infrastructure as a Service) services [3]
2. Their programming interface has become a *de facto* standard [14]
3. The different price offers for configurations allowed us to accommodate our needs in a more efficient way [3]

3.2   Private Cloud

There are several open source initiatives in the Private Cloud landscape. The most prominent ones are: Eucalyptus ©, CloudStack ©, OpenStack © and OpenNebula © [15].

In our case, we selected OpenNebula © for several reasons:

1. It is compatible with many Amazon Web Services © APIs (Application Programming Interfaces) [15]
2. It started in the scientific context and thus it was though for it [15]

3.3   Architecture Overview

As it is shown in Figure 1, the approach consists on connecting the Private Cloud, usually located in-house, to the Public Cloud, which is usually commercialized by third-party vendors. It includes:

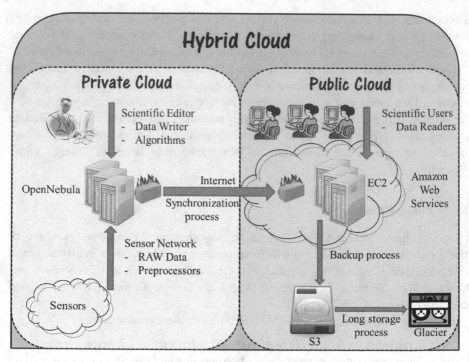

Fig. 1. Architecture Overview

Actors

1. *Scientific Editor*: It can write and edit data. It usually runs specific scientific algorithms to summary the data or to extract information from the raw data.
2. *Sensor Network*: It will output raw data directly into the servers. It may also preprocess some raw data already storing summaries of the data.
3. *Scientific Users*: They will consume the data. They usually outnumber by several degrees of magnitude the number of scientific editors.

Processes

1. *Synchronization process*: It will copy the contents of the private cloud to the public cloud for reliability, stability and assurance reasons. This process may run one or several times a day, especially during low-usage time frames of the network to minimize the transmission time.
2. *Backup process*: It will copy all the data stored in the public cloud several times a week to ensure that all data can be restored if any disaster may happen. It will use a quick access system, such as Amazon S3 so the amount of time needed to restore the last backup is as short as possible.
3. *Long storage process*: It will copy old backups to a slow and cheap storage system, such as tape storage, to ensure that if anything happens with the last backup or there is a need for comparison with old data, it can be done.

Technologies

1. *EC2*: Amazon Elastic Compute Cloud (Amazon EC2) is a web service that provides resizable compute capacity in the cloud. It is designed to make web-scale computing easier for developers [3].
2. *S3*: Amazon S3 is storage for the Internet. It provides a simple web services interface that can be used to store and retrieve any amount of data, at any time, from anywhere on the web [3].
3. *Glacier*: Amazon Glacier is an extremely low-cost storage service that provides secure and durable storage for data archiving and backup. In order to keep costs low, Amazon Glacier is optimized for data that is infrequently accessed and for which retrieval times of several hours are suitable [3].

4   Conclusions

The proposed architecture covers all use cases studied at the beginning of this paper:

1. **Big Data:** The sensor network is connected directly to the private cloud, so the first step will be to copy all raw data in real time. At a later step, the data will be copied to the public cloud when there is appropriate access to the network.
2. **Low Latency:** As happened with the big data use case, the sensor network is connected directly to the private cloud, meaning that there is a low latency between the sensor network and the private cloud, avoiding any kind of buffer overflow.
3. **High Availability:** There are two different providers of the data, the private and the public cloud, so everything is duplicated and ready to be accessed when needed. This resolves the concerns of Michael Armbrust et al. [9].
4. **Scalability:** All data is accessed by scientific users using the public cloud infrastructure. When peaks happen in the access of this data, automatic measures will take care and scale the infrastructure as required. This functionality is included in EC2 [3].
5. **Disaster Recovery:** All data is properly backed up several times a week using Amazon S3 [3]. Moreover, several old backups are also kept using Amazon Glacier [3] for possible later comparison and higher availability of data for disaster recovery.

References

[1] Benson, T., et al.: A first look at problems in the cloud. In: Proceedings of the 2nd USENIX Conference on Hot Topics in Cloud Computing, HotCloud 2010, p. 15. USENIX Association, Berkeley (2010), http://dl.acm.org/citation.cfm?id=1863103.1863118

[2] Mell, P., et al.: The NIST Definition of Cloud Computing. Recommendations of the National Institute of Standards and Technology. Special Publication 800-145 (September 2011)

[3] Amazon Elastic Compute Cloud (Amazon EC2) in Amazon Web Services, http://aws.amazon.com/ec2/ (retrieved February 6, 2013)

[4] Sotomayor, B., Montero, R.S., Llorente, I.M., Foster, I.: Virtual Infrastructure Management in Private and Hybrid Clouds. IEEE Internet Computing 13(5), 14–22 (2009)

[5] Data, data everywhere. The Economist (February 25, 2010) (retrieved February 6, 2013)

[6] Dumbill, E.: Big Data, ahead of print. "Making Sense of Big Data" (2013), doi:10.1089/big.2012.1503, ISSN: 2167-6461

[7] Fernandes, L., Michele, O., Weaver, V.: Big Data, Bigger Outcomes. Journal of AHIMA 83(10), 38–43 (2012)

[8] Aggarwal, N., et al.: Configurable isolation: building high availability systems with commodity multi-core processors. ACM SIGARCH Computer Architecture News 35(2), 470–481 (2007)

[9] Armbrust, M., et al.: A view of cloud computing. Communications of the ACM 53(4), 50–58 (2010)

[10] Tograph, B., Richard Morgens, Y.: Cloud computing. Communications of the ACM 51(7) (2008)

[11] Duranti, L.: Rethinking Appraisal - Conference Overview. In: DELOS International Conference, "Appraisal in the Digital World," in association with Digital Preservation Europe and InterPARES, November 15-16. Accademia Nazionale Dei Lincei, Rome (2007)

[12] Disaster Recovery: Best Practices. Technology White Paper. Cisco Systems (2008) (retrieved February 6, 2013)

[13] Strowd, H.D., Lewis, G.A.: T-Check in system-of-systems technologies: Cloud computing (2010)

[14] Clark, J.: Amazon Web Services: Rise of the utility cloud. ZDNET (June 6, 2012) (retrieved February 6, 2013)

[15] Open Nebula project, http://opennebula.org/ (retrieved February 6, 2013)

Formal Definition of Service Availability in Cloud Computing Using OWL

Mariam Rady

Christian Doppler Laboratory for Client-Centric Cloud Computing (CDCC)
Johannes Kepler University in Linz
m.rady@cdcc.faw.jku.at

Abstract. Fulfilling cloud customers needs entails describing a quality of service on top of the services functional description. Currently, the only guarantees that are offered by cloud providers are imprecise and incomplete Service Level Agreements (SLA). We present a model to describe one of the main attributes discussed in SLAs which is availability. The model is developed using Web Ontology Language OWL. And it aims at covering the different concepts of availability and availability-related attributes that should be present in a service contract in order to guarantee the quality of service the consumer is expecting.

1 Introduction

SLAs define assertions of a service provider, that the service he is providing meets a certain guaranteed IT-Level and business-process level service parameters. In addition, the service provider should deliver measures to be taken in the case he failed to meet these assertions [2]. Current SLAs are vague and do not offer solid guarantees for customers, on which they can rely on. If we take a look at how availability is promised in SLAs, it is usually presented as a percentage or rate value describing the total uptime to the total service agreement time. It is up to the customer to send claims of the downtime incidents, and the service provider checks if the claims are true. If the promised uptime percentage or rate is not met, then the customer gets compensation in form of service credit [4]. This is however, not a reliable guarantee for Quality of Service. In order for the customer to be able to rely on the Quality of the Service, quality attributes need to be well-described in SLAs. Their descriptions should be semantically complete and have a logical structure, to enable reasoning about and processing the information in the agreements. In this work, we focus on availability and we define it formally using the web ontology language OWL.

2 Background

In this section we will discuss how service availability is discussed in the literature. In addition we will also talk about OWL, the web ontology language we used to define our model.

R. Moreno-Díaz et al. (Eds.): EUROCAST 2013, Part I, LNCS 8111, pp. 189–194, 2013.
© Springer-Verlag Berlin Heidelberg 2013

2.1 Availability

The idea of this part of the literature review is to understand how availability is defined, and how it is monitored in different computing environments, in order to conclude a model that will both define availability as well as allow monitoring of the service contracts. Most of the work done on availability, is from the service providers point of view, to understand the behavior of their system and to act when unavailability occurs. Availability of a distributed computing system A(t), can be defined as the probability of a system to be functional at a given time t [6]. The model in [6] is a hierarchical one and models availability at the system level and the component level. At the system level the availability of tasks or processes is measured, whereas at the component level the availability of physical resources is assessed. Process availability modelling is complicated because the process execution involves the interaction of different types of resources. For the availability modelling at component level, for each resource a Markovian model is created, with the different states the resource can be in e.g. correct state, hardware failure, transient software failure or permanent software failure. In [7] system availability is also modelled using Markov models, representing the states of each host in the network. In some of the literature that we examined about availability we encountered that availability has been measured by observing the different resources and assessing their availability separately and then drawing conclusions about the availability of the entire system[6][7], some other measured the availability of the system as a whole[8]. As in our work we are considering a client-centric view of availability, we are trying to model availability in a way that would interest the client as well as allow us to monitor it. We decided to observe the whole service as a set of outcoming requests from the client's machine.

2.2 OWL

The Semantic web is aiming at giving information on the internet meaning, to make it easier for machines to automatically process the information. The Web Ontology Language OWL is used to define the semantics of a certain content instead of just presenting natural language. Therefore, it offers machine interpretability of web content.OWL is based on Description Logic(DL). DL is a family of formal knowledge representation language that is used for providing logical formalism for ontologies and the semantic web[9]. An ontology is a "formal explicit specification of a shared conceptualization"[10]. Our aim was to create an ontology to define availability.

3 Availability Model Using OWL

For the description of the service availability model we used OWL as the description language. In order to formally define availability we need to think about the different concepts that should be included in the definition. We identified several concepts `CommitmentValidity`, which expresses the amount of time the service will be available for use.

`MaintenanceTime` defines the time when maintenance will take place, causing the service to be unavailable. `ProbabilityDistribution` represents the probability distribution of the service resources availability. This concept will be very useful when we would like to monitor the claims of the service contracts. Last but not least, we defined the concept `MonitoringWindow` to specify the time period over which the monitoring of the resource availability is done. For better understanding we show part of the OWL ontology in Figure 1.

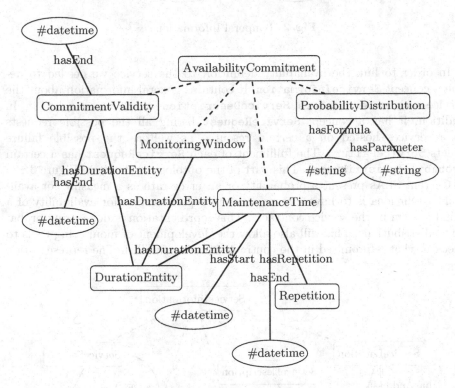

Fig. 1. AvailabilityCommitment

In order to complete the model we needed to define several concepts. `TemporalInformation`, which helps in defining information about time. We also needed to add information about the functionality of the service, to model the different resources and the different requests that are made to these resources, these are defined as `ServiceInformation`. OWL has a predefined datatype `datetime`, we used the concept `TemporalInformation` to include the definition of relative time in the model. The concept `DurationEntity` defines a duration of time, and `Repetition` defines if a certain action will be repeated after a certain amount of time(e.g. Maintenance will take place weekly). Figure 2 shows this part of the ontology.

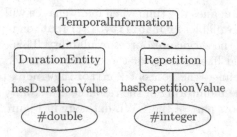

Fig. 2. Temporal Information

In order to link the availability definition to the service we needed to define a concept `ServiceInformation`. It contains general information about the service such as `ServiceName`, `ServiceDescription` and `ServiceLocation`. In addition, it has a concept `ServiceRequest` listing all the possible requests to a services hosted on a certain resource as well as the possible failure events `ServiceFailure`. The fulfilment of each `ServiceRequest` has a certain `ProbabilityDistribution`. This part of the ontology is shown in Figure 3.

Current SLAs present a probability or an error rate as a measure for availability. Our idea is to have a more concrete representation for availability of a cloud system in the service contracts. This representation is done using probability distributions. This will also allow the development of monitoring tools to check if what is promised in the contracts is being fulfilled. The representation

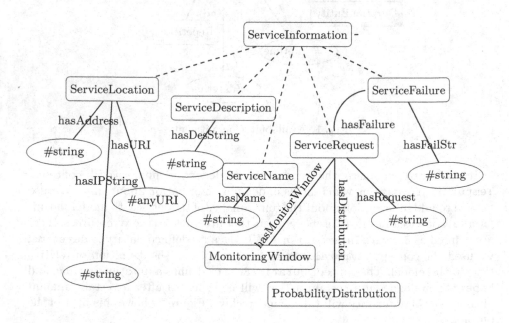

Fig. 3. ServiceInformation

of availability using probability distribution is done by gathering data sets for long periods of time for host and CPU availability of different networks and comparing them to the actual service availability data using either graphical analysis or Goodness-of-fit tests [3]. It is observable that in different networks, to have a best-fit, different distribution functions are needed [3][1][5]. This will possibly allow these contracts to be monitorable and give the consumers the courage to trust SLAs. For each of the in the ontology stated probability distribution functions we have different parameters that shape the distribution and different formulas. These are stored in the ontology as a string. After deciding which distribution is the best fit and the values of the different parameters, the distribution name and the parameters are stated "as-is" in the contract. And upon agreement these parameters should be checked every `MonitoringWindow` and if there are violations the customer should get a refund.

4   Conclusion

In this paper we presented a definition of service availability using the Web Ontology language OWL. We adopted a client centric view, trying to define service availability in a way that would be of interest to the client as well as monitorable. The general idea of the model is that for each service there are certain possible outgoing requests that can be made. The response to these requests can be modelled or fitted to a probability distribution function. The idea is not to bother the user with how the service will be monitored, but he will get an information about the probability a certain service request will be completed successfully at a certain instance. This way the cloud user can guarantee, that the claims that are stated in the SLAs are indeed true. For the future work, we plan on developing a monitoring tool, that would be placed either on the cloud user machine or as a middleware between the client and the service provider. This tool will monitor the outgoing requests and their responses and fit them to a probability distribution function, that will then be the reference for monitoring the SLAs.

References

1. Javadi, B., Kondo, D., Vincent, J.-M., Anderson, D.P.: Discovering statistical models of availability in large distributed systems: An empirical study of seti@home. IEEE Transactions on Parallel and Distributed Systems 22, 1896–1903 (2011)
2. Ludwig, H., Keller, A., Dan, A., King, R.P., Franck, R.: Web Service Level Agreement (WSLA) Language Specification, pp. 1–110 (2003)
3. Nurmi, D., Brevik, J., Wolski, R.: Modeling machine availability in enterprise and wide-area distributed computing environments. In: Cunha, J.C., Medeiros, P.D. (eds.) Euro-Par 2005. LNCS, vol. 3648, pp. 432–441. Springer, Heidelberg (2005)
4. Amazon Web Services. Amazon Web Services Customer Agreement (2008), http://aws-portal.amazon.com/gp/aws/developer/ terms-and-conditions.html (accessed August 29, 2012)

5. Wingstrom, J., Casanova, H.: Statistical Modeling of Resource Availability in Desktop Grids. Technical report (November 2007)
6. Hariri, S., Mutlu, H.: Hierarchical modeling of availability in distributed systems. IEEE Transactions on Software Engineering 21(1), 50–56 (1995)
7. Lai, C.D., Xie, M., Poh, K.L., Dai, Y.S., Yang, P.: A model for availability analysis of distributed software/hardware systems. Information and Software Technology 44(6), 343–350 (2002)
8. Goyal, A., Tantawi, A.N.: A Measure of Guaranteed Availability and its Numerical Evaluation. IEEE Transactions on Computers 37(1), 25–32 (1988)
9. W3C Recommendation, OWL Web Ontology Language Overview (February 10, 2004) (last retrieved: Mai 6, 2013)
10. Fensel, D., Lausen, H., Polleres, A., de Bruijn, J., Stollberg, M., Roman, D., Domingue, J.: Enabling Semantic Web Services: The Web Service Modeling, 1st edn. Springer-Verlag New York, Inc., Secaucus (2006)

Declarative Modeling and Bayesian Inference of Dark Matter Halos

Gabriel Kronberger

School of Informatics, Communications and Media,
University of Applied Sciences Upper Austria,
Softwarepark 11, 4232, Hagenberg
gabriel.kronberger@fh-hagenberg.at

Abstract. Probabilistic programming allows specification of probabilistic models in a declarative manner. Recently, several new software systems and languages for probabilistic programming have been developed in the on the basis of newly developed and improved methods for approximate inference in probabilistic models. In this contribution a probabilistic model for an idealized dark matter localization problem is described. We first derive the probabilistic model for the inference of dark matter locations and masses, and then show how this model can be implemented using BUGS and Infer.NET, two software systems for probabilistic programming. Finally, the different capabilities of both systems are discussed. The presented dark matter model includes mainly non-conjugate factors, thus, it is difficult to implement this model with Infer.NET.

Keywords: Declarative Models, Probabilistic Programming, Bayesian Inference, Dark Matter Localization.

1 Introduction

Recently, there has been a growing interest in declarative probabilistic modeling which has led to the development of several software systems for probabilistic modeling and Bayesian inference such as Stan [13], FACTORIE [8], Infer.NET [9], or PRISM [12]. Many of these systems provide a declarative modeling language for the definition of probabilistic models, which allows to define random variables and their relations in a way similar to computer programs. Thus, the term *probabilistic programming* is frequently used to refer to the implementation of probabilistic models in such systems. The common idea is to implement the probabilistic model declaratively, without specifying how inference should be performed in the model. Instead the underlying inference engine is responsible for the execution of an appropriate inference algorithm and can potentially adapt the inference procedure to specific models (e.g., to improve accuracy of efficiency).

This approach to probabilistic modeling is not a recent idea; BUGS [5], a software system for Bayesian modeling and inference using Gibbs sampling, is already more than twenty years old [6] and has become the de facto standard for

R. Moreno-Díaz et al. (Eds.): EUROCAST 2013, Part I, LNCS 8111, pp. 195–202, 2013.

probabilistic programming. BUGS defines its own modeling language, and relies on the fact, that Gibbs sampling is a very general Markov-chain Monte Carlo (MCMC) method and allows inference in a large class of probabilistic models. Thus, BUGS imposes almost no constraints on models and supports a large set of models, including analytically intractable models with non-conjugate or improper priors. However, MCMC methods often suffer from slow convergence especially for high-dimensional models or strongly correlated parameters. This drawback of Gibbs sampling has been a limiting factor for probabilistic programming with BUGS.

However, recent research results have led to several new and improved methods for approximate inference in probabilistic models, such as expectation propagation (EP) [10], variational message passing (VMP) [15], and improved sampling techniques including Hamiltonian Monte Carlo [11] and NUTS [2]. Several software systems have been developed, which incorporate these improved methods and can be used instead of BUGS.

In this contribution we discuss a Bayesian model for an idealized formulation of the dark matter localization problem, and show how this model can be implemented using BUGS and Infer.NET. The aim is to highlight and discuss the differences between BUGS and Infer.NET on the basis of a moderately complex model. A summary of the different capabilities of BUGS and Infer.NET, as well as a comparison of inference results, have also been given in [14].

1.1 Dark Matter Localization

A large fraction of the total mass in the universe is made up of so-called dark matter. Dark matter does not emit or absorb light but can be detected indirectly through its gravitational field. The existence and substance of dark matter is one of the unanswered questions of astrophysics, and a lot of effort is spent on improving methods to detect dark matter, and on studying its distribution in the universe. For instance in a recent publication a map of the distribution of dark mapper in the universe is discussed [7].

Dark matter can be detected through the gravitational lensing effect [4], which occurs because the gravitational force of large masses has a bending effect on light. Because of the gravitational lensing effect, objects behind a mass appear displaced to an observer and even multiple images of the same object might appear. Additionally, the apparent shape of larger objects such as galaxies is altered by the gravitational lensing effect.

The main aim of this contribution is to show, how a moderately complex probabilistic model, such as the dark matter localization model, can be implemented using software systems for probabilistic programming, in order to highlight and discuss the capabilities of such systems. We do not aim to derive a model that can be actually used for dark matter localization. However, it should be noted that e.g., LENSTOOL, a software system which has actually been used for calculating mass distribution profiles based on real images, also implements a Bayesian model and MCMC sampling [3].

1.2 Synthetic Data for Dark Matter Localization

We use a synthetic data set for the experiments presented in this contribution as we do not aim to improve on established models for dark matter localization. The data set has been generated for the "Observing Dark Worlds" competition hosted on Kaggle[1] by simulating dark matter halos, galaxies and the gravitational lensing effect. Distortions that would occur in real images e.g., through atmospheric effects or telescopic lenses, are ignored. For the purpose of the competition, real image data could not be used as it is necessary to compare solutions for dark matter halo locations. The data set is composed of 300 simulated skies and either one, two, or three dark matter halos. The data for each sky contains locations and ellipticities of between 300 and 740 galaxies. The ellipticity is specified using two components: the ellipticity along the x-axis e_1, and the ellipticity along a 45-degree angle to the x-axis e_2.

2 Model Formulation

In the following we describe the probabilistic graphical model for Bayesian inference of dark matter halo locations and masses from the observed locations and ellipticities of galaxies as specified in the synthetic data set.

It should be noted, that the model described below is the model that has been used by the author for the dark worlds competition. This model is very similar to the model used by the competition winner[2], but differs in relevant details. In particular, the model below uses different priors.

The goal in the dark matter localization problem is to determine probability distributions for halo locations $p(\text{loc}_h|\text{loc}_g, e_g)$ given observed galaxy locations $\text{loc}_g = (x,y)_h$ and ellipticities $e_g = (e_1, e_2)_g$. Using Bayes' theorem we can derive the posterior distribution of halo locations from the likelihood of observed locations and ellipticities times the prior. The mass of a halo determines the strength of the gravitational lensing effect. Therefore, the halo mass has to be included in the model as latent variable. This leads to the following model

$$p(\text{loc}_h, \text{mass}_h|\text{loc}_g, e_g) = \frac{p(\text{loc}_g, e_g|\text{loc}_h, \text{mass}_h)p(\text{loc}_h)p(\text{mass}_h)}{\int_{\text{mass}_h} \int_{\text{loc}_h} p(\text{loc}_g, e_g|\text{loc}_h, \text{mass}_h)p(\text{loc}_h)p(\text{mass}_h)}.$$

There is no prior information about the locations of halos, so a flat uniform prior $p(x_h) \sim U(0, 4200), p(y_h) \sim U(0, 4200)$ is used. For the halo mass a broad gamma prior is used: $p(\text{mass}_h) \sim \text{Gamma}(0.001, 0.001)$.

We assume that the galaxy locations are independent from halo locations and masses so the likelihood can be transformed:

$$p(\text{loc}_g, e_g|\text{loc}_h, \text{mass}_h) = p(e_g|\text{loc}_g, \text{loc}_h, \text{mass}_h)p(\text{loc}_g)$$

---

[1] Competition organizers: David Harvey and Thomas Kitching, Observing Dark Worlds Competition, http://www.kaggle.com/c/DarkWorlds/

[2] Tim Salimans' description of his model can be found at http://timsalimans.com/observing-dark-worlds/

The ellipticity is given as a vector with two components e_1, e_2 which are independent, and the empirical distribution of ellipticities is very close to a zero mean normal distribution with variance $\frac{1}{20}$. Therefore, the likelihood function for observed ellipticities e_g can be expressed as a normal likelihood with the mean given by the strength of the lensing effect and a constant variance $\sigma^2 = \frac{1}{20}$.

$$p(e_g|\text{loc}_g, \text{loc}_h, \text{mass}_h) = N(e_g|f(\text{loc}_g, \text{loc}_h, \text{mass}_h), \sigma^2)$$

We assume that the strength of the lensing effect can be modeled using a simple function, which increases linearly with the mass of the halo and inversely with the distance to the halo center.

$$f(\text{loc}_g, \text{loc}_h, \text{mass}_h) = \frac{\text{mass}_h}{||\text{loc}_g - \text{loc}_h||}$$

The final model is shown as a probabilistic graphical model in Figure 1, using plate notation to represent G galaxies and H halos. In the graphical representation several details that are necessary for the implementation, such as the distance of galaxies from halos and the angle of the force vector, are not shown.

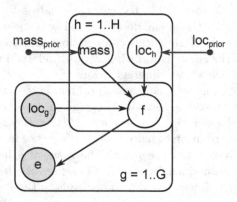

Fig. 1. Probabilistic graphical model for the gravitational lensing effect that can be used to infer dark matter locations and masses. The strength of the lensing effect f is a result of the masses and locations of H halos and effects the observed ellipticities of G galaxies.

For the implementation of the model the total force has to be allocated to the two components of ellipticity, which describe the elongation of the galaxy in the x-direction (e_1) and the elongation along a 45 deg angle. The gravitational lensing effect leads to tangential elongation of the ellipticity. Thus, we map the tangential force to the two components by multiplying with $-\cos(2\phi)$ and $-\sin(2\phi)$, respectively. ϕ is the angle of the vector from the halo to the galaxy.

$$e_1 \sim N(-f\cos(2\phi), \sigma^2), \quad e_2 \sim N(-f\sin(2\phi), \sigma^2), \quad \phi = \text{atan}\frac{y_g - y_h}{x_g - x_h}$$

2.1   Implementation Using BUGS

It is rather straightforward to transform the probabilistic model to BUGS syntax. The model can be defined as follows:

```
model{
  for( i in 1 : G ) {
    for( h in 1 : H ) {
      dx[i , h]    <- gx[i] - loc[h , 1]
      dy[i , h]    <- gy[i] - loc[h , 2]
      dist[i , h]  <- sqrt(dx[i , h] * dx[i , h] +
                           dy[i , h] * dy[i , h])
      phi[i , h]   <- atan2(dy[i , h], dx[i , h])
      iDist[i , h] <- 1.0 / dist[i , h]
      f[i , h]     <- mass[h] * iDist[i , h]
      f1[i , h]    <- -f[i , h] * cos(2 * phi[i , h])
      f2[i , h]    <- -f[i , h] * sin(2 * phi[i , h])
    }
    mu1[i] <- sum(f1[i , ])
    mu2[i] <- sum(f2[i , ])
    e1[i] ~ dnorm(mu1[i], 0.05)
    e2[i] ~ dnorm(mu2[i], 0.05)
  }
  for( h in 1 : H ) {
    mass[h]   ~ dgamma(0.001, 0.001)
    loc[h , 1] ~ dunif(0, 4200)
    loc[h , 2] ~ dunif(0, 4200)
  }
}
```

The only additional steps that are necessary to infer loc_h and $mass_h$ are loading initial values for all unobserved variables and loading the data for galaxy ellipticities e_1, e_2 and locations gx, gy. However, convergence is very slow when sampling this model within BUGS. Additionally, BUGS does not support the atan2() function in models. Fortunately, the source code of BUGS is available, so it is possible to add support for this function rather easily.

2.2   Implementation Using Infer.NET

Infer.NET[3] [9] allows declarative specification of probabilistic models and provides EP [10] and VMP [15] for approximate inference. Probabilistic models can be implemented directly in C#. The model is transformed transparently by the Infer.NET compiler to C# source code, which is then compiled to CLR byte code using the C# compiler. Compared to BUGS, it is much easier to use such models from existing code, as long as the application is based on the .NET platform. Additionally, inference is fast because the code for model inference is compiled. The model can be implemented in the following way:

---

[3] Infer.NET version 2.5 is available from http://research.microsoft.com/en-us/um/cambridge/projects/infernet/

```
// not shown: variable declarations
// [...]
sigma = Variable.New<double>();
evidence = Variable.Bernoulli(0.5);

IfBlock block = Variable.If(evidence);
using (Variable.ForEach(g)) {
  using (Variable.ForEach(h)) {
    // factors for the following are not implemented
    // dx[g][h].SetTo(g_x[g] - loc_x[h]);
    // dy[g][h].SetTo(g_y[g] - loc_y[h]);
    // phi.SetTo(Variable.Atan2(dy[g][h], dx[g][h]));
    // cos2phi[g][h].SetTo(Variable.Cos(2 * phi[g][h]));
    // sin2phi[g][h].SetTo(Variable.Sin(2 * phi[g][h]));
    // invDist[g][h].SetTo(1.0 / Variable.Sqrt(dx[g][h] * dx[g][h] +
    //                               dy[g][h] * dy[g][h]));
    f1[g][h].SetTo(-(mass[h] * invDist[g][h] * cos2phi[g][h]));
    f2[g][h].SetTo(-(mass[h] * invDist[g][h] * sin2phi[g][h]));
  }
  e1[g].SetTo(
   Variable.GaussianFromMeanAndPrecision(Variable.Sum(f1[g]), 20));
  e2[g].SetTo(
   Variable.GaussianFromMeanAndPrecision(Variable.Sum(f2[g]), 20));
}
block.CloseBlock();
```

Similarly to the BUGS implementation, arrays of random variables are used for galaxy locations and ellipticities, as well as for halo locations and masses. Looping over ranges can be accomplished with the `Variable.ForEach` factor; in the example two variants to handle blocks in Infer.NET are shown. Either the block is manually opened and closed, as shown for the `IfBlock`, or the using-syntax is used to manage blocks.

EP and VMP are able to exploit regularities in the model, so that inference can be performed much faster than would be possible with MCMC techniques. EP and VMP allow inference also for large scale models, such as document topic modeling with latent Dirichlet allocation. The drawback of both methods is that they are much less general than e.g., Gibbs sampling. Thus, the set of probabilistic models that can be used in Infer.NET is rather constrained [14]. However, in contrast to BUGS, Infer.NET also supports conditional blocks.

Even tough EP can potentially also be used to infer marginals when the factors are non-conjugate, this is in general not very efficient. So, Infer.NET typically does not contain such factors. Implementing custom factors for EP inference is rather difficult.

The model uses mainly non-conjugate factors. Thus, it is not possible to perform inference using the original model with the standard installation of Infer.NET. It would be necessary to implement new distribution types, factors and message operators to support inference for this model. Instead, the model is simplified, so that it basically represents a simple likelihood function. Infer.NET is only used to infer the likelihood (`evidence`). The parameters of the model, loc_h and $mass_h$ are optimized w.r.t. likelihood using the CMA-ES optimization algorithm [1]. Figure 2 shows locations and shapes of galaxies and the actual location of the dark matter halos for two skies. The predicted halo locations are marked with a green circle.

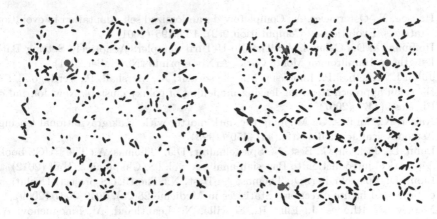

Fig. 2. Two simulated skies showing galaxies and the actual (red cross) and predicted (green circle) center location of the dark matter halos

3 Summary and Discussion

In this contribution a Bayesian model for gravitational lensing is described that the author used for the "Observing Dark Worlds" competition. The model is similar to the winning model but uses e.g., different priors. The gravitational lensing model can be easily implemented in BUGS. Only the atan2() function is missing, however, it is easy to add support for this function to the open-source version of BUGS. Sampling converges only slowly for this model in BUGS.

Infer.NET uses EP or VMP for approximate inference, and the models can be implemented directly e.g., in C#. Inference with EP and VMP is very efficient for certain types of models, but in general less flexible than e.g., Gibbs sampling. Because of these restrictions, it would be necessary to implement custom factors and distributions, to implement the full gravitational lensing model using Infer.NET. Instead, we performed simple ML optimization of dark halo locations and masses, based on a simplified implementation of the model in Infer.NET, using CMA-ES as optimization algorithm. The results are competitive, taking a spot in the top 10% of submitted solutions.

In this contribution we have only discussed the implementation of the model using BUGS and Infer.NET. However, several other software systems for probabilistic programming, e.g. Stan or FACTORIE, can also be used instead. It would certainly be interesting to implement the model also in these systems, and to compare the results and performance. Additionally, it would be interesting to discuss the implementation of factors, which are necessary for inference with EP, in more detail.

References

1. Hansen, N., Ostermeier, A.: Completely derandomized self-adaptation in evolution strategies. Evolutionary Computation 9(2), 159–195 (2001)
2. Hoffman, M.D., Gelman, A.: The No-U-Turn Sampler: Adaptively Setting Path Lengths in Hamiltonian Monte Carlo. ArXiv e-prints (November 2011)
3. Jullo, E., Kneib, J.P., Limousin, M., Eliasdottir, A., Marshall, P., Verdugo, T.: A Bayesian approach to strong lensing modelling of galaxy clusters. New Journal of Physics 9(447) (2007)
4. Kaiser, N., Squires, G.: Mapping the dark matter with weak gravitational lensing. Astrophysical Journal 404(2), 441–450 (1993)
5. Lunn, D., Jackson, C., Best, N., Spiegelhalter, D.J., Thomas, A.: The BUGS book: A practical introduction to Bayesian analysis, vol. 98. Chapman & Hall (2012)
6. Lunn, D., Spiegelhalter, D., Thomas, A., Best, N.: The BUGS project: Evolution, critique and future directions. Statistics in Medicine 28(25), 3049–3067 (2009)
7. Massey, R., Rhodes, J., Ellis, R., Scoville, N., Leauthaud, A., Finoguenov, A., Capak, P., Bacon, D., Aussel, H., Kneib, J.P., Koekemoer, A., McCracken, H., Mobasher, B., Pires, S., Refregier, A., Sasaki, S., Starck, J.L., Taniguchi, Y., Taylor, A., Taylor, J.: Dark matter maps reveal cosmic scaffolding. Nature 445, 286–290 (2007)
8. McCallum, A., Schultz, K., Singh, S.: FACTORIE: Probabilistic programming via imperatively defined factor graphs. In: Neural Information Processing Systems (NIPS) (2009)
9. Minka, T.P., Winn, J., Guiver, J., Knowles, D.: Infer.NET 2.5. Microsoft Research Cambridge (2012), http://research.microsoft.com/infernet
10. Minka, T.P.: Expectation propagation for approximate Bayesian inference. In: Proceedings of the Seventeenth Conference on Uncertainty in Artificial Intelligence, pp. 362–369. Morgan Kaufmann Publishers Inc. (2001)
11. Neal, R.M.: MCMC using Hamiltonian dynamics. In: Brooks, S., Gelman, A., Jones, G.L., Meng, X.L. (eds.) Handbook of Markov Chain Monte Carlo, pp. 113–162. Chapman and Hall/CRC (2011)
12. Sato, T., Kameya, Y.: New advances in logic-based probabilistic modeling by PRISM. In: De Raedt, L., Frasconi, P., Kersting, K., Muggleton, S. (eds.) ILP 2007. LNCS (LNAI), vol. 4911, pp. 118–155. Springer, Heidelberg (2008)
13. Stan Development Team: Stan: A C++ Library for Probability and Sampling, Version 1.3 (2013), http://mc-stan.org/
14. Wang, S., Wand, M.: Using infer.NET for statistical analyses. The American Statistician 65(2), 115–126 (2011)
15. Winn, J., Bishop, C.M.: Variational message passing. Journal of Machine Learning Research 6(1), 661 (2006)

Feature Selection for Unsupervised Learning via Comparison of Distance Matrices

Stephan Dreiseitl

Dept. of Software Engineering
Upper Austria University of Applied Sciences
A-4232 Hagenberg, Austria

Abstract. Feature selection for unsupervised learning is generally harder than for supervised learning, because the former lacks the class information of the latter, and thus an obvious way by which to measure the quality of a feature subset. In this paper, we propose a new method based on representing data sets by their distance matrices, and judging feature combinations by how well the distance matrix using only these features resembles the distance matrix of the full data set. Using articial data for which the relevant features were known, we observed that the results depend on the data dimensionality, the fraction of relevant features, the overlap between clusters in the relevant feature subspaces, and how to measure the similarity of distance matrices. Our method consistently achieved higher than 80% detection rates of relevant features for a wide variety of experimental configurations.

Keywords: Unsupervised feature selection, feature extraction, dimensionality reduction, distance matrix similarity.

1 Introduction

In many machine learning applications, feature selection constitutes an important data preprocessing step. The expected benefits of feature selection are numerous, and can be broadly separated into two groups [1]: First, machine learning algorithms benefit from the removal of noise in the form of irrelevant and redundant features, as this helps to avoid overfitting and thus allows the models to generalize better. Second, in many application domains (such as biomedical informatics) feature selection is an important endeavor in its own right, helping to identify and highlight key aspects of the data. Often, this form of exploratory data analysis is the basis of subsequent research efforts in the application domain (e.g., which of a set of biomarker candidates is relevant for a biomedical problem).

While there is a substantial amount of literature on feature selection methods for supervised learning tasks [2–4], there is considerably less on methods for unsupervised learning. The reason for this discrepency lies in the fact that supervised problems provide a target value to predict, and it is easy to measure the performance of an algorithm on a feature set by how well it performs this

R. Moreno-Díaz et al. (Eds.): EUROCAST 2013, Part I, LNCS 8111, pp. 203–210, 2013.

prediction. Features that achieve high performance are more important than those that do not. Consequently, filter and wrapper methods were developed to identify features that work well, either individually or as feature sets.

Feature selection for unsupervised learning is hard because it lacks a clear-cut performance measure. Some approaches, collectively known as *subspace clustering* [5], find feature sets that cluster well, although different sets may lead to different clusters. Other methods implement wrappers around clustering algorithms such as k-means or the EM algorithm, and maximize criteria based on intra- vs. intercluster separation [6]. Entirely different approaches are to identify features that cluster well by the entropy of the distribution of all between-points distances [7, 8], or to cluster the features themselves by their linear dependency, and then picking representative features from each cluster [9].

This work proposes a different and new direction for feature selection in unsupervised learning tasks by using distance matrices to assess the relevance of features. The basis of this work is the observation that the clustering of a data set is entirely dependent on its spatial arrangement, which — for clustering purposes — can be represented by its distance matrix. The distance matrix of the entire data set is therefore the "gold standard" against which we can measure the quality of feature subsets.

We present the derivation and details of our new method in the next section, and demonstrate its efficacy in Sec. 3. A discussion of these results, along with concluding remarks, is given in Sec. 4.

2   Concepts and Methods

Our research hypothesis is that the distance matrix of a data set can be used to identify features in the data set that cluster well. The idea behind this hypothesis is as follows: Because the spatial arrangement of a data set can be represented by its distance matrix, relevant features are those for which the restricted distance matrix (using only these features) closely matches the original distance matrix. We should then be able to identify these relevant features by a simple greedy search algorithm. Although this algorithm provides a feature *ranking*, we can perform feature *selection* by choosing only the top-ranked features. In Sec. 2.4, we propose a method to automatically determine how many of these top-ranked features to choose.

2.1   Feature Ranking

Throughout this paper, we use X to denote the $n \times m$ data matrix, i.e., X contains n rows of data points of dimensionality m. For an index set $S \subseteq \{1, \ldots, m\}$, let X_{-S} be the data set with the columns (features) in S removed. Let $D(x)$ denote the distance matrix of a data set x, i.e., a symmetric, non-negative matrix with entry $D(x)_{ij}$ denoting the distance between the ith and j^{th} entries in x.

A simple greedy backwards elimination algorithm for ranking features according to their relevance is given by following pseudocode:

1. Set $F \leftarrow \{1, \ldots, m\}$ to the set of all feature indices. Let $S \leftarrow \emptyset$ denote an initially empty set of feature indices. Calculate the full distance matrix $\tilde{D} \leftarrow D(X)$.

2. While $|F| > 1$ do:

   (a) For each $j \in F$, calculate $\tilde{D}_{-j} \leftarrow D(X_{-(S \cup \{j\})})$, the distance matrix with features $S \cup \{j\}$ removed.

   (b) Calculate $j^* \leftarrow \arg\min_{j \in F} \operatorname{sim}(\tilde{D}, \tilde{D}_{-j})$ as the feature for which the current distance matrix and the distance matrix with feature j removed have the smallest similarity as calculated by a similarity measure sim.

   (c) Set $F \leftarrow F \setminus \{j^*\}$, $S \leftarrow S \cup \{j^*\}$, and recalculate $\tilde{D} \leftarrow D(X_{-S})$.

3. The reverse order in which feature indices are entered into S gives an indication of their relevance.

In this algorithm, we recalculate the distance matrix for the remaining features after a feature is removed, rather than keeping one fixed distance matrix (the one for the entire data set). This is done to remove the contribution of features that are found to not be as relevant as the others.

2.2   Matrix Similarity Measures

In step 2(b) of the pseudocode above, we need to calculate the similarity between two distance matrices. There are a number of ways to accomplish this, most notably by

- the Pearson correlation coefficient ρ of the matrix entries;
- the R_V coefficient of matrix similarity [10], which for symmetric square matrices is given by

$$ R_V(A, B) := \frac{\operatorname{tr}(A \cdot B)}{\sqrt{\operatorname{tr}(A \cdot A) \operatorname{tr}(B \cdot B)}} , $$

  with $\operatorname{tr}(A) = \sum_{i=1}^{n} A_{ii}$ denoting the trace of a square matrix;
- the symmetric version of the Kullback-Leibler divergence [11], used for measuring the distance between two probability distributions (for this, matrix entries first have to be normalized to sum 1):

$$ \mathrm{KL}(A, B) := \sum_{j,k} A_{jk} \log \frac{A_{jk}}{B_{jk}} + \sum_{j,k} B_{jk} \log \frac{B_{jk}}{A_{jk}} . $$

Because the Kullback-Leibler divergence is a distance — rather than a similarity — measure, we modified the greedy search described in Sec. 2.1 to discard the *most* distant feature when using this measure for assessing matrix similarity.

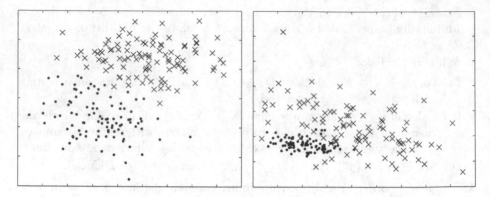

Fig. 1. Illustration of Bhattacharyya distance. Two features in five-dimensionals clusters with distance 50 (left), and two clusters with distance 10 (right).

2.3 Data Generation

In the experiments summarized in Sec. 3, we use artificial data so that we can control the data dimensionality and the ratio of relevant to irrelevant features. In particular, the relevant features comprise two multivariate Gaussians of varying overlap. The irrelevant features contain uniformly distributed noise. Both relevant and irrelevant features are subsequently scaled to zero mean and unit variance. All data sets contain 250 items in each of the two clusters.

In preliminary experiments, we observed that our algorithm is susceptible to the distance between the clusters in the data, with features more easily being recognized as relevant if the clusters are well separated. In order to quantify the contribution of this factor to our analyses, we constructed the relevant features as two multivariate Gaussians, for which the separation can be measured in the form of the *Bhattacharyya distance* [12, 13]

$$\text{dist}(G_1, G_2) = \frac{1}{8}(\mu_1 - \mu_2)^T \Sigma^{-1}(\mu_1 - \mu_2) + \frac{1}{2}\log\left(\frac{\det(\Sigma)}{\sqrt{\det(\Sigma_1)\det(\Sigma_2)}}\right).$$

Here, $G_1 = (\mu_1, \Sigma_1)$ and $G_2 = (\mu_2, \Sigma_2)$ are parametrizations of multivariate Gaussians, and $\Sigma = \frac{1}{2}(\Sigma_1 + \Sigma_2)$ is the arithmetic mean of the two covariance matrices. Fig. 1 provides an illustration of this notion of cluster distance.

2.4 Determining Relevant Features

When we plot the distance matrix similarity (or distance, in case of the Kullback-Leibler measure) vs. the removed features we can observe that there is a noticable difference between relevant and irrelevant features. Fig. 2 illustrates this observation for a 20-dimensional data set with 5 relevant features. There seems to be an exponential increase in the distance between distance matrices, as more and more features are removed from the data set. This progression no longer holds

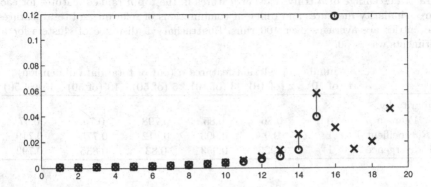

Fig. 2. Kullback-Leibler divergence between full distance matrix and distance matrix with the worst feature removed, shown as ×. The symbols o mark the predicted next value, assuming an exponential fit for the previous (left) values of ×. The feature at position 16 is the first that is deemed relevant by the heuristic of assessing the difference between × and o.

when the relevant features are reached at index 16 in the figure: An exponential fit to the previous values would predict a much larger distance than actually observed. Note that only 19 features are shown, because only that many features are removed from the original set of 20.

We therefore propose to select those features as relevant for which the exponential increase in similarity measure no longer holds. This process can be automated, with the first relevant feature being the one where there is more than 50% relative error between actual similarity measure and exponential model fit (calculated using the features up to this point). The value of 50% is a heuristic that seems to work reasonably well for various combinations of data dimensionality and number of relevant features.

3   Experiments

The experiments described here test the hypothesis that the greedy feature ranking algorithm in Sec. 2.1 is capable of identifying those features that belong to the artificially generated signal rather than to the noise. Within this broad setup, we investigate a number of experimental questions:

- Is one of the three methods for calculating the similarity of distance matrices (Pearson ρ, R_V coefficient, Kullback-Leibler divergence) better suited than the others?
- What effect does the data dimensionality, in particular the ratio of relevant to irrelevant features, have on the ability to detect relevant features?
- What influence does the distance between the clusters have on the results?

In the following, we will first rate combinations of these criteria by how well they can detect the relevant features, i.e., which percentage of the n truly relevant

Table 1. Percentage of n truly relevant features in the top n ranked features for each of three similarity measures and different combinations of relevant and total features. Table entries are averages over 100 runs. Bhattacharyya distance of clusters for all experiments was ~ 50.

| | number of relevant features n (out of total data dimension) | | | | | |
	1 (of 10)	2 (of 10)	3 (of 10)	5 (of 50)	10 (of 50)	15 (of 50)
similarity by:						
Pearson ρ	0	0.86	0.85	0.798	0.75	0.67
R_V coefficient	1	0.9	0.903	0.812	0.775	0.719
K-L divergence	1	0.935	0.953	0.83	0.835	0.792

features are in the top n features as ranked by the greedy search algorithm. We will then investigate the ability of the heuristic for automatically selecting relevant features that we described in Sec. 2.4. All experiments were repeated 100 times with different random numbers; the reported numbers are the averages over these 100 runs.

Table 1 gives a general impression of how well the three similarity/distance measures work in identifying the relevant features. One can observe that across all data dimensionalities and number of relevant features, the Kullback-Leibler divergence seems to be the best suited for measuring the difference between distance matrices in the greedy feature ranking algorithm. We therefore focus exclusively on this measure for the remainder of this paper. Furthermore, Table 1 also indicates that for constant data dimensionality (here 10 or 50), the percentage of truly relevant features among the highly-ranked features sometimes increase with the number of truly relevant features, and sometimes decreases. This is, for example, visible in the last row of this table, with the detection percentage rising from 0.935 to 0.953 for dimension 10, and falling from 0.835 to 0.792 for dimension 50.

To obtain a better understanding of the interaction between data dimensionality, number of relevant features, and cluster separation, we calculated the percentage of relevant features detected for all combinations of three data dimensions (10, 15, and 20), three number of relevant features (10%, 15%, and 20%), as well as seven different cluster overlaps (Bhattacharyya distances from 10 to 40), but now only for the Kullback-Leibler divergence as distance measure. The results of this comprehensive investigation is given in Table 2. As expected, increasing the cluster separation while keeping the dimensionality and number of relevant features constant (i.e., looking at each row in the table) generally results in higher numbers of detected relevant features, although there are a small number of fluctuations. Comparing entries in each 3×7 block of numbers for constant dimensionality with the corresponding entries in the other two such blocks, one can observe that the percentage of truly relevant features in the top ranked features mostly decreases with increasing data dimensionality. It thus becomes increasingly harder to identify relevant features in higher-dimensional spaces.

Table 2. Percentage of truly relevant features in the top ranked features for each of three data dimensions, in combination with different percentages of truly relevant features and Bhattacharyya distances. Table entries are averages over 100 runs.

	Bhattacharyya distance between clusters						
	10	15	20	25	30	35	40
dimensions = 10:							
relevant = 10%	0.99	1.00	1.00	1.00	1.00	1.00	1.00
relevant = 20%	0.62	0.69	0.70	0.68	0.81	0.74	0.69
relevant = 30%	0.74	0.80	0.79	0.78	0.81	0.80	0.79
dimensions = 20:							
relevant = 10%	0.84	0.84	0.91	0.89	0.90	0.91	0.92
relevant = 20%	0.82	0.86	0.85	0.89	0.84	0.87	0.85
relevant = 30%	0.81	0.83	0.85	0.87	0.86	0.90	0.91
dimensions = 30:							
relevant = 10%	0.78	0.82	0.82	0.86	0.90	0.89	0.90
relevant = 20%	0.71	0.77	0.81	0.83	0.83	0.86	0.84
relevant = 30%	0.69	0.74	0.79	0.83	0.86	0.88	0.88

Table 3. Percentage of times (out of 100 runs) that the heuristic of Sec. 2.4 was exactly correct, or off by at most one, when detecting the correct number of correct features in the data set. The percentage of relevant features was fixed to 30%.

	Bhattacharyya distance between clusters						
	10	15	20	25	30	35	40
exactly correct:							
dimensions = 10	0.56	0.54	0.57	0.48	0.53	0.53	0.61
dimensions = 20	0.32	0.36	0.43	0.49	0.45	0.48	0.51
dimensions = 30	0.05	0.16	0.21	0.26	0.35	0.36	0.24
approximately correct:							
dimensions = 10	1.00	1.00	1.00	1.00	1.00	1.00	1.00
dimensions = 20	0.69	0.73	0.81	0.85	0.82	0.83	0.82
dimensions = 30	0.22	0.24	0.48	0.57	0.77	0.77	0.75

The final part of our investigation consisted of checking how often the heuristic of Sec. 2.4 for determining the number of relevant features was correct. Since this may be too stringent a requirement, we checked both for the number of times where the heuristic was exactly correct, and for the number of times where it was off by at most one. We focused on a subset of the combinations in Table 2, looking only at the highest percentage of correct features (30%) for all three data dimensionalities. It can be seen that when settling for the approximate number of correct features, the heuristic is surprisingly accurate, with more than 75% correct for all data dimensionalities and large enough Bhattacharyya distances. The numbers for other percentages of relevant features are slightly lower (data not shown).

4 Conclusion

Without a clear-cut measure against which to assess a method's performance, unsupervised feature selection is generally harder than supervised feature selection, and less widely investigated. In this paper, we proposed a method for unsupervised feature selection that uses the distance matrix of a data set as a proxy for a gold standard against which to measure the performance of feature subsets. Although we implemented only a very crude greedy search mechanism for feature ranking, we nevertheless observed that relevant features can be distinguished from noise with high accuracy. More sophisticated search strategies, such as ones based on evoluationary computation, may lead to even better results.

References

1. Guyon, I., Elisseeff, A.: An introduction to variable and feature selection. Journal of Machine Learning Research 3, 1157–1182 (2003)
2. Saeys, Y., Inza, I., Larrañaga, P.: A review of feature selection techniques in bioinformatics. Bioinformatics 23, 2507–2517 (2007)
3. Yu, L., Liu, H.: Efficient feature selection via analysis of relevance and redundancy. Journal of Machine Learning Research 5, 1205–1224 (2004)
4. Liu, H., Motoda, H., Setiono, R., Zhao, Z.: Feature selection: An ever evolving frontier in data mining. In: Proceedings of the 4th International Workshop on Feature Selection in Data Mining, pp. 4–13 (2010)
5. Parsons, L., Haque, E., Liu, H.: Subspace clustering for high dimensinal data: A review. ACM SIGKDD Explorations 6, 90–105 (2004)
6. Dy, J., Brodley, C.: Feature selection for unsupervised learning. Journal of Machine Learning Research 5, 845–889 (2004)
7. Dash, M., Liu, H.: Feature selection for clustering. In: Terano, T., Liu, H., Chen, A.L.P. (eds.) PAKDD 2000. LNCS, vol. 1805, pp. 110–121. Springer, Heidelberg (2000)
8. Dash, M., Choi, K., Scheuermann, P., Liu, H.: Feature selection for clustering — a filter solution. In: Proceedings of the Second International Conference on Data Mining, pp. 115–122 (2002)
9. Mitra, P., Murthy, C., Pal, S.: Unsupervised feature selection using feature similarity. IEEE Transactions on Pattern Analysis and Machine Intelligence 24, 1–13 (2002)
10. Escoufier, Y.: Le traitement des variables vectorielles. Biometrics 29, 751–760 (1973)
11. Kullback, S., Leibler, R.: On information and sufficiency. Annals of Mathematical Statistics 22, 79–86 (1951)
12. Bhattacharyya, A.: On a measure of divergence between two statistical populations defined by their probability distribution. Bulletin of the Calcutta Mathematical Society 35, 99–109 (1943)
13. Fukunaga, K.: Introduction to Statistical Pattern Recognition. Academic Press, San Diego (1990)

Statistical Analysis of the Relationship between Spots and Structures in Microscopy Images[*]

Susanne Schaller[1], Jaroslaw Jacak[2], Rene Silye[3], and Stephan M. Winkler[1]

[1] University of Applied Sciences Upper Austria, Bioinformatics Research Group
Softwarepark 11, 4232 Hagenberg, Austria
{susanne.schaller,stephan.winkler}@fh-hagenberg.at
[2] Johannes Kepler University Linz, Institute for Applied Physics
Altenbergerstraße 69, 4020 Linz, Austria
jaroslaw.jacak@jku.at
[3] Wagner-Jauregg Hospital, Department of Neurosurgery
Wagner-Jauregg-Weg 15, 4020 Linz, Austria
silye@aon.at

Abstract. Fluorescence microscopy image analysis plays an important role in biomedical diagnostics and is an essential approach for researching and investigating the development and state of various diseases. In this paper we describe an approach for analyzing nanoscale microscopy images in which spots and background structures are identified and their relationship is quantified. A spatial analysis approach is used for identifying spots, then clustering of these spots is performed and those clusters are characterized using a series of here defined features. These cluster characteristics are used for comparing images via statistical hypothesis tests (using the Kolmogorov-Smirnov test for the equality of probability distributions). Moreover, to achieve a better distinction we additionally define features that quantify the relationship of clusters of spots and background structures. In the empirical section we demonstrate the use of this approach in the analysis of microscopy images of brain structures of patients potentially suffering from a neural disease (e.g., depression or schizophrenia). Using the here presented approach we will be able to investigate the development and state of various diseases in a better way and help to find more systematic medication of diseases in the future.

1 Introduction

Fluorescence microscopy on molecular level is one of the fastest growing fields in modern biomedical diagnostics; in this context, we here analyze microscopy images derived from a direct stochastic optical reconstruction microscopy

---

[*] The work described in this paper was done within the FIT-IT project "NanoDetect: A Bioinformatics Image Processing Framework for Automated Analysis of Cellular Macro and Nano Structures" (project number 835918) sponsored by the Austrian Research Promotion Agency (FFG).

R. Moreno-Díaz et al. (Eds.): EUROCAST 2013, Part I, LNCS 8111, pp. 211–218, 2013.

(dSTORM) for the examination of brain tissue samples [2]. This method is combined with immunocytochemistry using fluorescently labeled antibodies to mark serotonin receptors. The overall research goal described here is to find a statistical approach to analyze the relationship between structures and the arrangement of points. The structures might represent cells in the nervous system (e.g., glial cells); the spots correspond to single fluorescent molecules for, e.g., serotonin receptors (see microscopy images in Figure 2a).

The proposed approach (shown in Figure 1) consists of two major image analysis steps: First the relevant spots are detected ([6], [5]) and clustered [3]. Then, the so identified clusters are analyzed using predefined cluster characteristics described in Section 2. The statistical distribution of these characteristics of images is used for performing spatial analysis [8] in order to investigate whether a differentiation between different kinds of scenarios in images is possible (e.g., for distinguishing between ill and healthy patients on the basis of the arrangement of single molecule clusters). An additional characteristic is introduced to investigate whether there is a relationship between the clusters and background structures; these structures are differentiated from the image background using image segmentation and filtering methods (as discussed in Section 3). In Section 4 we show results of statistical tests using the Kolmogorov-Smirnov test to be able to assume inequality between different kinds of scenarios in microscopy images.

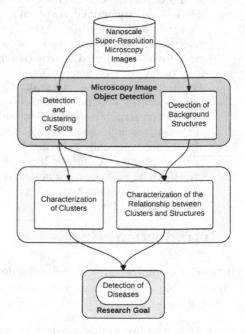

Fig. 1. An statistical approach for analyzing the relationship of hierarchically clustered spots and structures in microscopy images. Hypothesis testing is done to investigate whether there is a relationship between the arrangement of spots and background structures in nanoscale microscopy images.

2   Analysis of Clusters of Relevant Spots in Images

2.1   Detection of Single Molecules in Nanoscale Microscopy Images

In the context of analyzing nanoscale microscopy images, the detection of single molecules (serotonin receptors) is done using background estimation methods [5] (e.g., undecimated wavelet transformation) and Gaussian-based curves that are optimized using the Levenberg-Marquardt least-squares-method. Moreover, other pre-processing methods such as noise filtering and intensity normalization are essential for spot recognition ([7], [9]).

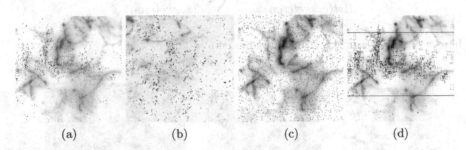

    (a)   (b)   (c)   (d)

Fig. 2. Microscopy images containing fluorescently labeled spots and structures. (a, b) Two different microscopy images (of patients A and B) with different distributions of spots and different background structures. The background structures represent glial cells, black spots visualize single molecules. (c) Randomly positioned spots over background structures. (d) Single molecules clustered after performing hierarchical clustering; the thin lines show the ranges in which single molecules are considered for building a cluster.

2.2   Definition of Characteristics of Clusters of Spots

The spots identified in nanoscale microscopy images are clustered [3], an example is shown in Figure 2d. We have defined four characteristics which are calculated for each cluster c:

- $size(c)$: the relative number of spots in cluster c to the total number of spots in the image
- $fluor(c)$: the relative number of fluorophores in c to the total number of fluorophores in the whole image segment
- $density(c)$: the relative number of spots within a cluster per cluster area
- $eccentricity(c)$: calculated as the mean of all distances $dist(a, b)$ of all pairs of spots a and b $(a, b \in c)$

3   Detection of Background Structures

In this section we focus on the definition of characteristics of the relationship of spots and background structures. The identification of the background structure is done using two different methods: Standard morphological filter operations (see Figure 3) can be used as well as thresholding and discretization methods.

When using morphological filter methods, the skeletons of background structures (see for example those shown in Figure 2a) are determined. Thus, the mean distance between the spots and the skeleton structure can be calculated for each cluster c:

$$dist(c, skeleton) = \frac{1}{n_c} \sum_{i=1}^{n_c} d(s, skeleton) \tag{1}$$

where s is a spot in c and n_c the number of spots in c.

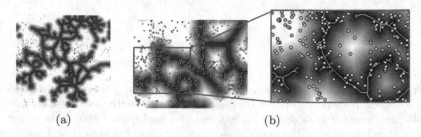

(a)   (b)

Fig. 3. Skeleton visualization of the background structure by using morphological filter operations. (a) Skeleton structure over the whole image segment. (b) Zoom view of the single molecule distances to the skeleton of the structure.

As an alternative, the layer based method uses thresholding and image segmentation approaches with respect to intensity values ([1], [10]).

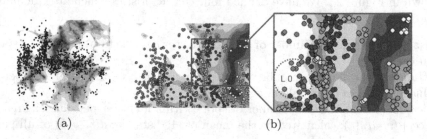

(a)   (b)

Fig. 4. Identification of layers in images; the structure is separated into a pre-defined number of layers

A set of of layers (which are segments in the image whose average intensity values are within a certain range) is formed, where the number of layers is pre-defined. The layer based characteristic is described as the number of spots in each layer and layering based coefficients are determined (as shown in Figure 4b). This structure information is used as shown later in Section 4 as an additional characteristic for more significant analysis if there is a relationship between clusters of spots and structures.

4 Empirical Study: Analysis of the Relationship between Spots and Structures in Brain Microscopy Images

Using the characteristics defined in the previous sections we here investigate in how far kinds of microscopy images can be differentiated; e.g., images of patients suffering from a neural disease have to be differentiated from images of healthy patients. Statistical hypothesis testing using the Kolmogorov-Smirnov (K–S test [4]) for the equality of probability distributions are performed in order to investigate whether the arrangement of clusters of spots provides enough information to differentiate between healthy and ill patients and whether the relationship between spots and background structures reveals more significant information.

4.1 Statistical Analysis of Cluster Characteristics

For the analysis presented in this section we have used a microscopy image in which spots are found near the structures and an image with randomly positioned spots over the structure areas (see Figure 2). The goal here is to find a statistically significant difference between those two microscopy images. We have used different mean cluster distance (ranging from 1 to 30) and characterized the so formed clusters using the four characteristics defined in Section 2.2. For each mean cluster distance the distribution of the characteristics of the microscopy images are compared and tested for equality using the Kolmogorov-Smirnov test: p-values over 0.05 indicate that the inequality of two different microscopy images can be assumed.

The results displayed in Figure 5 show that the inequality of the here analyzed images cannot be assumed using the cluster characteristics $size(c)$ and $fluor(c)$: Using both characteristics of clusters formed with distances from 1 to 30 the p-value does not reach 0.05 which indicates that a difference between original and randomly positioned spots in microscopy images cannot be detected. On the other hand, using the characteristics $density(c)$ and $eccentricity(c)$ the inequality can be detected since the p-value of the K-S-test of the cluster characteristic distributions exceeds 0.05 for the majority of cluster distance settings.

4.2 Statistical Analysis of Characteristics of Clusters and Structures

In previous tests we have used cluster characteristics that focus on the arrangement of spots; in order to identify whether there is a relationship between the

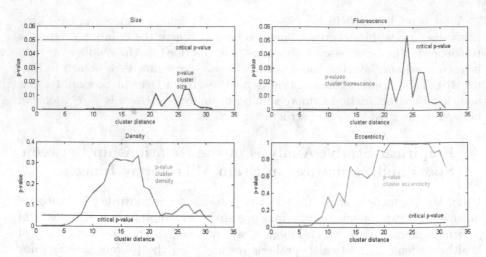

Fig. 5. Statistical hypothesis testing using cluster characteristics *size*, *fluorescence*, *density*, and *eccentricity*; for varying cluster distances the distributions of cluster characteristics are compared and their equalities are tested using K-S-tests. Inequality can be detected using the two cluster characteristics *density* and *eccentricity* as the calculated p-value is above 0.05 for cluster distances 5 – 30.

clusters of spots and the structure we now use the two structure characteristics defined in Section 3. In the context of brain tissue analysis, the assumption is that in patients who suffer from a neural disease the arrangement of spots to structures is significantly different than in healthy people. Thus, we have executed additional tests to gain more reliable results: We have tested whether inequality can be assumed using both structure characteristics separately on microscopy images (again using empirical and simulated data). As the plots seen in Figure 6 show, inequality can be detected using the skeleton method for detecting background structures as well as using the layer based method.

Moreover, we have also performed two-dimensional statistical hypothesis tests on the same microscopy images (original and random positioned spots as shown in Figure 2 (a) and (b)) using the density characteristic and the structure characteristics to show if a statistically significant difference can be detected. Neither a combination of the density and the skeleton of structure characteristic nor a combination of the density and layer-based characteristic lead to a statistically significant difference between those two microscopy images (p-value is nearly 0).

Thus, we have used a combination of the cluster density characteristic and both structure characteristics on two completely different microscopy images and performed two-dimensional tests to overcome the above mentioned problems. As we see in Figure 7, using this approach inequality can be detected using the combination of the cluster density and the skeleton based structure characteristic.

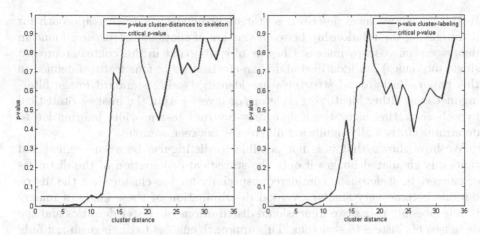

Fig. 6. Statistical hypothesis testing results (using Kolmogorov-Smirnov test) to compare two microscopy images, one original microscopy image (see also Figure 2a) and the other with random positioned spots (see also Figure 2c). The left plot represents the results of the equality test of cluster characteristic distributions using the skeleton based structure identification method, the right one the results using the layer-based method.

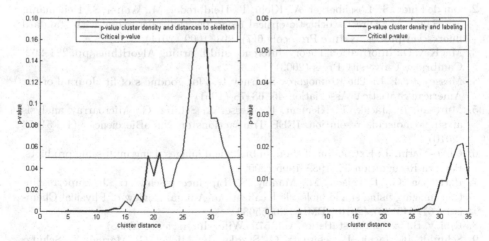

Fig. 7. Statistical hypothesis testing on two different microscopy images (patients A and B) using the density distance combined with the skeleton to structure characteristic (left image) as well as combined with the layer-based characteristic (right image). A statistically significant difference can be determined by analyzing a combination of the cluster density and the distance of clusters to skeletons.

5   Conclusion

In this paper we have described a statistical hypothesis testing approach for investigating the relationship between clusters of spots and structures found in fluorescent microscopy images. Clusters of spots (that in this context represent single molecules) are identified and characterized using four features defined in this paper. Background structures are identified using standard image filtering methods, either identifying skeletons or layers within the images. Statistical hypothesis testing using the Kolmogorov-Smirnov test provides information to determine statistically significant differences between samples.

We have shown that it is not possible to distinguish between original and randomly simulated images if only the statistical distribution of the distances of clusters to skeletons is considered; especially for big cluster sizes the distributions become very similar. A good discrimination of these kinds of images is only possibly using two-dimensional distributions of cluster densities and the distances of clusters to skeletons. This approach enables to distinguish not only between original and randomly generated images, but also between images of patients: Images of healthy patients can be differentiated from each other as well as diseased patients.

References

1. Comaniciu, D., Meer, P.: Robust analysis of feature spaces: color image segmentation. In: Proceedings of the IEEE Computer Society Conference on Computer Vision and Pattern Recognition, pp. 750–755 (1997)
2. van de Linde, S., Löschberger, A., Klein, T., Heidbreder, M., Wolter, S., Heilemann, M., Sauer, M.: Direct stochastic optical reconstruction microscopy with standard fluorescent probes. Nature Protocols 6(7), 991–1009 (2011)
3. MacKay, D.: Information Theory, Inference and Learning Algorithms, pp. 284–292. Cambridge University Press (2003)
4. Massey Jr., F.J.: The Kolmogorov-Smirnov test for goodness of fit. Journal of the American Statistical Association 46, 68–78 (1951)
5. Muresan, L., Jacak, J., Klement, E., Hesse, J., Schütz, G.: Microarray analysis at single-molecule resolution. IEEE Transactions on NanoBioscience 9(1), 51–58 (2010)
6. Olivo-Marin, J.: Extraction of spots in biological images using multiscale products. Pattern Recognition 35, 1989–1996 (2002)
7. Patterson, G., Davidson, M., Manley, S., Lippincott-Schwartz, J.: Superresolution imaging using single-molecule localization. Annual Review of Physical Chemistry 61, 345–367 (2010), PMID: 20055680
8. Ripley, B.D.: Spatial statistics, vol. 575. Wiley-Interscience (2005)
9. Schmidt, R., Jacak, J., Schirwitz, C., Stadler, V., Michel, G., Marmé, N., Schütz, G.J., Hoheisel, J.D., Knemeyer, J.: Single-molecule detection on a protein-array assay platform for the exposure of a tuberculosis antigen. Journal of Proteome Research 10(3), 1316–1322 (2011)
10. Zhang, Y., Brady, M., Smith, S.: Segmentation of brain MR images through a hidden Markov random field model and the expectation-maximization algorithm. IEEE Transactions on Medical Imaging 20(1), 45–57 (2001)

A Memetic Algorithm with Two Distinct Solution Representations for the Partition Graph Coloring Problem

Petrica C. Pop[1], Bin Hu[2], and Günther R. Raidl[2]

[1] Tech. Univ. Cluj-Napoca, North Univ. Center Baia-Mare
76 Victoriei, 430122 Baia-Mare, Romania
[2] Institute of Computer Graphics and Algorithms
Vienna University of Technology
Favoritenstraße 9–11/1861, 1040 Vienna, Austria
petrica.pop@ubm.ro, {hu,raidl}@ads.tuwien.ac.at

Abstract. In this paper we propose a memetic algorithm (MA) for the partition graph coloring problem. Given a clustered graph $G = (V, E)$, the goal is to find a subset $V^* \subset V$ that contains exactly one node for each cluster and a coloring for V^* so that in the graph induced by V^*, two adjacent nodes have different colors and the total number of used colors is minimal. In our MA we use two distinct solution representations, one for the genetic operators and one for the local search procedure, which are tailored for the corresponding situations, respectively. The algorithm is evaluated on a common benchmark instances set and the computational results show that compared to a state-of-the-art branch and cut algorithm, our MA achieves solid results in very short run-times.

1 Introduction

The partition graph coloring problem (PGCP) belongs to the class of problems usually referred to as generalized network design problems (GNDPs). This class of problems is obtained by generalizing in a natural way many network design problems by considering a related problem on a clustered graph, where the original problem's feasibility constraints are expressed in terms of the clusters, i.e., node sets instead of individual nodes.

In the literature, several GNDPs have already been considered such as the generalized minimum spanning tree problem, the generalized traveling salesman problem, the generalized vehicle routing problem, the generalized (subset) assignment problem, the generalized fixed-charge network design problem, etc. All such problems belong to the class of $\mathcal{NP}$-complete problems, are typically harder to solve in practice than their original counterparts and nowadays are intensively studied due to their interesting properties and important real-world applications in telecommunication, network design, resource allocation, transportation problems, etc. Nevertheless, many practitioners are still reluctant to use these models for modeling and solving practical problems because of the complexity of finding optimal or near-optimal solutions.

R. Moreno-Díaz et al. (Eds.): EUROCAST 2013, Part I, LNCS 8111, pp. 219–226, 2013.

The PGCP was introduced by Li and Simha [10] motivated by the wavelength routing and assignment problem in wavelength division multiplexing optical network. The authors proved that the problem is $\mathcal{NP}$-complete. In this context several approaches for solving the problem have been proposed: heuristic algorithms [10], a branch-and-price algorithm [9], and a tabu search algorithm [15]. Demange *et al.* [3,4] considered this type of graph coloring problem in the framework of GNDPs and named it selective graph coloring problem. They investigated some special classes of graphs and determined the complexity status of the PGCP in these classes. Extending our previous work [17], we propose a memetic algorithm (MA) which uses two different solution representations for the genetic operators and for the local search procedure.

2   Definition of the Partition Graph Coloring Problem

Formally, the partition graph coloring problem is defined on an undirected graph $G = (V, E)$ with the set of nodes V and the set of edges E. The set of nodes is partitioned into p mutually exclusive nonempty subsets, called clusters, $V_1, \ldots, V_p$ with $V_1 \cup \ldots \cup V_p = V$ and $V_i \cap V_j = \emptyset$ for all $i, j \in \{1, \ldots, p\}$ and $i \neq j$. The PGCP consists of finding a set $V^* \subset V$ such that $|V^* \cap V_i| = 1$, i.e., V^* contains exactly one node from each cluster V_i for all $i \in \{1, \ldots, p\}$, and the graph induced by V^* is k-colorable where k is minimal. The PGCP reduces to the classical graph coloring problem when all the clusters are singletons.

An illustration of the PGCP and an optimal solution with two colors is shown in Figure 1. In this example the graph $G = (V, E)$ has 10 nodes partitioned into 5 clusters. The optimal solution makes use of two colors: the first is used to color the nodes 3, 5 and 10 and the second for the nodes 2 and 8.

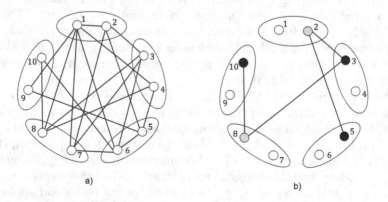

Fig. 1. a) An instance of PGCP and b) an optimal solution with two colors

3 The Memetic Algorithm

Memetic algorithms have been introduced by Moscato [13] and denote a family of metaheuristic algorithms that emphasis on the used of a population-based approach with separate individual learning or local improvement procedures for problem search. It is frequently also interpreted as a genetic algorithm (GA) hybridized with a local search procedure to intensify the search in the solutions space. GAs typically are not well suited for fine-tuning structures which are close to optimal solutions. Therefore, incorporating local improvement as an additional operator to the GA can be beneficial to obtain a competitive algorithm. MAs have been recognized as a powerful algorithmic paradigm, being applied successfully to solve many combinatorial optimization problems such as the vehicle routing problem [14], the generalized traveling salesman problem [1], etc. We use a memetic algorithm for solving the PGCP. In the following we will describe the solution representations, genetic operators and the local search procedure.

Genetic Representation: It is known that a good representation scheme is important for the performance of the GA and it should define noteworthy genetic operators to the problem in order to minimize the computational effort within these procedures. In order to meet this requirement, an individual is represented based on the color classes, i.e., $U = \{U_1, U_2, \ldots, U_k\}$ where U_i, $i \in \{1, \ldots, k\}$ consists of all nodes assigned to color i. Obviously, $U_1 \cup U_2 \cup \ldots \cup U_k = V^* \subseteq V$.

Initial Population: In our MA we use a randomized version of the *onestepLF* algorithm introduced in [10]. The basic idea of onestepLF is to choose for each cluster the node with smallest degree to be in the solution. Then in each iteration among the uncolored nodes the one with largest degree is colored with the smallest possible color index so that no conflicts occur with its adjacent nodes. In our case we want to reach a certain level of diversity in the population, therefore we do not necessarily use for each cluster the node with the smallest degree, but choose it randomly.

Fitness Evaluation: Every solution has a fitness value assigned to it, which measures its quality. In our case, the fitness value is given by $|U|$, the total number of used color classes, which corresponds to k, the number of different colors necessary for coloring the solution graph. The aim is to find to find a partition into color classes that minimizes k. The selection is purely based on the fitness values and ties (i.e. solutions with equal k) are broken randomly.

Crossover: Two parents are selected from the population by the binary tournament method. Consider two parent solutions represented based on the color classes

$$U^1 = \{U_1^1, U_2^1, \ldots, U_k^1\} \text{ and } U^2 = \{U_1^2, U_2^2, \ldots, U_{k'}^2\},$$

then the crossover operator is defined as follows:

1. start from parent U^1 and select a color class (partition) and copy it to the offspring;
2. delete from both parents the selected nodes and all other nodes that belong to the same clusters as the selected ones;
3. from parent U^2, select a color class, move it to the offspring and then remove from both parents the corresponding nodes analogously to step 1;
4. we continue this process until all nodes from the parents U^1 and U^2 are assigned to the offspring or removed.

An example of how the crossover operator works on the sample instance in Figure 1 is illustrated in Table 1.

Table 1. Example for the crossover operator

Parent 1	Parent 2	Offspring	
$U_1^1 = \{3,5,10\}$	$U_1^2 = \{2,4,8\}$	{}	Select U_1^1 as partition with most nodes and
$U_2^1 = \{1\}$	$U_2^2 = \{6\}$	{}	copy to the offspring. Delete copied nodes
$U_3^1 = \{8\}$	$U_3^2 = \{9\}$	{}	and corresponding nodes from the selected
			clusters from both parents.
$U_1^1 = \{\}$	$U_1^2 = \{2,8\}$	$\{3,5,10\}$	Select U_1^2 as partition with most nodes and
$U_2^1 = \{1\}$	$U_2^2 = \{\}$	{}	copy to the offspring. Delete copied nodes
$U_3^1 = \{8\}$	$U_3^2 = \{\}$	{}	and corresponding nodes from the selected
			clusters from both parents.
$U_1^1 = \{\}$	$U_1^2 = \{\}$	$\{3,5,10\}$	A new solution to the PGCP making use of
$U_2^1 = \{\}$	$U_2^2 = \{\}$	$\{2,8\}$	two colors.
$U_3^1 = \{\}$	$U_3^2 = \{\}$		

During the steps 1 and 3, the choice of selecting a color class to be moved to the offspring can be done either randomly or according to their size and preferring the largest one. The latter strategy will likely generate offsprings with lower k, but the diversity will be lower. Since we use a local improvement procedure for intensification, we select the color classes randomly.

Mutation: Mutation is another important feature of genetic algorithms since it diversifies the search directions and avoids convergence to local optima. In our algorithm we randomly choose between these two procedures:

- Pick a random color class and try to move each of its nodes to another color class so that no conflicts occur. If this is not possible, the node stays in its original color class.
- Remove a randomly selected node from the color class where it is assigned to and insert it to a different color class so that no conflicts occur. If necessary, a new color class is created.

While the first method is generally able to modify the solution to a greater extent, it does not create new color classes, so the solution never gets worse.

Due to this restriction, in some situations this method is not able to cause any modifications. The second method changes the color assignment of one node only, but it is possible that a new color class is created. In our experiments these two mutation methods complement each other well.

Local Improvement Procedure: By solely relying on the genetic operators, experiments have shown that the algorithm converges too slowly and there is no guarantee that the final solution is even a local optimum. Therefore we apply a local improvement procedure on an offspring after it has been created by the genetic operators with certain probability.

For this purpose we consider the solution in a more compact representation than the genetic representation in order to reduce the search space. We only use the selection of nodes without specifying the coloring information here, i.e., solution $V^* = \{v_1, \ldots, v_p\}$, $v_i \in V_i$, $i \in \{1, \ldots, p\}$. This is a common approach for representing solutions in GNDPs [16]. The problem here is that evaluating the solution, i.e., computing the necessary number of colors by solving the classical graph coloring problem, is $\mathcal{NP}$-hard. Therefore we use the DANGER construction heuristic proposed by Glover *et al.* [7]. The central idea is to color one node in each iteration that has the highest node-danger value (which indicates how danger it is to keep it for later) with a color that has the lowest color-danger value. In a previous version we used the DSATUR heuristic [2] which is faster since it uses simpler node and color evaluations, but the results of the DANGER heuristic are clearly better. There certainly are lots of options to choose from when it comes to solving the classical graph coloring problem. Using exact approaches such as mixed integer programming or constraint programming [8,12] or even metaheuristics [11] would consume too much time since this process has to be done a multitude of times during local search when evaluating neighbor solutions. For this reason we chose the current evaluation algorithm that is focused on fast run-times.

A common drawback of an one-sided evaluation criterion is that there is always a large amount of solutions with equal k, i.e., they have the same number of colors. Therefore, we use an additional criterion that is commonly used in graph coloring problems: the number of conflicts. The idea is that if two solutions can be colored with k colors, we apply a modified version of DANGER heuristic that attempts to color these solutions with $k-1$ colors and minimizes the number of conflicts. Then the solution with less conflicts is considered the better one and will be used in the algorithm. However, we keep the original coloring information that uses k colors in order to avoid infeasible solutions being generated.

For local search we use a standard node exchange neighborhood structure, i.e., the neighborhood of a solution $V^* = \{v_1, \ldots, v_p\}$ consists of all node vectors in which for precisely one cluster V_i the node v_i is replaced by a different node v_i' of the same cluster. In preliminary tests we also tried changing nodes of two clusters, but the size of the neighborhood becomes too large and the run-time increases too drastically. We follow a best improvement strategy since solutions are distinguishable accurately due to the finely granulated evaluation.

4 Experimental Results

Our experiments were run as single threads on a Intel Core i7 PC with 3.4 GHz and 16 GB memory. We use the Rand-set of instances [5] that was also used in [6]. It contains randomized instances with 20 to 120 nodes partitioned into 10 to 60 clusters, respectively. We performed 30 independent runs for each instance and determined the average and standard deviations of the final objective values. Each run was terminated after generating 2000 solutions without improvements. The probability for local improvement was set to 30%. We compare two MA variants: one that only uses the number of colors as evaluation criterion (MA1) and one that uses number of colors and the number of conflicts for evaluation (MA2). Table 2 contains experimental results on instances with 20 – 120 nodes and an edge density of 0.5 while Table 3 contains results on instances with 90 nodes and an edge density of 0.1 – 0.9. Each line corresponds to a set of 5 different instances. Both tables show the instance characteristics, the lower and upper bounds obtained by the branch and cut (B&C) approach [6] within two hours run-time, followed by the average objective values of the final best solutions, their standard deviations, and the run-time in seconds for the MA variants.

Table 2. Experimental results on instances with different size

Instance set		B&C		MA1			MA2		
nodes	density	LB	UB	obj	sd	time	obj	sd	time
20	0.5	3	3	3.00	0.00	0.02s	3.00	0.00	0.14s
40	0.5	4	4	4.50	0.51	0.10s	4.00	0.00	0.60s
60	0.5	5	5	5.96	0.20	0.31s	5.63	0.49	2.00s
70	0.5	6	6	6.86	0.40	0.53s	6.06	0.24	3.33s
80	0.5	6	6	7.66	0.48	0.80s	6.94	0.29	4.90s
90	0.5	6	7	8.22	0.42	1.21s	7.55	0.50	7.49s
100	0.5	6	7	8.90	0.30	1.74s	7.93	0.30	11.04s
120	0.5	7	8	10.26	0.44	3.41s	9.22	0.43	21.05s

Table 3. Experimental results on instances with different density

Instance set		B&C		MA1			MA2		
nodes	density	LB	UB	obj	sd	time	obj	sd	time
90	0.1	2	3	3.13	0.33	0.22s	3.09	0.29	1.37s
90	0.2	3	4	4.71	0.45	0.52s	4.41	0.49	3.24s
90	0.3	4	5	6.06	0.24	0.78s	5.52	0.56	4.90s
90	0.4	5	6	7.59	0.49	1.07s	6.79	0.83	6.54s
90	0.5	6	7	8.22	0.42	1.21s	7.55	0.50	7.49s
90	0.6	8	8	10.98	0.34	1.88s	10.50	0.87	11.95s
90	0.7	10	10	12.93	0.38	2.37s	12.39	1.12	14.83s
90	0.8	12	12	15.55	0.51	3.38s	15.18	0.80	20.98s
90	0.9	16	16	17.69	0.86	7.38s	17.27	0.98	45.75s

We observe that while MA2 consumes more time than MA1, the results are significantly better, particularly on larger instances the difference is approximately one color. This underlines that using the number of colors alone as evaluation criterion is insufficient because the search process circles around plateau regions that contain equally good solutions. When we additionally aim at minimizing the number of conflicts, the MA gets valuable information of what it should focus on. Compared to B&C, MA2 is worse in terms of solution quality. However, we have to take into account that B&C has a time limit of two hours while MA2 finishes in less than one minute. Therefore, MA2 is a practical approach when it comes to time-critical applications and/or large instances due to its excellent scalability.

5   Conclusions and Future Work

We proposed a memetic algorithm (MA) for the partition graph coloring problem that uses two distinct solution representations. For maintaining a diverse population and to keep the computational effort for genetic operators low, we use a full solution representation for crossover and mutation. In contrast, we use a more compact and incomplete solution representation during local search. Both representations work well in combination in the MA. During local search, we observed that minimizing the number of colors results in many solutions of equal quality. Therefore, we use a second evaluation criterion based on the number of conflicts when using one color less. Computational experiments on common benchmark instances sets show that although the MA is not always able to find the optimal solutions, it produces solid results with very low run-times and therefore has excellent scalability when it comes to large instances.

For future work, we want to consider a further incomplete solution representation which is based on characterizing the colors of the clusters. The challenge will be to develop efficient algorithms for choosing the nodes in the clusters that are compatible with the color assignments. We also want to consider further evaluation criteria besides color and conflicts so that more fine-tuned measurements depending on specific situations are possible.

Acknowledgments. This work was supported by grant PHC BOSPHORE 2012 N 26284RB which is gratefully acknowledged.

References

1. Bontoux, B., Artigues, C., Feillet, D.: A memetic algorithm with a large neighborhood crossover operator for the generalized traveling salesman problem. Computers and Operations Research 37(11), 1844–1852 (2010)
2. Brélaz, D.: New methods to color the vertices of a graph. Communication of ACM 22(4), 251–256 (1979)
3. Demange, M., Monnot, J., Pop, P., Ries, B.: Selective graph coloring in some special classes of graphs. In: Mahjoub, A.R., Markakis, V., Milis, I., Paschos, V.T. (eds.) ISCO 2012. LNCS, vol. 7422, pp. 320–331. Springer, Heidelberg (2012)

4. Demange, M., Monnot, J., Pop, P., Ries, B.: On the complexity of the selective graph coloring problem in some special classes of graphs. Theoretical Computer Science (in press, 2013)
5. Frota, Y., Maculan, N., Noronha T.F., Ribeiro, C.C.: Instances for the partition coloring problem, www.ic.uff.br/~celso/grupo/pcp.htm
6. Frota, Y., Maculan, N., Noronha, T.F., Ribeiro, C.C.: A branch-and-cut algorithm for the partition coloring problem. Networks 55(3), 194–204 (2010)
7. Glover, F., Parker, M., Ryan, J.: Coloring by tabu branch and bound. DIMACS Series on Discrete Mathematics and Theoretical Computer Science 26, 285–308 (1996)
8. Gualandi, S., Malucelli, F.: Exact solution of graph coloring problems via constraint programming and column generation. INFORMS Journal on Computing 24(1), 81–100 (2012)
9. Hoshino, E.A., Frota, Y.A., de Souza, C.C.: A branch-and-price approach for the partition coloring problem. Operations Research Letters 39(2), 132–137 (2011)
10. Li, G., Simha, R.: The partition coloring problem and its application to wavelength routing and assignment. In: 1st Workshop on Optical Networks (2000)
11. Lü, Hao, J.: A memetic algorithm for graph coloring. European Journal of Operational Research 203, 241–250 (2010)
12. Mehrotra, A., Trick, M.A.: A column generation approach for graph coloring. INFORMS Journal on Computing 8, 344–354 (1996)
13. Moscato, P.: Memetic algorithms: A short introduction. In: Corne, D., et al. (eds.) New Ideas in Optimization, pp. 219–234. McGraw Hill (1999)
14. Ngueveu, S.U., Prins, C., Calvo, R.W.: An effective memetic algorithm for the cumulative capacitated vehicle routing problem. Computers and Operations Research 37(11), 1877–1885 (2010)
15. Noronha, T.F., Ribeiro, C.C.: Routing and wavelength assignment by partition colouring. European Journal of Operational Research 171(3), 797–810 (2006)
16. Pop, P.C.: Generalized network design problems. Modeling and Optimization. De Gruyter Series in Discrete Mathematics and Applications, Germany (2012)
17. Pop, P.C., Hu, B., Raidl, G.R.: A memetic algorithm for the partition graph coloring problem. In: Extended Abstracts of the 14th International Conference on Computer Aided Systems Theory, Gran Canaria, Spain, pp. 167–169 (2013)

DNA Base-Code Generation for Bio-molecular Computing by Using a Multiobjective Approach Based on SPEA2

José M. Chaves-González and Miguel A. Vega-Rodríguez

Univ. Extremadura. Dept. Computers and Communications Technologies,
Escuela Politécnica. Campus Universitario s/n. 10003. Cáceres, Spain
{jm,mavega}@unex.es

Abstract. The design of DNA strands suitable for bio-molecular computing involves several complex constraints which have to be fulfilled to ensure the reliability of operations. Two of the most important properties which have to be controlled to obtain reliable sequences are self-assembly and self-complementary hybridizations. These processes have to be restricted to avoid undesirable interactions which could produce incorrect computations. Our study is focused on six different design criteria that provide reliable and robust DNA sequences. We have tackled the problem as a multiobjective optimization problem in which there is not only an optimal solution, but a Pareto set of solutions. In this paper, we have used the Strength Pareto Evolutionary Algorithm 2 (SPEA2) to generate reliable DNA sequences for three different real datasets used in bio-molecular computation. Results indicate that our approach obtains satisfactory DNA libraries that are more reliable than other results previously published in the literature.

Keywords: DNA Sequence Design, Multiobjective Optimization, SPEA2.

1 Introduction

Deoxyribonucleic acid (DNA) computing refers to a computational model proposed by Adleman in 1994 [1] which uses DNA molecules as computer storage units and their biological reactions as the operators to perform computations. In this context, the hybridization between DNA sequences is crucial, because undesirable hybridizations usually lead to incorrect computations [2]. Thus, the design of reliable sequences which generate specific duplexes while avoiding other undesirable reactions involves several conflicting design criteria which cannot be managed by traditional optimization techniques [2]. In this case, a design based on multi-objective evolutionary algorithms represents the most suitable alternative. Typical existing approaches for DNA sequence design problem include a wide range of non-exact algorithms, such as evolutionary algorithms, dynamic programming, and heuristic methods [2]. However, a design based on multi-objective evolutionary algorithms (MOEAs) represents the most appropriate design alternative [3] because MOEAs take into account several conflicting objectives simultaneously without the artificial adjustments which are included in classical mono-objective optimization methods.

R. Moreno-Díaz et al. (Eds.): EUROCAST 2013, Part I, LNCS 8111, pp. 227–234, 2013.

In this paper, we consider six different conflicting criteria, two of them taken as restrictions and the other four managed as objectives, to generate reliable DNA sequences suitable for DNA computing by using the multiobjective standard: Strength Pareto Evolutionary Algorithm 2 (SPEA2) [4]. In addition, our results are validated by using other works published in the literature. As will be discussed, our MOEA generates very promising DNA sequences that surpass the results obtained with other relevant approaches previously published.

The rest of the paper is organized as follows: Section 2 describes the basic background on the problem and the multiobjective formulation followed. The SPEA2 adaptation developed is explained in Section 3. Section 4 is devoted to present and to analyze the results, as well as comparing our approach with other methods published in the literature. Finally, Section 5 summarizes the conclusions of the paper.

2   DNA Base-Code Generation for Reliable Computation

In recent years, there has been an increase in the technologies which are based on DNA molecules, such as nanotechnology, DNA sequencing or DNA computing [2]. In all those technologies, the design of reliable DNA libraries is a crucial task. One of the most important processes for DNA molecules is the Watson-Crick pairing [5], or the hybridization between a sequence and its basepairing complement. The problem here is to control undesirable hybridizations, because they can produce errors in the biological reactions, so they have to be avoided when sequences are designed.

DNA sequence design problem consists of designing sets of reliable sequences which form stable duplexes while avoiding undesirable interactions. Every sequence design criteria should contribute to improving reliability, because this property is a very important requirement for any system based on DNA sequences. There are several biological criteria that can be considered to achieve this purpose. According to their biological meaning, design criteria can be classified into four groups [6]. First, properties that avoid inconvenient reactions; second, criteria that control the generation of secondary structures; third, properties that control the biochemical characteristics of DNA sequences; and finally, criteria that restrict the sequences composition. From the first group, we have taken the *similarity* and the *h-measure* objectives. Similarity calculates the inverse Hamming distance between two sequences, while h-measure tests the possibility of unintended DNA basepairing. Both criteria are checked by considering shifts in sequences under study. Regarding to the second category, secondary structures formation, we have included the objectives: *hairpin*, which indicates the probability that the sequence under study can generate secondary structures and *continuity*, which counts the repetitions of identical bases. This is important because if one base is repeated several times, an unusual secondary structure could be formed. The third category refers to the biochemical characteristics of the sequences. It is important to control that every sequence have similar chemical features. We have included the following two restrictions from this category: *melting temperature*, which is the temperature at which half of the DNA strands are in the double-helical state and half are in a random coil state (dissociated), and *GC ratio*, which indicates the percentage of cytosine (C) and guanine (G) in a sequence.

2.1   Multiobjective Formulation

DNA base-code generation can be naturally formulated as a multiobjective optimization problem in which the objectives and constraints are the design criteria that every sequence has to satisfy to ensure reliability. We have considered six different design criteria to cover a wide range of aspects which contribute to reliability [6]. Four are considered as objectives: *Similarity* and *h-measure* avoid inconvenient reactions between sequences. On the other hand, *continuity* and *hairpin* control the generation of secondary structures. Finally, *melting temperature* and *GC ratio* are considered as constraints for the problem and they assure that DNA sequences are in the similar bio-chemical ranges. The four objectives have to be minimized, so the problem can be described as follows.

$$\text{Minimize } F(X) = (f_1(X), f_2(X), f_3(X), f_4(X))$$
$$\text{subject to } c_1(X) \text{ and } c_2(X) \tag{1}$$

where $f_i(X)$ are the objectives previously mentioned (similarity, h-measure, continuity and hairpin), $c_i(X)$ are the melting temperature and the GC ratio constraints, and X is the set of DNA sequences under study.

A formal definition of each design criterion included in equation (1) is given below.

1) Similarity: This objective computes the similarity in the same direction of two given sequences to keep each sequence as unique as possible, including position shifts. For a more complete comparison, the target sequence is extended by adding its own sequence to the 3'-end with gaps. Moreover, we consider continuous (s_{cont}) and discontinuous (s_{disc}) similarities. The mathematical definition for this measure is described in (2).

$$f_{similarity}(x, y) = Max_{g,i}(s_{disc}(x, shift(y, g, i)) + \\ + s_{cont}(x, shift(y, g, i))) \tag{2}$$

where x and y are parallel sequences and *shift* indicates a shift of sequence y by i bases and g gaps. s_{disc} is a real value between 0 and 1, and s_{cont} is an integer between 1 and the length of the sequences. Finally, we have to indicate that similarities have to surpass a threshold that has to be established by experimentation to be considered.

2) H-measure: This objective is similar to similarity, but instead of considering sequences in parallel, they are managed as complementary. H-measure prevents cross hybridization between DNA strands. We consider elongated sequences with gaps for a more reliable measure. The mathematical definition is given in (3).

$$f_{h\_measure}(x, y) = Max_{g,i}(h_{disc}(x, shift(y, g, i)) + \\ + h_{cont}(x, shift(y, g, i))) \tag{3}$$

where x and y are anti-parallel sequences and *shift* indicates a shift as in the similarity case. h_{disc}, h_{cont} and the threshold have also analogous values to the similarity measure.

3) Continuity: This measure calculates the degree of successive occurrences of the same base in a sequence. The measure prohibits consecutive runs of the same base over a given threshold. For example, if the threshold is 3, in the sequence AGGCAATAAAACGAAATGGGC, only the third subsequence of adenines (A) violates the continuity. The mathematical definition for this measure is given in (4).

$$f_{continuity}(x) = \sum_{i=1}^{max} \sum_{a \in \{A,C,G,T\}} T(c_a(x,i),t)^2 \tag{4}$$

where x is the sequence under study, *max* is the difference between the length of the sequence and the threshold (T), $c_a(x,i)$ is equal to ε if $\exists \varepsilon$ s.t. $x_i \neq a$, $x_i+1=a$ for $1 \leq j \leq \varepsilon$, $x_{i+\varepsilon+1} \neq a$, and 0 otherwise.

4) Hairpin: This restriction represents the probability of secondary structures creation. For simplicity, it is calculated through the Hamming distance by considering the length of hairpin loop and the number of hybridized pairs. It is assumed that a hairpin has at least R_{min} bases as a loop and a minimum of P_{min} base pairs as a stem. It is also considered the penalty for formation of hairpins of various sizes at every position in the sequence. In (5) are considered hairpins with r-base loop and p-base pairs stem to be formed at position i in the sequence x, if more than half bases in the subsequence $x_{i-p}...x_i$ hybridize to the subsequence $x_{i+r}...x_{i+r+p}$. The number of matches in these subsequences is defined as the penalty for this hairpin.

$$f_{hairpin}(x) = \sum_{p=P\min}^{max\,l} \sum_{r=R\min}^{max\,R} \sum_{i=1}^{max\,l} T(hp(x,p,r,i), \frac{pinlen(p,r,i)}{2})$$

$$hp(x,p,r,i) = \sum_{j=1}^{pinlen(p,r,i)} bp(x_{p+i+j}, x_{p+i+r+j}) \tag{5}$$

where the function *pinlen* $(p,r,i) = min(p+i, l-r-i-p)$ and denotes the maximum number of possible basepairs when a hairpin is formed at center $p+i+r/2$.

5) GC content: This criterion indicates the percentage of bases C and G in the sequence. This is important because the GC content affects to the chemical properties of DNA sequences. For example, the GC% of the DNA sequence ACGTT is 40.

6) Melting temperature, T_m: This measure predicts DNA thermal denaturation, which is a key factor for DNA computing. Both sequence and base composition are important determinants of DNA duplex stability. There are many ways to calculate this relevant feature, but we use the nearest neighbour (NN) model [7]. The mathematical description for this measure is provided in (6).

$$Tm(x) = \Delta H°(x) / \Delta S°(x) + R\ln(|C_T|/4) \tag{6}$$

where x is the DNA sequence studied, R is a gas constant and $|C_T|$ is the total sequence concentration. $\Delta H°$ and $\Delta S°$ refer to predicted enthalpies and entropies. Those values were taken from [7].

3   Multiobjective Approach

We have generated reliable DNA sequences suitable for molecular computing by using an adapted version of the Strength Pareto Evolutionary Algorithm 2 (SPEA2), which is a population-based algorithm originally created by Zitzler et al. in [4]. The pseudocode of the proposed MOEA is shown in Algorithm 1.

Algorithm 1. Pseudocode of SPEA2

1: $P \Leftarrow$ generateRandomPopulation ($PSize$)
2: $A \Leftarrow \varnothing$ //Archive ($ArchiveSize$)
3: **while** not stop condition satisfied **do**
4:     FitnessAssignment (P, A)
5:     EnviromentalSelection (A, P) //Truncate A if necessary
6:     **for** i=1 to $PSize$ **do**
7:         $ind1, ind2 \Leftarrow$ tournamentSelection (A) // $ind1 \neq ind2$
8:         $P_i \Leftarrow$ recombination ($ind1, ind2, Pcr$)
9:         $P_i \Leftarrow$ mutation (P_i, Pm)
10:    **end for**
11: **end while**

SPEA2 uses a regular population, P, of $PSize$ individuals, and an archive (external set, A). The process starts with the random generation of the initial population and the initialization of the archive set (lines 1, 2). Each individual in the population is a valid DNA library which represents the solution for the specific problem instance which is being considered. A solution is composed of a set of n sequences. Each DNA strand is composed of m bases each (sequence length). The number of sequences and the number of bases per sequence depend on the problem instance. The data structure contains the DNA strands used by the genetic operators of our MOEA along with the values for each biochemical design criteria.

In each iteration, all non-dominated solutions (the best solutions) of both, population and archive, are copied into a new population, truncating it when the size of the new population exceeds $PSize$ solutions (line 5). Previously, a fitness value that is the addition of its strength raw fitness and a density estimation is assigned to each individual in P and in A (line 4). The raw fitness is based on the concept of Pareto dominance. The raw fitness of a solution, $R(i)$, is determined by the strengths of its dominators in both archive and population. It is a measure to be minimized, so $R(i) =$ 0 corresponds to a nondominated individual, while a high $R(i)$ value means that solution i is dominated by many individuals. A particular solution is of more quality than another if it is dominated by fewer solutions. A solution dominates another if it is better, at least, in one of the objectives and it is not worse in any of the others. In case of individuals having identical raw fitness, it is used a density estimation technique which is based on the distance (in the objective space) to the kth nearest solutions. SPEA2 uses binary tournament selection, crossover at two levels (at individual and sequence levels) and random mutation (lines 7-9) for improving the population in each generation.

4   Experimental Evaluation and Results

The algorithm developed has been adjusted to obtain optimal results by performing a complete set of experiments. The value of each parameter (population size *PSize*, archive size *ArchiveSize*, crossover probability *Pcr*, mutation probability *Pm* and parent selection strategy) has been fixed after executing 30 independent runs to ensure statistical significance. Table 1 shows the algorithm configuration. All experiments were performed by using a 2.3GHz Intel PC with 1GB RAM. The algorithm was compiled using gcc 4.4.5 compiler. For comparison with other authors [6], we have used the same population size and stop condition for the algorithm (3000 individuals and 200 iterations respectively).

Table 1. Algorithm configuration

SPEA2 configuration	
Archive size (*ArchiveSize*)	*PSize*/2
Crossover probability (*Pcr*)	0.3
Mutation probability (*Pm*)	0.5
Parent selection strategy	Binary tournament

We have used three different-sized sets of DNA sequences proposed by different authors [8], [9], and [10] which have been used for reliable DNA computing. This fact ensures that our algorithm works with several types of instances which have been tested to be used for bio-molecular computing. Moreover, we compare our results with sequences generated by Shin *et al.* [6], which use a multiobjective approach with the same data sets. We examine the quality of each design criterion for a set of sequences taken from the median Pareto front generated by our SPEA2. The comparison is not performed in terms of any multiobjective metrics, such as hypervolume, because unfortunately no studies have taken multiobjective indicators so far. Biochemical constraints and parametrical adjustments for the design criteria used in our study were established as explained in the literature [6]. Thus, for H-measure (H) and similarity (S), we set lower limits for the continuous case equal to six bases and 17% for the discontinuous case. For continuity (C), the threshold value was 2. Hairpin (P) formation requires at least six basepairings and a six base loop. The melting temperature (T_m) was calculated with 1 M salt concentration and 10nM DNA concentration. Furthermore, the T_m and the GC ratio are considered constraints whose values were taken from the literature. For the results in [8] and in [9], sequences have the GC ratio restricted to 50% and the melting temperature between 46 and 53 degrees. On the other hand, for the work in [10], the range of the GC ratio is between 40% and 50% and the melting temperature between 31 and 39 degrees. Shin *et al.* [6] uses the same restrictions. Comparative results are given in Fig. 1 for the three data sets under study. Furthermore, in Table 2, we show the comparison of sequences generated in [8], sequences generated in [6] and an example taken from the median Pareto front of the sequences generated by our approach. Due to the limit in the number of pages, we cannot show a similar table for the other two instances (but Fig. 1 summarizes these comparisons).

Table 2. Comparison of the sequences in [8], [6] and sequences obtained by our proposal

Seq. (5'→ 3')	C	P	H	S	Tm	GC
Sequences obtained in [8]						
ATAGAGTGGATAGTTCTGGG	9	3	55	64	52.6522	45
CATTGGCGGCGCGTAGGCTT	0	0	69	51	69.2009	65
CTTGTGACCGCTTCTGGGGA	16	0	60	63	60.8563	60
GAAAAAGGACCAAAAGAGAG	41	0	58	45	52.7111	40
GATGGTGCTTAGAGAAGTGG	0	0	58	54	55.3056	50
TGTATCTCGTTTTAACATCC	16	4	61	50	48.4451	35
TTGTAAGCCTACTGCGTGAC	0	3	75	55	56.7055	50
Sequences obtained in [6]						
CTCTTCATCCACCTCTTCTC	0	0	43	58	46.6803	50
CTCTCATCTCTCCGTTCTTC	0	0	37	58	46.9393	50
TATCCTGTGGTGTCCTTCCT	0	0	45	57	49.1066	50
ATTCTGTTCCGTTGCGTGTC	0	0	52	56	51.1380	50
TCTCTTACGTTGGTTGGCTG	0	0	51	53	49.9252	50
GTATTCCAAGCGTCCGTGTT	0	0	55	49	50.7224	50
AAACCTCCACCAACACACCA	9	0	55	43	51.4735	50
Sequences obtained with SPEA2						
CAACAGATGAGTAACTCCCC	0	0	57	44	47.214	50
TTCCTTGTTCCTGCTTCCTC	0	0	41	57	49.576	50
CTTCTCTCCTTCTCTCCTTG	0	0	37	61	46.266	50
ATGGTTAGTGTAGGAGTGGG	0	0	58	42	48.126	50
TCTCGTCGTAGTAGTCTTCG	0	0	52	57	47.901	50
TTCAACCTGCTGTCTTCCCT	0	0	45	55	51.112	50
TTCTTGTGTTCTGCACTCCC	0	0	48	58	50.125	50

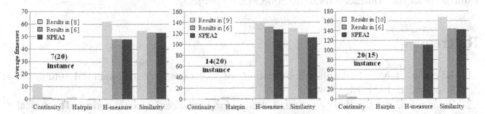

Fig. 1. Average fitness comparison between our approach (SPEA2) and other relevant works for the three instances tackled. Y axis indicates the average values of each fitness objective.

In [8], authors proposed a genetic algorithm to design good sequences for Adleman's graph. Shin *et al.*, in [6], proposed NACST/Seq algorithm to improve those sequences. Results given in Table 1 and Fig. 1 show that our approach obtains sequences with lower similarity (S) and h-measure (H) values, while obtaining minimal values for hairpin (P) and continuity (C). This means that sequences obtained by our SPEA2 have higher probability to hybridize with its correct complementary sequences. Besides, secondary structures are virtually prohibited because values for hairpin and continuity are reduced to zero. Moreover, ranges for melting temperature and GC ratio are also better, which means more stable sequences. On the other hand, results obtained in [9] and in [10] generated sequences to solve other problems (travelling salesman problem and knight movement problem) by using other methods. Fig. 1 shows that for those instances our approach also obtains sequences with lower similarities and h-measures, while obtaining minimal continuities and hairpins.

This means that sequences obtained by SPEA2 are more reliable. Secondary structures are virtually prohibited because hairpin and continuity are reduced to zero. Moreover, ranges for GC ratio and T_m are also better, which means more stable sequences.

5   Conclusions and Future Work

In this paper, we present SPEA2 for the design of DNA sequences that can be applied to reliable molecular computing. SPEA2 can obtain high quality sets of sequences which simultaneously minimize similarity, h-measure, hairpin and continuity while controlling T_m and GC content. We have used three different real-world instances proposed by different authors to ensure the effectiveness of our approach. These data sets include different number of sequences, number of bases and bio-chemical restrictions, and all of them have been used for reliable computation. After our study, we can conclude that our version of SPEA2 can generate better sequences than other approaches previously published in the literature. As future work, we are studying other multiobjective approaches and restrictions which can contribute to generate more reliable sequences for DNA computing.

Acknowledgments. This work was partially funded by the Spanish Ministry of Economy and Competitiveness and the ERDF (European Regional Development Fund), under the contract TIN2012-30685 (BIO project).

References

1. Adleman, L.M.: Molecular computation of solutions to combinatorial problems. Science 266, 1021–1024 (1994)
2. Brenneman, A., Condon, A.: Strand design for biomolecular computation. Theoretical Computation Science 287, 39–58 (2002)
3. Coello, C.A., Van Veldhuizen, D.A., Lamont, G.B.: Evolutionary Algorithms for Solving Multi-Objective Problems. Genetic Algorithms and Evol. Computation. Kluwer (2002)
4. Zitzler, E., et al.: SPEA2: Improving the Strength Pareto Evolutionary Algorithm. In: Proceedings of EUROGEN 2002, pp. 95–100 (2002)
5. Garzon, M.H., Deaton, R.J.: Biomolecular computing and programming. IEEE Trans. Evol. Computation 3, 236–250 (1999)
6. Shin, S.-Y., et al.: Multiobjective Evolutionary Optimization of DNA Sequences for Reliable DNA Computing. IEEE Trans. Evolutionary Computation 9(2), 143–158 (2005)
7. Santa Lucia Jr., J.: A unified view of polymer, dumbbell, and oligonucleotide DNA nearest-neighbor thermodynamics. Proc. Nat. Acad. Sci. U.S.A. 95, 1460–1465 (1998)
8. Deaton, R., et al.: Good encodings for DNA-based solutions to combinatorial problems. In: Proceedings of 2nd Annual Meeting on DNA Based Computers, pp. 247–258 (1996)
9. Tanaka, F., et al.: Toward a general-purpose sequence design system in DNA computing. In: Proceedings of the IEEE Congress on Evolutionary Computation (CEC), pp. 73–78 (2002)
10. Faulhammer, D., et al.: Molecular computation: RNA solutions to chess problems. Proceedings of the National Academy of Sciences 97, 1385–1389 (2000)

A Multiobjective SFLA-Based Technique for Predicting Motifs in DNA Sequences

David L. González-Álvarez* and Miguel A. Vega-Rodríguez

University of Extremadura,
Department of Technologies of Computers and Communications,
ARCO Research Group,
Escuela Politécnica, Campus Universitario s/n, 10003, Cáceres, Spain
{dlga,mavega}@unex.es

Abstract. In recent years design of new evolutionary techniques for addressing optimization problems is being a booming practice. Furthermore, considering that the vast majority of real optimization problems need to simultaneously optimize more than a single objective function (Multiobjective Optimization Problem - MOP); many of these techniques are also adapted to this multiobjective context. In this paper, we present a multiobjective adaptation of one of the last proposed swarm-based evolutionary algorithms, the Shuffle Frog Leaping Algorithm (SFLA), named Multiobjective Shuffle Frog Leaping Algorithm (MO-SFLA). To evaluate the performance of this new multiobjective algorithm, we have applied it to solve an important biological optimization problem, the Motif Discovery Problem (MDP). As we will see, the structure and operation of MO-SFLA makes it suitable for solving the MDP, achieving better results than other multiobjective evolutionary algorithms and making better predictions than other well-known biological tools.

Keywords: Shuffle frog leaping algorithm, evolutionary algorithm, multiobjective optimization, motif discovery, DNA.

1 Introduction

Biology is a natural science that studies the life by analyzing the structure, function, origin, and evolution of living organisms. Biology has many subdisciplines unified in several axioms. One of them is related to genes, which are the basic unit of heredity. A gene corresponds to a region of DNA that influences the function of an organism in a specific way. All organisms share the same basic machinery to copy and translate DNA into proteins. This transcriptional process occurs as a consequence of the genetic expression process which is activated or deactivated

* This work was partially funded by the Spanish Ministry of Economy and Competitiveness and the ERDF (European Regional Development Fund), under the contract TIN2012-30685 (BIO project). Thanks also to the Fundación Valhondo for the economic support offered to David L. González-Álvarez.

R. Moreno-Díaz et al. (Eds.): EUROCAST 2013, Part I, LNCS 8111, pp. 235–242, 2013.

by certain binds between small DNA substrings and proteins called Transcription Factors (TF). Identifying these Transcription Factor Binding Sites (TFBS) could provide valuable information about the complexity and evolution of living organisms. In this paper, we find over-represented DNA patterns, known as motifs [2], that may have biological significance such as be a TFBS. This problem is known as Motif Discovery Problem (MDP). For doing this, and considering that the MDP has been defined as a Multiobjective Optimization Problem (MOP), we have adapted a new evolutionary technique, more concretely, a new swarm-based metaheuristic, to the multiobjective context. The selected algorithm is a recently proposed technique inspired by the collective behavior of frogs called Shuffle Frog Leaping Algorithm (SFLA) [3]. SFLA was designed taking into account the benefits provided by the memetic genetic algorithms (MA) and the social-based techniques. More specifically, SFLA simulates the memetic evolution of a population of frogs which represent the solutions of the addressed optimization problem. Since this algorithm has never been applied to discover motifs, we thought it would be interesting to study its behavior when solving the MDP. To analyze the operation of the multiobjective SFLA version (MO-SFLA) we have used as benchmark a set of real biological instances selected from TRANSFAC database [8] with genetic information belonging to four organisms. In order to check the quality of the obtained results, we have compared them with those achieved by other two swarm-based algorithms as Multiobjective Artificial Bee Colony (MOABC, [6]) and Multiobjective Gravitational Search Algorithm (MO-GSA, [6]); and with those achieved by other two standard multiobjective evolutionary algorithms such as NSGA-II [1] and SPEA2 [9]. In addition, we also compare the predictions made with those predicted by thirteen well-known biological tools among which we highlight AlignACE, MEME, and Weeder. As we will see, the results obtained by the proposed algorithm show that it is suitable for solving the MDP, outperforming the results achieved by other algorithms and making better predictions than other biological tools.

The rest of the paper is organized as follows. Section 2 defines the mathematical formulation of the MDP. In Section 3, we include the description of the applied metaheuristic, the MO-SFLA. Section 4 is devoted to the experimentation, including the parameter settings and the methodology adopted in the tests. In this section we also conduct a discussion of the results, analyzing the biological relevance of the motifs discovered by the proposed technique. Finally, some conclusions and possible future lines are presented in Section 5.

2   Motif Discovery Problem

Given a set of sequences $S = \{S_i | i = 1, 2, ..., D\}$ of nucleotides defined on the alphabet $B = \{A, C, G, T\}$. $S_i = \{S_i^j | j = 1, 2, ..., w_i\}$ is a sequence of nucleotides, where w_i is its sequence width. The set of all the subsequences contained in S is $\{s_i^{j_i} | i = 1, 2, ..., D, j_i = 1, 2, ..., w_i - l + 1\}$, where j_i is the binding site of a possible motif instance s_i^j on sequence S_i, and l is the motif length. We refer to the number of motif instances as $|A| = \sum_{i=1}^{D} \sum_{j=1}^{w_i} A_i^j$. To obtain the objective values we have to build the consensus motif, which is a string abstraction of the motif instances. To compose this motif we have to take into account the dominant bases (A, C, G, or T) of the motif instance nucleotides. $S(A) = \{S(A)_1, S(A)_2, ..., S(A)_{|A|}\}$ is a set of $|A|$ motif instances, where $S(A)_i = S(A)_i^1 S(A)_i^2...S(A)_i^l$ is the ith motif instance in $|A|$. $S(A)$ can also be expanded as $(S(A)^1, S(A)^2, ..., S(A)^l)$, where $S(A)^j = S(A)_i^j \ S(A)_2^j \ ... \ S(A)_{|A|}^j$ is the list of nucleotides on the jth position in the motif instances. To obtain the objective values we have also to build the Position Count Matrix (PCM) $N(A)$ with the numbers of different nucleotide bases on each position of the candidate motifs (A) which have passed the threshold marked by the support. $N(A) = \{N(A)^1, N(A)^2, ..., N(A)^l\}$, and $N(A)^j = \{N(A)_b^j | b \in B\}$, where $N(A)_b^j = |\{S(A)_i^j | S(A)_i^j = b\}|$; and the Position Frequency Matrix (PFM) $\widehat{N} = \frac{N(A)}{|A|}$, where the dominant nucleotides of each position are normalized.

Given these considerations, we have defined the MDP as a multiobjective optimization problem $f_1(x)$, $f_2(x)$, $f_3(x)$ subjected to $C_1(x)$, $C_2(x)$, $C_3(x)$, $C_4(x)$:

Motif length $f_1(x)$: which maximizes the number of nucleotides that compose the motifs.

Support $f_2(x)$: which maximizes the number of sequences used to compose the final motif. Only those sequences that achieve a motif instance of certain quality, with respect to the consensus motif, were taken into account in this objective, and so, when we compose the final motif.

Similarity $f_3(x)$: which maximizes the similarity among the subsequences that compose the final solution. To calculate its value we have to average all dominance values of each PFM column, as is indicated in the following expression:

$$Similarity(Motif) = \frac{\sum_{i=1}^{l} max_b\{f(b,i)\}}{l} \tag{1}$$

where $f(b,i)$ is the score of nucleotide b in column i in the PFM and $max_b\{f(b,i)\}$ is the dominance value of the dominant nucleotide in column i.

Subject to certain constraints. We have restricted the motif length to the range [7,64] - $C_1(x)$. We have set a minimum support value of 2 for the motifs of the instances composed by 4 sequences or less, and of 3 for the other ones - $C_2(x)$. We have also set a minimum similarity value of 0.50 - $C_3(x)$. Finally, we apply the complexity concept [5] expanded with the improvements suggested in [4] - $C_4(x)$ - in order to avoid low complexity solutions by using the following expression:

$$Complexity = \log_{10} \frac{l!}{\prod (n_i!)} \tag{2}$$

where l is the motif length and n_i is the number of nucleotides of type $i \in \{A, C, G, T\}$.

3 Multiobjective Shuffle Frog Leaping Algorithm

In this paper we present a new multiobjective adaptation of the Shuffled Frog Leaping Algorithm (SFLA) [3], named Multiobjective Shuffle Frog Leaping Algorithm (MO-SFLA). Both swarm-based optimization techniques define a set of populations (memeplexes) which represent different frog species. After a given algorithm steps, some frogs migrate from a population to another, enriching the evolutionary process with new genetic information. MO-SFLA defines six important parameters: the population size (PS), the number of sub-populations $(MEMEPLEX)$, the size of each sub-population (Q), an evolutionary acceleration factor (P), a mutation probability (MP), and the number of partial generations during which evolves each sub-population (GEN). The MO-SFLA pseudocode is shown in Algorithm 1.

The first steps of the algorithm are dedicated to initialize the solution archive, generate and evaluate the initial population (lines 1 to 3 of Algorithm 1). Once

---

Algorithm 1. Multiobjetive Shuffle Frog Leaping Algorithm (MO-SFLA)

Require: $PS, MEMEPLEX, Q, P, MP,$ and GEN
Ensure: Set of non-dominated solutions (PF)
1: $PF \leftarrow \emptyset$
2: $P \leftarrow$ generateInitialPopulation(PS)
3: $P \leftarrow$ evaluateInitialPopulation(P,PS)
4: **while** no finalization condition **do**
5:     $Xg \leftarrow$ selectBestPopulationSolution(P,PS)
6:     $P \leftarrow$ sortPopulation(P,PS)
7:     **for** $i = 1 : MEMEPLEX$ all sub-populations **do**
8:         $Mem[i] \leftarrow$ buildSubpopulations(P,PS)
9:         $Mem[i]_{prob} \leftarrow$ assignProbabilities$(Mem[i])$
10:    **end for**
11:    **for** $i = 1 : MEMEPLEX$ all sub-populations **do**
12:        **for** $j = 1 : GEN$ all generations **do**
13:            **for** $k = 1 : Q$ all selected solutions **do**
14:                $MemFinal[i][k] \leftarrow$ selectSolutionAccordingToProbability$(Mem[i],Mem[i]_{prob})$
15:            **end for**
16:            $Xb \leftarrow$ selectBestSubpopulationSolution$(MemFinal[i],Q)$
17:            $Xw \leftarrow$ selectWorstSubpopulationSolution$(MemFinal[i],Q)$
18:            /* We mutate Xw to try to improve it */
19:            **for** $k = 1 : chromosomeNumber$ all chromosomes **do**
20:                **if** rand$(0,1) < MP$ **then**
21:                    $NewXw_k \leftarrow P \times$ rand$(0,1) \times (Xb_k - Xw_k)$
22:                **end if**
23:            **end for**
24:            $NewXw \leftarrow$ evaluateSolution$(NewXw)$
25:            **if** $NewXw$ is not better than Xw **then**
26:                **for** $k = 1 : chromosomeNumber$ all chromosomes **do**
27:                    $Xw_k \leftarrow P \times$ rand$(0,1) \times (Xg_k - Xw_k)$
28:                **end for**
29:            **end if**
30:            $NewXw \leftarrow$ evaluateSolution$(NewXw)$
31:            **if** $NewXw$ is not better than Xw **then**
32:                $NewXw \leftarrow$ randomTwoPointsCrossover(Xb,Xw)
33:            **end if**
34:            $NewXw \leftarrow$ evaluateSolution$(NewXw)$
35:            $MemFinal[i] \leftarrow$ greedySelectionProcess$(NewXw,Xw)$
36:        **end for**
37:    **end for**
38:    $PF \leftarrow$ updateSolutionArchive(PF,P)
39: **end while**

done this, the algorithm starts its operation until the finalization condition is met. In each loop iteration (which represents each evolutionary step), the best population solution is selected (Xg, line 5) and the entire population is sorted by quality (line 6). The best individual is randomly selected from all the non-dominated solutions, and the population is sorted taking into account the Pareto front to which each individual belongs (non-dominated sorting function). With the population properly sorted, the algorithm generates the sub-populations (*memeplexes*) by alternating solutions, i.e., considering for example three sub-populations, the first solution will belong to the first sub-population, the second solution to the second sub-population, the third to the third, and the fourth solution will belong to the first sub-population again, the fifth solution to the second, and so on. Thus, the algorithm defines m sub-populations composed by k solutions ($PS = m \times k$). Focusing on line 9 of Algorithm 1, we can see how when the algorithm builds the sub-populations, it also establishes different selection probabilities to the processed solutions. These probabilities are calculated by applying a linear bias b_r on each element r by using the following expression: $b_r = 1/r$. At this point, each *memeplex* begins to evolve independently during GEN generations. To this end, small populations composed by Q solutions of each *memeplex* are build by using the previously calculated probabilities (lines 13 to 15). After this, the worst solution of each sub-population (Xw) is located and the algorithm tries to improve it by applying the expression described on line 21 (which uses X_b). If applying this expression the quality of the Xw does not improve, it is applied again but this time with Xg. If, again, the algorithm fails to improve the quality of Xw, it applies a random two points crossover function considering Xw and Xb (all this process is described in lines 16 to 35). This steps are repeated for each subpopulation during GEN generations. When these evolutionary steps are completed, the algorithm sorts the entire population and it starts again all the process until the finalization condition is met.

4   Experimental Results

In this section we present and analyze the MO-SFLA experimental results. To measure the quality of the solutions obtained by the proposed algorithm we use the hypervolume, which is a widely used quality metric in multiobjective optimization. All the conducted experiments have been repeated in 31 independent runs to ensure certain statistical significance in the results; and have been executed on an Intel Xeon E5410 2.33Ghz 1GB of RAM with Scientific Linux 6.1. The individual representation is the same on all algorithms and includes the necessary information to form a motif, i.e., its length and the starting locations of each candidate motif in each sequence. As we have previously mentioned, we have compared the results obtained by MO-SFLA with those achieved by other four algorithms: MOABC, MO-GSA, NSGA-II, and SPEA2. Before starting the comparative analysis, it is important to note that the proposed algorithm has been properly configured to obtain the best possible results in the solved set of instances. All tested parameters values and the best performing ones are indicated

Table 1. Instance properties

	#Seq.	Size	#Nucl.	Time (s)
dm01g	4	1500	6000	20
dm04g	4	2000	8000	20
dm05g	5	2500	12500	20
hm03r	10	1500	15000	30
hm04m	13	2000	26000	30
hm16g	7	3000	21000	20
mus02r	9	1000	9000	20
mus03g	4	1500	6000	20
mus07g	12	500	6000	30
yst03m	8	500	4000	20
yst04r	7	1000	7000	20
yst08r	11	1000	11000	30

Table 2. MO-SFLA parameters

Parameter	Tested values (best value in bold)
Population size (PS)	50, 75, **100**, 125, 150, 175, 200
Sub-populations ($MEMEPLEX$)	1, 2, **4**, 5, 10
Sub-population size (Q)	1, 5, **10**, 15, 20, 25
Evol. acceleration factor (P)	10%, **25%**, 50%, 75%, 90%
Mutation probability (MP)	10%, 25%, **50%**, 75%, 90%
Generations (GEN)	10, 50, **100**, 250, 500, 1000

in Table 2. After configuring the algorithm we can analyze the obtained results. The solved instances have been selected from TRANSFAC database [8] and include genetic information belonging to four organisms: drosophila melanogaster (dm), homo sapiens (hm), mus musculus (mus), and saccharomyces cerevisiae (yst). Their properties are detailed in Table 1. The results achieved by the five compared algorithms when they solve four instances of each organism are shown in Table 3. Analyzing the results obtained by the five compared multiobjective evolutionary algorithms, we can see how MO-SFLA achieves good results. In eleven of the twelve solved instances the proposed algorithm obtains the highest hypervolume, also getting an average value of 77.96%, 3.55% more than the second best algorithm (MOABC) and 8.42% more than the worst algorithm (NSGA-II). Given that the hypervolume is an indicator used to measure the quality of one approximation to the Pareto front (set of solutions), we can conclude that this increase in hypervolume represents a significant improvement in the quality of the solutions found.

Finally, in this section we also analyze the biological significance of the predictions made by the designed algorithm, comparing them with those predicted by

Table 3. Median hypervolumes and Interquartile Range (IQR) achieved by the algorithms

Instances	MO-SFLA $\bar{HV}_{IQR}$	MOABC $\bar{HV}_{IQR}$	MO-GSA $\bar{HV}_{IQR}$	NSGA-II $\bar{HV}_{IQR}$	SPEA2 $\bar{HV}_{IQR}$
dm01g	**84.63%** 0.60%	83.24% 0.70%	81.79% 0.81%	81.56% 0.74%	83.17% 0.70%
dm04g	**85.56%** 0.59%	84.14% 0.78%	81.82% 0.66%	81.06% 1.16%	82.67% 1.06%
dm05g	**87.54%** 0.66%	86.43% 0.78%	84.26% 0.78%	84.41% 0.86%	86.13% 1.14%
hm03r	**70.00%** 2.04%	61.48% 1.30%	61.86% 2.37%	47.40% 4.02%	53.22% 1.56%
hm04m	**61.56%** 2.53%	56.50% 1.73%	53.38% 2.54%	43.32% 3.40%	46.59% 0.94%
hm16g	**84.09%** 3.02%	81.91% 3.15%	77.83% 4.74%	68.12% 1.02%	72.40% 1.70%
mus02r	**70.41%** 1.48%	64.17% 1.78%	61.13% 2.31%	59.24% 1.20%	59.68% 1.48%
mus03g	**80.51%** 0.50%	79.69% 0.61%	76.35% 2.55%	77.18% 0.47%	77.69% 0.53%
mus07g	86.80% 1.27%	88.29% 2.32%	83.57% 2.28%	87.01% 1.95%	**89.50%** 0.52%
yst03m	**74.26%** 0.69%	69.73% 1.63%	63.30% 3.15%	65.52% 2.08%	66.45% 1.13%
yst04r	**79.22%** 0.52%	75.57% 1.02%	71.12% 2.68%	74.80% 0.50%	71.72% 0.56%
yst08r	**70.96%** 2.74%	61.81% 1.55%	66.20% 2.35%	64.87% 1.74%	57.22% 1.12%
Mean	77.96%	74.41%	71.88%	69.54%	70.54%

Table 4. Comparison between the solutions of MO-SFLA and the results predicted by thirteen well-known biological tools ("-" when no tool is able to find solutions)

(a) Sensitivity (nSn).

Instance	Best tool	Result	MO-SFLA
dm01g	SeSiMCMC	0.344000	**0.408000**
dm04g	MotifSampler	0.022222	**0.214815**
dm05g	MEME	0.037500	**0.237500**
hm03r	MEME	0.063726	**0.213235**
hm04m	AlignACE	0.005952	**0.291667**
hm16g	-	0.000000	**0.317073**
mus02r	MEME	0.094828	**0.189655**
mus03g	AlignACE	0.281690	**0.492958**
mus07g	ANN_Spec	0.040000	**0.400000**
yst03m	Improbizer	**0.340136**	0.210884
yst04r	Consensus	**0.335878**	0.328244
yst08r	AlignACE	**0.387097**	0.197133

(b) Positive Predictive Value (nPPV).

Instance	Best tool	Result	MO-SFLA
dm01g	SeSiMCMC	0.344000	**0.980769**
dm04g	MotifSampler	0.032967	**0.725000**
dm05g	MEME	0.026667	**0.703704**
hm03r	MEME	0.108333	**0.453125**
hm04m	AlignACE	0.006061	**0.291667**
hm16g	-	0.000000	**0.444444**
mus02r	MEME	0.142857	**0.550000**
mus03g	AlignACE	0.256410	**0.598291**
mus07g	ANN_Spec	0.020942	**0.606061**
yst03m	YMF	**0.700000**	0.645833
yst04r	MITRA	0.357143	**0.671875**
yst08r	MotifSampler	**0.786408**	0.491071

(c) Performance Coefficient (nPC).

Instance	Best tool	Result	MO-SFLA
dm01g	SeSiMCMC	0.207730	**0.404762**
dm04g	MotifSampler	0.013453	**0.198630**
dm05g	MEME	0.015831	**0.215909**
hm03r	MEME	0.041801	**0.169591**
hm04m	AlignACE	0.003012	**0.170732**
hm16g	-	0.000000	**0.227074**
mus02r	MEME	0.060440	**0.164179**
mus03g	AlignACE	0.155039	**0.370370**
mus07g	ANN_Spec	0.013937	**0.317460**
yst03m	oligodyad	**0.261905**	0.189024
yst04r	Consensus	0.202765	**0.282895**
yst08r	MotifSampler	**0.269103**	0.163690

(d) Correlation Coefficient (nCC).

Instance	Best tool	Result	MO-SFLA
dm01g	SeSiMCMC	0.330043	**0.628421**
dm04g	MotifSampler	0.013401	**0.389724**
dm05g	MEME	0.006491	**0.402169**
hm03r	MEME	0.063601	**0.298153**
hm04m	AlignACE	-0.000400	**0.287060**
hm16g	MEME	-0.005204	**0.371283**
mus02r	MEME	0.097480	**0.313275**
mus03g	AlignACE	0.222480	**0.518377**
mus07g	ANN_Spec	0.006056	**0.485545**
yst03m	oligodyad	**0.437304**	0.356772
yst04r	Consensus	0.322430	**0.462990**
yst08r	MotifSampler	**0.470596**	0.300415

thirteen well-known biological tools: AlignACE, ANN_Spec, Consensus, GLAM, Improbizer, MEME, MITRA, MotifSampler, Oligo/Dyad-Analysis, QuickScore, SeSiMCMC, Weeder, and YMF. The biological indicators used in these comparisons are the Sensitivity (nSn), the Positive Predictive Value (nPPV), the Performance Coefficient (nPC), and the Correlation Coefficient (nCC). These four indicators are calculated by using the TP (True-Positives), TN (True- Negatives), FP (False-Positives), and FN (False-Negatives) values, obtained by comparing the real binding site positions with the predictions made by each tool or algorithm, and their values are in the range [-1,1], where 1 represents a perfect correlation between the real binding site and the prediction made (all nucleotides successfully identified), and -1 a minimum correlation (no nucleotide identified). Due to space constraints we can not give more information about the biological tools and indicators, further information can be found in [7].

The results of this comparison between the predictions made by the proposed approach and those predicted by the thirteen biological tools (only results of the best tool are shown) are included in Table 4. As we can note, the predictions made by MO-SFLA present good biological results in the four used indicators, getting a good correction with respect to the position of the real binding sites. On the other hand, it is important to know that while many tools are highly specialized in solving some instances (for example, 'yst' instances), the proposed approximation is able to make good predictions in all instances, regardless of the organism to which they belong.

5 Conclusions and Future Lines

In this work we have presented the Multiobjective Shuffle Frog Leaping Algorithm (MO-SFLA) for solving the Motif Discovery Problem (MDP). For analyzing the operation of this algorithm, we have solved a set of twelve real sequence data sets with biological information belonging to four organisms. The conducted experiments demonstrate that this algorithm achieves better results than other swarm-based algorithms such as MOABC and MO-GSA; and than other standard multiobjective algorithms such as NSGA-II and SPEA2. In addition, we have also demonstrated the biological significance of the predictions made by comparing them with those discovered by other well-known biological tools.

As future work we will test the designed approach for solving more complex instances that require more computational resources. In this case, if necessary, we may also incorporate parallelism to speed up its execution time.

References

1. Deb, K., Pratap, A., Agarwal, S., Meyarivan, T.: A fast and elitist multiobjective genetic algorithm: NSGA-II. IEEE Transactions on Evolutionary Computation 6, 182–197 (2002)
2. D'haeseleer, P.: What are DNA sequence motifs? Nature Biotechnology 24(4), 423–425 (2006)
3. Eusuff, M., Lansey, K.: Optimization of water distribution network design using the shuffled frog-leaping algorithm. Journal of Water Resources Planning & Management 129(3), 210–225 (2003)
4. Fogel, G.B., Porto, V.W., Varga, G., Dow, E.R., Craven, A.M., Powers, D.M., Harlow, H.B., Su, E.W., Onyia, J.E., Su, C.: Evolutionary computation for discovery of composite transcription factor binding sites. Nucleic Acids Research 36(21), e142 (2008)
5. Fogel, G.B., Weekes, D.G., Varga, G., Dow, E.R., Harlow, H.B., Onyia, J.E., Su, C.: Discovery of sequence motifs related to coexpression of genes using evolutionary computation. Nucleic Acids Research 32(13), 3826–3835 (2004)
6. González-Álvarez, D.L., Vega-Rodríguez, M.A., Gómez-Pulido, J.A., Sánchez-Pérez, J.M.: Comparing multiobjective swarm intelligence metaheuristics for DNA motif discovery. Engineering Applications of Artificial Intelligence 26(1), 314–326 (2012)
7. Tompa, M., et al.: Assessing computational tools for the discovery of transcription factor binding sites. Nature Biotechnology 23(1), 137–144 (2005)
8. Wingender, E., Dietze, P., Karas, H., Knuppel, R.: TRANSFAC: a database on transcription factors and their DNA binding sites. Nucleic Acids Research 24(1), 238–241 (1996)
9. Zitzler, E., Laumanns, M., Thiele, L.: SPEA2: Improving the strength pareto evolutionary algorithm. Technical report tik-report 103, Swiss Federal Institute of Technology Zurich, Switzerland (2001)

Optimizing the Location Areas Planning in the SUMATRA Network with an Adaptation of the SPEA2 Algorithm

Víctor Berrocal-Plaza*, Miguel A. Vega-Rodríguez, and Juan M. Sánchez-Pérez

Dept. Technologies of Computers & Communications, University of Extremadura
Escuela Politécnica, Campus Universitario S/N, 10003, Cáceres, Spain
{vicberpla,mavega,sanperez,jangomez}@unex.es

Abstract. This paper presents our adaptation of the Strength Pareto Evolutionary Algorithm 2 (SPEA2, a Multi-Objective Evolutionary Algorithm) to optimize the Location Areas Planning Problem. Location Areas is a strategy widely used to manage one of the most important issues of the Public Land Mobile Networks: the mobile location management. In contrast to previous works, we propose a multi-objective approach with the goal of avoiding the drawbacks associated with the linear aggregation of the objective functions. The main advantage of a multi-objective approach is that this kind of algorithm provides a wide range of solutions among which the network operator could select the solution that best adjusts to the network real state at each moment. Furthermore, in order to obtain realistic results, we apply our proposal to the SUMATRA network, a test network that stores real-time information of the users' mobile activity in the San Francisco Bay (USA). Experimental results show that our proposal outperforms the results obtained in other works and, at the same time, it achieves a great spread of solutions.

Keywords: Location Areas Planning Problem, Mobile Location Management, Multi-objective Optimization, Stanford University Mobile Activity Traces, Strength Pareto Evolutionary Algorithm 2.

1 Introduction

The Public Land Mobile Networks (PLMNs) must provide mobile communications to a huge number of subscribers with few radioelectric resources [1]. For it, the desired coverage area is divided into several smaller regions (also known as cells) among which the available resources are distributed and reused. Therefore, any mobile communication network requires of a system for tracking and

* The work of Víctor Berrocal-Plaza has been developed under the Grant FPU-AP2010-5841 from the Spanish Government. This work was partially funded by the Spanish Ministry of Economy and Competitiveness and the ERDF (European Regional Development Fund), under the contract TIN2012-30685 (BIO project).

R. Moreno-Díaz et al. (Eds.): EUROCAST 2013, Part I, LNCS 8111, pp. 243–250, 2013.

locating the subscribers. This system is known as Location Management System and it must control two main tasks: the location update and paging [2]. The Location Update (LU) is used to track the subscriber's movement. This procedure is initiated by the mobile station (MS) according to a predefined method (e.g. distance-based, movement-based, time-based, velocity-based, and zone-based). And the Paging (PA) is used to know the exact cell in which the callee user is located when he/she has an incoming call. This last procedure is initiated by the network and it can be classified into two main groups: probabilistic and non-probabilistic [3]. In this work, we study one of the most used method for managing the location update and the paging: the Location Areas scheme (a zone-based location update) with a probabilistic paging of two sequential cycles in which the cells within the last updated LA are grouped into two paging areas. The first paging area is the last updated cell of the callee subscriber, and the second paging area will be composed by the rest of cells of that LA.

In the literature, this problem is called Location Areas Planning Problem (LAPP) and it has recently been researched with different metaheuristics. P. R. L. Gondim defines in [4] the LAPP as an NP-hard combinatorial optimization problem due to the huge size of the objective space, and he proposes a Genetic Algorithm (GA) for finding quasi-optimal configurations of LAs. P. Demestichas et al. [5] study the LAPP in different environments with three different metaheuristics (Tabu Search (TS), Simulated Annealing (SA), and GA). J. Taheri and A. Y. Zomaya develop four test networks in which the user's call and mobility patterns are similar to those than we can find in current mobile networks. In their works, they propose several optimization algorithms: Hopfield Neural Network (HNN [6]), GA [7], SA [8], and combinations of GA with HNN (GA-HNNs [9]). R. Subrata and A. Y. Zomaya study in [10] the behavior of the Location Management System in the test network developed by the Stanford University (SUMATRA [11]: Stanford University Mobile Activity TRAces) with different location update strategies. This last test network is also studied in [12,13], where S. M. Almeida-Luz et al. implement the algorithms Differential Evolution (DE) and Scatter Search (SS).

It should be noted that in all of these works, the two objective functions of the LAPP are combined into a single objective function with the aim of optimizing this problem with Single-objective Optimization Algorithms (SOA). This allows the use of optimization algorithms with less computational complexity but has several drawbacks. Firstly, a very accurate knowledge of the problem is required to configure the weight coefficient (which is a real number). Secondly, the proper value of the weight coefficient might vary in time due to the dynamic behavior of the signaling network load. And thirdly, a SOA must perform an independent run for each configuration of the weight coefficient.

The main contribution of this work is the adaptation of the Strength Pareto Evolutionary Algorithm 2 (SPEA2, a Multi-Objective Evolutionary Algorithm or MOEA) to optimize the LAPP in the SUMATRA network. By using a Multi-objective Optimization Algorithm (MOA), we obtain a set of solutions among which the network operator could select the one that best meets the real state of the signaling network, and at the same time, we avoid the drawbacks associated with the linear aggregation of the objective functions.

The rest of the paper is organized as follows. Section 2 defines the Location Areas Planning Problem and shows a brief description of the SUMATRA network. Section 3 presents our adaptation of the Strength Pareto Evolutionary Algorithm 2 to optimize the LAPP. Experimental results are discussed in Section 4. Our conclusions and future work are summarized in Section 5.

2   Location Areas Planning Problem

The Location Areas (LAs) scheme is a zone-based strategy which is being widely used in current mobile networks to automatically manage the subscribers' location update. In this strategy, the network is divided into logical areas (or Location Areas) such that every Location Area is a continuous and non-overlapped group of cells. In doing so, the mobile station only updates its location (the cell in which it is currently located) when it moves to a new location area. Moreover, the paging procedure is only performed in the cells within the last updated location area (the network knows the exact location area in which every subscriber is located). Therefore, the main challenge of this strategy is to find the configurations of Location Areas that minimize the number of location updates and the number of paging messages simultaneously.

Note that these two objective functions are conflicting: the number of location updates is reduced to a minimum when all the network cells belong to the same location area (i.e. there is no location update), but in this case the number of paging messages achieves its maximum because the paging procedure must be performed in the whole network whenever a subscriber has an incoming call. And vice versa, the paging cost is minimized when the network knows the exact cell in which every subscriber is located (i.e. when every network cell belongs to a different location area), leading to a maximum location update cost because a location update is performed whenever a subscriber moves to a new cell. Therefore, the Location Areas Planning Problem can be formulated as a multi-objective optimization problem with the following objective functions:

$$f_1 = min\{LU_{cost}\}, LU_{cost} = \sum_{t=T_{ini}}^{T_{fin}} \sum_{i=1}^{N_{user}} \gamma_{t,i}, \qquad (1)$$

$$f_2 = min\{PA_{cost}\}, PA_{cost} = \sum_{t=T_{ini}}^{T_{fin}} \sum_{i=1}^{N_{user}} \rho_{t,i}(\alpha_{t,i} + (1 - \alpha_{t,i})NA[LA_t[i]]). \qquad (2)$$

Equation (1) shows the first objective function: minimize the number of location updates (or location update cost, LU_{cost}). In this equation, $\gamma_{t,i}$ is a binary variable that is equal to 1 when the MS_i moves to a new LA in the time t, otherwise $\gamma_{t,i}$ is equal to 0. N_{user} is the number of mobile subscribers. And $[T_{ini}, T_{fin}]$ is the time interval during which the LU_{cost} and PA_{cost} are calculated. The second objective function is defined in Equation (2). In this last equation, $\rho_{t,i}$ is a binary variable that is equal to 1 when the MS_i has an incoming call in the time t, otherwise $\rho_{t,i}$ is equal to 0. $\alpha_{t,i}$ is a binary variable that is equal to 1 when the MS_i is located in its last updated cell in the time t, otherwise $\alpha_{t,i}$ is equal to 0. NA is a vector in which we store the number of cells of each LA. And LA_t is a vector that stores the LA associated with each user in the time t.

In previous works, these two objective functions are linearly combined (see Equation (3)) with the aim of optimizing the LAPP by using Single-objective Optimization Algorithms (SOAs). However, in this work we propose a multi-objective approach in order to avoid the drawbacks associated with the linear aggregation of the objective functions. This strategy also provides a set of solutions among which the network operator could select the one that best meets the real state of the signaling network at each moment.

$$f^{SOA}(\beta) = \beta f_1 + f_2. \tag{3}$$

2.1   Stanford University Mobile Activity Traces

In this work, we study a realistic mobile network with 90 cells and 66,550 subscribers. This network has a mobile activity trace developed by the Stanford University (Stanford University Mobile Activity TRAces or SUMATRA [11]), which is a chronological list of events that stores the real-time mobile activity of the San Francisco Bay (USA) during 24 hours. The study of this network is very interesting because we can validate the behavior and the quality of our proposal in a realistic mobile environment.

3   Strength Pareto Evolutionary Algorithm 2

The Strength Pareto Evolutionary Algorithm 2 is a population-based meta-heuristic in which the typical operators of biological evolution (recombination of parents or crossover, mutation, and natural selection) are applied iteratively with the aim of improving a set of solutions. This algorithm is proposed by E. Zitzler et al. in [14]. Basically, SPEA2 is an elitist genetic algorithm with an archive of configurable size in which the best solutions found so far are stored.

Fig. 1 shows the task decomposition of SPEA2. As we can see, the first operation is to initialize and evaluate the population (a detailed explanation of the individual initialization is discussed in Section 3.1). And then, an iterative method is applied until the stop condition is reached. In this work, we use the same stop condition as in [12,13]: the *maximum number of generations*. The first operation of this iterative method is the crossover or recombination of parents. By using this operation (see Section 3.2), a new population of offspring is generated from the parent population (stored in the archive). Secondly, the mutation operation is applied with the aim of exploring unknown zones of the objective space (see Section 3.3). After these two evolutionary operators, a chromosomal repair function is always applied to transform invalid solutions into feasible solutions. Finally, we use the natural selection to store the fittest individuals (solutions) in the

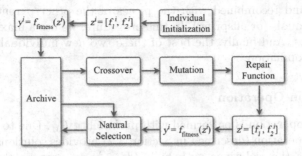

Fig. 1. Task decomposition of SPEA2

archive, where the best individuals are those that minimize the fitness function. This algorithm defines a fitness function with two main terms: the raw fitness and the density estimation (see Equation (4), where P_t and P_t^{arch} are the set of solutions stored in the population and in the archive in the time t). The raw fitness of a solution or objective vector z^i is defined as the sum of "strengths" of its dominating solutions ($z^j \prec z^i$), where the "strength" of a solution z^j ($S(z^j)$) is defined as the number of its dominated solutions. Note that the objective vector z^i is the vector that stores the values of the objective functions of the solution i, and that the solution or objective vector z^j is said to dominates the solution or objective vector z^i when $\forall n \in N = \{1,2\}, z_n^j \leq z_n^i \wedge \exists n \in N : z_n^j < z_n^i$. On the other hand, the density estimation associated with the solution z^i is calculated by means of the Euclidean distance between z^i and its k-th nearest objective vector ($d(z^i, z^k)$), where k is equal to the square root of the sum of the archive and population sizes.

$$f_{fitness}(z^i) = (2 + d(z^i, z^k))^{-1} + \sum_{j \in P_t + P_t^{arch}, z^j \prec z^i} S(z^j). \tag{4}$$

3.1 Individual Initialization

In this work, every individual of the population is a vector that stores the LA associated with each network cell. Therefore, in order to obtain the first population, every vector is filled with a random pattern of 0s and 1s. And then this random pattern is used to determine the configuration of LAs: every LA is composed by a continuous and non-overlapped group of network cells with the same value of vector.

3.2 Crossover Operation

The crossover operation is performed with probability P_C. In this paper, we have defined an elitist crossover with four main steps. Firstly, four individuals grouped in pairs are randomly selected. Secondly, we use elitism to select the two parents (i.e. each parent is the best individual of each group). Thirdly, each parent is

cut in pieces and recombined with the pieces of the other parent to generate
two new individuals (or offspring). In this procedure, we use a maximum of four
crossover points. And finally, the best of these two new individuals is stored in
the offspring population.

3.3 Mutation Operation

The mutation operation is performed with probability P_M. Due to the fact that
the crossover operation (described in Section 3.2) provides solutions with a high
number of LAs (i.e. solutions with high LU_{cost}), we propose the use of two
mutation operations that allow us to explore regions of the objective space with
high PA_{cost} (i.e. solutions with less number of LAs). The first mutation operation
is called *Gene Mutation*, and it consists in merging a boundary cell (a cell which
is border among two or more LAs) with its neighboring LA of lower size (in
terms of number of network cells). And the second mutation operation is called
Merge-LA Mutation. In this last operation, we merge the smallest LA with its
neighboring LA of lower size.

4   Experimental Results

With the aim of knowing the behavior and the quality of our proposal in a realistic environment, we study the test network developed by the Stanford University
(SUMATRA [11]). This test network is a trace that stores the real-time mobile
activity of the San Francisco Bay (USA) during 24 hours. Furthermore, we compare our results with those obtained by other authors, who propose the use of
the linear aggregation of the objective functions with the purpose of optimizing
the LAPP with Single-objective Optimization Algorithms (SOAs): Differential
Evolution (DE) [12] and Scatter Search (SS) [13]. For it, we must search in our
set of non-dominated solutions (also known as *Pareto front*) the one that best
fits the objective function used in [12,13], which is the Equation (3) with β equal
to 10 (this solution is represented by an open dot in Fig. 2.a). And then, we compare this solution with the best solution achieved by the DE [12] and the SS [13]
(see Fig. 2.b).

   In order to perform a fair comparison, we use the same population size
($N_{POP} = 300$) and the same stop condition (*Maximum Number of Generations*
$= 1000$) as in [12,13]. The other parameters of SPEA2 have been configured
by means of a parametric study of 31 independent runs per experiment. The
parameter configuration that achieves the highest *Hypervolume* (I_H) value is:
$P_C = 0.90$, $P_M = 0.26$, and $N_{arch} = 300$. The I_H is a multi-objective indicator which is used to know the quality of a multi-objective algorithm [15]. If
we assume a multi-objective optimization problem with two objective functions,
the I_H indicator measures the area of the objective space that is dominated
by the *Pareto front* and is bounded by the reference points, where the reference points are calculated by means of the solutions with the maximum and
minimum values of each objective function. Furthermore, we have calculated

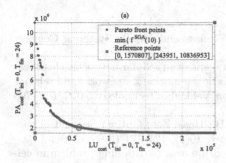 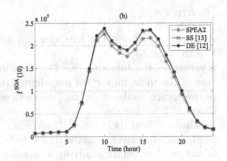

Fig. 2. Experimental results: (a) Median *Pareto front*. (b) Comparison between the solution associated with the open dot of Fig. 2.a with the best solution found in [12, 13]

statistical data of the I_H (of 31 independent runs): $median(I_H(\%)) = 92.96\%$ and $iqr(I_H(\%)) = 0.36\%$. Fig. 2 shows a graphic representation of our *Pareto front* with the median I_H (Fig. 2.a), and a comparison with the best results obtained in [12,13] (Fig. 2.b). As we can see in this figure, our algorithm achieves a great spread of the *Pareto front* and finds at least one solution that outperforms the best results obtained by the DE [12] and the SS [13] in the hours with higher mobile activity (8:00h-20:00h), which is far from trivial because we compare a multi-objective approach with algorithms specializing in finding only one solution. Numerical results of the Fig.2.b are: $\sum_{t=0h}^{t=24h} f^{SOA}(10) = 2{,}619{,}519$ (SPEA2), 2,756,836 (SS [13]), and 2,799,289 (DE [12]).

5   Conclusions and Future Work

This paper presents our adaptation of the Strength Pareto Evolutionary Algorithm 2 (SPEA2) to optimize the Location Areas Planning Problem in a realistic mobile network (SUMATRA [11], a test network that stores the real-time mobile activity of the San Francisco Bay (USA) during 24 hours). Owing to the fact that there is no other authors that address this problem with a multi-objective approach, we must compare with Single-objective Optimization Algorithms (SOAs). Applying a multi-objective optimization strategy in this problem is very interesting due to the dynamic behavior of the network load. With a multi-objective optimization algorithm, we obtain a wide set of solutions among which the network operator could select the one that best meets the real state of the signaling network at each moment. Results show that our proposal achieves a great spread of the *Pareto front*, and it outperforms the best solution found by the SOAs proposed in [12,13], which is far from trivial because we compare with algorithms specializing in finding only one solution.

   In a future work, we propose the study of the LAPP with other multi-objective optimization algorithms. Furthermore, it could be a good challenge to optimize the LAPP with different paging procedures.

References

1. Agrawal, D., Zeng, Q.: Introduction to Wireless and Mobile Systems. Cengage Learning (2010)
2. Kyamakya, K., Jobmann, K.: Location management in cellular networks: classification of the most important paradigms, realistic simulation framework, and relative performance analysis. IEEE Transactions on Vehicular Technology 54(2), 687–708 (2005)
3. Krishnamachari, B., Gau, R.H., Wicker, S.B., Haas, Z.J.: Optimal sequential paging in cellular wireless networks. Wirel. Netw. 10(2), 121–131 (2004)
4. Gondim, P.: Genetic algorithms and the location area partitioning problem in cellular networks. In: Procedings of the IEEE 46th Vehicular Technology Conference on Mobile Technology for the Human Race, vol. 3, pp. 1835–1838 (1996)
5. Demestichas, P., Georgantas, N., Tzifa, E., Demesticha, V., Striki, M., Kilanioti, M., Theologou, M.E.: Computationally efficient algorithms for location area planning in future cellular systems. Computer Communications 23(13), 1263–1280 (2000)
6. Taheri, J., Zomaya, A.Y.: The use of a hopfield neural network in solving the mobility management problem. In: Proceedings of the IEEE/ACS International Conference on Pervasive Services, pp. 141–150 (2004)
7. Taheri, J., Zomaya, A.Y.: A genetic algorithm for finding optimal location area configurations for mobility management. In: The IEEE Conference on Local Computer Networks 30th Anniversary, pp. 568–577 (2005)
8. Taheri, J., Zomaya, A.Y.: A simulated annealing approach for mobile location management. In: Proceedings of the 19th IEEE International Parallel and Distributed Processing Symposium, p. 194 (2005)
9. Taheri, J., Zomaya, A.Y.: A combined genetic-neural algorithm for mobility management. J. Math. Model. Algorithms, 481–507 (2007)
10. Subrata, R., Zomaya, A.Y.: Dynamic location management for mobile computing. Telecommunication Systems 22(1-4), 169–187 (2003)
11. Stanford University Mobile Activity TRAces (SUMATRA), http://infolab.stanford.edu/sumatra (accessed in 2013)
12. Almeida-Luz, S., Vega-Rodríguez, M.A., Gómez-Pulido, J.A., Sánchez-Pérez, J.M.: Applying differential evolution to a realistic location area problem using sumatra. In: Proceedings of the Second International Conference on Advanced Engineering Computing and Applications in Sciences, ADVCOMP 2008, pp. 170–175. IEEE Computer Society, Washington, DC (2008)
13. Almeida-Luz, S.M., Vega-Rodríguez, M.A., Gómez-Pulido, J.A., Sánchez-Pérez, J.M.: Solving a realistic location area problem using sumatra networks with the scatter search algorithm. In: Proceedings of the Ninth International Conference on Intelligent Systems Design and Applications, ISDA 2009, pp. 689–694. IEEE Computer Society, Washington, DC (2009)
14. Zitzler, E., Laumanns, M., Thiele, L.: SPEA2: Improving the strength pareto evolutionary algorithm for multiobjective optimization. In: Giannakoglou, K.C., Tsahalis, D.T., Périaux, J., Papailiou, K.D., Fogarty, T. (eds.) Evolutionary Methods for Design Optimization and Control with Applications to Industrial Problems, Athens, Greece, pp. 95–100. International Center for Numerical Methods in Engineering (2001)
15. Coello, C.A.C., Lamont, G.B., Veldhuizen, D.A.V.: Evolutionary Algorithms for Solving Multi-Objective Problems (Genetic and Evolutionary Computation). Springer-Verlag New York, Inc., Secaucus (2006)

Efficient Multi-Objective Optimization Using 2-Population Cooperative Coevolution⋆

Alexandru-Ciprian Zăvoianu[1,3], Edwin Lughofer[1],
Wolfgang Amrhein[2,3], and Erich Peter Klement[1,3]

[1] Department of Knowledge-based Mathematical Systems/Fuzzy Logic Laboratory
Linz-Hagenberg, Johannes Kepler University of Linz, Austria
[2] Institute for Electrical Drives and Power Electronics,
Johannes Kepler University of Linz, Austria
[3] ACCM, Austrian Center of Competence in Mechatronics, Linz, Austria

Abstract. We propose a 2-population cooperative coevolutionary optimization method that can efficiently solve multi-objective optimization problems as it successfully combines positive traits from classic multi-objective evolutionary algorithms and from newer optimization approaches that explore the concept of differential evolution. A key part of the algorithm lies in the proposed dual fitness sharing mechanism that is able to smoothly transfer information between the two coevolved populations without negatively impacting the independent evolutionary process behavior that characterizes each population.

Keywords: continuous multi-objective optimization, evolutionary algorithms, cooperative coevolution, differential evolution.

1 Introduction and State-of-the-Art

Part of our general research tasks are aimed at optimizing design parameters of electrical drives and deal with highly-dimensional multiple-objective optimization problems (MOOPs) that also display very lengthy run-times [17]. This is because our optimization scenarios require time-intensive design (fitness) evaluation functions that are based on finite element simulations. As such, having a robust and generally efficient (in number of required fitness evaluations) optimization algorithm is very important as it would significantly reduce the optimization run-times.

Like most MOOPs, the problems that we deal with rarely have a single solution and solving them means finding (an approximation of) a set of non-dominated solutions called the *Pareto-optimal set* [1]. Because of their inherent

---

⋆ This work was conducted in the frame of the research program at the Austrian Center of Competence in Mechatronics (ACCM), a part of the COMET K2 program of the Austrian government. The work-related projects are kindly supported by the Austrian government, the Upper Austrian government and the Johannes Kepler University Linz. The authors thank all involved partners for their support. This publication reflects only the authors' views.

R. Moreno-Díaz et al. (Eds.): EUROCAST 2013, Part I, LNCS 8111, pp. 251–258, 2013.

ability to produce complete Pareto-optimal sets over single runs, multi-objective evolutionary algorithms (MOEAs) have emerged as one of the most successful soft computing techniques for solving MOOPs [1].

Among the early MOEAs, NSGA-II [3] and SPEA2 [16] proved to be quite effective and are still widely used in various application domains. At a high level of abstraction, both algorithms can be seen as MOOP orientated implementations of the same paradigm: *the $(\mu + \lambda)$ evolutionary strategy*. Moreover, both algorithms are highly elitist and use a two-tier selection for survival function based on Pareto and crowding indices. Canonically, both algorithms also use the same classic evolutionary operators: SBX crossover operator [2] and polynomial mutation [5];

More modern MOEAs (e.g., DEMO [13] and GDE [8]) wanted to exploit the very good performance exhibited by differential evolution (DE) operators [12] and replaced the SBX and polynomial mutation operators with various DE variants. Convergence benchmark tests [13] [9] show that differential evolution can help MOEAs to explore the decision space far more efficiently for several classes of MOOPs. Also, DE-based algorithms seem to be quite stable, as premature convergence can usually be avoided by choosing a good parameterization that stimulates a minor increase in population diversity [14].

For some problems though, MOEAs that use the SBX and polynomial mutation operators still significantly outperform DE-based algorithms. SBX and polynomial mutation also seem to be quite robust with regards to their parameterization as standard values are able to produce good results on a wide range of test problems.

In the next sections of this paper we shall describe our attempt to efficiently combine the two different search paradigms in order to obtain a hybrid optimization method that retains to a good extent all of the above described positive traits: efficient exploration of the search space, stability with regards to premature convergence, and robustness to parameterization.

2   Our Approach

In order to achieve our goal and create an optimization method that has the robustness of classic MOEA algorithms and also profits from the very good performance exhibited by DE operators, we use coevolution. More precisely, we apply 2-population cooperative coevolution where the first population, P, is evolved using the SPEA2 model, while the second population, Q, uses the DEMO/GDE3 evolutionary model coupled with a survival strategy based on *environmental selection* [16]. The general state of our differential evolution-based, coevolutionary multi-objective optimization algorithm (**DECMO**) at a given generation is obtained by constructing $A = P \cup Q$.

Unsurprisingly, empirical results have shown that the way in which fitness is shared among the two coevolved populations has a crucial impact on the overall success of the method. We obtained the most stable behavior and the best results when using a dual fitness sharing mechanism based on the interleave between,

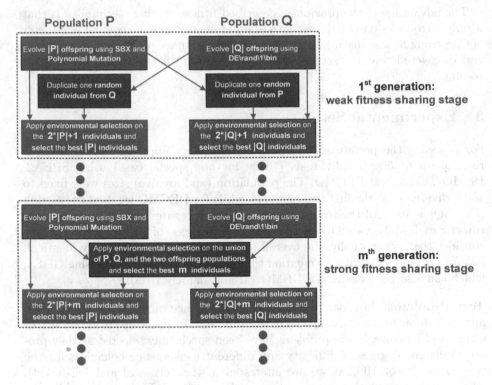

Fig. 1. Diagram of the proposed fitness sharing mechanism

generational, *weak sharing* stages and, fixed interval, *strong sharing* stages. As shown in Figure 1, the weak fitness sharing stage consists of trying to insert in each population one random offspring generated from the complementary population. In the strong sharing stage, which takes place every m generations, an elite subset is constructed by performing the union of A with the two offspring populations and extracting, via environmental selection, the best m individuals. Afterwards, environmental selection is again applied in an attempt to reintroduce (some of) these elite individuals in populations P and Q.

We make extensive use of the environmental selection operator because it inherently has two features that are, by default, beneficial to a coevolutionary process:

- a primary Pareto-based selection criterion - acts both as an inter and intra population fitness indicator
- a secondary crowding-based filtering mechanism - helps to preserve population diversity.

The above two features also characterize the non-dominated sorting [3] survival strategy proposed with NSGA-II. Choosing one method over the other for our initial DECMO prototype was simply a matter of personal preference on behalf of the authors.

The advantage of the previously described fitness sharing mechanism is that it only introduces one extra configuration parameter: m - the control parameter of the strong fitness sharing stage. Furthermore, we have performed several tests and discovered that the setting $m = (|P| + |Q|)/20$ is stable and yields good results.

3   Experimental Setup

For assessing the performance of our coevolutionary approach, we have made runs of up to 50000 individuals (75000 for one special case) using SPEA2, DEMO/DGE3, and DECMO. The population (and archive) sizes were fixed to 200 individuals for the first two methods, while for DECMO we used the setting $|P| = |Q| = 100$. All the results we report are aggregated from 50 independent runs for each MOEA - MOOP combination. In the case of DEMO and GDE3 we consider that conceptually, the overall evolutionary process is nearly identical, but for the sake of clarity we mention that we performed the tests using GDE3, which can also be considered a DEMO variant, namely $DEMO^{NS-II}$.

Test Problems. In order to assess the performance of the three MOEAs we apply them on 10 standard, artificial, test problems from the evolutionary multi-objective literature. These problems have been specifically selected as they propose different degrees of difficulty and different convergence behaviors for the two categories of MOEAs we are interested in (i.e., classical and DE-based). The first five problems we use are selected from the DTLZ set [4], while the other five are KSW10 (based on Kursawe's function [10]), LZ09-F1 and LZ09-F2 - part of the LZ09 problem set [11], which is particularly difficult for classic MOEAs, WFG1[7], and ZDT6 - a problem with a non-uniform search space [15].

MOEA Parameterization. We selected the standard parameterization for SPEA2: 0.9 for the crossover probability, 20 for the crossover distribution index, $1/L$ for the mutation probability (where L is the number of variables) and 20 for the mutation distribution index. In the case of DEMO/GDE3, we use a DE/rand/1/bin operator with the settings CR=0.3 and F=0.5 (recommended in [13]). The DE repair strategy we apply replaces any candidate value that is violating a boundary constraint with the boundary value. It should be noted that this particular repair strategy is biased as it offers an advantage in the case of problems where the true Pareto front lies on one of the bounds of the decision space. These settings are also used to parameterize the individual populations P and Q of DECMO. The m-parameter is set, according to the description at the end of Section 2, to a value of 10.

Assessment of Solution Quality. The hypervolume associated with a solution set, has the advantage that it is the only Pareto front quality estimation metric for which there is a theoretical proof [6] of a monotonic behavior. For any optimization problem, the *true Pareto front* has the highest achievable hypervolume value. As for our test problems, where the true Pareto front is known, we assess the performance of a MOEA after a given number of fitness evaluations by reporting the hypervolume of the current population to the hypervolume of the true Pareto front.

4   Results - Comparative Performance

The plots in Figure 2 present the average convergence behavior of the three optimization methods. On all the test problems, DECMO displays a search performance that is similar, or even slightly better, than that of the best performing stand-alone strategy. It is noteworthy to highlight the average performance of DECMO on the LZ09-F1 problem where the coevolutionary approach initially displays the same rapid convergence as SPEA2 but switches to a DEMO/GDE3 convergence behavior as the latter seems to be more efficient in the final stage of the runs.

Table 1. Mean and standard deviation information regarding the number of function evaluations (nfe) required in order to reach a late-stage of convergence. The values are computed by considering only those individual runs that are able to reach a late-stage of convergence. The best result for each problem is highlighted and selected by considering only those MOEAs that are able to achieve a successful run ratio (srr) of 1.0 for that problem.

Problem	SPEA2 nfe μ	σ	srr	GDE3 nfe μ	σ	srr	DECMO nfe μ	σ	srr
DTLZ1	27908	3489.3	1.00	15068	810.8	1.00	12688	983.3	1.00
DTLZ2	7216	735.0	1.00	10348	923.9	1.00	7576	513.7	1.00
DTLZ4	5573	396.8	0.90	6164	337.3	1.00	5626	356.0	1.00
DTLZ6	69578	1712.0	0.94	4884	259.0	1.00	5980	271.8	1.00
DTLZ7	22364	1247.2	1.00	11940	622.4	1.00	13048	769.4	1.00
KSW10	6872	600.4	1.00	12564	735.9	1.00	7576	831.7	1.00
LZ09-F1	12416	2484.2	1.00	16728	930.9	1.00	12184	866.5	1.00
LZ09-F8	-	-	0.00	-	-	0.00	-	-	0.00
WFG1	39720	8289.1	0.40	21012	1131.7	0.98	21596	1669.2	1.00
ZFT6	33416	909.7	1.00	6884	433.5	1.00	7800	557.0	1.00

In [18] it has been argued that after reaching a solution set that accounts for over 85% of the true hypervolume, a MOEA reaches a *late-stage of convergence* where improvements generally come at a greater cost in terms of fitness evaluations. Because we consider that knowing the number of fitness evaluations (nfe) that are required in order to reach such a late-stage of convergence is very helpful in characterizing the search behavior of a multi-objective optimization algorithm, we have also measured this data and present the aggregated values in Table 1.

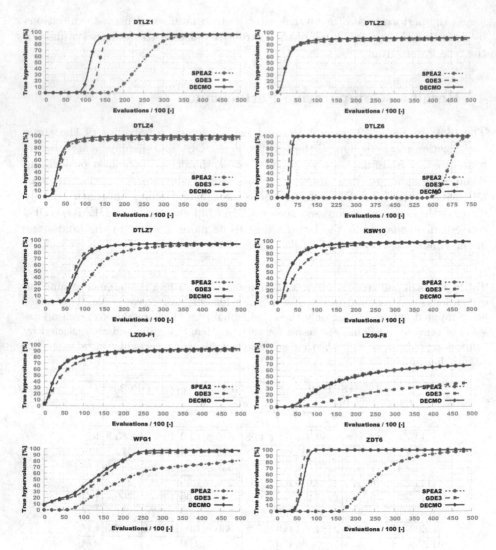

Fig. 2. The convergence behavior of the three MOEAs averaged over 50 runs

The results from Table 1 further underline the tendency that DECMO has to replicate the search behavior of the most successful strategy. This seems to be the case even on problems where both search strategies are having difficulties (e.g., LZ09-F8 and WFG1) as all or some of the runs are unable to reach a late-stage of convergence (i.e., srr < 1.0). For every test problem except LZ09-F1 (SPEA2 vs. DECMO), the observed differences between the performance of the MOEAs that were able to achieve a successful run ratio (srr) of 1.0 are also statistically significant (one-sided Mann-Whitney-Wilcoxon test with a considered significance level of 0.05).

5 Conclusions and Future Work

The results we obtained on 10 benchmark MOOPs indicate that coevolution is quite successful at its aim of constructing a robust average between SBX and DE based methods when using an appropriate fitness sharing mechanism. Furthermore, in general, this combination of two different evolutionary search paradigms also seems to be quite stable and efficient as it is able to perform very well on different optimization scenarios.

Future work will revolve around studying in more depth the qualitative differences between the two coevolved populations and how to use this information in order to improve the overall optimization method. We also plan to develop a steady state asynchronous version of DECMO and to test the performance of the algorithm on MOOPs from the field of electrical drive design.

References

1. Coello, C., Lamont, G., Van Veldhuisen, D.: Evolutionary Algorithms for Solving Multi-Objective Problems. Genetic and Evolutionary Computation Series. Springer (2007)
2. Deb, K., Agrawal, R.B.: Simulated binary crossover for continuous search space. Complex Systems 9, 115–148 (1995)
3. Deb, K., Pratap, A., Agarwal, S., Meyarivan, T.: A fast and elitist multiobjective genetic algorithm: NSGA-II. IEEE Transactions on Evolutionary Computation 6(2), 182–197 (2002)
4. Deb, K., Thiele, L., Laumanns, M., Zitzler, E.: Scalable multi-objective optimization test problems. In: IEEE Congress on Evolutionary Computation (CEC 2002), pp. 825–830. IEEE Press (2002)
5. Deb, K., Goyal, M.: A combined genetic adaptive search (geneas) for engineering design. Computer Science and Informatics 26, 30–45 (1996)
6. Fleischer, M.: The measure of Pareto optima. applications to multi-objective meta-heuristics. In: Fonseca, C.M., Fleming, P.J., Zitzler, E., Deb, K., Thiele, L. (eds.) EMO 2003. LNCS, vol. 2632, pp. 519–533. Springer, Heidelberg (2003)
7. Huband, S., Hingston, P., Barone, L., While, L.: A review of multiobjective test problems and a scalable test problem toolkit. IEEE Transactions on Evolutionary Computation 10(5), 477–506 (2006)
8. Kukkonen, S., Lampinen, J.: GDE3: The third evolution step of generalized differential evolution. In: IEEE Congress on Evolutionary Computation (CEC 2005), pp. 443–450. IEEE Press (2005)
9. Kukkonen, S., Lampinen, J.: Performance assessment of Generalized Differential Evolution 3 with a given set of constrained multi-objective test problems. In: IEEE Congress on Evolutionary Computation (CEC 2009), pp. 1943–1950. IEEE Press (2009)
10. Kursawe, F.: A variant of evolution strategies for vector optimization. In: Schwefel, H.-P., Männer, R. (eds.) PPSN 1990. LNCS, vol. 496, pp. 193–197. Springer, Heidelberg (1991)
11. Li, H., Zhang, Q.: Multiobjective optimization problems with complicated Pareto sets, MOEA/D and NSGA-II. IEEE Transactions on Evolutionary Computation 13(2), 284–302 (2009)

12. Price, K., Storn, R., Lampinen, J.: Differential evolution. Springer (1997)
13. Robič, T., Filipič, B.: DEMO: Differential evolution for multiobjective optimization. In: Coello Coello, C.A., Hernández Aguirre, A., Zitzler, E. (eds.) EMO 2005. LNCS, vol. 3410, pp. 520–533. Springer, Heidelberg (2005)
14. Zaharie, D.: A comparative analysis of crossover variants in differential evolution. In: Proceedings of the International Multiconference on Computer Science and Information Technology, IMCSIT 2007, pp. 171–181. PTI, Wisla (2007)
15. Zitzler, E., Deb, K., Thiele, L.: Comparison of multiobjective evolutionary algorithms: Empirical results. Evolutionary Computation 8(2), 173–195 (2000)
16. Zitzler, E., Laumanns, M., Thiele, L.: SPEA2: Improving the strength Pareto evolutionary algorithm for multiobjective optimization. In: Evolutionary Methods for Design, Optimisation and Control with Application to Industrial Problems (EUROGEN 2001), pp. 95–100. International Center for Numerical Methods in Engineering (CIMNE) (2002)
17. Zăvoianu, A.-C., Bramerdorfer, G., Lughofer, E., Silber, S., Amrhein, W., Klement, E.P.: A hybrid soft computing approach for optimizing design parameters of electrical drives. In: Snasel, V., Abraham, A., Corchado, E.S. (eds.) SOCO Models in Industrial & Environmental Appl. AISC, vol. 188, pp. 347–358. Springer, Heidelberg (2013)
18. Zăvoianu, A.C., Lughofer, E., Koppelstätter, W., Weidenholzer, G., Amrhein, W., Klement, E.P.: On the performance of master-slave parallelization methods for multi-objective evolutionary algorithms. In: Rutkowski, L., Korytkowski, M., Scherer, R., Tadeusiewicz, R., Zadeh, L.A., Zurada, J.M. (eds.) ICAISC 2013, Part II. LNCS, vol. 7895, pp. 122–134. Springer, Heidelberg (2013)

Solving a Vehicle Routing Problem with Ant Colony Optimisation and Stochastic Ranking

Alexander Hämmerle and Martin Ankerl

Profactor GmbH
Im Stadtgut A2, 4407 Steyr-Gleink, Austria
{alexander.haemmerle,martin.ankerl}@profactor.at

Abstract. In our contribution we are concerned with a real-world vehicle routing problem (VRP), showing characteristics of VRP with time
windows, multiple depots and site dependencies. An analysis of transport
request data reveals that the problem is over-constrained with respect
to time constraints, i.e. maximum route durations and time windows for
delivery at customer sites. Our results show that ant colony optimisation combined with stochastic ranking provides appropriate means to
deal with the over-constrained problem. An essential point in our investigations was the development of problem-specific heuristics, guiding
ants in the construction of solutions. Computational results show that
the combination of a refined distance heuristic, taking into account the
distances between customer sites when performing pickup operations at
depots, and a look-ahead heuristic, estimating the violation of maximum
route durations and delivery time windows when performing pickup operations, provides the best results for the VRP under consideration.

Keywords: logistics, heuristics, routing, ant colony optimisation, constraint satisfaction.

1 Introduction

In their daily business, forwarding companies are confronted with the necessity
to minimise transport cost. Capacity utilisation of vehicles has to be maximised,
while total travel times have to be minimised. The real-world problems can
be abstracted into vehicle routing problems (VRPs), providing the models to
study the efficiency of optimisation algorithms. In its basic variant the VRP is
concerned with assigning transport requests to a homogeneous fleet of vehicles
starting from a single depot and to construct optimal routes for these vehicles.
The introduction of constraints gives rise to a whole family of VRP variants,
considering vehicle capacities, time windows for deliveries, multiple depots, site
dependencies etc. In this paper we are concerned with a real-world VRP, showing characteristics of three general types of vehicle routing problems as classified
by [8]: vehicle routing problem with time windows (VRPTW), multi-depot vehicle routing problem (MDVRP) and side dependent vehicle routing problem
(SDVRP). In the VRPTW, time windows are assigned to customer sites, con-
straining the possible delivery dates. In the MDVRP, vehicles start their routes

R. Moreno-Díaz et al. (Eds.): EUROCAST 2013, Part I, LNCS 8111, pp. 259–266, 2013.

from multiple depots, and SDVRP imposes constraints on the accessibility of customer sites - a customer site requires specific vehicle types and excludes others. All of these VRP variants consider vehicle capacities. The vehicle routing problem with multiple depots and time windows MDVRPTW has been tackled by [2,9,4]. To the best of our knowledge there is no existing research paper on MDVRPTW with site dependencies.

In order to solve real-world VRPs, a variety of metaheuristic approaches have been proposed, amongst them ant colony optimisation (ACO). In a number of research publications ACO showed good performance when applied to large-scale and real-world instances. [3] used a multi ants colony system to solve time dependent VRP and tested their algorithm on a real-world case. [10] enhanced a savings based ant system by decomposing the VRP into smaller sub-problems. [11] investigated into the application of ACO to real-world VRP instances exhibiting characteristics of VRP with time windows, time dependent VRP, dynamic VRP and VRP with pickup and delivery. They conclude that "... ACO has been shown to be one of the most successful metaheuristics for the VRP and its application to real-world problems demonstrates that it has now become a fundamental tool in applied operations research."

Real-world VRP are characterised by a considerable amount of constraints that have to be observed during vehicle routing optimisation. Therefore, ACO has been integrated with several constraint handling mechanisms, amongst them constraint programming and penalty-based techniques. Of particular interest is the approach presented by [7] and [5] where ACO has been combined with stochastic ranking, a constraint handling mechanism originally proposed by [12]. In stochastic ranking a stochastic bubble sort algorithm ranks solutions according to their objective value or their amount of constraint violation, respectively. Top ranked solutions, including feasible and infeasible solutions, pass information to the next iteration (via pheromones in the case of ACO). [7] used ACO in combination with stochastic ranking to solve single machine job scheduling problems. Despite its low computational complexity stochastic ranking showed good performance when applied to weakly or moderately constrained problems.

In this paper we use an ACO algorithm integrated with stochastic ranking in order to solve a real-world VRP. To the best of our knowledge the application of ACO combined with stochastic ranking to VRP has not been reported before. The remainder of this paper is structured as follows. In section 2 we describe the real-world VRP under consideration. Our problem solving approach is outlined in section 3. In section 4 we discuss computational results, pointing out the importance of strong, problem-specific heuristics guiding the ACO algorithm in the construction of solutions. Our conclusions are presented in section 5.

2   Problem Description

Throughout the paper we discuss a particular real-world VRP instance, where 398 customers have to be supplied from two depots. The optimisation objective is the minimisation of travel times. We investigate a static planning problem with single day planning horizons, i.e. at the time of optimisation all transport requests to be scheduled for the next day are known in advance. Each customer may request several shipments per day. In the considered problem instance we are dealing with 789 transport requests. A fleet of 265 vehicles is available to supply the customers. The fleet is inhomogeneous: four types of vehicle are available, with many different vehicle capacities within each type. Each vehicle is assigned to a depot, at the beginning and at the end of a route the vehicle has to be located at its depot.

2.1 Data Model

In the following we describe the core entities making up the data model for our VRP instance. A *vehicle* is characterised through its type, capacity (measured in pallet spaces), a list of up to 3 shifts and the distance matrix relevant for the vehicle. Examples for vehicle types are semitrailer or road train. A shift is specified through an origin (the site where the vehicle starts its shift), a destination (the site where the vehicle has to be at the end of the shift), a shift start time and a shift end time. In the considered problem instance the origin as well as the destination of a shift is the depot where the vehicle is assigned to. Each entry in a distance matrix specifies the travel time between a pair of sites. We are using two different distance matrices, reflecting vehicle type specific travel times.

A *customer site* or *depot* is characterised through its geographic coordinates, up to 2 time windows, a service time and a list of supported vehicle types. Time windows specify the opening hours of a site, whereas the service time defines the average time required for a loading/unloading operation. The list of supported vehicle types specifies which vehicle types are able to access the site for loading/unloading operations. Finally a *transport request* is characterised through an origin, a destination and the amount of pallet spaces the load requires.

2.2 Constraints

Four types of constraints narrow the space of feasible solutions: (1) Loading/unloading operations should not be performed outside of specified time windows, (2) vehicle shifts limit the maximum duration of routes, (3) the supported vehicle types of a customer site / depot impose site dependency constraints on vehicles and (4) the total load of a vehicle must not exceed its capacity.

An analysis of transport request data reveals that the problem is over-constrained. We looked at the duration of transport for individual requests, i.e. the travel time from depot to customer site and back to the depot, plus service times for loading at depot and unloading at customer site. By comparing transport times with duration of vehicle shifts we noticed that in the worst case 146 transport requests cannot be fulfilled without violation of shift constraints. Worst case means that only vehicles using the distance matrix with longer travel times are used to fulfil requests with long transport times. In the best case 108 transport requests violate shift constraints, employing as much as possible vehicles using the distance matrix with shorter travel times.

3 Solving the Vehicle Routing Problem

3.1 Solution Construction

ACO algorithms are constructive solution methods, where a number of artificial ants move through a construction graph, that represents a particular problem. In our application a vertex in the construction graph corresponds to a logical customer site or to a logical depot. A logical depot represents the pickup location of a specific transport request, the origin of a vehicle's shift or the destination of a vehicle's shift. Examples: two requests with pickup at the same physical depot result in two different logical depots. Two vehicles with a single shift and shift origins / destinations at the same physical depot give rise to four different logical depots, two for shift origins and two for shift destinations. Due to the fact that customers may request multiple transports we had to introduce logical customer sites, one for each request. Example: a physical customer site requests three transports, resulting in three logical customer sites with the same geographic coordinates. With the above definition of a vertex in the construction graph at hand, a solution generated by an ant corresponds to a path through the construction graph connecting all vertices.

Ants generate solutions iteratively by following artificial pheromone trails through the construction graph. At each iteration, ants re-enforce "good solutions" (according to an objective function) with additional pheromone deposits, thus increasing the probability for segments of good solutions to be re-used in subsequent iterations. However, it is not just pheromone trails that guide ants during the construction of solutions. A problem-specific heuristic function also influences the choices made by ants. Such a heuristic is especially important in early iterations, when sufficient pheromone information is not yet available. The importance of pheromones and heuristics is expressed in equation 1, describing an ant's probability to move from vertex i to vertex j in the construction graph.

$$p_{i,j} = \frac{\tau_{i,j}^{\alpha} \cdot \eta_{i,j}^{\beta}}{\sum_{k \in N_i} \tau_{i,k}^{\alpha} \cdot \eta_{i,k}^{\beta}} \tag{1}$$

In equation 1, $\tau_{i,j}$ denotes the pheromone value on the edge from vertex i to vertex j, and $\eta_{i,j}$ is the heuristic value associated with the move from vertex i to vertex j. The parameters α and β are weights for the influence of pheromones and heuristic values. The neighbourhood of vertex i, i.e. all vertices reachable with a single move, is denoted by N_i.

Our ACO implementation is based on the MAX-MIN ant system originally proposed by [13]. To avoid pre-mature convergence of search the MAX-MIN algorithm introduces upper and lower boundaries on pheromone values, thus limiting differences in pheromone trail intensities. We modified the MAX-MIN algorithm with adaptive values for α and β, resulting in faster convergence and better solution qualities [1]. Solution construction in ACO algorithms conceptually supports concurrent computation, with ants determining solutions in parallel. We have exploited this feature with the implementation of a concurrency mechanism, based on the Reduction design pattern described in [6].

3.2   Heuristics

To study the influence of different heuristics on solution quality and convergence we have implemented the following standard heuristics: tightest time window, earliest due date, earliest start time and shortest distance (travel time). Applying these heuristics or combinations thereof to the problem specified in section 2 we noticed that the results are not very satisfactory, as the standard heuristics are not able to ensure that transport requests with deliveries to customer sites in close proximity to each other are grouped together in as few routes as possible. This is achieved with a *refined distance heuristic*, considering the travel time between customer sites when evaluating pickups at depots.

Time windows at customer sites and vehicle shifts constrain the space of feasible solutions. An efficient heuristic should consider these time constraints when guiding ants in the construction of solutions. Pickup operations are of particular interest, as they increase the vehicle's workload. We have implemented a *look-ahead heuristic* for the evaluation of pickup operations, estimating the time of arrival at the shift destination and calculating the violation of time constraints. Due to the over-constrained nature of the problem we had to introduce a tolerance with respect to delays. A move whose look-ahead return value exceeds the tolerance is discarded as infeasible.

3.3   Stochastic Ranking of Solutions

In stochastic ranking, the evaluation of a solution s generated by an ant takes into account the objective function $O(s)$ and the amount of constraint violation of s. After each iteration, the solutions constructed by the ants in the iteration are added to a fixed size ranking list. A stochastic bubble sort algorithm sorts the ranking list, where a probability parameter P_f denotes the probability for a pair of solutions to be compared according to their objective values, cf. [7,12]. Hence with probability $1 - P_f$ the pair of solutions is compared according to their respective amount of constraint violation. After the ranking procedure the list is pruned, i.e. all solutions with a rank higher than the size of the list are removed. The remaining solutions in the list will deposit pheromones, influencing ants' decisions in future iterations. The amount of a pheromone deposit is given by equation 2, with L denoting the size of the ranking list.

$$\Delta\tau_{i,j} = 1/\left(L \cdot O(s)\right) \; if(i,j) \in s; \; 0 \, otherwise \tag{2}$$

4   Discussion of Computational Results

Two questions were guiding our computational experiments. (1) What is the influence of different heuristics on algorithm performance, and (2) what is the relationship between solution quality and computation time. All experiments used the problem instance described in section 2 and they were performed on an Intel Core Duo CPU with 1.99 GHz running under Windows XP. The parameter P_f was set to 0.4, as this value yielded the best results.

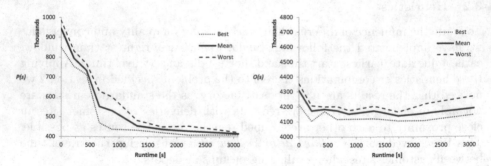

Fig. 1. Runtime performance for solutions with globally best $P(s)$ and $O(s)$ with look-ahead and refined distance heuristic. Look-ahead tolerance set to 5400 s.

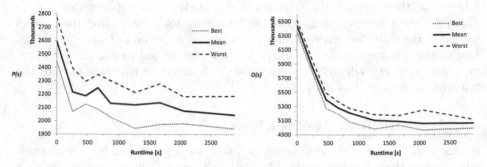

Fig. 2. Runtime performance for solutions with globally best $P(s)$ and $O(s)$ .with look-ahead and simple distance heuristic. Look-ahead tolerance set to 5400 s.

To examine the runtime performance all experiments were carried out with the following numbers of iterations: 1, 50, 100, 150, 200, 300, 400, 500 and 700. Solutions found in the first iteration are especially interesting, as the quality of these solutions solely depends on the chosen heuristics. For each number of iterations we performed 5 independent runs, calculating mean values as well as worst/best values for globally best $O(s)$ and $P(s)$, where $P(s)$ denotes the amount of constraint violation for solution s. Figure 1 reports the results for the best heuristics we have found, namely a combination of look-ahead and refined distance heuristic. The look-ahead tolerance was set to 5400 s, yielding the best results for our problem instance. We notice a strong reduction in constraint violation with increasing runtime, whereas the objective function does not show such a reduction.

Figure 2 shows a different picture. It depicts results obtained with a combination of look-ahead (tolerance set to 5400 s) and a simple distance heuristic with $\eta_{i,j} = 1/t_{i,j}$, where $t_{i,j}$ denotes the time required for travelling from vertex i to vertex j. The reduction of $O(s)$ in figure 2 is significant, and we note a strong reduction in $P(s)$. However, looking at the initial values for $O(s)$ and $P(s)$, found in the first iteration, we notice that the simple distance heuristic

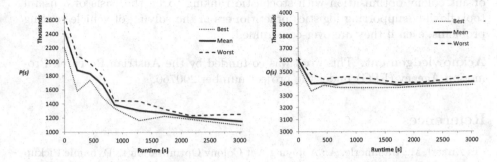

Fig. 3. Runtime performance for solutions with globally best $P(s)$ and $O(s)$ with look-ahead and refined distance heuristic. Look-ahead tolerance set to 14400 s.

produces very bad initial solutions compared to the refined distance heuristic. Starting from these low quality solutions the optimisation algorithm is able to reduce $O(s)$ and $P(s)$ simultaneously. With good initial cost values found by the refined distance heuristic, the algorithm, with $P_f = 0.4$ biased towards reduction of constraint violation, significantly reduces the amount of constraint violation while maintaining the quality level of objective values from early iterations.

This finding is also reflected in figure 3, where we report results obtained with a relaxed look-ahead (tolerance set to 14400 s) and a refined distance heuristic. Again the refined distance heuristic is able to produce good initial values for $O(s)$, being further reduced in the first iterations, but steadying throughout the remainder of the optimisation. Due to the relaxed look-ahead the values for $O(s)$ are lower than in figure 1: the algorithm uses the larger space of feasible solutions, i.e. solutions not violating the look-ahead tolerance, to produce solutions with lower values for $O(s)$. However, this comes at the expense of increased constraint violation.

5   Conclusions

When choosing ant colony optimisation to solve real-world VRP, tailored heuristics are an important aspect in order to achieve satisfactory results. Our investigations showed that the application of problem-specific heuristics significantly improved the quality of solutions, compared to the usage of simple heuristics like shortest distance. In our experiments with a real-world, over-constrained VRP we focussed on the evaluation of globally best solutions with respect to objective value or constraint violation, respectively. However, the algorithmic approach presented in this paper provides more solutions than just globally best ones. The ranking list allows a user to choose from a multitude of solutions, balancing the trade-off between low objective value and low constraint violation in a different way. The probability parameter P_f provides the simple means to adjust the bias of the optimisation algorithm towards reduction of objective value or constraint violation. Based on our results we consider the combination of ant colony optimisation with stochastic ranking to be the basis of a useful tool, flexibly supporting logistics practitioners in the solving of vehicle routing problems, even if they are over-constrained.

Acknowledgement. This work was co-funded by the Austrian Research Promotion Agency (FFG) under the project number 200760.

References

1. Ankerl, M., Hämmerle, A.: Applying Ant Colony Optimisation to Dynamic Pickup and Delivery. In: Moreno-Díaz, R., Pichler, F., Quesada-Arencibia, A. (eds.) EUROCAST 2009. LNCS, vol. 5717, pp. 721–728. Springer, Heidelberg (2009)
2. Cordeau, J.F., Laporte, G., Mercier, A.: A Unified Tabu Search Heuristic for Vehicle Routing Problems with Time Windows. Journal of the Operational Research Society 52, 928–936 (2001)
3. Donati, A.V., Montemanni, R., Casagrande, N., Rizzoli, A.E., Gambardella, L.M.: Time Dependent Vehicle Routing Problem with a Multi Ant Colony System. European Journal of Operational Research 185(3), 1174–1191 (2008)
4. Dondo, R., Cerdá, J.: A cluster-based optimization approach for the multi-depot heterogeneous fleet vehicle routing problem with time windows. European Journal of Operational Research 176(3), 1478–1507 (2007)
5. Held, M.: Analysis and Improvement of Constraint Handling in Ant Colony Algorithms. Thesis, Clayton School of Information Technology, Monash University (2005)
6. Intel^{TM}: Threading Building Blocks Design Patterns V1.0, Text file (2010), http://threadingbuildingblocks.org/ (last accessed April 27, 2011)
7. Meyer, B.: Constraint Handling and Stochastic Ranking in ACO. Evolutionary Computation 3, 2683–2690 (2005)
8. Pisinger, D., Ropke, S.: A general heuristic for vehicle routing problems. Computers & Operations Research 34(8), 2403–2435 (2007)
9. Polacek, M., Hartl, R.F., Doerner, K.: A Variable Neighborhood Search for the Multi Depot Vehicle Routing Problem with Time Windows. Journal of Heuristics 10, 613–627 (2004)
10. Reimann, M., Doerner, K., Hartl, R.F.: D-Ants: Savings Based Ants divide and conquer the vehicle routing problem. Computers & Operations Research 31, 563–591 (2004)
11. Rizzoli, A.E., Montemanni, R., Lucibello, E., Gambardella, L.M.: Ant colony optimization for real-world vehicle routing problems. Swarm Intelligence 1, 135–151 (2007)
12. Runarsson, T.P., Yao, X.: Stochastic Ranking for Constrained Evolutionary Optimization. IEEE Transactions on Evolutionary Computation 4(3), 284–294 (2000)
13. Stützle, T., Hoos, H.H.: MAX-MIN Ant System. Future Generation Computer Systems 16(8), 889–914 (2000)

The Influence of Routing on Lateral Transhipment

Richard F. Hartl and Martin Romauch

Department of Business Administration, University of Vienna,
Bruennerstrasse 72, 1021 Vienna, Austria
{richard.hartl,martin.romauch}@univie.ac.at.com

Abstract. We propose a model for lateral transhipments in a supply chain [6] that considers to use one vehicle to combine the transhipments in a tours to improve the overall costs. The corresponding problem is an extension of the One-Commodity Pickup and Delivery Traveling Salesman and the Pickup and Delivery Vehicle Routing Problem. In general we have to consider a maximum tour length and capacity limits, hence the problem also has aspects of an orienteering problem. The main contribution is the discussion of the tour planning aspects for lateral transhipments which may be valuable for an in-house planning but also for price negotiations with external contractors. We will introduce a mixed integer mathematical model for the single route and single commodity version and a LNS. heuristic to solve the problem.

Keywords: lateral transhipment, orienteering, team orienteering, vehicle routing, pickup and delivery.

1 Introduction

Previous research has analyzed deterministic and stochastic models of lateral transhipments in a supply chain, e.g. between different retailers [6]. These models propose fixed transhipment costs for shifting inventory between retailers and it is determined in which situations transhipment is profitable. However, in reality, we may consider to combine transhipments by using one ore more pickup & delivery routes to redistribute inventories. Therefore, in situations where routing is considered and where profits are dependent on the retailer it is more realistic to reflect routing and redistribution decisions in terms of profitability at the same time. If all retailers are visited, the One-Commodity Pickup and Delivery Traveling Salesman [7,8] and the Pickup and Delivery Vehicle Routing Problem represent suitable modeling approaches. In general, we need to select which retailers are included and therefore the problem has aspects of the (team) orienteering problem [3,11]. We claim that the aspect of routing in lateral transhipments can be valuable for an in-house planning but also for price negotiations with external contractors. In Section 2 we will introduce a mixed integer mathematical model for the single route version. A LNS based heuristic to solve the problem in presented in Section 3 and in Section 4 we present a computational study on the

R. Moreno-Díaz et al. (Eds.): EUROCAST 2013, Part I, LNCS 8111, pp. 267–275, 2013.

performance of the heuristic that is based on the benchmark instances derived from instances for the orienteering problem.

2   Mathematical Model

In this section we will formulate the lateral transhipment problem with one vehicle tour for the distribution. We start with defining the parameters and decision variables in the Subsection 2.1 and Subsection 2.2. In Subsection 2.3 we propose the mathematical model, which is based on the formulation for the Pickup and Delivery TSP [8] and the team orienteering formulation with time windows [11]. We also refer to the Prize Collecting TSP [2] and profitable tour problem [5,4]. We also want to mention the Static Bike Sharing Problem ([9] and [10]) which also combines the Orienteering Problem and the Pickup and Delivery Problem.

2.1   Parameters

Each retailer $i \in V$ has an available quantity in stock and a certain demand. If the demand of retailer i is higher than the delivered quantity then the demand balance q_i is negative (sink). For retailers that have a surplus we get a positive balance and we can consider transporting these quantities to retailers with a negative balance. The profitability is dependent on the price per unit $\bar{p}_i$ at location i and the transportation costs. Dependent on the balance of the node we have different interpretations of $\bar{p}_i$. If the balance is negative $q_i < 0$ then $\bar{p}_i$ (> 0) is the revenue for selling one additional unit at retailer i. If $q_i > 0$ then $\bar{p}_i$ (≥ 0) is the salvage value for one missing unit at retailer i. Suppose we are able to make a direct transhipment from a surplus retailer i $(q_i > 0)$ that compensates all the negative balance at retailer j, then we would get $\bar{p}_j q_j$ monetary units and we would lose the salvage value of $-\bar{p}_i q_j$ monetary units. Obviously we need a sufficient number of units at retailer i $(q_i > -q_j)$ to do so and the transhipment should be profitable, and without considering the transportation costs $\bar{p}_i$ should be smaller than $\bar{p}_j$. We also introduce the aggregated profit p_i which is the maximum possible salvage value at a surplus location or the maximum additional profit for a deficit location, i.e.: $p_i = \bar{p}_i q_i$. To formulate the tour costs and the duration of the tour we introduce the cost matrix (c_{ij}) and the time consumption matrix (t_{ij}). The capacity of the vehicle is limited to Q_{max} units and the duration of the tour should not exceed T_{max}.

2.2   Decision Variables

In our model we allow to have one vehicle (with fixed costs F) to make a pickup an delivery route that visits nodes with a surplus and deficit nodes to increase the overall profit. We declare the binary decision variable z which is equal to one if a profitable tour exists and equal to zero else. The binary variables (x_{ij}) are used to select the corresponding tour which starts and ends at the depot 0. The corresponding transportation costs are dependent on the cost matrix

(c_{ij}). The binary decision variable z_i will be used to identify nodes that are visited in the tour. For modeling the load capacity constraint we introduce the continuous variable Q_i, which will be used to describe the load of the vehicle when leaving the node i. To model the pick up or delivery intensity we introduce the continuous variable y_i ($0 \leq y_i \leq 1$), therefore $y_i q_i$ holds the number of units that are picked up or delivered at location i.

2.3 Linear Program

$$\max \sum_{i \in V} p_i y_i - \sum_{i,j \in V \cup \{0\}} c_{ij} x_{ij} - Fz \tag{1}$$

$$\text{s.t.} \quad \sum_{j \in V \cup \{0\} \setminus \{i\}} x_{ij} = \sum_{j \in V \cup \{0\} \setminus \{i\}} x_{ji} = z_i \qquad \forall i \in V \cup \{0\} \tag{2}$$

$$\sum_{i \in V} z_i \leq Mz; \quad \sum_{j \in V} x_{0j} = \sum_{j \in V} x_{j0} = z \tag{3}$$

$$y_i \leq z_i \tag{4}$$

$$s_i + t_{ij} \leq s_j + M(1 - x_{ij}) \qquad \forall i \in V \cup \{0\}, j \in V \tag{5}$$

$$Q_j \leq Q_i + q_j y_j + M(1 - x_{ij}) \qquad \forall i \in V, j \in V \cup \{0\} \tag{6}$$

$$Q_i + q_j y_j \leq Q_j + M(1 - x_{ij}) \qquad \forall i \in V, j \in V \cup \{0\} \tag{7}$$

$$Q_0 = 0 \tag{8}$$

$$0 \leq Q_i \leq Q_{max} \qquad \forall i \in V \cup \{0\} \tag{9}$$

$$\sum_{i,j \in V \cup \{0\}} t_{ij} x_{ij} \leq T_{max} \tag{10}$$

$$x_{ij}, z_i, z \in \{0, 1\} \qquad \forall i, j \in V \cup \{0\} \tag{11}$$

$$s_i, Q_i \geq 0 \quad 0 \leq y_i \leq 1 \qquad \forall i \in V \tag{12}$$

The set of constraints (2) are the flow balance in each node, the constraints (3) are used to model the variable z which is equal to one if we decide to start a tour in the origin. The variable y_i contains the portion of q_i that is used. Due to the constraints in (4) we know that $z_i = 1$ if $y_i > 0$. The constraints (5) are used for the subtour elimination and (6,7) are used to model the balance of the vehicle load $x_{ij} = 1 \Rightarrow Q_j = Q_i + q_j y_j$ and (9) implements the maximum capacity Q_{max}. Finally, the constraint (10) is limiting the tour length.

3 Metaheuristic

The proposed is a construction heuristic that uses variable neighborhood descent (VND) elements in a large naighborhood search (LNS) framework. In the main loop we iteratively add new customers to augment the solution. The augmented solution is then locally improved by a couple of subsequent local improvements

(VND). The VND is followed by an optimization of the pickup and delivery quantities. If the augmentation process stops we start to destroy parts of the solution and we continue augmenting the solution.

3.1   Basic Structure of the Algorithm

The structure of the algorithm is outlined in Figure 3.1. The termination criterion is given by a time limit or a maximum number of iterations, and if the termination criterion is not fulfilled we try to augment the partial solution. In the augmentation step we randomly select a pick up customer according to a probability distribution that is dependent on rough estimations of profitability and detour length. Once a pickup customer is selected, we insert it at the closest position in the tour and we then continue with inserting delivery customers until there is no possibility to insert profitable delivery customers anymore. Throughout the whole construction process we always stick to feasibility.

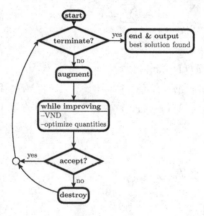

Fig. 1. Heuristic framework

3.2   Augmentation

If we consider to insert a new pickup customer i we may improve the partial solution by also adding one ore more delivery customers that are associated it, or we may use the new source to satisfy additional demand in the route by optimizing the pickup and delivery quantities. In the first case we consider inserting pairs of pickup and delivery customers and we choose them with a certain probability that is proportional to the estimated additional profit p and the detour length. We also implemented an aggregation mechanism where two or more retailers of the same type that are very close are considered as a big retailer with aggregated parameters - this kind of smoothing mechanism is used in the early stage when the tour duration/length buffer are relatively large.

After the augmentation step we try to improve the solution with a VND consisting of a two-opt and neighborhoods that switch customers within the tour (complete and partial) and neighborhoods that consider exchanging customers from the tour with customers that were not yet selected (complete and partial). We also include the optimization of pickup and delivery quantities for a given solution and we repeat the process until we are stuck in a local optimum. If we accept the solution we may continue with the augmentation, otherwise we will destroy parts of the solution beforehand. The destroy mechanism decides randomly on three alternative strategies that are equally likely. The first one randomly deletes up to 10% percent of the customers and the second respects the contribution to the profit. The third one randomly selects up to three centers with respect to the profit loss, and deletes up to 10% of customers that are close to the centers.

3.3 Optimization of the Pickup and Delivery Quantities

Since one of the more time consuming parts in the algorithm is the optimization of pickup and delivery quantities we want to give some more details about the implementation. First, we will formulate the corresponding sub problem that needs to be solved to get the optimal quantities for a tour τ. Without loss of of generality, we will assume that the tour and the set of vertices are given in the following form: $\tau = (1, 2, 3, \ldots n)$ and $V = \{1, 2, 3 \ldots n\}$. According to (1-12) we can derive the following LP:

$$\max \sum_{i \in V} p_i y_i \tag{13}$$

$$s.t. Q_0 = 0; \quad Q_{i+1} = Q_i + q_{i+1} y_{i+1} \qquad \forall i : \in V \cup \{0\} \tag{14}$$

$$0 \leq y_i \leq 1; 0 \leq Q_i \leq Q_{max}; \quad 0 \leq y_i \leq 1 \qquad \forall i \in V \cup \{0\} \tag{15}$$

We can interpret the contraints (14) as a flow balance equations. If the node $i + 1$ is a pickup customer the quantity $q_{i+1} y_{i+1}$ and Q_i are positive flows into the node $i + 1$ and the quantity Q_{i+1} leaves the node. If $i + 1$ is a delivery customer the quantity $q_{i+1} y_{i+1}$ is negative and therefore it will be interpreted as a negative flow. In Figure 3.3 we illustrate an example, the nodes 1, 3 and 4 are pickup customers and the nodes 2 and 5 are delivery customers. We note that f_{si} and f_{it} should be interpreted as $y_i q_i$ for pickups and deliveries. For each arc, the cost and the upper bound can be found inside the brackets under the variable name. We observe that this equivalent problem is a minimum cost flow problem, which can be solved very efficiently with a variant of the simplex method [1].

We now discuss the performance of the proposed Algorithm in Section 4.

4   Computational Experiment

We adapted instances for the orienteering problem that are presented in [3] and [12]. For selecting delivery and pickup nodes we randomly choose the nodes

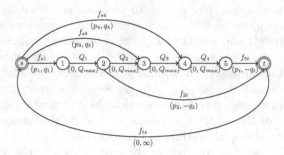

Fig. 2. Min Cost Flow with negative and positive costs. If the node on position i in the tour is a pickup customer then $f_{s,i}$ is the corresponding pickup quantity . If the node is a delivery customer then $f_{i,t}$ is the corresponding delivery quantitiy. transformation: $(y_i = \frac{f_{s,i}}{q_i})$

Table 1. Absolute values for LNS and CPLEX compared for different Q_{max} for the adapted Chao instances. Average and Maximum is reported for three LNS runs. The asterisk marks the best found solution.

class	group	Tmax	60 max LNS	60 avg LNS	60 CPLEX	120 max LNS	120 avg LNS	120 CPLEX	300 max LNS	300 avg LNS	300 CPLEX
set	64	15	4,587.17*	4,587.17	2,475.42	4,587.17*	4,587.17		4,587.17*	4,587.17	
		20	11,326.20*	11,326.20	9,790.21	11,326.20*	11,326.20	9,826.21	11,326.20*	11,326.20	7,432.11
		25	14,981.00*	14,385.27	13,433.03	15,167.40*	14,957.13	13,865.03	15,167.40*	14,957.13	12,137.62
		30	17,676.20*	17,164.40	15,804.20	18,012.10*	18,002.10	15,054.20	17,982.10*	17,982.10	
		35	19,705.00*	19,659.17	19,477.03	23,503.00*	22,977.07	19,621.15	23,011.00*	22,861.00	17,893.15
		40	23,864.80*	23,595.20	20,924.45	26,888.10*	26,828.17	20,282.13	27,956.40*	27,956.40	21,494.22
		45	30,663.00*	30,061.27		33,837.20*	33,783.20	31,023.48	34,701.60*	34,267.47	22,269.40
		50	29,758.40*	29,006.43	27,532.31	32,968.30*	32,684.43	29,794.72	33,808.30*	33,686.37	19,324.31
		55	32,813.40*	32,759.37	25,829.50	37,403.10*	37,151.43	34,547.83	38,435.10*	37,941.10	29,219.16
		60	37,056.30	36,728.30	38,004.08*	41,394.20*	41,258.33	39,840.51	42,324.20*	41,960.33	39,132.75
		65	45,937.90*	45,682.43	39,782.75	49,603.10*	49,563.50	44,395.25	50,101.40*	49,915.40	36,787.25
		70	46,244.20*	45,586.53	39,741.59	51,518.30*	51,476.50	46,461.34	53,174.00*	52,760.57	29,829.10
		75	43,593.10*	43,114.83	38,445.03	48,447.80*	48,374.17	40,971.33	49,467.30*	49,273.30	37,965.11
		80	37,810.10*	37,746.10	31,127.43	42,946.20*	42,894.50	32,974.28	45,766.00*	45,746.30	30,130.22
	66	5	520.76	520.76	520.76	520.76	520.76	520.76	520.76	520.76	520.76
		10	1,596.12	1,596.12	1,596.13	1,596.12	1,596.12	1,596.13	1,596.12	1,596.12	1,596.13
		15	3,820.01*	3,820.01	3,465.72	3,820.01*	3,820.01	3,465.44	3,820.01*	3,820.01	2,240.37
		20	8,145.11*	8,145.11	7,175.43	8,180.68*	8,156.97	5,625.92	8,145.11*	8,145.11	3,803.00
		25	11,745.40*	11,745.40	11,355.36	12,545.50	12,545.50	11,030.03	12,545.50*	12,545.50	12,035.84
		30	15,495.90	15,034.03	15,700.33*	17,715.50*	17,622.17	15,570.18	17,716.00*	17,715.67	12,106.76
		35	19,330.30	19,330.30	19,400.36*	21,130.80*	20,887.20	19,650.10	21,530.40*	20,528.60	15,705.70
		40	20,265.30*	20,063.50	19,500.07	25,360.20*	25,360.20	18,252.28	25,360.20*	25,360.20	18,310.09
		45	24,015.30*	24,015.30	21,970.28	30,470.30*	30,470.30	26,665.28	30,470.30*	30,470.30	23,980.63
		50	27,880.50*	27,822.03	27,295.12	31,771.00*	31,520.83	25,935.40	33,760.50*	33,503.83	21,525.29
		55	30,810.40*	29,118.93	27,200.11	33,820.10*	33,408.67	32,795.62	33,465.70*	33,213.67	29,030.05
		60	31,305.10*	30,775.33	29,925.40	33,545.50*	33,363.77	32,306.92	34,960.60*	34,815.40	28,445.97
		65	30,865.30	30,783.63	32,375.49*	36,835.90*	36,648.97	27,885.22	39,370.40*	38,355.33	24,755.18
		70	35,565.30*	35,141.10	30,420.40	39,915.10*	39,781.77	36,425.13	40,780.10*	40,425.07	27,920.46
		75	38,980.30*	38,368.80	37,820.57	44,140.10*	44,043.60	39,380.16	46,015.20*	45,762.00	33,100.22
		80	49,530.70*	49,068.57	37,785.08	55,240.30*	54,806.90	45,955.32	55,140.10*	54,950.27	33,026.06
		85	36,150.00*	36,000.37	30,255.66	43,225.40*	43,136.93	34,726.76	45,960.30*	45,838.60	30,210.15
		90	48,445.30*	47,443.90	37,184.30	54,590.00*	54,026.83	44,420.77	56,230.00*	56,066.83	37,136.01
		95	43,681.40*	43,374.43	41,825.29	52,740.10*	52,536.83	46,705.36	55,405.20*	55,287.07	37,355.60
		100	49,930.50*	49,376.13	49,487.74	58,210.30*	57,987.60	50,120.25	61,330.50*	61,158.50	45,135.34
		105	42,122.60*	41,563.13	39,466.73	52,620.10*	51,771.90	42,515.76	55,825.80*	55,575.87	43,775.20
		110	45,125.30	44,916.17	46,571.17*	55,920.10*	55,705.50	47,965.63	59,285.20*	58,582.13	37,205.14
		115	50,961.00*	50,700.83	44,450.37	59,885.60*	59,711.10	43,950.37	61,391.60*	61,226.03	42,030.82
		120	58,745.10*	58,460.73	52,545.27	68,220.80*	67,755.40	53,710.58	70,045.10*	69,666.77	57,358.44
		125	51,460.30*	50,718.93	42,436.33	57,590.50*	57,477.20	50,300.15	59,210.10*	59,033.83	43,115.09
		130	47,902.20*	46,965.80	44,515.27	49,069.70*	49,069.33	46,932.97	49,070.50*	49,070.50	46,086.00

with a probability of 50%. The oiriginal price of the node will be interpreted as the maximum available quantity and the costs and the profit are randomly generated. We choose $c_{ij} = t_{ij}$ and we considered different values for Q_{max}. The

Table 2. Absolute values for LNS and CPLEX compared for different Q_{max} for the adapted Tsiligirides instances. Average and Maximum is reported for three LNS runs. The asterisk marks the best found solution.

			60			120			300		
class	group	Tmax	max LNS	avg LNS	CPLEX	max LNS	avg LNS	CPLEX	max LNS	avg LNS	CPLEX
tsiligirides	1	10	560.24	560.24	560.24	560.24	560.24	560.24	560.24	560.24	560.24
		15	1,205.98	1,205.98	1,205.98	1,205.98	1,205.98	1,205.98	1,205.98	1,205.98	1,205.98
		20	1,430.73	1,430.73	1,430.73	1,430.73	1,430.73	1,430.73	1,430.73	1,430.73	1,430.73
		25	4,195.79*	4,195.79	3,630.32	4,195.79	4,195.79	4,195.79	4,195.79*	4,195.79	3,771.88
		30	4,820.44	4,820.44	4,820.45	4,820.44	4,820.44	4,820.45	4,820.44	4,820.44	4,820.45
		35	5,875.32*	5,875.32	5,310.15	5,875.32*	5,875.32	4,615.13	5,875.32*	5,875.32	4,581.48
		40	5,866.66*	5,866.66	4,970.29	5,866.66*	5,866.66	5,515.83	5,866.66	5,866.66	5,866.66
		46	6,274.14*	6,274.14	6,144.94	6,274.14*	6,231.07	6,004.57	6,274.14*	6,231.07	5,751.15
		50	7,691.74	7,691.74	7,740.26*	7,740.26*	7,724.06	7,640.63	7,740.26*	7,724.06	7,470.09
		55	8,085.02*	7,965.29	8,040.21	8,085.02	8,085.02	8,245.12*	8,085.02*	8,085.02	7,505.35
		60	8,260.02*		7,266.08	8,260.02*	8,260.02	7,165.21	8,260.02*	8,260.02	7,790.26
		65	8,000.02*	7,926.92	7,075.40	8,000.02*	7,913.38	7,460.57	8,000.02*	7,913.38	5,085.45
		70	7,685.39*	7,685.10	7,466.16	7,685.10*	7,685.10	6,883.10	7,685.10*	7,685.10	6,240.60
		73	10,007.60*	10,007.60	9,747.06	10,007.60*	10,007.60	9,847.42	10,007.60*	10,007.60	9,002.39
		75	10,245.90*	10,245.90	9,576.60	10,245.90*	10,245.90	9,320.09	10,245.90*	10,245.90	7,305.27
		80	10,090.80*	10,090.80	9,516.54	10,090.80*	10,090.77	10,087.44	10,090.80*	10,090.73	9,395.48
		85	7,886.46*	7,886.46	7,869.78	7,886.46*	7,886.46	7,797.59	7,886.46*	7,886.46	7,684.66
	2	15	4,410.08	4,410.08	4,410.08	4,410.08*	4,410.08	4,130.41	4,410.08	4,410.08	4,410.08
		20	6,580.28	6,580.28	6,580.28	6,580.28	6,580.28	6,580.28	6,580.28	6,580.28	6,580.28
		23	7,557.50	7,557.50	7,557.50	7,557.50	7,557.50	7,557.50	7,557.50	7,557.50	7,557.50
		25	8,860.18*	8,860.18	8,206.34	8,860.18*	8,860.18	8,206.34	8,860.18*	8,860.18	8,270.20
		27	10,058.70	10,058.70	10,058.74	10,058.70	10,058.70	10,058.74	10,058.70*	10,058.70	9,239.81
		30	10,895.00	10,895.00	10,895.02	11,205.00*	11,205.00	10,890.10	11,205.00*	11,205.00	10,890.10
		32	8,449.99	8,449.99	8,468.15*	8,588.19*	8,588.19	8,469.41	8,588.19*	8,588.19	8,053.05
		35	11,576.30	11,576.30	11,576.30	12,545.40*	12,545.40	11,845.47	12,545.40*	12,545.40	11,576.30
		38	12,972.00*	12,972.00	12,692.56	13,337.10	13,337.10	13,337.08	13,337.10*	13,337.10	11,648.72
		40	12,705.60	12,705.60	12,705.58	15,050.30	15,050.30	15,050.35	15,050.30	15,050.30	15,050.35
		45	11,722.50	11,722.50	11,722.53	11,822.00	11,822.00	11,822.02	11,821.70	11,821.70	11,822.02*
	3	15	7,045.01	7,045.01	7,045.01	7,045.01	7,045.01	7,045.01	7,045.01	7,045.01	7,045.01
		20	6,370.08	6,370.08	6,370.08	6,370.08	6,370.08	6,370.08	6,370.08	6,370.08	6,370.08
		25	9,615.61	9,615.61	9,615.61	9,615.61	9,615.61	9,615.61	9,615.61	9,615.61	9,615.61
		30	11,490.30	11,490.30	11,490.27	13,820.00	13,820.00	13,820.03	13,820.00*	13,820.00	13,740.29
		35	8,575.08	8,575.08	8,575.08	8,575.08	8,575.08	8,575.08	8,575.08*	8,575.08	8,456.44
		40	14,010.60*	13,896.93	13,781.69	15,340.00	15,213.40	15,340.04	15,340.00*	15,340.00	13,111.59
		45	13,565.10	13,565.10	13,585.51*	17,575.50*	17,575.50	17,545.00	17,935.00*	17,935.00	17,635.40
		50	17,450.10	17,306.87	18,240.56*	18,830.50*	18,703.80	18,400.36	18,670.40*	18,526.97	18,260.89
		55	17,775.30*	17,749.00	17,055.68	18,785.30*	18,785.30	18,225.49	18,785.30*	18,785.30	18,236.06
		60	20,791.90	20,697.70	20,960.65*	22,030.80*	21,783.90	22,030.57	21,830.00*	21,670.37	21,700.36
		65	24,005.00*	24,005.00	23,537.22	24,825.20	24,645.33	24,825.17	24,825.20*	24,825.20	22,795.30
		70	22,463.00*	22,463.00	21,040.40	25,270.10*	25,156.80	22,070.72	26,180.00*	26,180.00	24,410.89
		75	21,165.10*	20,932.10	20,415.64	23,975.80*	23,972.20	23,885.36	24,675.50*	24,675.50	24,555.02
		80	23,000.50	23,000.50	23,000.54	25,290.30*	24,923.57	24,031.77	25,250.60*	24,910.33	25,200.05
		85	27,206.90	26,643.80	27,305.27*	29,777.00*	29,769.43	29,397.39	29,805.50*	29,787.90	29,715.96
		90	28,281.20	28,281.20	28,441.02*	31,240.10*	31,240.10	27,720.38	31,240.90*	31,240.90	29,680.15
		95	28,205.80*	28,165.83	27,816.72	29,975.40*	29,975.40	27,365.42	30,475.50*	30,465.43	22,795.30
		100	26,672.40*	26,672.40	26,150.81	30,621.00*	30,620.97	29,522.33	31,104.20*	31,104.20	30,912.36
		105	32,950.00*	32,875.43	30,787.30	34,850.10*	34,850.10	31,253.03	34,856.70*	34,856.70	34,853.42
		110	22,981.90*	22,980.70	22,970.82	22,987.10*	22,987.10	22,975.41	22,987.10*	22,987.10	22,985.82

instances can be found at http://homepage.univie.ac.at/martin.romauch/ PDOP/dat01.zip .

To get information about the performance of the solution methods we take different sizes of Q_{max}, i.e. $Q_{max} \in \{60, 120, 300\}$, where the load 300 is reached in only very few cases and serves as unconstrained case. We start with some details about the computer and the computing paradigms. We were using a Windows PC with a i7-260QM CPU @ 2.2 GHz, 4 Cores, 8 logical processors and 8GB RAM. CPLEX takes full advantage of parallel computing and generates a 100% CPU utilization. LNS is running on single logical processor with a utilization of 12-13%. For CPLEX to behave like a heuristic we activated the options 'feasibility pump' and 'polishing'. For each instance the LNS was running for 5 minutes and CPLEX was running for 20 minutes in parallel mode. In Figure 3 we compare the overall average performance of the methods for all adapted instances. For the primary axis (black) we can see the average gap dependent on the CPU time, i.e. we consider the best nontrivial solutions found so far. For the secondary axis we can see the percentage of instances where a nontrivial solution

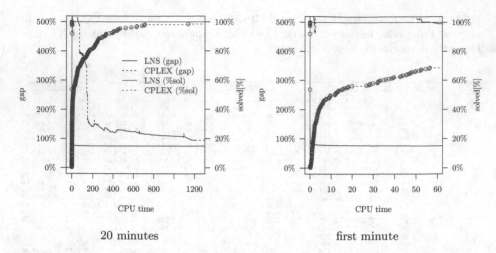

20 minutes   first minute

Fig. 3. Time dependent GAP for LNS and CPLEX for all adapted instances. The GAP for LNS is the average of three runs. If no nontrivial solution was found by CPLEX then the GAP is not reported.

was found. The dashed lines correspond to the CPLEX results while the solid ones correspond to the LNS results. You can also find the 60 seconds magnified, which is a drastically shows the benefit of a heuristic. The Tables 1 and 2 report the results for CPLEX after 20 minutes (parallel computing) and the results for the LNS after 5 minutes for each instance. We can see that the overall performance of the heuristic is in average better, especially for large Q_{max}. We also note that the CPLEX results are better for some instances especially for the smaller Tsiligirides instances.

We also experimented with the original orienteering instances, applying the following transformation: we can setting $c_{ij} = 0$, $p_i = 1$ and we are adding sufficient pickup quantities to the origin, and therefore we can use the algorithms for the PDOP to solve the orienteering instances presented in [3] and [12]. We note that in the PDOP the vector y is continuous, but due to the maximization of the profit we can find an optimal binary solution. In our experiment with a 5 minutes time limit we always found the optimum.

5   Conclusion and Outlook

We presented a LNS based heuristic for the single commodity lateral transhipment problem with one vehicle. Computational Experiments show that the proposed Algorithm yields to high quality results in a reasonable time. We also want to mention that for evaluating a fair price (or an interesting price range) for negotiations with external contractors it is therefore of practical interest to extend the model accordingly. We also want to note that there are several extensions like stochastic demands, mulitple visits and the multi commodity case that will be interesting future research topics.

References

1. Ahuja, R.K., Magnanti, T.L., Orlin, J.B.: Network Flows: Theory, Algorithms, and Applications. Prentice-Hall, Inc. (1993)
2. Balas, E.: The prize collecting traveling salesman problem. Networks 19, 621–636 (1989)
3. Chao, I.M., Golden, B., Wasil, E.A.: The team orienteering problem. European Journal of Operational Research 88, 474 (1996)
4. Dell'Amico, M., Maffioli, F., Värbrand, P.: On prize-collecting tours and the asymmetric travelling salesman problem. Internet. Trans. Oper. Res. 2(3), 297–308 (1995)
5. Feillet, Dejax, Gendreau: Traveling salesman problems with profits. Transportation Science 39(2), 188–205 (2005)
6. Herer, Y.T., Tzur, M., Yücesan, E.: The multilocation transhipment problem. IIE Transactions 38, 186–200 (2006)
7. Hernández-Pérez, H., Salazar-González, J.J.: The multi-commodity one-to-one pickup-and-delivery traveling salesman problem. European Journal of Operational Research 196(3), 987–995 (2009)
8. Parragh, S.N., Doerner, K.F., Hartl, R.F.: A survey on pickup and delivery problems. Part ii: Transportation between pickup and delivery locations. Journal für Betriebswirtschaft 58, 81–117 (2008)
9. Rainer-Harbach, M., Papazek, P., Hu, B., Raidl, G.R.: Balancing bicycle sharing systems: A variable neighborhood search approach. In: Middendorf, M., Blum, C. (eds.) EvoCOP 2013. LNCS, vol. 7832, pp. 121–132. Springer, Heidelberg (2013)
10. Raviv, T., Tzur, M., Forma, I.A.: Balancing bicycle sharing systems: A variable neighborhood search approach evolutionary computation in combinatorial optimization. EURO Journal on Transportation and Logistics (2012)
11. Tricoire, F., Romauch, M., Doerner, K.F., Hartl, R.F.: Heuristics for the multiperiod orienteering problem with multiple time windows. Computers & Operations Research 37, 351–367 (2010)
12. Tsiligirides, T.: Heuristic methods applied to orienteering. Journal of the Operational Research Society 35(9), 797–809 (1984)

Structural Synthesis of Dispatching Rules
for Dynamic Dial-a-Ride Problems

Stefan Vonolfen, Andreas Beham, Michael Kommenda, and Michael Affenzeller

Heuristic and Evolutionary Algorithms Laboratory
School of Informatics, Communications and Media
University of Applied Sciences Upper Austria
Softwarepark 11, 4232 Hagenberg, Austria
stefan.vonolfen@fh-hagenberg.at

Abstract. The dial-a-ride problem consists of designing vehicle routes in the area of passenger transportation. Assuming that each vehicle can act autonomously, the problem can be modeled as a multi-agent system. In that context, it is a complex decision process for each agent to determine what action to perform next. In this work, the agent function is evolved using genetic programming by synthesizing basic bits of information. Specialized dispatching rules are synthesized automatically that are adapted to the problem environment. We compare the evolved rules with other dispatching strategies for dynamic dial-a-ride problems on a set of generated benchmark instances. Additionally, since genetic programming is a whitebox-based approach, insights can be gained about important system parameters. For that purpose, we perform a variable frequency analysis during the evolutionary process.

Keywords: Dispatching Rules, Genetic Programming, Dynamic Dial-a-ride Problem.

1 Introduction and Related Work

The dial-a-ride problem (DARP) is a well-known model about the transportation of people between origins and destinations using a fleet of vehicles [8]. The main objective is to achieve the best service quality possible given a certain amount of vehicles. The service quality is determined by the user inconvenience which can be modeled as the number of unserved requests or the average lead time of all requests. In the dynamic variant of the DARP, the requests are not known in advance but arrive during the planning process [4]. Practical applications include door-to-door transportation of elderly people and taxi-cabs.

Solution concepts for the dynamic DARP include approaches that plan ahead as well as dispatching-based scheduling. A planning-based approach tries to construct a set of routes given the currently known requests. For that purpose, static algorithms can be adapted and incorporated in a rolling-horizon framework. The adaption of static algorithms is based on extensive research on algorithms for the static DARP [5] [7] [11]. In the field of metaheuristics, especially local search

R. Moreno-Díaz et al. (Eds.): EUROCAST 2013, Part I, LNCS 8111, pp. 276–283, 2013.

techniques have been applied successfully to dynamic variants such as variable neighborhood search [15] or tabu search [2].

On the contrary, dispatching approaches do not use a-priori planning and only schedule one step in advance. This approach has been proven to be applicable especially in very dynamic and volatile environments where a short reaction time is required and thus planning ahead might be infeasible. For the single-vehicle case, dispatching rules have been derived and analyzed based on queuing theory [6] [12]. In the multi-vehicle case, dynamic planning and autonomous acting of vehicles makes it feasible to model the environment in terms of a multi-agent system where each vehicle is modeled as an autonomous agent. Multi-agent systems provide a de-central decision mechanism for environments where only local and incomplete information can be used [13]. Specialized dispatching rules are one way of implementing the decision mechanism on an agent level.

In that context, Beham et al. [3] have proposed a multi-agent system for dynamic DARP that is based on a linear combination of various atomic bits of dispatching information. The weights of this linear combination are tuned by a simulation-based evolutionary optimization process. The optimized rules were compared among each other in different problem situations. We extend their work by not using a fixed structure in the form of a linear combination, but by synthesizing the basic bits of dispatching information to complex rules.

The most closely related work was done by van Lon et al. [13]. To the best of our knowledge, this is the only work that exists where genetic programming (GP) is applied to solve the dynamic DARP by synthesizing priority rules. Extending the approach, we use 18 different bits of information and analyze their influence, while they used three different bits (distance, time left, nearby requests). In their work, they did not incorporate any communication between the vehicles while we also incorporate self-organization between the agents. Also, the vehicles in their multi-agent system had a capacity of one single customer while we consider a larger capacity.

In this work, we combine different atomic bits of information which include spatial, temporal, and also agent information. The synthesis is done using GP which has been proven to find solutions to structurally complex problems [10]. The structural synthesis should yield advantages compared to the linear combination and simple dispatching rules in terms of achieved service quality, i.e. total lead time. Experiments are carried out on previously defined benchmark instances [3]. The core assumption is, that a more powerful model should be able to capture non-linearities in the problem characteristics.

The main contribution of this paper is a comparison of the complex priority rules that have been evolved using GP with other dispatching rules for dynamic DARP. By exploring a more powerful solution space, the algorithm should be able to identify non-linearities and the rules should be better adapted to the problem environment. Additionally, we want to estimate the gap to a planning-based approach that considers all available information. Another interesting aspect of our work is the inclusion of many diverse bits of information for dispatching. The structural synthesis process should yield valuable insights on the important influence factors and parameters by means of a variable impact analysis.

The remainder of this paper is organized as following. In Section 2 we give a problem definition, in Section 3 we detail our methodology including the algorithm environment and the GP process, in Section 4 we perform experiments on benchmark instances and compare the individual dispatching rules and in Section 5 we summarize our findings and give an outlook on future research.

2   Problem Definition

In the following, we will focus on a shared taxi system where users can dynamically place requests between pre-defined service points and a fleet of buses can carry multiple people at the same time. The main objective to be optimized is the customer inconvenience. We model our problem as a dynamic DARP. A formal problem formulation is provided for example by [2].

The requests arrive dynamically at predefined vertices in the Euclidean plane during the planning horizon. We assume, that the requests can be serviced immediately after they appeared. For each request, an origin and a target vertex is given as well as the demand and the required service time. In our case, the demand specifies the number of people that want to be transfered and the service time is the time needed to get in and step out of the vehicle. Each vehicle has a predefined capacity (i.e. people it can carry) and we consider a fleet of homogeneous vehicles and a fixed fleet size.

The objective is to minimize the average lead time which represents the total time a request is in the system. A request enters the system when it is placed and leaves the system when it was delivered at the target location. To avoid starving of individual requests, we additionally impose a fixed time limit for the lead time. If a request remains in the system longer than this limit, we impose an exponential penalty.

$$\min f(L) = \frac{\sum_{i=1}^{|R|} l_{r_i}}{|R|} + \sum_{i=1}^{|R|} \exp(\max(0, l_{r_i} - b)) \tag{1}$$

The objective function is given in equation 1. For each request $r_i \in R$ its lead time l_{r_i} is given. We assume that $|R|$ requests appeared during the planning period and aim at minimizing the average lead time of all requests considering the operational constraints. The lead time is the total time between the appearance of the request and its completion. For requests that were active in the system longer than the predefined time limit b, an exponential penalty is added.

3   Methodology

As stated earlier, we model our system as a multi-agent system. Each vehicle is an agent which acts autonomously which means that there is no central decision mechanism. The decision which order to pickup next and where to go next is based on bits of information that are available to the agent for each waiting request. They include general properties of the request, information about the location of the request and also information about other agents. They are based on the work of [3]. A summary about the different bits of information is given in Table 1.

Table 1. Bits of information available to the agent about each request

Name	Description
Demand	Number of people to be transported.
StartDate	Time the request arrived in the system.
DueDate	Time the request is due.
LeadTime	Lead time of the request if it would by served immediately.
EarliestArrival	Earliest arrival time of the agent at the location.
Distance	Distance to the current agent.
Remoteness	Min./avg./max distance to other locations.
PickupRequests	Pickup requests waiting at that location.
PickupDemand	Total pickup demand waiting at that location.
DropoffRequests	Dropoff requests waiting at that location.
DropoffDemand	Total dropoff demand waiting at that location.
DropoffDueDate	Due date of a carried request heading to the same destination.
AgentDistance	Min./avg./max distance to the other agents.
CommonTarget	Number of agents heading to the same location.

To utilize the available information about the requests, the different bits are synthesized to a dispatching rule which represents the agent function. Each agent utilizes the same function which is adapted for a certain problem environment. The outcome of the agent function is a priority value for each request. The request with the highest priority is carried out by the agent. If multiple agents are competing for a waiting request, the agent with the highest priority function value wins.

To calculate a priority value for a given request, we need to synthesize the basic bits of information. For the synthesis process we use a tree representation with a fixed grammar. The grammar includes arithmetic (addition, subtraction, multiplication, division, average, exponential, logarithm), conditional (if, greater, less, and, or, not) and terminal symbols. The terminal symbols are numerical constants or most importantly the different bits of information which are listed in Table 1.

Previous work has shown that specialized dispatching rules are needed for different problem environments [3]. To evolve such rules, simulation optimization is a powerful technique [9]. The solution process is separated into two phases: the training and the test phase. In the training phase, the rules are evolved and adapted using test problem instances. In the test phase, the rules are applied to previously unseen instances.

The training phase is carried out using a extended genetic programming process with offspring selection [1]. Each individual in the population represents a candidate dispatching rule which is evaluated on a number of training scenarios. We use a population size of 100, a maximum of 100 generations, a maximum selection pressure of 200, a mutation rate of 15%, 1 elites and a success ration of 90%. A tree length limit of 25 and a depth limit of 15 have been applied. This parameterization has been proven to be successful in a similar approach applied to production logistics [14]. The comparably low population size stems from the fact that the simulation optimization of dispatching rules is a computationally complex task.

The simulation and optimization environment has been implemented in HeuristicLab [16]. To evaluate the performance of the evolved rules, this implementation was used for our experiments.

4   Results

We test our approach on different scenarios that consist of 1000 request with an average number of 4 requests per minute. The requests arrive according to a Poisson process and are placed at 26 predefined service points. The source and target service points are chosen according to a uniform distribution. We assume a homogeneous fleet of 5 taxi buses that can carry up to 10 people. We set a time limit of 15 minutes. Within that time, each customer has to arrive at the specified destination after placing the request.

For our numerical experiments we randomly generated 7 different instances as a training and 3 instances as a test set. We compare our approach to both dispatching and planning based algorithms. The lower bound is represented by a static tabu search (TS) algorithm. In that case all the requests are known in advance leading to a static DARP. In the case of the ad-hoc TS the requests arrive dynamically. Whenever new requests arrive, the routes are planned according to the new situation.

We compare 4 different dispatching strategies. The earliest-due-date (EDD) always serves the request that is the most urgent one. The first-come-first-serve (FCFS) strategy serves the requests in the sequence they are placed. The linear strategy is a linear dispatching rule which has been proposed by [3]. We compare all rules with the tree-based dispatching approach proposed in this work. The evolved dispatching rule is illustrated in Figure 1.

The results of our experiments are summarized in Table 2. The quality is given as the average lead time and penalty over all instances. The next columns indicate the gap to the static solution and the best solution on the dynamic problem obtained by applying the tabu search algorithm. Additionally, the average runtime required for solving a problem instance is given in minutes.

The first observation is, that there is a large gap between the solution to the static problem and the dynamic variant. Generally, the planning-based approaches (TS) perform best, however they have a higher runtime than the dispatching-based approaches. In terms of simple dispatching rules, the EDD performs better than the FCFS. This is due to the fact that our main target is the optimization of customer satisfaction in this case.

Table 2. Comparison of different algorithms on the training and test set

Training	Lead Time	Penalty	Quality	Gap(static)	Gap(ad hoc)	Runtime
TS (static)	3412.52	0.40	3412.92	0.00%	-24.89%	46.97
TS (ad hoc)	4543.69	0.24	4543.93	33.14%	0.00%	50.86
FCFS	6344.03	515.94	6859.97	101.00%	50.97%	0.63
EDD	6223.24	42.03	6265.27	83.57%	37.88%	0.60
Linear	4733.25	5.18	4738.44	38.84%	4.28%	0.66
Tree	4640.11	5.39	4645.50	36.12%	2.24%	0.70
Test	**Lead Time**	**Penalty**	**Quality**	**Gap(static)**	**Gap(ad hoc)**	**Runtime**
TS (static)	3295.92	0.69	3296.61	0.00%	-26.25%	46.52
TS (ad hoc)	4470.21	0.04	4470.25	35.60%	0.00%	56.90
FCFS	5809.30	268.81	6078.12	84.37%	35.97%	0.719
EDD	5632.76	17.28	5650.04	71.39%	26.39%	0.71
Linear	4680.94	9.29	4690.23	42.27%	4.92%	0.75
Tree	4633.07	12.22	4645.29	40.91%	3.92%	0.72

Comparing the Tree dispatching to the planning-based approach, there is a gap of 3.92% on the dynamic instances. However, less runtime is used during the test phase which makes the dispatching approach applicatable to highly volatile environments where decisions have to be taken quickly.

The Tree dispatching rule performs around 2% better on the training set and around 1% better on the test set than the linear dispatching rule. This indicates, that it is advantegous to synthesize complex rules. The evolved rule is illustrated in Figure 1 and indicates that non-linearities were identified in the system.

In general, the evolutionary process is more complex for the tree-based rule. It took 3204 evaluations to evolve the linear rule, while it took 29072 evaluations to evolve the tree-based rule. This means, that the training phase is much more complex for the tree-based dispatching rule compared to the linear rule. In the test phase, however, a better quality can be achieved and there is no significant runtime overhead compared to the other approaches.

Since the GP process is a white-box approach, conclusions can be drawn on the problem environment based on the evolutionary process. For that purpose, we performed variable frequency analysis as described in [10]. When we analyze the top 5 variables we can observe, that there are three important influence factors in the problem environment. The first one is related to the time a customer is already waiting in the system and also the time that is left to serve the request (*DueDate, LeadTime*). The second one is related to the distance of the customer to the agent and also to already carried requests to minimize transportation cost (*Distance, DropoffDemand*). The third factor is the self-organization aspect (*AvgAgentDistance*).

One could also come to a similar conclusion by intelligent reasoning that time, distance and self-organization are important aspects of the system. However, the weighting and combination (i.e. synthesis) of the different influence factors is a much more challenging task which has been achieved by the GP process.

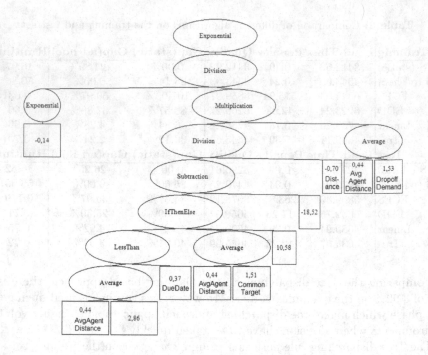

Fig. 1. Evolved dispatching rule

5 Conclusions

Summarizing, we have applied genetic programming for the synthesis of specialized dispatching rules for the dynamic dial-a-ride problem. The rules are adapted to a certain problem environment using training scenarios and can then be applied to similar previously unseen scenarios. The complex dispatching rule performs around 4% worse than a planning-based approach having a considerably lower runtime. This makes it applicatable in volatile and highly dynamic environments where planning might not be feasible.

The GP process led to better dispatching rules than the other approaches. A possible explanation is, that it can identify non-linearities in the system. However, the search space and the evolutionary process are complex. An advantage of GP is, that it is a white-box approach and the resulting models can be used to gain insights about the system. For that purpose we have applied a variable frequency analysis. We have identified the most important influence factors of the system.

For future work, there is still a large gap between the dynamic and the static solutions. Thus it would be interesting to include information about future requests in the model. This could lead to online stochastic problem formulations where the dispatching rules can be incorporated. Additionally, we want to compare our approach to additional methods from the literature and test it on more standard benchmark instances.

Acknowledgments. The work described in this paper was done within the Regio 13 program sponsored by the European Regional Development Fund and by Upper Austrian public funds.

References

1. Affenzeller, M., Winkler, S., Wagner, S., Beham, A.: Genetic Algorithms and Genetic Programming: Modern Concepts and Practical Applications (Numerical Insights), 1st edn. Chapman & Hall (April 2009)
2. Attanasio, A., Cordeau, J., Ghiani, G., Laporte, G.: Parallel tabu search heuristics for the dynamic multi-vehicle dial-a-ride problem. Parallel Computing 30(3), 377–387 (2004)
3. Beham, A., Kofler, M., Wagner, S., Affenzeller, M.: Agent-based simulation of dispatching rules in dynamic pickup and delivery problems. In: 2nd International Logistics and Industrial Informatics, LINDI 2009, pp. 1–6. IEEE (2009)
4. Berbeglia, G., Cordeau, J., Laporte, G.: Dynamic pickup and delivery problems. European Journal of Operational Research 202(1), 8–15 (2010)
5. Berbeglia, G., Cordeau, J.F., Gribkovskaia, I., Laporte, G.: Static pickup and delivery problems: a classification scheme and survey. Top 15(1), 1–31 (2007)
6. Bertsimas, D.J., Van Ryzin, G.: A stochastic and dynamic vehicle routing problem in the euclidean plane. Operations Research 39(4), 601–615 (1991)
7. Cordeau, J.F., Laporte, G.: The dial-a-ride problem: models and algorithms. Annals of Operations Research 153(1), 29–46 (2007)
8. Cordeau, J., Laporte, G.: The dial-a-ride problem (darp): Variants, modeling issues and algorithms. 4OR: A Quarterly Journal of Operations Research 1(2), 89–101 (2003)
9. Fu, M.C., Glover, F.W., April, J.: Simulation optimization: a review, new developments, and applications. In: 2005 Proceedings of the Winter Simulation Conference, 13. p. IEEE (2005)
10. Kronberger, G.: Symbolic Regression for Knowledge Discovery – Bloat, Overfitting, and Variable Interaction Networks. No. 64 in Johannes Kepler University, Linz, Reihe C, Trauner Verlag+Buchservice GmbH (2011)
11. Laporte, G.: Recent algorithms for the dial-a-ride problem. In: Operations Research for Complex Decision Making, p. 13 (2010)
12. Larsen, A., Madsen, O., Solomon, M.: Partially dynamic vehicle routing-models and algorithms. Journal of the Operational Research Society, 637–646 (2002)
13. van Lon, R., Holvoet, T., Vanden Berghe, G., Wenseleers, T., Branke, J.: Evolutionary synthesis of multi-agent systems for dynamic dial-a-ride problems. In: Proceedings of the Fourteenth International Conference on Genetic and Evolutionary Computation Conference Companion, pp. 331–336. ACM (2012)
14. Pitzer, E., Beham, A., Affenzeller, M., Heiss, H., Vorderwinkler, M.: Production fine planning using a solution archive of priority rules. In: 2011 3rd IEEE International Symposium on Logistics and Industrial Informatics (LINDI), pp. 111–116. IEEE (2011)
15. Schilde, M., Doerner, K.F., Hartl, R.F.: Metaheuristics for the dynamic stochastic dial-a-ride problem with expected return transports. Computers & Operations Research 38(12), 1719–1730 (2011)
16. Wagner, S.: Heuristic Optimization Software Systems - Modeling of Heuristic Optimization Algorithms in the HeuristicLab Software Environment. Ph.D. thesis, Johannes Kepler University, Linz, Austria (2009)

On the Evolutionary Behavior of Genetic Programming with Constants Optimization

Bogdan Burlacu, Michael Affenzeller, and Michael Kommenda

University of Applied Sciences Upper Austria
Heuristic and Evolutionary Algorithms Laboratory
Softwarepark 11, 4232 Hagenberg, Austria
bogdan.burlacu@fh-hagenberg.at

Abstract. Evolutionary systems are characterized by two seemingly contradictory properties: robustness and evolvability. Robustness is generally defined as an organism's ability to withstand genetic perturbation while maintaining its phenotype. Evolvability, as an organism's ability to produce useful variation. In genetic programming, the relationship between the two, mediated by selection and variation-producing operators (recombination and mutation), makes it difficult to understand the behavior and evolutionary dynamics of the search process. In this paper, we show that a local gradient-based constants optimization step can improve the overall population evolvability by inducing a beneficial structure-preserving bias on selection, which in the long term helps the process maintain diversity and produce better solutions.

Keywords: Genetic Programming, Evolutionary Behavior, Constant Optimization, Symbolic Regression, Algorithm Analysis.

1 Introduction

Genetic programming is a well-established and widely used meta-heuristic optimization technique. The main reason behind its success is the inherent high robustness of darwinian evolution as an optimization engine and the flexibility it offers with regard to the representation scheme, making it suitable for many problem domains [2].

Individual genotypes often harbor large amounts of hidden genetic variation (or potential variation), that is only expressed when the genetic background changes [8]. Genes may have an effect on the phenotype, but this effect strongly depends on other genes in the genome; hence, genetic effects can be larger in one genetic background and smaller in another. Robustness protects phenotypes from genetic perturbations but by doing so, it reduces evolvability and promotes evolutionary stasis. Mechanisms allowing release from such buffering increase evolvability and may be crucial to evolutionary change [6].

At population level, robustness is manifested as a redundancy of the genotype-phenotype mappings. That is, many genotypes fold into identical or equivalent phenotypes (in terms of fitness). This non-injective mapping between genotypes

R. Moreno-Díaz et al. (Eds.): EUROCAST 2013, Part I, LNCS 8111, pp. 284–291, 2013.

and phenotypes can lead to loss of diversity as it makes the selection mechanism "blind" to some potentially useful variation (since selection is based only on fitness).

Two main causes for the loss of population diversity follow from the above. On the one hand, if there are many individuals sharing the same fitness, variation is lost because selection is unable to discriminate between more or less evolvable individuals. On the other hand, if genotypes do not express the optimal (fittest possible) phenotype (for example, because of poor constants), their potentially good structural properties might be ignored during selection and thus, they might be lost. A similar idea is expressed in [5], although in their case the fitness of a tree was weighted according to its size, thus also potentially limiting good structures.

In this paper, we investigate the behavior of the standard GP in conjunction with a local optimization technique designed to improve the weights and constant values of symbolic expression trees. By optimizing the genotypes in the population, we allow potentially good structure to further take part in the evolutionary process. This leads to changes in the dynamics of the algorithms, which will be detailed below. In the following sections we introduce the idea of GP hybridisation with a local search (Section 2), discuss the results on a standard benchmark problem (Section 3) and present our conclusions and development plans (Section 4).

2   Genetic Programming with Constants Optimization

Hybrid GP results from the combination with other optimization algorithms, meant to improve quality of the solutions. Hybridisations of this kind have been attempted several times before; for instance STROGANOFF [1] performs a tree optimization step after recombination. In [5], "whenever a new constant is introduced into the predictive expression, a non-linear least squares optimization is performed to obtain the 'best' value of the constant(s) in the expression".

Another effort in this direction uses a gradient descent method for the optimization of numeric leaf values [7]. The better performance of the resulting algorithm is explained in terms of adaptability to local learning, such that the optimization changes the fitness distribution in the population, directly affecting the selection outcome. The authors note that individuals in the GP population appear to acquire a growing number of constants within their structure, therefore becoming more able to adapt to local learning modifications. They promote the Baldwin effect as the main reason for this behavior, which can be described as the effect resulting from the interaction of two adaptive processes: the genotypic evolution of the population (global search) and the phenotypic plasticity (or flexibility) of individual organisms (local search). The optimization method used in this paper is described in detail in [3].

In our experiments, the constant optimizing GP (COGP) was tested against the standard GP (SGP) and two specialized variants, using a standard benchmark dataset for symbolic regression. To analyze the effects of constants optimization

Table 1. Experimental configurations

#	Pop. size	Gen.	Crossover	Mut. prob.	Max depth	Max length	CO %
A	500	100	Subtree swap	25%	12	50	25%
B	500	100	Subtree swap	25%	12	50	50%
C	500	100	Subtree swap	25%	12	50	100%
D	500	100	Subtree swap	25%	12	50	—
E	500	100	Context-aware	25%	12	50	—
F	500	100	Deterministic-best	25%	12	50	—

on the evolutionary dynamics of GP, we tested different run configurations which are detailed in Table 1. The "CO %" parameter in the table indicates the percentage of constant-optimized individuals in the population. Additionally, configurations E and F include specialized *context-preserving* crossover operators, described below. Considering parents P_0 and P_1, the *context-aware* crossover [4] deterministically finds the best insertion point in P_0 for a randomly selected subtree from P_1. while the *deterministic-best* crossover finds the best subtree from P_1 to be inserted in a randomly selected point from P_0. This operator was developed independently by the authors during their work on HeuristicLab [9].

While they do not guarantee fitter offspring, these two specialized operators are able to minimize the destructive effect of crossover so that whatever good structures initially present in the population may also be preserved. Therefore, they provide a good basis for comparison with COGP.

In order to characterize the evolutionary behavior of the algorithms, the average and best individual qualities, the average tree length, and the average fragment size were measured, where a *fragment* is defined as the portion of a tree that was affected by mutation or crossover. Larger fragments indicate better progress in the exploratory phase of the algorithm, while small fragments indicate convergence and the beginning of the local search phase.

For investigating the Baldwin effect, the average number of leafs for the population of trees was also measured. Finally, the following measures were used to quantify the *evolvability* of the population:

Reproductive success. The percentage of 'successful' offspring in a generation (offspring with a fitness better than both their parents). A 'successful' offspring may be produced by a genetic operator or it may become better than its parents after the constant optimization step.

Average improvement. The average fitness difference (Pearson's R^2) between the best parent and the offspring obtained by crossover or mutation.

In the case of COGP, the operator improvement values were measured both *before* and *after* the optimization step, and compared to the values obtained without any constants optimization at all. In what follows, the results are averaged over 50 repetitions of each run configuration.

3   Experimental Results

Our experiment consists of a number of symbolic regression runs on the *Poly-10* problem, in which the objective is to find a good approximation for the function:

$$f(\mathbf{x}) = x_1 x_2 + x_3 x_4 + x_5 x_6 + x_1 x_7 x_9 + x_3 x_6 x_{10}.$$

It is usual that in this synthetic benchmark problem, the standard algorithm does not perform very well. Figure 1a shows that SGP is unable, on average, to obtain a training quality greater than ≈ 0.6. Comparing the average and the best qualities from the different run configurations (Figure 1b), we notice that the best solution of COGP is $35 - 48\%$ better than SGP (average quality $29 - 74\%$ better). In the context-preserving GP variants, the values for the average and best solution quality are very close, indicating a loss of diversity during the runs but also a steeper convergence.

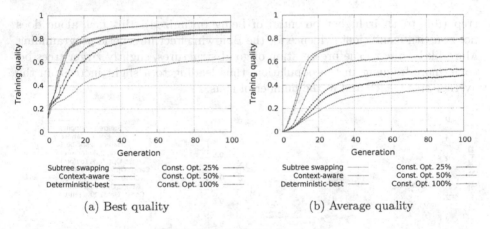

(a) Best quality   (b) Average quality

Fig. 1. Best and average quality

As the local optimization step biases selection, we are interested to see the degree to which this bias affects the overall genotypic structure of the population, and consequently, its evolvability. We first take a look at the average tree size and notice that the constants optimization does produce a slight increase in average tree length (Figure 2a). This increase ($4.2–8.8\%$) however, is negligible and compensated by higher quality. By comparison, the increase in size produced by the context-preserving crossover operators (context-aware and deterministic-best) is much larger. A similar picture, considering the average number of leafs per individual is shown in 2b where again we notice very small differences between SGP and COGP and a larger number of leafs for the context-preserving variants.

Therefore, we can conclude that even if larger programs (with more constants in their structure) may be favored by selection post the constants optimization

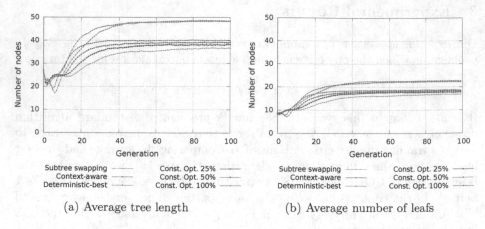

(a) Average tree length   (b) Average number of leafs

Fig. 2. Average tree length and number of leaf nodes

step (due to their higher potential of being optimized), this fact alone does not constitute sufficient evidence for the Baldwin effect in genetic programming. More likely, due to the preservation of good structures, slightly larger trees become more frequent in the population, thus leading to a slight increase in the average tree length and in the number of leafs.

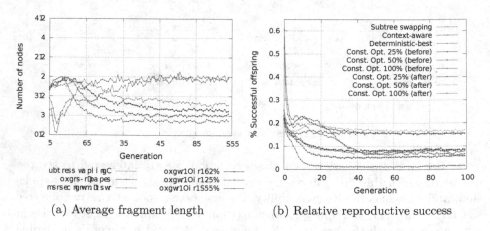

(a) Average fragment length   (b) Relative reproductive success

Fig. 3. Average fragment sizes and relative reproductive success

The variation of average fragment sizes (subtrees affected by mutation or swapped by crossover) supports our claim that COGP exhibits better evolutionary behavior. Figure 3a shows that in the beginning of the search progress is achieved by changing and replacing larger fragments; towards the end fragments become smaller, indicating convergence and a transition to the exploitative or local search phase. This transition becomes more obvious if we consider the decrease of average fragment size in conjunction with the increase of average tree size in the population. The evolution of average fragment size has a more

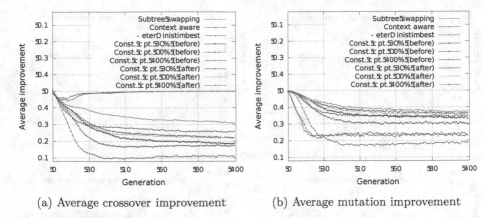

(a) Average crossover improvement   (b) Average mutation improvement

Fig. 4. Average crossover and mutation operator improvement

pronounced decrease in the case of COGP, suggesting a shorter, more efficient exploratory phase and a more localized search towards the end.

By contrast, the context preserving crossover variants start with small fragments which increase gradually in size. This can be explained by the combination of local search (deterministically choosing which fragments to swap) and selection, which leads to a decreased diversity and a large amount of buffering within the population. These crossover operators will inevitably become unable to produce better offspring, becoming neutral (no change in fitness), as can be seen in Figure 4a.

In the case of COGP, the average operator improvement is relative to the average quality of the population, which in turn is correlated to the "CO %" parameter. In the case of crossover, the curves in Figure 4 show a more pronounced negative improvement for COGP (compared to SGP), while in the case of mutation the curves for SGP and COGP after the CO step are similar. Clearly, the higher the CO%, the higher the quality and the lower the curves (as a high quality individual is more likely to be disrupted). In this context, the fact that COGP is able to achieve comparable improvement clearly indicates superior evolutionary dynamics.

We see that the CO step is able to produce a significant improvement even as the average quality of the population increases on every generation. This behavior can also be observed in Figure 3b, where the reproductive success (measured as the percentage of offspring that outperform their parents) is shown for each algorithm configuration. To get an even clearer picture, we averaged the improvement brought by CO on each individual. Figures 5a, 5b and 5c show the increase in fitness brought by CO, recorded separately for crossover and mutation.

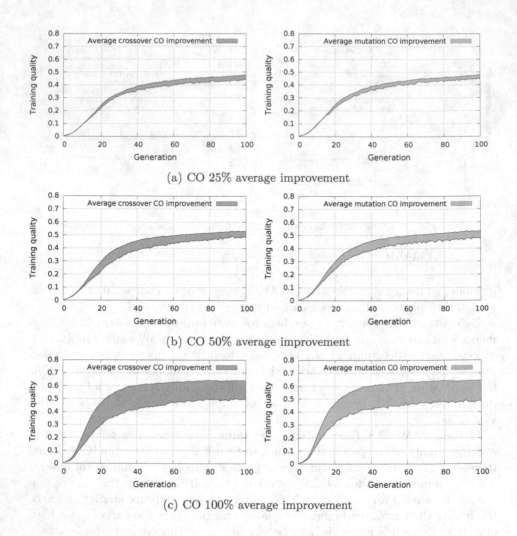

(a) CO 25% average improvement

(b) CO 50% average improvement

(c) CO 100% average improvement

4   Conclusions and Future Work

In this paper, we analyzed the evolutionary behavior of a hybrid GP system in which a gradient-based algorithm was used to improve the variable weights and constants of tree individuals. We saw that COGP can improve the overall population evolvability, by inducing a structure-preserving bias on selection. It is able to better preserve and exploit the existing diversity and exhibits better dynamics: short and efficient exploratory phase, followed by gradual improvement (with smaller fragments). Our investigation of tree lengths and number of leafs has provided no definite proof regarding the occurrence of the Baldwin effect in COGP.

Regarding performance, COGP was able to outperform the standard GP and variants in all cases. The context-preserving GP variants also performed well, but exhaust diversity, while creating bloat.

Further research ideas involve extending the analysis and tracking framework, and investigating further aspects of GP evolutionary dynamics such as individual ancestries, fragments and building blocks and constructional aspects of selection.

References

1. Iba, H., Sato, T., de Garis, H.: Recombination guidance for numerical genetic programming. In: 1995 IEEE Conference on Evolutionary Computation, November 29-December 1, vol. 1, pp. 97–102. IEEE Press, Perth (1995)
2. Koza, J.R.: Genetic Programming: On the Programming of Computers by Means of Natural Selection. MIT Press, Cambridge (1992)
3. Kommenda, M., Affenzeller, M., Kronberger, G., Winkler, S.: Nonlinear Least Squares Optimization of Constants in Symbolic Regression (2013)
4. Majeed, H., Ryan, C.: Using context-aware crossover to improve the performance of gp. In: GECCO 2006: Proceedings of the 8th Annual Conference on Genetic and Evolutionary Computation, pp. 847–854. ACM Press (2006)
5. McKay, B., Willis, M., Barton, G.: Using a tree structured genetic algorithm to perform symbolic regression. In: First International Conference on Genetic Algorithms in Engineering Systems: Innovations and Applications, GALESIA (Conf. Publ. No. 414), pp. 487–492 (September 1995)
6. Rutherford, S.L.: From genotype to phenotype: buffering mechanisms and the storage of genetic information. BioEssays 22(12), 1095–1105 (2000)
7. Topchy, A., Punch, W.F.: Faster genetic programming based on local gradient search of numeric leaf values. In: Proceedings of the Genetic and Evolutionary Computation Conference (GECCO 2001), pp. 155–162. Morgan Kaufmann (2001)
8. de Visser, J.A.G.M., Hermisson, J., Wagner, G.P., Meyers, L.A., Bagheri-Chaichian, H., Blanchard, J.L., Chao, L., Cheverud, J.M., Elena, S.F., Fontana, W., Gibson, G., Hansen, T.F., Krakauer, D., Lewontin, R.C., Ofria, C., Rice, S.H., von Dassow, G., Wagner, A., Whitlock, M.C.: Perspective: Evolution and detection of genetic robustness. Evolution 57(9), 1959–1972 (2003)
9. Wagner, S.: Heuristic Optimization Software Systems - Modeling of Heuristic Optimization Algorithms in the HeuristicLab Software Environment. Ph.D. thesis, Institute for Formal Models and Verification, Johannes Kepler University, Linz, Austria (2009)

Fitness Landscape Based Parameter Estimation
for Robust Taboo Search

Andreas Beham, Erik Pitzer, and Michael Affenzeller

University of Applied Sciences Upper Austria
School of Informatics, Communications and Media
Softwarepark 11, 4232 Hagenberg, Austria
{andreas.beham,erik.pitzer,michael.affenzeller}@fh-hagenberg.at

1   Introduction

Metaheuristic optimization algorithms are general optimization strategies suited
to solve a range of real-world relevant optimization problems. Many metaheuristics expose parameters that allow to tune the effort that these algorithms are
allowed to make and also the strategy and search behavior [1]. Adjusting these
parameters allows to increase the algorithms' performances with respect to different problem- and problem instance characteristics. The difficulty in exposing
parameters of metaheuristics is that these parameters *need* to be set and *should*
be adjusted for good performance. Also, choosing a reasonable default value is
not an easy task for algorithm developers. The purpose of this work is, on the
one hand to explore the effect of parameter settings and provide more suited
default values, and on the other hand to introduce a new method to use fitness
landscape analysis (FLA) for the prediction of algorithm parameterization. An
overview of fitness landscape analysis is given in [6]. The scope of such a study
can in general be extended to any algorithm and problem combination, but this
paper is restricted to the robust taboo search (RTS) when applied to problem
instances of the quadratic assignment problem library (QAPLIB). With a similar intention [2] used fitness landscape analysis to choose the best algorithm to
solve instances out of the BBOB benchmark set. In [7] a study was made that
predicted the hardness of a problem instance using FLA fingerprints.

Quadratic Assignment Problem

The quadratic assignment problem (QAP) can be described by an $N \times N$ matrix
W with elements w_{ik} denoting the weight between facility i and facility j and
an $N \times N$ matrix D with elements d_{xy} denoting the distance between location
x and location y. The goal is to find a permutation π with $\pi(i)$ denoting the
element at position i so that the objective given in equation (1) is achieved [5].

$$\min \sum_{i=1}^{N} \sum_{k=1}^{N} w_{ik} * d_{\pi(i)\pi(k)} \tag{1}$$

The permutation is a feasible representation and is interpreted as assigning
exactly one facility to exactly one location.

R. Moreno-Díaz et al. (Eds.): EUROCAST 2013, Part I, LNCS 8111, pp. 292–299, 2013.
© Springer-Verlag Berlin Heidelberg 2013

2   Robust Taboo Search

Tabu search is a metaheuristic that was introduced by Glover [4] and which was studied by many others including Taillard who introduced the robust taboo search (RTS) variant [8]. The search strategy of tabu search incorporates a short term memory which remembers and forbids to revert moves that have been previously made. A *tabu tenure* parameter governs the time a certain move should not be undone. Additionally, a parameter called *aspiration tenure* was introduced in robust taboo search. Instead of picking the best move in each iteration, the algorithm would pick a move it has not made for a certain time. A move in RTS consists of a swap of two elements in the permutation. This is interpreted as exchanging the location between two facilities i and j.

2.1   Parameter Impacts

The parameters mainly affect the balance between exploration and intensification. A high tabu tenure would augment diversification as moves are kept tabu for a longer time and cannot be undone. The search is thus not allowed to return to previously visited solutions. A small tabu tenure on the other hand would allow the search to remain in a smaller depression of the search space leading to an intensified search in a smaller part. On the other hand a small aspiration tenure would lead to a higher diversification. This parameter controls the time after which not the best non-tabu move is made, but one that diversifies the search by performing moves that have not been made previously. The shorter these times are, the more diversifying moves will be made. As can be seen in Figure 1 when the tabu tenure is low and the aspiration tenure is high the search intensifies, meaning it will often return to a very similar solution. If the tabu tenure is set to a higher value the search is going to diversify to a larger degree. However, the aspiration tenure has a much bigger influence on the search. The effect of the tabu tenure is barely noticeable when the aspiration is set to a low value. The effects become more obvious when we also take into account the diversity with respect to the solution quality as indicated in Figure 2. It can be seen that the most diverse setting also visits worse solutions than any other setting.

3   Parameter Estimation

In a large experiment that involves 90 different combinations of tabu tenure and aspiration tenure and 20 repetitions for each combination we estimated the performance of RTS applied to the QAPLIB. We measured the number of iterations it was necessary to reach the best known solution (as given in the QAPLIB) as well as the deviation to the best known quality in case the best known solution was not discovered. In the results it was observed that the aspiration criteria depends to a certain degree on the problem dimension. However, it was also observed that for certain instances the parameters need to be set much higher or lower. In this work we attempt to find better models

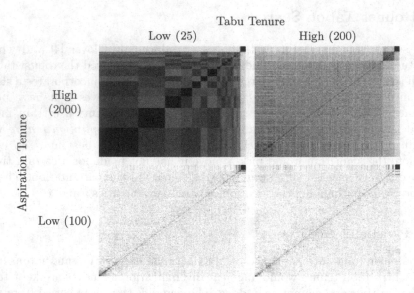

Fig. 1. Showing the similarity of all solutions along the trajectory of RTS applied to the els19 instance. The plots show the similarity matrix of permutations in the trajectory against each other. The darker the pixels in the matrix the more similar two permutations are. The Hamming distance has been used to determine permutation similarity.

for choosing this parameter by taking fitness landscape analysis (FLA) features into account. These features describe a problem instance with respect to further dimensions than just the problem size allowing us to come to a more informed and hopefully better decision.

However, our goal in this case is to make use of as little FLA information as possible. We aim to enhance models that can be solely based on the problem size by adding another feature-dimension to each instance that results from FLA studies. Often, the problem size is the only guidance one can exploit when applying metaheuristics as it is a pregiven property of a concrete problem instance. In this work we show how to improve those models by including additional features.

3.1   Fitness Landscape Measurements

As stated in [6] a fitness landscape $\mathcal{F}$ is composed of a solution space S and a fitness function $f : S \to \mathbb{R}$ that assigns a fitness to every solution candidate $x \in S$. Additionally, a fitness landscape contains a notion of connectivity $\mathcal{X}$ between different solution candidates. This connectivity is often implicitly assumed in the form of a neighborhood relation $N : S \to \mathcal{P}(S)$, where $\mathcal{P}(S)$ is the power set of S, or a distances function $d : S \times S \to \mathbb{R}$ that is used to compare solution candidates. This connectivity gives rise to notions of locality inside the solution space and, hence, inside the fitness landscape.

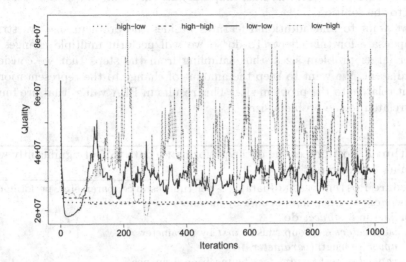

Fig. 2. Plot of RTS progress applied to the els19 in the configurations mentioned in Figure 1. The plot shows the current quality at each iteration. The amount of diversification with respect to the height in the fitness landscape becomes obvious.

The measurements that we obtained from the fitness landscape stem from a variety of different perspectives on that landscape. In particular, we used sampling based techniques which can be, principally, obtained from any fitness landscape. That considered data can be obtained from random walks in those landscapes, as well as up-down walks. Random walks are sequences of solutions $s \in S$ obtained through randomly choosing among the available connections for each solution s. The qualities $f(s)$ that can be attributed to each solution s in the sequence then form the so called *quality trail* which is used to calculate many of the landscape properties. These properties, i.e. the autocorrelation coefficient [3] measure the ruggedness of these landscapes and further properties such as the steepness of local optima. The total list of features that we considered is described in [6] in more detail.

Compensation for Problem Size. As was discussed previously, the connectivity that we considered in the QAP is the so called swap-neighborhood. This neighborhood is well-suited to solve the quadratic assignment problem, however, as is typical for neighborhoods of combinatorial optimization problems, the amount of change to the representation is a constant value that is independent of the representation size. For instance, in the traveling salesman problem a 2-opt would exchange two edges, in the QAP the swap exchanges two facilities. As the problem size grows this change in the solution becomes relatively small and much of the representation, and thus of the fitness, remains constant. The impression from walks on problems of bigger size is thus that they appear to be much smoother. However, this smoothness is only the result of a smaller relative change to the solution.

As we want to find additional features besides the problem size, we strive to compensate for this effect. To do so we will perform multiple changes at once for larger problem sizes, thus sampling from the steps that we consider to be adjacent. We want to keep the amount of change to the representation a constant relative to the problem size. This results in FLA values that are much less correlated to the problem size.

Algorithm 1. Post-processing of the performance data to find significantly well performing parameters

---

    procedure POSTPROCESSING(data)   ▷ per run: instance, parameter, performance
        instances ← group lines in *data* by instance
        for *inst* in *instances* **do**
            parameters ← group runs in *inst* by parameter
            upper ← length(*parameters*)
            ranked ← sort *parameters* by mean performance
            p ← ANOVA(*parameters*)
            if $p < 0.01$ **then**   ▷ post-hoc analysis with Holmes adjustment
                adj ← 1
                for i ← *ranked.worst* to *ranked.best* **do**
                    $\hat{p}$ ← TTEST(*ranked.i*, *ranked.best*)
                    if $\hat{p} > 0.01/adj$ **then**   ▷ Insignificant result
                        upper ← i
                    end if
                    adj ← *adj* + 1
                end for
                Write *inst* and smallest parameter from *ranked.best* to *ranked.upper*
            end if   ▷ No significant difference
        end for
    end procedure

3.2 Modeling Parameters

We performed a large parameter variation experiment in which we divided the parameter space into a total of 90 different configurations. Each configuration was evaluated 20 times on each of the problem instances to account for stochastic variance of the algorithms' results.

Given the obtained performance data and the FLA fingerprint information we want to find models that would indicate how to parameterize the robust taboo search. To do so the problem of choosing a good parameter value is transformed to a machine learning problem where the goal is to take the input values and find a model that would result in the specified output. We thus aim to find models with a better correlation between the estimated parameters and those that have been observed to work well in the experiments. More specifically, we examined a regression-based approach as well as a classification-based approach to represent our machine learning problem. We then aim to solve these problems using simple linear techniques and compare the models that we obtain using only problem size with models that we obtain using problem size and FLA fingerprint information.

In order to proceed with this task the performance data first has to be processed. It contains many measurements from the execution of the algorithm on the problem instances, however, we would like to know for each problem instance the best parameter that we should choose. For this purpose we perform a hypothesis test for the performance measurements on every problem instance to find out if a certain parameterization is significantly better than other parameterizations. In reality however, we will often obtain a group of parameters that are significantly better to the rest and thus make an a priori choice in which we use the smallest parameters in the insignificant group. The post-processing procedure is given as pseudo code in Algorithm 1.

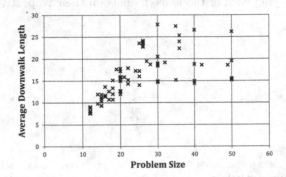

Fig. 3. A scatter plot showing problem size vs average down-walk length. For larger problem sizes these two values are not correlated anymore.

The inputs for our parameters constitute the fingerprint information described above. The target however is different in the approaches that we investigated. In the regression-based approach the goal is to find models that would exactly predict the value of the parameter given the fingerprint information. Whereas in the classification-based approach the parameter values are categorized into low and high values, and those that are deemed insignificant by the hypothesis test. The goal is to find models that are able to predict the correct category for each problem instance. When doing regression we would get an exact value of a parameter that we should choose, while in classification we just know that the parameter should be set, e.g. high, but have to come up with a reasonable value ourselves.

4   Results

Using the problem size as well as at most one other fitness landscape characteristic we found improved models when using the average down-walk length.
This information gives an insight into the depth of the fitness landscape, if it
contains rather steep holes or is rather flat. In Figure 3 a scatter plot between
the problem size and this value is shown.

  If we are going to reason about this result, it would indicate that there should
be different parameter settings for very rugged problem instances in contrast
to those that are rather flat. If we examine the linear regression models more
closely, it is visible that the down-walk length has a negative influence which
means that instances which allow larger down-walks tend to be solved better
if more aspiration is being used. This would mean that instances which require
a lot of steps to also get out of the local optima should use more aspiration.
The tabu search using only the tabu list thus is not enough to really explore the
landscape in those problems. We used 3-fold crossvalidation and calculated the
test error by applying each of the folds' models on their respective test data.

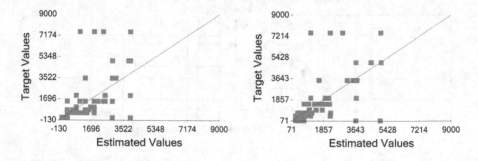

Fig. 4. Comparison of the standard model that would set the aspiration tenure according to the problem size only and the improved model that takes into account the average
down-walk length. The difference in test error is an R^2 of 0.338 vs 0.416 resulting from
a 3-fold crossvalidation on 89 problem instances.

  Comparing the regression and the classification results in Figure 4 and Table 1, we see that in both cases the improved models are able to make slightly
better predictions. In the classification example the instances where there was
no significant difference between the results could be better classified. Those are
problem instances that may be very easy and thus can be solved with all parameter settings equally well or may be very hard and cannot be solved with any
parameter setting.

Table 1. Results from applying linear-discriminant analysis to the classification problem using only the problem size on the left vs using the problem size and the average down-walk length on the right

	Actual				Actual		
Predicted	Low	Insig.	High Total	Predicted	Low	Insig.	High Total
Low	38	2	9	Low	36	0	7
Insig.	0	12	1	Insig.	1	14	1
High	2	0	20	High	3	0	22
Accuracy	95%	85.7%	66.7% **70%**	Accuracy	90%	100%	73.3% **75%**

5 Conclusions

We showed that fitness landscape measurements can be used to enhance the models that we use to predict the parameter values of metaheuristic algorithms. In the classical approach only the problem size would be considered as a guidance, as well as implicit expert knowledge by those who apply the algorithms. We can use FLA to account for some of that implicit knowledge by learning about the different fingerprints of problem instances. The improved models are not difficult to implement and will require some sampling before they can be applied. Additionally, in conducting such studies we can learn more about the algorithm's behavior. There is potential that we can use FLA measures even in problem overarching analysis as we are able to make these fingerprints universally comparable for different problems.

References

1. Affenzeller, M., Winkler, S., Wagner, S., Beham, A.: Genetic Algorithms and Genetic Programming - Modern Concepts and Practical Applications. Numerical Insights. CRC Press (2009)
2. Bischl, B., Mersmann, O., Trautmann, H., Preuss, M.: Algorithm selection based on exploratory landscape analysis and cost-sensitive learning. In: Proceedings of the Genetic and Evolutionary Computation Conference (GECCO 2012), pp. 313–320 (2012)
3. Chicano, F., Luque, G., Alba, E.: Autocorrelation measures for the quadratic assignment problem. Applied Mathematics Letters 25, 698–705 (2012)
4. Glover, F.: Tabu search – part I. ORSA Journal on Computing 1(3), 190–206 (1989)
5. Koopmans, T.C., Beckmann, M.: Assignment problems and the location of economic activities. Econometrica, Journal of the Econometric Society 25(1), 53–76 (1957)
6. Pitzer, E., Affenzeller, M.: A Comprehensive Survey on Fitness Landscape Analysis. In: Fodor, J., Klempous, R., Araujo, C.P.S. (eds.) Recent Advances in Intelligent Engineering Systems. SCI, vol. 378, pp. 161–191. Springer, Heidelberg (2011)
7. Pitzer, E., Beham, A., Affenzeller, M.: Generic hardness estimation using fitness and parameter landscapes applied to robust taboo search and the quadratic assignment problem. In: Companion Publication of the 2012 Genetic and Evolutionary Computation Conference, pp. 393–400 (2012)
8. Taillard, E.D.: Robust taboo search for the quadratic assignment problem. Parallel Computing 17, 443–455 (1991)

Bridging the Gap between Rich Supply Chain Problems and the Effective Application of Metaheuristics through Ontology-Based Modeling

Corinna Engelhardt-Nowitzki[1], Stefan Rotter[1], and Michael Affenzeller[2]

[1] Upper Austria University of Applied Sciences,
Campus Steyr, Wehrgrabengasse 1-3, 4400 Steyr, Austria
[2] Upper Austria University of Applied Sciences,
Campus Hagenberg, Softwarepark 11, 4232 Hagenberg, Austria
{corinna.engelhardt,stefan.rotter}@fh-steyr.at,
michael.affenzeller@fh-hagenberg.at

Abstract. Supply chains (SC) are exposed to dynamic markets and enlarged network structures. This induces abundant decision complexity and the need to frequently adapt decisions. Metaheuristics are most suitable for rich SC optimization problems. However, effectiveness and adaptability of these approaches are impaired through extensive modeling efforts and intricate data representation issues. Therefore we propose using ontological modeling to mitigate these disadvantages.

Keywords: Supply Chain Optimization, Metaheuristics, Supply Chain Ontology.

1 Introduction

Due to high demand volatility, supply chain management (SCM) faces high uncertainty. Material, information and financial flows are highly integrated across company borders. Hence, supply chain (SC) decisions rely on manifold complex and fluctuating parameters from different SC entities [1] and have to handle multidimensional, possibly conflicting objectives. This requires the processing of dynamically changing or stochastic input-data, often together with the need to use estimates, instead of exact values [2]. With growing problem intricacy it becomes more important while more difficult to deploy capable problem solving algorithms that enable computational processing despite abundant time-complexity. Even if divided into less complex sub-problems, SC decision problems are large scale problems. Besides, these disentangled sub-problems have interdependencies. Thus, the literature has increasingly investigated recursively interrelated sub-problems (e.g., vehicle routing [3]).

Increasingly, metaheuristics are applied to such problems [4]. However, problem solving in a SC context typically relies on arbitrarily structured data of non-trivial structure. As SC optimization involves more than one company,

R. Moreno-Díaz et al. (Eds.): EUROCAST 2013, Part I, LNCS 8111, pp. 300–307, 2013.
© Springer-Verlag Berlin Heidelberg 2013

the required knowledge representation has to be retrieved from heterogeneous datasets, fraught with poor cross-company interoperability [5]. Semantic differences, e.g. a differing use of SC terms or key indicators have to be harmonized. For example, part systematization and related numerical coding might differ: while the supplier refers to 'tons of steel' (geometric and metallurgical attributes), the buyer refers to 'number of sold cars' (model attributes). In principle, the buyer's bill of materials could facilitate the transformation of measurement units between these SC parties. However, in a real life SC this might regard hundreds of parts and as many companies. Hence, continuous information sharing requires huge effort and is often fault-prone. SC participants are linked via m:n relations (e.g., m suppliers - n customers). Thus, the amount of SC interfaces that require data transition is immense and increases with growing network density. Even if limiting an analysis to the most relevant SC parties, the remaining interoperability lacks impair algorithmic solving.

In changing environments that require frequent decision taking and revision, solution parameters have to be modified accordingly. Reasoning mechanisms must be advanced towards the capability of being applied frequently. In this respect, it is not sufficiently answered how to design cross-company data representations that (i) validly reflect complex real world SC coherences, (ii) are sufficiently harmonized for being processed by, e.g., metaheuristic algorithms and (iii) are easy to adapt for repeated processing.

This paper proposes using SC ontologies to advance the effectiveness of metaheuristics in SCM. A SC ontology is a formal specification of particular conceptualizations, relevant for SC decision making. It is an explicit, abstracted and hierarchically structured representation of real world SC phenomena that is semantically harmonized across SC parties and consensually shared among involved decision makers [6]. The paper is structured as follows: section two provides an extended problem characterization. Section three explains potential benefits from ontological modeling. Section four presents exemplary SC scenarios for a facility location and resource allocation problem. Concluding, we provide tentative assumptions and questions for future research.

2   Problem Statement

As stated above, SC complexity inhibits formalized modeling as required for computational processing. Additionally to interoperability lacks, three further issues are influential: (i) the determination of adequate data granularity, (ii) information asymmetries between SC parties together with behavioral biases and (iii) the widely supposed domain-dependency of SC problems.

The degree of *(i) data granularity* refers to e.g., product hierarchies or planning itemization. While exaggerated itemization unduly increases complexity, too low granularity yields inferior solutions. For instance, a demand forecast might be smooth on a product group level. When, however, inspecting singular product variants, the same demand could remarkably alternate. In this case it depends on the ability to substitute variants against each other, whether this variety causes difficulties for the underlying logistics system and SC decisions. The same applies for operational issues, e.g., when determining, whether demand changes will affect a company's daily operations. A capable data representation has to be able to change the level of detail (hierarchical drill-down and roll-up).

In a SC context these questions have to be extended towards SC parties. Assuming volatile demand and hence a fluctuating product mix, also the supply side is affected, e.g., when seeking to determine volatility impacts on delivery schedules for purchased parts with adequate granularity. The same applies for transport matters and other SC activities. With changed demand patterns, new optimization runs have to be executed regarding e.g., vehicle routing, production scheduling or resource allocation. Provided that decision makers can be enabled to quickly model and reconfigure complex SC problems, they could examine planned or actual business settings on varying granularity levels to determine relevant elastic forces in their supply network. However, most operational research contributions are not concerned with granularity and leave parameter scaling issues to the user's disposal. A scalable SC ontology offers two advantages: the ability of quick modeling and model reconfiguration and further, the capability to process different levels of detail.

(ii) Information asymmetries, opportunism [7] and other behavioral deviations [8] from rational reasoning cause decision biases. Due to lacking abilities to model such phenomena, most optimization approaches neglect such influences. SC decisions have to be taken without formalized reasoning mechanisms (creating human decision biases) or based on simplified (i.e., also biased) models. Reversely, repeated algorithm processing based on modified parameters would allow exploring "what-if" scenarios. A SC ontology could enable this by means of reduced modeling and model reconfiguration effort.

A further aspect is the often assumed (iii) domain-dependency of SC problems. The literature widely inspects particular SC cases and solutions. Though, the same problem matters elsewhere, poor generalization capability and domain-dependency obviate a cross-domain transfer of used models. For practitioners this inhibits the reusability of useful solutions. Researchers face lacking abilities to generalize from singular cases. This impairs theory-building. Ontological modeling could advance both concerns through semantic harmonization.

Concluding, a SC ontology has to provide an explicit, sufficiently abstracted, domain-independent representation of real world SC phenomena (entities, relations, attributes, flows, indicators, rules, etc.) that ideally is machine-readable ([9], [10]). A SC ontology has to be hierarchically structured [11] and scalable to facilitate a flexible granularity level for computational problem solving.

Algorithmic problem solving takes course sequentially. Starting with problem description and system delineation, objectives, constraints and relations between the system and adjacent areas are defined. This determines data gathering efforts and solution quality. A mathematical model (objective function(s), decision variables, sets, parameters, constraints) is formulated and fed with collected data. However, data gathering is often time-consuming because of insufficient data structure, quality and incompleteness. Next, a computational procedure (e.g., metaheuristics) is applied and validated to derive initial solutions. Finally, managerial implications are drawn to prepare real world decision taking [12]. Ontological modeling could remarkably accelerate such approaches.

3 Applying SC Ontologies to Computational Problem Solving

SC operations follow divergent, linear, convergent or blended network topologies. Assuming each company to be represented through a network node, relations and value flows are constituted through connecting edges. SC decisions are taken de-centrally in each node, establishing a heterarchical [13] and constantly fluctuating value network. Accordingly, a unique value network conceptualization that is shared by all SC participants, can't exist. In fact, each decision maker establishes an own, subjective network perception that overlaps with other, possibly contradictory conceptions [5]. Material, information and financial flows will be examined at differing granularity levels, incorporating different entities, flows and influence factors and using varied descriptors. A primary motivation to develop ontological SC conceptualizations is to enable SC parties to construct their particular view and still to facilitate mutual interoperability through dynamic and integrated description means [15]. Accordingly, the concept of enterprise ontologies has been extended towards a SC perspective (cp. [5], [10]). Some authors (e.g., [16]) explicitly assume that ontologies improve SC agility. However, this research field is far from having matured. Semantic precision and cross-company rule consistency are major issues [14].

Ontology concepts establish *classes* (hierarchically structured sets of instances) with defined *properties* (data-type and object-type, based on recursive heritage) and *rules* (e.g., for class membership, instance interaction or consistency validation; [17], [18], [19]). These data definition elements provide a meta-data model. Reasoning mechanisms that are build upon this model instead of upon instantiated, context-specific data, allow developing domain independent, adaptive software [5]. Thus, SC disturbances (e.g., demand fluctuations) could be timely integrated in adaptive scenario analyses (represented through modified parameters) across affected SC segments. Particularly, the cross-company unification of terms and nomenclatures (part numbers, product identifiers, scheduling data, etc.) by means of ontological modeling could remarkably improve SC optimization and decision making. Previous research ([5]) has proposed a generic SC ontology that was subsequently applied on a real case.

Advantages of this generic structure are simplicity and scalability from heterogeneous SC perspectives. In SCM, often the same (uniquely defined) entity "Unit" is considered to be a sold product from the vendor's view, while the customer refers to it as a supplied part. On a company-specific level numerical codes and attributes could differ (e.g., a supplier assigns material details that are not known to the customer). Still, interoperability can be achieved as long as the generic SC ontology provides a consistently harmonized overall conceptualization and each SC party integrates their individual views into the generic reference

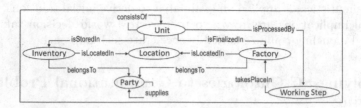

Fig. 1. Generic SC ontology (prototype - partial model) [5]

ontology. The hierarchical class concept enables different granularity levels, e.g., a part hierarchy at the vendor's site. The same applies for a "Factory", belonging to a "Party" and being located in a geographic "Location". The same entity will be referred to with different attributes, depending on whether a company treats a factory as internal unit or external supplier / customer. Relations between companies are established via the "Party supplies Party" coherence. Assuming first, that most problem solving algorithms - especially metaheuristics - are capable to work with parameters that can be implemented in a generic SC ontology and second, that companies can integrate their instantiated data in this SC ontology, the benefits of scalability and data abstraction can be exploited.

4   Selected Case Examples

This subsection discusses three exemplary multi-echelon SC scenarios, each facing a facility location and resource allocation problem. This commonly represents a complex combinatorial optimization problem. Metaheuristics are considered as powerful solution mechanism for these problems [4].

4.1   Case A: A Four-Echelon Industrial Supply Chain

Scenario A [20] examines a multi-objective optimization problem in a four-echelon network (suppliers - production plants - distributions centers (DCs) - customers) regarding the minimization of total SC costs. At the same time a maximum of customer demand has to be fulfilled. Costs have to be spent for facilities, labor, transport, material supply and inventory. The setting necessitates location and allocation decisions. The produced products need three raw materials. Costs (material, transport, production, distribution, DCs, inventory) and capacities (suppliers, plants, DCs) are fix. These facts are used to determine the number and location of plants and DCs, the material flow from suppliers to plants, the product flow from plants to DCs, and the allocation of customers to DCs. The formal problem includes mathematical model and network graph.

This mathematical model is *specific* in the way that 3 suppliers deliver to 1-5 plants, 1-6 DCs, etc. It is, however easy, to create a more generic model using broader parameterization (e.g., not assuming 3 suppliers as fixed). Using a generic ontology would require such generic models for existing reasoning mechanisms - e.g., the facility location and capacity allocation problem. On the other hand, the given mathematical model is *generic* from the view of each SC party. A supplier, plant or DC has to determine cost and capacity based on individual measurement units and costing systems. Whereas a supplier's unit for a material might be "tons", the second supplier might deliver "pieces", the third "meters". One DC may charge per m plus a flat service charge, another may base their prices on occupied storage shelves. From the manufacturer's perspective the capacity may fluctuate with changing product mix, due to differing machine occupation times.

In case, the optimization problem has to be solved once, the required data has to be retrieved from the involved SC parties. This may last weeks. In case of changes - e.g., additional locations, changed demands or costs - at least parts of the data acquisition have to be repeated. Modeling and data acquisition efforts will remarkably slow down the problem solving process. Introducing a SC ontology as communication and harmonization layer between real world data acquisition and optimization runs offers notable advantages. We assume that integrating a new SC party in a generic SC ontology once will in most cases create similar efforts compared to instantiated integration in a reasoning algorithm. As soon as changes occur, the instantiated solution requires time-consuming adaptation. Contrariwise, the ontology-based solution could simply update parameterized values, hence saving time and cost. Even if the initial effort for using a ontology is higher than instantiated data integration, a break-even is reached as soon as an algorithm is used more than once.

4.2   Case B: A Two-Echelon Bioenergy Carrier Production SC

The second case is engaged in biomass-based energy carrier production. Here, a supply network is designed for converting biogenic residues (sewage sludge, municipal organic waste) into biocoal through hydrothermal carbonization (HTC). This technology aims at substituting fossil fuels in the near future. When building commercial plants, profitability and SCM are critical issues.

Rotter examines a facility location and allocation problem within a two-echelon supply network for bioenergy carrier production [21]. By maximizing profit, the decision model defines the optimal number and locations for HTC plants and allocated transport flows between feedstock sources and conversion plants under plant capacity restrictions. Before setting up the mathematical model (MILP), potential HTC plant locations and feedstock locations were geocoded. A transport distance matrix was compiled. Modeling supply networks for bioenergy carrier production implies data collection difficulties due to diverse measuring units among SC actors. Biogenic residues are indicated differently pertaining to moisture and cubature. For instance, woody biomass can be characterized as 'fresh' or 'dry' matter. Further, there are solid, stacked and bulk cubic meters. Thus, conversion factors are required along the SC. Further peculiarities arise from obnoxious facility location and hazmat transportation.

Compared to case A, problem statement and mathematical model are similar. Still, this case requires a modified data representation and specific parameter setting. In the absence of a standardized reference ontology, the model was developed from scratch with high effort and low prospect of reusability.

4.3   Case C: Cross-Domain Harmonization

SCM is rarely limited to one SC domain. For example, a steel producer purchases ore, coal and scrap metal from several suppliers and delivers steel to e.g., car manufacturers or (here) agricultural machinery producers [5]. All parties take SC decisions depending on the other parties' behavior. Currently, problem solving takes place company-internally, despite problem dependencies. In case of limited data exchange, ontological modeling benefits can primarily result from utilizing standardized reference models and algorithms.

As soon as this steel producer seeks to exploit joint SCM-approaches - e.g. collaborative planning, forecasting and delivery coordination - the ability arises to integrate company-specific sub-problems through cross-company data-exchange. The cooperating parties could integrate their heterogeneous sub-models into the generic SC ontology with an initial effort that is in most cases comparable to instantiated modeling. Integrated once, repeated parameter adaptation and algorithm execution advances SC interoperability and hence facilitates conceptual SCM approaches on an operational level.

5   Conclusion and Outlook

Summarizing, algorithmic problem solving in complex, dynamic SC settings requires the ability to quickly model large scale optimization problems through adequate data representation. "Adequate" refers to the capability to integrate and harmonize heterogeneous, incomplete and arbitrarily structured data from semantically differing real word SC sources. To ensure reusability and adaptability, modeling and reconfiguration efforts must be low. Applying a generic, scalable SC reference ontology as communication layer between real world datasets and computational problem solving offers promising potentials. In particular, manifold modeling biases could be mitigated through adaptive scenario exploration. Thorough parameterization of reasoning mechanisms within future research should advance domain-independency and solution portability. With regard to previous research, three examples have tentatively indicated feasibility and have illustrated how future case-based research could develop this conceptual proposal further.

Moreover, future problem solving with e.g., metaheuristics, could be extended from current isolated sub-problem perspectives towards a more holistic modeling approach that is able to handle recursively interrelated sub-problems. In this regard, the use of ontological modeling is a strong enabler to avoid suboptimal local solutions to the advantage of an essentially integrated SC perspective.

References

1. Benyoucef, L., Jain, V.: Editorial note for the special issue on 'Artificial Intelligence Techniques for Supply Chain Management'. Engineering Applications of Artificial Intelligence 22(6), 829–831 (2009)
2. Mirzapour Al-e-hashem, S.M.J., Malekly, H., Aryanezhad, M.B.: A multi-objective robust optimization model for multi-product multi-site aggregate production planning in a supply chain under uncertainty. International Journal of Production Economics 134(1), 28–42 (2011)
3. Schmid, V., Doerner, K.F., Laporte, G.: Rich routing problems arising in supply chain management. European Journal of OR 224(3), 435–448 (2013)
4. Affenzeller, M., et al.: Genetic Algrothims and Genetic Programming - Modern Concepts and Practical Applications. CRC Taylor & Francis Group (2009)
5. Arthofer, K., et al.: Servicing Individual Product Variants within Value Chains with an Ontology. In: Modelling Value. Selected Papers of the 1st International Conference on Value Chain Management, pp. 333–354 (2012)
6. Gruber, T.R.: A translation approach to portable ontology specifications. Knowledge Acquisition 5(2), 199–220 (1993)
7. Williamson, O.E.: The economic institutions of capitalism. Firms, markets, relational contracting. Free Press, Collier Macmillan, New York, London (1985)
8. Bendoly, E., et al.: Bodies of Knowledge for Research in Behavioral Operations. Production & Operations Management 19(4), 434–452 (2010)
9. Studer, R., Fensel, D.: Knowledge engineering: Principles and methods. Data & Knowledge Engineering 25(1-2), 161–197 (1998)
10. Grubic, T., Fan, I.-S.: Supply Chain Ontology: Review, analysis and synthesis. Computers in Industry 61(8), 776–786 (2010)
11. Swartout, B., et al.: Toward Distributed Use of Large-Scale Ontologies. In: AAAI 1997 Spring Symposium on Ontological Engineering, Stanford University, CA, USA, pp. 138–148 (1997)
12. Hillier, F.S., Lieberman, G.: Introduction to Operations Research. McGraw-Hill International Edition, New York (2010)
13. Ahlert, K.-H., Corsten, H., Gössinger, R.: Capacity management in order-driven production networks - A flexibility-oriented approach to determine the size of a network capacity pool. Int. Journal of Production Economics 118(2), 430–441 (2009)
14. Lee, J., et al.: Design of product ontology architecture for collaborative enterprises. Expert Systems with Applications 36(2), 2300–2309 (2009)
15. Brock, D.L., et al.: An Introduction to semantic modeling for logistical systems. Journal of Business Logistics 26(2), 97–117 (2005)
16. Chi, Y.-L.: Rule-based ontological knowledge base for monitoring partners across supply networks. Expert Systems with Applications 37(2), 1400–1407 (2010)
17. Horridge, M., et al.: A Practical Guide to Building OWL Ontologies using the Protege-OWL Plugin and CO-ODE Tools Edition 1.0 (2004)
18. Lacy, L.W.: Owl: Representing Information Using the Web Ontology Language. Trafford Publishing, Victoria (2005)
19. Prud'hommeaux, E., Seaborne, A.: SPARQL Query Language for RDF (2008)
20. Latha Shankar, B., et al.: Location and allocation decisions for multi-echelon supply chain network - A multi-objective evolutionary approach. Expert Systems with Applications 40(2), 551–562 (2013)
21. Rotter, S.: Supply Chain Network Design - A Facility Location and Allocation Model for Biomass-based Energy Carrier Production in Upper Austria (2012)

Evolution of Covariance Functions for Gaussian Process Regression Using Genetic Programming

Gabriel Kronberger and Michael Kommenda

School of Informatics, Communications and Media,
University of Applied Sciences Upper Austria,
Softwarepark 11, 4232, Hagenberg
{gabriel.kronberger,michael.kommenda}@fh-hagenberg.at

Abstract. In this contribution we describe an approach to evolve composite covariance functions for Gaussian processes using genetic programming. A critical aspect of Gaussian processes and similar kernel-based models such as SVM is, that the covariance function should be adapted to the modeled data. Frequently, the squared exponential covariance function is used as a default. However, this can lead to a misspecified model, which does not fit the data well.

In the proposed approach we use a grammar for the composition of covariance functions and genetic programming to search over the space of sentences that can be derived from the grammar.

We tested the proposed approach on synthetic data from two-dimensional test functions, and on the Mauna Loa CO_2 time series. The results show, that our approach is feasible, finding covariance functions that perform much better than a default covariance function. For the CO_2 data set a composite covariance function is found, that matches the performance of a hand-tuned covariance function.

Keywords: Gaussian Process, Genetic Programming, Structure Identification.

1 Introduction

The composition of covariance functions is a non-trivial task and has been described as a black art [2]. On the one hand, it is critical to tune the covariance function to the data set, that should be modeled, because this is the primary option to integrate prior knowledge into the learning process [10]; on the other hand a lot of experience and knowledge about the modeled system is required to do this correctly. Frequently, and especially for multi-dimensional data sets it is far from obvious how the covariance function should be structured.

In this work we discuss the composition of covariance functions for Gaussian processes, that can be used for nonparametric machine learning tasks e.g., for regression or classification [10]. In this context a Gaussian process is used as a Bayesian prior over functions, relating the input variables to the target variable. Gaussian process regression allows modeling of non-linear functional dependencies through different covariance functions, and produces posterior probability distribution estimates for the target values instead of point estimates only.

R. Moreno-Díaz et al. (Eds.): EUROCAST 2013, Part I, LNCS 8111, pp. 308–315, 2013.

1.1   Our Contribution

The aim of this paper is to describe the idea of using a grammar for covariance functions and genetic programming to search for a good covariance function for a given data set. We also describe our prototype implementation using grammar-guided tree-based GP, and finally, present results as a proof-of concept. We have not yet evaluated the difficulty of this problem for genetic programming, and in particular, if GP suited well for this kind of problem. The results of our experiments indicate that the idea is feasible, producing good covariance functions for low-dimensional data sets.

1.2   Previous Work

In a very recent contribution, the problem of structure identification for covariance functions has been approached using a grammar, or rather a set of rewriting rules, as a basis for searching over composite covariance functions for Gaussian processes [2]. This approach is actually very similar to our work; the main difference is, that in our work we use genetic programming to search over the set of possible structures, while Duvenaud et al. enumerate over composite functions, starting with standard functions.

Another recent contribution discusses more flexible families of covariance functions, instead of composing covariance functions from simple terms [12]. Also related is earlier work that describes additive Gaussian processes [3], which are equivalent to a weighted additive composition of base kernels, but can be calculated efficiently.

Genetic programming has been used previously to evolve kernel functions for SVMs with mixed results [4], [6]. The latest contribution found that genetic programming was able to *"rediscover multiple standard kernels, but no significant improvements over standard kernels were obtained"* [7]. These results can, however, not be transfered directly to Gaussian processes because of several major differences between Gaussian processes and SVMs. In particular, in the case of Gaussian processes hyper-parameters are optimized using a ML-II approach, in contrast to SVMs, where hyper-parameter values are usually tuned using cross-validation and grid-search. Additionally, in contrast to all other previous work, simple embeddings of covariance functions by masking dimensions are supported.

2   Gaussian Processes

A Gaussian process is a non-parametric model that produces predictions solely from the specified mean and covariance functions and the available training data [10]. The inference of function values f^* for observed input values X^* based on observations of y and X involves the calculation of the covariance matrices $K(X, X)$ and $K(X, X^*)$ and inference from the multi-dimensional Gaussian shown in Equation 1.

$$\begin{bmatrix} y \\ f^* \end{bmatrix} \sim N \left(\begin{bmatrix} m(X) \\ m(X^*) \end{bmatrix}, \begin{bmatrix} K(X,X) + \sigma^2 I & K(X,X^*) \\ K(X^*,X) & K(X^*,X^*) \end{bmatrix} \right) \tag{1}$$

The term $\sigma^2 I$ is necessary to account for Gaussian distributed noise with variance σ^2. From this definition it follows that the posterior for f^* is again a multi-dimensional Gaussian. For model selection and hyper-parameter learning the marginal likelihood $p(y|X)$ must be calculated. The model is a multi-dimensional Gaussian so an analytical form of the likelihood can be derived.

Calculation of the marginal likelihood requires a matrix inversion and, thus, has asymptotic complexity $O(n^3)$. Usually, the covariance function $K(x, x')$ has hyper-parameters that must optimized. This is often accomplished in a simple ML-II fashion, optimizing the hyper-parameters w.r.t. the likelihood using a quasi-Newton method (e.g., BFGS). Since the gradients of the marginal likelihood for the hyper-parameters can be determined with an additional computational complexity of $O(n^2)$ for each hyper-parameter, it is feasible to use gradient-based methods. The drawback is that the likelihood is typically multimodal, and especially for covariances with many hyper-parameters (e.g., ARD) the optimizer can converge to a local optimum. Thus, it is typically suggested to execute several random restarts. A better solution would be to include priors on the hyper-parameters and optimizing w.r.t. posterior distribution (MAP). However, this can only be accomplished using a MCMC approach which is computationally expensive.

Frequently used covariance functions for Gaussian processes include the linear, polynomial, squared exponential (SE), rational quadratic (RQ) and the Matérn function. Covariance functions can be combined to more complex covariance functions, for instance as products or sums of different covariance functions [10].

3   Genetic Programming

Genetic programming generally refers to the automatic creation of computer programs using genetic algorithms [8]. The basic principle is to evolve variable-length structures, frequently symbolic expression trees, which represent potential solutions to the problem. One of the most prominent applications of genetic programming is symbolic regression, the synthesis of regression models without a predetermined structure. Genetic programming makes it possible to optimize the structure of solutions in combination with their parameters. Thus, it should also be possible to synthesize composite covariance functions with genetic programming. In the following, we use a grammar-guided genetic programming system to make sure that only valid covariance functions are produced. A good survey of grammar-guided genetic programming is given in [9].

4   Grammar for Covariance Functions

The grammar for covariance functions has been derived from the rules for the composition of kernels as e.g., discussed in [10]. It should be noted that the grammar shown below is not complete, meaning that several constructions that would lead to a valid covariance function are not possible[1]. The following represents the grammar $G(\text{Cov})$ for covariance functions in EBNF notation[2]:

```
Cov          -> "Prod" "(" Cov { Cov } ")" | "Sum"  "(" Cov { Cov } ")" |
                "Scale" Cov | "Mask" BitVector Cov | TerminalCov  .
TerminalCov -> "SE" | "RQ" | "Matern1" | "Matern3" | "Matern5" |
                "Periodic" | "Linear" | "Constant" | "Noise" .
BitVector   -> "[" {"0" | "1" } "]" .
```

The functions Prod and Sum produce the product and sum of multiple covariance functions, which can again be composite covariance functions. The scale operator can be used to add a scaling factor to any covariance function. The Mask operator selects a potentially empty subset of input variables from all possible input variables. The non-terminal symbol BitVector can be derived to a list of zeros and ones. The bit vector is used to mask selected dimensions in the data set, effectively reducing the dimensionality. The length of the bit mask has to match the total number of dimensions; this is checked when the resulting covariance function is evaluated.

Finally, the non-terminal symbol TerminalCov can be derived to a range of default covariance functions. Currently, we only included isometric covariance functions, but other covariance functions can be added to the grammar easily. The grammar does not include the hyper-parameters, because they are not optimized by genetic programming. Instead, hyper-parameters are optimized for each potential solution, using a gradient-descent technique.

5   Experiments

For the experiments we implemented Gaussian processes, a set of commonly used covariance functions, and the grammar for covariance functions in HeuristicLab[3] [11] which already provides an implementation of grammar-guided tree-based genetic programming.

The aim of the experiments presented in this contribution is mainly to test the feasibility of the idea. Two different types of data sets are used for the experiments, and the forecasts of the synthesized covariance functions are compared to a set of default covariance functions and also to hand-tuned covariance functions. The first data set is the univariate Mauna Loa atmospheric CO_2 time series. This data set has been chosen, because a hand-tuned covariance function for this data set is presented in [10]. For the second experiment we created several synthetic data sets sampled randomly from two-dimensional Gaussian process priors shown in Equation 2. The data generated from these functions are difficult to model with a single isometric covariance function. Multiple covariance

---

[1] One example is vertical scaling of covariance functions: $K'(x,x') = a(x)K(x,x')a(x')$
[2] The grammar is largely based on the capabilities of the GPML package by Rasmussen and Nickisch, http://gaussianprocess.org/gpml/code.
[3] HeuristicLab version 3.3.8 is available from http://dev.heuristiclab.com/

functions have to be combined and the correct dimension masking vectors have to be identified. Each data set contains 882 samples of the function on a regular two-dimensional grid.

$$\text{SE+RQ}(\boldsymbol{x}, \boldsymbol{x}') = \text{SE}(x_0, x_0') + \text{RQ}(x_1, x_1')$$
$$\text{SE+Matérn}(\boldsymbol{x}, \boldsymbol{x}') = \text{SE}(x_0, x_0') + \text{Matérn1}(x_1, x_1') \qquad (2)$$
$$\text{SE+Periodic}(\boldsymbol{x}, \boldsymbol{x}') = \text{SE}(x_0, x_0') + \text{RQ}(x_1, x_1')$$

5.1   Genetic Programming Parameter Settings

Training of Gaussian processes is computationally expensive, and because it is necessary to optimize the hyper-parameters for each evaluated covariance function the run time of the genetic programming algorithm grows quickly. Therefore, we used very restrictive parameter settings, in particular a small population size of only 50 individuals. All other parameter settings are shown in Table 1.

Table 1. Genetic programming parameter settings for all experiments

Parameter	Value
Population size	50
Max. length / height	25 / 7
Initialization	PTC2
Parent selection	gender-specific (proportional + random)
Mutation rate	15%
ML-II iterations	50
Offspring selection [1]	strict (success ratio = 1, comparison factor = 1)
Max. selection pressure	100
Max. generations	20

5.2   Results on Mauna Loa CO_2 Data Set

The results for the CO_2 time series are positive. The algorithm was able to consistently find covariance functions that fit well in the training period (1958 – 2004), accurate forecasts over the testing period (2004 – 2012). The structures of two exemplary solutions are shown in Equation 3. The first solution ($K1$) is actually very similar to the hand-tuned covariance solution proposed in [10]. The second covariance function is more complex and has only a slightly better likelihood. Unfortunately, genetic programming often leads to overly complex solutions which is a critical drawback of our approach. Both solutions have been found after only 800 evaluated solution candidates and achieve a negative log-likelihood of 129.8 and 116, respectively. The correlation coefficients for the forecasts in the test partition are above 0.99. Figure 1 shows the output of the first model.

$$K1(x, x') = \text{SE}(x, x') + \text{Periodic}(x, x') + \text{Matérn1}(x, x') +$$
$$\text{SE}(x, x') + \text{Matérn5}(x, x') + \text{Const}$$
$$K2(x, x') = \text{Matérn3}(x, x') * \text{Perioric}(x, x') * \text{RQ}(x, x') *$$
$$(\text{Matérn1}(x, x') + \text{Matérn3}(x, x') + \text{Matérn5}(x, x') +$$
$$\text{Perioric}(x, x') + \text{Linear}(x, x')) * \tag{3}$$
$$(\text{Matérn1}(x, x') + \text{Matérn3}(x, x') + \text{RQ}(x, x'))$$

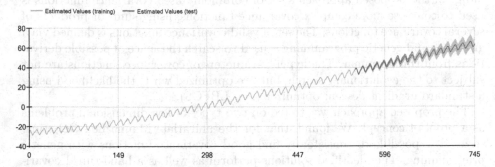

Fig. 1. The output and forecast for the Mauna Loa CO_2 time series of a Gaussian process using the first evolved covariance function ($K1$) shown in Equation 3

5.3   Results on Synthetic Data Sets

The results for the synthetic two-dimensional data set are shown in Table 2. In this experiment we trained multiple Gaussian process models using several frequently used covariance functions. We trained many models using random restarts for each data set and covariance function, and report the best negative log-likelihood for each pair. As expected, the models with the isometric covariance functions do not fit well. In contrast, the composite covariance functions produced by genetic programming fit much better. For comparison, we also

Table 2. Best negative log-likelihood achieved for the three synthetic two-dimensional test functions, with default covariance functions and with evolved composite covariance functions

		Problem instance		
		SE+RQ	SE+Matérn	SE+Periodic
Covariance	SE	-204	-492	440
	RQ	-272	-492	103
	Periodic	-221	-492	479
	Matérn	-27	31	304
	Evolved	-803	-760	-640
	Optimal	-2180	-2187	-2131

report the negative log-likelihood, that can be achieved with the optimal covariance function for each data set. In these experiments, the exact structure of the covariance could not be rediscovered, thus, the evolved functions are worse than the optimal solution.

6   Summary and Discussion

In this contribution we described an approach for the synthesis of composite covariance function for Gaussian processes using grammar-guided genetic programming. In the proposed approach a set of commonly used covariance functions is used to compose more complex covariance functions, using sums or products of several covariance functions. The set of valid covariance functions is defined via a grammar and genetic programming is used to search the space of possible derivations from this grammar. The hyper-parameters of covariance functions are not subject to the evolutionary search, but are optimized w.r.t. the likelihood using a standard gradient-descent optimizer (i.e., LBFGS).

The proposed approach was tested on two types of low-dimensional problems as a proof of concept. We found, that for the univariate Mauna Loa CO_2 time series it is possible to consistently find good covariance functions with genetic programming. The identified solutions perform as well as a hand-tuned covariance function for this problem. The results for our two-dimensional synthetic functions show that it is possible to find composite covariance functions, which perform much better than default covariance functions on these data sets.

In contrast to previous work by the genetic programming community [7], which focused mainly on kernel synthesis for SVMs, this contribution discusses kernel synthesis for Gaussian processes, which are non-parametric fully Bayesian models. For Gaussian process models the hyper-parameters can be optimized with a standard gradient-descent approach, and it is not strictly necessary to execute cross-validation [10]. Previous work either used grid-search and cross-validation to tune hyper-parameters, which is very computationally expensive, or did not consider hyper-parameter optimization at all. Additionally, we are using a grammar to compose covariance functions from simple covariance functions instead of evolving the full function.

In the statistics community, a very recent contribution has also discussed the usage of grammars for the composition of covariance functions [2]. The main difference to this work is that here genetic programming is used to search over the derivations of the grammar. Another relevant difference is that the grammar in this contribution also supports simple embeddings through the masking function. It should be noted, that we have not yet analyzed if genetic programming is well suited for this task, and in particular we did not compare the approach to simple enumeration or random search.

One question that remains for future work is whether composed covariance functions also work well for data sets with more variables. We have observed that simple covariance functions often work very well, and tuned covariance functions do not have a strong beneficial effect for these data sets.

Another interesting topic for future research is to look at alternative ways for searching over the space of covariance functions defined by a grammar. Recently, an interesting approach has been described that uses variational methods for Bayesian learning of probabilistic context free grammars for this task [5]. This idea could be especially useful for Bayesian models such as Gaussian processes.

Acknowledgments. The authors would like to thank Jeffrey Emanuel for the initial idea leading to this contribution. This work has been supported by the Austrian Research Promotion Agency (FFG), on behalf of the Austrian Federal Ministry of Economy, Family and Youth (BMWFJ), within the program "Josef Ressel-Centers".

References

1. Affenzeller, M., Winkler, S., Wagner, S., Beham, A.: Genetic Algorithms and Genetic Programming: Modern Concepts and Practical Applications. Numerical Insights. CRC Press, Singapore (2009)
2. Duvenaud, D., Lloyd, J.R., Grosse, R., Tenenbaum, J.B., Ghahramani, Z.: Structure Discovery in Nonparametric Regression through Compositional Kernel Search. ArXiv e-prints (February 2013)
3. Duvenaud, D., Nickisch, H., Rasmussen, C.E.: Additive Gaussian processes. arXiv preprint arXiv:1112.4394 (2011)
4. Gagné, C., Schoenauer, M., Sebag, M., Tomassini, M.: Genetic programming for kernel-based learning with co-evolving subsets selection. In: Runarsson, T.P., Beyer, H.-G., Burke, E.K., Merelo-Guervós, J.J., Whitley, L.D., Yao, X. (eds.) PPSN IX. LNCS, vol. 4193, pp. 1008–1017. Springer, Heidelberg (2006)
5. Hasegawa, Y., Iba, H.: Latent variable model for estimation of distribution algorithm based on a probabilistic context-free grammar. IEEE Transactions on Evolutionary Computation 13(4), 858–878 (2009)
6. Howley, T., Madden, M.G.: An evolutionary approach to automatic kernel construction. In: Kollias, S.D., Stafylopatis, A., Duch, W., Oja, E. (eds.) ICANN 2006. LNCS, vol. 4132, pp. 417–426. Springer, Heidelberg (2006)
7. Koch, P., Bischl, B., Flasch, O., Beielstein, T., Weihs, C., Konen, W.: Tuning and evolution of support vector kernels. Evolutionary Intelligence 5, 153–170 (2012)
8. Koza, J.R.: Genetic programming: on the programming of computers by means of natural selection. MIT Press, Cambridge (1992)
9. McKay, R.I., Hoai, N.X., Whigham, P.A., Shan, Y., O'Neill, M.: Grammar-based genetic programming: a survey. Genetic Programming and Evolvable Machines 11(3/4), 365–396 (2010)
10. Rasmussen, C.E., Williams, C.K.: Gaussian Processes for Machine Learning. MIT Press (2006)
11. Wagner, S.: Heuristic optimization software systems – Modeling of heuristic optimization algorithms in the HeuristicLab software environment. Ph.D. thesis, Institute for Formal Models and Verification, Johannes Kepler University, Linz (2009)
12. Wilson, A.G., Prescott Adams, R.: Gaussian Process Covariance Kernels for Pattern Discovery and Extrapolation. ArXiv e-prints (February 2013)

Improving the Accuracy of Cancer Prediction by Ensemble Confidence Evaluation[*]

Michael Affenzeller[1], Stephan M. Winkler[1], Herbert Stekel[2],
Stefan Forstenlechner[1], and Stefan Wagner[1]

[1] Heuristic and Evolutionary Algorithms Laboratory, Bioinformatics Research Group
School of Informatics, Communications and Media
Upper Austria University of Applied Sciences, Hagenberg Campus
Softwarepark 11, 4232 Hagenberg, Austria
{michael.affenzeller,stephan.winkler,stefan.forstenlechner,
stefan.wagner}@fh-hagenberg.at
[2] Central Laboratory, General Hospital Linz
Krankenhausstraße 9, 4021 Linz, Austria
herbert.stekel@akh.linz.at

Abstract. This paper discusses a novel approach for the prediction of breast cancer, melanoma and cancer in the respiratory system using ensemble modeling techniques. For each type of cancer, a set of unequally complex predictors are learned by symbolic classification based on genetic programming. In addition to standard ensemble modeling, where the prediction is based on a majority voting of the prediction models, two confidence parameters are used which aim to quantify the trustworthiness of each single prediction based on the clearness of the majority voting. Based on the calculated confidence of each ensemble prediction, predictions might be considered uncertain. The experimental part of this paper discusses the increase of accuracy that can be obtained for those samples which are considered trustable depending on the ratio of predictions that are considered trustable.

1 Introduction: Identification of Classifiers Using Medical Data Sets

The research described in this paper is based on real world data collected from the central laboratory of the general hospital of Linz. Datasets from thousands of patients have been collected containing standard blood parameters as well as tumor marker values as well as corresponding cancer diagnoses according to the ICD-10 standard for the classification of diseases. From this data pool several data sets have been extracted for certain cancer types which contain a sufficient number of samples for modeling purposes. Each of these data-sets is dedicated to a certain cancer type which is modeled as a two-class classification problem

[*] The work described in this paper was done within the Josef Ressel Centre for Heuristic Optimization *Heureka!* (http://heureka.heuristiclab.com/) sponsored by the Austrian Research Promotion Agency (FFG).

R. Moreno-Díaz et al. (Eds.): EUROCAST 2013, Part I, LNCS 8111, pp. 316–323, 2013.
© Springer-Verlag Berlin Heidelberg 2013

(cancer vs. no cancer). Those samples are considered representative for the cancer type which contain blood parameters and corresponding tumor marker values that have been measured within a time window of three weeks before the first cancer diagnosis.

In previous publications we have used real world data-sets and discussed the achievable accuracies for predicting certain cancer types using several machine learning techniques such as genetic programming (GP), artificial neural networks, and support vector machines. These predictors were trained using either solely standard blood parameters or standard blood parameters in combination with tumor marker values. In [6] the use of standard blood parameters as well as the use of standard blood parameters in combination with real and estimated tumor marker values have been discussed for the prediction of breast cancer. In [7] the use of evolutionary modeling in combination with feature selection techniques has been discussed for the prediction of cancer. [3] focused on the analysis of achievable prediction accuracies for certain cancer types with symbolic classification analyzing the effects of additional tumor marker information for different model complexities. In [2] a first approach considering the integration of ensemble modeling and corresponding confidence measures has been described analyzing the confidence of correct prediction versus incorrect prediction results.

2   Ensemble Modeling and Genetic Programming

Especially in the field of medical data mining, not only the ratio of correct classifications (accuracy) is of concern, but also the the confidence in a prediction is essential. In order to support this claim, the present contribution uses the concept of ensemble modeling in order to calculate confidence parameters for each prediction result based on the clearness of the ensemble prediction. The basic idea of ensemble modeling is to apply not only a single hypothesis for predicting a certain sample, but rather a collection of independent models; the result of an ensemble prediction is usually calculated by a majority decision. Basically, this concept of ensemble modeling can be combined with any machine learning technique that may be used for supervised learning of classifiers.

One of the first and best known ensemble modeling techniques is given by random forests which is based on tree learning [4]. Random forests learn many trees using different subsets of the given input variables and consolidate the learned results in a common evaluation of the tree ensembles (e.g., via majority voting). However, the general concept of ensemble modeling can be combined also with other machine learning techniques such as genetic programming based symbolic classification [5].

The combination of ensemble modeling and genetic programming has also been discussed in [2] where two new confidence measures stated below (cm_1 and cm_2) have been introduced which consider the clearness of the prediction confidence in order to calculate normalized confidence values. The results of this study show that the confidence of correct classifications is significantly higher than the confidence of incorrect classifications as shown in Fig.2 for unseen test data samples [2].

$$cm_1 := 2 \cdot \left(\frac{|votes(winnerclass)|}{|votes|} - 0.5 \right) \in [0, 1] \tag{1}$$

$$cm_2 := min\left(\frac{\Delta(m(t), m(e))}{\Delta(m(t), class)}, 1 \right) \in [0, 1] \tag{2}$$

The distribution properties indicated in Fig.2 motivate the introduction of a confidence threshold which defines the level of confidence that has to be reached in order to consider a prediction result trustable. This transforms the original two-class classification problem into a three-class interpretation introducing a third class – samples for which the confidence threshold is not reached are considered *uncertain*.

Detailed analysis focuses on the introduced confidence measures and the increase in prediction accuracy that can be obtained when only considering those samples that surpass certain confidence levels with respect to the ratio of samples that can still be predicted. These analyses are shown for the prediction of breast cancer, melanoma, and cancer in the respiratory system based on standard blood parameters as well as on standard blood parameters in combination with tumor marker information.

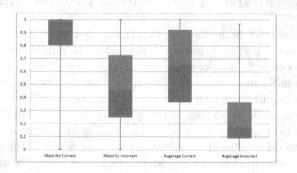

Fig. 1. Distribution of the two confidence measures for correct and incorrect predictions for the modeling of breast cancer with standard blood parameters and tumor markers

3 Results

The results shown in this section have been achieved with offspring selection programming [1]. For each cancer prediction 300 independent ensemble runs have been performed using 3 different model complexities, i.e. for each prediction 100 small (20 nodes), 100 medium size (35 nodes) and 100 larger (50 nodes) GP models have been learned for ensemble interpretation. The results have been evaluated using a 5-fold cross validation. The detailed algorithm settings and their motivation are described in [2]

Table 1. Best model accuracy and ensemble accuracy

	Breast cancer with TM	Breast cancer without TM	Melanoma with TM	Melanoma without TM	Respiratory system with TM	Respiratory system without TM
Best model accuracy	79.32%	70.96%	73.26%	72.27%	88.45%	85.15%
Ensemble accuracy	81.44%	76.49%	76.46%	74.14%	90.18%	87.18%

Table 1 shows test qualities of the model with best training accuracy for the considered cancer prediction tasks as well as the ensemble accuracy of all ensemble models (300 for each prediction) based on majority voting on the cross validation results. The results in Table 1 already show the positive effects of ensemble interpretation concerning a significant increase of achieved prediction accuracy which is a well documented effect of GP ensemble modeling [5].

However, in this contribution we aim to go one step further in the interpretation of ensemble modeling results by utilizing the unambiguousness of the ensemble predictors quantified by the two confidence measures defined in section 2 in order to classify only that subset of data samples which exceed a certain confidence. Table 2 - Table 13 show the classification accuracies for different confidence thresholds as well as the relative amount of samples which are still covered for the analyzed cancer types with and without additional tumor marker information. Obviously, the higher the claimed value of confidence is set, the lower the sample coverage. But even more important, the results in Table 2 - Table 13 clearly show the gain in accuracy that can be achieved by increasing the confidence threshold. In other words, increasing the confidence threshold significantly increases achievable accuracy while still explaining a reasonable percentage of the data samples. This property is especially important in the field of cancer prediction where a prediction, if stated, should be as clear as possible. The gains in accuracy that could be achieved range between 10 and 20 percent while still covering between half to a quarter of the data. Furthermore, the results reported in Table 2 - Table 13 also show that the properties of the two considered confidence measures seem to be very similar in terms of accuracy gains in relation to coverage losses.

The tradeoff between accuracy gain and coverage loss can he shown graphically by plotting the accuracy against the coverage for the confidence threshold ranging between 0 to 1. Fig. 2 exemplarily shows this visualization for the case of respiratory cancer prediction without tumor marker information for both considered confidence measures.

Especially in medical data mining not only the achieved accuracy is of interest but also the distribution of false positive and false negative predictions which is commonly represented in confusion matrices. Table 14 - Table 16 exemplarily

Table 2. Breast cancer with tumor marker (cm_1)

Confidence	Accuracy	Covered
0.1	0.817236256	0.95325779
0.3	0.834670947	0.882436261
0.5	0.86569873	0.780453258
0.7	0.898785425	0.699716714
0.9	0.929292929	0.560906516
0.95	0.954545455	0.467422096
1	0.98	0.354107649

Table 3. Breast cancer with tumor marker (cm_2)

Confidence	Accuracy	Covered
0.01	0.81186686	0.978753541
0.1	0.8304	0.885269122
0.3	0.892215569	0.709631728
0.5	0.936868687	0.560906516
0.7	0.95970696	0.386685552
0.75	0.970212766	0.33286119
0.8	0.972093023	0.304532578
0.9	0.988023952	0.236543909

Table 4. Breast cancer without tumor marker (cm_1)

Confidence	Accuracy	Covered
0.1	0.760646109	0.964589235
0.3	0.775	0.906515581
0.5	0.787826087	0.814447592
0.7	0.836065574	0.69121813
0.9	0.877358491	0.450424929
0.95	0.900452489	0.313031161
1	0.919463087	0.211048159

Table 5. Breast cancer without tumor marker (cm_2)

Confidence	Accuracy	Covered
0.01	0.765140325	0.958923513
0.1	0.774143302	0.909348442
0.3	0.855895197	0.648725212
0.5	0.871323529	0.385269122
0.7	0.880733945	0.154390935
0.75	0.862068966	0.123229462
0.8	0.913793103	0.082152975

Table 6. Melanoma with tumor marker (cm_1)

Confidence	Accuracy	Covered
0.1	0.756482525	0.980110497
0.3	0.768948655	0.903867403
0.5	0.785234899	0.82320442
0.7	0.804281346	0.722651934
0.9	0.829218107	0.537016575
0.95	0.835227273	0.388950276
1	0.86440678	0.19558011

Table 7. Melanoma with tumor marker (cm_2)

Confidence	Accuracy	Covered
0.01	0.756179775	0.983425414
0.1	0.766431925	0.941436464
0.3	0.797101449	0.762430939
0.5	0.838709677	0.445303867
0.7	0.952941176	0.093922652
0.77	0.94	0.055248619
0.8	0.933333333	0.033149171

show the confusion matrices for the three considered cancer types using tumor marker information for breast cancer interpreted with $cm1$ and for melanoma and cancer in the respiratory system interpreted with $cm2$. Those tables oppose standard ensemble evaluation with enhanced confidence interpretation showing a significant decrease of positive samples which are predicted as negative.

Table 8. Melanoma without tumor marker (cm_1)

Confidence	Accuracy	Covered
0.1	0.740950226	0.97679558
0.3	0.759371221	0.913812155
0.5	0.779947917	0.848618785
0.7	0.797919762	0.743646409
0.9	0.812244898	0.541436464
0.95	0.805882353	0.375690608
1	0.835227273	0.194475138

Table 9. Melanoma without tumor marker (cm_2)

Confidence	Accuracy	Covered
0.01	0.741321389	0.986740331
0.1	0.755077658	0.924861878
0.3	0.809022556	0.73480663
0.5	0.831134565	0.41878453
0.6	0.869767442	0.237569061
0.7	0.901098901	0.100552486
0.8	0.913043478	0.025414365

Table 10. Respiratory system with tumor marker (cm_1)

Confidence	Accuracy	Covered
0.1	0.900342173	0.750561798
0.3	0.908252853	0.731300161
0.5	0.91839495	0.712038523
0.7	0.929610511	0.684109149
0.9	0.945945946	0.62953451
1	0.960106383	0.48282504

Table 11. Respiratory system with tumor marker (cm_2)

Confidence	Accuracy	Covered
0.01	0.903170523	0.749277689
0.1	0.905979203	0.740930979
0.3	0.917493237	0.712038523
0.5	0.931636021	0.680898876
0.7	0.952224053	0.58459069
0.8	0.98067287	0.44847512

Table 12. Respiratory system without tumor marker (cm_1)

Confidence	Accuracy	Covered
0.1	0.869957082	0.986034702
0.3	0.88130299	0.948370715
0.5	0.887898687	0.902242912
0.7	0.913283208	0.844265764
0.9	0.940199336	0.764282691
0.95	0.955621302	0.715192552
1	0.963752665	0.595429539

Table 13. Respiratory system without tumor marker (cm_2)

Confidence	Accuracy	Covered
0.01	0.871728872	0.986457893
0.1	0.883156966	0.959796868
0.3	0.901559454	0.868387643
0.5	0.944623656	0.787134998
0.7	0.962116657	0.703766399
0.8	0.963487332	0.567922133
0.9	0.985270049	0.258569615

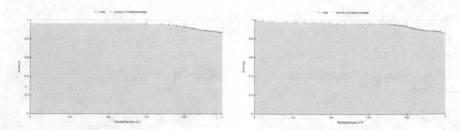

Fig. 2. Accuracy gain in relation to covered samples for the prediction of cancer in respiratory system without tumor marker information achieved by using $cm1$ (left) and $cm2$ (right)

Table 14. Confusion matrix for breast cancer with tumor marker (cm_1) with a confidence above or equal to 1

	Standard interpretation		Enhanced interpretation		
	Estimated pos.	Estimated neg.	Estimated pos.	Estimated neg.	Not estimated
Pos.	347	35	94	1	287
Neg.	106	218	4	151	169

Table 15. Confusion matrix for melanoma without tumor marker (cm_2) with a confidence above or equal to 0.6

	Standard interpretation		Enhanced interpretation		
	Estimated pos.	Estimated neg.	Estimated pos.	Estimated neg.	Not estimated
Pos.	275	145	58	16	346
Neg.	94	391	12	129	344

Table 16. Confusion matrix for respiratory system without tumor marker (cm_2) with a confidence above or equal to 0.9

	Standard interpretation		Enhanced interpretation		
	Estimated pos.	Estimated neg.	Estimated pos.	Estimated neg.	Not estimated
Pos.	745	251	164	7	825
Neg.	69	1298	2	438	927

4   Summary

In this contribution GP-based ensemble modeling has been applied to real world medical data-sets for the prediction of three cancer types. In addition to standard ensemble modeling two confidence measures have been introduced which aim to quantify the clearness of ensemble predictions. By applying confidence thresholds a significant increase of achievable accuracy could be shown for all considered modeling scenarios. This interpretation seems especially meaningful for medical data mining. Future investigations will apply the proposed methodology on medical benchmark data sets. Also it is planned to further develop algorithmic strategies in order to support the diversity of the ensemble members.

References

1. Affenzeller, M., Wagner, S.: Offspring selection: A new self-adaptive selection scheme for genetic algorithms. In: Ribeiro, B., Albrecht, R.F., Dobnikar, A., Pearson, D.W., Steele, N.C. (eds.) Adaptive and Natural Computing Algorithms, pp. 218–221. Springer Computer Science, Springer (2005)
2. Affenzeller, M., Winkler, S., Forstenlechner, S., Kronberger, G., Kommenda, M., Wagner, S., Stekel, H.: Enhanced confidence interpretations of gp-based ensemble modeling results. In: Proceedings of the 24th European Modeling & Simulation Symposium, pp. 340–345 (2012)
3. Affenzeller, M., Winkler, S., Jacak, W., Stekel, H.: Cancer prediction models based on blood data with and without tumor marker information. In: Symposium 2011 of the German, Austrian, and Swiss Societies for Hematology and Onkology (2011)
4. Breman, L.: Random forests. Machine Learning 45, 5–32 (2001)
5. Keijzer, M., Babovic, V.: Genetic programming, ensemble methods and the bias/variance tradeoff - introductory investigations. In: Poli, R., Banzhaf, W., Langdon, W.B., Miller, J., Nordin, P., Fogarty, T.C. (eds.) EuroGP 2000. LNCS, vol. 1802, pp. 76–90. Springer, Heidelberg (2000)
6. Winkler, S., Affenzeller, M., Kronberger, G., Kommenda, M., Wagner, S., Dorfer, V., Jacak, W., Stekel, H.: On the use of estimated tumor marker classifications in tumor diagnosis prediction - a case study for breast cancer. Accepted to be published in: International Journal of Simulation and Process Modelling (2012)
7. Winkler, S., Jacak, M.A.W., Stekel, H.: Identification of cancer diagnosis estimation models using evolutionary algorithms - a case study for breast cancer, melanoma, and cancer in the respiratory system. In: Proceedings of the Genetic and Evolutionary Computation Conference, GECCO 2011 (2011)

Optimization of Container Terminal Problems: An Integrated Solution Approach

Christopher Expósito-Izquierdo, Eduardo Lalla-Ruiz, Belén Melián Batista, and J. Marcos Moreno-Vega

Department of Statistics, Operations Research and Computation
University of La Laguna
38271 La Laguna, Spain
{cexposit,elalla,mbmelian,jmmoreno}@ull.es

Abstract. Over the last decades, a great effort has been done in order to achieve a suitable management of international sea freight trade. The maritime container terminals are intermediate points aimed at exchanging containers within multimodal transport networks. The large number of decision problems brought together in these facilities and the way they are related to each other constitute a challenge for their managers. The goal of this work is to overview the most outstanding logistic processes in maritime container terminals and provide some general guidelines for designing integration approaches.

Keywords: Maritime Container Terminal, Seaside, Storage Yard, Landside, Integration Approach.

1 Introduction

The United Nations Conference on Trade And Development (UNCTAD)[1] publishes annually a review on the current state of maritime transport worldwide. One of its main assertions remarks that the global container trade has grown over the last decades. In order to face the logistic requirements stemming from the increasing volume of containers transported around the world, freight shipping companies and public institutions have funded the building of maritime container terminals as elements of investment and engines of economic development (Coto-Millán et al. [3]).

A maritime container terminal is an infrastructure aimed at exchanging containers among different means of transportation within a multimodal transport network. The most extended means of transportation in this type of facilities are container vessels, trucks and trains. In general terms, the layout of a common maritime container terminal is split into three functional areas: the seaside, the yard and the landside (Vis and de Koster [18]). Firstly, the seaside provides the set of services required by the container vessels. The yard is a temporal storage area for the containers incoming toward the port. Finally, the landside is

---

[1] http://unctad.org

R. Moreno-Díaz et al. (Eds.): EUROCAST 2013, Part I, LNCS 8111, pp. 324–331, 2013.

an interface for exchanging containers between the terminal and the mainland transports.

The decision problems found at maritime container terminals are closely related to each other and, therefore, having proper knowledge-based systems that integrate them is highly advised in order to provide an adequate service level. Several approaches based on simulation have been developed to analyze the impact that the operational decisions have on the performance of the terminal (Sun et al. [17]). Furthermore, as indicated by Meisel [11], functional integration and deep integration are general-purpose strategies widely used to solve the logistical problems found at container terminals. These strategies define the sequence of decision problems to address and the set of data to exchange at each step with the goal of finding a suitable operational balance between the different areas of the terminal.

This work is aimed at providing an overview of the main logistical problems appeared in a common maritime container terminal, describing the relationships among them and indicating some general guidelines for further research within the integration approaches.

The remainder of this work is organized as follows. Firstly, Section 2 studies the main seaside problems appeared in maritime container terminals. Section 3 describes the management of the containers in storage yards. Finally, Section 4 extracts the main conclusions from the work and indicates several lines for further research.

2   Seaside Operations

The freight shipping companies are interested in those terminals which ensure certain service level. In this context, the turnaround time of the container vessels in the port is the main indicator of the overall productivity of a terminal (Wiegmans [19]). A great effort is currently being carried out with the goal of increasing the efficiency of the seaside operations, that is, those operations aimed at serving the container vessels arrived toward the port. In addition, the seaside operations pursue to maximize the productivity of the handling equipment used to serve the vessels. In this context, three relevant logistical problems could be highlighted: Berth Allocation Problem, Quay Crane Allocation Problem and Quay Crane Scheduling Problem. An exhaustive description of the seaside decision problems is provided by Meisel [11].

The first step concerning the service of a given container vessel is to provide it a specific position alongside the quay according to its particular characteristics (dimensions, expected service time, vessel draft, water depth, etc.). This decision problem is known as Berth Allocation Problem (BAP). Its goal is to allocate and schedule incoming vessels to berthing positions in order to optimize some cost function. Multitude of formulations for this problem have been published in the literature, for which different spatial, temporal and planning constraints have been considered. The BAP is closely related to other seaside problems in the terminal and, therefore, high efficient approaches are required in order to solve more general problems in which the BAP is involved. Lalla-Ruiz et al. [9] present an effective and efficient algorithm for solving the dynamic arrival version subject to berths and vessels time windows.

Once each incoming vessel is assigned to a given position alongside the quay, a subset of the available quay cranes at the terminal must be allocated in order to load/unload containers to/from them. This problem is referred to as Quay Crane Allocation Problem (QCAP). The number of allocated quay cranes is determined on the basis of the technical characteristics of each container vessel and, therefore, this problem is usually tackled at the same time as the BAP. According to Bierwirth et al. [1], the QCAP is easily solvable when it is considered in an isolated way. Nevertheless, it gains in importance when is considered in integrated approaches with the BAP due to the severe impact it has on the vessels service time. A well-defined example of these integration approaches is the so-called Tactical Berth Allocation Problem presented by Giallombardo et al. [7]. It consists in assigning and scheduling incoming vessels to berthing positions and allocating a subset of quay cranes to them in order to reduce the costs associated with the transfer of transshipment containers and exploit fully the use of the quay cranes.

The container cargo of a container vessel is defined by means of its stowage plan. It determines the position of each container according to the bays, containers priority, type and route. In this context, a hard scheduling problem to determine the loading and unloading operations for a set of allocated quay cranes arises in container terminals. This problem is known as Quay Crane Scheduling Problem (QCSP), whose goal is to determine the sequence of tasks performed by each quay crane. The most extended optimization criterion in the related literature is to minimize the overall service time of the vessel and minimize the usage of the quay cranes. The QCSP has been addressed in the literature by using both approximate and exact approaches (Bierwirth et al. [1]). Moreover, this problem becomes even more interesting for researchers and practitioners since the service time of the vessels depends on its appropriately solving and, consequently, it might provide a highlighted feedback for an integrated approach with the BAP. An evolutionary proposal is presented in the work by Expósito-Izquierdo et al. [4], which develops a high competitive algorithm for solving the QCSP.

Addressing the seaside operations in an isolated way through dividing them into well-defined decision problems is useful for reducing the complexity of the decision-making systems. However, this division simplifies and limits the use of the input data. This fact may cause in practical scenarios poor quality or even non-realistic solutions since it is not considered the interrelation between the operations. In this regard, the relation among these problems is given by the use of the common resources among them. In practice, starting from the berthing operation, the service time of each vessel depends on the number of the quay cranes assigned and the quality of service they provide. Moreover, to determine the amount of quay cranes and establish the quay cranes schedule of the vessels loading/unloading tasks is necessary to know in advance the vessel workload and its stowage plan. This exchange of information among these operations and their proper incorporation into integrated models can tackle the berthing process at container terminals. Furthermore, it allows terminal managers to provide a high quality service and increase the overall productivity of the terminal through the appropriate use of the seaside resources.

In the related literature there are already several integration approaches for the seaside operations of a maritime container terminal. They address the joint consideration of the aforementioned decision problem. A detailed overview of the integration schema for the seaside problems is reported by Bierwirth et al. [1]. However, according to Meisel [11], many of these integrations fail for practical reasons, the required input data for solving the QCSP is not available due to the fact that the stowage plans of the container vessels are not known until the seaside operations are about to be planned. Moreover, most of the integration approaches between the BAP and QCSP treat them at an operational level, namely, the planning horizon ranges from one to several days (Vis and de Koster [18]). Few studies consider them at a tactical level, where the planning horizon ranges from one week to several months. The study of integration schemes at this level can address other issues surrounding the seaside operations, that is, the container transshipment operations, negotiations between the terminal and the freight shipping company, etc. This issue is proposed for further research as an interesting consideration for tackling relevant logistic aspects arising in maritime container terminals.

3   Storage Yard Operations

The yard is the main functional area of a maritime container terminal due to the fact that it allows the temporary storage for the containers until their later retrieval through some of the means of transportation brought together at the terminal (Vis and de Koster [18]). In general terms, the yard is divided into a set of homogeneous blocks organized in parallel along the quay and spaced wide apart by lanes for the yard vehicles. A block is a three dimensional storage split into bays with a limited number of stacks and tiers in which containers are piled up on the basis of the Last In First Out (LIFO) policy. The number, dimension and distribution of blocks on the yard have a great impact on the container handling operations. As discussed below, the reasons are found in the time required to access to a specific container buried below other ones in a stack and the logistic problems derived from the interoperability of the handling equipment. The work by Petering [15] studies the effect of yard layout on the overall performance of the terminal.

The relevance of the yard derives from the fact that it must handle the main flows of containers found in the terminal, those established between the quay and the landside. Firstly, the containers unloaded from the vessels and those arriving by means of mainland transports should be located into a suitable position of the yard such that its later retrieval could be performed efficiently. The location (block, bay, stack and tier) of an incoming container on the yard must be adapted to its physical and cargo characteristics, type, retrieval time and destination.

A stacking policy determines the location of each container arrived to the port with the goal of optimizing some given criterion: minimizing the handling cost, minimizing the distance to its retrieval point, etc. Park et al. [14] propose an algorithm to adjust dynamically the stacking policy of a container terminal in order to enhance the operational productivity. The unloaded containers from a vessel can be involved in a transshipment operation between a pair of vessels or being stored on the yard until its later retrieval through a landside mean of transportation. In transshipment operations, the incoming containers are usually assigned to locations found near the berthing position of their target vessels. Integration approaches aimed at berthing the vessels alongside the quay and locating the transshipment containers on the yard are scarce in the literature. The work by Lee and Jin [10] is one of these few examples. Finally, the quay and landside can exchange containers using the yard as an intermediate storage.

In order to satisfy the aforementioned flows of containers the maritime terminals usually use specific-purpose transport vehicles. Among them, yard trucks, straddle carriers and AGVs are highlighted types of vehicles (Vis and de Koster [18]). Their purpose is to move the containers from the quay cranes toward the blocks. In addition, they are aimed at moving the container from the blocks toward the landside of the terminal (Wu et al. [20]). The main objectives pursued by terminal managers in this field are to minimize the number of transport vehicles and maximizing their performance. The work by Nishimura et al. [13] addresses a routing problem in which the objective is to fulfill the demand of containers from the yard requested by the quay cranes during the loading/unloading operations. A review on the main vehicle routing problems in container terminals is provided by Stahlbock and Voβ [16].

The throughput capacity of a container terminal derives from the number of containers that it can handle over a given period of time. Therefore, as pointed out by Wiegmans [19], improving the speed of response of the handling equipment is the main focus of interest for terminal managers. Different types of gantry cranes such as Rail-Mounted Gantry Cranes (RMGCs), Rubber-Tyred Gantry Cranes (RTGCs), etc. are being currently used in the major container terminals with the goal of performing the stacking and retrieval operations. However, non-crossing and interference constraints inherit to multi-crane systems in the same block must be suitably addressed with the goal of ensuring the safety of cranes. An exhaustive study on the main planning problems associated with using a RMGC-based system in a container yard is provided by Nils [8]. In this context, the Yard Crane Scheduling Problem (YCSP) pursues to assign the container handling tasks associated with the blocks to the allocated gantry cranes. The involved tasks can be delivering or retrieving a container to/from a given block. Several objectives have been addressed in the related literature. Maximizing the usage of the gantry cranes in order to perform the tasks and minimizing the waiting time of trucks and container vessels are the most extended ones. The work by Ng and Mak [12] presents a mixed integer programming model aimed at modelling the YCSP. In addition, this work analyzes a Branch and Bound algorithm with several lower bounds in order to find high-quality schedules by means of reasonable computational times on real-world instances.

As briefly mentioned above, delivering/retrieving and forecast information concerning future container requests should be properly exploited in order to anticipate the handling operations. In this regard, a large number of strategies has been proposed to relocate the containers into the blocks, in such a way that, they can be accessible from the top of the stacks in which they have been located. Caserta et al. [2] review the main rehandling problems. The Pre-Marshalling Problem (PMP, Expósito et al. [5]) pursues to arrange the containers on the basis of their retrieval order before they are requested in order to avoid future relocation movements. The Blocks Relocation Problem (BRP, Forster and Bortfeldt [6]) determines the shortest sequence of movements to perform by a gantry crane to retrieve a subset of containers from the yard.

In spite of the large number of logistical problems concerning the yard, there is still a lack of integration approaches that provide a complete management of the containers located on the yard in the medium to large term and allow to evaluate the overall performance of the terminal. The relationships among problems can be suitable exploited in order to obtain the pursued integration approaches. At tactical planning level, the yard layout and deployment of technical equipment must be addressed. In this regard, the distribution of the cranes on the yard is highly influenced by the arrangement of blocks and their dimensions. At operational planning level, the handling operations performed by the gantry cranes should be in accordance with the deliveries of containers. As indicated in the previous section, the time in which the container have to be loaded/unloaded to/from each vessel is determined by the QCSP but the availability of these containers is subject to keeping a steady flow of containers from/to the yard. The YCSP and the distribution of container by transport vehicles should be therefore studied simultaneously with the QCSP with the objective of evaluating the feasibility of providing the containers to the vessels when these are scheduled. The speed of response of the gantry cranes when delivering a given container is determined by the position in which is currently located. However, the sequence-dependent structure of the rehandling problems (PMP, BRP, etc.) limits the estimation of the future workload due to the fact that a wrong decision has a great impact on the future handling operations. This means that the YCSP should be tackled considering the processing times of the handling operations derived from the access toward the container.

4   Conclusions and Future Works

The maritime container terminals are huge infrastructures aimed at managing the increasing volume of containers within transport multimodal networks. The large number of logistical problems that take place in them and their interrelation constitute a challenge for practitioners. The overview reported in this work shows the relevant role of the optimization techniques on the overall performance of a container terminal. In this regard, a great effort have being performed by the researching community with the goal of improving the effectiveness of the container handling operations.

The related literature has been traditionally focused on the individual impact of the logistical problem on the performance of the terminal. Unfortunately, these approaches give rise to unrealistic or poor quality solutions in most of real scenarios. The reason is found in that they do not take into account the inter-relations among them. In this regard, a deep research of integration proposals within the seaside and yard area logistical problems is essential to increase and maintain a high productivity as well as produce real-context planning solutions.

The challenges of the integration approaches are the study and identification of the operations with conflicting objectives regarding the different areas and planning levels. Moreover, further research in providing flexible solutions by including real-context aspects arising container terminals is presented as an attractive study area. In this regard, the consideration of stochastic and dynamic approaches which take into account the quay crane breakdowns, vessel delay, changes of container priorities, etc. have a practical economical benefits pursued by terminal managers.

Acknowledgements. This work has been partially funded by the European Regional Development Fund, the Spanish ministry of Science and Technology (project TIN2012-32608). Christopher Expósito Izquierdo and Eduardo Lalla Ruiz thank CajaCanarias and the Canary Government the financial support they receive through their respective grants.

References

1. Bierwirth, C., Meisel, F.: A survey of berth allocation and quay crane scheduling problems in container terminals. European Journal of Operational Research 202(3), 615–627 (2010)
2. Caserta, M., Schwarze, S., Voβ, S.: Container rehandling at maritime container terminals. In: Böse, J.W. (ed.) Handbook of Terminal Planning. Operations Research/Computer Science Interfaces Series, vol. 49, pp. 247–269. Springer, New York (2011)
3. Coto-Millán, P., Pesquera-González, M.Á., Castanedo, J. (eds.): Essays on port economics. Contributions to economics. Physica-Verlag, Berlin (2010)
4. Expósito-Izquierdo, C., González-Velarde, J.L., Melián-Batista, B., Marcos Moreno-Vega, J.: Estimation of distribution algorithm for the quay crane scheduling problem. In: Pelta, D.A., Krasnogor, N., Dumitrescu, D., Chira, C., Lung, R. (eds.) NICSO 2011. SCI, vol. 387, pp. 183–194. Springer, Heidelberg (2011)
5. Expósito-Izquierdo, C., Melián-Batista, B., Marcos Moreno-Vega, J.: Pre-marshalling problem: Heuristic solution method and instances generator. Expert Systems with Applications 39(9), 8337–8349 (2012)
6. Forster, F., Bortfeldt, A.: A tree search procedure for the container relocation problem. Computers & Operations Research 39(2), 299–309 (2012)
7. Giallombardo, G., Moccia, L., Salani, M., Vacca, I.: Modeling and solving the tactical berth allocation problem. Transportation Research Part B: Methodological 44(2), 232–245 (2010)

8. Kemme, N.: Operational rmgc-planning problems. In: Design and Operation of Automated Container Storage Systems. Contributions to Management Science, pp. 117–202. Physica-Verlag HD (2013)
9. Lalla-Ruiz, E., Melián-Batista, B., Marcos Moreno-Vega, J.: Artificial intelligence hybrid heuristic based on tabu search for the dynamic berth allocation problem. Engineering Applications of Artificial Intelligence 25(6), 1132–1141 (2012)
10. Lee, D.-H., Jin, J.G.: Feeder vessel management at container transshipment terminals. Transportation Research Part E: Logistics and Transportation Review 49(1), 201–216 (2013)
11. Meisel, F.: Integration concepts for seaside operations planning. In: Seaside Operations Planning in Container Terminals. Contributions to Management Science, pp. 47–54. Physica-Verlag HD (2009)
12. Ng, W.C., Mak, K.L.: Yard crane scheduling in port container terminals. Applied Mathematical Modelling 29(3), 263–276 (2005)
13. Nishimura, E., Imai, A., Papadimitriou, S.: Yard trailer routing at a maritime container terminal. Transportation Research Part E: Logistics and Transportation Review 41(1), 53–76 (2005)
14. Park, T., Choe, R., Kim, Y.H., Ryu, K.R.: Dynamic adjustment of container stacking policy in an automated container terminal. International Journal of Production Economics 133(1), 385–392 (2011)
15. Petering, M.E.H.: Effect of block width and storage yard layout on marine container terminal performance. Transportation Research Part E: Logistics and Transportation Review 45(4), 591–610 (2009)
16. Stahlbock, R., Voβ, S.: Vehicle routing problems and container terminal operations - an update of research. In: Golden, B., Raghavan, S., Wasil, E. (eds.) The Vehicle Routing Problem: Latest Advances and New Challenges. Operations Research/Computer Science Interfaces, vol. 43, pp. 551–589. Springer US (2008)
17. Sun, Z., Lee, L.H., Chew, E.P., Tan, K.C.: Microport: A general simulation platform for seaport container terminals. Advanced Engineering Informatics 26(1), 80–89 (2012)
18. Vis, I.F.A., de Koster, R.: Transshipment of containers at a container terminal: An overview. European Journal of Operational Research 147(1), 1–16 (2003)
19. Wiegmans, B.W., Rietveld, P., Nijkamp, P.: Container terminal services and quality. Serie Research Memoranda 0040, VU University Amsterdam, Faculty of Economics, Business Administration and Econometrics (2001)
20. Wu, Y., Luo, J., Zhang, D., Dong, M.: An integrated programming model for storage management and vehicle scheduling at container terminals. Research in Transportation Economics 42(1), 13–27 (2013)

An Improved Heuristic for the Probabilistic Traveling Salesman Problem with Deadlines Based on GPGPU

Dennis Weyland, Roberto Montemanni, and Luca Maria Gambardella

IDSIA - Dalle Molle Institute for Artificial Intelligence / USI / SUPSI
Galleria 2, 6928 Manno, Switzerland
{dennis,roberto,luca}@idsia.ch

Abstract. Stochastic combinatorial optimization problems have received increasing attention in recent years. These problems can be used to obtain more realistic models for real world applications. The drawback is that stochastic combinatorial optimization problems are usually much harder to solve than their non-stochastic counterparts and therefore efficient heuristics for these problems are of great importance. In this paper we focus on the PROBABILISTIC TRAVELING SALESMAN PROBLEM WITH DEADLINES, a well-known stochastic vehicle routing problem. This problem can be efficiently solved using a heuristic based on general-purpose computing on graphics processing units. We show how such a heuristic can be further improved to allow a more efficient utilization of the graphics processing unit. We extensively discuss our results and point out how our techniques can be generalized for solving other stochastic combinatorial optimization problems.

1 Introduction

In recent decades stochastic combinatorial optimization problems [10, 14, 5] have received an increasing amount of attention. Here the input is (partially) modeled in a stochastic way, which allows for more realistic models of real world problems. The drawback is that stochastic combinatorial optimization problems are usually much harder to solve than their non-stochastic counterparts, both in practice and also from a computational complexity point of view [24]. For many such problems only very small instances can be solved to optimality with reasonable computational resources. Therefore, heuristics are of great importance for the optimization of stochastic combinatorial optimization problems [6, 21–23].

An important class of stochastic combinatorial optimization problems are so-called two-stage stochastic combinatorial optimization problems [16, 20, 19]. Here the decision process is divided into two stages. The first stage decision has to be taken before the actual realizations of the stochastic input data are known. After the actual realizations of the random events are known, a second stage decision can be performed. The costs caused by decisions on the first stage are usually smaller than those caused by decisions on the second stage, but due to

R. Moreno-Díaz et al. (Eds.): EUROCAST 2013, Part I, LNCS 8111, pp. 332–339, 2013.

the uncertainty in the problem formulation it is not always possible to perform all decisions in the first stage. In particular, the second stage can be used to guarantee feasibility of the final solution. The class of two-stage stochastic combinatorial optimization problems in which the major part of the decision process is already performed in the first stage are called a-priori stochastic combinatorial optimization problems [4, 17, 18, 7]. Here the second stage decisions are only used to modify the final solution slightly, for example to guarantee feasibility.

In this work we focus on stochastic vehicle routing problems. These are problems arising in the field of transportation and logistics. Many such problems belong to the class of two-stage stochastic combinatorial optimization problems and a-priori optimization problems. The most famous problems in this field are the PROBABILISTIC TRAVELING SALESMAN PROBLEM [15, 3, 6], the VEHICLE ROUTING PROBLEM WITH STOCHASTIC DEMANDS [2, 1, 11], the VEHICLE ROUTING PROBLEM WITH STOCHASTIC DEMANDS AND CUSTOMERS [12, 13] and the PROBABILISTIC TRAVELING SALESMAN PROBLEM WITH DEADLINES (PTSPD, [8, 9, 23, 25, 26]). The methods of choice for the optimization of these problems are heuristic approaches [6, 21, 22]. Recently, heuristics using the enormous parallel computational power of modern graphics cards have been introduced [23]. They have proven to be very efficient and in this paper we discuss several enhancements for these heuristics in the context of the PROBABILISTIC TRAVELING SALESMAN PROBLEM WITH DEADLINES.

The remaining part of the paper is organized as follows. In section 2 we give a formal definition of the PTSPD and discuss relevant literature. Section 3 contains a careful analysis of the state-of-the-art method for the PTSPD. Based on this analysis we propose several enhancements. We perform an extensive computational study with the resulting approach and show that the proposed enhancements lead to major improvements with respect to the efficiency. We finish the paper with a discussion of our results and with conclusions in section 4.

2   The Probabilistic Traveling Salesman Problem with Deadlines

In this section we give a formal definition of the PROBABILISTIC TRAVELING SALESMAN PROBLEM WITH DEADLINES (PTSPD). We then discuss related literature and give an overview about known facts and algorithms for the PTSPD.

The PTSPD is an a-priori stochastic vehicle routing problem in which the presence of the customers are modeled in a stochastic way and additionally time constraints in terms of deadlines are imposed. The task is to find a so-called a-priori tour starting at the depot, visiting all the customers exactly once, and returning to the depot, such that the expected costs of the a-posteriori tour is minimized. For a given realization of the random events (the presence of the customers) the a-posteriori tour is derived from a given a-priori tour in the following way. The vehicle starts at the depot and visits the customers which are present in the order defined by the given a-priori tour. The customers which do not require to be visited are just skipped. The costs of such an a-posteriori tour are then the travel costs plus penalties for missed deadlines.

More formally, the PTSPD is defined as follows. We have given a set of locations $V = \{v_0, v_1, \ldots, v_n\}$. Here v_0 is the depot and the set $V' = V \setminus \{v_0\}$ is the set of customers. Additionally, we have given a function $d : V \times V \to \mathbb{R}^+$ representing travel times between the different locations, a function $p : V' \to [0, 1]$ representing the presence probabilities of the customers, a function $t : V' \to \mathbb{R}^+$ representing the deadlines of the customers and a function $h : V' \to \mathbb{R}^+$ representing the penalties for deadlines violations for the customers. The task is to find a so-called a-priori tour starting at the depot and visiting all the customers exactly once, such that the expected costs over the a posteriori tours (with respect to the given probabilities) is minimized. For a given realization of the customers' presence an a-posteriori tour is derived by visiting the present customers in the order defined by the a priori tour while skipping the other customers. The costs for such an a posteriori tour is the sum of the travel times plus the penalties for violated deadlines. Figure 1 illustrates the relation between a-priori and a-posteriori tours for a specific input instance. A more detailed definition of this problem, including a thorough motivation, is given in [8].

The PTSPD has been introduced in 2008 [8]. Some fundamental properties of the four different models of this problem are discussed in [8, 9]. In [24, 26] the computational complexity of the PTSPD has been examined. Here it has been shown that several computational tasks related to the PTSPD, including the evaluation of the objective function, are #P-hard (which implies NP-hardness). Therefore, heuristics are of great importance for this problem. In particular, methods which are based on an approximation of the objective function. Such methods have been introduced in [9, 25, 23]. The method in [23] is currently the state-of-the-art approach for the PTSPD. Here the evaluation of solutions is performed in parallel on the graphics processing unit (GPU) using an approximation based on Monte Carlo sampling.

3   An Improved Heuristic for the PTSPD

In this section we perform a careful analysis of the current state-of-the-art approach for the PTSPD. In this way we are able to identify four bottleneck components which account for around 97% of the total computational time. We then propose enhancements for these four bottleneck components and evaluate the effects of these enhancements. After that we compare the resulting approach (using all the enhancements together) with the current state-of-the-art method in an extensive computational study.

3.1   Profiling

To understand the distribution of the computational time between different components of the current state-of-the-art approach for the PTSPD we performed some careful profiling. For this purpose we split the whole algorithm into nine

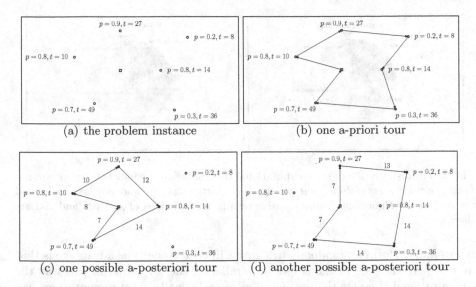

(a) the problem instance

(b) one a-priori tour

(c) one possible a-posteriori tour

(d) another possible a-posteriori tour

Fig. 1. Example of how a-posteriori tours are derived from a given a-priori tour for the PTSPD. Part (a) shows the given PTSPD instance and (b) shows the given a-priori tour. Parts (c) and (d) represent two particular realizations of the random events. Here the filled circles represent the customers that require a visit. These customers are visited in the order specified by the a-priori tour, while the other customers are just skipped. Note that penalties for missed deadlines are not visualized here.

components: the initialization of the host (CPU) data structures, the initialization of the device (GPU) data structures, the computation of permutations, the general setup, the exact evaluation of the local optimal solutions (at the end of the algorithm), the cleanup and the three core components of the algorithm *put solutions*, *evaluate solutions* and *process results*. For further details about the algorithm, we refer to the original publication [23].

The results of the profiling were quite surprising. As expected, the three core components of the heuristic, *put solutions*, *evaluate solutions* and *process results*, contribute significantly to the total computational time. More surprising, the computation of permutations was another component which required a lot of computational time. These four components account for around 97% of the total computational time for most of the instances and we will therefore refer to them as the bottleneck components. This is also visualized in Figure 2. We continue in the next section with proposing enhancements for these bottleneck components.

3.2   Enhancements

Let us start with the computation of the permutations. In the original implementation the Fisher-Yates shuffle algorithm was used to compute permutations used in the local search. This method requires a computational time of $\mathcal{O}(n)$ to permute a set of n elements. We propose an approach running in $\mathcal{O}(\log n)$

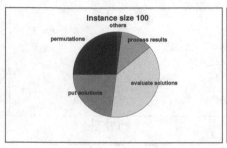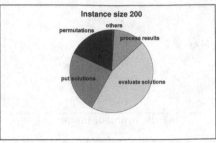

Fig. 2. The distribution of the computational time between the four bottleneck components *compute permutations*, *put solutions*, *evaluate solutions* and *process results* and the rest of the algorithm. Representative results for instances of size 100 and 200 are shown.

stages and performing randomly $n/2$ swaps in each stage. The advantage is that we can perform each of the stages in parallel on the GPU and in this way the computational time for the computation of realistically sized permutations can be reduced by a factor of around 10.

The next enhancement is for the component *put solutions*. Here the idea is to put the workload onto the GPU and to perform the computations in parallel. Using a large number of solutions good results are obtained in this way. Unfortunately, it results only in minor improvements using a realistic number of solutions.

For the evaluation of solutions we tried two different enhancements. The first is an implementation of the existing method which utilizes the GPU in a much better way. The computational time for this component could be reduced by almost an order of magnitude. The second idea was to use the quasi-parallel evaluation of samples [25] on the GPU. This approach resulted in slightly smaller improvements, mainly because the solutions are evaluated in rather small packages of samples due to the statistical tests. Therefore, we decided to use the first of the new approaches.

The last enhancement is for the component *process results*. Here the idea is to perform the computations in parallel on the GPU. In contrast to the component *put solutions* we are able to obtain major runtime improvements even for a realistic number of solutions. In practice the computational time can be reduced by around an order of magnitude.

All in all, the proposed enhancements reduce the computational time of the bottleneck components significantly and it seems promising that the overall computational time of the current state-of-the-art algorithm for the PTSPD can be reduced as well. To be able to give a more precise statement, we will perform computational studies in the next section.

3.3   Computational Studies

To assess the performance of our new approach we run the algorithm on 80 common benchmark instances of the PTSPD. For the details about the benchmark instances we refer to [8]. We perform 25 independent runs for each instance of size 40, 60 and 100 and 5 independent runs for each instance of size 150 and 200. For each instance we measure the average computational time and the average costs of the final solution.

The aggregated results are depicted in Table 1. Here we see the average relative costs and the average relative runtime of the new approach with respect to the state-of-the-art approach for the PTSPD. Here a value smaller than 1 indicates an improvement. We can see that over all classes of instances the costs of the final solution are competitive and in most cases even slightly better. Additionally, the computational time is reduced by about 25% in average. In particular, the computational time is reduced significantly for the practically relevant instance classes: 61.5% for the largest instances and 48.4% for instances with small presence probabilities.

Table 1. The average relative costs and the average relative runtime of the new approach with respect to the state-of-the-art approach for the PTSPD, averaged over different instance classes

instances	average relative costs	average relative runtime
all	0.997	0.758
size 40	0.992	0.638
size 60	1.001	0.668
size 100	1.000	0.976
size 150	1.004	1.124
size 200	0.989	0.385
prob. 0.1	0.999	0.516
prob. 0.9	1.000	0.987
prob. ranged	0.996	0.788
prob. mixed	0.994	0.743
deadl. early	0.999	0.762
deadl. late	0.996	0.755
penalty 5	0.998	0.789
penalty 50	0.997	0.727

4   Discussion and Conclusions

In this work we have carefully analyzed the state-of-the-art approach for the optimization of the PROBABILISTIC TRAVELING SALESMAN PROBLEM WITH DEADLINES. We could identify four bottleneck components of this approach and proposed several enhancements. We first examined the effect of each of our proposed enhancements on its own. These results were very promising. We then compared the resulting approach with the current state-of-the-art method in an extensive computational study. Here we could show that the approach using our enhancements significantly outperforms the state-of-the-art method.

Although we applied our enhancements for a specific problem, the PROBABILISTIC TRAVELING SALESMAN PROBLEM WITH DEADLINES, we believe that it can be generalized to many other stochastic combinatorial optimization problems as well. In fact, the former state-of-the-art method for the PTSPD is based mainly on a very general framework for the optimization of stochastic combinatorial optimization problems and it is promising that we can obtain similar enhancements for other approaches which are based on this framework.

The runtime behavior of the PTSPD heuristic has been optimized in a way which does not leave a lot of space for further improvements based on similar techniques. Nonetheless, we believe that many practical stochastic combinatorial optimization problems can be solved in a satisfiable way with our approach. We suspect that new conceptual ideas are necessary to further improve the performance of heuristics for stochastic combinatorial optimization problems. Parallelization seems very promising here and in particular the usage of cloud resources, maybe also in combination with GPGPU.

Acknowledgments. The first author's research has been supported by the Swiss National Science Foundation, grant 200020-134675/1.

References

1. Bastian, C., Rinnooy Kan, A.H.G.: The stochastic vehicle routing problem revisited. European Journal of Operational Research 56(3), 407–412 (1992)
2. Bertsimas, D.J.: A vehicle routing problem with stochastic demand. Operations Research 40(3), 574–585 (1992)
3. Bertsimas, D.J., Howell, L.H.: Further results on the probabilistic traveling salesman problem. European Journal of Operational Research 65(1), 68–95 (1993)
4. Bertsimas, D.J., Jaillet, P., Odoni, A.R.: A priori optimization. Operations Research 38(6), 1019–1033 (1990)
5. Bianchi, L., Dorigo, M., Gambardella, L.M., Gutjahr, W.J.: A survey on metaheuristics for stochastic combinatorial optimization. Natural Computing 8(2), 239–287 (2009)
6. Campbell, A.M.: Aggregation for the probabilistic traveling salesman problem. Computers and Operations Research 33(9), 2703–2724 (2006)
7. Campbell, A.M., Thomas, B.W.: Challenges and advances in a priori routing. In: The Vehicle Routing Problem: Latest Advances and New Challenges, pp. 123–142 (2008)
8. Campbell, A.M., Thomas, B.W.: Probabilistic traveling salesman problem with deadlines. Transportation Science 42(1), 1–21 (2008)
9. Campbell, A.M., Thomas, B.W.: Runtime reduction techniques for the probabilistic traveling salesman problem with deadlines. Computers and Operations Research 36(4), 1231–1248 (2009)
10. Carraway, R.L., Morin, T.L., Moskowitz, H.: Generalized dynamic programming for stochastic combinatorial optimization. Operations Research 37(5), 819–829 (1989)
11. Dror, M., Laporte, G., Louveaux, F.V.: Vehicle routing with stochastic demands and restricted failures. Mathematical Methods of Operations Research 37(3), 273–283 (1993)

12. Gendreau, M., Laporte, G., Séguin, R.: An exact algorithm for the vehicle routing problem with stochastic demands and customers. Transportation Science 29(2), 143–155 (1995)
13. Gendreau, M., Laporte, G., Séguin, R.: A tabu search heuristic for the vehicle routing problem with stochastic demands and customers. Operations Research 44(3), 469–477 (1996)
14. Immorlica, N., Karger, D., Minkoff, M., Mirrokni, V.S.: On the costs and benefits of procrastination: Approximation algorithms for stochastic combinatorial optimization problems. In: Proceedings of the Fifteenth Annual ACM-SIAM Symposium on Discrete Algorithms, pp. 691–700. Society for Industrial and Applied Mathematics (2004)
15. Jaillet, P.: Probabilistic traveling salesman problems. PhD thesis, M. I. T., Dept. of Civil Engineering (1985)
16. Klein Haneveld, W.K., van der Vlerk, M.H.: Stochastic integer programming: General models and algorithms. Annals of Operations Research 85, 39–57 (1999)
17. Laporte, G., Louveaux, F.V., Mercure, H.: A priori optimization of the probabilistic traveling salesman problem. Operations Research 42(3), 543–549 (1994)
18. Murat, C., Paschos, V.T.: A priori optimization for the probabilistic maximum independent set problem. Theoretical Computer Science 270(1), 561–590 (2002)
19. Schultz, R., Stougie, L., Vlerk, M.H.: Two-stage stochastic integer programming: A survey. Statistica Neerlandica 50(3), 404–416 (2008)
20. Uryasev, S., Pardalos, P.M.: Stochastic optimization: Algorithms and applications. Springer (2001)
21. Weyland, D., Bianchi, L., Gambardella, L.M.: New heuristics for the probabilistic traveling salesman problem. In: Proceedings of the VIII Metaheuristic International Conference (MIC 2009) (2009)
22. Weyland, D., Montemanni, R., Gambardella, L.M.: Using statistical tests for improving state-of-the-art heuristics for the probabilistic traveling salesman problem with deadlines. In: Moreno-Díaz, R., Pichler, F., Quesada-Arencibia, A. (eds.) EUROCAST 2011, Part I. LNCS, vol. 6927, pp. 448–455. Springer, Heidelberg (2012)
23. Weyland, D., Montemanni, R., Gambardella, L.M.: A metaheuristic framework for stochastic combinatorial optimization problems based on GPGPU with a case study on the probabilistic traveling salesman problem with deadlines. Journal of Parallel and Distributed Computing (2012)
24. Weyland, D., Montemanni, R., Gambardella, L.M.: Hardness results for the probabilistic traveling salesman problem with deadlines. In: Mahjoub, A.R., Markakis, V., Milis, I., Paschos, V.T. (eds.) ISCO 2012. LNCS, vol. 7422, pp. 392–403. Springer, Heidelberg (2012)
25. Weyland, D., Montemanni, R., Gambardella, L.M.: Heuristics for the probabilistic traveling salesman problem with deadlines based on quasi-parallel Monte Carlo sampling. Computers and Operations Research (2012) (to appear)
26. Weyland, D., Montemanni, R., Gambardella, L.M.: On the computational complexity of the probabilistic traveling salesman problem with deadlines (2012) (submitted)

Measurement of Anisotropy
in Fitness Landscapes

Erik Pitzer and Michael Affenzeller

University of Applied Sciences Upper Austria
Softwarepark 11, 4232 Hagenberg, Austria
{erik.pitzer,michael.affenzeller}@fh-hagenberg.at

Abstract. In this work we elaborate on the measurement of anisotropy
in fitness landscapes by defining an extension over arbitrary base measures. This rather pragmatic method's soundness is justified by statistical argument and tested on several existing and new fitness landscapes.
Moreover, new variants of the popular NK landscapes are introduced
that exhibit varying degrees of anisotropy.

Keywords: fitness landscapes, anisotropy, stationarity, NK landscapes.

1 Introduction

In the past several years, fitness landscape analysis has developed from an academic metaphor for the understanding of problem structure [13], to a practically
applicable methodology for the empirical analysis of real-world problems.[3,7].
During the course of its development, it was often assumed that fitness landscapes were—or should be—*isotropic* or stationary[11,10]. In part, this was assumed to facilitate and generalize the analysis and because many real-world
examples seem to be isotropic. However, the analysis of isotropy itself and especially the empirical measurement of isotropy has received little attention in the
past. One notable exception is in [8] where a definition for empirical anisotropy
is introduced and applied to the free energy landscape of RNA.

Within the perspective of fitness landscape analysis, only a very abstract and
general view of optimization problems is used. In particular, only the solution
space, the fitness function as a black box and a notion of connectivity between
solution candidates is used for these analysis types. Therefore, a fitness landscape
is formally defined as $\mathcal{F} := \{\mathcal{S}, f, \mathcal{X}\}$, where $\mathcal{S}$ is the set of solution candidates,
$f : \mathcal{S} \to \mathbb{R}$ is the fitness function, and $\mathcal{X}$ is a connectedness, very often a distance
function $d : \mathcal{S} \times \mathcal{S} \to \mathbb{R}$, or a neighborhood definition $N : \mathcal{S} \to 2^{\mathcal{S}}$. Using only
this limited view of optimization problems allows convenient reuse of analysis
methods across different problems and facilitates a more abstract understanding
of problem structure and applicable optimization methods.

2 Previous Definitions of Isotropy

For fitness landscape analysis, isotropy is the property of a landscape to "look
the same" everywhere. In other words, an isotropic landscape will yield very

R. Moreno-Díaz et al. (Eds.): EUROCAST 2013, Part I, LNCS 8111, pp. 340–347, 2013.

similar analysis results no matter the staring point or direction of the analyzed subsample. While conceptually, we can talk about an isotropic landscape, there is no way of directly measuring it. As isotropy is the "measure" of homogeneity of this sample, repeated measurements of different parts of the landscape can be taken and compared to each other.

This first formulation of isotropy can be found in [8] where it is defined based on the average fitness difference over pairs of solution candidates at a certain distance. In an isotropic landscape this average would be the same for every partition of the landscape as well as for the overall landscape. Finally, the *coefficient of anisotropy* is derived in [8], as shown in Equation 1 and captures the amount to which isotropy is violated. Here, the variance of the average in each individual partition is divided by the overall variance minus the average correlation. Or even simpler, the relative variance of the average fitness in different areas of the solution space.

$$\alpha = \frac{\text{var}_B[\langle f \rangle_A]}{\text{var}_S[f]} - \overline{\rho}_B \tag{1}$$

3 Practical Isotropy Analysis

To quantify isotropy, it has to be specified in which way it should be isotropic. Luckily, there are many ways of measuring fitness landscapes as shown in e.g. [6] or [5] such as auto correlation [12] or information conent [10]. The basic idea is to take these measurements confined to different regions and compare them. In [8], these subspaces are non-intersecting partitions of the solution space. However, for practical problem sizes the probability of intersection even of larger samples is vanishingly small as explained in the next section.

3.1 Subsample Overlap Probabilities

To illustrate the low probabilities of overlaps, the birthday paradox [4] can be used. For most of the measurements, a connected trajectory is used to generate the underlying sample for further analysis. It can be assumed that a trajectory-based sample is more connected, or more local, than a random sample. For simplicity of the argument, a random sample will be assumed that can, therefore, serve as an upper bound of the true overlap probability between trajectories.

If a random walk of length l is performed and repeated s times, a total number of $w = l \cdot s$ walk samples is obtained. So, there are $\binom{w}{2}$ pairs of points that could potentially overlap. Using an approximation formula for calculating the chance of overlaps as given in Equation 2, it is easy to see that the maximum overlap probability is very small for realistic solution space sizes.

$$p(w, n) = 1 - \exp\left(\frac{-w \cdot (w - 1)}{2 \cdot n}\right) \tag{2}$$

For combinatorial solution spaces of size 30 the number of samples can be as high as $700 \cdot 10^{12}$ to have an overlap probability around 0.1%. Similarly, for binary vector solution spaces of size 100, the number of samples can be up to $50 \cdot 10^{12}$ with similar overlap probability. Even for the very tightly coupled combinatorial landscapes, it is therefore, extremely unlikely, that two or more continuous random samples are overlapping. This yields the pragmatic approach to repeat a measurement over several different regions of a fitness landscape and to compare whether "they look the same".

3.2 Measurement of Isotropy

Finally, we arrive at a surprisingly simple concept for describing isotropy as shown in Equation 3, where $\mathcal{M}$ is any fitness landscape measure over a subset S' of S which is then compared with the result on the whole solution space. If these measures substantially deviate from each other, the landscape is not isotropic. Moreover, Equation 4 can be derived which might seem more difficult to check, however, as we are interested in its violation it might be easier to find examples in a sampling based approach and it does not need to be evaluated over the whole solution space.

$$\forall (S' \subseteq S) \quad \mathcal{M}\left(\{S', f, \mathcal{X}\}\right) \cong \mathcal{M}\left(\{S, f, \mathcal{X}\}\right) \tag{3}$$

$$\forall (S_1, S_2 \subseteq S) \quad \mathcal{M}\left(\{S_1, f, \mathcal{X}\}\right) \cong \mathcal{M}\left(\{S_2, f, \mathcal{X}\}\right) \tag{4}$$

A simple approach to *measure* anisotropy would be to define the violation of the equality in Equation 4 as the extent of anisotropy. If a comparison of different isotropy measures is desired, however, it seems more natural to take inherent variance into account and focus on the variations that stem from different "locations". Equation 5 shows a simple definition of anisotropy as the variance of a measure over different subsets of the landscape $S' \subseteq \mathcal{P}(S)$, ideally, where $\forall (S_i, S_j \in S') |S_i| = |S_j|$.

$$\widetilde{\mathcal{I}_{\mathcal{M}}}\left(\{S', f, \mathcal{X}\}\right) := \mathrm{Var}\left[\left\{\mathcal{M}\left(\{S_i, f, \mathcal{X}\}\right) \middle| S_i \in S'\right\}\right] \tag{5}$$

This definition is similar to the previous definition in [8] insofar as the isotropy is described by the variance of another, substrate measure. To exclude outliers, a slightly different formulation is proposed in Equation 6, where the difference between the 95th and the 5th percentile are used instead.

$$\mathcal{I}_{\mathcal{M}}\left(\{S', f, \mathcal{X}\}\right) := \mathrm{QDiff}_{.05}^{.95}\left[\left\{\mathcal{M}\left(\{S_i, f, \mathcal{X}\}\right) \middle| S_i \in S'\right\}\right] \tag{6}$$

3.3 Subsample Selection

The choice of S' should ideally be in a way, where all subsamples have the same size. Additionally, to be able to analyze the variance of *local* properties the subsample should be locally confined and separated from other subsamples, as shown in Equation 7, where $\overline{d}$ is either a unary function defining the average distance of pairs within a subset, or a binary function defining the average distance between one element from one subset and one from an other.

$$\forall (S_i \neq S_j \in S') \, \overline{d}(S_i) < \overline{d}(S_i, S_j) \tag{7}$$

3.4 Multi-trajectory Analysis

The basis for the analysis of isotropic features is the analysis of a distribution over several subsamples of a solution space. In its simplest form, this is just the analysis of several trajectories from different starting points in the landscape.

As the lengths of the individual walks increase, the statistical accuracy of each of the walks increases and all of them measure more or less the same. This important insight might seem slightly discouraging as it implies that the more significant the results become the less we are able to observe isotropy at all. It would be desirable to see measurements for very short walks as these would exhibit very local features, however, these results would be quite insignificant and mostly attributable to inherent variation instead of location dependent variation.

For the measurement of anisotropy the *variance*, as stated in Equation 5, is relevant. In Figure 1 these anisotropy values using the auto correlation function as base are compared with variance corrected values: As the walks of different lengths have different inherent variances, this effect has to be accounted for by multiplying the differences with the corresponding standard error, which is the square root of the samples' sizes.

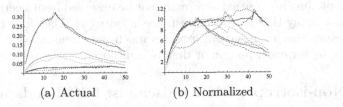

(a) Actual   (b) Normalized

Fig. 1. Quantile Spread Analysis of the Auto Correlation Function: The difference of quantiles 95 and 5. The lines groups on the left are from top to bottom for 10^3, 10^5, and 10^6 steps in each walk, while the dotted lines are for 10, dashed for 100 and continuous lines for 10^3 different locations.

With at least 100 starting locations throughout the landscape, the different analysis results are quite stable and comparable. The apparent peaks in the individual curves are due to the cut-off of insignificant correlations, which are different for different walk lengths. Therefore, the individual isotropy measures can only be compared up to this point. However, most frequently, only $\rho(1)$, or the auto correlation after one step is used. The apparent match of different walk lengths, especially for the first few steps of the auto correlation functions in combination to the quantile spread or confidence interval size, gives solid repeatable results in these cases.

Combination with Repeated Local Analysis. As described in Section 3.4, random restarts alone have the problem of either insufficient significance or insufficient locality. One possibility of increasing locality would be to force the random walk to return to the starting point after some time, this, however, would make this walk less random. Therefore, another simple possibility is to restart the walk from the same staring point and combine the results from several iterations from the same starting point. This gives analysis trajectories with good locality and, with sufficient repetitions, enough statistical power to provide useful measurements. Now, the analysis of underlying values has to undergo two aggregation steps, first over the local repeats into an analysis that resembles a single, longer analysis, followed by a variability analysis using an anisotropy measure.

3.5   Combined Isotropy Measures

Ideally, *the* isotropy of a certain problem instance would be described by a single value. However, form the existing tests, this does not seem to be immediately possible (not shown). In fact even the base measures currently lack normalization that would make them directly comparable. This is a non-trivial issue, since solution space space size, neighborhood size and the distribution characteristics of the measurements are all involved.

The second question, even if it is assumed that different isotropy measures based on different base measures are able to obtain comparable estimates of isotropy, it is questionable whether an average or weighted average would be sufficient. Just because anisotropy cannot be observed from a certain perspective does not imply that a problem instance is isotropic. Therefore, once normalization issues have been settled, it seems much more reasonable to combine them using a higher order p-norm or the uniform norm.

4   Non-isotropic NK Landscapes: NKi Landscapes

With the popularity of NK landscapes and the history of introduction of variants as a showcase for new measures, it was attempted in this work to create a variation of NK landscapes with varying isotropy. These *NKi landscapes* are designed to introduce anisotropy into the extremely isotropic NK landscapes.

Before we begin to modify NK landscapes, or actually the more general block model introduced in [1], let us recall Equation 8 which gives the general structure.

$$f(x) := \frac{1}{n} \sum_{i=1}^{n} f_i(n_{i,1}(x), n_{i,2}(x), \ldots, n_{i,k_i}(x)) \tag{8}$$

The basic idea of NKi landscapes is to introduce differences, so that different locations on the bit vectors exhibit different properties. This has been tried with several different configurations. There are two aspects of NK landscapes that can be modified to achieve anisotropy: On the one hand, the component selection functions $n_{i,j}$, which determine the epistatic structure, can be modified to group certain solution candidate components x_i together. So that, on the other hand, the component functions f_i and the magnitude of their contribution to the overall fitness can differentiate between different "areas" of the solution candidates. In such a tightly coupled landscape this is relatively difficult as every solution candidate component, or in other words, every dimension is only a binary value.

The following modifications where examined for the component selection functions to influence the epistatic setup: The basic *random interaction* model randomly assigns solution candidate components, or genes, to fitness component functions. This is the default and equals the generalized block model. With a *limited range interaction*, a model similar to the adjacent neighborhood structure has been introduced, where not only directly adjacent neighbors but neighbors up to a certain maximum distance are assigned to each component function. With a *deliberate interaction size* the number of epistatic interactions of different fitness component functions has been directly selected so that f_i has exactly i input values. Similarly, a *sorted random interaction* model first assigns random interactions to all fitness components but then sorts the genes according to their component function affinity. This does not change the interaction structure but relies on a systematic change of fitness component function magnitude which is described in the following paragraph.

The fitness component functions themselves cannot easily be influenced, as these random tables are not actually tangible. The random tables are in general too large to be available and have, therefore, been replaced by a pseudo-random number generator as described in [2]. For this reason, the only accessible aspect are artificial weights for each of the fitness component functions as shown in Equation 9, which were already part of the original NK landscapes but have been subsequently removed from the generalized block model.

$$f(x) := \sum_{i=1}^{n} c_i \cdot f_i(n_{i,1}(x), n_{i,2}(x), \ldots, n_{i,k_i}(x)) \qquad (9)$$

By systematically assigning component function weights in concert with the modified neighborhood interactions, described above, it was tried to introduce some anisotropy. The default assignment is an *equal weight* to each of the fitness component functions and should, conceptually, not cause any anisotropy. However, by assigning *linearly increasing weights* with $c_i = i$ it was attempted to disturb the equal distribution of landscape features. An even more disruptive change of the fitness landscape was attempted by using *exponential weights* for the different fitness component functions, where $c_i = 2^i$. Together these two modifications can create skewed NK landscapes, where e.g. the first dimensions have much more influence on the overall fitness than the later ones.

5   Results

To validate the usefulness of the new measures, they are compared and put in relation to their existing base measures. As can be seen from Figure 2a, the values of auto correlation and its anisotropy measurement are strongly correlated with an $r^2 = 0.757$. Here, where the relatively isotropic quadratic assignment problem is analyzed, only those instances that exhibit anisotropy stand out.

To validate the new measurement, it was tested on different real vector functions that should conceptually exhibit different levels of an isotropy. On the one

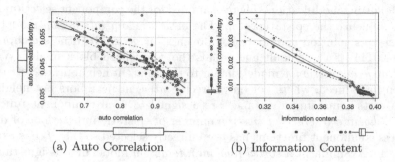

(a) Auto Correlation   (b) Information Content

Fig. 2. Existing Measures and Their Dependent Isotropy Values: While most instance of the QAPLIB show very high correlation of isotropy measures to their corresponding base measures, some special cases such as the nearly flat `esc` or `tai` instances stand out

hand, the relatively smooth but multimodal Rastrigin test function [9] is compared to a simple function with very high anisotropy, $f(x,y) := \sin(x^y)$. This function, while relatively smooth near the axes, is increasingly oscillating and therefore has high anisotropy. As shown in Figure 3a, this function exhibits a very large amount of measurable anisotropy, in contrast to the quite smooth Rastrigin test function. This can serve as a first validation of the introduced anisotropy measure. Figure 3b shows the auto correlation isotropy measure for several different variants of the NK and NKi landscapes. While the default NK landscapes exhibit very low anisotropy, especially for low values of k and only a slight increase as k increases, all variants including an exponential weight distribution for the fitness components show a very high value of anisotropy. Interestingly, the isotropy decreases as k increases, reversing the trend as seen in the NK landscapes. The effect of increased anisotropy is only clearly visible for values of $k \leq 5$. From this point on, it seems that the effects of epistasis overlay the individual components enough to make the landscape more and more isotropic again.

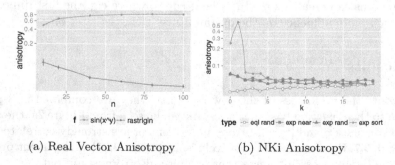

(a) Real Vector Anisotropy   (b) NKi Anisotropy

Fig. 3. Examples of Anisotropy Measurement

6   Conclusions

The analysis of isotropy is a delicate subject. In many practical cases, problem instances are highly isotropic. In these cases, isotropy measurement might seem superfluous and not worth the effort. However, to discover that these instances are isotropic is an important reassurance for the validity of many other analysis results. Currently, it is relatively easy to detect the presence of significant isotropy which can have observable impacts on both other measurements as well as optimization attempts. However, the exact measurement of isotropy requires careful attention to details such as inner walk length and used neighborhood definitions to become observable. Using one particular neighborhood a landscape can seem just rugged, while, on closer examination the underlying anisotropy can be discovered.

Acknowledgments. This work has been supported by the Josef-Ressel Centre "Heureka!" funded by the Austrian Resarch Funding Agency (FFG).

References

1. Altenberg, L.: Evolving better representations through selective genome growth. In: CEC 1994, vol. 1, pp. 182–187 (1994)
2. Altenberg, L.: NK Fitness Landscapes. In: The Handbook of Evolutionary Computation, vol. 1–2, pp. B2.7.2:1–B2.7.2:11. Oxford University Press (1997)
3. Jones, T.: Evolutionary Algorithms, Fitness Landscapes and Search. Ph.D. thesis, University of New Mexico, Albuquerque, New Mexico (1995)
4. Naus, I.I.: An extension of the birthday problem. Am. Stat. 22, 27–29 (1968)
5. Pitzer, E.: Applied Fitness Landscape Analysis. Ph.D. thesis, Johannes Kepler University Linz, Austria (2013)
6. Pitzer, E., Affenzeller, M.: A Comprehensive Survey on Fitness Landscape Analysis. In: Fodor, J., Klempous, R., Suárez Araujo, C.P. (eds.) Recent Advances in Intelligent Engineering Systems. SCI, vol. 378, pp. 161–191. Springer, Heidelberg (2012)
7. Pitzer, E., Beham, A., Affenzeller, M.: Automatic algorithm selection for the quadratic assignment problem using fitness landscape analysis. In: Middendorf, M., Blum, C. (eds.) EvoCOP 2013. LNCS, vol. 7832, pp. 109–120. Springer, Heidelberg (2013)
8. Stadler, P.F., Grüner, W.: Anisotropy in fitness landscapes. J. Theor. Biol. 165(3), 373–388 (1993)
9. Törn, A., Žilinskas, A. (eds.): Global Optimization. LNCS, vol. 350. Springer, Heidelberg (1989)
10. Vassilev, V.K., Fogarty, T.C., Miller, J.F.: Information characteristics and the structure of landscapes. Evol. Comput. 8(1), 31–60 (2000)
11. Weinberger, E.D.: Local properties of kauffman's n-k model, a tuneably rugged energy landscape. Physical Review A 44(10), 6399–6413 (1991)
12. Weinberger, E.: Correlated and uncorrelated fitness landscapes and how to tell the difference. Biological Cybernetics 63(5), 325–336 (1990)
13. Wright, S.: The roles of mutation, inbreeding, crossbreeding and selection in evolution. In: Int. Congr. Genet. 6, vol. 1, pp. 356–366 (1932)

Optimization as a Service: On the Use of Cloud Computing for Metaheuristic Optimization

Sebastian Pimminger, Stefan Wagner,
Werner Kurschl, and Johann Heinzelreiter

University of Applied Sciences Upper Austria
School of Informatics, Communications and Media
Softwarepark 11, 4232 Hagenberg, Austria
{sebastian.pimminger,stefan.wagner,werner.kurschl,
johann.heinzelreiter}@fh-hagenberg.at

Abstract. Cloud computing has emerged as a new technology that provides on-demand access to a large amount of computing resources. This makes it an ideal environment for executing metaheuristic optimization experiments. In this paper, we investigate the use of cloud computing for metaheuristic optimization. This is done by analyzing job characteristics from our production system and conducting a performance comparison between different execution environments. Additionally, a cost analysis is done to incorporate expenses of using virtual resources.

1 Introduction

Cloud computing provides a flexible, on demand computing infrastructure [1]. It provides instant access to a massive pool of computational resources which are dynamically managed, monitored, and maintained. Clouds are often seen as alternatives for custom local cluster and grid computing systems since they eliminate the problem of inadequate hardware dimensioning accompanied with high acquisition and maintenance costs [7].

With its characteristics, cloud computing gets increasingly popular in the scientific community. A number of research papers examined the benefits of running computation and data intensive applications in the cloud [5]. However, there are only little studies about executing large scale experiments of metaheuristic optimization in cloud environments. Nevertheless, they would be quite suitable for such environments regarding their resource and runtime characteristics.

In this paper we explore the use of cloud computing for metaheuristic optimization scenarios. This is done from a perspective of researchers and domain experts. The distributed computation environment HeuristicLab Hive (section 2) is used for the analysis. We examine how cloud computing can support these types of applications (section 3) and analyzed the applicability of cloud computing in the field of metaheuristic optimization (section 4). The results include typical usage characteristics, a performance comparison of different computation environments, and a cost analysis (section 5).

R. Moreno-Díaz et al. (Eds.): EUROCAST 2013, Part I, LNCS 8111, pp. 348–355, 2013.
© Springer-Verlag Berlin Heidelberg 2013

2   HeuristicLab Hive

HeuristicLab Hive is part of the open source HeuristicLab[1] optimization environment for heuristic and evolutionary algorithms [13]. It is an easy to use, elastic, scalable and secure infrastructure for distributed computing [9] and speeds up the execution of algorithms by distributing the computation jobs to multiple computers. HeuristicLab Hive takes care of managing computation resources and deploying the jobs. It follows the master-slave model. The server queues the uploaded jobs and distributes them to the computation resources if they are available and meet certain constraints. A running jobs can be paused and redeployed to a different resource. These calculation resources, also called Hive slaves, execute the jobs and store the results back on the server. Recently, HeuristicLab Hive Server has been migrated to the Windows Azure Platform.

3   Execution Environments for Metaheuristic Optimization

With the rise of cloud computing, traditional execution environments like local systems and clusters can now be extended to incorporate on demand virtual resources. Users may choose between multiple execution environments, ranging from local distributed environments over hybrid approaches to full cloud environments. In the following, we discuss the characteristics of these execution environments (see also Figure 1).

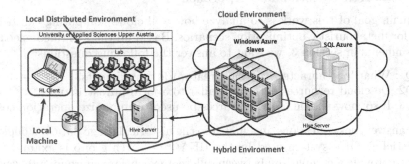

Fig. 1. Execution Environments

- **Local Machine.** Experiments are executed on the local machine. This means no data transfer is needed and the performance is restricted to the power of this machine.
- **Local Distributed Environment.** Experiments are executed on the local infrastructure. The computing power is restricted to local resources and data is transferred locally.

---

[1] http://dev.heuristiclab.com

- **Hybrid Environment.** Experiment are distributed among the local and cloud infrastructure. This implies a dependency on internet connectivity. Either the server can be hosted in the cloud or in the local infrastructure. Outbound cloud traffic accrues while computing and retrieving results.
- **Cloud Environment.** Experiments are executed exclusively on virtual resources from the cloud provider. The cloud provider fully operates the infrastructure and offer elasticity and scalability features. Typically the services are offered with a pay-as-you-go pricing model. Outbound traffic is only necessary for retrieving results.

Many frameworks for executing metaheurics experiments are available [11], but they often lack support for parallelization and distribution. In [2], Cahon et al. present ParadisEO, a framework that uses MPI for executing parallel and distributed metaheuristics. An extension for grid computing technologies, called ParadisEO-CMW, was presented in [3]. Kim et al. proposed PADO, a distributed and parallel metaheuristics framework that can utilize heterogeneous computing and communications resources [8]. Similar to that, Vecchiola et al. proposed in [12] a plug-in based environment for executing evolutionary algorithms on distributed computing environments. Recently, Derby et al. described in [6] a system called FlexGP, that is specifically design to run efficiently in cloud environments. FlexGP is a large-scale distributed system using genetic programming for machine learning on the cloud.

4   Experiments and Setup

4.1   Research Question and Approach

The main goal of this work is to analyze how well cloud computing can be utilized for metaheuristic optimization scenarios. Based on the identified execution environments in section 3, we want to answer the following questions:

- Q1: What job characteristics have real world experiments?
- Q2: Do cloud resources perform similar to a local infrastructure?
- Q3: If so, how should cloud resources be used to minimize operation costs?

To answer these questions, in a first step the historical usage data of a deployed HeuristicLab Hive system used by the HEAL[2] research group is examined. In order to provide a comparison between different execution environments, various jobs with different predefined runtimes are executed to test overall differences in runtime behavior and overhead costs. The used test data and setup are described in section 4.2 and section 4.3, respectively. Additionally, a cost analysis is performed to answer whether it makes sense to completely move to the cloud or only cover peaks of utilization.

The experiments were conducted from the perspective of a researcher and domain expert in metaheuristic optimization. Hence, the experiments are done from a high level perspective and no detailed comparison of performance aspects of virtual machines or HPC infrastructure.

---

[2] http://heal.heuristiclab.com

4.2 Test Data

The runtime experiments were conducted with a modified version of the Whetstone benchmarking algorithm [4] which is part of HeuristicLab and allows to set a predefined runtime and to allocate a specified size of data junk. This gives us the advantage to mimic and simulate real world scenarios. For investigating usage statistics, data from the HeuristicLab Hive deployment at the University of Applied Sciences Upper Austria is used. The data was collected between 01.12.2011 and 06.02.2013 (14 months). It includes 725 jobs, which in turn consist of 52,283 tasks (the actual computation units). When jobs are deleted, only aggregated statistics remain in the system. This historical data comprise 41,076 entries.

4.3 Test Environment

The experiments run in a mixed environment comprising on-premises and cloud infrastructure. Each environment consists of a Hive Server, which distributes the jobs, and Hive slaves, where the actual computation happens. The local test environment consists of resources located in the University of Applied Sciences Upper Austria, Campus Hagenberg. A detailed overview of the test environment and the specifications of the used systems are shown in Figure 2.

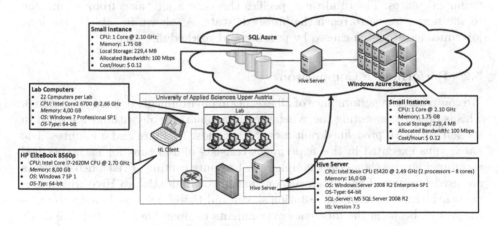

Fig. 2. Test Evironment

5   Results and Analysis

5.1   Job Characteristics

To get a better understanding of how users work with HeuristicLab Hive, an analysis of the usage statistics was done. A detailed description of the available test data can be found in section 4.2. When analyzing the usage statistics, it

Table 1. Job Characteristics of HeuristicLab Hive Usage Data

	Min	Q1	Median	Q3	Max
No. of Tasks in a Job	1	1	3	60	1224
Calculation Times	00:00:09	00:01::33	00:09:33	00:52:55	2399:56:35
Transfer Times	00:00:01	00:00::04	00:00:07	00:00:26	01:56:35
Execution Times	00:00:01	00:00::08	00:01:46	00:09:51	17054:43:32
Total Times	00:00:12	00:00::54	00:02:52	00:07:10	133081:13:33

turns out that most jobs contain very few tasks (Table 1). About 85% contain between 1 and 100 tasks, 13% are between 101 and 1000, and only 2% are above.

Another interesting aspects are calculation and transfer times for tasks. Calculation time defines the time to prepare and execute an algorithm. The transfer time specifies the time a task in transferred between HeuristicLab Hive Server and slave. As shown in table 1, most of the tasks calculation times are less than an hour. High calculation times may be caused by pausing a running algorithm, which is time intensive. The transfer times are mainly determined by the network connection between the server and slave. High transfer times can be caused by slaves located in different network zones, far away.

When looking at the execution times and total times of the historical data, very long job runtimes can be observed. The execution time is the time an algorithm calculates. The total time specifies the time a job takes from submitting to the server queue to reach the 'finished' state. As shown in table 1, the long job runtimes are often caused by pausing and rescheduling tasks.

5.2 Performance Comparison

We compared the performance of all execution environments defined in section 3. This is done by executing the Whetstone benchmarking algorithm (described in section 4.2) with predefined runtimes of 5 seconds, 1 minute and 5 minutes. The batch runs executed in this experiment consists of 100 runs for each specified runtime. Figure 3 shows the example with 1 minute runtime. Predefined runtimes are used because of the heterogeneous nature of HeuristicLab Hive which supports arbitrary types of computation slaves and therefore a mechanism to make the results between the different environments comparable is needed. We don't want to compare the runtime of jobs on individual slaves, but rather benchmark the execution of the whole environment.

Another aspect we have encountered is the communication and calculation overhead depending on the chosen execution environment (Figure 4). It clearly points out, that communication between zones is expensive and depends on variable WAN conditions [10].

When comparing the local environment and the cloud environment also cloud platform specific aspects have to be kept in mind. Beside virtualization overhead, the allocated network bandwidth is limited for each instance. Additionally, bigger instances provide higher I/O and network performance.

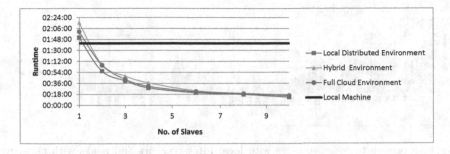

Fig. 3. Performance comparison of different execution environments

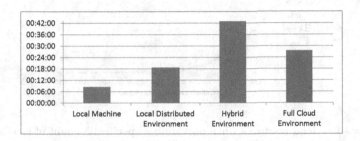

Fig. 4. Communication and calculation overhead for 100 runs with 5 sec. runtime

5.3 Cost Analysis

When conducting cost analysis, platform specific aspects and pricing details have to be considerd accordingly. Therefor, the following calculations are based on the pricing model of Windows Azure[3].

In a first step, the costs for completely replacing the local infrastructure with cloud resources are considered. This includes (Figure 2): A server (medium instance, a SQL Azure database with 150 GB storage and 41 cores for Hive slaves (based on average number of available cores in usage statistics). Costs for storage transactions and outbound data (for obtaining results) are considered but only estimated since they take a very low share in the resulting costs. Based on this specification the costs would sum up to a total of approximately $54,040.00 for 14 months or $3,860.00 per month.

A second approach would be a hybrid model where a defined load is covered with the local infrastructure and peak loads with additional cloud resources. Especially, this makes sense when looking at the general usage statics. It can be observed that there is a high demand for computing resource before important events (e.g. conferences and project deadlines), while for the remaining period of time an over-dimensioning is observable. Therefore it makes clear sense to make use of scalability features. Figure 5 shows an example of covering 40 cores with local infrastructure and the peaks with cloud resources. The peaks correspond

---

[3] http://www.windowsazure.com/en-us/pricing/calculator/

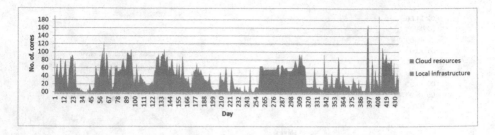

Fig. 5. Example to cover 40 cores with local infrastructure and peaks with cloud resources

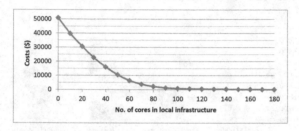

Fig. 6. Costs for cloud resources when providing a specified amount of local resources

to approximately $16,030.00 for 14 months ($1,145.00 per month). In general, Figure 6 shows the remaining costs for cloud resources when providing a specified amount of local resources based on the usage statistics.

6   Conclusion

In this paper, the authors aimed to identify and analyze various aspects of executing metaheuristic optimization scenarios using cloud computing environments. The analysis included a study of typical job characteristics, a performance comparison with different execution environments, and a cost analysis.

Over a long period of time, the usage data revealed fluctuating demand for computation resources and the system showed an over-dimensioning. Therefore, the use of hybrid computing environments is beneficial. The basic load should be covered with local infrastructure and peaks with additional cloud resources. When considering hybrid, and cloud environments in general, the server and the computational units should be placed as close as possible. This is especially important for data intensive applications. Additionally, is it useful to process short running tasks locally, since the overhead for distribution can be too high.

Acknowledgments. This research was partially supported by a grant from Microsoft. Special thanks goes to Andreas Schabus und Jürgen Mayrbäurl from Microsoft Austria for their great support. Any opinions, findings and conclusions in this paper are those of the authors and do not necessarily represent the views of the research sponsors.

References

1. Armbrust, M., Fox, A., Griffith, R., Joseph, A.D., Katz, R., Konwinski, A., Lee, G., Patterson, D., Rabkin, A., Stoica, I., Zaharia, M.: A View of Cloud Computing. Commun. ACM 53, 50–58 (2010)
2. Cahon, S., Melab, N., Talbi, E.G.: ParadisEO: A framework for reusable design of parallel and distributed metaheuristics. Journal of Heuristics 10(3), 357–380 (2004)
3. Cahon, S., Melab, N., Talbi, E.G.: An enabling framework for parallel optimization on the computational grid. In: Proceedings of the Fifth IEEE International Symposium on Cluster Computing and the Grid (CCGrid 2005), pp. 702–709. IEEE Computer Society (2005)
4. Curnow, H.J., Wichmann, B.A., Si, T.: A Synthetic Benchmark. The Computer Journal 19, 43–49 (1976)
5. Deelman, E., Singh, G., Livny, M., Berriman, B., Good, J.: The Cost of Doing Science on the Cloud: The Montage Example. In: Proceedings of the 2008 ACM/IEEE Conference on Supercomputing, vol. 50, pp. 1–12. IEEE Press (2008)
6. Derby, O., Veeramachaneni, K., O'Reilly, U.-M.: Cloud Driven Design of a Distributed Genetic Programming Platform. In: Esparcia-Alcázar, A.I. (ed.) EvoApplications 2013. LNCS, vol. 7835, pp. 509–518. Springer, Heidelberg (2013)
7. Foster, I., Zhao, Y., Raicu, I., Lu, S.: Cloud Computing and Grid Computing 360-Degree Compared. In: 2008 Grid Computing Environments Workshop, pp. 1–10. IEEE (2008)
8. Kim, J., Kim, M., Stehr, M.O., Oh, H., Ha, S.: A parallel and distributed metaheuristic framework based on partially ordered knowledge sharing. J. Parallel Distrib. Comput. 72(4), 564–578 (2012)
9. Neumüller, C., Scheibenpflug, A., Wagner, S., Beham, A., Affenzeller, M.: Large Scale Parameter Meta-Optimization of Metaheuristic Optimization Algorithms with HeuristicLab Hive. In: Actas del VIII Español sobre Metaheurísticas, Algoritmos Evolutivos y Bioinspirados (MAEB), Albacete, Spain (2012)
10. Palankar, M.R., Iamnitchi, A., Ripeanu, M., Garfinkel, S.: Amazon s3 for science grids: a viable solution? In: Proceedings of the 2008 International Workshop on Data-Aware Distributed Computing, pp. 55–64. ACM (2008)
11. Parejo, J.A., Ruiz-Cortés, A., Lozano, S., Fernández, P.: Metaheuristic optimization frameworks: A survey and benchmarking. Soft Computing 16(3), 527–561 (2011)
12. Vecchiola, C., Pandey, S., Buyya, R.: High-performance cloud computing: A view of scientific applications. In: Proceedings of the 2009 10th International Symposium on Pervasive Systems, Algorithms, and Networks, pp. 4–16. IEEE Computer Society (2009)
13. Wagner, S.: Heuristic Optimization Software Systems: Modeling of Heuristic Optimization Algorithms in the HeuristicLab Software Environment. Ph.D. thesis, Johannes Kepler Universität Linz (2009)

Yard Storage Assignment Optimisation
with Neutral Walks

Monika Kofler, Andreas Beham, Erik Pitzer,
Stefan Wagner, and Michael Affenzeller

University of Applied Sciences Upper Austria,
Heuristic and Evolutionary Algorithms Laboratory
{monika.kofler,andreas.beham,erik.pitzer,
stefan.wagner,michael.affenzeller}@heuristiclab.com
http://dev.heuristiclab.com

Abstract. In this paper we investigate how to stack products on a storage yard for efficient retrieval. The objective is to minimise both the transport distance and the number of stack shuffles. Previous research on yard storage assignment indicated that the fitness landscape of the problem features a high degree of neutrality, meaning that there are many neighbouring solutions with identical objective value. We exploit this property and couple local search, tabu search and evolution strategy with neutral walks and extrema selection. A small benchmark instance can be solved to optimality with all three modified algorithm variants while the standard algorithms got stuck in local optima.

Keywords: local search, fitness landscapes, neutral walk, storage location assignment.

1 Fitness Landscape Analysis and Neutrality

Fitness landscape analysis (FLA) was first introduced and applied in the field of evolutionary biology. Sewall Wright, one of the founding fathers of theoretical population genetics, developed the metaphor of *fitness landscapes* or *fitness surfaces* to describe the relationship between an individual's genotype or phenotype and its fitness [1]. Wright observed that mutation and natural selection would ideally lead to a population climbing the nearest fitness peak while excessive mutation, cross- or inbreeding can lead to or evolutionary stagnation or extinction of a species.

The fitness landscape metaphor has since been successfully transferred to the field of heuristic and evolutionary optimisation. Among other things FLA can be used to analyse why some problem instances are harder to solve for certain algorithms than others. Landscape characteristics such as the number of local optima, landscape ruggedness, basins of attraction, barriers or neutrality can assist the user in selecting and parameterising the most appropriate optimisation algorithm. A comprehensive survey of FLA can be found in [2].

R. Moreno-Díaz et al. (Eds.): EUROCAST 2013, Part I, LNCS 8111, pp. 356–363, 2013.

In this paper we focus on the property of *neutrality*. Neutral areas or *plateaus* are connected neighbourhood structures that have the same fitness. A high degree of neutrality can be found in real-world problems such as flow-shop scheduling [3], digital circuit evolution [4] or the yard storage optimisation problem [5].

Pronounced neutral plateaus are usually seen as a challenge in algorithm development due to the absence of a fitness gradient to guide the search. However, some researchers have attempted to actively exploit neutral plateaus as a shortcut to other regions of the solution space and to effectively escape from local optima. Figure 1 illustrates this hypothesis as originally depicted and described in [6].

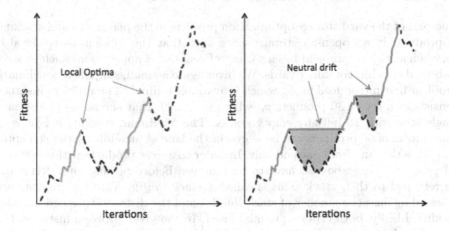

Fig. 1. Some researchers incorporate neutral drift into their algorithms to improve optimisation results. (left) A multi-start algorithm that accepts a moderate amount of non-improving solutions is used. However, each run converges to a local optimum and is effectively stuck there. (right) Neutral drift is added to the algorithm as a means to escape local optima and cross larger "fitness valleys". The graph was adapted from [6].

The Netcrawler algorithm, which is a variety of hillclimber, was one of the first algorithms that tried to utilise neutral drift [7]. In 2004, Verel, Collard and Clergue developed Scuba Search, which uses fitness landscape characteristics associated with neutral plateaus to guide the search, and showed that it outperformed Netcrawler on certain benchmark problems [8]. Marmion et al. used random walks as diversification strategy in iterated local search [3] and Owen and Harvey adapted particle swarm optimisation to accept neutral moves [9].

For population-based approaches, such as genetic algorithm, evolution strategy or swarm optimisation, Stewart introduced the mechanism of *extrema selection* [10]. If multiple solution of equal fitness are present in the population, extrema selection picks the individuals which are most distant from the population centroid or current best solution.

One could argue that a multitude of algorithmic approaches already incorporate strategies to effectively escape from local optima. Humeau et al. [11] differentiate between four categories of approaches, namely those who a) iterate from different initial solutions, b) accept non-improving neighbours, c) change the neighbourhood and d) change the objective function. Some algorithms combine multiple approaches. Using neutral drift in optimisation falls into category b. More well-known algorithms in that category include tabu search and simulated annealing. We will show in subsequent sections that neutral walk can be easily be incorporated into existing algorithms as a complementary strategy to improve performance.

2 Yard Storage Optimization Problem

The goal of the yard storage optimization problem is the placement and stacking of products in an open-air storage space such that the subsequent retrieval is very efficient. The problem has a variety of real-world applications such as steel slab yards or ship container yards. We investigate a small, simplified benchmark problem first introduced in [5], which is available online[1]. The problem instance consists of a set of 30 products p_i, where $i = 0..29$, that should be placed in a single lane with 10 initially empty stacks. The maximum stacking height is 6, thus a total of 60 products can be stored in the lane. A straddle carrier can enter and leave the lane from one end only. In order to access products within a stack, all products lying above it have to be removed before picking and afterwards be returned to their stack. This is called a *stack shuffle*. Yard assignments are assessed against the number of stack shuffles and the distance travelled in order picking. Ideally, both criteria are minimised. In the given problem instance, the following three orders o_1, o_2 and o_3 need to be retrieved consecutively from the yard:

$$o_1 = 4 \rightarrow 6 \rightarrow 11 \rightarrow 15 \rightarrow 16 \rightarrow 17 \rightarrow 25$$
$$o_2 = 3 \rightarrow 7 \rightarrow 13 \rightarrow 14 \rightarrow 18 \rightarrow 19 \rightarrow 26 \rightarrow 27$$
$$o_3 = 1 \rightarrow 2 \rightarrow 8 \rightarrow 12 \rightarrow 20 \rightarrow 23 \rightarrow 24 \rightarrow 28$$

We assume that the capacity of the picking vehicle is sufficient to retrieve all products of an order in a single tour. Products with index $i \in \{0, 5, 9, 10, 21, 22, 29\}$ are not assigned to an order and remain on the yard during the planning period.

As depicted in Figure 2, the best solution of this problem can be readily found with a simple construction heuristic that assigns products top-down in order of retrieval. However, if additional constraints are added to the problem - such as different product sizes, stack stability constraints or stochastic delivery - this is not possible anymore. Since the algorithmic analysis in this paper is meant as a pre-study for a real-world yard storage problem we aim to find (meta-)heuristic algorithms that can perform well on such a problem instance instead.

Six different, problem-specific move operators, which generate only feasible solutions, were implemented. Tests with local search and simulated annealing

---

[1] http://dev.heuristiclab.com/trac/hl/core/wiki/AdditionalMaterial

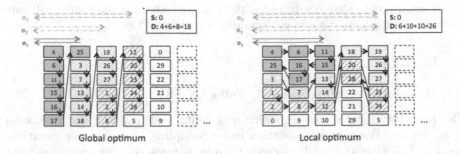

Fig. 2. The graphic illustrates the known best solution (left) and a sample local optimum (right) as well as the required stack shuffles (S) and distance (D) for the investigated benchmark problem instance

predominately terminated in local optima. Implementation details and results can be found in [5]. One such local optimum generated with local search and an exhaustive *insertion move* operator is shown on the right side of Figure 2. In this situation, no improving moves can be made.

We conducted fitness landscape analysis on the given yard storage problem instance and found pronounced neutral plateaus with all move operators. We modified a standard local search, tabu search and evolution strategy in an attempt to exploit the existing neutrality in the search space.

3   Experimental Setup

Multiple algorithms from the literature, which actively explore neutral plateaus, are tested in this study. First of all we combine local search with neutral walks, which is equivalent to the Netcrawler [7] algorithm. Second, we create a new tabu search variant which also performs neutral walks. Third, we use extrema selection [10] and couple it with evolution strategy.

Usually, algorithms are compared by their runtime and sometimes storage requirements. However, the efficiency of the algorithm implementation has to be considered as well. Therefore we evaluate the results based on the number of evaluated moves, all created with the *insertion move* operator described in [5]. No crossover operator was used in the evolution strategy runs to facilitate a better comparison of the total optimisation efforts. The ability of the different algorithms to cross neutral plateaus fast can thus be compared very well.

The parameter settings for each algorithm were tuned empirically as detailed in Section 4. The most suitable settings were subsequently used to compare the three algorithms. For each algorithm a batch of 100 runs was conducted to account for stochastic variability. A random initial assignment is generated at the beginning of each run. The insertion move operator was employed to generate children/neighbours in each iteration. Due to the size of the neighbourhood 30 neighbours were sampled randomly per iteration instead of enumerating the entire neighbourhood.

All experiments were conducted with HeuristicLab, an open-source software environment for heuristic and evolutionary algorithms [12].

4   Results

4.1   Local Search Plus Neutral Walks (N-LS)

The neutrality local search algorithm was configured to perform a maximum of 40,000 iterations, to use insertion move (sampling 30 moves per iteration) and best selection. If a neighbourhood sample contains no improving moves but neutral neighbours one of these is picked randomly. Each of the 100 runs with a random initial solution reached the known optimal quality of zero shuffles and a travel distance of 18. On average, a run performed 1262 iterations and evaluated more than 37,000 moves until the optimum was reached. The minimum number of iterations was 169 or 5070 moves. Details can be found in Table 1.

To get a better understanding about the difficulty of the problem, we investigated the distribution and size of neutral plateaus. On average 19.4 neutral plateaus had to be crossed per local search optimisation run. The maximum number of steps required to find a portal to a better solution varied considerably. In the initial algorithm stages the number of neutral steps might be just one or two, indicating that the neighbourhood sample did not contain an improving move but that subsequent sampling would probably have yielded a better solution without performing an intermediate neutral move. 57% of all neutral walks required 10 steps or less until a portal was reached. On the contrary, the largest walk length per run ranged between 66 and 1806 steps, with a median of 482 steps. As a rule of thumb, the neutral walk lengths increased towards the end of the local search run and in 75% of all runs the largest neutral walk was encountered in the last 20% of total neutral plateaus encountered. Therefore, using an optimisation approach such as classical simulated annealing, which allows non-improving moves in the beginning and gradually reduces the likelihood of such moves towards the end, is not appropriate for this kind of fitness landscape.

4.2   Tabu Search Plus Neutral Walks (N-TS)

Since neutral walks performed very well in conjunction with local search, we also modified a standard tabu search algorithm to accept neutral moves if no improving move can be found and if the move is not tabu. The maximum number of iterations was set to 40,000. The tabu criterion is that a slab may not be moved twice directly in sequence. We tested tabu list lengths from 0 to 10 and found that for this very small sample sample instance, a tabu length of 1 yielded the best results. As shown in Table 1 and Figure 3 the average number of evaluated moves could be reduced by about 5% compared to N-LS. The downside is that the best quality was not reached in 13 of 100 test runs because a large number of moves is tabu in each iteration due to the restrictive tabu criterion. Since the insertion move is not a simple swap operator and thus not symmetric [5] a more refined tabu criterion would be required for further experiments.

4.3 Evolution Strategy with Extrema Selection (E-ES)

E-ES required by far the most parameter tuning due to the difficulty of balancing population size and and evaluation effort. Larger populations offer more solution diversity but also require more evaluations per iteration. We tested a variety of settings, with population sizes in the range 1-5, a number of children per iteration of 1, 2, 5, 10, 20, 25, 30, 35, 50 and 100 and employed either comma and plus selection. The maximum number of iterations was set to 10,000 in all test runs and since no no crossover operator was used, each child had to be created by mutating one parent with the stochastic insertion move operator. The distance between solutions was calculated as the number of slabs that are not in the same position.

Surprisingly, E-ES performed worse than N-LS on this test instance. This is at odds with Terry Stewart's argument that extrema selection allows the algorithms to cross neutral plateaus much faster than randomly drifting across with

Table 1. The table shows statistics about the number of evaluated moves until the best quality was reached for different algorithms. N-LS and E-ES reached the global optimum in all tests. For tabu search (N-TS) only 87/100 runs that reached the global optimum were considered.

		N-LS	N-TS	E-ES
Runs where optimum was found		100	87/100	100
	Minimum	5070	4410	5218
	Maximum	150840	115050	184243
	Average	37857.3	36025.9	42142.3
Evaluated moves	Median	33210	31890	34583
per run	Standard Deviation	22633.2	21334.6	27127.2
	Variance	5.12E+08	4.55E+08	7.36E+08
	25th Percentile	22522.5	20940	25535.5
	75th Percentile	47205	45720	50324.3

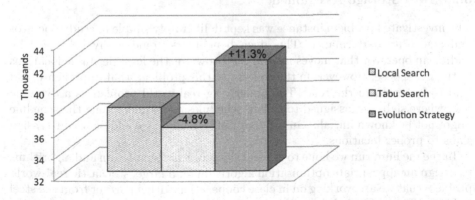

Fig. 3. The chart shows the average number of evaluations per 100 runs and algorithm variant, as detailed in Table 1

a neutral walk. His argument was based on the results of comparing a genetic algorithm with extrema selection versus Netcrawler for NKp fitness functions [10]. Further tests will need to be conducted but we believe that the most efficient way to cross a neutral plateau is fitness landscape specific and depends on the number and distribution of portals. In this problem instance the average length of the largest neutral walk per run was actually much longer for E-ES than LS-N.

5   Conclusions and Outlook

5.1   Algorithmic Performance

We showed that coupling classic local or tabu search algorithms with neutral walks leads to better performance on a small yard storage assignment instance. Extrema selection can infuse diversity into populations without loss of fitness but did not perform quite as well as hoped on the test instance. We plan to experiment with different distance measures between solutions and also with larger problem instances that cannot be solved as quickly. Whether a general strategy or an indicator can be devised on how to best approach movement across a neutral plateau remains to be seen.

All three algorithmic variants can be used without prior analysis of the degree of neutrality of a problem. Since neutral solutions are only considered if no improving solution can be found in the (sampling) neighbourhood or population, the algorithmic adjustments have no negative performance impact on problems with a small degree of neutrality.

We found that the required neutral walk lengths to find a portal can be rather long and there is a need for research on how to control the effort put into neutral exploration. One option would be to introduce a maximum walk length but this parameter would need to be tuned for each problem or even problem instance.

5.2   Yard Storage Assignment

The investigated problem instance was kept deliberately simple to study operator and algorithm performance. The given benchmark could easily be solved by adding an operator that moves *neutral slabs* towards the least desirable locations in the warehouse. However, in the context of this problem, that approach would lead to issues down the road. The underlying real-world problem is a dynamic one, where slabs get assigned to rolling schedules over time. While the schedule might not be known initially, an estimator of slab affinity could be used to assign slabs to proper locations.

In the medium run we hope to expand the problem formulation and algorithms to design an appropriate optimisation algorithm for a large, stochastic real-world problem that we are working on in close cooperation with a partner from the steel industry. This extended scenario contains more than 300,000 storage locations, additional stacking constraints and stochastic orders.

References

1. Wright, S.: The roles of mutation, inbreeding, crossbreeding and selection in evolution. In: Proceedings of the Sixth International Congress on Genetics, vol. 1, pp. 356–366 (1932)
2. Pitzer, E., Affenzeller, M.: A comprehensive survey on fitness landscape analysis. In: Fodor, J., Klempous, R., Suárez Araujo, C.P. (eds.) Recent Advances in Intelligent Engineering Systems. SCI, vol. 378, pp. 161–191. Springer, Heidelberg (2012)
3. Marmion, M.-E., Dhaenens, C., Jourdan, L., Liefooghe, A., Verel, S.: On the neutrality of flowshop scheduling fitness landscapes. In: Coello, C.A.C. (ed.) LION 2011. LNCS, vol. 6683, pp. 238–252. Springer, Heidelberg (2011)
4. Vassilev, V.K., Miller, J.F.: The advantages of landscape neutrality in digital circuit evolution. In: Miller, J.F., Thompson, A., Thompson, P., Fogarty, T.C. (eds.) ICES 2000. LNCS, vol. 1801, pp. 252–263. Springer, Heidelberg (2000)
5. Kofler, M., Beham, A., Vonolfen, S., Wagner, S., Affenzeller, M.: Modelling and optimizing storage assignment in a steel slab yard. In: Szakal, A. (ed.) 2012 4th IEEE International Symposium on Logistics and Industrial Informatics (LINDI), pp. 101–106. IEEE (September 2012)
6. Forst, C.V.: Molecular evolution: A theory approaches experiments. Journal of Biotechnology 64(1), 101–118 (1998)
7. Barnett, L.: Netcrawling-optimal evolutionary search with neutral networks. In: Proceedings of the 2001 Congress on Evolutionary Computation, vol. 1, pp. 30–37. IEEE (2001)
8. Verel, S., Collard, P., Clergue, M.: Scuba search: when selection meets innovation. In: Congress on Evolutionary Computation (CEC 2004), vol. 1, pp. 924–931. IEEE (2004)
9. Owen, A., Harvey, I.: Adapting particle swarm optimisation for fitness landscapes with neutrality. In: Swarm Intelligence Symposium, SIS 2007, pp. 258–265. IEEE (April 2007)
10. Stewart, T.: Extrema selection: Accelerated evolution on neutral networks. In: Proceedings of the 2001 Congress on Evolutionary Computation (CEC 2001), vol. 1, pp. 25–29. IEEE (2001)
11. Humeau, J., Liefooghe, A., Talbi, E.G., Verel, S.: ParadisEO-MO: From fitness landscape analysis to efficient local search algorithms. Technical Report (February 2012), http://hal.inria.fr/docs/00/66/54/21/PDF/RR-7871.pdf
12. Wagner, S.: Heuristic Optimization Software Systems - Modeling of Heuristic Optimization Algorithms in the HeuristicLab Software Environment. PhD thesis, Institute for Formal Models and Verification, Johannes Kepler University, Linz, Austria (2009)

An Analysis of the Intensification and Diversification Behavior of Different Operators for Genetic Algorithms

Andreas Scheibenpflug and Stefan Wagner

Heuristic and Evolutionary Algorithms Laboratory (HEAL)
School of Informatics, Communications and Media
University of Applied Sciences Upper Austria, Campus Hagenberg
Softwarepark 11, 4232 Hagenberg, Austria
{ascheibe,swagner}@heuristiclab.com

Abstract. Intensification and diversification are two driving forces in genetic algorithms and are frequently the subject of research. While it seemed for decades that a genetic operator can be classified as either the one or the other, it has been shown in the last few years that this assumption is an oversimplified view and most operators exhibit both, diversification and intensification, to some degree. Most papers in this field focus on a certain operator or algorithm configuration as theoretical and generalizable foundations are hard to obtain. In this paper we therefore use a wide range of different configurations and behavior measurements to study the intensification and diversification behavior of genetic algorithms and their operators.

1 Introduction

Metaheuristics are usually applied to problems that cannot be solved in polynomial time. Because of the frequent use of stochastic processes, theoretical foundations are hard to obtain and are often limited to a certain algorithm configuration for a certain problem instance [9]. In [10] we have therefore proposed behavior measurements with the goal of defining a framework that allows to empirically study the behavior of metaheuristics and gain insights into the inner workings of these algorithms. In this paper the authors will present results obtained from empirical tests with genetic algorithms and the traveling salesman problem. We will focus on the interplay of intensification and diversification as these are driving forces in genetic algorithms.

This paper is organized as follows: Section 2 introduces the concepts of intensification and diversification as well as an overview of previous works in this area of algorithm analysis. Section 3 gives an introduction to algorithm behavior measurements and how they are computed. Section 4 first describes how the empirical tests are conducted and then presents the results. Finally, Section 5 concludes this work.

R. Moreno-Díaz et al. (Eds.): EUROCAST 2013, Part I, LNCS 8111, pp. 364–371, 2013.
© Springer-Verlag Berlin Heidelberg 2013

2 Intensification and Diversification

Metaheuristics iteratively apply a set of operators to solution candidates with the goal of improving these solutions until a satisfactory result is computed. More sophisticated metaheuristics use several types of operators that pursuit different goals. Most often these goals are diversification (exploration) and intensification (exploitation) as they are the two most essential aspects in metaheuristics. Diversification is responsible for exploring the search space and identifying regions with high quality solutions while intensification further improves solutions by exploiting the accumulated search experience [11]. But as mentioned in [8], it is essential for the performance of a metaheuristic to find an optimal balance between diversification and intensification. Furthermore, when considering genetic algorithms, there needs to be operators (e.g. mutation) that inject diverse solutions into the population as the crossover operator heavily relies on diversity in the population [6]. Blum et. al. [2] mention that for a long time the common assumption was that diversification is done by mutation and crossover while intensification is achieved with the selection operator. Eiben an Schippers [4] were the first to question this view. It is argued that while mutation introduces new material (diversification) it also preserves most information from the parent and is thus also an intensification operator. Similarly, crossover creates a new solution (diversification) but also preserves most material (intensification). This view is also shared in other publications [5] and as remarked in [3], the line between selection, crossover and mutation is blurred and it is difficult to distinguish between intensification and diversification. Another point that is mentioned is that other parameters of the GA (e.g. population size) also have an influence on the behavior of an operator and therefore on the intensification and diversification ratio. Despite the amount of work that has been published in this field there is no clear and coherent definition of what intensification and diversification is. As mentioned in [4], most authors leave their definition implicit and use the intuitive meaning of the concepts to explain the working of EAs. This makes it hard to measure the intensification and diversification that an operator exhibits. In this paper we will use the term diversification in the sense that operators should introduce new material to a solution while the resulting quality can be neglected. We define the concept of intensification as the reuse of existing material to improve solution quality, while the amount of diversification should be kept to a minimum.

3 Behavior Measurements

Behavior measurements [10] were introduced as a tool for analyzing metaheuristics. By calculating a range of measurements while executing a metaheuristic, information about the behavior and the inner workings of the algorithm is captured and can then be analyzed. While there are papers that investigate the performance and behavior of operators [7,13] for the traveling salesman problem, they are often theoretical or only show very limited experimental results.

A theoretical or synthetic empirical study in isolation often only highlights certain aspects and falls short to capture the dynamics of the genetic algorithm and the population. Crepinsek et. al. [3] describe this problem by stating that *"it is almost impossible to study a particular feature in isolation"*. Therefore we use empirical tests with a wide range of tested configurations and behavior measurements for algorithm analysis (see [10] for a detailed description), some of which are described in the following:

- Child/Mutation diversity: Diversity of a child generated by crossover or mutation compared to the parent(s).
- Unwanted mutations: Counts the broken edges generated by a crossover.
- Crossover/Mutation performance: Tracks the average scaled fitness change that a crossover/mutation operator exhibits.
- Parent diversity and quality difference: A measure for diversity and scaled quality difference between selected solutions. Additionally, the number of equal parents is tracked as well.
- Selection Pressure: Scaled quality difference of selected solutions compared to average population quality.
- Quality/Diversity difference to population after crossover/mutation: Compares a child generated by crossover or mutation to the average population quality or diversity.
- Beneficial Crossovers/Mutations: Counts beneficial crossovers (based on a comparison factor as described in [1]) or beneficial mutations.

4   Empirical Tests

All tests described in the following are conducted using the HeuristicLab[1][12] optimization environment and it's implementation of the genetic algorithm and it's operators. Parameter configurations for the GA are chosen randomly within certain bounds as defined in Table 1. This results in 167,400 possible configurations where samples of size 1,000 are drawn multiple times. The goal of this approach is to draw a group of samples that is representative for the space of possible parameter configurations within the given bounds. To verify that the sample sizes are representative, the groups are compared for equality using statistical hypothesis testing. Furthermore, the stopping criterion of the genetic algorithm

Table 1. Parameter configurations

Parameter	Variations
Population size	[50, 3000], Step size: 50
Mutation probability	[0.01, 0.6], Step size: 0.02
Crossover	OX, CX, ERX, PMX, PBX, ULX
Mutation	Insertion, Inversion, Scramble, Swap2, Translocation
Selection	Proportional, Tournament (group size: 2), Linear Rank
Evaluated solutions	350,000
Elites	1

---

[1] http://dev.heuristiclab.com

is fixed to the number of evaluated solutions. This allows to limit runtime to a reasonable amount of time as well as making the comparison between configurations fairer. The boundary has been chosen to match to a population size - generation ratio that would be considered by most researchers as a plausible configuration (e.g. population size: 100, generations: 3500).

4.1   Results

In this section the results of the empirical tests with different genetic operators on four different TSPLIB problem instances (berlin52, ch130, a280, att532) are analyzed using algorithm behavior measurements. Figure 1 shows the scaled quality difference between the parent(s) and the offspring.

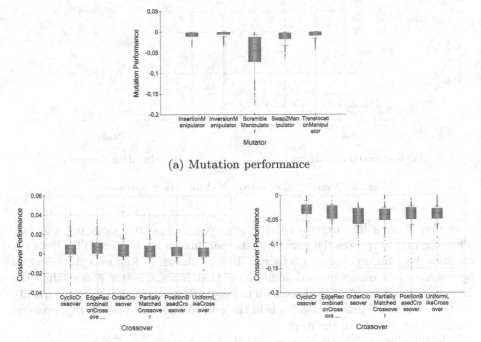

(a) Mutation performance

(b) Crossover performance (worse parent) (c) Crossover performance (better parent)

Fig. 1. Performance of crossover and mutation operators

It shows that mutation operators generally generate worse offspring while the crossover operator most of the time produces children that are at least better than their worse parent, but on an average seldom surpass the fitness of the better parent. While most mutation operations only produce a slight decrease in quality of the solution candidate, scramble mutation can decrease the solution quality quite heavily. The reason for this behavior is that it modifies the solution to a high degree which results in a bigger diversity (Figure 2). Crossover performance compared to the better parent shows some differences in the variance of the operators. The reason for this behavior can be found in the unwanted mutations that an operator exhibits (Figure 2). It shows that the ERX operator has very little unwanted mutations which also results in a very stable performance behavior. Figure 2 also shows that PBX and UX are the crossover operators that have the highest unwanted mutations rate. This can be traced back to the fact that these operators are originally designed for the quadratic assignment problem and not for the traveling salesman problem. When comparing the diversity that the mutation and crossover operators produce, the charts show that crossover often produces more diverse solutions through unwanted mutations than mutation operators.

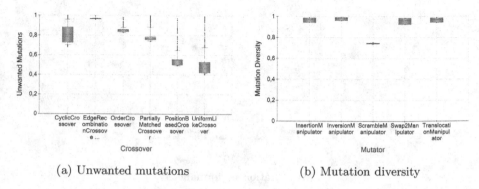

(a) Unwanted mutations   (b) Mutation diversity

Fig. 2. Diversity of crossover and mutation operators

It may seem a bit surprising that the crossover operator does not generate offspring that surpasses the quality of the parents on an average. This begs the question how improvement is achieved. But as shown in Figure 3 the selection operators select on an average individuals that have a better fitness than the average population. And as also shown in Figure 3, when compared to the quality of the population, this process leads in the end to an slight overall improvement from one generation to the next.

Additionally, the charts also show that, for example, the CX operator has a higher intensification component than the PBX operator as it performs better while producing less unwanted mutations. The behavior of an operator changes with different parameter settings. For example when increasing population size, the diversity that a crossover produces compared to the population increases as well. For example for population size of 50, the diversity is on an average 0.5 while with population sizes of 3,000 it increases to 0.07 (a value of 0 means highest diversity, a value of 1 means no diversity). Increasing the mutation rate has a similar effect. For example a mutation rate of 2% leads on average to a diversity of 0.34 while a rate of 60% leads to 0.08. Operators also change their behavior with different problem instances.

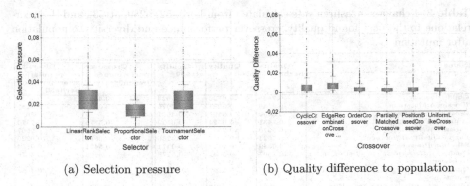

(a) Selection pressure   (b) Quality difference to population

Fig. 3. Selection pressure and quality difference to population after crossover

Table 2. Change of operator behavior with different problem instances

Measurement	berlin52	ch130	a280	att532
ERX Performance	0.0103	0.0062	0.0051	0.0044
ERX Quality difference to population	0.0105	0.0064	0.0050	0.0045
CX Performance	0.0095	0.0044	0.0027	0.0026
CX Quality difference to population	0.0122	0.0054	0.003	0.0022
Inversion Performance	-0.0100	-0.0025	-0.0011	-0.0005
Parent Diversity Tournament	0.2031	0.1286	0.1061	0.0804

Table 2 shows that if problem size is increased, the influence of the operators on quality decreases while diversity produced by selection increases. Mutation operators do not increase the amount of changes with bigger problems and therefore they do not influence the quality of the solution (and also the diversity) so much. Crossover operators also have less impact since the search space increases with higher problem dimensions and it is getting more difficult to produce better offspring. Table 3 shows correlations for the berlin52, a280, att532 problem instances between the best achieved quality and different measurements using Spearman's rank correlation coefficient. It shows that diversity (e.g. child diversity or parent diversity) very well correlates with the best found solution. The higher diversity (a value nearer 0 than 1) the worse the quality (the TSP is a minimization problem). Because the generated experiments can contain very high population sizes and mutation rates, diversity is an important influence for the algorithm. The table additionally shows that higher crossover performance and mutation performance correspond to a higher quality, though mutation performance correlates better, again resulting from the generated configurations. Comparing the correlations between the three problem instances, most correlations decrease with increased population size. An exception are the quality difference to population values as well as unwanted mutations which seem to be measures that could get more important with increasing problem size.

Comparing correlations between algorithm behavior measures, crossover performance correlates very well with the measurements of the selection operator. The higher the quality difference and the higher the diversity between selected solutions, the harder it is for the crossover operator to improve solutions. Table 3

Table 3. Behavior measurements calculated from berlin52, a280, att532 and their correlations to the best found quality, crossover performance and diversity to population after mutation

Name	Quality berlin52	Quality a280	Quality att532	Crossover performance berlin52	Diversity to population after mutation berlin52
Child Diversity	-0.7688	-0.6726	-0.6624	0.4691	0.7543
Unwanted Mutations	-0.5946	-0.6301	-0.6076	0.3371	0.5285
Crossover Performance	-0.5592	-0.5501	-0.4601	—	0.5823
Mutation Performance	0.7435	0.6524	0.6129	-0.5775	-0.7373
Parent Diversity	-0.8970	-0.7443	-0.7465	0.5534	0.9967
Parent Quality Difference	0.5524	0.5017	0.4286	-0.6584	-0.6220
Selection Pressure	0.0689	0.1828	0.0471	-0.5421	-0.0854
Quality difference to population after crossover	-0.4597	-0.5641	-0.5273	0.4603	0.4076
Quality difference to population after mutation	-0.4582	-0.5507	-0.5176	0.4552	0.4068
Diversity to population after mutation	-0.8968	-0.7588	-0.7582	0.5823	—
Beneficial Crossovers (Comparison Factor: 1.0)	0.3555	0.1544	0.1836	0.2382	-0.3562
Beneficial Mutations	0.8613	0.8437	0.7518	-0.5897	-0.8348

shows how the measurements, the operators and parameter settings they result from correlate and influence each other. Interestingly, the diversity between the parents correlates very well with the diversity of the generated child to the population. If two diverse solutions are selected, the generated offspring is again very different to the whole population.

5   Conclusion

In this paper genetic algorithms were analyzed concerning intensification and diversification using algorithm behavior measurements. It was shown in empirical tests that, as literature suggest, operators cannot be defined as either an intensification or a diversification mechanisms. Most of the tested mutation operators (except scramble mutation) only modify solution candidates very little. Additionally, mutation works on individuals that have been evolved over generations and therefore uses accumulated search experience which represents the intensification part of the operator. But an important aspect as well is that mutation generally does not improve solution quality but decreases it on average. Scramble mutation is the exception as it generates very diverse solutions based on heavy modifications where the accumulated information is nearly completely destroyed. Scramble mutation has therefore a very high diversification ratio.

In contrast to mutation, crossovers generally do not produce worse individuals but, on an average only surpass the quality of the worse individual and rarely produce children that are superior to the better parent. As crossovers also use accumulated search information, crossovers would very well suit the definition of an intensification operator. But when looking at unwanted mutations, it is clear that some crossovers produce even more diversity than some mutation operators and therefore crossovers also have a strong diversification component.

The investigated selection operators tend to select solutions which have a fitness higher than the average population. But when selecting diverse solutions, it has been shown that crossovers and mutations will also be more likely to produce diverse children. So selection does intensification as it selects fitter individuals but is indirectly responsible for diversification when selecting diverse solutions.

Furthermore, it was shown using correlations how algorithm behavior measurements correlate with the best found solution and with each other. As the measurements are the result of different parameter configurations, the behavior of some operators very well correlate with other operators. How an operator and how the ratio of intensification and diversification therefore behaves is depending on the problem, the state of the population, the parameters and the used operators.

References

1. Affenzeller, M., Winkler, S., Wagner, S., Beham, A.: Genetic Algorithms and Genetic Programming - Modern Concepts and Practical Applications. Numerical Insights. CRC Press (2009)
2. Blum, C., Roli, A.: Metaheuristics in combinatorial optimization: Overview and conceptual comparison. ACM Computing Surveys 35(3), 268–308 (2003)
3. Crepinsek, M., Liu, S.H., Mernik, M.: Exploration and exploitation in evolutionary algorithms: A survey. To be pubished in ACM Computing Surveys 45(3) (2013)
4. Eiben, A.E., Schippers, C.A.: On Evolutionary Exploration and Exploitation. Fundamenta Informaticae 35(1-4), 35–50 (1998)
5. Hansheng, L., Lishan, K.: Balance between exploration and exploitation in genetic search. Wuhan University Journal of Natural Sciences 4(1), 28–32 (1999)
6. Kötzing, T., Sudholt, D., Theile, M.: How crossover helps in pseudo-boolean optimization. In: Proceedings of the 13th Annual Conference on Genetic and Evolutionary Computation, GECCO 2011, pp. 989–996. ACM (2011)
7. Larranaga, P., Kuijpers, C.M.H., Murga, R.H., Inza, I., Dizdarevic, D.: Genetic algorithms for the travelling salesman problem: A review of representations and operators. Artificial Intelligence Review 13, 129–170 (1999)
8. Mitchell, M.: An Introduction to Genetic Algorithms. MIT Press (1998)
9. Reeves, C.R., Rowe, J.E.: Genetic algorithms: principles and perspectives; a guide to GA theory. Kluwer Academic Publishers (2004)
10. Scheibenpflug, A., Wagner, S., Pitzer, E., Burlacu, B., Affenzeller, M.: On the analysis, classification and prediction of metaheuristic algorithm behavior for combinatorial optimization problems. In: Proceedings of the 24th European Modeling and Simulation Symposium, EMSS 2012 (2012)
11. Stützle, T.: Local search algorithms for combinatorial problems: analysis, algorithms, and new applications. Ph.D. thesis, TU Darmstadt (1999)
12. Wagner, S.: Heuristic Optimization Software Systems: Modeling of Heuristic Optimization Algorithms in the HeuristicLab Software Environment. Ph.D. thesis, Johannes Kepler Universität Linz (2009)
13. Whitley, L.D., Starkweather, T., Fuquay, D.: Scheduling problems and traveling salesmen: The genetic edge recombination operator. In: Proceedings of the 3rd International Conference on Genetic Algorithms. pp. 133–140. Morgan Kaufmann Publishers Inc. (1989)

A PILOT/VND/GRASP Hybrid for the Static Balancing of Public Bicycle Sharing Systems[*]

Petrina Papazek, Günther R. Raidl, Marian Rainer-Harbach, and Bin Hu[**]

Institute of Computer Graphics and Algorithms
Vienna University of Technology
Favoritenstraße 9–11/1861, 1040 Vienna, Austria
{papazek,raidl,rainer-harbach,hu}@ads.tuwien.ac.at

Abstract. Due to varying user demands in bicycle sharing systems, operators need to actively shift bikes between stations by a fleet of vehicles. We address the problem of finding efficient vehicle tours by an extended version of an iterated greedy construction heuristic following the concept of the PILOT method and GRASP and applying a variable neighborhood descend (VND) as local improvement. Computational results on benchmark instances derived from the real-world scenario in Vienna with up to 700 stations indicate that our PILOT/GRASP hybrid especially scales significantly better to very large instances than a previously proposed variable neighborhood search (VNS) approach. Applying only one iteration, the PILOT construction heuristic followed by the VND provides good solutions very quickly, which can be potentially useful for urgent requests.

1 Introduction

Public bicycle sharing systems (BSSs) emerge worldwide in various cities. Such systems augment public transport very well, reduce the amount of motorized traffic, congestions, parking problems, and last but not least are an incentive for sports, thereby contributing to public health [4]. Typically, modern BSSs offer automated rental stations distributed over the city, where users may rent or return bicycles anytime. Operators face one important issue: most stations show asymmetric usage patterns, e.g., people tend to rent bikes at topographically higher stations and return them at lower stations. Other frequent influences are commuting patterns across working days and the weather situation [9]. In order to avoid critical situations where stations run completely empty or full, operators actively move bikes between stations, usually by a fleet of cars with trailers. The Balancing Bicycle Sharing System (BBSS) Problem deals with optimizing these vehicle tours together with corresponding loading or unloading directions.

2 The Balancing Bicycle Sharing System Problem

The BBSS problem is defined on a complete directed graph $G_0 = (V_0, A_0)$, with node set $V_0 = V \cup \{0\}$ consisting of the nodes for rental stations V and the vehicles' depot 0.

[*] This work is supported by the Austrian Research Promotion Agency (FFG) under contract 831740.

[**] We thank the Austrian Institute of Technology (AIT) and Citybike Wien for the collaboration in this project.

R. Moreno-Díaz et al. (Eds.): EUROCAST 2013, Part I, LNCS 8111, pp. 372–379, 2013.
© Springer-Verlag Berlin Heidelberg 2013

Arcs $(u,v) \in A_0$ connecting all $v \in V$ are weighted with a time value $t_{u,v} > 0$ that consists of the time needed for driving from u to v and for servicing v. Let the subgraph induced by the bike stations V only be $G = (V,A)$, $A \subset A_0$. For each station $v \in V$ we are given the bike capacity $C_v \geq 0$, the number of present bikes when beginning the rebalancing process p_v, as well as a target number of bikes q_v, with $0 \leq p_v, q_v \leq C_v$. The BSS operator employs a fleet of vehicles $L = \{1,\ldots,|L|\}$ for moving bikes. Each vehicle $l \in L$ starts empty at the depot 0, has a capacity of Z_l bikes and may visit an arbitrary number of stations before returning empty to the depot again as long as the total tour length t_l does not exceed an available time budget $\hat{t}$.

Solutions to the BBSS problem consist of a route for each vehicle $l \in L$ specified by an ordered sequence of visited stations $r_l = (r_l^1,\ldots,r_l^{\rho_l})$ with $r_l^i \in V$, $i = 1,\ldots,\rho_l$, and ρ_l being the number of visited stations. Note that each station may be visited multiple times by several vehicles. Each visit has associated loading instructions $y_l^i \in \{-Z_l,\ldots,Z_l\}$ with $l \in L$, $v \in V$, and $i = 1,\ldots,\rho_l$, specifying how many bikes are to be picked up ($y_l^i > 0$) or delivered ($y_l^i < 0$) at that visit.

Let a_v be the final number of bikes at each station $v \in V$ after rebalancing and let $\delta_v = |a_v - q_v|$, $\forall v \in V$. Our objective function is given by

$$
\min \quad \omega^{\text{bal}} \sum_{v \in V} \delta_v + \omega^{\text{load}} \sum_{l \in L} \sum_{i=1}^{\rho_l} |y_l^i| + \omega^{\text{work}} \sum_{l \in L} t_l. \tag{1}
$$

Scaling factors $\omega^{\text{bal}}, \omega^{\text{load}}, \omega^{\text{work}} \geq 0$ control the relative importance of the respective terms. The primary objective is to minimize deviations δ_v and only secondarily the number of loading activities as well as the overall tour lengths. We use the setting $\omega^{\text{bal}} = 1$ and $\omega^{\text{load}} = \omega^{\text{work}} = 1/100\,000$ in all our tests.

We simplify the problem by restricting the fill levels of stations to *monotonicity*. Let $V_{\text{pic}} = \{v \in V \mid p_v > q_v\}$ denote *pickup stations* and $V_{\text{del}} = \{v \in V \mid p_v < q_v\}$ denote *delivery stations*. A vehicle must only load bikes at pickup stations and unload bikes at delivery stations. As shown in previous work, this restriction has only a minimal impact on the theoretically achievable best solution quality [8].

3   Related Work

The BBSS problem is related to variants of the vehicle routing problem (VRP). Significant differences, however, include allowing multiple visits of stations, even by different vehicles, and the possibility of loading or unloading an arbitrary number of bikes. BBSS can be regarded as a capacitated single commodity split pickup and delivery VRP.

Each approach deals with different application characteristics, making a direct comparison difficult. In particular, Chemla et al. [2] require achieving perfect balance as a hard constraint. Their approach is designed for a single vehicle and consists of a branch-and-cut algorithm on a relaxed MIP model in conjunction with a tabu search for the local improvement of solutions. Benchimol et al. [1] focus on approximation algorithms for selected special situations. Their approaches also assume balancing as a hard constraint and are limited to a single vehicle. Raviv et al. [9] propose MIP models for the multiple-vehicle case. They consider a convex penalty objective function minimizing user dissatisfaction and tour lengths, but ignore the number of loading operations.

The assets and drawbacks of the models are compared on instances with up to 104 stations, two vehicles and a time horizon of up to five hours. Contardo et al. [3] investigate the dynamic scenario where user activities during rebalancing are taken into account. They describe a hybrid MIP approach utilizing Dantzig-Wolfe and Benders decomposition. Upper and lower bounds can be derived relatively quickly for instances up to 100 stations, but significant gaps remain. Schuijbroek et al. [11] decompose the problem into separate single-vehicle routing problems by solving a clustering problem. The routing problems are handled by a clustered MIP heuristic or a constraint programming approach.

In [8], we propose a greedy construction heuristic followed by a variable neighborhood search/variable neighborhood descent (VNS/VND) metaheuristic for efficiently finding vehicle routes. Three alternative auxiliary algorithms calculate meaningful loading instructions for given tours. In [7] we develop a forth alternative for deriving loading instructions and describe an effective way for applying all of them in a hybrid fashion. The current work extends our methods by applying the PILOT method [12] in the construction heuristic and GRASP as an alternative to the VNS, as well as by performing experiments on larger instances of up to 700 stations.

4   Construction Heuristics

We employ two alternative construction heuristics for creating initial solutions: a greedy construction heuristic (GCH) and an extended version following the PILOT method.

4.1   Greedy Construction Heuristic

The greedy construction heuristic, which is in detail described in [8], sequentially constructs vehicle tours in a pure greedy manner following a local best successor strategy. First, we compute the maximum number of bicycles γ_v that can be picked up or delivered at any station v in the set of feasible, i.e., not yet balanced, successor stations F:

$$\gamma_v = \begin{cases} \min(a_v - q_v, Z_l - b_l) & \text{for } v \in F \cap V_{\text{pic}} \text{ and} \\ \min(q_v - a_v, b_l) & \text{for } v \in F \cap V_{\text{del}}, \end{cases} \tag{2}$$

where b_l expresses the final load of vehicle l so far and a_v the final number of bikes at station v in the partial tour. Next, we evaluate the ratio $\gamma_v/t_{u,v}$ for all $v \in F$. As vehicles need to return empty to the depot, we additionally apply a correction at pickup stations: We restrict the number of pickups at a station by potential deliveries after this stop. Eventually, we append the station offering the highest ratio to the tour r_l and derive loading instructions as follows:

$$y_l^{\rho_l} = \begin{cases} \gamma_v & \text{if } v \in V_{\text{pic}} \text{ and} \\ -\gamma_v & \text{if } v \in V_{\text{del}}. \end{cases} \tag{3}$$

After updating b_l and a_v, the procedure continues with the next extension.

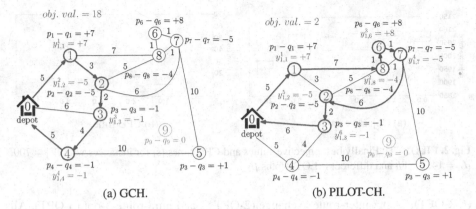

(a) GCH.   (b) PILOT-CH.

Fig. 1. Exemplary solutions of GCH vs. PILOT-CH with $|L| = 1$ and $\hat{t} = 30$min.

4.2 PILOT Construction Heuristic

The drawbacks of the fast GCH – always choosing the single locally best successor – are possible shortsighted results, e.g., we might never service a more distant cluster of stations offering a substantial balance gain. The PILOT (Preferred Iterative LOok ahead Technique) method addresses this issue by looking ahead in order to escape this greedy trap [12]. Consequently, the PILOT construction heuristic (PILOT-CH) extends GCH by evaluating each potential successor in a deeper way by constructing a complete temporary route. For this purpose, we utilize the objective function value as evaluation criterion and select the candidate station with the highest benefit. Figure 1 demonstrates an example where PILOT-CH surpasses GCH. For simplicity we merely visualize the most lucrative connections weighted with symmetric traveling times. Due to the recursive evaluation of candidates the time complexity of PILOT-CH is higher than GCH by a factor of $O(|V|)$. To speed up the computation we may limit the *PILOT depth β*, i.e., restrict the number of successor stations of the recursive look-ahead. In this case we adopt the evaluation criterion of GCH, i.e., the ratio of the balance gain and the time for the whole extension, as the objective function only makes sense for complete solutions. Figure 2 illustrates obtained objective values and computation times for varying β on benchmark instances, where $\beta = 0$ represents GCH and $\beta = \infty$ unrestricted depth. For details on the instances and hardware see Section 7. As $\beta = \infty$ runs fast compared to our other approaches while yielding significantly better results than all depth-restricted cases, we use it in all further experiments in this article.

5   Variable Neighborhood Descent

For locally improving candidate solutions, we employ a Variable Neighborhood Descent (VND) [5] with several classical neighborhood structures that were successfully applied in VRPs [6] as well as new neighborhood structures specific to BBSS. The neighborhoods are described in detail in our previous work [8]: Remove station (REM-VND), insert unbalanced station (INS-U), replace station (REPL), intra or-opt

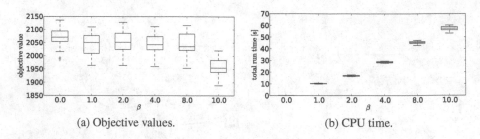

(a) Objective values.   (b) CPU time.

Fig. 2. PILOT-CH: Finally best objective values and CPU times [s] for instances with $|V| = 700$, $|L| = 14$, $\hat{t} = 8h$ and different PILOT depths β

(OR-OPT), 2-opt* inter-route exchange (2-OPT*), and intra-route 3-opt (3-OPT). All neighborhoods are searched using the best improvement strategy, and they are applied in random order, which turned out to work better in conjunction with PILOT-CH than the static order from [8].

The VND only searches the space of vehicle routes, while loading instructions are calculated for each candidate solution by an auxiliary heuristic following the greedy strategy from GCH; see also [8], Chemla et al. [2].

6 Greedy Randomized Adaptive Search Procedure

For optimizing solutions further, we realized a *Greedy Randomized Adaptive Search Procedure* (GRASP) [10] by iteratively applying randomized versions of either the GCH or PILOT-CH, locally improving each solution with the VND, and finally returning the overall best solution. In the randomized construction heuristics we select a random successor station from a restricted candidate list $RCL \subseteq F$ instead of always picking the best candidate:

$$RCL = \{v \in F \mid g(v) \geq g_{max} - \alpha\,(g_{max} - g_{min})\}, \tag{4}$$

where $g(v)$ is the greedy value of candidate station v, while $g_{max} = \max\{g(v) \mid v \in F\}$ and $g_{min} = \min\{g(v) \mid v \in F\}$ are the maximum and minimum evaluation values in F, respectively. Accordingly, $\alpha \in [0,1]$ controls the strength of the randomization, with $\alpha = 0$ representing a pure greedy and $\alpha = 1$ a completely random construction method. In this context, we may choose either a fixed α, i.e., remaining constant throughout all GRASP iterations, or a randomized $\alpha \in [0, \alpha_{max}]$, changing in a random manner at each iteration. Evaluating both variants of α on the benchmarks instances disclose that the randomized version is more robust, and thus we employ it in all further tests. Moreover, the tests indicate that large instances w.r.t. $|V|$, $|L|$, and $\hat{t}$ require smaller values for α than small instances. Figure 3 shows the impact of different values for α exemplarily for GCH-based GRASP (GCH-GRASP) on large instances. Based on many preliminary tests, we finally decided to choose $\alpha = 0.11 \cdot e^{-\frac{|V|}{187}}$.

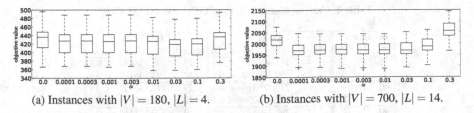

(a) Instances with $|V| = 180$, $|L| = 4$.   (b) Instances with $|V| = 700$, $|L| = 14$.

Fig. 3. GCH-GRASP: Final objective values in dependence of α; $\hat{t} = 8h$

7   Computational Results

We performed computational tests on benchmark instances[1], which range from 10 to 700 stations and are derived from real-world data provided by Citybike Wien, which operates a BSS of 92 stations in Vienna, Austria. For larger instances the Austrian Institute of Technology (AIT) supplied us with another 664 artificial stations placed at reasonable locations. For the following tests we consider $|V| \in \{30, 60, 90, 180, 300, 400, 500, 600, 700\}$ and a shift length $\hat{t}$ for all vehicles ranging from 2 to 8 hours. We set $|L|$ between 1% and 12% of $|V|$ depending on $\hat{t}$. All instance sets include 30 instances and represent unique combinations of $|V|$, $|L|$, and $\hat{t}$. We implemented and ran each test on a single core of an Intel Xeon E5540 machine with 2.53 GHz. For a fair comparison we terminate our algorithms after a defined run time t_{max} depending on the instance size.

Note that the scaling factors $\omega^{bal} = 1$, $\omega^{load} = \omega^{work} = 1/100\,000$ induce that an improved balance always effects the objective values more than a decrease in tour lengths or number of loading operations. Since the values of ω^{load} and ω^{work} cause small differences of objective values, these small values are still crucial for evaluating the quality of solutions. In order to ease these comparisons we also list the number of runs for which the variant yields the best results of all variants in the #best column.

As indicated by the mean objective values $\overline{obj}$ and #best in table 1 and confirmed by Wilcoxon signed-rank test with an error probability of 5%, the PILOT construction heuristic (PILOT-CH) clearly outperforms the simple greedy construction heuristic (GCH) on each instance set. Naturally, PILOT-CH consumes more median computation time as listed in the column $\widetilde{t_{tot}}$. Nevertheless, it is still faster than the more complex optimization methods and consequently a good compromise between solution quality and computation time. PILOT-CH might be a good option for practical applications requiring short computation times. Table 2 includes the final results of selected instance sets for VNS as proposed in our previous work [8], GCH-GRASP (GRASP with randomized GCH), and PILOT-GRASP (GRASP with randomized PILOT-CH). According to a Wilcoxon signed-rank test (with less than 5% error probability), PILOT-GRASP yields significantly better results than GCH-GRASP. When comparing our VNS with PILOT-GRASP, we observe that all approaches perform almost equally good on small instances with 30 stations. However, while VNS dominates the medium-sized instances with 60 to 180 stations, PILOT-GRASP is superior on large instances with 400 or more stations.

---

[1] Available at: https://www.ads.tuwien.ac.at/w/Research/Problem_Instances

Table 1. Computational results of GCH and PILOT-CH

Instance set			GCH			PILOT-CH		
$\|V\|$	$\|L\|$	$\hat{t}$ [h]	#best	$\overline{\text{obj}}$	$\widetilde{t_{\text{tot}}}$ [s]	#best	$\overline{\text{obj}}$	$\widetilde{t_{\text{tot}}}$ [s]
30	1	2	4	141.401410	< 0.1	29	138.134850	< 0.1
30	1	4	1	99.203000	< 0.1	30	93.536490	< 0.1
60	1	4	3	279.136470	< 0.1	29	271.136660	< 0.1
.60	2	2	2	302.936050	< 0.1	29	291.603090	< 0.1
90	2	4	1	390.739620	< 0.1	29	379.273230	< 0.1
90	2	8	1	236.545910	< 0.1	29	220.812930	0.2
180	4	4	1	760.812500	< 0.1	29	735.146480	0.3
180	4	8	0	448.825240	< 0.1	30	421.425890	1.2
300	6	4	0	1361.285300	< 0.1	30	1310.753180	1.1
300	6	8	0	865.571370	< 0.1	30	819.039150	5.0
400	8	4	0	1833.891260	< 0.1	30	1760.959600	2.3
400	8	8	0	1161.650440	< 0.1	30	1096.118750	11.3
500	10	4	0	2294.297610	< 0.1	30	2213.966180	4.5
500	10	8	0	1452.530120	< 0.1	30	1378.665150	22.2
600	12	4	0	2783.170230	< 0.1	30	2672.506080	6.9
600	12	8	0	1762.409230	< 0.1	30	1658.011680	35.9
700	14	4	0	3255.442790	0.1	30	3125.779220	10.3
700	14	8	0	2068.555330	0.1	30	1957.891110	57.6
		Total	13	21498.403880	0.2	534	20544.759720	158.8

Table 2. Computational results of VNS and two GRASP variants

Instance set				VNS		GCH-GRASP		PILOT-GRASP	
$\|V\|$	$\|L\|$	$\hat{t}$ [h]	$t_{\max}$ [s]	#best	$\overline{\text{obj}}$	#best	$\overline{\text{obj}}$	#best	$\overline{\text{obj}}$
30	1	2	900	28	137.13486	27	137.13617	29	136.93617
30	1	4	900	29	89.26988	28	89.34470	30	89.27799
60	1	4	1800	30	267.00340	19	268.01137	25	267.27850
60	2	2	1800	24	287.40315	12	288.67231	24	287.47238
90	2	4	1800	28	368.00672	0	370.35554	4	369.42263
90	2	8	1800	27	205.21311	2	210.95327	2	210.75318
180	4	4	3600	27	714.21342	0	723.57714	3	719.04451
180	4	8	3600	28	396.82615	0	412.56891	2	408.03814
300	6	4	3600	27	1287.42007	0	1304.53134	4	1294.80010
300	6	8	3600	17	798.57261	3	813.78571	10	803.72637
400	8	4	3600	19	1737.75980	0	1762.41566	11	1743.21898
400	8	8	3600	1	1087.31864	0	1094.79654	29	1077.87467
500	10	4	3600	12	2193.83297	0	2217.90432	18	2192.24287
500	10	8	3600	0	1383.19814	1	1381.35180	29	1359.56638
600	12	4	3600	2	2664.17266	0	2691.98787	28	2651.39459
600	12	8	3600	0	1675.21100	0	1675.89018	30	1641.57620
700	14	4	3600	0	3128.84563	0	3150.20618	30	3102.14626
700	14	8	3600	0	1979.89031	0	1974.83820	30	1938.92603
		Total	52200	299	20401.29252	92	20568.32721	338	20293.69595

8   Conclusions and Future Work

We presented and tested two GRASP approaches iterativly employing randomized versions of the construction heuristics and compared them to our previously proposed VNS approach. Computatinal results indicate that the PILOT-GRASP variant surpasses the

GCH-GRASP and the VNS on large instances up to 700 stations. However, the VNS yields the best results on medium instances. Hence, we conclude that PILOT-GRASP scales better with respect to instance size and complexity.

In future work we will adapt our methods to the dynamic case of BBSS considering prognosis of demands involving stochastic aspects and investigate the hybridization of VNS with MIP approaches for computing lower bounds.

References

1. Benchimol, M., Benchimol, P., Chappert, B., De la Taille, A., Laroche, F., Meunier, F., Robinet, L.: Balancing the stations of a self service bike hire system. RAIRO – Operations Research 45(1), 37–61 (2011)
2. Chemla, D., Meunier, F., Calvo, R.W.: Bike sharing systems: Solving the static rebalancing problem. Discrete Optimization 10(2), 120–146 (2013)
3. Contardo, C., Morency, C., Rousseau, L.M.: Balancing a Dynamic Public Bike-Sharing System. Tech. Rep. CIRRELT-2012-09, Montreal, Canada (2012)
4. DeMaio, P.: Bike-sharing: History, impacts, models of provision, and future. Journal of Public Transportation 12(4), 41–56 (2009)
5. Mladenović, N., Hansen, P.: Variable neighborhood search. Computers and Operations Research 24(11), 1097–1100 (1997)
6. Pirkwieser, S., Raidl, G.R.: A variable neighborhood search for the periodic vehicle routing problem with time windows. In: Proceedings of the 9th EU/MEeting on Metaheuristics for Logistics and Vehicle Routing, Troyes, France (2008)
7. Raidl, G.R., Hu, B., Rainer-Harbach, M., Papazek, P.: Balancing bicycle sharing systems: Improving a VNS by efficiently determining optimal loading operations. In: Blesa, M.J., Blum, C., Festa, P., Roli, A., Sampels, M. (eds.) HM 2013. LNCS, vol. 7919, pp. 130–143. Springer, Heidelberg (2013)
8. Rainer-Harbach, M., Papazek, P., Hu, B., Raidl, G.R.: Balancing bicycle sharing systems: A variable neighborhood search approach. In: Middendorf, M., Blum, C. (eds.) EvoCOP 2013. LNCS, vol. 7832, pp. 121–132. Springer, Heidelberg (2013)
9. Raviv, T., Tzur, M., Forma, I.A.: Static repositioning in a bike-sharing system: models and solution approaches. EURO Journal on Transportation and Logistics, 1–43 (2013)
10. Resende, M., Ribeiro, C.: Greedy randomized adaptive search procedures. In: Glover, F., Kochenberger, G. (eds.) Handbook of Metaheuristics, pp. 219–249. Kluwer Academic Publishers (2003)
11. Schuijbroek, J., Hampshire, R., van Hoeve, W.J.: Inventory Rebalancing and Vehicle Routing in Bike Sharing Systems. Tech. Rep. 2013-E1, Tepper School of Business, Carnegie Mellon University (2013)
12. Voß, S., Fink, A., Duin, C.: Looking ahead with the Pilot method. Annals of Operations Research 136, 285–302 (2005)

Enhancing a Genetic Algorithm with a Solution Archive to Reconstruct Cross Cut Shredded Text Documents*

Benjamin Biesinger, Christian Schauer, Bin Hu, and Günther R. Raidl

Institute of Computer Graphics and Algorithms
Vienna University of Technology
Favoritenstraße 9–11/1861, 1040 Vienna, Austria
{biesinger,schauer,hu,raidl}@ads.tuwien.ac.at

Abstract. In this work the concept of a trie-based complete solution archive in combination with a genetic algorithm is applied to the Reconstruction of Cross-Cut Shredded Text Documents (RCCSTD) problem. This archive is able to detect and subsequently convert duplicates into new yet unvisited solutions. Cross-cut shredded documents are documents that are cut into rectangular pieces of equal size and shape. The reconstruction of documents can be of high interest in forensic science. Two types of tries are compared as underlying data structure, an *indexed trie* and a *linked trie*. Experiments indicate that the latter needs considerably less memory without affecting the run-time. While the archive-enhanced genetic algorithm yields better results for runs with a fixed number of iterations, advantages diminish due to the additional overhead when considering run-time.

Keywords: genetic algorithm, solution archive, reconstruction.

1 Introduction

A common weakness of most genetic algorithms is the generation of duplicate solutions, i.e., solutions that have already been visited. As Mauldin showed in [3] maintaining diversity in the population significantly improves the performance of genetic algorithms. Although duplicate detection in stochastic search methods has been studied thoroughly [8,11], complete solution archives are a rather new approach to fulfill this task. In addition to storing the solution, solution archives are able to efficiently transform an already visited solution into a guaranteed new one. This avoids duplicate solutions, hence unnecessary solution evaluations, as well as premature convergence due to loss of diversity. Ronald has shown in [8] that diversity loss due to duplicate solutions is a weakness of genetic algorithms. In the same paper he introduced hash tagging for duplicate detection. Yuen and Chow used a binary tree in [11] to store all visited solutions. Solution archives have already been successfully applied to several benchmark problems by Raidl

---
* This work is supported by the Austrian Science Fund (FWF) under grant P24660.

R. Moreno-Díaz et al. (Eds.): EUROCAST 2013, Part I, LNCS 8111, pp. 380–387, 2013.

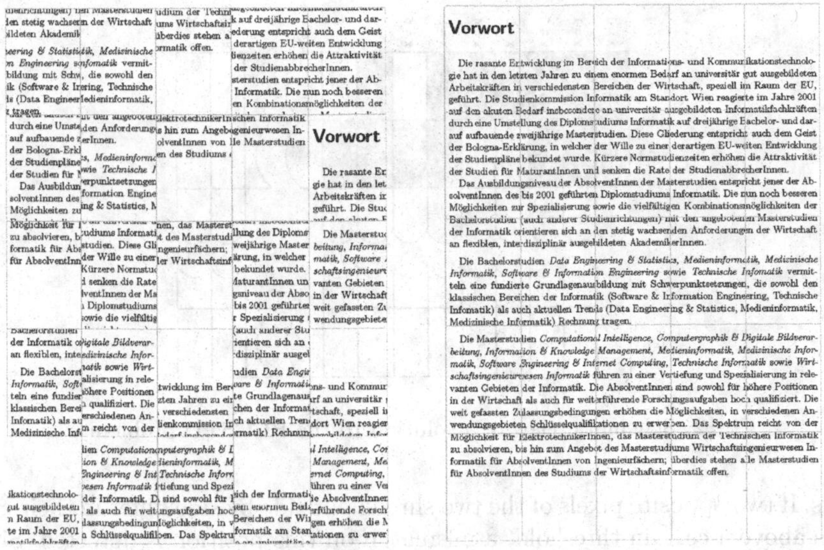

Fig. 1. A shredded document (left) and the fully reconstructed document (right)

and Hu in [7] and to the generalized minimum spanning tree problem in [2]. In this work we will investigate this concept in combination with a genetic algorithm for a more advanced and practical problem, the Reconstruction of Cross-Cut Shredded Text Documents (RCCSTD) problem, which Prandtstetter proved to be $\mathcal{NP}$-complete in [5].

Document shredding is a frequently used method to obfuscate data printed on paper, like personal or sensitive information (e.g., passwords, signatures, PINs). The reconstruction of such data is of high interest especially in the fields of forensic science. Figure 1 shows a sample cross-cut shredded document and its correct reconstruction.

The RCCSTD problem is defined as follows: Let $S = \{1, ..., n\}$ be the set of shreds that belong to one document and let $X \times Y$ be its grid-shaped cutting pattern. A shred $s \in S$ is a non-blank piece of a document. All blank shreds are substituted by a single virtual shred V since there is no exploitable information available on these shreds. A solution to the problem is an injective mapping $\Pi = S \rightarrow \mathbb{D}^2$. In this mapping each shred $s \in S$ is assigned to exactly one position (x, y) in the Euclidean space, where $x \in \{0, ..., X - 1\}$ and $y \in \{0, ..., Y - 1\}$. The remaining positions are filled with the virtual blank shred. See Figure 2 for a schematic view of a candidate solution, where the white rectangles stand for the virtual shred, which is allowed to be used more than once. Further, we assume here that the document is only printed on one side and the orientation of the shreds is already known.

As a cost function to determine if two shreds should be placed side by side we take the metric from Schauer *et al.* [9] for approximately indicating this likelihood, which is based on the gray value of the pixels along the edges of the

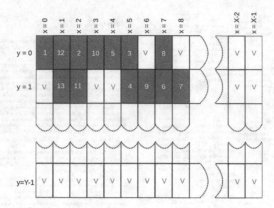

Fig. 2. Schematic view of a solution to the RCCSTD problem

shreds. If two opposite pixels of the two shreds put side by side differ in their gray values above a certain threshold, a mismatch on this position is detected. Since we focus in this work on the combinatorial aspect of the problem we use this simple metric, which could be replaced by more advanced pattern recognition techniques, e.g., [4]. The objective is to find an injective mapping such that the weighted sum of gray-value mismatches is minimal.

Prandtstetter and Raidl developed an ant colony optimization and a variable neighborhood search for RCCSTD in [6]. Schauer *et al.* described a memetic algorithm to solve the RCCSTD problem in [9], which is modified and extended with a solution archive in this work. A different approach for RCCSTD, which is based on iteratively building clusters of shreds, is described by Sleit *et al.* in [10]. In their approach they merge two clusters that fit well together, while possibly occurring conflicts are repaired.

The rest of the paper is organized as follows. In Section 2 the genetic algorithm and its operators are described. A detailed presentation of the solution archive is given in Section 3. Finally, the computational results are presented in Section 4 and conclusions are drawn in Section 5.

2   Genetic Algorithm

This section gives a short overview of the genetic algorithm (GA). For a detailed description of the operators used within the GA we refer to [9].

Solution Representation: A solution with n shreds is represented as an $X \times Y$ matrix storing for each position the assigned shred. Note that all empty positions are filled with the virtual shred V. This representation is used for all operators of the GA.

Initial Population: To create an initial population the *Row Building Heuristic* and the *Prim-Based Heuristic* are used, which were introduced by Prandtstetter *et al.* in [6], but slightly changed to restrict the solutions to the given format.

Recombination: To exploit the two-dimensional structure of the problem standard crossover operators were adapted for RCCSTD. Preliminary tests showed that modified versions of the 1-point crossover perform best. Instead of choosing a splitting point in the one-dimensional case, for RCCSTD a random splitting line is computed that cuts the solution apart. This line is drawn either horizontally or vertically. In the *Horizontal Block Crossover* a top and a bottom block from two different individuals are recombined to create the offspring, while the *Vertical Block Crossover* recombines a left and a right block. Note that when using these operators invalid solutions could be created. To ensure that each shred is used exactly once, shreds that are already in the solution are replaced by the virtual shred and in the end all missing shreds are inserted using a greedy heuristic.

Mutation: The solution splitting of the block crossover is also performed in the mutation operators. In this case a single solution is either cut apart horizontally (*Horizontal Flop Mutation*) or vertically (*Vertical Flop Mutation*) and then the top/bottom or the left/right parts are exchanged. The *Swap Two Mutation* swaps two shreds randomly.

Selection and Replacement Strategy: We pass the best 10% of individuals with regard to the objective value directly to the next population. The other 90% are generated by applying the genetic operators to uniformly selected individuals of the current population. For a detailed discussion about the selection and generation replacement strategy we refer to [9].

3   A Solution Archive for the RCCSTD

Our primary concern in this work is the following solution archive for duplicate detection. The underlying data structure for our solution archive is a trie, a tree data structure commonly used for storing strings, e.g., for dictionaries in highly compact ways as explained in [1]. Raidl *et al.* argue in [7] that a trie is a very well suited data structure for solution archives in their applications because the operations *search*, *insertion* and *conversion* can be performed in $\mathcal{O}(l)$ time, where l is the length of the solution representation, and thus independent of the number of already stored solutions. Therefore, tries are also used in this work.

3.1   Solution Insertion / Conversion

For inserting a solution of the GA into the trie, the solution is transformed into a more compact one-dimensional array. This is done by adding a special character for line breaks. Blank shreds at the end of lines and empty lines at the bottom are skipped. At the top of Figure 3 two sample transformations are shown. In this example the numbers correspond to actual shreds, the V stands for the virtual shred and the ↵-symbol is interpreted as a line break.

Then, this array is stored in the trie, where the i-th level of the trie corresponds to the i-th entry of the solution vector. During insertion, *invalid*-flags (denoted as I) are placed to avoid invalid (i.e., that are not in the given format) solutions

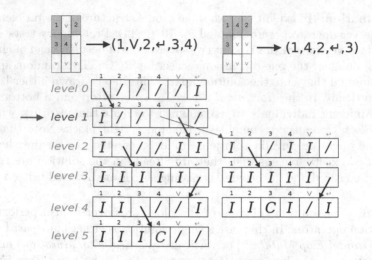

Fig. 3. Solution conversion after detecting a duplicate

to be stored in the trie. The /-symbols represent not yet explored subtries, i.e., areas of the solution space that have not been visited before. After the last element of the solution has been inserted, a *complete*-flag is placed at the last trie node (denoted as C) to indicate that this solution is in the trie.

Whenever a *complete*-flag is visited during solution insertion, a duplicate is detected and a conversion is performed. In Figure 3 a sample conversion is sketched. Suppose that the solution on the top left of the figure would be inserted twice. Eventually the *complete*-flag is reached and a level to deviate from the existing solution is chosen randomly; in this example level 1 is picked. Then, a different feasible element is chosen at this level and the remaining solution is inserted into the trie with as few changes as possible. The converted solution can be seen on the top right of the figure.

3.2 Adaption of the Trie Data Structure

In preliminary tests we noticed that the trie using standard arrays to realize trie-nodes, the so-called *indexed trie*, needs a huge amount of memory. Hence, in order to reduce the memory consumption we switched to a *linked trie* by replacing the arrays with linked lists. This obviously saves memory especially in the case of sparsely used nodes since the linked lists do not have to allocate space for all possible children at the time when the node is created. A disadvantage of the *linked trie* is that the worst case run-time for the *search* operation in a trie node increases to $\mathcal{O}(k)$ for a node containing k elements.

3.3 Integration of the Solution Archive into the GA

In each iteration the solutions generated by the GA are inserted into the solution archive after mutation. If the solution already exists then the conversion procedure as described above is applied and this operation can also be considered as *intelligent mutation*. The resulting new solution replaces the original solution in the population.

4   Computational Results

We performed our tests on the benchmark instances from [9]. These instances are based on five different text documents cut into nine different patterns ranging from 9×9 to 15×15. We implemented our approach in Java 1.6 and performed all tests on a single core of an Intel Xeon Quadcore CPU with 2.53 GHz and 70 GB RAM.

By using the *indexed trie* as data structure, memory consumption increased quickly after a relatively small number of iterations. Our testing platform ran out of memory and stopped the GA before it converged, which led to worse results than the GA without the archive. By switching to the *linked trie* we are able to drastically reduce the memory usage by about 75% without affecting the run-time of the algorithm. Therefore, only the GA using the *linked trie* as underlying data structure for the solution archive is considered in the following.

The configuration of the GA is similar to the one used in [9]. It uses both recombination operators, see Section 2, with a probability of 50% but only the better of the two offspring individuals created each time is transferred into the next generation. The mutation rate is set to 15%, where each operator is applied with 5%.

To compare the results of the GA with (column "GA-SA") and without (column "GA-time") the archive we performed 30 runs for each configuration and test instance and used a run-time of 300 seconds. Additionally we performed tests where the GA with and without the solution archive run the same number of generation (column "GA-gen"). The results are shown in Table 1. The first two columns refer to the cutting pattern; the number of mismatches of the original document is given in column "orig"; in the columns "gap" and "sd" the gap values are given, which describe the relative difference of the objective values of the reconstructed and the original document and their associated standard deviations. Note that due to inexactness of the cost function, these gap values can sometimes be negative, i.e., a certain reconstruction can have a better fitness value than the original document. To verify the statistical significance of differences in the results of the GA with and without archive, Wilcoxon signed-rank tests with an error probability of 5% were performed as well. The outcome is given in column "p", where "<" means that the algorithm on the left-hand side performed significantly better, an ">" indicates significantly better results for the algorithm on the right-hand side. Whenever a cell is empty the statistical test was not able to make a statement about significant differences.

Unfortunately, even with the improvement of using a *linked trie* the solution archive could not improve the solution quality of the GA when using the same amount of time as stopping criterion. The reason is that the solution archive in this case is not able to fully compensate its overhead by saving the effort for

Table 1. The average percentage gaps and standard deviations of the GA with (GA-SA) and without the solution archive over 30 runs with a run-time of 300 seconds (GA-time) and with the same number of generations (GA-gen)

	x	y	orig	GA-time gap/sd [%]/[%]	p	GA-SA gap/sd [%]/[%]	p	GA-gen gap/sd [%]/[%]
instance p01	9	9	2094	24.8/22.8		33.5/19.1		37.8/19.1
	9	12	3142	31.9/3.9		31.6/5.3	<	34.1/4.7
	9	15	3223	34.0/3.8		33.4/6.1	<	36.9/6.3
	12	9	2907	24.0/10.3		26.3/6.3		29.4/6.4
	12	12	3695	35.4/5.9		33.7/5.4	<	38.8/5.0
	12	15	3825	36.8/5.1		35.5/4.5	<	40.5/5.1
	15	9	2931	32.2/14.4	<	38.0/9.9		37.0/7.3
	15	12	3732	37.8/5.5		37.9/3.1	<	42.0/4.4
	15	15	3870	42.7/4.0	>	40.4/4.0	<	45.7/4.1
instance p02	9	9	1434	-16.0/8.9	<	-8.5/12.6	>	-14.7/10.7
	9	12	1060	21.9/13.1		23.3/10.5		22.2/12.7
	9	15	1978	7.7/4.1		7.3/5.2	<	11.9/4.7
	12	9	1396	-10.0/8.6		-7.8/9.3		-7.6/8.9
	12	12	1083	22.8/10.7	<	28.4/12.1		30.7/9.5
	12	15	1904	7.6/5.9	<	10.4/5.3		11.1/7.1
	15	9	1658	-1.6/8.1		1.8/7.9		5.9/11.9
	15	12	1503	21.3/13.5		22.6/10.6		22.0/11.7
	15	15	2283	15.6/7.6		17.1/5.3		20.1/7.2
instance p03	9	9	2486	5.2/9.0	<	11.5/10.5		11.6/8.4
	9	12	2651	31.3/6.8	<	36.5/8.9		33.1/9.3
	9	15	2551	24.8/11.4	<	33.9/9.7	>	27.0/8.9
	12	9	3075	20.2/4.6		20.3/5.6		19.0/5.3
	12	12	3377	26.8/7.1		29.9/7.3		32.0/6.6
	12	15	3313	31.8/6.0		30.0/6.4	<	35.0/9.1
	15	9	3213	21.5/8.0		22.8/6.9		23.7/7.0
	15	12	3278	44.0/6.9	>	41.4/5.2	<	47.6/5.6
	15	15	3308	37.6/5.7	>	34.4/4.4	<	42.5/5.2

	x	y	orig	GA-time gap/sd [%]/[%]	p	GA-SA gap/sd [%]/[%]	p	GA-gen gap/sd [%]/[%]
instance p04	9	9	1104	-1.7/12.9		1.2/19.0		4.8/19.5
	9	12	1463	3.0/7.1		3.3/7.4		4.6/9.3
	9	15	1589	-2.8/7.8		-3.6/9.7		-1.8/9.0
	12	9	1515	39.1/9.0	>	33.8/10.4		35.5/8.9
	12	12	2051	16.4/5.5		18.3/4.8		19.0/6.4
	12	15	2146	0.7/4.3		1.8/4.2		3.3/5.2
	15	9	1567	41.5/11.7		43.7/15.5		47.1/12.9
	15	12	1752	34.0/8.6		35.0/8.4		34.1/8.8
	15	15	2026	8.3/5.7		9.5/5.7		9.5/5.5
instance p05	9	9	690	2.2/3.6	>	0.0/0.0	<	0.8/1.2
	9	12	888	58.1/31.4		50.1/28.7		55.4/25.1
	9	15	1623	37.7/13.9		40.7/11.3		44.8/10.4
	12	9	1016	16.5/15.2	>	8.3/12.4	<	17.5/15.8
	12	12	1325	30.9/16.5	<	43.1/14.8		43.5/17.8
	12	15	1986	44.0/7.1		43.3/7.3	<	48.5/9.5
	15	9	1010	2.5/13.1		4.0/18.0		1.7/17.9
	15	12	1156	65.1/15.5		59.9/12.7	<	68.4/12.7
	15	15	1900	52.2/10.9		49.9/9.4	<	62.1/7.4

re-evaluating duplicate solutions. However, as can be seen in Table 1, when using numbers of generations as stopping criterion, the GA with solution archive outperforms the GA without the solution archive and achieved statistically better results in 15 out of 45 instances.

5   Conclusions and Future Work

In this work we investigated a solution archive for a genetic algorithm (GA) for the reconstruction of cross-cut shredded text documents problem. We used a solution archive for duplicate detection and a solution conversion method was presented such that no invalid solutions are generated. The first approach of using an *indexed trie* for the archive consumed a huge amount of memory. Therefore, we proposed an alternative data structure, the *linked trie*, in which the trie nodes are stored as linked lists instead of arrays. This modification reduced memory consumption significantly without affecting the run-time in a negative way. The solution archive was able to improve the performance of the GA when run-time is of minor importance. The use of a *linked trie* was essential for this success. However, compared to state-of-the-art algorithms our approach could not compete because we did not use any pattern recognition technique, which would likely improve results.

Possible future work for the RCCSTD problem should be the incorporation of a more elaborate cost function that uses pattern recognition techniques and to further reduce the memory overhead, e.g., by calculating bounds in order to cut off search areas that evidently do not contain optimal solutions. We will also investigate the concept of solution archives on other problems where we can take considerable advantage of this extension.

References

1. Gusfield, D.: Algorithms on strings, trees, and sequences: computer science and computational biology. Cambridge University Press, New York (1997)
2. Hu, B., Raidl, G.R.: An evolutionary algorithm with solution archives and bounding extension for the generalized minimum spanning tree problem. In: Proceedings of the 14th Annual Conference on Genetic and Evolutionary Computation (GECCO), pp. 393–400. ACM Press, Philadelphia (2012)
3. Mauldin, M.L.: Maintaining Diversity in Genetic Search. In: National Conference on Artificial Intelligence, vol. 19, pp. 247–250. AAAI, William Kaufmann (1984)
4. Perl, J., Diem, M., Kleber, F., Sablatnig, R.: Strip shredded document reconstruction using optical character recognition. In: 4th International Conference on Imaging for Crime Detection and Prevention 2011 (ICDP 2011), pp. 1–6 (2011)
5. Prandtstetter, M.: Hybrid Optimization Methods for Warehouse Logistics and the Reconstruction of Destroyed Paper Documents. Ph.D. thesis, Vienna University of Technology (2009)
6. Prandtstetter, M., Raidl, G.R.: Meta-heuristics for reconstructing cross cut shredded text documents. In: Proceedings of the 11th Annual Conference on Genetic and Evolutionary Computation, GECCO 2009, pp. 349–356. ACM Press, New York (2009)
7. Raidl, G.R., Hu, B.: Enhancing genetic algorithms by a trie-based complete solution archive. In: Cowling, P., Merz, P. (eds.) EvoCOP 2010. LNCS, vol. 6022, pp. 239–251. Springer, Heidelberg (2010)
8. Ronald, S.: Duplicate genotypes in a genetic algorithm. In: IEEE World Congress on Computational Intelligence, Evolutionary Computation Proceedings, pp. 793–798 (1998)
9. Schauer, C., Prandtstetter, M., Raidl, G.R.: A memetic algorithm for reconstructing cross-cut shredded text documents. In: Blesa, M.J., Blum, C., Raidl, G., Roli, A., Sampels, M. (eds.) HM 2010. LNCS, vol. 6373, pp. 103–117. Springer, Heidelberg (2010)
10. Sleit, A., Massad, Y., Musaddaq, M.: An alternative clustering approach for reconstructing cross cut shredded text documents. Telecommunication Systems, 1–11 (2011)
11. Yuen, S.Y., Chow, C.K.: A non-revisiting genetic algorithm. In: IEEE Congress on Evolutionary Computation, CEC 2007, pp. 4583–4590 (2007)

An Integrated Clustering
and Classification Approach
for the Analysis of Tumor Patient Data[*]

Stephan M. Winkler[1], Michael Affenzeller[1], and Herbert Stekel[2]

[1] Heuristic and Evolutionary Algorithms Laboratory; Bioinformatics Research Group
University of Applied Sciences Upper Austria, Hagenberg Campus
Softwarepark 11, 4232 Hagenberg, Austria
{stephan.winkler,michael.affenzeller}@fh-hagenberg.at
[2] Central Laboratory, General Hospital Linz
Krankenhausstraße 9, 4021 Linz, Austria
herbert.stekel@akh.linz.at

Abstract. Standard patient parameters, tumor markers, and tumor diagnosis records are used for identifying prediction models for tumor markers as well as cancer diagnosis predictions. In this paper we present a hybrid clustering and classification approach that first identifies data clusters (using standard patient data and tumor markers) and then learns prediction models on the basis of these data clusters. The so formed clusters are analyzed and their homogeneity is calculated; the models learned on the basis of these clusters are tested and compared to each other with respect to classification accuracy and variable impacts.

1 An Integrated Clustering and Classification Approach for the Identification of Predictors for Tumor Diagnoses

The overall goal of the research described here is to identify prediction models for tumor markers (TM) and tumor diagnoses. In previous work ([13], [16]) we have identified classification models that can be used as virtual tumor markers for estimating TM values on the basis of standard blood parameters. Tumor markers are substances (found in blood and/or body tissues) that can be used as indicators for certain types of cancer ([4], [14]). Moreover, in [14] and [15] we have published research results achieved in the identification of prediction models for tumor diagnoses. As described in [15], the use of TM prediction models as virtual tumor markers increases the achievable classification accuracy.

The here proposed analysis approach (schematically shown in Figure 1) integrates clustering and classification algorithms:

First, the available patient data are clustered; this clustering is done on the one hand only for standard blood data and on the other hand for standard

---

[*] The work described in this paper was done within the Josef Ressel Centre for Heuristic Optimization *Heureka!* (http://heureka.heuristiclab.com/) sponsored by the Austrian Research Promotion Agency (FFG).

R. Moreno-Díaz et al. (Eds.): EUROCAST 2013, Part I, LNCS 8111, pp. 388–395, 2013.

data plus tumor markers. The so identified clusters of samples are analyzed and compared with each other; we especially analyze the size of the clusters and to which extent samples which are assigned the same clusters regarding standard data are also assigned to the same clusters on the basis of standard and tumor marker data. Within the *Heureka!* research project we have applied several clustering approaches including k-means clustering and soft k-means clustering ([9], [8]) as well as the identification of Gaussian mixture models using expectation maximization techniques [18]. As simpler models are to be preferred over more complex ones, the quality of clusterings is calculated considering not only their quantization error, but also the number of clusters formed; the Davies-Bouldin index [3] as well as the Akaike information criterion [2] can be used, e.g.

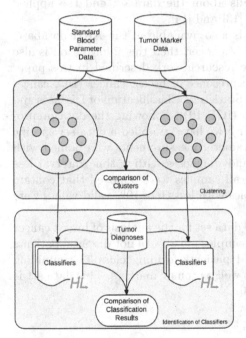

Fig. 1. An integrated clustering and classification approach for the analysis of medical data: Data clusters are formed using standard data and optionally also tumor marker data; these clusters are the basis for the identification of classifiers that can be used as predictors for cancer diagnoses

The so clustered data are subsequently (in combination with tumor diagnosis data) used for learning tumor diagnosis predictors; each cluster is used individually for training these models. We use the following two modeling methods for identifying predictors for tumor markers and cancer diagnoses: Hybrid modeling using machine learning algorithms and evolutionary algorithms (that optimize feature selection and the modeling algorithms' parameters) as well as genetic programming.

The so identified models are analyzed and compared to each other with respect to classification accuracy and variable impacts.

2 Empirical Test Study: Clustering and Classification of Breast Cancer Patient Data

2.1 Data Basis

Data of thousands of patients of the General Hospital (AKH) Linz, Austria, have been analyzed in order to identify mathematical models for cancer diagnoses. We have used a medical database compiled at the central laboratory of AKH: 28 routinely measured standard values of patients are available as well as several tumor markers. In total, information about 20,819 patients is stored in 48,580 samples. Please note that of course not all values are available in all samples; there are many missing values simply because not all blood values are measured during each examination. Further details about the data set and the applied preprocessing methods can be found in [13] and [14].

Information about cancer diagnoses is also available in the AKH database: If a patient is diagnosed with any kind of cancer, then this information is also stored in the database. Our goal in the research work described in this paper is to identify estimation models for the presence of breast cancer (BC, cancer class C50 according to the International Statistical Classification of Diseases and Related Health Problems 10th Revision (ICD-10)). Following the data preprocessing approach described in [13] and [14] we have compiled a data set specific for this kind of tumor: First, blood parameter measurements were joined with diagnosis results; only measurements and diagnoses with a time interval less than a month were considered. Second, all samples were removed that contain less than 15 valid values. Finally, variables with less than 10% valid values were removed from the data base.

This procedure results in a specialized data set for the analysis of breast cancer patient data; this data set contains 706 samples (45.89% of not diseased patients forming class 0 and 54.11% of diseased patients forming class 1) containing routinely measured values of patients as well as tumor markers. This data set is the same as the BC data set used in [14].

2.2 Clustering Results

The so compiled data set of patients was clustered using k-means algorithm ([9], [8]) with varying numbers of clusters k: The cluster centers are initially set at random and then iteratively adapted until the quantization error is minimized; each sample is assigned to the cluster whose center has the minimum distance to the sample (distance is here calculated using the Euclidean distance function). As on the one hand the optimal number of clusters is unknown and different values for k have to be tried, and on the other hand simpler models are to be preferred over more complex ones, the quality of clusterings is calculated considering not only their quantization error, but also the number of clusters formed; the Davies-Bouldin index [3] is used in this context. Information about the samples' classification (as diseased or not diseased) is of course not available for the clustering algorithm.

The mean quantization error (MQE) of $cluster_i$ is defined as the average distance of its samples to its center ce_i, and the Davies-Bouldin Index (DBI) for a complete clustering hypothesis takes into account the compactness of the formed clusters (via their MQE) as well as their distance:

$$MQE_i = \frac{\sum_{s_j \in cluster_i} dist(s_j, ce_i)}{|cluster_i|} \tag{1}$$

$$DBI = \frac{1}{k} \cdot \sum_i (max_{j,i \neq j} \frac{MQE_i + MQE_j}{dist(ce_i, ce_j)}) \tag{2}$$

We assume that optimal clustering minimizes the DBI, i.e., we will eventually use that number of clusters k that leads to minimal DBI-values.

Additionally, we also analyze how well this unsupervised clustering approach solves the original classification task by calculating the homogeneity of $cluster_j$ as the ratio r of the samples of the most prominent class in the cluster:

$$r(class_i, cluster_j) = \frac{|s:class(s)=class_i \wedge s \in cluster_j|}{|cluster_j|} \tag{3}$$

$$homogeneity(cluster_j) = max_i (r(class_i, cluster_j)) \tag{4}$$

As we are interested in the total homogeneity of a whole clustering (i.e., a set of clusters formed for a given data collection), we calculate $homogeneity_{total}$ as the weighted average of all homogeneities:

$$homogeneity_{total}(clusters) = \frac{\sum_{c \in clusters} (homogeneity(c) \cdot |c|)}{n} \tag{5}$$

where n is the total number of samples.

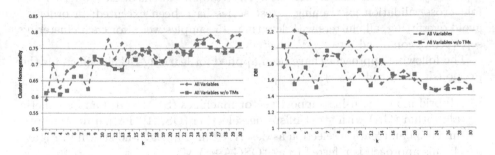

Fig. 2. Progress of cluster homogeneity (left) and DBI (right) for clusterings with varying numbers of clusters

In Figure 2 we show the progress of the clusters' homogeneity over k as well as the progress of the DBI over k (averages of 5 independent clusterings for each k and data partition are shown). We see that setting $k = 25$ seems to yield optimal clustering results as the DBI is minimized and the cluster homogeneity

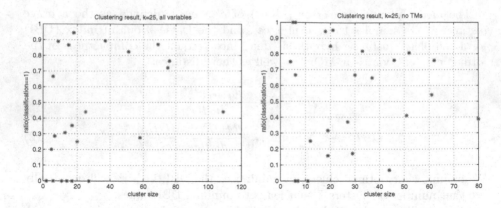

Fig. 3. Clustering result for $k = 25$: Size and homogeneity of clusters formed by k-means clustering using all variables (left) and all variables except tumor markers (right)

reaches relatively high values using all variables as well as using all variables except tumor makers; tumor diagnoses were not used for clustering. These results are consistent with result presented in [17]. In Figure 3 we show an overview of exemplary clustering results achieved for $k = 25$; the sizes as well as the homogeneity of the formed clusters are shown (each spot represents one cluster).

2.3   Identification of Classifiers Using Clustered Data

Finally, using the previously identified clusters we have performed machine learning in order to learn classifiers for the given samples. All clusters were used separately, i.e., each cluster was used for training classification models. Five-fold cross-validation [5] training / test series have been executed; in order to avoid overfitting, all clusters with less than 45 samples were (for each clustering separately) combined into "rest" clusters.

The following approaches have been applied for learning BC classifiers for the previously identified clusters:

– Hybrid modeling using support vector machines (SVMs, [10]) and a genetic algorithm (GA) with strict offspring selection (OS, [1]) for parameter optimization and feature selection as described in [14], e.g., and shown in Figure 4; this approach is referred to as "OSGA+SVM".
– Genetic programming (GP) ([6], [7], [12]) in combination with strict offspring selection as shown in Figure 5, referred to as "OSGP".

The implementations of these approaches in HeuristicLab[1] [11] have been applied; for the evolutionary process the population sizes were set to 10 and 100, respectively, and for evolutionary feature selection the parsimony pressure α was set to 0.1.

---

[1] http://dev.heuristiclab.com

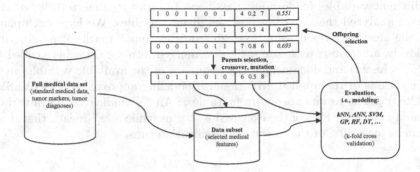

Fig. 4. A hybrid evolutionary algorithm for feature selection and parameter optimization in data based modeling

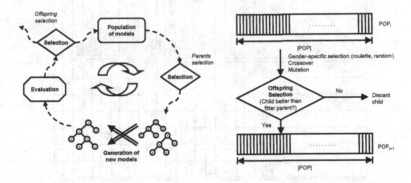

Fig. 5. The genetic programming cycle [7] (left) including strict offspring selection [1] (right)

In [14] we have documented that using all variables except tumor markers up to ∼ 75% of the given samples in the BC data set can be classified correctly; using the here discussed clustering and classification approach we are able to reach the following classification rates:

– Hybrid modeling (OSGA+SVM, $\alpha = 0.1$): 78.136% (±3.08)
– Genetic programming with offspring selection (OSGP): 77.787% (±4.81)

Please note that each method was applied 5 times using 5-fold cross validation and that the here stated numbers are averages of weighted averages (calculated as the average of the classification accuracies on the given clusters multiplied with their relative size); no tumor markers were used for clustering or learning classifiers. More result details shall be presented in [17].

One of the major advantages of the here discussed approach is that it first clusters the data in groups of rather similar samples and is then able to separate the classes within these groups; for different clusters the algorithms are able to use different variables for forming classifiers. In order to analyze this behavior we have analyzed the importance of the given variables: We have exemplarily used the clusters formed using $k = 25$ (and no tumor markers; as described previously, all clusters with size <45 were merged into a cluster here called the "REST" cluster) and documented the frequency of the available variables in the final solutions of the applied evolutionary modeling approaches (OSGA+SVM and OSGP). The results are shown in Table 1: An "X" indicates that a variable was used in at least 80% of the executed test runs while a "x" means that it was used in at least 40% of the executed classification runs.

Table 1. Relevant variables for classifying pre-clustered samples

Cluster index	Modeling method	ALTER	ALT & AST	BSG1	BUN	CBAA	CEOA	CHOL	CLYA	CMOA	CNEA & WBC	CRP	FER	GT37	HB & HKT & RBC	HDL	HS	KREA	LD37	MCV	PLT	TBIL	TPS
1	OSGA+SVM	x	x		X							x		x							x		
	OSGP	x	X		x		X					x	x	X			x		x				
2	OSGA+SVM											X		x	x							x	
	OSGP			x								X		x	x								X
3	OSGA+SVM	x	X	x	X	x								X	x							X	
	OSGP	x	x					x			X			x	x							x	
4	OSGA+SVM	x	x								X					X							
	OSGP						X	x		X				x									
9	OSGA+SVM										x			x			x	x	x		x		
	OSGP								x	x	x			x				X	x		X		
16	OSGA+SVM										x	x		x				x					x
	OSGP												x				x		x	x			
REST	OSGA+SVM		X		X		X	x						x		x	x		x				
	OSGP		X				X	X	x					x		x			x				

3   Conclusion

As we clearly see in the classification results section, the here applied approach of using pre-clustered data and evolutionary modeling techniques leads to better results than those reported in previous test series: The classification accuracy of potential breast cancer patients (without considering tumor markers) can be increased to ~78% using evolutionary modeling (hybrid modeling or genetic programming). Furthermore, we see that there are significant differences regarding the importance of variables for classifying pre-clustered data: Some variables are essentially important for classifying samples of certain clusters while they might be irrelevant for forming classifiers for other clusters.

Further research shall focus on the capability of this approach to lead to better results on other data sets (real world as well as benchmark data collections). Furthermore, we plan to use an evolutionary algorithm for optimizing the sets of features for clustering the data in order to even further improve the resulting cluster homogeneities and classification rates.

References

1. Affenzeller, M., Winkler, S., Wagner, S., Beham, A.: Genetic Algorithms and Genetic Programming - Modern Concepts and Practical Applications. Chapman & Hall / CRC (2009)
2. Akaike, H.: A new look at the statistical model identification. IEEE Transactions on Automatic Control 19, 716–723 (1974)
3. Davies, D.L., Bouldin, D.: A cluster separation measure. IEEE Transactions on Pattern Analysis and Machine Intelligence 2, 224–227 (1979)
4. Koepke, J.A.: Molecular marker test standardization. Cancer 69, 1578–1581 (1992)
5. Kohavi, R.: A study of cross-validation and bootstrap for accuracy estimation and model selection, pp. 1137–1143. Morgan Kaufmann (1995)
6. Koza, J.R.: Genetic Programming: On the Programming of Computers by Means of Natural Selection. The MIT Press (1992)
7. Langdon, W.B., Poli, R.: Foundations of Genetic Programming. Springer, Heidelberg (2002)
8. MacKay, D.: Information Theory, Inference and Learning Algorithms, pp. 284–292. Cambridge University Press (2003)
9. Press, W., Teukolsky, S., Vetterling, W., Flannery, B.: Gaussian Mixture Models and k-Means Clustering. Cambridge University Press, New York (2007)
10. Vapnik, V.: Statistical Learning Theory. Wiley, New York (1998)
11. Wagner, S.: Heuristic Optimization Software Systems – Modeling of Heuristic Optimization Algorithms in the HeuristicLab Software Environment. Ph.D. thesis, Johannes Kepler University Linz (2009)
12. Winkler, S.: Evolutionary System Identification - Modern Concepts and Practical Applications. Ph.D. thesis, Institute for Formal Models and Verification, Johannes Kepler University Linz (2008)
13. Winkler, S., Affenzeller, M., Jacak, W., Stekel, H.: Classification of tumor marker values using heuristic data mining methods. In: Proceedings of the Genetic and Evolutionary Computation Conference, GECCO 2010 (2010)
14. Winkler, S., Affenzeller, M., Jacak, W., Stekel, H.: Identification of cancer diagnosis estimation models using evolutionary algorithms - a case study for breast cancer, melanoma, and cancer in the respiratory system. In: Proceedings of the Genetic and Evolutionary Computation Conference, GECCO 2011 (2011)
15. Winkler, S., Affenzeller, M., Kronberger, G., Kommenda, M., Wagner, S., Dorfer, V., Jacak, W., Stekel, H.: On the use of estimated tumor marker classifications in tumor diagnosis prediction - a case study for breast cancer. Accepted to be published in: International Journal of Simulation and Process Modelling (2013)
16. Winkler, S., Affenzeller, M., Kronberger, G., Kommenda, M., Wagner, S., Jacak, W., Stekel, H.: On the use of estimated tumor marker classifications in tumor diagnosis prediction - a case study for breast cancer. In: Proceedings of the 23rd European Modeling & Simulation Symposium (2011)
17. Winkler, S., Affenzeller, M., Stekel, H.: Evolutionary identification of cancer predictors using clustered data - a case study for breast cancer, melanoma, and cancer in the respiratory system. In: Proceedings of the Genetic and Evolutionary Computation Conference, GECCO 2013 (2013)
18. Xu, L., Jordan, M.I.: On convergence properties of the EM algorithm for Gaussian mixtures. Neural Computation 8, 129–151 (1995)

An Efficient and Self-adaptive Model Based on Scatter Search: Solving the Grid Resources Selection Problem

María Botón-Fernández[1], Miguel A. Vega-Rodríguez[2],
and Francisco Prieto-Castrillo[1]

[1] Ceta-Ciemat, Dept. Science and Technology
Trujillo, Spain
{maria.boton,francisco.prieto}@ciemat.es
[2] University of Extremadura,
Dept. Technologies of Computers and Communications
Cáceres, Spain
mavega@unex.es

Abstract. Grid computing environments are distributed systems formed by a heterogeneous and geographically distributed resource set. In spite of the advantages of such paradigm, several problems related to resources availability and resources selection have become a challenge extensively studied by the grid community in last years.

The aim of this work is to provide an intelligent and self-adaptive model for selecting grid resources during applications execution. This adaptive capability is obtained by applying during the selection process an evolutionary method known as *Scatter Search* (it is based on quality and diversity criteria).

Finally, the model is evaluated in a real grid infrastructure. The results show that the infrastructure throughput is enhanced. Even more, a reduction in the applications execution time and an improvement of the successfully finished tasks rate are also achieved. As a conclusion, the proposed model is a feasible solution for grid applications.

Keywords: Grid Computing, Scatter Search, Adaptability, Resources Selection, Optimization.

1 Introduction

Grid Computing environments [1][2] are distributed systems comprised of heterogeneous resources with a different geographical location. All these resources are used in a collaborative way to perform computationally large tasks; this type of infrastructure emerges for solving massive computation problems. The set of experiments developed within the Large Hadron Collider[1] (*LHC*) is a paradigmatic example of massive computing applications deployed in a grid infrastructure.

---

[1] http://lhc.web.cern.ch/lhc/

R. Moreno-Díaz et al. (Eds.): EUROCAST 2013, Part I, LNCS 8111, pp. 396–403, 2013.

The architecture of grid infrastructures is constituted by 4 main layers: the lowest layer is known as **Network Layer** and it is responsible for connecting grid resources. Over this layer is located the **Resources Layer** which contains the computational elements, storage systems, digital data catalogues, etc. Next, the **Middleware Layer** provides tools that allow grid resources to work as a single powerful computer. Finally, at the top of grid architecture is situated the **Application Layer** consisting of scientific applications, frameworks and development tools.

Despite the advantages of these systems, the grid dynamic nature along with the heterogeneous and changing characteristics of resources lead to tasks management constraints. The availability, performance and efficiency of grid resources vary over time because of these constraints, resulting in an applications execution detriment. That is the reason why it has become a challenge to solve these restrictions. In this regard, an alternative increasingly used by the grid community is to provide a self-adaptive ability to applications.

As described in Section 2, there are several solutions that design frameworks, define new scheduling policies, present new notifications algorithms etc. for allowing applications to face the environmental changes. In this work we focus on providing this adaptive capability from a different point of view. In particular, the model is defined from the user point of view: it guides application during their execution by selecting the most efficient resources. However, the model does not control, change or modify grid resources behaviour. Within the selection process the *Scatter Search (SS)* methodology [3]-[5] is applied for choosing grid resources based on quality and diversity criteria. The approach is denoted as *Efficient Resources Selection (ERS)* model based on *SS (ERS-SS)*.

The article is structured as follows: In Section 2 it is exposed the related work concerning adaptive solutions in grid computing environments. The *ERS-SS* model is described in Section 3. The evaluation phase, which has been performed in a real grid infrastructure [6] [7], is discussed in Section 4. Section 5 concludes the paper.

2   Related Work

As stated, there are several studies within the grid community addressing the *adaptation* concept to face the dynamic nature of such infrastructures. In this regard, the work in [8] proposes an adaptive framework based on GLOBUS[2] for managing tasks in an efficient way. The research in [9] is focussed on improving the discovery and monitoring processes. A new Grid Information System (*GIS*) is also defined in this work. The study in [10] presents the design of a new software system which is dynamically adjusted to the application parallelism. The migration framework developed within that system includes two scheduling policies:one for governing tasks suspension and another for handling the migration process.

---

[2] http://www.globus.org/toolkit/

The main idea in [11] is to collect information about resources communication and resources processing times during applications execution. This way, resources are added or deleted by considering this information. The aim of that work is to resolve bottleneck problems and to avoid resources overload. A similar research is described in [12], in which an alternative for managing grid applications autonomously is exposed. This approach is based on the infrastructure status and also on certain information gathered from external sensors; both types of information are used to select resources. The concept of *living application* is introduced and it involves performing migration processes as needed. Finally, a survey of adaptive grid systems is discussed in [13].

The studies mentioned above have a common purpose: improving the infrastructure performance by using solutions defined at the system level (i.e. by designing scheduling techniques, reducing bottlenecks fails, avoiding resources overload, etc.). However, the present contribution proposes an *Efficient Resources Selection* Model focuses on improving the infrastructure throughput, by providing a self-adaptive ability to applications. The model is defined from the user point of view, without modifying resources characteristics or resources behaviour. Moreover, the *ERS* model only applies basic grid concepts and the user command set; during applications execution the approach selects resources based on their efficiency.

3   Efficient Resources Selection Model Based on the Scatter Search

The *ERS* model applies the *Scatter Search SS* to determine the resources involved in the application execution. As stated, this version of the model is denoted as *ERS-SS* (*Efficient Resources Selection Model Based on the Scatter Search*). The following evolutionary mechanisms are included in the strategy: *mutation, recombination and selection*. Before describing the model, an introduction to the *Scatter Search* method is exposed.

The *Scatter Search SS* [3]-[5] is an evolutionary methodology used for solving a wide range of optimization problems. *SS* is primarily based on combining solutions to create new enhanced solutions. By applying several systematic selections over a *Reference Set* R_f (small set of solutions) the corresponding combination of solutions is obtained. Notice that the *Reference Set* registers the best solutions found within the search process. Quality and diversity criteria are used for determining the *goodness* of a solution. Now, the main components of *SS* are summarized:

- *Diversification Generation Method*: the resulting set of diverse solutions - labelled as G - is used for composing the *Reference Set*.
- *Reference Set Update Method*: it generates the *Reference Set* in which solutions have different quality and diversity values. In general terms, half of the solutions are selected by considering quality criteria. The remaining solutions are chosen according to diversity criteria.

- *Subset Generation Method*: it is used for creating combined solutions by forming several subsets from R_f.
- *Solution Combination Method*: two or more subsets $S \subset R_f$ are combined following a specific strategy.
- *Improvement Method*: a local search is performed for achieving higher quality solutions.

3.1   Model Description

The *ERS* model is based on the mapping between two spaces: a task space J with the n independent and parallel application tasks, and a heterogeneous resource space R composed by the m available resources from the grid infrastructure used. In particular, these resources are a type of schedulers denoted as Computing Element (*CE*) in grid computing. A *CE* decides the best computing node to send tasks. It must also be highlighted that in *ERS-SS* each task t_α has associated a *lifetime lt*, i.e., it is the time that the corresponding resource Rt_α has for performing t_α. Thus, for every task t_α a resource Rt_α is efficiently selected (*tasks-resources* allocation is a *many-to-one* relationship).

Next, the mathematical formulation for measuring the resources efficiency is described. Concerning the fitness value of a particular resource i, the first step is to calculate its *processing time* T_i (Eq.1). It is based on the *communication time* $Tcomm_i$ between the resource and other grid services and on the *computation time* $Tcomp_{j,i}$ of task j in the resource. NT_i is the set of assigned tasks to this resource.

$$T_i = Tcomm_i + \sum_{j \in NT_i} Tcomp_{j,i} \ . \tag{1}$$

Next, the time consumed θ_i by resource i with regard to the *lifetime* is obtained as shown in Eq.2.

$$\theta_i = (lt - T_i)/lt \ . \tag{2}$$

Finally, the fitness F_i is calculated by using this θ_i time along with other three parameters (Eq. 3). On the one hand, the percentage of success ϵ_i during execution of tasks (percentage of successfully finished tasks in the resource i). On the other hand, two relevance parameters a and b are also included. This way, users can specify the priority conditions of their experiments.

$$F_i = (a \cdot \epsilon_i + b \cdot \theta_i)/(a + b) \ . \tag{3}$$

As mentioned, the present work proposes an *ERS* model focused on improving the infrastructure throughput and on solving the grid selection problem. It is defined from the user point of view, which means that the model has no control over grid components and it does not change their behaviour. Moreover, the efficient selection process applied during application execution is based on *SS*. Furthermore, the main elements that constitute our particular *SS* version are specified below.

- Quality set Q_S: composed by the top 5 resources at efficiency level.
- Diversity set D_S: includes the 5 most diverse resources with respect to the Q_S set. The value of diversity is calculated taking into account geographical (physical location) and efficiency criteria. That is to say, each resource has associated its site identifier. By using this identifier, the diversity value is calculated for those resources which do not belong to Q_S. The resulting set is ordered from higher to lower diversity values. The D_S is formed with the first 5 resources that exceed the threshold U_E (defined below).
- Efficiency threshold U_E: is the average value of the fitness of all evaluated resources at a given instant of time. It is used in the creation of the diversity set (efficiency criterion).

Regarding the *ERS-SS* execution flow, the main steps are represented in Figure 1. Once the model determines the elements of spaces J and R, a task subset $P_\alpha \subset J$ is constituted. For performing this subset, several resources are randomly chosen (at the beginning of application execution there are no efficiency metrics). The tasks *lifetime lt* is initialized and P_α is launched into execution. Then, tasks are monitored in an independent way. When a task ends its execution or its lifetime is finished, the efficiency value of Rt_α is updated. Next, the different components of *SS* are also updated and a new resource is efficiently selected for executing a new task. There is a selection condition which determines that the new resource must belong to Rt_α set (if $Rt\alpha$ belonged to Q_S, then the new resource belongs to Q_S; in the same way, if Rt_α belonged to D_S, the new resource will belong to D_S). This way, the model exploits the efficient resources while it explores other new unevaluated *CE*.

PSEUDOCODE: ERS-SS ALGORITHM

Input: application tasks, infrastructure resources
Output: set of solutions

1. Determine spaces J and R;
2. Prepare set P_α;
3. Launch P_α into execution;
4. **while** there are unprocessed tasks **do**
      4.1. Monitor tasks;
      4.2. If a task ends its execution **then**
         4.2.1. Update resource efficiency value;
         4.2.2. Update threshol U_E;
         4.2.3. Update Q_S and D_S;
         4.2.4. Apply SS selection process;
         4.2.5. Launch a new task;
5. **End** while

Fig. 1. Main rules that govern the *ERS-SS* model

Finally, all these processes of selection, execution and monitoring of tasks are repeated until the whole space J is processed. All the information generated during the application execution is gathered in output files.

4   Performance Evaluation

The model has been tested in a real grid infrastructure belonging to the National Grid Initiative [6][7]. Concerning the testing applications, it is based on the Runge-Kutta method [14]. Notice that we focus on providing a self-adaptive capability to parametric sweep applications, in which there is not communication between tasks.

During the evaluation phase two scenarios are defined for verifying the next two objectives: an execution time reduction and an improvement of the successfully finished tasks. The implemented version *ERS-SS* is compared with the traditional resources selection in grid (denoted as *TRS*), in which the selection criteria are based on resources availability and proximity. In every scenario a range of tests is fulfilled, so that, each test performs about 10 real experiments with both versions, *TRS* and ERS-SS, respectively.

4.1   Scenario 1: Model Learning

In this first scenario we want to determine the influence of P_α size in the model learning. We expect that the number of tasks launched at the beginning will accelerate such learning, so that, we want to determine the minimum value of P_α size that achieves a significant execution time reduction. 5 tests have been defined, every of them with a space J of 200 tasks. Moreover, in these tests the size of P_α varies from 5 to 40 tasks (5, 10, 13, 20, 40). Finally, parameters a and b (Eq. 3) were established at 60% and 40% respectively.

Regarding the results shown in Figure 2 it is possible to conclude that the proposed model achieves a execution time reduction with regard to *TRS*. It must also be highlighted that the execution time of *ERS-SS* involves not only the application execution time but also the time used by the model for monitoring and selecting resources in an efficient way. The time difference between both versions grows when the size of P_α is increased. In these cases (sizes of 20 and 40) the number of tasks launched initially is larger, so that, more resources are evaluated at the beginning (faster learning).

The *ERS-SS* also achieves an improvement in the successfully finished tasks rate. *TRS* executes a 73% of tasks in a successful way while *ERS-SS* reaches a rate of 96%.

4.2   Scenario 2: Increasing the Number of Tasks

The objective in this scenario is to specify the range of applications in which it is feasible to apply the *ERS* model. For that reason, in this case the size of J is varied in the different tests (50, 100, 200, 300 400, 500). Furthermore, in every test the size of P_α is fixed at 10 tasks. It is assumed that for higher values of J the model will get better execution times due to a deeper learning of the infrastructure status.

In Figure 3 the resulting data of this scenario are shown, in which the *ERS-SS* obtains again better results than *TRS*. For example, in point $J = 500$ tasks the

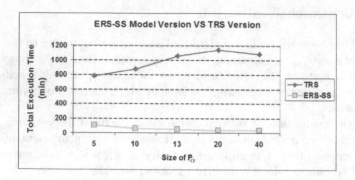

Fig. 2. Execution times obtained within the first scenario. *ERS-SS* improves the execution time with respect to *TRS*.

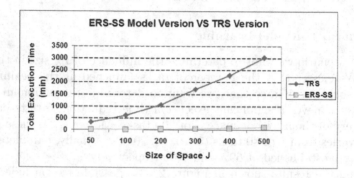

Fig. 3. Results obtained in scenario 2. *ERS-SS* performs properly for applications with large number of tasks.

TRS version spent 3019 minutes (more than 2 days) while *ERS-SS* used only 108 minutes (less than 2 hours). Thus, the initial assumptions within this scenario have been accomplished.

Finally, from the results obtained in both scenarios it is concluded that the *ERS-SS* model achieves a significant execution time reduction while increasing the rate of successfully completed tasks in a 23%.

5   Conclusions and Future Work

The present work is focused on solving the grid resources selection problem by providing a self-adaptive capability to applications. To carry out this strategy the fitness and efficiency values are continuously monitored. During the evaluation phase the *ERS-SS* version is compared with the *TRS*. From the obtained results is deduced that such efficient selection is a feasible solution to the problem.

Future work will involve studying new algorithms, improving some model functionalities and considering other grid services that impact negatively on applications performance.

Acknowledgement. María Botón-Fernández is supported by the PhD research grant of the Spanish Ministry of Economy and Competitiveness at the Research Centre for Energy, Environment and Technology (CIEMAT). The authors would also like to acknowledge the support of the European Funds for Regional Development.

References

1. Foster, I.: What is the Grid? A three Point Checklist. GRIDtoday 1(6), 22–25 (2002)
2. Foster, I.: The Anatomy of the Grid: Enabling Scalable Virtual Organizations. In: Sakellariou, R., Keane, J.A., Gurd, J.R., Freeman, L. (eds.) Euro-Par 2001. LNCS, vol. 2150, pp. 1–4. Springer, Heidelberg (2001)
3. Laguna, M., Martí, R.: Scatter Search: Methodology and Implementations in C. Kluwer Academic Publishers (2003)
4. Laguna, M., Martí, R.: Scatter Search. In: Alba, E., Martí, R. (eds.) Metaheuristic Procedures for Training Neural Networks, pp. 139–152. Springer (2006)
5. Resende, M., Ribeiro, C., Glover, F., Martí, R.: Scatter Search and Path Relinking: Fundamentals, Advances and Applications. In: Gendreau, M., Potvin, J.Y. (eds.) Handbook of Metaheuristics. Springer (2009)
6. National Network of e-Science, http://www.e-ciencia.es/grid.jsp
7. National e-Science Grid Portal, http://www.e-ciencia.es/wiki/index.php/Portal:Grid
8. Huedo, E., Montero, R.S., Llorente, I.M.: A Framework for Adaptive Execution in Grids. Software-Practice & Experience 34(7), 631–651 (2004)
9. Keung, H.N.L.C., Dyson, J.R.D., Jarvis, S.A., Nudd, G.R.: Self-adaptive and Self-optimising Resource Monitoring for Dynamic Grid Environments. In: Proceedings of the 15th International Workshop on Database and Expert Systems Applications, DEXA 2004, pp. 689-693. IEEE Computer Society (2004)
10. Vadhiyar, S.S., Dongarra, J.J.: Self Adaptivity in Grid Computing. Concurrency and Computation: Practice & Experience 17(2-4), 235–257 (2005)
11. Wrzesinska, G., Maasen, J., Bal, H.E.: Self-adaptive Applications on the Grid. In: 12th ACM SIGPLAN Symposium on Principles and Practice of Parallel Programming, pp. 121–129 (2007)
12. Groen, D., Harfst, S., Portegies Zwart, S.: On the Origin of Grid Species: The Living Application. In: Allen, G., Nabrzyski, J., Seidel, E., van Albada, G.D., Dongarra, J., Sloot, P.M.A. (eds.) ICCS 2009, Part I. LNCS, vol. 5544, pp. 205–212. Springer, Heidelberg (2009)
13. Batista, D.M., Da Fonseca, L.S.: A Survey of Self-adaptive Grids. IEEE Communications Magazine 48(7), 94–100 (2010)
14. Press, W.H., Flannery, B.P., Teukolsky, S.A., Vetterling, W.T.: Numerical Recipies in C. Press Syndicate of the University of Cambridge, New York (1992)

A Parallel Two-Level Multiobjective Artificial Bee Colony Approach for Traffic Grooming*

Álvaro Rubio-Largo** and Miguel A. Vega-Rodríguez

Department of Technologies of Computers and Communications,
University of Extremadura, Polytechnic School, Cáceres, 10003 Spain
{arl,mavega}@unex.es

Abstract. A parallel two-level approach based on the behaviour of honey bees is proposed in this paper for Traffic Grooming in optical networks. In this Telecommunication problem, the complexity increases exponentially depending on either the size of the network or the amount of low-speed traffic. Therefore, the use of a parallel evolutionary algorithm is a promising option for facing this optical problem in a suitable amount of time. In this way, we present a multiobjective evolutionary algorithm based on swarm intelligence, the Multiobjective Artificial Bee Colony (MO-ABC) algorithm. Furthermore, we design a parallel two-level MO-ABC by using OpenMP and MPI with the aim of exploiting several multi-core systems in the same interconnecting data network. After testing the parallel performance of the parallel proposal in a machine with four 8-core nodes (32 cores), we observe that it is able to obtain around 80% of average efficiency with 32 cores.

Keywords: OpenMP+MPI, Multiobjective optimization, Artificial Bee Colony, Traffic Grooming, WDM optical networks.

1 Introduction

In the last years, optical networks have gained more and more attention from telecommunication industry. Our present-day data networks do not provide enough bandwidth for the enormous number of current traffic requests; however, the huge optical fiber bandwidth (Tbps) easily solves this drawback.

In Wavelength Division Multiplexing (WDM) optical networks each optical fiber link (Tbps) is divided into several wavelengths of light (λ) or channels (Gbps) [3]. In this way, each end-to-end connection from one node to another over a specific wavelength of light is known as lightpath.

---

* This work was partially funded by the Spanish Ministry of Economy and Competitiveness and the ERDF (European Regional Development Fund), under the contract TIN2012-30685 (BIO project).

** Álvaro Rubio-Largo is supported by the research grant PRE09010 from Gobierno de Extremadura (Consejería de Economía, Comercio e Innovación) and the European Social Fund (ESF).

R. Moreno-Díaz et al. (Eds.): EUROCAST 2013, Part I, LNCS 8111, pp. 404–411, 2013.

Since the vast majority of current data requests only require a few Mbps, a waste of bandwidth at each lightpath is produced as a result [5]. However, by using access station at each optical network, we can groom or multiplex several low-speed requests onto high-speed lightpaths, making the most of the bandwidth. This problem is known as the Traffic Grooming problem [6] and it is considered an NP-hard problem.

In this work we present a parallel approach based on swarm intelligence for solving the Traffic Grooming problem in mesh optical networks. The selected algorithm is the Artificial Bee Colony algorithm, but adapted to the multiobjective domain (MO-ABC). The parallel approach proposed in this paper has been parallelized by using a two-level OpenMP+MPI model in order to exploit several multi-core systems interconnected through the same data network. By using a machine with four 8-core nodes, we compare the parallel performance of our parallel two-level proposal with a pure message-passing version of the MO-ABC approach (one-level parallelism). In this performance comparison, we measure the efficiency and speedup of the two parallel approaches when solving the Traffic Grooming problem in two different sized real-world optical networks.

The rest of this paper is organized as follows. A description of the Traffic Grooming problem is presented in Section 2. Section 3 is devoted to describe the parallel two-level Multiobjective Artificial Bee Colony algorithm. In Section 4, we compare the parallel performance of our parallel two-level MO-ABC with a pure message-passing MO-ABC in different Traffic Grooming scenarios. Finally, we summarize the conclusions of the work and discuss possible lines of future work in Section 5.

2 Traffic Grooming Problem

In this paper, we consider an optical network topology as a directed graph $G=(N, E)$, where N is the set of nodes and E is the set of physical links connecting nodes. In the first place, we enumerate the assumptions for modeling the problem:

- *Multi-hop grooming facility* [6]. A low-speed traffic request may use more than one concatenated lightpath in order to be accommodated.
- The number of wavelengths (W), the propagation delay (d), and capacity (C) is exactly the same for all the links $(m,n) \in E$. Note that, we assume that the propagation delay is equal to one $(d_{mn}=1)$.
- *Wavelength continuity constraint* [2]. All the physical links traversed in a lightpath must be routed through in the same channel or wavelength of light (λ). Thus, none of the nodes in N supports *wavelength conversion*.
- *Static traffic pattern*. The set of low-speed traffic requests is known in advance and cannot be split into lower speed requests and routed separately. Note that, the granularity of each low-speed request is OC-x, $x \in \{1, 3, 12,$ and $48\}$, where $x \times 51.84Mb/s$.
- The number of outgoing links is equal to the number of incoming links for all nodes in N. Furthermore, at each node the number of transceivers $(T_i/R_i$ or $T)$ will be greater than or equal to one.

Then, we list the main parameters of the traffic grooming problem:

- Λ: traffic demand matrix

$$\Lambda^x = [\; \Lambda^x_{sd}; \; s, d \in N \;]_{|N| \times |N|},$$

  where Λ^x_{sd} is the number of OC-x requests between node pair (s, d).
- S^x_{sd}, $x \in \{1, 3, 12, \text{and } 48\}, \forall s, d \in N$: number of OC-$x$ streams requested from node s to node d that are successfully routed.
- P_{mn}, $\forall m, n \in N$: number of fibers interconnecting nodes m and n.
- V^w_{ij}, $\forall w \in \{1 \ldots W\}, \forall i, j \in N$: number of lightpaths from node i to node j on wavelength w (Virtual Topology).
- $P^{ij,w}_{mn}$, $\forall w \in \{1 \ldots W\}, \forall i, j, m, n \in N$: number of lightpaths between node i to node j routed through fiber link (m, n) on wavelength w (Physical Topology route).

Hence, given an optical network topology, a set of connection requests with different bandwidth granularity, a fixed number of available wavelengths per fiber, a capacity of each wavelength, and a fixed number of transmitters and receivers at each node, the Traffic Grooming problem may be stated as a Multiobjective Optimization Problem (MOOP) [1], where the objective functions are:

- *Traffic Throughput* (y_1): Maximize the total successfully routed low-speed traffic demands on the virtual topology.
- *Number of Transceivers or Ligthpaths* (y_2): Minimize the total number of transceivers used or the number of lightpaths established.
- *Average Propagation Delay* (APD, y_3). Minimize the average hop count of lightpaths established, due to we assume $d_{mn} = 1$ in all physical fiber links (m, n).

For a complete formulation of the Traffic Grooming problem, including all parameters, variables, constraints, objective functions, and an illustrative example, please see [4].

3   Parallel Two-Level MO-ABC

The Artificial Bee Colony (ABC) algorithm is a population-based evolutionary algorithm inspired by the intelligent behavior of honey bees. In the ABC algorithm, the population of individuals is defined as a colony with three groups of bees: *employed bees, onlooker bees,* and *scout bees.* Since we are dealing with a MOOP, we have adapted the standard ABC algorithm to the Multiobjective domain (MO-ABC).

Figure 1 shows the sequential operational scheme of the MO-ABC algorithm. Note that the different tones of grey represents the different steps within each generation. As we may observe in Figure 1, a single process is in charge of generating the new employed bees, onlooker bees, and scout bees at each generation.

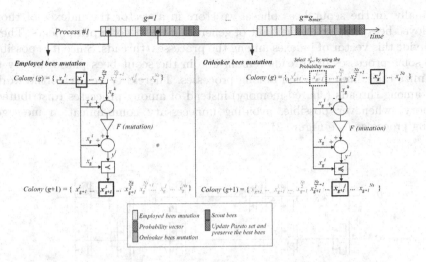

Fig. 1. Operational scheme of the MO-ABC algorithm

In this way, in the design of the parallel operation scheme of the MO-ABC, we can distinguish three regions: *Employed Bees Region*, *Onlooker Bees Region*, and *Scout Bees Region*. These regions are perfectly suitable for being parallelized because there are no dependencies among the tasks carried out by threads/processes in the same region.

As we may observe in Figure 1, the number of bees that reach the limit of iterations with no improvements (Scout bees) is different at each generation. Therefore, in order to minimize the communication overhead, we divide the scout bees among the available computational resources dynamically.

In this work, we present a parallel two-level MO-ABC algorithm by using OpenMP and MPI jointly. In this way, the parallel approach has been designed like a master-slave model in the main three regions: mutation of the employed bees, generation of the onlooker bees, and generation of the scout bees.

In the employed bees phase, a master process broadcasts the first half of the colony to the slave processes by using message passing; therefore, $\lceil \frac{NS/2}{M} \rceil$ bees to each slave process. Then, the workload of each process is divided among a set of threads by using OpenMP directives. Each thread at each process mutates its corresponding employed bees in the range $[a + 1, \ a + b]$; where N_s is the population size, NTh is the total number of threads, NPr is the total number of processes, a is $(thread\_id - 1) + ((process\_id - 1) * b)$, $b = \lceil \frac{N_s}{2} \rceil$, $M = (NTh * NPr)$, $thread\_id \in [1 \ldots NTh]$, and $process\_id \in [1 \ldots NPr]$. Once all the threads of a slave process finish, the $\lceil \frac{N_s/2}{M} \rceil$ mutated employed bees are sent to the master process.

In the onlooker bees phase, when the master process has computed the probability vector, it broadcasts not only all the mutated bees to all the slave processes, but also the probability vector. Then, the same parallel procedure followed for mutating the employed bees is applied for generating the onlooker bees in the range $[\frac{N_s}{2} + a + 1, \ \frac{N_s}{2} + a + b]$.

Finally, in the scout bees phase, we store in a vector the indexes of those employed bees that reach the limit of generations with no improvements. Then, we divide this vector of indexes among the processes/threads. Since it is possible that some processes or threads remain idle in the scout bees phase, we try to minimize the communication among processes. Therefore, we divide the workload among threads (shared-memory) instead of among processes (distributed-memory) whenever possible, avoiding unnecessary communication messages among processes (see Figure 2).

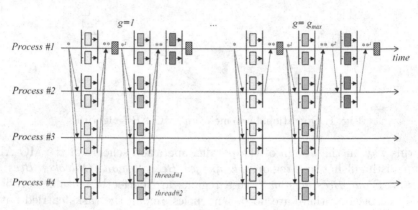

*   MPI_Bcast (Employed bees); therefore, Ns/2 bees are sent to each process

** MPI_Recv (Partial Employed/Onlooker bees); therefore, $\left\lceil \frac{Ns/2}{NPr} \right\rceil$ bees are sent to the master from each slave process.

*   MPI_Bcast (Employed bees, Probability vector); therefore, Ns/2 bees and probabilities are sent to each slave process.

*   MPI_Bcast (Scout index vector); therefore, S indexes to each process, where S is in the range [1 ... Ns/2].

** MPI_Recv (Partial Scout bees); therefore $\left\lceil \frac{S}{NPr} \right\rceil$ random bees are sent to the master from each slave process.

Fig. 2. Operational scheme of the parallel two-level MO-ABC algorithm by using MPI and OpenMP in a machine with four 2-core nodes.

4   Experimental Results

In this section, we compare the parallel performance of the two-level OpenMP+MPI MO-ABC approach presented in Section 3, with a pure MPI version of the MO-ABC (one-level parallelism). The operational scheme of the pure MPI version is almost identical to the parallel scheme of the hybrid version; the main difference is that in this version the slave processes do not divide their workload into different threads.

The performance of a parallel algorithm is commonly measured by computing the *speedup* and *efficiency*. In this work, we use the notation $\overline{T}_m$, S_m, and E_m to denote the the *mean runtime*, *speedup*, and *efficiency* obtained on m processors; respectively. Note that, we report the efficiency as a percentage.

Table 1. Mean runtime, speedup, and efficiency for the *OpenMP+MPI* and *MPI* versions of the MO-ABC algorithm with 1, 2, 4, 8, 16, and 32 cores in 30 runs.

	T W	1 core MO-ABC T_1	2 cores OpenMP+MPI T_2	S_2	E_2	MPI T_2	S_2	E_2	4 cores OpenMP+MPI T_4	S_4	E_4	MPI T_4	S_4	E_4
6-node	3 3	54.66	27.52	1.986	99.30%	28.34	1.929	96.43%	13.95	3.919	97.98%	15.10	3.620	90.50%
	4 3	56.19	28.19	1.993	99.65%	28.66	1.960	98.02%	14.07	3.994	99.86%	15.25	3.686	92.14%
	5 3	55.79	27.98	1.994	99.69%	28.67	1.946	97.29%	14.10	3.956	98.89%	15.15	3.682	92.04%
	7 3	55.75	28.13	1.982	99.11%	28.72	1.942	97.08%	14.12	3.948	98.71%	15.17	3.675	91.87%
	3 4	54.64	27.49	1.988	99.38%	28.25	1.934	96.71%	13.96	3.914	97.85%	15.16	3.604	90.10%
	4 4	56.27	28.33	1.987	99.33%	28.89	1.948	97.39%	14.28	3.941	98.53%	15.46	3.639	90.98%
	5 4	55.32	27.80	1.989	99.47%	28.50	1.941	97.05%	14.10	3.923	98.08%	15.11	3.662	91.55%
		55.52	**27.92**	**1.988**	**99.42%**	**28.58**	**1.943**	**97.14%**	**14.08**	**3.942**	**98.56%**	**15.20**	**3.652**	**91.31%**
NSF	3 3	384.17	194.22	1.978	98.90%	196.76	1.953	97.63%	100.31	3.830	95.74%	103.13	3.725	93.12%
	4 3	448.52	226.35	1.981	99.07%	231.27	1.939	96.97%	115.11	3.896	97.41%	120.21	3.731	93.28%
	5 3	484.72	244.51	1.982	99.12%	249.77	1.941	97.03%	127.45	3.803	95.08%	129.60	3.740	93.51%
	4 4	504.11	253.70	1.987	99.35%	258.36	1.951	97.56%	131.73	3.827	95.67%	136.94	3.681	92.03%
	5 4	580.78	293.71	1.977	98.87%	305.19	1.903	95.15%	153.00	3.796	94.90%	160.87	3.610	90.26%
	6 4	620.76	312.10	1.989	99.45%	322.60	1.924	96.21%	162.09	3.830	95.75%	170.44	3.642	91.05%
		503.84	**254.10**	**1.983**	**99.13%**	**260.66**	**1.935**	**96.76%**	**131.62**	**3.830**	**95.76%**	**136.87**	**3.688**	**92.21%**

	T W	8 cores OpenMP+MPI T_8	S_8	E_8	MPI T_8	S_8	E_8	16 cores OpenMP+MPI T_{16}	S_{16}	E_{16}	MPI T_{16}	S_{16}	E_{16}
6-node	3 3	7.08	7.717	96.46%	8.42	6.493	81.16%	3.84	14.223	88.89%	5.33	10.261	64.13%
	4 3	7.44	7.554	94.43%	8.69	6.466	80.83%	3.93	14.312	89.45%	5.47	10.264	64.15%
	5 3	7.29	7.656	95.70%	8.45	6.600	82.50%	3.96	14.096	88.10%	5.36	10.400	65.00%
	7 3	7.34	7.596	94.95%	8.43	6.611	82.64%	3.95	14.129	88.31%	5.36	10.406	65.04%
	3 4	7.12	7.674	95.93%	8.59	6.358	79.47%	3.82	14.297	89.35%	5.24	10.426	65.16%
	4 4	7.28	7.725	96.56%	8.71	6.461	80.76%	3.89	14.465	90.41%	5.31	10.604	66.27%
	5 4	7.22	7.657	95.71%	8.60	6.434	80.42%	3.90	14.198	88.74%	5.25	10.546	65.91%
		7.25	**7.654**	**95.68%**	**8.56**	**6.489**	**81.11%**	**3.90**	**14.246**	**89.04%**	**5.33**	**10.415**	**65.10%**
NSF	3 3	50.62	7.589	94.86%	58.24	6.596	82.46%	26.48	14.508	90.68%	31.44	12.218	76.36%
	4 3	59.44	7.546	94.32%	68.65	6.533	81.66%	30.98	14.479	90.49%	38.09	11.776	73.60%
	5 3	65.17	7.438	92.98%	74.82	6.478	80.98%	33.26	14.575	91.10%	42.12	11.508	71.92%
	4 4	68.40	7.370	92.13%	77.28	6.523	81.54%	34.61	14.565	91.03%	43.73	11.528	72.05%
	5 4	78.16	7.431	92.89%	90.10	6.446	80.57%	39.82	14.585	91.16%	53.97	10.761	67.25%
	6 4	83.85	7.404	92.54%	94.91	6.541	81.76%	42.33	14.664	91.65%	56.13	11.059	69.12%
		67.61	**7.463**	**93.29%**	**77.33**	**6.520**	**81.50%**	**34.58**	**14.563**	**91.02%**	**44.25**	**11.475**	**71.72%**

	T W	32 cores OpenMP+MPI T_{32}	S_{32}	E_{32}	MPI T_{32}	S_{32}	E_{32}
6-node	3 3	2.12	25.806	80.65%	2.87	19.044	59.51%
	4 3	2.18	25.779	80.56%	2.94	19.136	59.80%
	5 3	2.17	25.749	80.47%	2.93	19.031	59.47%
	7 3	2.15	25.936	81.05%	2.92	19.117	59.74%
	3 4	2.10	26.052	81.41%	2.97	18.400	57.50%
	4 4	2.16	26.043	81.38%	2.95	19.073	59.60%
	5 4	2.12	26.036	81.36%	2.99	18.494	57.80%
		2.14	**25.915**	**80.98%**	**2.94**	**18.899**	**59.06%**
NSF	3 3	14.52	26.450	82.66%	19.93	19.280	60.25%
	4 3	17.49	25.642	80.13%	22.85	19.626	61.33%
	5 3	18.87	25.683	80.26%	25.29	19.164	59.89%
	4 4	19.70	25.589	79.96%	25.90	19.464	60.82%
	5 4	22.62	25.680	80.25%	30.02	19.348	60.46%
	6 4	24.07	25.788	80.59%	31.74	19.557	61.11%
		19.55	**25.805**	**80.64%**	**25.96**	**19.407**	**60.65%**

We have used two different optical network topologies [4]. The first one is a small network with six nodes (6-node), a capacity (C) per link of OC-48, and a traffic matrix with a total amount of traffic of 988 OC-1 units. The second one is the large real-world National Science Foundation (NSF) network topology with 14 nodes, a capacity of OC-192, and a total amount of requested traffic of 5724 OC-1 units. We have tested different scenarios over these topologies, varying the number of transceivers per node (T) and the number of wavelengths (W) per link:

- 6-node Network: T={3,4,5,7} W={3} and T={3,4,5} W={4}.
- NSF Network: T={3,4,5} W=3 and T={4,5,6} W={4}.

We have performed 30 independent runs of each parallel version on a homogenous cluster which consists of 4 multi-core nodes, where each node is equipped with 8 cores; thus, we have a total of 32 cores. The stopping criterion was established to 3000 (6-node) and 7500 (NSF) generations.

Since we have four multi-core nodes interconnected through the same data network, we present different comparisons between the two aforementioned parallel versions of the MO-ABC in different scenarios with 2, 4, 8, 16, and 32 cores. The configuration used for the MO-ABC (in both parallel approaches) is: Population size (N_s)=100, Maximum Limit value ($limit_{max}$)=5, and Mutation rate (F)=25%.

In Table 1 we present the the mean runtime, speedup, and efficiency obtained by the OpenMP+MPI MO-ABC (two-level parallelism) and by the pure MPI MO-ABC (one-level parallelism) in different scenarios of the two network topologies (6-node and NSF).

As we can see in Table 1, the performance of the parallel versions of the MO-ABC remains almost constant independently of the optical network. Furthermore, we may observe how the efficiency of the MPI version decreases exponentially when the number of cores increases. As we may observe in Table 1, when we use 32 cores the efficiency of the parallel two-level MO-ABC (OpenMP+MPI) is very promising (over 80%), whereas in the case of the pure MPI version of the MO-ABC, the efficiency depends on the scenario and ranges between 59-61%.

Finally, in Figure 3, we summarize, for each optical network, the mean speedup obtained by each parallel approach in order to provide a global view of their parallel performance with different number of cores.

To sum up, we can say that the two-level OpenMP+MPI version is a good approach for solving efficiently the Traffic Grooming problem in a reasonable amount of time. In average, the hybrid OpenMP+MPI MO-ABC is able to obtain the same quality results than the sequential version nearly 26 times faster with 32 cores. For example, in the scenario NSF topology with T=3 and W=3, the sequential runtime is 384.17 seconds, whereas the runtime in the parallel two-level approach is 14.52 seconds.

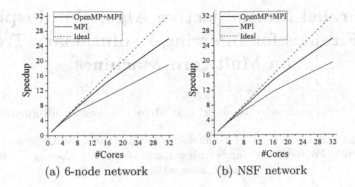

(a) 6-node network   (b) NSF network

Fig. 3. Summary of the mean speedup obtained by the parallel versions of the MO-ABC in the 6-node and NSF optical networks

5   Conclusions and Future Work

In this work, we have applied a parallel two-level Multiobjective Evolutionary Algorithm to a complex optical networking problem: Traffic Grooming problem, in order to solve it in a reasonable amount of time. We have tested the performance of a parallel two-level multiobjective version of the ABC algorithm (MO-ABC) in four 8-core nodes interconnected through the same data network (a total of 32 cores). After a parallel performance study with different scenarios (2, 4, 8, 16, and 32 cores), we can conclude that the parallel two-level MO-ABC is really promising for solving the Traffic Grooming problem in a reasonable amount of time for industry, as it is able to solve (in average) this problem 25 times faster with 32 cores than with a single-core system. As future work, we intend to solve the Traffic Grooming with larger optical networks as well as testing the parallel two-level MO-ABC in other real-world MOOPs.

References

1. Deb, K.: Multi-Objective Optimization Using Evolutionary Algorithms. John Wiley & Sons, Inc., New York (2001)
2. Gagnaire, M., Koubaa, M., Puech, N.: Network Dimensioning under Scheduled and Random Lightpath Demands in All-Optical WDM Networks. IEEE Journal on Selected Areas in Communications 25(S-9), 58–67 (2007)
3. Hamad, A.M., Kamal, A.E.: A survey of Multicasting Protocols for Broadcast-and-select Single-hop Networks. IEEE Network 16, 36–48 (2002)
4. Rubio-Largo, A., Vega-Rodríguez, M.A., Gómez-Pulido, J.A., Sánchez-Perez, J.M.: Multiobjective Metaheuristics for Traffic Grooming in Optical Networks. IEEE Transactions on Evolutionary Computation, 1–17 (2012) (available online since June 2012)
5. Zhu, K., Mukherjee, B.: A Review of Traffic Grooming in WDM Optical Networks: Architectures and Challenges. Optical Networks Magazine 4(2), 55–64 (2003)
6. Zhu, K., Mukherjee, B.: Traffic Grooming in an Optical WDM Mesh Network. IEEE Journal on Selected Areas in Communications 20(1), 122–133 (2002)

A Parallel Multiobjective Algorithm Inspired by Fireflies for Inferring Evolutionary Trees on Multicore Machines

Sergio Santander-Jiménez* and Miguel A. Vega-Rodríguez

Univ. of Extremadura, Dept. of Technologies of Computers and Communications,
Escuela Politécnica. Campus Universitario s/n, 10003. Cáceres, Spain
{sesaji,mavega}@unex.es

Abstract. Recent researches have pointed out the need to combine parallelism and bioinspired computing to address computationally intensive problems in bioinformatics. The inference of evolutionary histories represents one of the most complex problems in this field. Phylogenetic inference can be tackled by using multiobjective metaheuristics designed to resolve the problems that arise when different optimality criteria support conflicting evolutionary relationships. As the inference process becomes harder when we have to consider multiple criteria simultaneously, these new approaches must be defined on the basis of parallel computing. In this paper, we propose a parallel multiobjective approach inspired by fireflies to address the phylogenetic inference problem by using OpenMP to exploit the characteristics of multicore machines. Experimental results on four real biological data sets show significant parallel and biological performances with regard to other proposals from the literature.

Keywords: Swarm Intelligence, Parallel Computing, Multicore Architectures, Firefly Algorithm, Phylogenetic Inference.

1 Introduction

Recently, a wide range of research topics in bioinformatics has been formulated as multiobjetive optimization problems [1], involving two or more objective functions that must be optimized simultaneously. Most of these problems show a NP-hard complexity due to the fact that the search space grows exponentially with the size of the biological information to be processed. In addition, as multiple complex objective functions must be considered, the assessment of solutions will be hard from a computational perspective. These issues motivate a growing need for new approaches based on bioinspired computation and parallelism.

Recent research efforts in the field of phylogenetics have tried to apply parallel computing and metaheuristics to describe new hypotheses about the evolution

* This work was partially funded by the Spanish Ministry of Economy and Competitiveness and the ERDF (European Regional Development Fund), under the contract TIN2012-30685 (BIO project). Sergio Santander-Jiménez is supported by the grant FPU12/04101 from the Spanish Government.

R. Moreno-Díaz et al. (Eds.): EUROCAST 2013, Part I, LNCS 8111, pp. 412–419, 2013.
© Springer-Verlag Berlin Heidelberg 2013

of species [2]. In this sense, the availability of shared-memory multicore architectures has allowed biologists to address phylogenetic analyses on a growing
amount of biological data [3]. The need for parallelism grows when the problem
is tackled by using multiobjetive optimization. Phylogenetic searches can be conducted according to different principles about the way species evolve in nature,
giving as a result conflicting evolutionary relationships. By applying multiobjective metaheuristics, we aim to describe a set of Pareto solutions which represent
a compromise between multiple optimality criteria. As the inference process involving multiple objective functions becomes even harder, different strategies
can be used to parallelize multiobjective algorithms for inferring phylogenies [4].

In this paper, we apply OpenMP to parallelize the Multiobjective Firefly
Algorithm (MO-FA), a bioinspired proposal for inferring evolutionary histories
according to two criteria: parsimony and likelihood. By using swarm intelligence,
we can define an algorithmic design suitable to be parallelized on multicore architectures. We will evaluate the parallel performance achieved on four nucleotide
data sets by comparing speedup factors and efficiencies with other proposals from
the literature. In addition, we will study multiobjective performance by using
the well-known hypervolume metrics [5] and report, finally, biological results.

This paper is organized as follows. In Section 2 we introduce the fundamentals
of the problem and explain its complexity. Section 3 details our multiobjective
approach and introduces a parallel version for multicore architectures. Section 4
reports experimental results, in terms of parallel, multiobjective, and biological
performance. Finally, Section 5 provides conclusions and future research work.

2   Phylogenetic Inference Problem

Phylogenetic methods analyze aligned biological sequences composed by S sites
which contain the genetic information that characterize a set of N organisms with
the aim of inferring their ancestral evolutionary relationships [6]. By processing
these sequences, we can build a tree-shaped structure $T = (V, E)$ which describes
a hypothesis about the evolution of the input species. In a phylogenetic tree T,
ancestor-descendant relationships are modelled by connecting related organisms
in V using the branches defined in E.

With the availability of a growing amount of molecular data, new strategies
must be defined to overcome the NP-hard complexity of the problem [2], which
is motivated by two factors: firstly, the exponential growth of the number of
phylogenetic topologies with the number of species considered; and secondly,
the increase in the processing times required to assess phylogenetic trees under
optimality criteria, which depends on the number of sites in molecular sequences.

In this paper, we tackle the phylogenetic inference problem according to two
criteria: parsimony and likelihood. Maximum parsimony approaches seek to find
the phylogenetic tree that represents the simplest evolutionary hypothesis by
minimizing the amount of mutation events throughout its topology. Given a
phylogenetic trees $T = (V, E)$ inferred from a dataset composed by N sequences
with S sites per sequence, the parsimony score $P(T)$ is defined as follows [6]:

$$P(T) = \sum_{i=1}^{S} \sum_{(a,b)\in E} C(a_i, b_i) \tag{1}$$

where $(a, b) \in E$ represents an evolutionary relationship between two nodes $a, b \in V$, a_i and b_i are the state values at the ith character in the molecular sequences for a and b, and $C(a_i, b_i)$ the cost of evolving from a_i to b_i. Searching for the most parsimonious tree is a well-known NP-hard problem [7] due to the number of topologies that must be considered.

On the other hand, the maximum likelihood criterion was defined with the aim of finding the most likely evolutionary tree under the assumptions made by an evolutionary model about the reality of the evolutionary process. Let $T = (V, E)$ be a phylogeny inferred from a set of N sequences characterized by S sites, and m an evolutionary model. We define the likelihood $L[T, m]$ as [6]:

$$L[T, m] = \prod_{i=1}^{S} \prod_{j=1}^{E} (r_i t_j)^{n_{ij}} \tag{2}$$

where r_i is defined as the mutation probability for the ith site, t_j represents the evolutionary time given by the length of the branch $j \in E$, and n_{ij} is the number of changes observed between the nodes connected by j at the ith site. As well as maximum parsimony, maximum likelihood is considered as a NP-hard problem [8] which requires huge computational resources due to the large number of parameters involved in likelihood computations [2].

3   Parallel Multiobjective Firefly Algorithm

In this paper, we address the phylogenetic inference problem by applying a parallel multiobjective algorithm, Multiobjective Firefly Algorithm (MO-FA) [9]. This approach extends the Firefly Algorithm [10] to tackle multiobjective optimization problems. The behaviour of fireflies in nature is based on a bioluminescence system defined to attract potential partners. Fireflies will move towards the position of those fireflies with the brightest patterns of flashing lights, taking into account several factors: the distance between fireflies, the light intensity, and the environmental light absorption. By identifying the light intensity of a firefly with the quality of a solution, we can define an algorithmic design based on the well-known concept of dominance [5] to resolve multiobjective optimization problems. In order to address the inference of phylogenetic trees according to the parsimony and likelihood principles, we define an individual representation based on distance matrices which contain genetic distances between species [6].

Given a population F of $swarmSize$ fireflies, the algorithm operates as follows. Let F_r be a firefly dominated by, at least, other firefly F_s, with distance matrices $F_r.M$ and $F_s.M$. MO-FA will move F_r towards F_s by applying an attraction formula over all the entries $F_r.M[i, j]$, taking into account the distance between fireflies δ_{rs}, an attraction factor β_0, an absorption coefficient γ,

---

Algorithm 1. Parallel Multiobjective Firefly Algorithm

```
1.  F ← initializeAndEvaluatePopulation(swarmSize, dataset)
2.  #pragma omp parallel num_threads(nthreads)
3.  for i = 1 to maxGenerations do
4.      /* Compute the number of dominated fireflies */
5.      #pragma omp single
6.      idDominatedFireflies ← 0, numDominatedFireflies ← 0
7.      for j = 1 to swarmSize do
8.          if ∃ F[k]: F[k] ≻ F[j] then
9.              idDominatedFireflies[numDominatedFireflies] ← j
10.             numDominatedFireflies ← numDominatedFireflies + 1
11.         end if
12.     end for
13.     /* Saving the current state of the swarm */
14.     AuxPop ← F
15.     /* MO-FA movement loop */
16.     #pragma omp for num_threads(nthreads) schedule (scheduleType)
17.     for j = 1 to numDominatedFireflies do
18.         idDom ← idDominatedFireflies[j]
19.         F[idDom].M ← attractFirefly(F[idDom].M, AuxPop, β₀, γ, α)
20.         F[idDom].T ← generatePhylogeneticTree(F[idDom].M)
21.         F[idDom] ← setParsimonyAndLikelihoodScores(F[idDom].T, dataset)
22.     end for
23.     ParetoFront ← saveSolutions(F, ParetoFront)
24. end for
```

---

and a randomization factor α: $F_r.M[i,j] = F_r.M[i,j] + \beta_0 e^{-\gamma \delta_{rs}^2}(F_s.M[i,j] - F_r.M[i,j]) + \alpha(rand[0,1] - \frac{1}{2})$. Once $F_r.M$ has been updated, we infer the corresponding phylogenetic topology $F_r.T$ by using a tree-building distance method [6], evaluating the solution afterwards according to parsimony and likelihood. This movement step is applied over all the dominated fireflies, updating the set of Pareto solutions with the best nondominated solutions found at each iteration.

As fireflies in the swarm are modelled as independent agents, MO-FA can benefit from parallel computing techniques. For this purpose, we propose a coarse-grained parallel implementation for shared-memory multicore architectures by using the OpenMP libraries. In order to design this parallel version of MO-FA, we must consider two key issues. Firstly, as the movement step is applied over a variant number of dominated fireflies which will learn from several different fireflies, we must introduce load balancing techniques to make a proper distribution of tasks among threads, avoiding idle threads throughout the execution of the algorithm. Secondly, as multiple threads operate simultaneously over the swarm, we must consider additional data structures to handle possible read-write risks.

Algorithm 1 shows MO-FA parallel design. We enclose the main loop of the algorithm by using the #pragma omp parallel directive with the aim of minimizing the thread management overhead. The fireflies to be updated in the movement step (lines 16 to 22 in Algorithm 1) are distributed among *nthreads* execution threads by using #pragma omp for. In order to avoid load balance issues, we compute at the beginning of each generation the number of currently dominated fireflies in the swarm (lines 5-12). By using this strategy, we will consider *numDominatedFireflies* update tasks to be processed in the movement step. In addition, as dominated fireflies must learn from a changing number of fireflies in accordance with the dominance concept, we can apply OpenMP scheduling techniques to distribute new tasks among those threads that have completed their initial workload. Regarding read-write risks, we address this issue by introducing a backup population (line 14) defined with the aim of keeping the current state of the swarm, avoiding inconsistencies when updating fireflies.

4   Experimental Methodology and Results

In this section, we show the results obtained by MO-FA in terms of parallel, multiobjective, and biological performance. We have performed experiments on four real nucleotide data sets [4]: $rbcL\_55$, 55 sequences (1314 nucleotides per sequence) of the rbcL gene from green plants, $mtDNA\_186$, 186 sequences (16608 nucleotides) of human mitochondrial DNA, $RDPII\_218$, 218 sequences (4182 nucleotides) of prokaryotic RNA, and $ZILLA\_500$, 500 sequences (759 nucleotides) of rbcL plastid gene. The algorithm was configured according with the experimentation conducted in [9]. The values for the input parameters are $swarmSize$=100, $maxGenerations$=100, β_0=1, γ=0.5, and α=0.05.

Parallel Performance. We have carried out different sets of experiments composed by 10 independent runs for 1, 2, 4, 8, 16, and 24 OpenMP threads to evaluate the parallel performance of the proposal, considering the OpenMP scheduling mechanisms *static* and *guided*. All our experiments were performed on a machine composed by 2 processors AMD Opteron 12-core Magny-Cours 6174 at 2.2 GHz running Scientific Linux 6.1, and the algorithm was compiled using GCC 4.4.5.

Table 1. Speedup factors -SU- and efficiencies -EF- achieved by MO-FA

	\multicolumn{10}{c}{$rbcL\_55$ (mean sequential time = 5319.625s)}									
	\multicolumn{2}{c}{2 threads}	\multicolumn{2}{c}{4 threads}	\multicolumn{2}{c}{8 threads}	\multicolumn{2}{c}{16 threads}	\multicolumn{2}{c}{24 threads}
ScheduleType	SU	EF(%)	SU	EF(%)	SU	EF(%)	SU	EF(%)	SU	EF(%)
Static	1.847	92.359	3.591	89.765	6.673	83.411	11.613	72.580	15.772	65.718
Guided	**1.853**	**92.669**	**3.598**	**89.941**	**6.854**	**85.678**	**12.251**	**76.569**	**16.199**	**67.494**

	\multicolumn{10}{c}{$mtDNA\_186$ (mean sequential time = 35616.655s)}									
	\multicolumn{2}{c}{2 threads}	\multicolumn{2}{c}{4 threads}	\multicolumn{2}{c}{8 threads}	\multicolumn{2}{c}{16 threads}	\multicolumn{2}{c}{24 threads}
ScheduleType	SU	EF(%)	SU	EF(%)	SU	EF(%)	SU	EF(%)	SU	EF(%)
Static	1.877	93.872	3.627	90.666	6.646	83.079	11.800	73.751	16.202	67.507
Guided	**1.960**	**97.995**	**3.751**	**93.778**	**6.863**	**85.793**	**12.161**	**76.004**	**16.612**	**69.216**

	\multicolumn{10}{c}{$RDPII\_218$ (mean sequential time = 34822.043s)}									
	\multicolumn{2}{c}{2 threads}	\multicolumn{2}{c}{4 threads}	\multicolumn{2}{c}{8 threads}	\multicolumn{2}{c}{16 threads}	\multicolumn{2}{c}{24 threads}
ScheduleType	SU	EF(%)	SU	EF(%)	SU	EF(%)	SU	EF(%)	SU	EF(%)
Static	1.894	94.722	3.502	87.560	6.643	83.033	12.525	78.282	16.388	68.283
Guided	**1.968**	**98.420**	**3.830**	**95.761**	**7.097**	**88.711**	**12.956**	**80.977**	**16.956**	**70.650**

	\multicolumn{10}{c}{$ZILLA\_500$ (mean sequential time = 72083.350s)}									
	\multicolumn{2}{c}{2 threads}	\multicolumn{2}{c}{4 threads}	\multicolumn{2}{c}{8 threads}	\multicolumn{2}{c}{16 threads}	\multicolumn{2}{c}{24 threads}
ScheduleType	SU	EF(%)	SU	EF(%)	SU	EF(%)	SU	EF(%)	SU	EF(%)
Static	1.918	95.887	3.766	94.147	7.318	91.476	13.366	83.536	18.649	77.706
Guided	**1.984**	**99.184**	**3.875**	**96.868**	**7.416**	**92.705**	**13.676**	**85.477**	**19.819**	**82.579**

The parallel performance achieved under these two scheduling types has been evaluated by using two metrics: speedup and efficiency. For each configuration of number of threads and scheduling mechanisms, Table 1 shows the mean speedup factors and efficiencies obtained, introducing also the mean sequential times required to complete a phylogenetic analysis on each dataset. As shown in this table, we can obtain meaningful speedup factors for all the data sets by introducing a guided scheduling, improving the results achieved by the static scheduling mechanism. By analyzing these results, we can observe that MO-FA is able to improve the parallel performance when considering a large number of species. As we increase the complexity of the dataset, the amount of computation which takes place in the parallel regions grows significantly with regard to the critical sections. This fact explains the speedups observed on large data sets, obtaining an efficiency over 82% for 24 threads when analyzing the $ZILLA\_500$ dataset.

In order to assess the quality of these parallel results, we introduce a comparison with RAxML-PTHREADS [3], a POSIX-based proposal for maximum likelihood phylogenetic reconstruction, and PhyloMOEA [4], a multiobjective algorithm for maximum parsimony and maximum likelihood which was parallelized by using MPI-based and OpenMP-MPI schemes up to 16 cores. Table 2 reports the mean speedup factors observed when using RAxML to analyze the data sets considered in this study, comparing them with MO-FA under a guided scheduling. Figure 1 shows a graphical representation of the speedups achieved by both proposals with regard to the theoretical linear speedup. As shown in Table 2, MO-FA obtains improved results when considering 16 and 24 execution threads, especially on the dataset with the largest number of species. On the other hand, Table 3 suggests significant parallel results with regard to the values reported by PhyloMOEA in [4]. These comparisons with other authors' parallel proposals give account of the relevance of the performance obtained by MO-FA.

Table 2. Speedup comparison: MO-FA - RAxML

	2 threads	4 threads	8 threads	16 threads	24 threads
			$rbcL\_55$		
MO-FA	1.853	3.598	**6.854**	**12.251**	**16.199**
RAxML	**1.988**	**3.929**	6.630	9.331	10.151
			$mtDNA\_186$		
MO-FA	1.960	3.751	6.863	**12.161**	**16.612**
RAxML	**1.993**	**3.899**	**7.317**	11.175	12.700
			$RDPII\_218$		
MO-FA	1.968	3.830	7.097	**12.956**	**16.956**
RAxML	**1.981**	**3.902**	**7.271**	12.238	14.809
			$ZILLA\_500$		
MO-FA	**1.984**	**3.875**	**7.416**	**13.676**	**19.819**
RAxML	1.981	3.667	6.153	8.833	9.404

Table 3. Speedup comparison: MO-FA - PhyloMOEA (both with 16 execution threads)

	MO-FA	PhyloMOEA	
Dataset	OpenMP	MPI	MPI-OpenMP
$rbcL\_55$	**12.25**	7.30	8.30
$mtDNA\_186$	**12.16**	7.40	8.50
$RDPII\_218$	**12.96**	9.80	10.20
$ZILLA\_500$	**13.68**	6.70	6.30

Multiobjective and Biological Performance. Next, we evaluate the phylogenetic results generated by our proposal from a multiobjective point of view. For this purpose, we apply the hypervolume metrics [5] which defines the percentage of the solution space covered by our Pareto solutions. The mean hypervolume values computed from 30 independent runs for each dataset under the $HKY85 + \Gamma$ evolutionary model [6] are given by Table 4. This quality indicator suggests a significant multiobjective performance, covering over a 69.065% of the space bounded by the ideal and nadir reference points defined in this table.

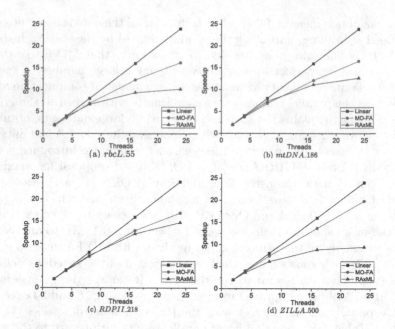

Fig. 1. Comparing MO-FA with RAxML-PTHREADS

Regarding biological performance, we compare MO-FA with several well-known multiobjective and biological methods from the literature: PhyloMOEA, RAxML, and TNT [11] (a single-criterion method for maximum parsimony). For this purpose, we report in Table 5 phylogenetic results from the execution which scored the closest value to the mean hypervolume for each dataset. According to this table, the parsimony scores obtained by our proposal improve the results reported by PhyloMOEA, matching the reference scores provided by TNT. In addition, the likelihood results under the models $HKY85 + \Gamma$ and $GTR + \Gamma$ [6] suggest a meaningful performance in comparison with PhyloMOEA and RAxML.

Table 4. Measuring multiobjective performance

	Hypervolume	
Dataset	Mean	Std. Dev.
rbcL_55	70.142%	0.047
mtDNA_186	69.659%	0.008
RDPII_218	74.078%	0.234
ZILLA_500	69.065%	0.055
	Ideal ref. point	
Dataset	Pars.	Like.
rbcL_55	4774	-21569.69
mtDNA_186	2376	-39272.20
RDPII_218	40658	-132739.90
ZILLA_500	15893	-79798.03
	Nadir ref. point	
Dataset	Pars.	Like.
rbcL_55	5279	-23551.42
mtDNA_186	2656	-43923.99
RDPII_218	45841	-147224.59
ZILLA_500	17588	-87876.39

Table 5. Comparison of biological results

	MO-FA					
	Best pars. tree(HKY85)		Best like. tree(HKY85)		Best like. tree(GTR)	
Dataset	Pars.	Like.	Pars.	Like.	Pars.	Like.
rbcL_55	**4874**	-21835.65	4892	**-21817.74**	4890	**-21786.88**
mtDNA_186	**2431**	-39979.10	2445	**-39888.86**	**2447**	**-39869.30**
RDPII_218	**41488**	-136356.51	42833	**-134179.88**	42813	-134088.93
ZILLA_500	**16218**	-81603.87	16308	**-80967.31**	16305	**-80606.79**
	Best parsimony		Best likelihood			
	TNT	PhyloMOEA	PhyloMOEA(HKY85)		RAxML(GTR)	
Dataset	Pars.	Pars.	Pars.	Like.	Pars.	Like.
rbcL_55	**4874**	**4874**		-21889.84	4893	-21791.98
mtDNA_186	**2431**	2437		-39896.44	2453	-39869.63
RDPII_218	**41488**	41534		-134696.53	42894	**-134079.42**
ZILLA_500	**16218**	16219		-81018.06	**16305**	-80623.50

5   Conclusions

In this paper, we have reported a parallel multiobjective approach to tackle one of the most challenging problems in bioinformatics, phylogenetic inference. Our approach was defined to take advantage of modern shared-memory multicore architectures with the aim of addressing the analysis of complex biological data. For this purpose, we proposed a parallel design based on OpenMP which introduces several algorithmic techniques to minimize load balance issues and read-write risks. Experiments on four nucleotide data sets have shown a significant performance in terms of parallel, multiobjective, and biological results with regard to other multiobjective and biological methods from the state-of-the-art.

The development of new parallel multiobjective approaches to phylogenetics represents one of the most promising lines of future work. GPU and cluster computing can be useful to exploit the characteristics of modern hardware architectures, allowing these techniques to carry out the inference of evolutionary histories on data sets with thousands of species. Parallelism can also be applied to improve biological results by using parallel teams of bioinspired algorithms.

References

1. Handl, J., Kell, D., Knowles, J.: Multiobjective Optimization in Computational Biology and Bioinformatics. IEEE/ACM Trans. Comput Biol. Bioinform. 4(2), 289–292 (2006)
2. Bader, D.A., Roshan, U., Stamatakis, A., Tseng, C.-W.: Computational Grand Challenges in Assembling the Tree of Life: Problems and Solutions. In: Advances in Computers, pp. 128–179. Academic Press, Elsevier (2006)
3. Stamatakis, A., Ott, M.: Exploiting Fine-Grained Parallelism in the Phylogenetic Likelihood Function with MPI, Pthreads, and OpenMP: A Performance Study. In: Chetty, M., Ngom, A., Ahmad, S. (eds.) PRIB 2008. LNCS (LNBI), vol. 5265, pp. 424–435. Springer, Heidelberg (2008)
4. Cancino, W., Jourdan, L., Talbi, E.-G., Delbem, A.C.B.: Parallel Multi-Objective Approaches for Inferring Phylogenies. In: Pizzuti, C., Ritchie, M.D., Giacobini, M. (eds.) EvoBIO 2010. LNCS, vol. 6023, pp. 26–37. Springer, Heidelberg (2010)
5. Coello, C., Veldhuizen, D.V., Lamont, G.: Evolutionary algorithms for solving multi-objective problems. In: Genetic Algorithms and Evolutionary Computation, vol. 5. Kluwer Academic Publishers (2002)
6. Felsenstein, J.: Inferring phylogenies. Sinauer Associates, Sunderland (2004)
7. Day, W.E., Johnson, D.S., Sankoff, D.: The Computational Complexity of Inferring Rooted Phylogenies by Parsimony. Mathematical Biosciences 81, 33–42 (1986)
8. Chor, B., Tuller, T.: Finding a Maximum Likelihood Tree is Hard. Journal of the ACM 53(5), 722–744 (2006)
9. Santander-Jiménez, S., Vega-Rodríguez, M.A.: A Multiobjective Proposal Based on the Firefly Algorithm for Inferring Phylogenies. In: Vanneschi, L., Bush, W.S., Giacobini, M. (eds.) EvoBIO 2013. LNCS, vol. 7833, pp. 141–152. Springer, Heidelberg (2013)
10. Yang, X.-S.: Firefly Algorithm, Stochastic Test Functions and Design Optimisation. Int. J. Bio-Inspired Computation 2(2), 78–84 (2010)
11. Goloboff, P.A., Farris, J.S., Nixon, K.C.: TNT, a free program for phylogenetic analysis. Cladistics 24(5), 774–786 (2008)

Nonlinear Least Squares Optimization of Constants in Symbolic Regression

Michael Kommenda, Michael Affenzeller,
Gabriel Kronberger, and Stephan M. Winkler

Heuristic and Evolutionary Algorithms Laboratory
School of Informatics, Communications and Media
University of Applied Sciences Upper Austria
Softwarepark 11, 4232 Hagenberg, Austria
{michael.kommenda,michael.affenzeller,
gabriel.kronberger,stephan.winkler}@fh-hagenberg.at

Abstract. In this publication a constant optimization approach for symbolic regression by genetic programming is presented. The Levenberg-Marquardt algorithm, a nonlinear, least-squares method, tunes numerical values of constants in symbolic expression trees to improve their fit to observed data. The necessary gradient information for the algorithm is obtained by automatic programming, which efficiently calculates the partial derivatives of symbolic expression trees.

The performance of the methodology is tested for standard and off-spring selection genetic programming on four well-known benchmark datasets. Although constant optimization includes an overhead regarding the algorithm runtime, the achievable quality increases significantly compared to the standard algorithms. For example, the average coefficient of determination on the Poly-10 problem changes from 0.537 without constant optimization to over 0.8 with constant optimization enabled. In addition to the experimental results, the effect of different parameter settings like the number of individuals to be optimized is detailed.

Keywords: Constant Optimization, Symbolic Regression, Genetic Programming, Levenberg-Marquard Algorithm, Automatic Differentiation

1 Introduction

Symbolic regression is the task of learning a model in form of a mathematical formula, which describes the relation between a dependent variable y and several independent variables x and the according weights w given as $y = f(x, w) + \epsilon$. Contrary to other regression tasks the structure of the model as well of the variables used in the final model are not predetermined, but rather evolved during the optimization process. Thus not all independent variables x present in the dataset are required to be used in the obtained formula. The focus of this publication is how weights w are obtained for a given model and how this step can be further improved.

R. Moreno-Díaz et al. (Eds.): EUROCAST 2013, Part I, LNCS 8111, pp. 420–427, 2013.
© Springer-Verlag Berlin Heidelberg 2013

Symbolic regression problems are commonly solved by genetic programming [6] using a tree-based encoding where every inner tree node describes a mathematical function (e.g., addition or division) and every leaf node represents either an independent variable multiplied by a constant (weight) or solely a constant. These constants are randomly initialized according to a normal distribution $\mathcal{N}(\mu, \lambda)$ during the tree creation. After this initialization phase, the only possibilities to find better suited values for the constants are either random mutation, or the combination of existing constants. As both ways of obtaining new constant values are undirected, the progress of the genetic programming algorithm might be unnecessarily hampered; even if the correct model structure is found, its fitness value is small as long as the model parameters are not set correctly.

In the last few years different ways of optimizing constants in symbolic regression have been studied using multi-dimensional optimization techniques [8,2,15,12]. A promising approach was developed by Topchy and Punch [12] by performing differentiation of candidate models and using a gradient-based algorithm to find optimal constant values. However, in [5] it is indicated that this constant optimization technique is outperformed by scaled symbolic regression. The reason is that without linear scaling [5] the algorithm must first find models in the range of the dependent variable before its characteristics are fitted.

In this paper a new constant optimization approach is presented, which helps the evolutionary algorithm to obtain the right numerical values for constants and thus improves the achievable quality. Section 2 describes the methodology for tuning the numerical constants of a model. In Section 3 the experimental setup to demonstrate the usefulness of constant optimization is described and in Section 4 the obtained results are stated and discussed. Finally, Section 5 concludes the publication and gives an outlook of further research directions.

2   Methods

Constants optimization is performed by treating every constant as a parameter that should be tuned by a nonlinear optimization algorithm. As it can also be regarded as a least squares fitting problem, the Levenberg-Marquard (LM) algorithm [7] is especially suited for performing constant optimization. The LM algorithm minimizes an objective function $Q(\beta)$ (Equation 1), which is the sum of squared errors (nonlinear least squares optimization) between the predictions of the symbolic expression tree $f(x, \beta)$ and the observed data y, by modifying the parameter vector β according to a supplied gradient. Hence, a requirement for the whole procedure to work is that the symbolic expression tree encoding a mathematical formula must consist of differentiable functions, because otherwise the gradient calculation would fail.

$$Q(\beta) = \sum_{i=0}^{m} (y_i - f(x_i, \beta))^2 \tag{1}$$

Before the gradient can be calculated the tree encoding a mathematical formula must be transformed and the initial numerical values of constants extracted. Equation 2 shows an example of the tree transformation where every constant is replaced by an according parameter β_i and two artificial scaling terms (β_3 and β_4 in the example) are inserted to account for the linear scaling.

$$\begin{aligned} f(x) &= 1.2x_0 + x_2(3 + 0.5x_1) \\ f(x,\beta) &= (\beta_0 x_0 + x_2(\beta_1 + \beta_2 x_1))\beta_3 + \beta_4 \end{aligned} \tag{2}$$

The gradient ∇f of the transformed tree $f(x,\beta)$ consists of all partial derivations of $f(x,\beta)$ according to its parameters β (Equation 3) and is calculated by automatic differentiation [10]. The reason why automatic differentiation was chosen for gradient calculation is that it provides faster results than symbolic differentiation and more accurate ones compared to numerical differentiation.

$$\nabla f = \left(\frac{\partial f}{\partial \beta_0}, \frac{\partial f}{\partial \beta_1}, ..., \frac{\partial f}{\partial \beta_n} \right) \tag{3}$$

The LM algorithm uses the calculated gradient and the extracted constant values to iteratively modify the constants and stops if a certain number of iterations were performed or no further improvements could be achieved. After the LM algorithm stops, the original tree is updated with the optimized constants.

The constant optimization approach was incorporated in the genetic programming algorithm directly before the evaluation of symbolic expression trees. Furthermore, an additional parameter was introduced to allow constant optimization to be applied on parts of the current population, either the best or random $x\%$ of the population so that the effects of constant optimization can be studied.

2.1 Implementation

The whole approach for constant optimization was implemented in HeuristicLab [13]. HeuristicLab is an open-source heuristic optimization system with comprehensive experiment design and analysis capabilities, as well as a graphical user interface and distributed computation support. Since its beginning in 2002 HeuristicLab offers support for genetic programming and symbolic regression with a symbolic expression tree encoding.

The LM-algorithm which tunes the constants was not implemented anew, but is provided by the numerical analysis and data processing library ALGLIB [3]. The calculation of gradients with automatic differentiation is supplied by AutoDiff [11], which drastically minimizes the implementation effort. The whole constant optimization approach consisting of the symbolic tree transformation, gradient calculation and LM-optimization is available, as source code as well as ready-to-use program, at http://dev.heuristiclab.com.

3   Experiments

The effectiveness of constant optimization was tested on four benchmark problems that are listed in Table 1. The Pagie-1 and Tower problem have recently been recommended as benchmark problems for symbolic regression in [14] and the Poly-10 was introduced in [9]. The Friedman-II problem [4] was additionally included, to have another test problem beside the Tower problem, that is not exactly solvable due to its noise term.

Table 1. Definition of benchmark problems, training and test ranges and the best achievable quality

Name	Training	Test	Variables	Best Quality
Poly-10	250	250	10	1.00
Pagie-1	676	1000	2	1.00
Friedman-II	500	5000	10	0.96
Tower	3136	1863	25	unknown

For every benchmark problem, 50 repetitions of a standard genetic programming for 100 generations with a population size of 500, one elite individual, tournament selection (group size of 4), subtree swapping crossover, a mutation rate of 25%, and tree limits of length 50 and depth 12 were performed. Additionally, 50 runs with strict offspring selection [1] were performed to show the effects of constant optimization for different algorithms. For the offspring selection genetic programming the same settings as for the standard genetic programming algorithm were used, with the exception that gender specific selection (proportional and random) and a maximum selection pressure of 100 were used. The result of an algorithm run is the best individual on the training partition and the detailed results in terms of the R^2 on the test partition are stated in the following.

4   Results

The possible improvement with constant optimization was tested on all four benchmark problems to demonstrate the effectiveness. The improvement is calculated as the change in the coefficient of determination R^2 of a symbolic expression tree after and before constant optimization was applied. Figure 1 shows the average and maximum improvement on the training partition per generation averaged over all 50 genetic programming algorithm repetitions. It can been that the maximum improvement is very high, whereas the average improvement stays rather low. An explanation for this behavior is that offspring of high quality individuals gets a much worse quality by crossover events and their quality can be brought up again by constant optimization.

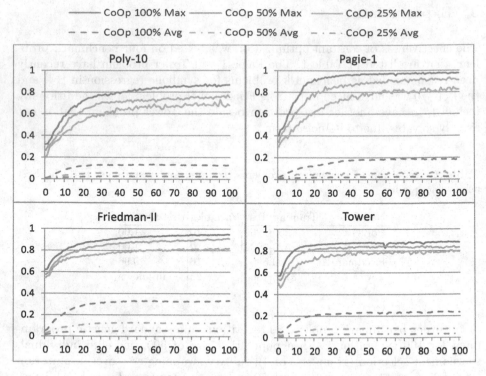

Fig. 1. Maximum and average improvement (in terms of the increase in the R^2) per generation obtained by varying constant optimization probabilities with standard genetic programming. The displayed lines are averages of 50 algorithm repetitions on all four benchmark problems.

4.1   Selection Strategies for Constant Optimization

After demonstrating the effectiveness of constant optimization, different selection strategies for the individuals whose constants are to be optimized were investigated. The research question was whether it gives an advantage if the best proportion of a generation in contrast to randomly chosen individuals are optimized. The results obtained with the two different strategies are stated in Table 2, where success is defined as an $R^2 \geq 0.99$ of the best training model on the test partition. For the two problems, where this can not be achieved, the median test R^2 is stated.

The results are only stated for a constant optimization probability of 25% and 50% as there would be no difference between the two different selection strategies if 0% or 100% of the population were selected for constant optimization. Although, there is a slight advantage of optimizing the best 50% of a population on the Poly-10 and Pagie-1 problem, the results are not conclusive. Therefore, we retain to choose the individuals randomly for further experiments.

Table 2. Test qualities obtained by different selection strategies for constant optimization with a standard genetic programming algorithm

Problem		CoOp 25%		CoOp 50%	
		Random	Best	Random	Best
Poly-10	Success rate	0.08	0.12	0.18	0.24
Pagie-1	Success rate	0.12	0.06	0.18	0.26
Friedman-II	Median R^2	0.870	0.864	0.957	0.957
Tower	Median R^2	0.885	0.876	0.898	0.899

4.2 Standard and Offspring Selection Genetic Programming Results

Finally, we had a detailed look on the results obtained on the test partition for the standard and offspring selection genetic programming algorithm with varying constant optimization probabilities. As a reference runs without any constant optimization applied (CoOp 0%) were included.

The results for standard genetic programming are stated in Table 3. For all benchmark problems better results were obtained with higher probabilities for constant optimization. However, for the Pagie-1 problem overfit models were produced (CoOp 50% and 100%) which is indicated by the high standard deviation. Another interesting fact is, that on the two noisy benchmark problems (Friedman-II and Tower) overfitting is no issue.

Table 3. Average and standard deviation ($\mu \pm \sigma$) of the best training individual on the test partition for 50 repetitions of the standard genetic programming algorithm.

Problem	CoOp 0%	CoOp 25%	CoOp 50%	CoOp 100%
Poly-10	0.537 ± 0.188	0.824 ± 0.110	0.861 ± 0.127	0.912 ± 0.073
Pagie-1	0.553 ± 0.363	0.712 ± 0.398	0.558 ± 0.476	0.581 ± 0.470
Friedman-II	0.672 ± 0.153	0.844 ± 0.133	0.916 ± 0.095	0.947 ± 0.052
Tower	0.844 ± 0.021	0.884 ± 0.015	0.896 ± 0.011	0.906 ± 0.007

Table 4 shows the results obtained with offspring selection genetic programming. In general, the achieved quality is higher compared to standard genetic programming, due to the different evolutionary behavior of the algorithm. Furthermore, the algorithm evaluates more individuals per generation, because with the here used strict offspring selection, only child individuals surpassing the quality of their parents are allowed to participate in the next generation.

As in the case of standard genetic programming the results get better the higher the probability of constant optimization. However, the quality increase between 50% and 100% constant optimization is negligible. It is especially noteworthy, that the Poly-10 problem was solved almost every time if constant optimization was applied. The overfitting on the Pagie-1 problem is not as strong as with standard genetic programming, but with a probability of 100% for constant optimization, overfit models were produced on the Friedman-II problem.

Table 4. Average and standard deviation ($\mu \pm \sigma$) of the best training individual on the test partition for 50 repetitions of the offspring selection genetic programming algorithm.

Problem	CoOp 0%	CoOp 25%	CoOp 50%	CoOp 100%
Poly-10	0.737 ± 0.225	0.967 ± 0.062	0.992 ± 0.031	0.991 ± 0.035
Pagie-1	0.820 ± 0.277	0.597 ± 0.463	0.857 ± 0.316	0.875 ± 0.293
Friedman-II	0.805 ± 0.107	0.871 ± 0.151	0.920 ± 0.086	0.864 ± 0.142
Tower	0.875 ± 0.009	0.916 ± 0.007	0.921 ± 0.006	0.927 ± 0.005

5   Conclusion

In this publication a gradient-based method for optimizing numerical constants of symbolic expression trees solving symboling regression problems was presented. Partial derivatives of the trees were calculated by automatic differentiation and the Levenberg-Margquardt (LM) algorithm for nonlinear least square optimization iteratively altered the constant values. The approach is algorithm-independent and works with every genetic programming variant that encodes individuals as symbolic expression trees.

Results regarding the improvement by constant optimization, the influence of the selection strategy and the achievable quality were detailed on four benchmark problems. Constant optimization increases the obtained quality significantly and thus it can be deducted the algorithm learns better from the data. A drawback is that overfitting is encountered more frequently and measures to counter over-fitting, like use of a validation partition, or sampling, should be included in the modeling.

Another not discussed aspect is the effect of constant optimization on the algorithm runtime, which is clearly increased with the use of constant optimization depending on its probability. The here performed experiments were not tune for performance and the focus was on the achievable quality. Nevertheless, ways of minimizing the overhead of constant optimization, like data sampling, or limiting the number of iterations for the LM algorithm, should be investigated in the future.

Summarizing, the achieved results with constant optimization are encouraging for further research on that topic. Constant optimization seems to directly affect the evolutionary search behavior of the genetic programming algorithms by its additional local optimization step. However, the detailed changes in the algorithm dynamics are an open topic.

Acknowledgments. The here presented work was mostly performed within the Josef Ressel Center for heuristic optimization *Heureka!*, sponsored by the Austrian Research Promotion Agency (FFG).

References

1. Affenzeller, M., Winkler, S., Wagner, S., Beham, A.: Genetic Algorithms and Genetic Programming - Modern Concepts and Practical Applications, Numerical Insights, vol. 6. CRC Press, Chapman & Hall (2009)
2. Alonso, C.L., Montaña, J.L., Borges, C.E.: Evolution strategies for constants optimization in genetic programming. In: ICTAI, pp. 703–707. IEEE Computer Society (2009),
   http://dblp.uni-trier.de/db/conf/ictai/ictai2009.html#AlonsoMB09
3. Bochkanov, S., Bystritsky, V.: Alglib, http://www.alglib.net/
4. Friedman, J.H.: Multivariate adaptive regression splines. The Annals of Statistics, 1–67 (1991)
5. Keijzer, M.: Improving symbolic regression with interval arithmetic and linear scaling. In: Ryan, C., Soule, T., Keijzer, M., Tsang, E.P.K., Poli, R., Costa, E. (eds.) EuroGP 2003. LNCS, vol. 2610, pp. 70–82. Springer, Heidelberg (2003)
6. Koza, J.R.: Genetic Programming: On the Programming of Computers by Means of Natural Selection. MIT Press, Cambridge (1992)
7. Levenberg, K.: A method for the solution of certain non-linear problems in least squares. Quarterly Journal of Applied Mathmatics II(2), 164–168 (1944)
8. Mukherjee, S., Eppstein, M.J.: Differential evolution of constants in genetic programming improves efficacy and bloat. In: Proceedings of the Fourteenth International Conference on Genetic and Evolutionary Computation Conference Companion, GECCO Companion 2012, pp. 625–626. ACM, New York (2012),
   http://doi.acm.org/10.1145/2330784.2330891
9. Poli, R.: A simple but theoretically-motivated method to control bloat in genetic programming. In: Ryan, C., Soule, T., Keijzer, M., Tsang, E.P.K., Poli, R., Costa, E. (eds.) EuroGP 2003. LNCS, vol. 2610, pp. 204–217. Springer, Heidelberg (2003),
   http://dl.acm.org/citation.cfm?id=1762668.1762688
10. Rall, L.B.: Automatic Differentiation: Techniques and Applications. LNCS, vol. 120. Springer, Heidelberg (1981)
11. Shtof, A.: Autodiff, http://autodiff.codeplex.com/
12. Topchy, A., Punch, W.F.: Faster genetic programming based on local gradient search of numeric leaf values. In: Spector, L., Goodman, E.D., Wu, A., Langdon, W.B., Voigt, H.M., Gen, M., Sen, S., Dorigo, M., Pezeshk, S., Garzon, M.H., Burke, E. (eds.) Proceedings of the Genetic and Evolutionary Computation Conference (GECCO-2001), July 7-11, pp. 155–162. Morgan Kaufmann, San Francisco (2001),
   http://www.cs.bham.ac.uk/~wbl/biblio/gecco2001/d01.pdf
13. Wagner, S.: Heuristic Optimization Software Systems - Modeling of Heuristic Optimization Algorithms in the HeuristicLab Software Environment. Ph.D. thesis, Institute for Formal Models and Verification, Johannes Kepler University, Linz, Austria (2009)
14. White, D.R., McDermott, J., Castelli, M., Manzoni, L., Goldman, B.W., Kronberger, G., Jaskowski, W., O'Reilly, U.M., Luke, S.: Better GP benchmarks: community survey results and proposals. Genetic Programming and Evolvable Machines 14(1), 3–29 (2013)
15. Zhang, Q., Zhou, C., Xiao, W., Nelson, P.C.: Improving gene expression programming performance by using differential evolution. In: Proceedings of the Sixth International Conference on Machine Learning and Applications, ICMLA 2007, pp. 31–37. IEEE Computer Society, Washington, DC (2007),
   http://dx.doi.org/10.1109/ICMLA.2007.55

Algorithm for Computing Unfoldings of Unbounded Hybrid Petri Nets

Petr Novosad and Milan Češka

Faculty of Information Technology, Brno University of Technology,
Božetěchova 2, 612 66 Brno, Czech Republic
{novosad,ceska}@fit.vutbr.cz

Abstract. The paper formalizes the concept of the unfolding for unbounded hybrid Petri nets and introduces the algorithm for its computing. The unfolding is a useful partial-order based method for analysis and verification of the Petri net properties. This technique can cope well with the so-called state space explosion problem, especially for the Petri nets with a lot of concurrency.

Keywords: Hybrid Petri net, unfolding.

1 Introduction

Petri nets are a mathematical and graphical tool for modeling concurrent, parallel and/or distributed systems. An unfolding is a useful structure for checking properties of the Petri nets. Our goal it to update the algorithm for computing unfolding for discrete Petri nets to continuous and unbounded hybrid Petri nets.

This article extends our previous work [14] by introducing unfoldings for ordinary unbounded hybrid Petri nets. Unbounded hybrid Petri nets have infinite state space and thus similar set of problems with reachability arises as for unbounded discrete Petri nets [12].

The article consists of the following. The definitions and notations of the hybrid Petri nets are given in Section 2. Section 3 contains definitions and notations of unfoldings. Section 4 presents algorithm for unfolding construction with examples. Section 5 concludes the paper.

2 Hybrid Petri Nets

The concept of the continuous and hybrid Petri nets has been presented by David and Alla in 1987 [3,5,6,4]. It is a fluidification of the discrete Petri net. Some places can hold a real valued marking. This paper assumes that the reader is familiar with the basic theory of the Petri nets [1,2]. The Petri net is *persistent* when enabled transitions can only be disabled by its own firing.

2.1 Continuous Petri Nets

Continuous Petri net [6] is defined as a 5-tuple $R_C = (P, T, Pre, Post, M_0)$, where P is a finite set of places and T is a finite set of transitions. $P \neq \emptyset$,

R. Moreno-Díaz et al. (Eds.): EUROCAST 2013, Part I, LNCS 8111, pp. 428–435, 2013.

$T \neq \emptyset$ and $P \cap T = \emptyset$. $Pre : P \times T \rightarrow \mathbb{Q}^+$ is the input incidence matrix. $Post: P \times T \rightarrow \mathbb{Q}^+$ is the output incidence matrix. $M_0 : P \rightarrow \mathbb{R}^+$ is the initial marking[1]. Let $p \in P, t \in T : Pre(p, t)$ is the weight of the arc $p \rightarrow t$; $Post(p, t)$ is the weight of the arc $t \rightarrow p$. If the arc does not exist, the weight is 0. In a graphical representation of the continuous Petri net places are represented by double circles and transitions are represented by empty rectangles (Fig. 1).

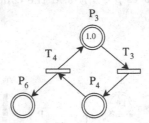

Fig. 1. The unbounded continuous Petri net

The *continuous marking* $m \in (\mathbb{R}^+)^{|P|}$ is a vector of non-negative real numbers. A transition $t \in T$ is *enabled* in a marking m, iff $\forall p \in {}^\bullet t : m(p) > 0$. Enabling of the transition does not depend on the arc weight, it is sufficient that every input place has a non-zero marking. The *enabling degree* q of the transition t for the marking m is the maximal amount that the transition can fire in one go, i.e. $q(t, m) = \min_{p \in {}^\bullet t} (m(p)/Pre(p, t))$. Firing the transition t with a quantity $\alpha < q(t, m), \alpha \in \mathbb{R}^+$ is denoted as $m \overset{\alpha t}{\rightarrow} m'$. $[t]^\alpha$ represents $\alpha \in \mathbb{R}^+$ firings of the transition t at one go. The new marking $m' = m + \alpha.C(P, t)$, where $C = Post - Pre$ is a token-flow matrix. The marking m' is *reachable* from the marking m.

Let m be a marking. The set P of places may be divided into two subsets: $P^+(m)$ the set of places $p \in P$ such that $m(p) > 0$, and the set of places p such that $m(p) = 0$. A *continuous macro-marking* is the union of all markings m with the same set $P^+(m)$ of marked places. Since each continuous macro-marking is based on the Boolean state of every place (marked or not marked), the number of continuous macro-markings is less than or equal to 2^n, where n is the number of places.

2.2 Hybrid Petri Nets

Hybrid Petri net [6] is a 6-tuple $R_H = (P, T, Pre, Post, M_0, h)$, where P is a finite set of discrete and continuous places, T is a finite set of discrete and continuous transitions. $P \neq \emptyset$, $T \neq \emptyset$ and $P \cap T = \emptyset$. $Pre : P \times T \rightarrow \mathbb{Q}^+$ or $\mathbb{N}$ is the input incidence matrix. $Post: P \times T \rightarrow \mathbb{Q}^+$ or $\mathbb{N}$ is the output incidence matrix.

---

[1] Notation $\mathbb{Q}^+$ corresponds to the non-negative rational numbers and notation $\mathbb{R}^+$ corresponds to the non-negative real numbers (both including zero).

Let $p \in P, t \in T$: $Pre(p,t)$ is the weight of the arc $p \to t$; $Post(p,t)$ is the weight of the arc $t \to p$. If the arc does not exist, the weight is 0. A graphical representation of the hybrid Petri net is shown in Fig. 2. $M_0 : P \to \mathbb{R}^+$ or $\mathbb{N}$ is the *initial marking*. A function $h : P \cup T \to \{D, C\}$ is called a *hybrid function*, that indicates for every node whether it is a discrete node (sets P_D and T_D) or a continuous one (sets P_C and T_C). In the definitions of Pre, $Post$ and m_0, the set $\mathbb{N}$ corresponds to the case where $p \in P_D$ and the set $\mathbb{Q}^+$ to the case where $p \in P_C$. For the discrete places $p \in P_D$ and the continuous transitions $t \in T_C$ must hold $Pre(p,t) = Post(p,t)$.

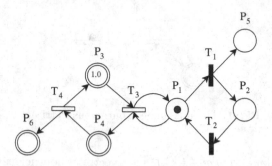

Fig. 2. The unbounded hybrid Petri net

The *hybrid marking* for the hybrid Petri net is a couple $m = (m_D, m_C)$, where m_D denotes the marking of the discrete places and m_C denotes the continuous macro-marking of the continuous places. The discrete transition $t \in T_D$ is *enabled* in a marking m, iff $\forall p \in {}^\bullet t : m(p) \geq Pre(p,t)$. The *enabling degree* q of the discrete transition t for the marking m is integer $q(t,m) = \min_{p \in {}^\bullet t} (m(p)/Pre(p,t))$. For continuous places $p \in {}^\bullet t \wedge p \in P_C$ the edge $p \to t$ is a treshold for marking in the place p for enabling the discrete transition t. A continuous transition $t \in T_C$ is *enabled* in a marking m, iff $\forall p \in {}^\bullet t \wedge p \in P_D : m(p) \geq Pre(p,t)$ and $\forall p \in {}^\bullet t \wedge p \in P_C : m(p) > 0$. The *enabling degree* q of the continuous transition t for the marking m is $q(t,m) = \min_{p \in {}^\bullet t} (m(p)/Pre(p,t))$.

3   Unfoldings

The unfolding [9,7,8,10,11] is a useful partial-order method for analysis and verification of the Petri net properties. This technique can cope well with the so-called state space explosion [12], specially for the Petri nets with a lot of concurrency. The state space of the Petri net is represented by an acyclic net with a simpler structure than the Petri net. The unfolding represents all reachable states of the Petri net and can be infinite if the Petri net has a cycle. However it can be truncated before it starts to repeat.

Our approach combines the macro-markings from the so-called case graph for the continuous Petri nets [6,13] with the idea of the coverability unfolding for the unbounded discrete Petri nets [15]. Continuous conditions in the unfolding can have associated a symbol representing the macro-marking thus some nonzero real marking. Discrete conditions in the unfolding can have associated a symbol ω representing that the corresponding place is unbounded.

A *net* is a triple $N = (P, T, F)$, where P is a finite set of places and T is a finite set of transitions. $P \neq \emptyset$, $T \neq \emptyset$ and $P \cap T = \emptyset$. $F \subseteq (P \times T) \cup (T \times P)$ is a flow relation.

An *occurrence net* is a net $O = (B, E, G)$, where B is a set of occurence of places, E is a set of occurrence of transitions. O is acyclic and G is the acyclic flow relation, i.e. for every $x, y \in B \cup E : xG^+y \Rightarrow \neg yG^+x$, where G^+ is a transitive closure of G. Let us denote $x < y$, iff xG^+y, and $x \leq y$, iff $x < y$ or $x = y$. The relation $<$, resp. $\leq$ is a partial order relation. Nodes $x, y \in (P \cup T)$ are in a *conflict* relation, denoted by $x \# y$, iff $\exists t_1, t_2 \in T : t_1 \neq t_2 \wedge {}^{\bullet}t_1 \cap {}^{\bullet}t_2 \neq \emptyset \wedge t_1 \leq x \wedge t_2 \leq y$. Nodes $x, y \in (P \cup T)$ are in a *concurrency* relation, denoted by x *co* y, if neither $x < y$ nor $y < x$ nor $x \# y$. For every $b \in B : |{}^{\bullet}b| \leq 1$. For every $x \in (B \cup E) : \neg(x \# x)$, i.e. no element is in confict with itself. The set of elements $\{y \in (B \cup E) | y < x\}$ is finite, i.e. O is finitely preceded. $Min(O)$ denotes the set of minimal elements of $B \cup E$ with respect to the relation $\leq$, i.e. the elements with an empty preset.

A *homomorfism* from the occurrence net O to the hybrid Petri net $R_H = (P, T, Pre, Post, M_0, h)$ is a mapping $p : B \cup E \to P \cup T$ such that $p(B) \subseteq P$ and $p(E) \subseteq T$, i.e. preserves the nature of nodes. For every $e \in E : p({}^{\bullet}e) = {}^{\bullet}p(e) \wedge p(e^{\bullet}) = p(e)^{\bullet}$, i.e. p preserves the environment of transitions. The restriction of p to $Min(O)$ is a bijection between $Min(O)$ and M_0.

A *hybrid branching process* of the unbounded hybrid Petri net R_H is a quadruple $\pi_H = (B, E, G, p, d, w) = (O, p, d, w)$, where O is the labelled occurrence net and $p(x) = y$ denotes labelling element x as element y. A mapping $d : E \to \{m_1, \ldots, m_{|P|}\} \cup \{0\}$ labels transitions occurrences with symbol m_i indicating maximal firing degree or with 0 indicating arbitrary lower degree (that will not be depicted). A mapping $w : B \to \{\omega, 1\}$ labels discrete places occurrences with symbol ω indicating an unbounded discrete place or with 1 otherwise (that will not be depicted). The type of the node determines its graphical representation. Every node $e \in E : p(e) \in T_C$ is represented by double rectangle and every node $b \in B : p(b) \in P_C$ is represented by double circle with the name of the corresponding marking.

A hybrid branching process $\pi'_H = (O', p', d', w')$ is a *prefix* of π_H, denoted by $\pi'_H \sqsubseteq \pi_H$, if $O' = (B', E', G')$ is a subnet of O satisfying $Min(O)$ belongs to O'; if $e \in E'$ and $(b, e) \in G$ or $(e, b) \in G$ then $b \in B'$; if $b \in B'$ and $(e, b) \in G$ then $e \in E'$; p' is the restriction of p to $B' \cup E'$. For every R_H there exists a unique (up to isomorphism) maximal (w.r.t. $\sqsubseteq$) branching process that is called *unfolding*.

A *configuration* of the occurrence net O is a set of the transitions occurrences $C \subseteq E$ such that for all $e_1, e_2 \in C : \neg(e_1 \# e_2)$, i.e. C is conflict-free. For every $e_1 \in C : e_2 \leq e_1 \Rightarrow e_2 \in C$, i.e. C is causally closed. A *local configuration* $[e]$ for the transition occurrence $e \in E$ is a set $[e] = \{e' \in E | e' \leq e\}$.

A set of places occurrences $D \subseteq B$ is called a *co-set*, iff for all distinct $d_1, d_2 \in D : d_1 \ co \ d_2$. A *cut* is the maximal (w.r.t. set inclusion) co-set. For every $d_1, d_2 \in D$, if $p(d_1) = p(d_2)$ then $d_1 = d_2$. Let C be the finite configuration of the hybrid branching process π_H. Then $Cut(C) = (Min(O) \cup C^\bullet) \setminus {}^\bullet C$ is a cut. A set $Mark(C) = p(Cut(C))$ is the reachable hybrid macro marking of the hybrid Petri net R_H.

An *adequate order* $\lhd$ is a strict well-founded partial order on the local configurations such that for two transitions occurrences $e_1, e_2 \in E : [e_1] \subset [e_2] \Rightarrow [e_1] \lhd [e_2]$. The transition occurrence $e_1 \in E$ is a *cut-off* transition induced by $\lhd$, iff there is a corresponding transition $e_2 \in E$ with $Mark([e_1]) = Mark([e_2])$ and $[e_2] \lhd [e_1]$. The order $\lhd$ is a refined partial order from [9]. For the hybrid branching process π_H and every $e_1, e_2 \in E : p(e_1) \in T_D \land p(e_2) \in T_C \Rightarrow [e_1] \lhd [e_2]$. For every $e_1, e_2 \in E : d(e_1) \neq 0 \land d(e_2) = 0 \Rightarrow [e_1] \lhd [e_2]$.

The hybrid branching process is *complete*, iff for every reachable hybrid macro marking $M \in [M_0 >$ of the hybrid Petri net R_H there is the configuration C of π_H such that $M = Mark(C)$ and for every transition $t \in T$ enabled in M there is the finite configuration C and the transition occurrence $e \in C$ such that $M = Mark(C)$, $p(e) = t$ and $C \cup \{e\}$ is the configuration.

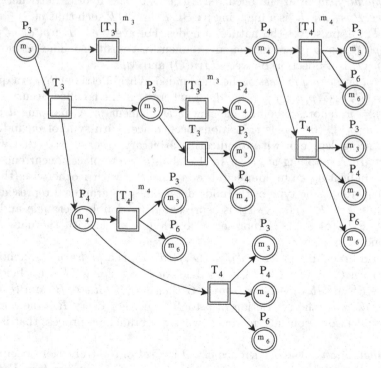

Fig. 3. The prefix of the unfolding of the unbounded continuous Petri net from Fig. 1

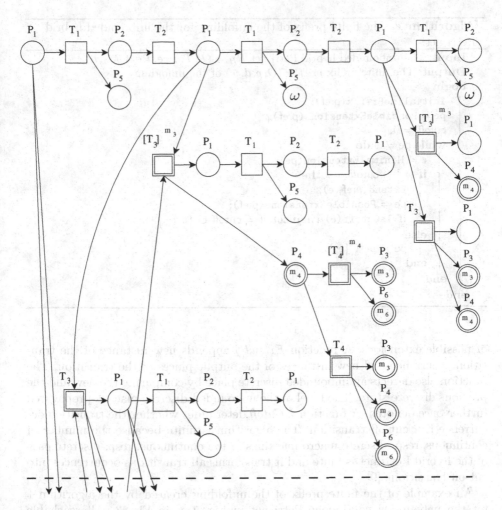

Fig. 4. The main segment of the finite prefix of the unfolding of the unbounded hybrid Petri net from Fig. 2. The whole prefix is not depicted because of size limitations.

4   Algorithm

The algorithm 1 is a modified and extended algorithm presented in [8]. It constructs the finite and complete prefix of the unfolding of the unbounded hybrid Petri net. A function *InitializePrefix()* initializes the prefix *pref* with instances of the places from M_0. A function *PossibleExtensions()* finds the set of possible extensions of the hybrid branching process *pref* using possible transitions firings for the hybrid Petri net, including continuous transitions firings with the maximal degree. The decision version of this function is NP-complete in the size of the prefix *pref*. A function *MinimalExtension()* chooses the transition occurrence with minimal local configuration with respect to the order ⊲ from the set

---

Algorithm 1. The finite prefix of the unfolding for the unbounded hybrid Petri net.

Input: The unbounded hybrid Petri net $R_H = (P, T, Pre, Post, M_0, h)$
Output: The finite prefix $pref = (O, p, d, w)$ of the unfolding
begin

    InitializePrefix(pref);
    pe = PossibleExtensions(pref);
    cutoff = $\emptyset$;
    while pe $\neq \emptyset$ **do**
        e = MinimalExtension(pe);
        if [e] $\cap$ cutoff = $\emptyset$ **then**
            Extend(pref, e);
            pe = PossibleExtensions(pref);
            if IsCutoff(e) **then** cutoff = cutoff $\cup$ {e };
        else
            | pe = pe \ {e };
        end
    end
end

---

of possible extensions. A function *Extend()* appends new instance of the transition occurrence and new instances of the output places of the transition. The function also detects an unbounded discrete place by comparing the new and the previous discrete state. The label of the unbounded discrete place is propagated further once denoted. A function *IsCutoff* determines whether the transition occurrence is a cut-off transition. The algorithm is finite because the number of continuous, resp. discrete macro markings in the continuous, resp. discrete part of the hybrid Petri net is finite and it transforms all transitions occurrences into cut-off transitions [9].

An example of the finite prefix of the unfolding created by the algorithm 1 for the unbounded continuous Petri net in Fig. 1 is in Fig. 3. All reachable continuous macro markings are represented by cuts.

The image in Fig. 2 shows very simple, yet typical example from the application domain of the hybrid Petri nets, where the discrete part enables or disables the continuous transitions. An example of the complete and finite prefix of the unfolding created by the algorithm 1 for the unbounded hybrid Petri net in Fig. 2 is in Fig. 4. The image shows only the most interesting part of the whole prefix because of size limitations. It can be seen how the unbounded discrete place is detected and propagated further.

5   Conclusion and Future Work

We have introduced the algorithm for computation of the unfolding for the ordinary unbounded hybrid Petri nets and shown the corresponding definitions. Some information regarding reachability is lost due to the abstraction in the continuous and discrete macro markings. Nevertheless, advantages of the unfolding remain. Analysis of the partial order between the transitions occurrences and checking on persistency by analysing the conflicts between the transitions occurrences in the unfolding is simpler due to absence of cycles. It preserves concurrency and explicitly represents conflicts.

In the future we plan to develop algorithms for analysing properties of the hybrid Petri nets from the unfolding.

Acknowledgements. This work was supported by the Czech Science Foundation (P103/10/0306), the Czech Ministry of Education (MSM 0021630528) and the EU/Czech IT4Innovations Centre of Excellence project CZ.1.05/1.1.00/02.0070.

References

1. Reisig, W.: Petri Nets - an Introduction, Berlin (1985)
2. Desel, J., Juhás, G.: What Is a Petri Net? In: Ehrig, H., Juhás, G., Padberg, J., Rozenberg, G. (eds.) APN 2001. LNCS, vol. 2128, pp. 1–25. Springer, Heidelberg (2001)
3. David, R., Alla, H.: Continuous Petri nets. In: Proc. of the 8th European Workshop on Application an Theory of Petri Nets, Zaragoza, Spain, pp. 275–294 (1987)
4. Recalde, L., Teruel, E., Silva, M.: Autonomous Continuous P/T Systems. In: Donatelli, S., Kleijn, J. (eds.) ICATPN 1999. LNCS, vol. 1639, pp. 107–126. Springer, Heidelberg (1999)
5. David, R., Alla, H.: Continuous and hybrid Petri nets. Journal of Circuits, Systems, and Computers (1998)
6. David, R., Alla, H.: Discreet, Continuous and hybrid Petri nets. Springer, Berlin (2005)
7. McMillan, K.L.: A Technique of State Space Search Based on Unfolding. Formal Methods in System Design 6, 45–65 (1995)
8. Esparza, J., Romer, S., Vogler, W.: An Improvement of McMillan's Unfolding Algorithm. Formal Methods in System Design 20 (2002)
9. Esparza, J., Heljanko, K.: Unfoldings - a partial-order approach to model checking. EATCS Monographs in Theoretical Computer Science. Springer (2008)
10. Khomenko, V., Koutny, M.: Towards an Efficient Algorithm for Unfolding Petri Nets. In: Larsen, K.G., Nielsen, M. (eds.) CONCUR 2001. LNCS, vol. 2154, pp. 366–380. Springer, Heidelberg (2001)
11. Weidlich, M., Elliger, F., Weske, M.: Generalised Computation of Behavioural Profiles Based on Petri-Net Unfoldings. In: Bravetti, M., Bultan, T. (eds.) WS-FM 2010. LNCS, vol. 6551, pp. 101–115. Springer, Heidelberg (2011)
12. Valmari, A.: The State Explosion Problem. In: Reisig, W., Rozenberg, G. (eds.) APN 1998. LNCS, vol. 1491, pp. 429–528. Springer, Heidelberg (1998)
13. Novosad, P., Češka, M.: Algorithms for Computing Coverability Graphs for Hybrid Petri Nets. In: MEMICS, pp. 177–183. MUNI, Brno (2008)
14. Novosad, P., Češka, M.: Unfoldings of Bounded Hybrid Petri Nets. In: Moreno-Díaz, R., Pichler, F., Quesada-Arencibia, A. (eds.) EUROCAST 2011, Part I. LNCS, vol. 6927, pp. 543–550. Springer, Heidelberg (2012)
15. Desel, J., Juhás, G., Neumair, C.: Finite Unfoldings of Unbounded Petri Nets. In: Cortadella, J., Reisig, W. (eds.) ICATPN 2004. LNCS, vol. 3099, pp. 157–176. Springer, Heidelberg (2004)

Petri Net Dynamic Partial Reconfiguration in FPGA

Arkadiusz Bukowiec and Michał Doligalski

Institute of Computer Engineering and Electronics, University of Zielona Góra,
Zielona Góra, Poland
{a.bukowiec,m.doligalski}@iie.uz.zgora.pl
http://www.iie.uz.zgora.pl/

Abstract. The rigorous digital design of embedded Application Specific
Logic Controllers starts from algorithm designed with concurrent hierarchical control interpreted Petri net and then implemented into FPGA.
But, there could be required to have several contexts of work mode of
such device. The classic design flows includes all contexts in one control
algorithm together with switching handling. The design flow proposed in
this paper uses feature of dynamic partial reconfiguration of new FPGA
devices. There is proposed a way of design of a top level Petri net and
subnets describing particular contexts and its connections. The rules of
implementation are also formed.

Keywords: FPGAs, Logic controllers, Petri nets, Reconfiguration.

1 Introduction

Concurrent logic controllers [3,16] have many fields of industrial applications.
The digital design of such controllers can be implemented in many ways, for
e.g., with use of microprocessors [18], as embedded systems [5,15] or using programmable logic devices [3,6]. On the other hand, concurrent logic controllers
could have several contexts of work mode. In case of classical design flow there
is required to include all contexts in control algorithm together with switching
handling. Very often it makes that control algorithm is complicated. The main
feature of contexts is fact that there is no need to switch between them very
often. In such a situation the design of one huge control algorithm is no effective. Regarding to the classical design flow the option is to design one control
algorithm for each context and reprogram the logic controller in aim to switch
between contexts. Such solution is not efficient because control algorithms differs
in small parts, it also required to stop the controller for reprogramming process
and the reprogramming process is time consuming.

The new idea is to apply partial reconfiguration of control algorithm. It is
possible how long the modern FPGAs have such feature [12]. But, it required to
elaborate new design methodology. Such methodology with application of Petri
net as a models of concurrent logic controllers [3] is presented in this paper.

R. Moreno-Díaz et al. (Eds.): EUROCAST 2013, Part I, LNCS 8111, pp. 436–443, 2013.

2   Control Interpreted Petri Net

An interpreted Petri net [1,10] is an extension of a simple Petri net [17] about a feature for information exchange. This exchange is made by use of binary signals. It is required for a models of concurrent logic controllers [13,2] to establish communication with enviroment.Such Petri net is defined as a 7-tuple

$$PN = (P, T, F, M_0, X, Y, Z),   \tag{1}$$

where:

P is a finite non-empty set of places,
   $P = \{p_1, \ldots, p_M\}$,
T is a finite non-empty set of transitions,
   $T = \{t_1, \ldots, t_S\}$,
F is a set of arcs from places to transitions and from transitions to places:

$$F \subseteq (P \times T) \cup (T \times P),$$
$$P \cap T = \varnothing,$$

M_0 is an initial marking,
X is a set of input variables, $X = \{x_1, \ldots, x_L\}$,
Y is a set of output variables, $Y = \{y_1, \ldots, y_N\}$,
Z is a set of internal communication variables, typically it is not used and $Z = \varnothing$.

Sets of input and output transitions of a place $p_m \in P$ are defined respectively as follows:

$$\bullet p_m = \{t_s \in T : (t_s, p_m) \in F\},$$
$$p_m \bullet = \{t_s \in T : (p_m, t_s) \in F\}.$$

Sets of input and output places of a transition $t_s \in T$ are defined respectively as follows:

$$\bullet t_s = \{p_m \in P : (p_m, t_s) \in F\},$$
$$t_s \bullet = \{p_m \in P : (t_s, p_m) \in F\}.$$

A marking of a Petri net is defined as a function:

$$M : P \to \mathbb{N}.$$

It describes a number of tokens $M(p_m)$ situated in a place p_m. When a place or a set of places contain a token it is marked. The initial marking M_0 defines positions of tokens when the algorithm is started.

A transition t_s can be fired if all its input places are marked and a condition φ_s returns value true. Firing of a transition removes tokens from its input places and puts one token in each output place. The condition φ_s is defined as Boolean function of the input or internal variables form sets X and Z. In particular case the condition φ_s can be simple equal to true.

In case of Moore type interpreted Petri net, ψ_m is an elementary conjunction of affirmation of some output variables form the set Y. Each such conjunction ψ_m is associated to place p_m. If the place p_m is marked the output variables from corresponding conjunction ψ_m are being set otherwise they are being reset.

In case of Mealy type interpreted Petri net ψ_s is an elementary conjunction of affirmation or negation of some output variables form the set Y. When transition t_s is fired variables from corresponding conjunction ψ_s are being set if their affirmation belongs to this conjunction and they are being reset if their negation belongs to this conjunction. The value of non used variables in corresponding conjunction ψ_s remain unchanged.

An interpreted Petri net can be extended with a hierarchy by application of macroplaces [11,7]. A macroplace correspond to a part of a net. The macroplaces theory is well developed and includes many classes of macroplaces. In this article we make frequent use of macroplaces, that are limited to have one input and one output.

3   Method Overview

The control algorithm of concurrent logic controller have to be designed as a Petri net. The parts of the net that should have several contexts of work should be closed in macroplace [11]. Then the content of macroplace should be designed as a subnet. Each context should be described be separate subnet. It means that there could be designed several contexts for each macroplace.

After designing the control algorithm with all contexts the synchronization between top-level Petri net and subnets should be done. This synchronization works in such manner:

- the transition of top-level net that fires the macroplace should generate Mealy output signal $y_{start(mp_m)}$,
- the subnet have additional place pw to represent no operation state,
- the transition of subnet that take token from the place pw should have condition with signal x_{start}, the source of this signal is the signal $y_{start(mp_m)}$,
- the subnet have place pe to represent the end of its operation, it could be last place of original algorithm or it have to be added as additional place, there is generated Moore signal y_{end} to inform top-level net about the fact of finishing of operation,
- the transition of top-level net that take token from the place mp_m should have condition with signal $x_{end(mp_m)}$, the source of this signal is the signal y_{end}, this transition should also generate acknowledgment Mealy output signal $y_{ack(mp_m)}$,
- the transition of subnet that take token from the place pe should have condition with signal x_{ack}, the source of this signal is the signal $y_{ack(mp_m)}$, this transition moves token to the place pw.

Then, Petri nets can be described in HDLs on behavioral level [9] or logic level [4]. There have to be created top-level module for macro Petri net and one module for each context. The modules that describe different contexts of the same macro place should have the same name. These modules should also have the same list of input and output signals. If some of output signals are not used in particular context they should be set to constant logic value 0. If some of input signals are not used in particular context they should be ignored in algorithm description but they have to appear on input list. Then, such module should be instantiated as a component in the top-level module.

Such described model of a concurrent logic controller can be passed into third party synthesis tool. It is very important to synthesis top-level module without any context and contexts separately. During synthesis of top-level module the components for reconfigurable macro place are treated as black-boxes. During synthesis of contexts the inserting of input/output buffers should be turned off. Such received netlists are base to create a configurations of FPGA device. There is created full configuration for each context based on top-level netlist and particular context(s) netlist(s). The full configuration is used for initial programming of the device. There is also created partial configuration for each context netlist. It can be used for partial reconfiguration of the FPGA.

4   Sample Application

The method of Petri net partial reconfiguration, described in the previous section, is illustrated by designing the control algorithm for industrial mixer of aggregate content and water (Fig. 1a) [8,14]. The control algorithm is extended with the possibility of heating the water (Fig. 1b) in the second context of work. The example Petri net PN$_1$ (Fig. 2a) describes this algorithm.

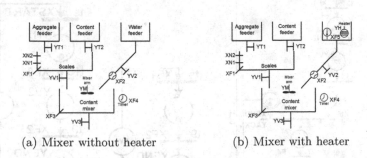

(a) Mixer without heater   (b) Mixer with heater

Fig. 1. Industrial mixer

There is extracted one macroplace mp_1. This macroplace represents the part of control algorithm that is responsible for adding and possibility of heating water. It going to be described be two contexts. First context only add required amount of water (Fig. 2b) and the second one first heat water and then add it

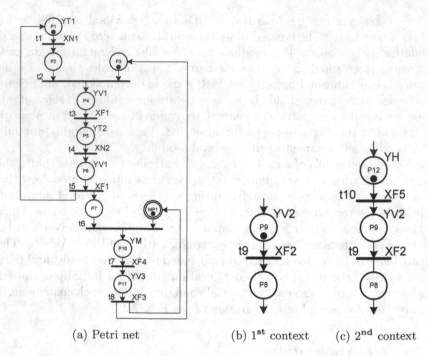

(a) Petri net   (b) 1st context   (c) 2nd context

Fig. 2. An example of Petri net with two contexts of macroplace

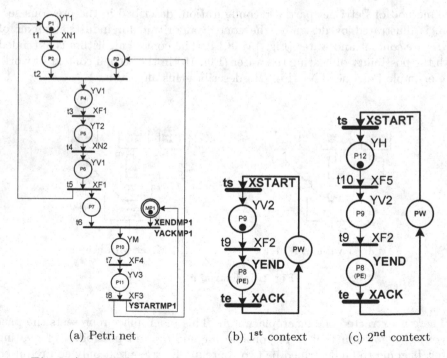

(a) Petri net   (b) 1st context   (c) 2nd context

Fig. 3. An example of Petri net with two contexts with synchronization

(Fig. 2c). Outputs of the controller are connected into valves of tanks and engine of mixer. Inputs gives information about state of tanks, scale, timer, flow meter and temperature.

Such designed control algorithm have to be extended with synchronization (Fig. 3). Because, there is only one macroplace mp_1 designed for reconfiguration there are addend two Mealy output signals $y_{start(mp_1)}$ (transition t_8) and $y_{ack(mp_1)}$ (transition t_6) to top-level net (Fig. 3a) and they are marked by bold in the figure. The subnets were also modified (Figs. 3b, 3c). There was added additional place pw and there have to be added additional two transitions t_s and t_e to fire and leave this place and there were added two input signals x_{start} (transition t_s) and x_{ack} (transition t_e) and one Moore output signal y_{end} (place p_8) to each context subnet. In this case, in both contexts, the place p_e is represented by the last place of the algorithm p_8. In this approach, top-level net and subnets were described on behavioral level in VHDL by method oriented on transitions. The top-level net is described as typical Petri net with one process but additionally it has instantiation of component **pn1mp1** (Fig. 4). It is responsible for operation of particular context and its algorithm is under reconfiguration. To handle the synchronization there are defined internal signals and they are mapped with component. Subnets are also described with one process. The example control algorithm was tested with XUPV5-LX110T Development System. The design was synthesized with Xilnix XST in Xilnix ISE and the implemented in Xilnix PlanAhead. There were also setup all contexts during implementation (Fig. 5). For the testing purpose the design was extended with onchip generator of stimuators and then it was analyzed with use of logic analyzer. The sample captured waveform is shown in figure 6. There is shown one cycel of control algrithm forking in first mode. There are visible additional signals CFG_A, CFG_B, and *trigger*. First two signals indicate wich context of the controller is activ and the last one idicates the start of simulation and triggs the logic analizer to the capture mode.

```
architecture pn1top of pn1top is
  (...)
  signal YackMP1, YstartMP1, XendMP1: std_logic;
  component pn1mp1
    port(CLK, RESET, XF2, XF5, Xack, Xstart : in STD_LOGIC;
         YH, YV2, Yend : out STD_LOGIC);
  end component;
begin
  CMP1: pn1mp1 port map(CLK => CLK, RESET => RESET,
      XF2 => XF2, XF5 => XF5, Xack => YackMP1, Xstart => YstartMP1,
      YH => YH, YV2 => YV2, Yend => XendMP1);
  OT: process (CLK)
  (...)
  end process;
end pn2top;
```

Fig. 4. Part of VHDL description of top-level net

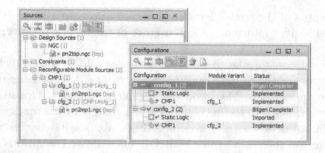

Fig. 5. Contexts configuration in PlanAhead

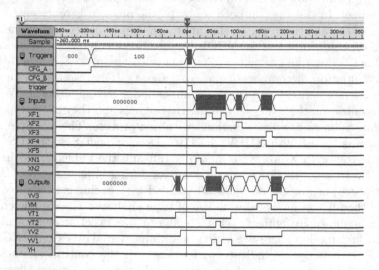

Fig. 6. Waveform of first context

5 Summary

The presented methodology shorts the time of changing the context of concurrent logic controller. Additionally the reconfiguration can be made dynamically, it means that there is no need to stop the control algorithm because other parts of device works continuously. Because the implemented control algorithm (with one context) is less complicated that the control algorithm with all contexts it consume less hardware elements of FPGA device and it is also less power consuming.

References

1. Adamski, M., Monteiro, J.L., Fengler, W., Wendt, A.: A distributed Petri net-based discrete controller system. In: Proceedings of the Conference on Automatic Control, Control 1996, Porto, Portugal, vol. 2, pp. 777–782 (1996)

2. Adamski, M., Węgrzyn, M.: Petri nets mapping into reconfigurable logic controllers. Electronics and Telecommunications Quarterly 55(2), 157–182 (2009)
3. Biliński, K., Adamski, M., Saul, J., Dagless, E.: Petri-net-based algorithms for parallel-controller synthesis. IEE Proceedings – Computers and Digital Techniques 141(6), 405–412 (1994)
4. Bukowiec, A., Adamski, M.: Synthesis of Petri nets into FPGA with operation flexible memories. In: Proceedings of the IEEE 15th International Symposium on Design and Diagnostics of Electronic Circuits and Systems, DDECS 2012, Tallinn, Estonia, pp. 16–21 (2012)
5. Bukowiec, A., Węgrzyn, M.: Design of logic controllers for safety critical systems using FPGAs with embedded microprocessors. In: Colnaric, M., Halang, W.A., Węgrzyn, M. (eds.) Real-Time Programming 2004. A Proceedings Volume from the 28th IFAC/IFIP Workshop, WRTP 2004, pp. 97–102. Elsevier, Oxford (2005)
6. Chang, N., Kwon, W.H., Park, J.: Hardware implementation of real-time Petri-net-based controllers. Control Engineering Practice 6(7), 889–895 (1998), http://www.sciencedirect.com/science/article/pii/S0967066198000768
7. Esparza, J., Silva, M.: On the analysis and synthesis of free choice systems. In: Rozenberg, G. (ed.) APN 1990. LNCS, vol. 483, pp. 243–286. Springer, Heidelberg (1991)
8. Gniewek, L., Kluska, J.: Hardware implementation of fuzzy Petri net as a controller. IEEE Transactions on Systems, Man, and Cybernetics – Part B: Cybernetics 34(3), 1315–1324 (2004)
9. Gomes, L., Costa, A., Barros, J., Lima, P.: From Petri net models to VHDL implementation of digital controllers. In: 33rd Annual Conference of the IEEE Industrial Electronics Society, IECON 2007, pp. 94–99. IEEE, Taipei (2007)
10. Karatkevich, A.: Dynamic Analysis of Petri Net-Based Discrete Systems. LNCIS, vol. 356. Springer, Berlin (2007)
11. Karatkevich, A.: On macroplaces in Petri nets. In: Proceedings of IEEE East-West Design & Test Symposium, EWDTS 2008, pp. 418–422. IEEE, Lviv (2008)
12. Koch, D.: Partial Reconfiguration on FPGAs. LNCIS, vol. 153. Springer, New York (2013)
13. Kozłowski, T., Dagless, E., Saul, J., Adamski, M., Szajna, J.: Parallel controller synthesis using Petri nets. IEE Proceedings – Computers and Digital Techniques 142(4), 263–271 (1995)
14. Łabiak, G., Adamski, M., Doligalski, M., Tkacz, J., Bukowiec, A.: UML modelling in rigorous design methodology for discrete controllers. International Journal of Electronics and Telecommunications 58(1), 27–34 (2012)
15. Ma, L., Xia, F., Peng, Z.: Integrated design and implementation of embedded control systems with scilab. Sensors 8(9), 5501–5515 (2008)
16. Milik, A., Hrynkiewicz, E.: Reconfigurable logic controller, architecture, programming, implementation. In: Ciazynski, W., Hrynkiewicz, E., Klosowski, P. (eds.) Programmable Devices and Systems 2001. A Proceedings Volume from the 5th IFAC Workshop, PDS 2001, pp. 163–168. Pergamon, London (2002)
17. Murata, T.: Petri nets: Properties, analysis and applications. Proceedings of the IEEE 77(4), 541–580 (1989), http://ieeexplore.ieee.org/lpdocs/epic03/wrapper.htm?arnumber=24143
18. Nhivekar, G.S., Nirmale, S.S., Mudholker, R.: Implementation of fuzzy logic control algorithm in embedded microcomputers for dedicated application. International Journal of Engineering, Science and Technology 3(4), 276–283 (2011)

Operating System for Petri Nets-Specified Reconfigurable Embedded Systems

Tomáš Richta and Vladimír Janoušek

Brno University of Technology, Faculty of Information Technology,
IT4Innovations Centre of Excellence
Božetěchova 2, 612 66 Brno, The Czech Republic
{irichta,janousek}@fit.vutbr.cz

Abstract. This paper describes an operating system (OS) and supporting development tools for Petri nets-specified dynamically reconfigurable embedded control systems construction. We use nets-within-nets paradigm formalized by Reference Nets. This formalism allows for layered architecture that enables the dynamic reconfigurability of the modeled system. Our specific contribution is the idea of code generation for a virtual machine (VM), which is able to interpret a model composed of a set of Petri nets. This VM is part of the OS for the target microcontroller. The proposed OS and application architecture then enables incremental changes within the system specification and implementation during its life-time.

Keywords: model-based design, Reference Nets, nets-within-nets, embedded systems, code generation.

1 Introduction and Motivation

The development and deployment of safe and reliable software for embedded control systems remains the actual challenge to the computer scientists. The most important part of the system development process is testing and verification of the system before its final deployment. Also very important remains the possibility of the system to flexible reflect the changes in requirements after the software deployment. For that it is necessary to enable the incremental changes to the running system and thus modify its behavior. At the same time we need to maintain the model of the system throughout the whole system development process, to keep the testing and verification possible. Prevalent approach to the dynamic reconfigurability within embedded systems nowadays reside in FPGA partial reconfiguration [1]. This approach assume the possibility of partial reconfiguration of the FPGA design, but skips the problem of dynamic reconfigurability of software within microcontrollers that is our area of research.

We use Petri Nets for the system specification, because they can serve as an executable model that allows for the specification debugging, testing, simulation and verification. The main goal of the presented architecture and development process is to provide for dynamic system reconfigurability, which means propagation of the system specification changes to the system implementation while

R. Moreno-Díaz et al. (Eds.): EUROCAST 2013, Part I, LNCS 8111, pp. 444–451, 2013.
© Springer-Verlag Berlin Heidelberg 2013

it is in its run-time. In order to allow the reconfigurability, there is a necessity to decompose the application to some parts, that together represent the whole system functionality. Because we are using Petri nets-based specification, we needed proper decomposition of the system model to a set of subnets, which is called partitioning problem [2]. Our solution to this problem is based on nets-within-nets paradigm [3] formalized as Reference Nets [4]. It is a kind of high-level Petri nets where tokens can represent other Petri Nets. Nets can migrate among various places and each net can use functionality of other nets. Consequently, placing a net to a place of a subsystem may change behavior of the subsystem. This approach is described in [5] and used for modeling a multilayered multi-agent architecture. We use similar, but simplified layered architecture, which is oriented towards the distributed control systems modeling and implementation.

The proposed process of system construction starts with forming the model of the system, which is then used for simulation-based debugging and verification of the specification. An automated lossless transformation of the model into the interpretable code then follows. Finally, the execution of the model on the target platform takes place, as well as its testing using the platform simulator. Dynamic reconfigurability of the target system then lies on the possibility of changing any of the decomposed parts of the system within the system run-time. This approach considers dynamic exchange of chunks of code which can be placed as a data to the memory of the microcontrollers during their run-time. For that purpose we decided to directly interpret the Petri Net-based models. Each net is represented by a sequence of bytes (so called bytecode). Bytecode represents instructions for a virtual machine installed on the target hardware as a part of the operating system.

The next section describes used formalism and the whole process of system development and deployment. Section Operating System describes the proposed platform for reconfigurable applications. The last section concludes the achieved results.

2   The Formalism and the Development Process

2.1   Reference Nets

We use Reference Nets as a formalism for model specification. The formalism is based on nets-within-nets concept introduced by Valk [3]. This concept enables the nets to be nested in other nets in the form of tokens. As in other high-level Petri nets e.g. Coloured Petri Nets introduced by Jensen [7], there are places and transitions interconnected by arcs. Places may contain tokens. There are quite simple rules for transition execution: if its input places contain tokens specified on its input arcs, it can be executed (fired). Execution of a transition is an event, atomically changing state of the system: tokens specified on transition input arcs are removed from the corresponding places and tokens specified on its output arcs are put to the corresponding places. A transition could also have a guard restricting its fireability and an action allowing to do arbitrary computations as part of transition execution. Reference Nets allow to instantiate net templates and to use the net instances as tokens. More precisely, references to nets are used as tokens. Thus, a token can be either simple object such as a number or a character, as well as a reference to some other net instance. Nets are able to communicate with each other using so-called downlinks and uplinks. An uplink is a special kind of transition which can be executed only as part of another transition which calls it. For example, uplink :foo() can be called by downlink net:foo() which can be specified as part of an action of another transition. Data can be exchanged in both directions during the call. More detailed explanation of r Reference Nets can be found in [4].

Reference Nets allow to construct a system hierarchically, in several levels. Nets can migrate among places in other nets and thus it is possible to dynamically modify functionality of system components, specified by this kind of nets [5]. This is exactly what we need for the specification of potentially reconfigurable systems.

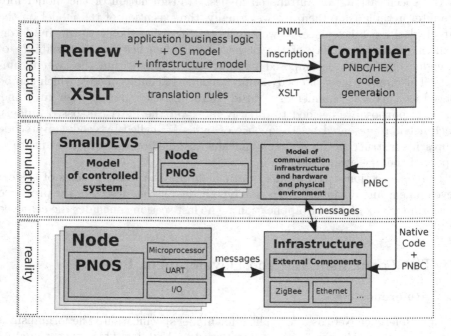

Fig. 1. Application development process

2.2 The Development Process

The development process is described in Figure 1. It starts with the system specification using Reference Nets framework Renew [6] which is then followed by the transformation of the models to the Petri Net Byte Code (PNBC). It is also possible to generate native code, and deploy it directly to the chip, but this approach dramatically reduces the level of reconfigurability. After the bytecode was prepared it is then used for the target system simulation within the SmallDEVS

[8] environment. SmallDEVS can be used for realistic simulation of the whole system with its surroundings. Statistics gathered from simulation experiments can be used for verification purposes and also can support decisions about type of hardware for target system implementation. Then, the hardware components for the target implementation are installed with the Petri Net Operating System (PNOS) and then the nets can be sent to those subsystems. They can also be reinstalled later. This is how the deployment and maintenance of the system is achieved.

3 Operating System

We consider distributed control systems based on Wireless Sensor Networks as a targeted application area. Each node of a distributed control system contains an operating system (PNOS) which is able to host Petri nets-specified applications. PNOS comprise the PNOS kernel and the platform net. PNOS kernel contains PNVM (Petri Net Virtual Machine) which interprets Petri nets that are installed in the system in form of a bytecode (PNBC). PNOS also supports access of the application program to the hardware inputs and outputs including parallel digital and analog inputs and outputs (which are obviously connected to sensors and actuators), as well as serial communication port (which is obviously connected to Zigbee radio module).

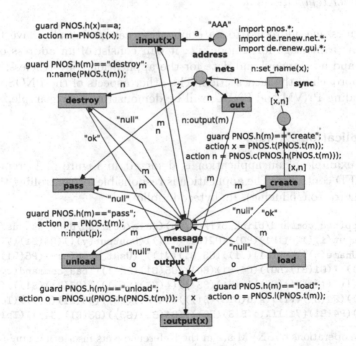

Fig. 2. Platform net

3.1 Platform

The root net (first process) interpreted in PNOS is the Platform Net (see Figure 2). Platform Net is responsible for interpretation of commands which are read from buffered serial line. Using primitive operations of PNVM,[1] it preforms the commands for installation, instantiation, and uninstallation of other Petri nets. The Platform net also allows to pass messages to the other layers of the system which are responsible for application-specific functionality. Since we need reconfigurability in all levels, the installation and uninstallation functionality has to be implemented in each level which is responsible for it.

Thanks to the Platform functionality, a node can understand to and perform commands specified by messages which can be sent to the node via serial line (obviously connected to radio). General form of a message is:

$$< address > < command > < data >$$

Address is the name of the node (and platform). Command and data can be any of the following ones:

load *net_template_bytecode*,
create *net_template_name net_instance_name*,
pass *message_for_an_application*,
destroy *net_instance_name*,
unload *net_template_name*,
dump.

A nested message addressed to an application can potentially have the same structure as a message for a node, i.e. it can consist of an address of an application, and a command and data for the application. Nevertheless, we use a simpler approach in the next section. The other aspects of the PNOS functionality, including PNVM and PNBC, will be demonstrated by example.

3.2 Application Example

A simple example of an application is depicted in Figure 3. It represents a blinking LED controller. The application is responsible for controlling the status of the LED (on/off/blinking). Its bytecode follows.

```
(Nblink-app(bad_command/blink/off/ok/on)(idle/command/done/status/blinker
/name)(Uinput(x)()(P1(B1)(B0))(O2(B1)(V1)))(Uoutput(y)()(P3(B1)(V1))(O1(B
1)(B0)))(Uname(n)()(P6(B1)(V1))(O6(B1)(V1)))(Uset_name(n)()(P6(B1)(B1))(O
6(B1)(V1)))(I(O1(B1)(B0))(O4(B1)(B0))(O5(B1)(B0)))(Tbad_command(cmd)(P2(B
1)(V1))(G(!(|(|(|(=(V1)(S2))(=(V1)(S3)))(=(V1)(S5)))))(O3(B1)(S1)))(Ton(x)(
P2(B1)(S5))(P4(B1)(V1))(A(o(B13)(B1)))(O4(B1)(S5))(O3(B1)(S4)))(Toff(x)(P
2(B1)(S3))(P4(B1)(V1))(A(o(B13)(B0)))(O4(B1)(S3))(O3(B1)(S4)))(Tblink(x)(
```

---

[1] Primitive operations of PNVM are in the Reference Nets inscription language available as PNOS.*operation*, e.g., PNOS.o(13,1) sets i/o pin 13 to value 1, PNOS.h(m) gets first space-separated substring from string m, and PNOS.t(m) returns the rest of the string m without the first substring.

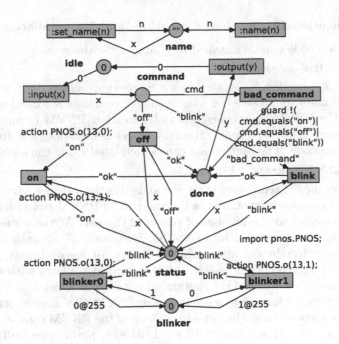

Fig. 3. Application net

P2(B1)(S2))(P4(B1)(V1))(04(B1)(S2))(03(B1)(S4)))(Tblinker0()(P4(B1)(S2))(
P5(B1)(B1))(A(o(B13)(B0)))(04(B1)(S2))(Y5(B1)(B0)(I255)))(Tblinker1()(P4(
B1)(S2))(P5(B1)(B0))(A(o(B13)(B1)))(04(B1)(S2))(Y5(B1)(B1)(I255))))

It is a text representation of the bytecode. In this representation, numbers are represented as a text and also some spaces and line breaks are added. This means that the actual contents of the code memory is a bit more condensed. Each byte of the code is either an instruction for PNVM, or a data.

The bytecode contains symbols (strings) definition and places declaration, followed by a code for each uplink (U), initialization (I), and each transition (T). Each transition or uplink description consists of preconditions (P), guard (G), action (A) postconditions (O), and delayed postconditions (Y) in a form of instructions for the PNVM. Transition pre- and postconditions are specified as tuples containing a data and a place index. Action or guard is specified as a primitive operation call in a LISP-like notation, i.e. arguments can be also function calls. Each data element is a tuple consisting of a type (B - byte, I - integer, S - symbol/string index, V - variable index) and a value. Variables are declared as part of each transition code. Uplinks have parameters declaration. Initialization contains only postconditions.

Names of transitions, places and variables in the bytecode are not necessary for code execution. The are used for logging and debugging purposes only. Primitive operations in the example are identified as !, |, =, :, o. In general, they implement arithmetic, logic, string, and simple input/output operations.

3.3   Application Installation, Execution, and Uninstallation

An application code can be installed to a node using the message

AAA load *ApplicationByteCode.*

It loads the application bytecode (shown in previous subsection) to the node identified by name AAA. Once the code of the net template is loaded to the code memory of the PNVM, it is indexed in order to allow PNVM to quickly access particular parts of the bytecode, especially places declaration, the uplinks, and the transitions code. The application can be activated using the message

AAA create blink-app blinker1.

It instantiates the net template blink-app and gives the instance name blinker1. Once the blink-app is instantiated, a specific part of PNVM runtime memory is allocated according to the number of places of the net. At the same time, the net transitions are scheduled for execution. Execution of a transition consists of reading its bytecode and attempting to satisfy all preconditions, downlinks and guards using a recursive backtracking algorithm conform with the Reference Nets semantics. Places may contain all data types which can be specified in bytecode, plus a reference to a net instance. PNVM also maintains a calendar for delayed postconditions. Main execution loop of the PNVM consists of testing and execution of all transitions in all net instances, performing buffered serial input/output (data are exchanged by calling the platform's :input and :output uplinks), and execution of previously scheduled delayed postconditions. In the case of no change in the object memory during last iteration of the main loop, PNVM goes into the sleep state. It is woken up when hardware input occurs, or at the time of the next scheduled event in the calendar.

The complete status of the execution of the application instance together with the status of the OS including input/output buffers can be dumped using message

AAA dump.

As a response, the OS of the node AAA sends the complete dump of the code memory, runtime object memory, input/output serial line buffers and input/output ports.

It is possible to communicate with the running application using a message AAA pass followed by a command for the application, i.e. on, off, or blink. In this simple example, we omited name of application (it does not check it), but in more complex situations, it would be necessary to use names, of course. The running application can be stopped and its template can be uninstalled using messages

AAA destroy blinker1,
AAA unload blink-app.

4   Conclusion

In this paper, we proposed a method for dynamically reconfigurable embedded systems software development based on the formal specification of the system behavior using Reference Nets, which can be directly interpreted in the target implementation. Nets are interpreted in and maintained by PNOS. This approach makes the dynamic reconfigurability of the running system possible. As an expectant application area for described approach we see the smart house or smart city solutions where is a strong need for the possibility to easily change the control system behavior and also to prove that the specification is correctly assembled to serve the intended purposes. This is achieved by the debugging and simulation of the system specification in its executable form.

Acknowledgment. This work has been supported by the European Regional Development Fund in the IT4Innovations Centre of Excellence project (CZ.1.05/1.1.00/02.0070), by BUT FIT grant FIT-S-11-1, and by the Ministry of Education, Youth and Sports under the contract MSM 0021630528.

References

1. Rana, V., Santambrogio, M., Sciuto, D.: Dynamic reconfigurability in embedded system design. In: IEEE International Symposium on Circuits and Systems, ISCAS 2007. IEEE (2007)
2. Girault, C., Valk, R.: Petri Nets for System Engineering: A Guide to Modeling, Verification, and Applications. Springer-Verlag New York, Inc., Secaucus (2001)
3. Valk, R.: Petri Nets as Token Objects: An Introduction to Elementary Object Nets. In: Desel, J., Silva, M. (eds.) ICATPN 1998. LNCS, vol. 1420, pp. 1–25. Springer, Heidelberg (1998)
4. Kummer, O.: Introduction to petri nets and reference nets. In: von Lude, R., Moldt, D., Valk, R. (Hrsg.) SozionikAktuell 1:2001 (2001)
5. Cabac, L., Duvigneau, M., Moldt, D., Rölke, H.: Modeling dynamic architectures using nets-within-nets. In: Ciardo, G., Darondeau, P. (eds.) ICATPN 2005. LNCS, vol. 3536, pp. 148–167. Springer, Heidelberg (2005)
6. Kummer, O., Wienberg, F., Duvigneau, M., Köhler, M., Moldt, D., Rölke, H.: Renew - the Reference Net Workshop. In: Veerbeek, E. (ed.) Tool Demonstrations. 24th International Conference on Application and Theory of Petri Nets, ATPN 2003 (2003)
7. Jensen, K.: Coloured Petri Nets. Basic Concepts, Analysis Methods and Practical Use, 3 vols. Springer (1997)
8. Janoušek, V., Kironský, E.: Exploratory Modeling with SmallDEVS. In: Proceedings of ESM 2006, Toulouse, France, pp. 122–126 (2006) ISBN 90-77381-30-9

Notification Concept for BPMN Workflow Interpreter Using the ASM Method

Jan Kubovy and Josef Küng

Institute for Application Oriented Knowledge Processing (FAW)
Johannes Kepler University in Linz
{jkubovy,jkueng}@faw.jku.at
http://www.faw.jku.at

Abstract. In this paper we focus on filling the gap between the formal Business Process Model and Notation (BPMN) Abstract State Machine (ASM) ground model[1, 3] and a Workflow Interpreter (WI) implementation. For that purpose we use an execution *context* concept and *notification* concept, a refinement of triggers (event definitions)[4].

1 Introduction

The motivation for this paper is to fill the gab between abstract Business Model and Notation (BPMN) Abstract State Machine (ASM) ground model defined in [1, 3] and the Workflow Interpreter (WI). The basic idea of how a WI can be seen in [3] as `rule WorkflowTransitionInterpreter`, which is firing the `rule WorkflowTransition : flowNodes`. This abstract rule handles the traversal of a token through all the instances of all the processes deployed to the Workflow Engine (WE), which the WI is the core part of. The `WorkflowTransition : flowNodes` is further refined in [1] for the concrete flow node types such as activities, gateways and events. The communication between the process run and the WI is refined in this paper by defining the rules and locations left abstract in [1] as the communication between processes using messages or signals.

Starting with defining the execution *context tree* in section 2, where the root of that three is the *static context* present only once. Its immediate children are *root contexts* created for each running top-level process. The rest of the *context tree* is formed by *sub contexts* which are created for every new activity instance. After building a *context tree*, *notifications*, defined in section 3, can carry triggers to their destination through it. These *notifications* are ordered according to their time of occurrence and are processed in that order. *Implicit triggers*, defined in section 4, that are triggered when certain conditions occur in the work-flow, automatically throw corresponding *notifications* in such case. Inter-process communication is in [4] possible using messages and signals. For those we define in section 5 the creation of the corresponding *notifications*. Finally, in section 6 and 7, the rest of the forwarding concepts[4], the *publication* concept to forward the *notifications* down the *context tree* and the *propagation* to forward the *notification* up, are formally defined.

R. Moreno-Díaz et al. (Eds.): EUROCAST 2013, Part I, LNCS 8111, pp. 452–459, 2013.

2   Context

The environment communicates with the WI through existing contexts. There are three types of context (*Static Context*, *Root Context* and *Sub Context*) but only two (*Static Context* and *Root Context*) are allowed to be accessed by the environment. By environment we mean here the rest of the Workflow Engine (WE) of an arbitrary execution platform.

Static Context exists only once and is created as soon as the WE is started. All existing deployments expose their defined top-level start events of their rootProcessOfDeployment : Deployments → Processes, which are those with no defined tigger or with "Message", "Timer", "Conditional" or "Signal" trigger [4], to the *static context* waiting for a corresponding *notification* to be fired (see section 3).

Root Context is a context created for each new rootProcessOfDeployment → Processes instance. The environment can communicate with such instance by sending *notifications* to existing events or by evaluating Completed : Instances → Boolean[1] to true as soon as the corresponding task is finished. The rules for finishing the different task types will be defined further in this paper. The instance of a context, for which it was created, can be obtained from the instanceOfContext : Contexts → Instances location.

Sub Context is a context created for every new activity instance inside a running process instance. This context is not visible to the environment but may populate some uncatched events to the parentContext : Contexts → Contexts. Notifications sent by the environment to the *root context* may be populated down to the *sub contexts*.

3   Notifications

We define a *notification* as an object similar to a token but carrying Event Definition or trigger through the *context tree*. The environment puts all *notifications* to the notifications → List, an ordered list, where the *notifications* are ordered by their monitored timeOfOccurrence : Notifications → Time. Such timestamp is created by an arbitrary *time authority machine*, i.e. neither by the environment nor by the WI machine, which can only read this value. Therefore, for both it is a monitored dynamic location[2].

Notifications fire a concrete trigger (or event definition see [4, sec. 10.4.5]) of a defined event. It specifies the shared contextOfNotification : Notifications → Contexts where the *notification* happened. Since a *notification* can be created by both, the environment and the WI this function is shared.

A *notification* may also define a concrete flow node the *notification* is meant for. This is optional and shared nodeOfNotification : Notifications → FlowNodes may be left *undef*. The case we want to assign a concrete event to a *notification* is e.g. in the case when the *notification* is created by the environment to start a new process instance. Using this location we can select a concrete event with undefined (none) trigger to start the process. Other *notifications* may not specify a concrete flow node. Concrete flow node will be assigned by a *context* as soon as the *notification* reaches the *context* where an appropriate flow node is present. For example if a error event happens a corresponding *notification* is created but the catching event is not know yet and therefore the shared `nodeOfNotification : Notifications → FlowNodes` is *undef*. The WI then searches for the catching event using the *propagation* concept[4] in this case, further defined in section 7. This way we implement the different forwarding concepts[4, sec. 10.4.1] of event triggers. Eventually, every *notification* will be assigned to a concrete flow node or removed from the `notifications → List`. See section 6 and 7 for details about the assignment of flow nodes to *notifications* and their removal from the `notifications → List`.

The trigger of a *notification* may be defined using the shared `triggerOf-Notification : Notifications → Triggers` location. If this location is left *undef* it represents the "None" trigger.

The `notifications → List` is processed by the `rule ProcessNotificationList` shown in listing 1. Since the list is ordered by monitored `timeOf-Occurrence : Notifications → Time` the `select` construct will always return the oldest *notification*. This way is assured that older *notifications* will be processed before newer ones. The `rule ProcessNotificationList` will wait till the selected *notification* is assigned to a concrete flow node (see section 6 and 7). Unassigned *notifications* have to be first forwarded by other rules defined further in this paper.

Listing 1. ProcessNotificationList

```
rule ProcessNotificationList =
  ∀ notification ∈ notifications |
      nodeOfNotification(notification) = undef do
    ForwardNotification(notification)

  select notification ∈ notifications do
    if nodeOfNotification(notification) ≠ undef then
      let trigger ← triggerOfNotification(notification),
          node ← nodeOfNotification(notification) in
        if flowNodeType(node) ∈ Events then
          TriggerOccurs(trigger, node) ← true
        else if flowNodeType(node) = "Receive"
          Received(trigger, node) ← true
      remove notification from notifications
    else
      skip
```

4   Implicit Triggers

Concept of implicitly thrown events is defined here to enable the WI control also the implicit events. The rule ThrowImplicitNotification, shown in listing 2, is then responsible for observing conditional and timer triggers and throw corresponding *notifications* if their conditions were met. The assumption made is that every timer can be generalized as a conditional trigger and the attributes: timeDate, timeCycle and timeDuration[4, table 10.101] can be expressed by a condition[4, table 10.95].

Listing 2. rule ThrowImplicitNotifications

```
rule ThrowImplicitNotifications =
  ∀ process ∈ Processes do
     ∀ event ∈ flowNodes(process) |
          flowNodeType(event) ∈ {"Conditional", "Timer"} do
        ∀ instance ∈ instances(process) do
        if eventCondition(event, instance) = true then
           let context ← choose {context | context ∈ Contexts
              ∧ instanceOfContext(context) =instance} in
              let n ← new Notifications in
              contextOfNotification(n) ← context
              nodeOfNotification(n) ← event
                 triggerOfNotification(n) ← trigger(event)
```

As the nodeOfNotification : Notifications → FlowNodes is defined with the creation of the *notification* this forwarding concept is in [4] referred to as "direct resolution".

5   Message and Signal Pools

For the purpose of inter process communication the BPMN standard defines Messages and Signals[4]. The main difference is that a Message specifies a target but Signal broadcasts to all Signal Catch events. The second most significant difference is that Signals just trigger the corresponding catch events but Messages usually carry more complex content and also may call a Service operation[4, sec. 8.4.3, fig. 8.30, 10.89].

The source and the target event of a Message are linked by a Message flow defined in collaboration[4, ch.9], but this is out of the execution scope. First, collaboration is not required for **Business Process Model and Notation (BPMN) Process Execution Conformance** nor for **BPMN BPEL Process Execution Conformance** [4, p. 109]. Second, implementation of message flows will require loading all communicating processes into the WI which is not always possible, since different processes may be running on different WE and still be communicating. For this purpose we define a messagePool → Set and a signalPool → Set. Messages or Signals arriving from the environment are converted to notifications (see section 3) as defined in the rule ProcessMessagePool, shown in listing 3, and similarly for Signals in the rule ProcessSignalPool, shown in listing 4.

Listing 3. `rule ProcessMessagePool`

```
rule ProcessMessagePool =
  ∀ message ∈ messagePool do
    let notification ← new Notifications ,
    let trigger ← new triggers ("Message") in
      messageOfTrigger (trigger) ← message
      triggerOfNotification (notification) ← trigger
      contextOfNotification (notification) ← "StaticContext"
    remove message from messagePool
```

Listing 4. `ProcessSignalPool`

```
rule ProcessSignalPool
  ∀ sig ∈ signalPool do
    let notification ← new Notifications ,
    let trigger ← new triggers ("Signal") in
      signalOfTrigger (trigger) ← signal
      triggerOfNotification (notification) ← trigger
      contextOfNotification (notification) ← "StaticContext"
    remove sig from signalPool
```

6   Event Publication

Publication forwarding concept defined in [4] applies for message and signal
events. The creation of *notifications* for such events coming from the environment
is shown in section 5. Here, the publication of those *notifications* is defined in
listing 5.

As communicating processes can be running on different WE the proposal
is to define the message flow as a matching concept based on the name of the
message (see [4, figure 10.89]). After a message event with the corresponding
name is found, it will be fired and the *notification* will be consumed. Similarly
for signals[4, figure 10.93] but with the exception that the corresponding *notification* will not be consumed which allows multiple signal catch events to catch
the signal. For this purpose we define `name : Message` $\rightarrow$ `String` and `name :
Signal` $\rightarrow$ `String`.

Listing 5. `rule PublishNotification : Notifications`

```
rule PublishNotification (n) = ForwardNotification (n) where
  let context ← contextOfNotification (n) in
  ∀ node ∈ flowNodes (context) |
      flowNodeType (node) ∈ {"Message","Signal","Receive"} do

    if flowNodeType (node) ∈ {"Message", "Signal"}
    ∧ name (trigger (node)) = name (triggerOfNotification (n))
    ∨ flowNodeType (node) = "Receive"
```

```
        ∧ name(message(node)) = name(triggerOfNotification(n))
    then
      if flowNodeType(node) ∈ {"Message", "Receive"} then
        nodeOfNotification(n) ← node
      else if flowNodeType(node) = "Signal" then
        let duplicate ← Clone(n) in
          nodeOfNotification(duplicate) ← node

    // Publish only yet unassigned notifications
    if nodeOfNotification(n) = undef then
      ∀ child ∈ contexts | parent(child) = context do
      let duplicate ← Clone(n) in
        contextOfNotification(duplicate) ← child
    remove n from notifications // lifetime ends
```

The **abstract rule Clone** : **Notifications** duplicates the original *notification* with preserving the original **timeOfOccurrence** : **Notifications**. Creating a new *notification* with the **new** construct would generate new timestamp.

Additionally the fact that all messages in a process have unique names is checked as shown in listing 6.

Listing 6. constraint UniqueMessageNames

```
∀ process ∈ Processes holds
  ∀ first ∈ flowNodes(process) |
    flowNodeType(first) = "Message" holds
    ∄ second ∈ flowNodes(process) |
      flowNodeType(second) = "Message"
      ∧ name(second) = name(first)
```

7 Event Propagation

Additionally, events from running process instances may be propagated [4, sec. 10.4.1] up to their innermost *context* containing an event which can catch them. If no such event is defined those *notifications* may be propagated up to their *Root Context* or to the common *Static Context*, e.g. error, escalation, cancel or terminate.

The corresponding *notifications* are created in the refined **rule Throw** : **Flow-Nodes** × **Instances**[1] shown in listing 7.

Listing 7. rule Throw : FlowNodes × Instances

```
rule Throw(node, instance) =
  let notification = new Notifications in
    choose context ∈ Contexts |
      instanceOfContext(context) = instance do
      contextOfNotification(notification) ← context
      triggerOfNotification(notification) ← trigger(node)
```

If such a *notification* is not caught by any enclosing activity the process instance will terminate in case of error and terminate trigger[4, tab. 10.88]. In case of other triggers nothing will happen as this is defined as the common behavior in [4] and may be refined in a concrete implementation, as shown in listing 8.

Listing 8. rule `PropagateNotification` : `Notifications`

```
rule  PropagateNotification(n) = ForwardNotification(n) where
  let  context ← contextOfNotification(n) in
    let  i ← instanceOfContext(context) in
      let  boundary ← { b |
          b ∈ boundaryNodes(instantiatingFlowNode(i)) |
          flowNodeType(boundary) ∈ BoundaryEventTypes
          ∧ trigger(boundary) = triggerOfNotification(n)} in

        if  |boundary| = 1 ∧ flowNodeType(boundary) ≠ "Cancel"
          nodeOfNotification(n) ← boundary
        else if  |boundary| = 0
          local  parent ← parentContext(context) in
          if  parent ≠ undef
            contextOfNotification(n) ← parent
          else  // No parent - Static Context
            if  triggerOfNotification(n) = "Terminate"
                ∨ triggerOfNotification(n) = "Error"
              TerminateProcess
        else
          // Exception may be thrown in concrete impl.
```

8 Summary

The *notification* concept, shown in this paper, allows the Workflow Interpreter (WI) to control and observe the processes deployed to it. It implements the communication concept using messages or signals with other processes. It also enables the Workflow Interpreter (WI) to instantiate new processes and to react to some events, e.g. unhandled error, escalation or terminate events. The *context* concept, defined in section 2, is used as a communication medium to forward the *notifications* to different parts of running processes and activities in the WI.

The event forwarding concepts[4] were formally defined in section 4, 6 and 7. The link events were left out since they are used only to break sequence flows to solve some graphical presentation limitations in the same process level[4, section 10.4.5] and this can be handled by the rule `WorkflowTransition` : `FlowNodes`[3].

In section 5 we have shown the creation of *notifications* for incoming messages and signals using pools. One can see the similarity between a message and a signal. The two apparent differences are that a message specifies a concrete target (i.e. catching event) and carries a more complex payload[4, figure 8.30, table 8.48], while a signal can be caught by any, and possibly more than one, catching event and does not carry any additional payload[4, figure 10.93]. Since we cannot model a message flow across different processes possibly running in different WIs we match the message target in section 6 using the name of the message. Another possibility is to define `messageFlowNameOfMessage` and match the target flow node by that parameter, since a message flow also specifies a name[4, figure 8.30]. We chose to match the target by the name of the message and not message flow to demonstrate the similarity between messages and signals and because message flow is a part of collaboration[4, section 9] which is not necessary to claim neither *Process Execution Conformance*[4, section 2.2] nor *BPEL Process Execution Conformance*[4, section 2.3].

The concepts presented in this paper, the *context concept* and the *notification concept*, are the core concepts currently used for our work-in-progress abstract specification of a Workflow Engine (WE).

References

[1] Börger, E., Sörensen, O.: BPMN core modeling concepts: Inheritance-based execution semantics. In: Embley, D., Thalheim, B. (eds.) Handbook of Conceptual Modeling: Theory, Practice and Research Challenges. Springer (2011)

[2] Börger, E., Stärk, R.: Abstract state machines: a method for high-level system design and analysis. Springer (2003)

[3] Börger, E., Thalheim, B.: Modeling workflows, interaction patterns, web services and business processes: The ASM-based approach. In: Börger, E., Butler, M., Bowen, J.P., Boca, P. (eds.) ABZ 2008. LNCS, vol. 5238, pp. 24–38. Springer, Heidelberg (2008)

[4] OMG, Business process model and notation (BPMN) 2.0 (2011), http://www.omg.org/spec/BPMN/2.0

An Abstraction of Multi-port Memories
with Arbitrary Addressable Units*

Lukáš Charvát, Aleš Smrčka, and Tomáš Vojnar

Brno University of Technology, FIT, IT4Innovations Centre of Excellence
Božetěchova 2, 612 66 Brno, Czech Republic
{icharvat,smrcka,vojnar}@fit.vutbr.cz

Abstract. The paper describes a technique for automatic generation of abstract models of memories that can be used for efficient formal verification of hardware designs. Our approach is able to handle addressing of different sizes of data, such as quad words, double words, words, or bytes, at the same time. The technique is also applicable for memories with multiple read and write ports, memories with read and write operations with zero- or single-clock delay, and it allows the memory to start with a random initial state allowing one to formally verify the given design for all initial contents of the memory. Our abstraction allows large register-files and memories to be represented in a way that dramatically reduces the state space to be explored during formal verification of microprocessor designs as witnessed by our experiments.

1 Introduction

As the complexity of hardware is growing over the last decades, automation of its development is crucial. This also includes automation of the process of verification of the designed systems. Verification of current microprocessor designs is typically performed by simulation, functional verification, and/or formal verification (often using various forms of model checking or theorem proving). The complexity of the verification process is usually significantly influenced by the presence and size of the memories used in the design because of an exponential increase in the size of the state space of the given system with each additional memory bit. Therefore the so-called *efficient memory modeling* (EMM) techniques that try to avoid explicit modeling of the memories are being developed.

In this work, we present an approach to automatic generation of abstract memory models whose basic idea comes from the fact that formal verification often suffices with exploring a limited number of accesses to the available memory, and it is thus possible to reduce the number of values that are to be recorded to those that are actually stored in the memory (abstracting away the random contents stored at unused memory locations). Around this basic idea, we then build an approach that allows one to

---

* The work was supported by the Czech Science Foundation (project P103/10/0306), the Czech Ministry of Education (project MSM 0021630528), the Czech Ministry of Industry and Trade (project FR-TI1/038), the EU/Czech IT4Innovations Centre of Excellence project CZ.1.05/1.1.00/02.0070, and the internal BUT projects (FIT-S-11-1 and FIT-S-12-1).

R. Moreno-Díaz et al. (Eds.): EUROCAST 2013, Part I, LNCS 8111, pp. 460–468, 2013.
© Springer-Verlag Berlin Heidelberg 2013

represent memories with various advanced features, such as different kinds of endianness (big or little), read and write delays, multiple read and write ports, and different sizes of addressable units (e.g., bytes, words, double words). As far as we know, the ability to handle all of the above mentioned features differentiates our approach from the currently used ones. Moreover, our technique is applicable in environments requiring a very high level of automation (e.g., processor development frameworks), and it is suitable for formal verification approaches that aim at verifying a given design for an arbitrary initial contents of the memory. Moreover, our abstract memory models can be used within formal verification in a quite efficient way as proved by our experiments.

2 Related Work

Numerous works have focused on memory abstraction, notably within the area of formal verification. Some of the proposed abstractions are tightly coupled with the verification procedure used: for instance, many of them rely on that SAT-based bounded model checking (BMC) [1] or BDD-based model checking [2] are used.

More general approaches, i.e., approaches not tailored for a specific verification procedure, often exploit theories for reasoning about safety properties of systems with arrays, such as [3,4] and especially the work on an extensional theory of arrays [5]. Intuitively, this theory formalizes the idea that two arrays are equivalent if they have the same value at each index. An example of such an approach has been presented in [7]. In the work, an automatic algorithm for constructing abstractions of memories is presented. The algorithm computes the smallest sound and complete abstraction of the given memory.

In [6], the authors introduce a theory of arrays with quantifiers which is an extension of [5]. Moreover, they define the so-called *array property fragment* for which the authors supplement a decision procedure for satisfiability. A modification of the decision procedure for purposes of correspondence checking is proposed in [8] and implemented in [9].

Another method of large memory modeling is described in [10]. The memory state is represented by an ordered set containing triples composed of (i) an expression denoting the set of conditions for which the triple is defined, (ii) an address expression denoting a memory location, and (iii) a data expression denoting the contents of this location. For this set, a special implementation of write and read operations is provided. The abstracted memory interacts with the rest of the circuit using standard *enable*, *address*, and *data* signals. The size of the set is proportional to the number of memory accesses. Further, in [11], the same author extends the approach such that it can be used for correspondence checking by applying the so-called shadowing technique for read operations (we will get back to this issue in Section 3.4).

A recently published work [12] formally specifies and verifies a model of a large memory that supports efficient simulation. The model is tailored for Intel x86 implementations only in order to offer a good trade-off between the speed of simulation and the needed computational resources.

A common disadvantage of [7,8,10,11] is the fact that they omit a support for addressing of different sizes of data which is considered, e.g., in [12]. On the other hand,

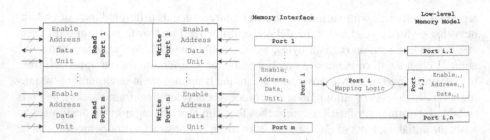

Fig. 1. Memory interface   **Fig. 2.** Memory mapping

in [12], the authors assume starting from the nullified state of the memory, not from a random state.

Some of the other proposed works describe a smarter encoding of formulas, including a description of memories, into CNF [13,14]. In this work, the problems linked to the CNF transformation are not discussed, however, the ideas in [13,14] can be potentially applied here. An example of a tool based on the method coupled with CNF is the *Bit Analysis Tool* [13] (BAT) which automatically builds abstraction of memories to be used in BMC of a certain depth. As its input, BAT uses a custom LISP-based language. A model of the verified system using abstracted memories is created in the following steps: (1) The design to be verified is simplified through pre-defined rewrite rules applied on the level of terms of the BAT language. (2) An *equality test relation* that relates memories that are directly compared for equality is built over the set of memory variables. (3) The transitive closure of the test relation is computed. The closure is an equivalence relation. (4) An *address set* is computed for each of the equivalence classes. The address set contains only the addresses that are relevant for the given class. (5) For all addresses in an address set, a shorter bit vector for addressing the abstract memories is created. The size of the vector is proportional to the number of memory accesses. (6) The behavior of memories is changed to be compatible with the new addressing style. (7) Original memories and addresses are replaced with their abstract counterparts. A description of a system together with the checked properties is then efficiently transformed to a CNF formula. Similarly to previous approaches, there is no support for addressing different sizes of data.

To sum up, our approach can generate abstractions of memories that support addressing of arbitrary addressable units, such as bytes and words (unlike [7,8,10,11]), with multiple read and write ports (in contrast with [7,8]), and it allows the memory to start from a random initial state (not available in [12]). The algorithm is not bound to any specific verification technique (unlike [13,14]).

3 Large Memory Abstraction

We are now going to describe our technique of automated memory abstraction. As we have already said, its basic idea is to record only those values in the memory that are actually used (abstracting away the random contents stored at unused memory locations).

3.1 Memories To Be Abstracted

In our approach, we view a memory as an item of the verified design with the interface depicted in Fig. 1. The interface consists of (possibly multiple) read and write ports. Each port is equipped with Enable, Address, Data, and Unit signals. When the Enable signal is down, the value of the Data signal of a read port is undefined. When dealing with a write port, no value is stored into the memory through this port. On the other hand, when the Enable signal is up, the memory returns/stores data from/into the cell associated with the value of the Address signal. In the special case when multiple ports are enabled for writing into the same memory cell, the result depends on the implementation of the memory. We support two variants: (i) either a prioritized port is selected or (ii) an undefined (random) value is stored to the multiply addressed memory cell.

The size of the addressed unit can be modified by the Unit signal. When the size of the accessed unit is smaller than the size of the greatest addressable unit, the most significant bits of the Data signal are filled up with zeros. It is also assumed that the size of any addressable unit is divisible by the size of the least addressable unit, and thus for the Data signal it is sufficient to transfer the size of the addressed unit expressed as a multiple of the least addressable unit only (instead of the actual number of bits of the unit). Finally, if the memory allows addressing of a single kind of units only, then the Unit signal can be omitted.

3.2 Abstraction of the Considered Memories

Our abstraction preserves the memory interface, and hence concrete memories can be easily substituted with their abstract counterparts. We will first describe the basic principle of our abstraction on memories with a single addressable unit only. An extension of the approach for multiple addressable units will be discussed later. Moreover, we assume reading with no delay and writing with a delay of one cycle. An extension to other timings will be described in Section 3.4.

The abstract memory effectively remembers only the memory cells which have been accessed. Internally, the memory is implemented as a table consisting of some number d of couples of variables storing corresponding pairs of addresses and values (a, v). When using bounded model checking (BMC) as the verification technique, the needed number d of address-value pairs can be easily determined from the depth k of BMC as the following holds $d = k * (m + n)$ where m and n denote the number of read and write ports, respectively. For unbounded verification, the number d can be iteratively incremented until it is sufficient. The incrementation is finite since the number of memory cells is finite. The memory also remembers which of the pairs are in use by tracking the number $r \in \{0, ..., d\}$ of couples that were accessed (and hence the number of the rows of the table used so far).

When the memory is accessed for reading, the remembered address-value pairs $(a_1, v_1), ..., (a_r, v_r)$ that are in use are searched first. If a location a_{rd} that is read has been accessed earlier, then the value v_i associated with the appropriate address $a_i = a_{rd}$ is simply returned. On the other hand, if a location that has never been accessed is read, a corresponding pair is not found in the table, and a new couple (a_{rd}, v_{rd}) is allocated.

Its address part a_{rd} will store the particular address that is accessed while the value v_{rd} is initialized as unconstrained. However, the variable representing the value v_{rd} associated with the accessed location a_{rd} is kept constant in the future (unless there occurs a write operation to the a_{rd} address). This ensures that subsequent reads from a_{rd} return the same value. In case of writing, the address a_{wr} and value v_{wr} are both known. When writing to a location that has not been accessed yet, a new address-value pair (a_{wr}, v_{wr}) is allocated to store the given address-value pair. Otherwise, a value v_i associated with the given address $a_{wr} = a_i$ is replaced by v_{wr}.

3.3 Dealing with Differently Sized Data

In order to support dealing with different sizes of addressable data (including reading/writing data smaller than the contents of a single memory cell of the modeled memory), we split our abstract memory into a low-level memory model and a set of functions mapping accesses to ports of the modeled memory to ports of the low-level memory. The idea of this approach is shown in Fig. 2 and further discussed below.

The low-level memory consists of cells whose size equals the size of the least addressable unit of the modeled memory, and therefore, for low-level memory, the Unit signal can be omitted. In the low-level memory, values of units that are larger than the least addressable unit are stored on succeeding addresses. In order to allow for reading/writing the allowed addressable units (including the greatest one) in one cycle, the number of read and write ports of the low-level memory is appropriately increased. The resulting number of ports of the low-level memory is equal to $m * n$ where m is the number of interface ports and n is the number of distinct addressable units. The latter can be expressed as the quotient of bit-widths of the greatest (w_{gau}) and the least (w_{lau}) addressable unit. In other words, for each port of the memory interface there are n corresponding ports of the low-level memory model. Therefore, we use double indices for the low-level memory ports in our further description.

In particular, let $enable_i$, $data_i$, $address_i$, and $unit_i$ be values of signals of the port i of the memory interface, and let $enable_{i,j}$, $data_{i,j}$, and $address_{i,j}$ have the analogical meaning for the low-level memory port i, j. Then, the value of the $enable_{i,j} \in \mathbb{B}$ signal can be computed as $enable_i \wedge unit_i \geq j$ where $enable_i \in \mathbb{B}$ and $1 \leq unit_i \leq n$. This means that the required number of low-level memory ports are activated only. Next, the value of $address_{i,j}$ can be expressed as $address_i + j - 1$ for the little endian version of the memory and $address_i + unit_i - j$ for the big endian version, respectively. These expressions follow from the fact that larger units of the original memory are stored as multiple smallest addressable units stored at succeeding addresses in the low-level memory.

Further, for transfers of data, separate mappings for read ports and write ports must defined. In the case of a write port, the data flow into the low-level memory, and the value of the $data_{i,j}$ signal can be computed as $slice(data_i, unit_i * w_{lau} - 1, (unit_i - 1) * w_{lau})$ where $slice$ is a function extracting the part of the first argument (on the bit level) that lies within the range given by the second and third arguments (with the bit indices being zero-based). Finally, for a read port, for which data flow from the low-level memory, the value of the $data_i$ signal can be expressed as $concat(ite(enable_{i,n} \vee \neg enable_{i,1}, data_{i,n}, 0), ..., ite(enable_{i,2} \vee \neg enable_{i,1}, data_{i,2}, 0), data_{i,1})$ where *concat* is a bit concatenation and *ite* ("if-then-else") is the selection operator. Thus, the data value is composed from several ports of the low-level memory, and the most significant bits are zero-filled when the read unit is smaller than the greatest one. Note that according to the semantics of the Enable and Data signals (described in Section 3.1), in the case when $enable_{i,1}$ is false (i.e., no unit is read), the value of the $data_i$ signal is undefined.

3.4 Further Extensions of the Abstract Memory Model

To broaden the range of memories that we can abstract, we further added a support for more memory timing options, in particular for one-cycle-delay reading and zero-delay writing. The former can be achieved by simply connecting a unit buffer to the data signal of the memory interface. For the latter case, a special attention must be paid to the situation when both read and write operations over the same address are zero-delayed. In such a situation, it is required to append an additional logic that ensures that written data are propagated with zero delay to a given read port.

Moreover, for a practical deployment in correspondence checking, our model has also been extended by applying the shadowing technique described in [11]. In particular, during correspondence checking, both models are executed in a sequence. The shadowing technique deals with potential inconsistencies that can arise when both models read from the same uninitialized memory cell—indeed, in this case, a random value is to be returned, but the same one in both models. To ensure this, when shadowing is used, the return value of the read operation is obtained from the memory in the design executed first whenever the value is not available in the second design.

4 Implementation and Experiments

The memory abstraction that we generate in the above described way can be encoded in any language for which the user can provide templates specifying (i) how to express declarations of state and nonstate variables, (ii) how to encode propositional logic expressions over state and nonstate variables, (iii) and how to define initial and next states of state variables. We currently created these templates for the Cadence SMV language [15].

In order to prove usefulness of the described abstraction technique, we used our abstract memory generator within the approach proposed in [16] for checking correspondence between the ISA and RTL level descriptions of microprocessors, which we applied to several embedded microprocessors. Briefly, in the approach of [16], the ISA specification and VHDL model of a processor are automatically translated into behavioral models described in the language of a model checker (the Cadence SMV language in our case). These models are then equipped with an environment model, including architectural registers and memories, which can be abstracted using the technique proposed in this article. All these models are composed together, and BMC is used to check whether if both of the processor models start with the same state of their environment (including the same instruction to be executed), their environments equal after the execution too. The described approach was integrated into the Codasip IDE [17] processor development framework.

Table 1. Verification results

Processor	Reg. File Size	Memory Size	Explicit Memory	Abs. Reg. File	Abs. Memory	All Abs.
TinyCPU	4 x 8bit	-	0.151 s	0.41 s	-	-
SPP8	16 x 8bit	256 x 8bit	5.06 s	1.11 s	3.66 s	0.452 s
SPP16	16 x 16bit	2048 x 8bit	266 s	92.2 s	1.23 s	0.822 s
Codea2_single	32 x 16bit	32768 x 16bit	o.o.m.	o.o.m.	4.30 s	4.44 s
Codea2_mult	32 x 16bit	65536 x 8bit	o.o.m.	o.o.m.	4.75 s	4.89 s

Our approach was tested on three processors: *TinyCPU* is a small 8-bit test processor with 4 general-purpose registers and 3 instructions that we developed mainly for testing new verification approaches. *SPP8* is an 8-bit ipcore with 16 general-purpose registers and a RISC instruction set consisting of 9 instructions. *SPP16* is a 16-bit variant of the previous processor with a more complex memory model allowing one, e.g., to load/store both bytes and words from/to the memory. *Codea2* is a 16-bit processor with 4 pipeline stages partially based on the MSP430 microcontroller developed by Texas Instruments [18]. The processor is dedicated for signal processing applications. It is equipped with 16 general-purpose registers, 15 special registers, a flag register, and an instruction set including 41 instructions, where each may use up to 4 available addressing modes. Our experiments were evaluated for two modifications of the processor—using memory with and without multiple addressable units.

Our experiments were run on a PC with Intel Core i7-3770K @3.50GHz and 32 GB RAM using Cadence SMV (the build from 05-25-11) and GlueMinisat (version 2.2.5) [19] as an external SAT solver. The results can be seen in Table 1. The first three columns give the processor being verified, the size of its register file, and the size of the memory. The next columns give the results obtained from the verification—in particular, the average time needed for verification of a single instruction with the abstraction applied or not-applied in different combinations on the register file and the memory. In the first case, both the register file and the memory were modeled explicitly which, for larger designs such as Codea2, led to out-of-memory errors ("o.o.m."). Next, the abstraction was only used for register files. Even though better results were obtained this way for the SPP8 and SPP16 processor designs, the verification still ran out of system resources for Codea2 because of the explicitly modeled memory. In the last two cases when either only memories or both memories and register files of the verified processors were abstracted, verification was able to finish even for larger designs. We explain the 10 % deterioration between verification times for the Codea2 processor with and without presence of multiple addressable units by the complexity of the additional logic.

Finally, we note that for very small memories and memories with many possible accesses (caused by, e.g., a higher verification depth during BMC), the overhead brought by the abstraction can result in worse verification times as can be seen in the case of the register file of the TinyCPU and Codea2 processors. Moreover, for SPP8, where only a few instructions directly access the memory, and thus only a few instructions influence the average verification times, the overhead caused by the abstraction introduces worse than expected average verification time when abstracting the memory only. In practice, we deal with this problem by defining a heuristics that computes whether or not it is better to use an explicit or abstract description of a given memory.

5 Conclusion

We have presented an approach of memory abstraction that exploits the fact that formal verification often suffices with exploring a limited number of accesses to the available memory, and it is thus possible to reduce the number of values that are to be recorded to those that are actually stored in the memory. Our approach allows one to abstract memories with various advanced features, such as different kinds of endianness, read and write delays, multiple read and write ports, and different sizes of addressable units. The techniques is fully automated and suitable for usage within processor development frameworks where it can bring a significant improvement in verification times.

References

1. Biere, A., Cimatti, A., Clarke, E., Strichman, O., Zhu, Y.: Bounded Model Checking. Advances in Computers 58 (2003)
2. Burch, J.R., Clarke, E.M., McMillan, K.L., Dill, D.L., Hwang, L.J.: Symbolic Model Checking: 10^{20} States and Beyond. Information and Computation 98(2) (1992)
3. McCarthy, J.: Towards a mathematical science of computation. In: IFIP Congress (1962)
4. Nelson, G., Oppen, D.C.: Simplification by cooperating decision procedures. ACM Trans. Program. Lang. Syst. 1(2) (1979)
5. Stump, A., Barrett, C.W., Dill, D.L., Levitt, J.R.: A Decision Procedure for an Extensional Theory of Arrays. In: Proc. of Logic in Computer Science. IEEE Computer Society (2001)
6. Bradley, A.R., Manna, Z., Sipma, H.B.: What's decidable about arrays? In: Emerson, E.A., Namjoshi, K.S. (eds.) VMCAI 2006. LNCS, vol. 3855, pp. 427–442. Springer, Heidelberg (2006)
7. German, S.M.: A Theory of Abstraction for Arrays. In: Proc. of FMCAD, Austin, TX (2011)
8. Koelbl, A., Burch, J., Pixley, C.: Memory Modeling in ESL-RTL Equivalence Checking. In: Proc. of DAC. IEEE Computer Society (2007)
9. Koelbl, A., Jacoby, R., Jain, H., Pixley, C.: Solver Technology for System-level to RTL Equivalence Checking. In: Proc. of DATE. IEEE Computer Society (2009)
10. Velev, M.N., Bryant, R.E., Jain, A.: Efficient Modeling of Memory Arrays in Symbolic Simulation. In: Grumberg, O. (ed.) CAV 1997. LNCS, vol. 1254, pp. 388–399. Springer, Heidelberg (1997)
11. Bryant, R.E., Velev, M.N.: Verification of Pipelined Microprocessors by Comparing Memory Execution Sequences in Symbolic Simulation. In: Shyamasundar, R.K., Ueda, K. (eds.) ASIAN 1997. LNCS, vol. 1345, pp. 18–31. Springer, Heidelberg (1997)
12. Hunt Jr., W.A., Kaufmann, M.: A Formal Model of a Large Memory that Supports Efficient Execution. In: Proc. of FMCAD. IEEE Computer Society (2012)
13. Manolios, P., Srinivasan, S.K., Vroon, D.: Automatic Memory Reductions for RTL Model Verification. In: Proc. of ICCAD. ACM/IEEE Computer Society (2006)

14. Ganai, M.K., Gupta, A., Ashar, P.: Verification of Embedded Memory Systems using Efficient Memory Modeling. In: Proc. of DATE. ACM/IEEE Computer Society (2005)
15. McMillan, K.L.: Cadence SMV, http://www.kenmcmil.com/smv.html
16. Smrčka, A., Vojnar, T., Charvát, L.: Automatic Formal Correspondence Checking of ISA and RTL Microprocessor Description. In: Proc. of MTV (2012)
17. Codasip Studio for Rapid Processor Development, http://www.codasip.com
18. Codea2 Core IP in Codasip Studio, www.codasip.com/products/codea2/
19. Naneshima, H., Iwanuma, K., Inoue, K.: GlueMinisat, appeared in SAT Competition 2011 (2011), http://sites.google.com/a/nabelab.org/glueminisat/

Battery Internal State Estimation: Simulation Based Analysis on EKF and Auxiliary PF

V. Pathuri-Bhuvana, C. Unterrieder, and J. Fischer

Alpen-Adria University, Klagenfurt, Institute of Networked and Embedded Systems
venkata.pathuri@aau.at

Abstract. In battery management systems, the estimation of internal cell parameters has become an important research focus in the recent years. Exemplarily, this includes the tracking of parameters such as the internal cell impedances, the cell capacity, or the state-of-charge (SoC) of a battery. In general, the battery is considered to be a non-linear dynamic system. Hence, this paper compares the accuracy and the complexity of the extended Kalman filter (EKF) and the particle filter (PF), which are applied for the estimation of internal cell states such as the SoC and the battery's transient response. The comparison shows that the PF yields better accuracy compared to the EKF under the given conditions. However, the EKF is computationally less complex compared to the PF.

Keywords: PF, EKF, SoC estimation.

1 Introduction

The estimation of the internal states of a battery such as the state-of-charge (SoC), the open-circuit-voltage (OCV), and the internal impedances is a critical issue in battery management systems. In general, these quantities are estimated based on noisy measurements. Researchers have proposed SoC estimation methods using the Kalman filter (KF) [1]. The KF requires the battery to be described by a linear model with zero mean additive Gaussian noise. In contrast, many battery models show non-linear characteristics, for which the EKF [1], [2] is widely used for the state estimation.

However, more efficient but in general also more complex non linear filters such as the particle filters (PF) [3] are also possible candidates for the addressed problem. The PF is a Monte-Carlo based approximation method that uses a set of weighted random samples to approximate the states of a system. In [4], the authors presented a comparison of the EKF- and the PF-based SOC estimation methods. In addition, this paper also compares the EKF- and the PF-based battery internal state estimation methods by considering the dynamics of the battery transient response. The transient response of a battery mainly depends on the applied load current and the internal impedance of a battery [5]. Moreover, this paper uses the auxiliary resampling based PF which is less sensitive to the outliers when the process noise is small.

R. Moreno-Díaz et al. (Eds.): EUROCAST 2013, Part I, LNCS 8111, pp. 469–475, 2013.

The paper is organized as follows, Section 2 describes the considered three-state non-linear battery model. Section 3 discusses the battery internal state estimation methods based on the EKF and the PF. Section 4 presents the simulation results and Section 5 concludes the paper.

2   Battery Model

To characterize the behavior of a battery, different models have been proposed in the literature. In this paper, the battery model is considered as an electrical-equivalent-circuit [5] as shown in Fig. 1. In this model, the SoC, the battery capacity, and the battery runtime are modeled by the capacitor C_{CAP} and the current-controlled current source I_{batt}. The voltage-controlled voltage source describes the non-linear relation between the cell's SoC and its OCV,

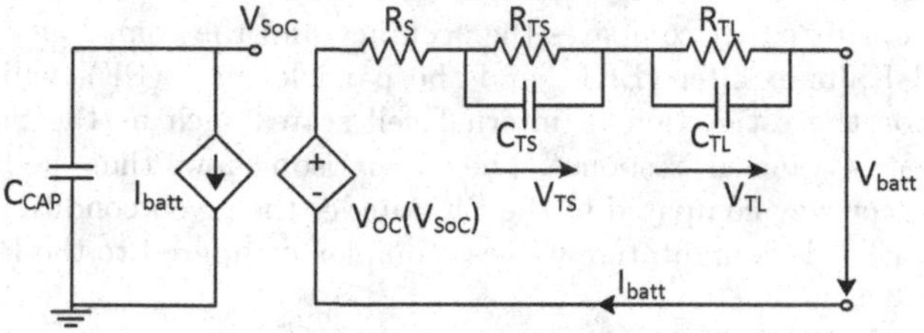

Fig. 1. Battery model

$$V_{OC}\left(V_{SoC}\right) = -1.031e^{-35SoC} + 3.685 + 0.2156SoC - 0.1178SoC^2 + 0.3201SoC^3. \tag{1}$$

The elements R_{TS}, C_{TS}, R_{TL}, and C_{TL} represent two RC networks which model the short and long time constants of the battery step response. The resistance R_S models the instantaneous voltage change in the battery step response.

Sequential SoC estimation requires a state-space model that accurately describes the behavior of the battery. In general, the process model characterizes the system's state transition, given by

$$\mathbf{x}_{k+1} = \mathbf{f}_k\left(\mathbf{x}_k, \mathbf{u}_k\right) + \mathbf{w}_k, \tag{2}$$

where $\mathbf{x}_k$ is the state vector at the time instant k and $\mathbf{w}_k$ is an independent and identically distributed (IID) process noise vector with covariance $\mathbf{Q}$. $\mathbf{x}_k$ is estimated from the measurements taken at each time instant up to k. The system's measurement equation is given by

$$\mathbf{y}_k = \mathbf{h}_k\left(\mathbf{x}_k, \mathbf{u}_k\right) + \mathbf{v}_k, \tag{3}$$

where $\mathbf{v}_k$ is an IID measurement noise vector with covariance $\mathbf{R}$. In this paper, we estimate the voltages across the two parallel RC networks V_{TS} and V_{TL} in addition to the SoC. Hence, the state vector at time k becomes $\mathbf{x}_k =$

$[SoC\ V_{TS}\ V_{TL}]_k^T$. According to the described battery model, the discretized process model is linear, given by

$$\begin{bmatrix} SoC \\ V_{TS} \\ V_{TL} \end{bmatrix}_{k+1} = \begin{bmatrix} 1 & 0 & 0 \\ 0 & e^{-\frac{T_s}{R_{TS}C_{TS}}} & 0 \\ 0 & 0 & e^{-\frac{T_s}{R_{TL}C_{TL}}} \end{bmatrix} \begin{bmatrix} SoC \\ V_{TS} \\ V_{TL} \end{bmatrix}_k$$
$$+ \begin{bmatrix} -T_s/C_{Cap} \\ R_{TS}(1 - e^{-(\frac{T_s}{C_{TS}R_{TS}})}) \\ R_{TL}(1 - e^{-(\frac{T_s}{C_{TL}R_{TL}})}) \end{bmatrix} I_{batt,k} + \mathbf{w}_k, \tag{4}$$

where $\mathbf{w}_k$ is assumed to be the zero mean Gaussian noise with covariance $\mathbf{Q}$ and T_S is the sampling time.

The only measurements available to estimate $\mathbf{x}_k$ is the measurements of the battery terminal voltage $V_{batt,k}$ The measurement equation is given by

$$V_{batt,k} = V_{OC}(V_{SoC}) - R_s I_{batt,k} - V_{TL} - V_{TS} + v_k, \tag{5}$$

where v_k is assumed to be the zero mean Gaussian noise with variance r.

3 Non-Linear State Estimation Methods for the Battery Internal State Estimation

In general, the EKF and the PF are used to approximate the states of a nonlinear system.

3.1 Extended Kalman Filter (EKF) Based Estimation

The EKF performs a local linearization of the state-space model. According to the used battery model, the process equation is already linear and it is in the form of

$$\mathbf{x}_{k+1} = \mathbf{F}_k \mathbf{x}_k + \mathbf{B}_k \mathbf{u}_k + \mathbf{w}_k.$$

The local linearization rewrites the measurement equation represented by (5) as

$$\mathbf{y}_k = \mathbf{H}_k \mathbf{x}_k + \mathbf{v}_k,$$

where $\mathbf{H}_k$ is obtained through the local linearization based on the Taylor series approximation. Then, the KF algorithm is used to estimate the states, as follows: Initialize the error covariance $\mathbf{P}_{0|0}$, and the prior state estimate $\hat{\mathbf{x}}_{0|0}$. At each time k,

– Predict the state from $\hat{\mathbf{x}}_{k-1|k-1}$

$$\hat{\mathbf{x}}_{k|k-1} = \mathbf{F}_k \hat{\mathbf{x}}_{k-1|k-1} + \mathbf{B}_k \mathbf{u}_k.$$

– Predict the error covariance

$$\mathbf{P}_{k|k-1} = \mathbf{Q} + \mathbf{F}_k \mathbf{P}_{k-1|k-1} \mathbf{F}_k^T.$$

– Calculate the gain

$$\mathbf{k}_k = \mathbf{P}_{k|k-1}\mathbf{H}_k^T \left(\mathbf{H}_k\mathbf{P}_{k|k-1}\mathbf{H}_k^T + r\right)^{-1}.$$

– Update the predicted state and the error covariance

$$\hat{\mathbf{x}}_{k|k} = \hat{\mathbf{x}}_{k|k-1} + \mathbf{k}_k \left(\mathbf{y}_k - \mathbf{h}_k \left(\hat{\mathbf{x}}_{k|k-1}\right)\right).$$

$$\mathbf{P}_{k|k} = \mathbf{P}_{k|k-1} - \mathbf{k}_k\mathbf{H}_k\mathbf{P}_{k|k-1}.$$

The EKF is computationally less complex but its efficiency is severely limited in highly non-linear systems due to inherent linearization errors.

3.2   Particle Filter (PF) Based Estimation

The PF is a sequential Monte Carlo method that is used as an approximation for the optimum Bayesian filtering. Point masses with the corresponding weights are used to approximate probability density functions (PDF). This method can be better empathized from the concept of sequential importance sampling (SIS).

Importance sampling is used to approximate the PDFs. Let $p(x)$ be the target PDF to be approximated with the support S_x, $q(x)$ be the proposal or importance density with $q(x) > 0$ for all $x \in S_x$. Let $\{x^i\}_{i=1}^N$ be the N IID samples drawn from the $q(x)$, then the approximated PDF $\hat{p}(x)$ is given by

$$\hat{p}(x) = \sum_{i=1}^N w\left(x^i\right) \delta\left(x - x^i\right), \tag{6}$$

where $w\left(x^i\right)$ is the normalized weight of the ith sample and the weights are given by

$$\tilde{w}\left(x^i\right) = \frac{p\left(x^i\right)}{q\left(x^i\right)}. \tag{7}$$

Let $\left\{\mathbf{x}_{0:k}^i, \mathbf{w}_k^i\right\}_i^N$ be the set of N random samples drawn from the importance density $q\left(\mathbf{x}_{0:k} \mid \mathbf{y}_{1:k}\right)$ and their associated weights. Then, the required PDF can be approximated as

$$p\left(\mathbf{x}_{0:k} \mid \mathbf{y}_{1:k}\right) \approx \sum_{i=1}^N \mathbf{w}_k^i \delta\left(\mathbf{x}_{0:k} - \mathbf{x}_{0:k}^i\right), \tag{8}$$

where the weights up to a constant are defined as

$$\mathbf{w}_k^i = \frac{p\left(\mathbf{x}_{0:k}^i \mid \mathbf{y}_{1:k}\right)}{q\left(\mathbf{x}_{0:k}^i \mid \mathbf{y}_{1:k}\right)}. \tag{9}$$

In the case of sequential importance sampling [3], the samples and the corresponding weights which approximate $p\left(\mathbf{x}_{0:k-1} \mid \mathbf{y}_{1:k-1}\right)$ are known at time k. If the importance density for approximating $p\left(\mathbf{x}_{0:k} \mid \mathbf{y}_{1:k}\right)$ is chosen in such a way that

$$q\left(\mathbf{x}_{0:k} \mid \mathbf{y}_{1:k}\right) = q\left(\mathbf{x}_k \mid \mathbf{x}_{0:k-1}, \mathbf{y}_k\right) q\left(\mathbf{x}_{0:k-1} \mid \mathbf{y}_{1:k-1}\right), \tag{10}$$

then the weight can be updated sequentially as

$$\mathbf{w}_k^i = \mathbf{w}_{k-1}^i \frac{p\left(\mathbf{y}_k \mid \mathbf{x}_k^i\right) p\left(\mathbf{x}_k^i \mid \mathbf{x}_{k-1}^i\right)}{q\left(\mathbf{x}_k^i \mid \mathbf{x}_{0:k-1}^i, \mathbf{y}_k\right)}. \tag{11}$$

The SIS algorithm recursively propagates the samples and their corresponding weights as the measurement is received. The SIS algorithm experiences a degeneracy problem after few iterations due to which all but a few particles have negligible weights. Due to the degeneracy, large computational effort is used for updating the particles with less contribution to the approximation of the required PDF. A potential solutions for the degeneracy problem is resampling. The resampling generates a set of new particles $\left\{\mathbf{x}_k^{i*}\right\}_{i=1}^N$ with the equal weights $1/N$. Then, the density function $p\left(\mathbf{x}_{0:k} \mid \mathbf{y}_{1:k}\right)$ can be approximated as

$$p\left(\mathbf{x}_{0:k} \mid \mathbf{y}_{1:k}\right) \approx \sum_i^N \delta\left(\mathbf{x}_k - \mathbf{x}_k^{*i}\right) \tag{12}$$

The PF algorithm proposed for the battery internal state estimation is an SIS based PF with auxiliary resampling. The state transition PDF $p\left(\mathbf{x}_k \mid \mathbf{x}_{k-1}\right)$ is used as proposal density. This choice highly simplifies the weight update equation (11) which then becomes

$$\mathbf{w}_k^i = \mathbf{w}_{k-1}^i p\left(\mathbf{x}_k^i \mid \mathbf{x}_{k-1}^i\right). \tag{13}$$

The auxiliary resampling is used because it is not very sensitive to the outliers when the process noise is small. The complete auxiliary resampling algorithm is provided in [3].

At time k, $\left\{\mathbf{x}_{k-1}^i, \mathbf{w}_{k-1}^i\right\}_{i=1}^N$ are known.

– Generate the new samples

$$\mathbf{x}_k^i \sim p\left(\mathbf{x}_k \mid \mathbf{x}_{k-1}^i\right)\big|_{i=1}^N.$$

– Update the weights

$$\tilde{\mathbf{w}}_k^i = p\left(\mathbf{y}_k \mid \mathbf{x}_k^i\right)\big|_{i=1}^N.$$

– normalizing the weights

$$\mathbf{w}_k^i = \frac{\tilde{\mathbf{w}}_k^i}{sum\left(\tilde{\mathbf{w}}_k^i\right)\big|_{i=1}^N}\bigg|_{i=1}^N.$$

– Resampling: The particles are resampled by using the auxiliary resampling [3].

$$\left\{\mathbf{x}_k^{i*}, 1/N\right\}\big|_{i=1}^N = AUX\_Resampling\left\{\mathbf{x}_k^i, \mathbf{w}_k^i\right\}\big|_{i=1}^N.$$

– The state estimate is given by the sample mean of the resampled particles $\mathbf{x}_k^{i*}$.

The PF is an efficient and simple algorithm for the battery internal state estimation. The disadvantage of the PF is its computational complexity compared to the EKF.

4   Simulation Results

The EKF- and PF- based state estimation methods discussed in the previous section are used to estimate the SoC and the transient response of a battery according to the model proposed in Section 2. The internal model parameters such as the RC elements are adapted from [5]. The simulated discharge scenario is as follows: The pulsated load current $I_{batt} = 2A$ with 50% duty cycle is applied to a fully charged battery. The process and the measurement noises are assumed to be IID Gaussian noises with covariance matices $Q =$ diag$\{10^{-6}, 0.25.10^{-6}, 0.25.10^{-6}\}$ and $r_{=}0.25$, respectively.

Fig. 2 shows the simulated estimation results of the three states SoC, V_{TS}, and V_{TL} for the applied non-linear state estimation methods. The true states (black solid lines) are simulated based on the process model described in Section 2 with the process noise covariance $Q = $ diag$\{10^{-6}, 0.25.10^{-6}, 0.25.10^{-6}\}$. The estimation results of the EKF-based method (red dotted lines) show significant errors at the initial stages of the estimation process due to the uncertainty in the prior information. The estimation results of the PF (N=300)-based method (blue dotted line) shows a significant improvement compared to the EKF-based estimation method.

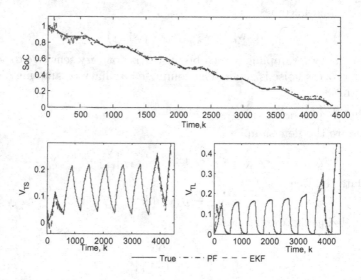

Fig. 2. Battery internal state estimation based on the EKF and the PF

Table 1 gives the average root mean square error (% RMSE) of the SoC, V_{TS}, and V_{TL} for the both methods. The RMSE is averaged over 300 simulation runs. The average The PF-based method achieves the root mean square error of approximately 3% for the SoC and 1% for V_{TS} and V_{TL}. Although, the PF-based method shows a better efficiency compared to that of the EKF-based method in terms of estimation error, it is computationally more complex. Table 2 shows the computational complexity of the both non-linear state estimation methods in

Table 1. Efficiency of the applied state estimation methods

Method	%RMSE (SoC)	%RMSE (V_{TS})	%RMSE (V_{TL})
EKF	4.71	2.84	2.48
PF	3.01	0.90	1.12

Table 2. complexity of the applied state estimation methods

Method	Computational time
EKF	0.45sec
PF	10.47sec(N=300)

terms of the computational time required in the Matlab environment. Thereby, the computational time is calculated as the time taken by the individual methods to estimate the battery states during one full discharge scenario.

5   Conclusions

In this paper, a comparison of non-linear battery internal state estimation methods based on the EKF and the PF is presented. The internal states comprises of the SoC and the battery transient response. The efficiency and the complexity of the these state estimation methods are compared based on a simulated-based evaluation. The simulation results show that the PF-based method is more efficient compared to the EKF-based method. However, the PF-based estimation method features a significantly higher computational complexity compared to the EKF.

References

1. Plett, G.L.: Kalman-filter SOC estimation for LiPB HEV cells. In: Proceedings of the 19th International Battery, Hybrid and Fuel Cell Electric Vehicle Symposium & Exhibition, Busan, Korea, pp. 527–538 (2002)
2. Plett, G.L.: Extended Kalman Filtering for Battery Management Systems of LiPB-based HEV Battery Packs: Part 3. State and Parameter Estimation. Journal of Power Sources, 277–292 (August 2004)
3. Sanjeev Arulampalam, M., Maskell, S., Gordon, N., Clapp, T.: A Tutorial on Particle Filters for Online Non linear/non-Gaussian Bayesian Tracking. IEEE Transactions on Signal Processing, 174–188 (February 2002)
4. Mingyu, G., Yuanyuan, L., Zhiwei, H.: Battery State of Charge Online Estimation based on Particle Filter. In: 4th International Congress on Image and Signal Processing, pp. 2233–2236 (October 2011)
5. Chen, M., Rincon-Mora, G.A.: Accurate Electrical Battery Model Capable of Predicting Runtime and I-V Performance. IEEE Transactions on Energy Conversion, 504–511 (June 2006)

Computer-Aided Optimization for Predictive Battery State-of-Charge Determination

C. Unterrieder[1], M. Lunglmayr[1], S. Marsili[2], and M. Huemer[1]

[1] Institute of Networked and Embedded Systems
Klagenfurt University
9020 Klagenfurt, Austria
christoph.unterrieder@aau.at
[2] Infineon Technologies Austria AG
9500 Villach, Austria
stefano.marsili@infineon.com

Abstract. Optimizing the battery management of today's portable electronic applications goes hand in hand with the reliable and accurate knowledge of the battery's state-of-charge (SoC). During periods of low load, usually the SoC is determined based on the measurement of the corresponding open-circuit voltage (OCV). This requires a battery to be in a well-relaxed state, which can take more than 3 hours depending on influence factors like the SoC itself and the temperature. Unfortunately, a well-relaxed state is rarely reached in real world scenarios. As an alternative, predicted OCV values can be used to estimate the SoC. In this work, we use a polynomial-enhanced model description for the OCV prediction process. After identifying the critical model parameters, a computer-aided parameter optimization methodology is applied to optimize the OCV prediction process. As a major result, the proposed methodology enables the possibility to optimize the OCV prediction process with respect to a specified SoC estimation accuracy.

Keywords: battery, state-of-charge, open-circuit voltage prediction, least-squares estimation, nonlinear optimization.

1 Introduction

In modern electronic applications, usually the battery state-of-charge (SoC) is updated based on the use of the so-called Coulomb counting- (CC) method [1], which mostly is re-initialized based on the measurement of the battery open-circuit voltage (OCV). The recalibration of the CC method is needed due to errors which inherently are included in the charge integration step, exemplary caused by current measurement offset errors or an inaccurate time base in integrated solutions. Typically, the OCV-based actualization of the SoC is applied during periods of low loads. To rely on the OCV, the battery is required to be in a well-relaxed state, which typically is reached after a time of about 3 to 5 hours (for e.g. Li-Ion accumulators) measured from the point in time when

R. Moreno-Díaz et al. (Eds.): EUROCAST 2013, Part I, LNCS 8111, pp. 476–482, 2013.
© Springer-Verlag Berlin Heidelberg 2013

the charge/discharge current drops below a pre-defined threshold value. Unfortunately, the time to reach a well-relaxed state, also called relaxation time, is not fixed and depends on factors like the SoC and the temperature. In general, the relaxation time is tending to increase for low temperatures, low SoC and high current rates. A more severe problem is that in today's typical use cases such long relaxation times are rarely reached. To obtain a reliable estimate of the SoC, a highly accurate predicted OCV, as well as reliable SoC-OCV tables are mandatory. In practice, the SoC-OCV tables are found during the battery characterization process.

In order to predict a battery's OCV, in this work a polynomial-enhanced relaxation voltage model description, in combination with sequential linear least squares (LS) based estimation schemes, is used. First, the OCV relaxation process is analyzed with respect to influence factors like the cell temperature, the battery aging, and the cell-to-cell or chemistry-to-chemistry deviation. Based on that, the critical parameters for the OCV prediction process are identified. Subsequently, a nonlinear programming based optimization methodology is applied to the predictive battery OCV estimation problem. Consequently, appropriate choices of the parameters of the OCV estimation process are identified based on simulation. In general, this work is structured as follows: Section 2 presents the chosen OCV modeling-, OCV estimation- and optimization strategy. In Section 3, simulation results based on measurements of a Sanyo UR18650 Li-Ion cell are presented. Section 4 concludes the work.

2   Modeling and Optimization

Recently, a polynomial-enhanced OCV prediction method has been proposed [2] based on the consecutive application of sequential linear least squares estimation approaches. It extends the following typical model [3,4] to predict the OCV $V_{OC,t}$ at a certain time step:

$$V_{OC,t} = V_\infty - \frac{\Gamma \gamma}{t^\alpha \log_e^\delta(t)} \exp(\frac{\varepsilon_t}{2}).$$

(1)

Here the parameters to be estimated are given by γ, α, δ and V_∞. ε_t represents a random error term and Γ equals to ± 1, depending if the relaxation occurs after charge or discharge. In [2], the usage of a polynomial-enhanced version of the model (1) has been proposed. It can be described schematically as depicted in Fig. 1. The whole relaxation is split into $(P+1)$ sections (in Fig. 1: $P = 2$), so-called *phases* p_k, with $k = 0 \ldots P$. The solid gray line represents the measured (true) relaxation process. The dash-dotted black line represents the predicted relaxation process using (1). The polynomial enhancement in phase p_2 is shown with two functions, one with a polynomial of degree one (solid black line) and one with a polynomial of degree two (dashed black line).

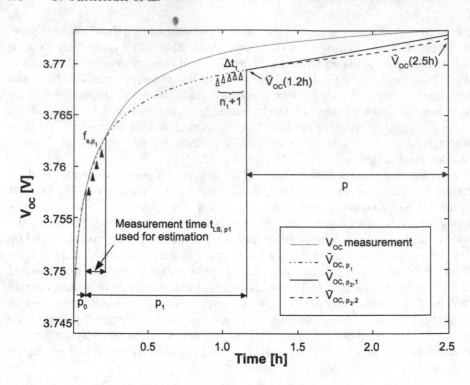

Fig. 1. Polynomial enhanced prediction of the OCV

For this enhancement, the coefficients of (1) are predicted based on the OCV measurements taken in the beginning of phase p_1. For the following phases p_k, $k > 1$, the predicted functions are polynomials of the form:

$$f_{p_k}(t) = \sum_{i=0}^{n_k} a_{i,k} t^i. \tag{2}$$

For phases p_k, $k > 1$, only values of the predicted function of the previous phase p_{k-1} are used to calculate the coefficients of $f_{p_k}(t)$. For the calculation of the individual coefficients, sequential linear LS based estimation schemes are applied for the time duration $t_{LS,pk}$, respectively. Consequently, this approach provides two degrees of freedom per phase p_k: the time distance Δt_k and a chosen reference time t_k, where the values $\tilde{V}_{OC}(t_k - i \cdot \Delta t_k)$, $i = 0 \ldots n_k - 1$, are used for the coefficient calculation of the next phase.

To guarantee a reliable OCV/SoC estimate, a constrained nonlinear optimization strategy is used. The scalar cost function to be minimized is formed by

$$g(\mathbf{x}) = |V_{OC}(2.5h) - \tilde{V}_{OC}(2.5h)|, \tag{3}$$

and the constrained optimization problem is defined as

$$\min_{\mathbf{x}} g(\mathbf{x}), \text{such that} \begin{cases} \mathbf{c}(\mathbf{x}) \le \mathbf{0} \\ \mathbf{c}_{eq}(\mathbf{x}) = \mathbf{0} \\ \mathbf{A} \cdot \mathbf{x} \le \mathbf{b} \\ \mathbf{A}_{eq} \cdot \mathbf{x} = \mathbf{b}_{eq} \\ \mathbf{lb} \le \mathbf{x} \le \mathbf{ub} \end{cases} \qquad (4)$$

In general, the vector $\mathbf{x} = [t_k, \Delta t_k, n_k, t_{LS,pk}]$ includes the parameters to be optimized by the applied nonlinear optimization strategy. $\mathbf{c}(\mathbf{x})$ and $\mathbf{c}_{eq}(\mathbf{x})$ represent nonlinear vector functions. $\mathbf{A}$, $\mathbf{b}$, $\mathbf{A}_{eq}$ and $\mathbf{b}_{eq}$ are matrices/vectors of appropriate size which form the linear equality and the inequality constraints. The vectors $\mathbf{lb}$ and $\mathbf{ub}$ define a set of lower and upper bounds on the variables of $\mathbf{x}$. To find the constrained minimum of $g(\mathbf{x})$, algorithms of various inherent characteristics may be applied. Examples are the trust region algorithm, which approximates $g(\mathbf{x})$ in the neighborhood of $\mathbf{x}$ or the active set algorithm [5], which uses the concept of sequential quadratic programming for the identification of $\min_{\mathbf{x}} g(\mathbf{x})$. As an alternative, an interior-point algorithm may be used. In this work, a quasi-Newton approximation based interior-point algorithm is used for the optimization step. Thereby, the interior-point algorithm is used such that the general optimization framework in (4) reduces to a form which uses only the upper and the lower bound of $\mathbf{x}$ as an optimization constraint.

3   Experimental Results

In this section, the performance of the proposed modeling and optimization strategy is evaluated based on measurements of a Sanyo UR18650 Li-Ion accumulator. First the results of the analysis of the OCV relaxation process with respect to influence factors like the cell temperature, the battery aging, and the cell-to-cell or chemistry-to-chemistry deviation are presented. Subsequently, simulation results are shown, which illustrate the performance of the proposed modeling and optimization strategy.

3.1   Analysis of the OCV Relaxation Process

In order to analyze the behavior of the OCV relaxation process, the following test procedure has been applied to the battery: First the cell has been charged to full. Then, a pulse discharge test has been applied, with the application of discharge steps of 5% of the SoC, followed by a $3h$ period of rest, respectively. This test has been repeated at different temperatures. The behavior of the OCV relaxation process can be summarized as follows:

- Chemistry-to-chemistry and cell-to-cell deviations play a minor role. In general, a similar behavior has been observed for different chemistries, as well as for different cells of the same chemistry.

– In general, the OCV relaxation process decelerates with decreasing SoC and decreasing temperature, as already found in [3]. Based on the pulse discharge test special SoC regions have been found around 30% to 40% SoC, as well as around 60% to 80% SoC, at which the OCV relaxation process significantly slows down. Moreover, a decreasing operating temperature causes the OCV relaxation process to become even more decelerated in this regions.

3.2   Modeling and Optimization

To evaluate the performance of the proposed modeling and optimization methodology, a polynomial-enhanced description is chosen which splits the overall relaxation curve in three phases, p_0 - p_2. For the polynomial enhancement of phase p_2, the polynomial function $f_{p_k}(t)$ is chosen as a linear function. The nonlinear optimization method targets the constrained minimization of the scalar function $g(\mathbf{x})$. Hence, the influence of the model and estimation parameters is analyzed as follows:

– As the goal is to predict $V_{OC}(2.5h)$, that means we are interested in the long-term trend of the OCV relaxation phase, the influence of $f_{s,p1}$ is negligible. In general, the choice of the sampling rate is a trade-off between the achievable estimation accuracy, and on the other hand the power consumption which is needed in an embedded implementation. As best compromise, $f_{s,p1}$ is chosen to $f_{s,p1} = 1Hz$.
– n_1 and Δt_1 are chosen to $n_1 \ll$ and $\Delta t_1 = 1s$. n_1 has to be chosen so that there is still an appropriate number of generated voltage samples available to solve the corresponding linear least squares estimation problem. Δt_1 is chosen to $1s$ to use the latest trend of phase p_1 for the polynomial extension by phase p_2.
– t_k and $t_{LS,pk}$ are expected to have the major impact on the proposed OCV extrapolation method, which therefore are chosen as the parameters to be optimized by the nonlinear optimization strategy.

In order to find the constrained minimum of $g(\mathbf{x})$ the following methodology is used: First choose reasonable initial values for the parameters to be optimized. Then, apply the proposed nonlinear optimization methodology which yields a local minimum of $g(\mathbf{x})$. Subsequently, choose a new set of initial parameter values and again apply the proposed optimization methodology.

In Fig. 2, the results for the application of the proposed constrained optimization strategy are shown. Thereby, the found set of local minimums of $g(\mathbf{x})$ is plotted in dependence of the chosen initial values of t_0 and $t_{LS,1}$ for different values of the SoC, at an operating temperature of $+10°C$. It can be concluded that the beginning of phase p_0 has to be skipped for the proposed OCV extrapolation process. Exemplary, the blue upward-pointing triangle marked plot (70% SoC) shows a worst-case error of more than $4mV$ for the predicted relaxation end value at very short durations of p_0. For the skin color circle marked (90% SoC) plot, the red downward-pointing triangle marked plot (50% SoC) and the

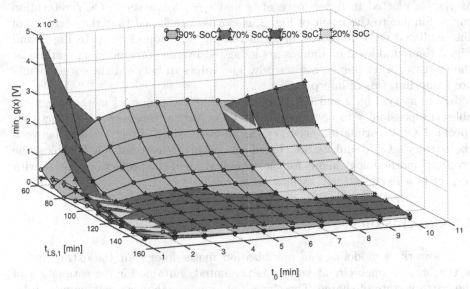

Fig. 2. Set of local minimums of $g(\mathbf{x})$ in dependence of t_0 and $t_{LS,1}$, for different SoCs

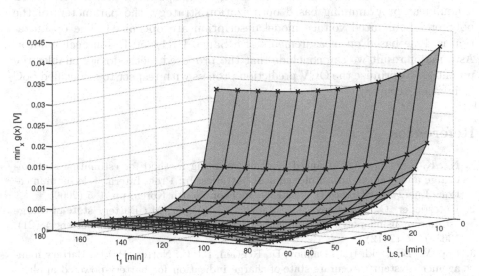

Fig. 3. Set of local minimums of $g(\mathbf{x})$ in dependence of t_1 and $t_{LS,1}$, for a single relaxation curve

yellow cross marked plot (20% SoC), the worst-case error lies around $2mV$. The application of the proposed modeling methodology should be as much independent of the SoC as possible, that's why we propose to skip the early phase of the relaxation process for the prediction of the OCV. Furthermore, it can be concluded from Fig. 2 that - as expected - an increasing duration of p_1 improves the accuracy of the OCV prediction. In Fig. 3, the found set of local minimums of $g(\mathbf{x})$ is plotted in dependence of t_1 and $t_{LS,1}$ for a single OCV relaxation curve. Similar to the result of Fig. 2, it can be concluded that the accuracy of the predicted OCV improves for an increasing duration of $t_{LS,1}$. In Fig. 2 and Fig. 3 the found local minimums are indicated by the corresponding markers at the raster's corner points, respectively. The values in between the corner points are found in terms of interpolation.

In summary, Fig. 2 and Fig. 3 illustrate that the proposed methodology enables the possibility to optimize the OCV prediction process with respect to a specified OCV estimation accuracy. As there exists a direct relation between the battery's OCV and its SoC based on the predefined SoC-OCV tables, the proposed methodology allows for the optimization of the prediction process with respect to a requested SoC estimation accuracy.

4   Conclusion

In this work, a modeling and optimization methodology for the extrapolation of the battery open-circuit voltage is presented, suitable for the estimation of the battery state-of-charge. Thereby, a polynomial-enhanced voltage model description is used for the open-circuit voltage extrapolation process. Based on a nonlinear programming based optimization strategy, the parameters of the polynomial-enhanced voltage model description are optimized. The optimization is done based on measurements of a Sanyo UR18650 Li-Ion accumulator. As a major result we can conclude that the proposed methodology enables the potential to optimize the OCV prediction process with respect to a specified SoC estimation accuracy.

References

1. Ng, K.-S., et al.: An enhanced coulomb counting method for estimating state-of-charge and state-of-health of lead-acid batteries. In: Proc. Intern. Telecommunications Energy Conference (INTELEC), Incheon, South Korea, pp. 1–5 (2009)
2. Unterrieder, C., Lunglmayr, M., Marsili, S., Huemer, M.: Battery state-of-charge estimation using polynomial enhanced prediction. IET Electronic Letters 48(21), 1363–1365 (2012)
3. Pop, V., Bergveld, H.J., Danilov, D., Regtien, P.P.L., Notten, P.H.L.: Battery management systems: Accurate state-of-charge indication for battery-powered applications, Eindhoven. Springer (2009)
4. Unterrieder, C., et al.: Comparative study and improvement of battery open-circuit voltage estimation methods. In: Proc. IEEE Mid. Symp. on Circuits and Systems (MWSCAS), Boise, Idaho, USA, pp. 1076–1079 (August 2012)
5. Nocedal, J., Wright, S.: Numerical Optimization, 2nd edn. Springer, Berlin (2006)

Application of Artificial Neuron Networks and Hurst Exponent to Forecasting of Successive Values of a Time Series Representing Environmental Measurements in an Intelligent Building

Andrzej Stachno and Andrzej Jablonski

Institute of Computer Engineering, Control and Robotics,
Wroclaw University of Technology, Wroclaw, Poland
{andrzej.stachno,andrzej.jablonski}@pwr.wroc.pl

Abstract. Control systems for intelligent buildings based on environmental measurements. The information contained in the measurement data in many cases are independent and chaotic. You can not interact with the control system, but only to monitor. In many cases, the use of measurement data for the purpose of building automation control, requires the use of forecasting systems. For the needs forecasting this type of measurement data apply artificial neural networks. Learning provides a mechanism to adjust its internal parameters of artificial neural network to characterize the trend of the time series reflects the measurement data. For time series with greater variability of smoothing is necessary. The intention initial clàssification time series smoothing and allows the use of artificial neural networks to forecast the next value of the time series irrespective of their volatility.

Keywords: Artificial Neuron Networks, FFT, Forecasting, Successive Values of a Time Series, Moving Window Fourier, Environmental Measurements in an Intelligent Building.

1 Intelligent Buildings and Environmental Analyzes

Measuring environmental in intelligent buildings (building automation) are a very important factor in the functioning of the autonomic system control. Of particular importance are the measurements of weather conditions, such as temperature, wind speed, gas concentration and light intensity. This information is completely independent and their inclusion significantly affect the operation of the building [1]. Based on these data, the building management system to decide on the scope and method of control. The control system can operate as a follower system, taking into account the measured parameters. However, due to the large inertia of this type of process (for example, solar light, which is affected by a rise in temperature in the room, regardless of the heating), this type of control can lead to erroneous control decisions (such as uncontrolled growth room temperature). The solution to this problem is to use forecasting systems that will be able to generate, respectively,

R. Moreno-Díaz et al. (Eds.): EUROCAST 2013, Part I, LNCS 8111, pp. 483–490, 2013.

accurate forecasts of parameters based on an analysis of trends (historical and current measurement) well in advance, so that the control system can react accordingly.

The parameters such as light intensity, wind speed and ambient temperature depends on many factors which control has no influence, however, must be taken into account in the control algorithm. Necessary here is an adaptive mechanism, setting out short-term forecasts of these parameters for the control system, adaptable to changing conditions in which it operates.

2   Application of Artificial Neural Networks to Forecasting

Very good forecasting system that satisfies the assumptions of adaptability are Artificial Neural Networks (ANN). Application of artificial neural network solves the main problem that meets the following value forecasting time series defining independent environmental parameters, or inability to determine the object model. Presentation at the input of the artificial neural network of the historical value of the time series, and an estimate of its output, allows you to adjust the internal structure of connections between neurons to the properties of the object generating the data (time series). Because the adaptation of artificial neural network accurately reflects the relationship between the presented data in a single step, it is necessary to cyclic learning neural network. Neural network undergone a process of learning in each cycle of historical data to assign the generated forecasts, automatically adjusts its internal structure (weight connections between neurons) to the changes that occur in the time series. On the basis of the behavior of the specified variety of internal structure of the network in each of learning cycles for different time series. On this basis, the theory has been formulated, assuming the initial classification of the time series needed to determine the quality of forecasts based on the time series of belonging to the group.

3   Classification of Time Series

Established, the initial classification of time series using Hurst exponent. It specifies a numerical measure of the range [0, 1] volatility time series. For the purpose of the investigations division of time series into three groups (Table 1). The time series for which the Hurst exponent is close to the value 0, it antipersistent series. They are characterized by high volatility following values. The second group consists of the time series for which the Hurst exponent is close to the value of 0.5. Series of this type illustrate the random walk. The third group, the time series defined Hurst exponent close to the 1. These time persistent series, characterized by a continuation of the trend and low volatility.

Assessed the studies performed, it was found that the time series for which the value of the Hurst exponent is close to 1, are the time series for the accuracy of the forecasts using neural networks and presentation of historical data is the highest. In addition, the analysis of the internal structure of a neural network learning in

Table 1. Classification of time series – Hurst exponent. Source: Own computations.

HURST EXPONENT VALUE	The behavior of neural network (the type of forecast)	Example of a time series
H < 0,5	Chaotic forecasts, large errors	
H = 0,5	The next values are forecast as the value of the previous step	
H > 0,5	The higher the value H, the more precise forecasts	

subsequent cycles of the network confirms its low volatility. This allows you to conclude that this type of time series are well suited to forecasting the next value by using artificial neural networks. For the time series in the other two groups, according to the proposed classification, forecasting accuracy is significantly smaller.

Because the in the real measuring of environmental parameters an intelligent building, dominated antipersistent and random time series, it is necessary to apply the method slight modification of the data series, so as not changing the nature of the measured data, showing it to adapt to the possibility of a time series forecasting using artificial neural network.

4   Smoothing Time Series

The basic method of modifying Hurst exponent of the time series to values close to unity is the smoothing of the time series. The most commonly used method to smooth time series rely on the analysis of historical data and averaging them or to isolate the most chaotic changes in order to reflect as accurately as possible the direction of the trend. The disadvantage of any method to smooth edges of this type is the delay between the smoothed and original data. An example would be smoothing using a moving average or eliminate harmonics when using fast Fourier transform.

4.1   Smoothing Time Series Using a Moving Average

Smoothing time series using the moving average [3] is based on cycles (moving) averaging the values of the time series according to equation (1):

$$S_{(n)}=1/k\sum(X_n+X_{n-1}+ \ldots +X_{n-(k+1)}) \tag{1}$$

where:

$S_{(n)}$ – moving average value at the point n,

X_n – the value of the time series at the point n,

k – quantity terms of the time series with the calculated value of $S_{(n)}$.

Subsequently received values create a new time series $S(n)$, whose volatility is modified by the parameter k The higher the k value, the more smoothed time series. The advantage of this method is low computational complexity. In this way it can be used for the series in which the data processing needs of small intervals. The disadvantage is the long delay between the original data, and the resulting time series.

4.2   Smoothing Time Series Using the Fast Fourier Transform

Elements of time series subjected to Fast Fourier Transform can be classified into two groups, reflecting the trend and disturbances [4]. Removing part of higher harmonics will filter out noise and leaving the components determining the trend (Fig. 1).

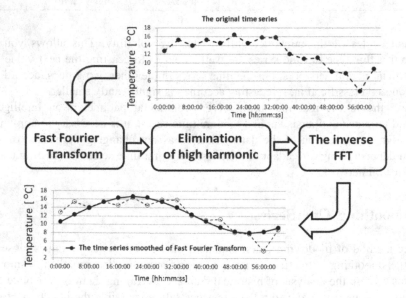

Fig. 1. Smoothing using Fast Fourier Transform with the elimination high harmonics

Filtration level disturbances and thereby change the Hurst exponent of unity in the direction determined by the number of harmonics removed.

The advantage of this method is the high accuracy of the resulting time series of the original series and the ability to adjust the level of smoothing by specifying the number of eliminated components.

The disadvantage, eliminating this method for the forecasting is the need for knowledge of all the elements of the time series when calculating the Fast Fourier Transform.

4.3   Smoothing Time Series Using Moving Window Fourier

Presented author's method of Moving Window Fourier allows accurate smoothing of the original time series, without having to know all of its components. The procedure for smoothing time series is presented in the form of an algorithm made up of five steps (Fig. 2):

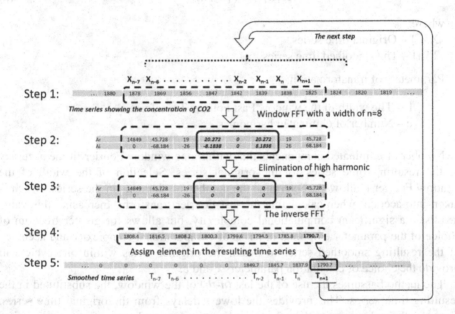

Fig. 2. The smoothing algorithm of the time series with the use of Moving Window Fourier (MWF)

Step 1: From the time series is extracted k consecutive elements. Window width k is selected experimentally based on the volatility of the time series. The range is more chaotic, the k should be larger (in the illustrated example k=8).
Step 2: From selected elements of the window width k is calculated fast Fourier transform.
Step 3: In the resulting set of numbers (coefficients of amplitudes and phases) that eliminated the higher harmonics. Number of harmonics eliminated is dependent on width of the window k and the variability of the time series. This value is selected experimentally so that the Hurst exponent of the resulting (smoothed) time series was close to unity as possible.

Step 4: For a modified frequency domain values is calculated inverse Fourier transform.

Step 5: With the so obtained, transcribed the value of the last element in the resulting (smoothed) time series. The calculations are repeated from *k-1* to the last element of the original series with an offset of one element in each cycle.

Additional assumption: the window width *k* and the number of the eliminated elements e remain the same for each cycle during the execution of the algorithm.

The above-described transformation set is a mapping of the original time series *X{n}* in the resulting series of *T{n}* (2):

$$X\{n\} => T\{n\} | k,e \tag{2}$$

where:

X{n} – Original time series,

T{n} – The smoothed time series.

Parameters of transformation:

k – The width of the window Fast Fourier Transform,

e – Number of eliminated harmonics.

Number of eliminated components that within one window Fourier fit the accuracy of the resulting time series for the original series. Selection of the width of the window Fourier k allows to determine the number of elements in the series, which is taken into account when calculating the fast Fourier transform. Increasing this value results in a significant computational complexity, but allows for greater freedom of choice of the parameter e optimal in terms of computational complexity and accuracy of the resulting smoothed series to match the original series within one cycle will provide the choice of calculation parameters *k* and *e*.

The method assumes the use of the last *(n-th)* of the window, the substituted in the resulting time series. This provides the lowest delays from the original time series. Use of other elements *(n-1, n-2, etc..)* improves smoothness of the time series, however, generate the method described in the moving average delay. It is less favorable when presenting historical data for the neural network. It is then forecasting the next value range with more advance. For the values *n-1* is projected the Fourier window element *n+2*, for the value *n-2*, *n+3* element, etc.

5   Forecasting of Environmental Parameters and Comparison of Smoothing Methods

The examples of the methods, smoothing effect on delays time series modified the original series. Comparison of methods for smoothing allows you to specify which of them has a beneficial effect on the accuracy of the forecasts successive values of the time series. Forecasting successive values of the time series according to the assumptions, is implemented using artificial neural networks. This method allows the preparation of measured data from the sensors, intelligent building systems for management and control systems affecting the comfort, operation and lower operating costs of automated building. Table 2 shows examples illustrate exemplary results of measurements of the parameters assigned to three groups of time series in accordance with the assumptions described in section 3.

Table 2. Compare the accuracy of forecasts for the original time series and the smoothed time series. Source: Own computations.

Type of input data for the Artifical Neural Network	Smoothing	Mean Absolute Deviation [%]
Wind speed [m/s]	Original time series	141,20
	Smoothed time series	**1,07**
Temperature [°C]	Original time series	17,95
	Smoothed time series	**15,73**
Concentration of CO2 [ppm]	Original time series	0,69
	Smoothed time series	**0,51**

6 Summary

Smoothing time series is necessary during forecasting the successive values using a neural network, which presents historical data. It causes a shift Hurst exponent determining the variability of the time series in the direction of unity, which is a modification and a change in the classification described in section 3. The accuracy of forecasts is highly dependent on the exact fit inside the parameters of artificial neural network, and they adapt to the fragment of time series. High volatility successive values of the time series requires continual modification of the internal parameters of artificial neural network, and does not guarantee the accuracy forecasts in subsequent cycles of learning. Smoothing time series eliminates this problem and allows the extension learning cycles of network and ensures stable results of forecasting at longer intervals of time. Alternatively, it is possible to achieve more accurate forecasts, cyclical matching network to the current value of the time series.

The exact determination parameters depending the presented method e and k Moving Window Fourier, a time series according to predetermined classification and forecasts accuracy of the successive values of the time series. It will also allow for accurate way to smoothing the time series forecasting for the next of its value.

According to the general measurement data processing algorithm for the automatic control system of intelligent building, the measurement data are transmitted directly to the management (BMS) [5]. Regulators analyze the data, and the result is a control signal actuators. The processing of information and the reaction of the actuators, and as a result the system reaction occurs with a time delay. For systems with a high inertia, the delay is significant and the system reaction occurs too late, the occurring conditions. An example of a security system monitoring the concentration of carbon dioxide in the room. The set threshold value of gas concentration above which runs a ventilation system to provide fresh air after some time, depending on the size of the room and the ventilation rate. More preferably, the system will apply the forecasting changes in the gas concentration measurement smoothing algorithm of the time series between the sensors measuring and control system (Fig. 3) and an early start the ventilation equipment. This will reduce costs through the use of devices with lower efficiency and also ensure a comfortable life of the building.

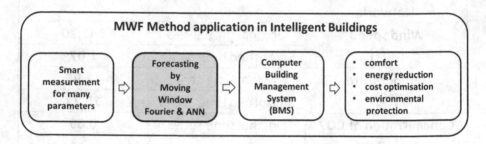

Fig. 3. MWF Method application in Intelligent Buildings

References

1. Stachno, A.: Inteligentne systemy pomiarowe w instalacji elektrycznej (Smart metering in the electricalinstallation). Fachowy Elektryk, Poznan (March 2013)
2. Peitgen, H.O., Jurgens, H., Saupe, D.: Introduction to Fractals and Chaos. PWN (2002)
3. Technical Analysis of the Financial Markets. WIG Press (1999)
4. Bernstein, J.: Cycles of profit. WIG Press (1996)
5. Jabłoński, A.: Intelligent buildings as distributed information systems. CASYS: International Journal of Computing Anticipatory Systems 21, s.385–s.394 (2008)

Data Improvement to Enable Process Mining on Integrated Non-log Data Sources

Reinhold Dunkl

University of Vienna, Austria
Faculty of Computer Science
reinhold.dunkl@univie.ac.at

Abstract. Process models derived using Process Mining (PM) are often very complex due to Data Quality Issues (DQIs). Some of those DQIs arise from integration of different data sources or the transformation of non-process oriented data, hence are structural and can be abstracted from the domain. Activity Sequencing and Activity Hierarchy are two concepts for improving certain DQIs in order to improve PM outcomes. The approaches are evaluated by showing the improvement of derived process models using a simplified real world scenario with simulated data.

Keywords: Data Enrichment, Data Quality Improvement, Data Integration, Process Mining.

1 Introduction

Process Mining (PM) – or more specific Process Discovery – aims at analyzing data in order to derive process models [1]. ProM is a PM framework that offers diverse mining algorithms to discover such models, e.g: apriori, heuristic or genetic algorithms. For any process discovery activity ProM expects as input process oriented data (event data) in a log file format. Normally the execution log files of information systems are used to derive the underlying process model that led to these log files. We will use the ProM framework and the heuristic miner to show the virtues of our approaches to improve the data quality and therefore the mined process models.

Data Quality issues (DQIs) – related to process oriented data – are manifold and arise from diverse real world situations like integration of diverse data sources or preparatory data transformations to generate process oriented data out of diverse structured data. Being confronted with such situation in the EBMC^2 project [3,6] we identified different DQIs related to process oriented data. We are facing diverse DQIs at once which heavily impairs PM outcomes. The combination of different DQIs makes analyzing of causation of one DQI to the outcome of PM intransparent. In order to generate meaningful process models we need to separate single DQIs and develop concepts to tackle each of them.

Section 2 motivates our research and connects it to related work followed by Section 3 which confines and abstracts DQIs within our setting. Concepts to

R. Moreno-Díaz et al. (Eds.): EUROCAST 2013, Part I, LNCS 8111, pp. 491–498, 2013.

improve data quality in order to overcome the identified DQIs are presented in
Section 4 whereas Section 5 evaluates how mined models improve by rectified
log data based on our proposed concepts. Section 6 summarizes the paper and
points out future and follow up work and research.

2   Motivation and Related Work

DQIs have different causes from obvious simple operational causes, like data
input errors, to more structural causes, like data model designs. In this paper we
want to deal with DQIs that can be abstracted and solved by adding knowledge
in order to improve existing data. Therefore we do not deal with errors arising
from operation but with errors based on structural differences.

One way to improve DQIs is by purging log data based on constraint violation
[7]. This way whole cases are purged which is not always intended. If we want
to preserve deviant cases we need to tackle DQIs in another way.

As mentioned before, we want to use PM to discover process models which
makes process oriented data necessary, expected in log file format. We know
from the EBMC^2 project on skin cancer treatment – as well as stated in the
Process Mining Manifesto [2] – that such process oriented data is not always at
hand when it comes to realistic data sources. Such data sources are designed
for a certain application without a particular process structure in mind and
therefore lacking in – for PM purpose – necessary details e.g.: detailed temporal
information.

The Process Mining Manifesto [2] categorizes the quality of data sources in
terms of PM from one to five starts (* - *****) where PM results from * and **
data sources are not trustworthy. Following this categorization we are dealing
with data sources that are categorized as * or **. In order to make those data
sources usable – deriving meaningful process models using PM – we aim to
raise the quality to at least ***. These categories are already aggregated and
therefore hard to use in order to identify single DQIs. Bose et al. [4] collected
and categorized a multitude of DQIs in this area, also covering the ones we
identified, but offers no solutions or concepts to improve data relating to theses
DQIs.

Any event stream is limited in the knowledge that is included – and therefore
also what can be derived from it – as it contains instantiations of the underlying
process which might not represent the whole process model at all. In order to
overcome DQIs that impede PM outcomes we need to extract more knowledge
and prepare or pre-process the log data. Or in other words, by adding some
knowledge we intend to raise the possibilities to derive further knowledge.

A PM project following a process model like the L* life-cycle model described
in the Process Mining Manifesto [2] or the PMMF approach [5] helps in avoiding
certain DQIs but do not guarantee to solve all of them, hence this process models
can be enhanced by adding data improvement based on additional knowledge.
E.g. the L* life-cycle model consists of four stages describing a PM project
where the first stage deals with extraction by understanding the available data

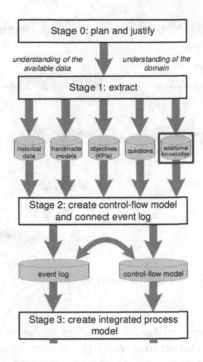

Fig. 1. Extended extract of the L* life-cycle model [2]

and the domain. Here we need to attach the extraction of additional knowledge for the concepts (cf. Subsection 4.1 and 4.2) we suggest to solve certain identified DQIs. The proposed concepts correspond to the second stage ("*create control-flow model and connect event logs*") that are dealing with filtering and adaption of the event log in order to improve results. Figure 1 shows an extended extract of the L* life-cycle model with the mentioned stages where our approach is embedded.

3 Abstractions from the Problem Setting

One aim of the EBMC² project is to derive patient treatment models for skin cancer treatment [3,6]. For that purpose we identified and integrated diverse databases and used them as a basis to generate process oriented data. After first attempts using this data for PM we were able to identify several DQIs that made the mining of meaningful process models impossible, especially because of combinations of different DQIs.

In order to provide PM with data we developed the Data Integration Layer for Process Mining (DIL/PM) – partially described in [3] – that eases integration and transformation steps. Figure 2 shows the central extract of the underlying data model. The entities "*case*", "*event*", "*attribute*" and "*attributeValue*" represent all necessary information to generate log files for PM. Meta information is stored

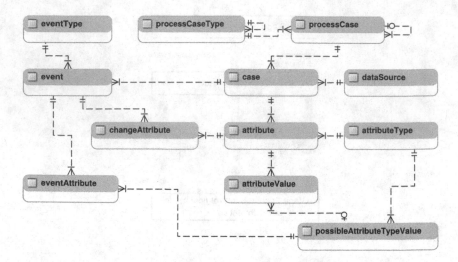

Fig. 2. Data model from the Data Integration Layer for Process Mining (DIL/PM)

in the corresponding type entities, hence allowing us to extend the model for holding additional information to solve DQIs. A transformation and/or filtering step can make use of this additional data to improve DQIs while generated required log files.

3.1   The Problem Environment and Setting

Some DQIs arise from the integration of different data sources, e.g.: Activities from one data source representing other activities from another data source or existing different granularity levels of activities within different data sources. Certain DQIs arise from the non-process orientation of data that makes transformations necessary, e.g.: Missing temporal information leading to incomplete process models or rough temporal granularity. Every data source holds attributes that are set at a certain point when an event happens. The information which events happened and the order they happened in is often missing in the data source.

3.2   DQI Confinement and Abstraction

Being confronted with actual diverse and non-log data sources raises actual problems [3,6]. Some of them are domain specific and need to be solved individually, others can be abstracted, solutions conceptualized and used for improving by pre-precessing or enriching data. In this paper we concentrate on two different domain independent DQIs. First the already mentioned rough temporal granularity that leads to parallelisms in the process model and second different granularity levels of activities leading to unnecessary overloaded process models.

To improve these DQIs we need additional knowledge that is not found within the data itself. The persons knowing the process itself or conducting the activities within the process are possessing the missing knowledge. In order to improve the data quality or enrich the data it is necessary to make use of this knowledge by identifying, extracting and storing it in a structured way so it can be used for processing. To overcome rough temporal granularity, meaning several activities have the same date and time even though they are conducted at different times, we need to know simple sequencing information on activities that allows us to correct time information. For solving different granularity levels of activities, meaning multiple different activities having a common denominator and can be represented by one activity, we need this hierarchical links between the activities. A filter using this information can generate log files with less activities leading to simpler and easier understandable process models.

4   Concept Design to Improve Data Quality

The last section presented some DQIs we identified. We now suggest to introduce parts of the wanted process model it self to improve these DQIs. This section presents two concepts to improve two of those DQIs: Activity Sequencing to improve rough temporal granularity and Activity Hierarchy to improve different granularity levels of activities. Both concepts are integrated into the DIL/PM model, cf. Figure 3.

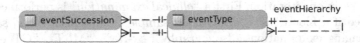

Fig. 3. Extension of the DIL/PM to hold information on Activity Sequencing and Activity Hierarchy

4.1   Activity Sequencing

Activity Sequencing aims for collecting basic information on the antecedent and subsequent activities (e.g.: wake up, breakfast, lunch, dinner, sleep) to resolve parallelisms caused by imprecise temporal information. Figure 3 (left side) shows how eventTypes (activities) can be extended with an additional entity eventSuccession that way allowing multiple succession eventTypes to be stored to one eventType. In a pre-processing step events with the same time stamp can be corrected by searching for a succession relation in eventSuccession. The time correction should be minimal just to allow PM to resolve parallelisms without changing the rest of the model. This very simple algorithm can be extended to find transitive eventTypes, in which case loops within the sequencing have to be recognized. Hence the usage of e.g. reachability algorithms will be necessary, especially if we want to resolve the DQI of missing temporal information. For this paper and the DQI of rough temporal granularity we stick to the simple algorithm as we want to show how the derived process models improve.

4.2 Activity Hierarchy

Activity Hierarchy aims for collecting subtype information on activities (e.g.: swimming with subtypes front crawl, back crawl, breaststroke) that way resolving overloaded process models caused by different granularity levels of activities. Figure 3 (right side) shows how eventTypes (activities) can be extended with an recursive relationship that way allowing to store a rooted tree hierarchy of eventTypes. In a filtering (choosing the level of granularity) and a pre-processing step the event name can be unified to parent eventType names. If we want to use more than one level of this hierarchy – transitive activity name unification – we need a more complex algorithm. For this paper and to be able to show how derived process models improve we stick to the simple case of one level.

5 Evaluation

For evaluation we take a closer look at a part of the skin cancer treatment process which is reflecting the problems we identified. The process starts with the first visit by the patient, hence with the activity "*medical history*". After that a "*skin check*" is performed followed by the "*surgical excision of primary tumor*". Some days later the "*histology of primary tumor*" is finished that decides about the further examination activities (some processes already end here, if no further follow-up examinations are necessary). The examination part that follows is a loop and the severeness of the illness defines which examinations will be performed in one iteration. First a "*clinical examination*" is performed where it is decided if a blood test ("*draw blood sample*" and "*check blood sample*") and/or imaging examinations ("*sonography*", "*x-ray*", "*MRT*", "*CT*", "*PET*" and/or "*PET-CT*") will be conducted in order to find distant metastases.

5.1 Simulation

Real world data we collected within the EBMC^2 project is to small in quantity and has diverse other DQIs. Therefore we use the developed simulation tool $iMine^{Sim}$ to generate a log file containing entries with imprecise temporal information as well as the six defined imaging examination activities. The activities *medical history*", "*skin check*" and "*surgical excision of primary tumor*" happen in this order but on the same day. The generated time stamps granularity is on a day basis, therefore all three activities have the same time stamp. Figure 4 (left side) shows the derived process model using the heuristic miner from the ProM 5.2 framework. As we can see the first visit activities that happened on the same day are assumed to be parallel. The found particular control flow is based on the order of the entries in the log file, which was randomized. Further we can see how examinations are conducted parallel which is represented with the four branches leaving "*histology of primary tumor*" to "*sonography*" which is the primary imaging examination that is used, "*draw blood sample*", "*check blood sample*" and "*clinical examination*". We can also see the loop of examinations with the backwards directed branches.

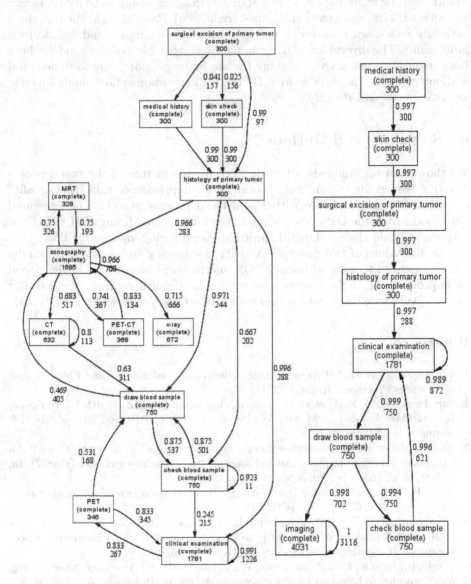

Fig. 4. Derived process models before (left) and after (right) DQIs improvement

5.2 Process Model Improvement

After specifying times stamps using Activity Sequencing and reducing the activities for imaging examinations to one activity *"imaging"* using Activity Hierarchy we can see the improvements in Figure 4 (right side). Parallelism at the first three activities have been resolved as well at *"draw blood sample"* and *"clinical examination"*. The diverse imaging examinations – that bloated the model – have been reduced to one activity making the model much more easy to understand without changing the data source. Different filter options allow single imaging activities to be added easily.

6 Summary and Outlook

We showed on a simplified real world example the virtues of the two concepts Activity Sequencing and Activity Hierarchy for improving certain Data Quality Issues (DQIs) and therefore with PM derived process models. The presented data model from the Data Integration Layer for Process Mining (DIL/PM) was extended to hold the additional knowledge for preparing log files for PM.

The algorithms of two concepts Activity Sequencing and Activity Hierarchy will be extended to solve additional DQIs and further concepts will be developed to improve other DQIs. Evaluations with future real data from the EBMC^2 project [3,6] as well as a data set on higher eduction system will be conducted.

References

1. van der Aalst, W.M.P.: Process Mining - Discovery, Conformance and Enhancement of Business Processes. Springer (2011)
2. van der Aalst, W.M.P., et al.: Process mining manifesto. In: Daniel, F., Barkaoui, K., Dustdar, S. (eds.) BPM 2011 Workshops, Part I. LNBIP, vol. 99, pp. 169–194. Springer, Heidelberg (2012)
3. Binder, M., et al.: On analyzing process compliance in skin cancer treatment: An experience report from the evidence-based medical compliance cluster (ebmc2). In: Ralyté, et al. (eds.) [8], pp. 398–413
4. Bose, J.C., Mans, R., van der Aalst, W.M.P.: Wanna improve process mining results? Tech. rep., BPM Center Report (2013)
5. De Weerdt, J., Schupp, A., Vanderloock, A., Baesens, B.: Process mining for the multi-faceted analysis of business processes: A case study in a financial services organization. Computers in Industry 64(1), 57–67 (2013)
6. Dunkl, R., Fröschl, K.A., Grossmann, W., Rinderle-Ma, S.: Assessing medical treatment compliance based on formal process modeling. In: Holzinger, A., Simonic, K.-M. (eds.) USAB 2011. LNCS, vol. 7058, pp. 533–546. Springer, Heidelberg (2011)
7. Ly, L.T., Indiono, C., Mangler, J., Rinderle-Ma, S.: Data transformation and semantic log purging for process mining. In: Ralyté, et al. (eds.) [8], pp. 238–253
8. Ralyté, J., Franch, X., Brinkkemper, S., Wrycza, S. (eds.): CAiSE 2012. LNCS, vol. 7328. Springer, Heidelberg (2012)

Comparing Some Estimate Methods
in a Gompertz-Lognormal Diffusion Process

Nuria Rico, Desiree Romero, and Maribel G. Arenas

Universidad de Granada, Spain
{nrico,deromero}@ugr.es, mgarenas@atc.ugr.es
http://www.ugr.es

Abstract. This paper compares four different methods to obtain maximum likelihood estimates of the parameters of a Gompertz-lognormal diffusion process, where no analytical solution for the likelihood equations exists. A recursive method, a Newton-Raphson algorithm, a Simulated Annealing algorithm and an Evolutionary Algorithm to obtain estimates are proposed. The four methods are compared using a simulated data set. The results are compared with simulated paths of the process in terms of several error measurements.

Keywords: Maximum likelihood estimate, optimization algorithm.

1 Introduction

Diffusion processes are frequently used for natural growth-pattern modeling and making forecast. For this aim researches usually consider the mean, mode or percentile functions of the process. The Gompertz-lognormal diffusion process [1] can be built like a mixture between a Gompertz-type process [2] and a lognormal process [3]. Thus, the Gompertz-lognormal diffusion process is defined through the infinitesimal moments:

$$A_1(x,t) = (me^{-\beta t} + c)x$$
$$A_2(x,t) = \sigma^2 x^2, \tag{1}$$

with $m > \beta > 0$, $c \in \mathbb{R}$.

The drift is a function depending on three parameters (m, β and c) and the infinitesimal variance is a function that includes σ^2. For $c = 0$ the process is a Gompertz-type and for $\beta = 0$ the process is an homogeneous lognormal diffusion process. If not, the process would have a shape that might show two inflection points, so it makes the process useful for modeling many situations with paths along time turning from increasing to decreasing or turning from concave to convex shape.

The transition density function is a lognormal distribution. Thus, for $t > s$, the distribution is one dimensional lognormal-type with first parameter:

$$\ln(y) - \frac{m}{\beta}\left(e^{-\beta t} - e^{-\beta s}\right) + \left(c - \frac{\sigma^2}{2}\right)(t - s) \tag{2}$$

R. Moreno-Díaz et al. (Eds.): EUROCAST 2013, Part I, LNCS 8111, pp. 499–506, 2013.

and second parameter:

$$(t - s)\sigma^2. \tag{3}$$

Since the process being considered is Markovian, the calculation of the finite-dimensional distributions only depends on the initial distribution and the transitions. The latter being known, the initial distribution must be imposed in order to obtain the finite-dimensional distributions. In the case of a degenerate initial distribution, namely $P[X(t_0) = x_0] = 1$, or a lognormal initial distribution, $X(t) \sim \Lambda(\mu_0; \sigma_0^2)$, the finite-dimensional distributions are certain to be lognormal.

The estimation of the set of parameters leads the estimation of the main features of the process. The most widely used, specifically for predicting purposes, are the mean, mode and quantile functions. Their expressions depend on the set of parameters $\{m, \beta, c, \sigma^2\}$ and, in the case of a lognormal initial distribution being considered, on the $\{\mu_0, \sigma_0^2\}$ set too.

The problem is to find the maximum likelihood estimation (MLE) for the parameters of the model, from which the estimation of the parametric functions can be found.

2   The Methods

In order to obtain the estimations, four different methods have been used. Firstly, two methods that try to solve the maximum likelihood equations are considered. Secondly, the other two algorithms, which optimize the likelihood function directly, are applied.

The estimation procedure takes some steps; the first is to consider only the variable part of the function, not the constant one. The second step is to change the sign in order to minimize the value. This function is optimized by minimizing it by the four methods.

2.1   Methods to Approximate the Solution of the Equation System

The first is an iterative or recursive method. It considers the relationship between parameters and uses it to find a solution in an iterative procedure. The second way is to find the solution using a numerical method such as the Newton-Raphson method.

The recursive (or iterative) method works in three steps. The first step is to obtain a value for β. With this value, the equation system can be solved and it gives an initial set of solutions. Then, the procedure uses the relationship between β and the point where the path shows the second inflection point, to get a better value of β. With this new β it solves the system. Then, it is repeated until a criterion of convergence is set.

In practice, when β is known, the process can be seen as a non-homogeneous lognormal diffusion process like the one studied in [4]. In such case the parameters can be estimated by solving the equation system.

This method is not difficult to program, and it is able to achieve a solution close to the real one in few seconds. The main problem of using this method is the calculation of the time of the second inflection point. Sometimes this is not an easy problem. The obtained solution is as precise as the calculation of this point is.

The second way to solve the equation system is to use a numerical method such as Newton-Raphson algorithm. This uses one initial value and calculates the root of the primitive function at this point as a better solution. Then it uses the root of the primitive function at the new point as a better solution, and so on, until an stop criteria is reached.

This is a good way to deal with the problem if there is not too much noise on the observed data and if the initial solution is good. Moreover, this method is applied because the likelihood equation system has enough regularity conditions. Applying this numerical approximation is easy in computational terms because a great deal of software with this approximation method have been developed. In few seconds a very good solution is obtained if a good initial solution is given. The problem arises when a bad initial solution for β is set. In this case the method does not work.

2.2   Methods to Optimize the Likelihood Function

These methods do not try to solve the equation system, but rather try to maximize the likelihood function. The two methods considered are the Simulated Annealing [5] algorithm and an Evolutionary Algorithm [6].

The first one, Simulated Annealing, needs a big set of parameters to work; initial and final temperature, number of iterations, cool method, etc. In short, the method evaluates a lot of sets of solutions. It looks for the best solution firstly with big changes in the proposed solution when the temperature is high enough or with very little steps for the solution when the temperature becomes cooler.

The main problem of using this method is that it is not easy to tune because there are a lot of parameters to be defined. It must be tuned to find good solutions and actually it takes much more time than the other two methods previously mentioned. An advantage of this method is it might offer a good set of solutions even if the noise is high and the program can always be run again to try to obtain a better solution, because it is not deterministic.

The second optimization method carried out is an Evolutionary Algorithm. This kind of method is designed to find a solution evolving one initial solution, that is, a population of solutions is the starting point and it gives a new generation of solutions using natural based reproduction and mutation among the individuals of the population. The method simulates a generational evolution of the population along a number of iterations. This process is repeated until the number of generations is reached.

This method takes much more time than Newton-Raphson method does. On the other hand, this method gives the best results when there is a big noise in the data.

3   Simulated Paths Study

In order to compare the four different ways to estimate the set of parameters we carried out a simulation of the Gompertz-lognormal diffusion process based on the algorithms derived from the numerical solution of stochastic differential equations (Kloeden et al. [7], Rao et al. [8]).

The simulation allows us to find paths that validate the estimation procedures proposed. To this end, several different paths are generated. Since the algorithm is recursive, an initial value is required for x_0. Said value is determined by the initial distribution being considered as either degenerate or lognormal. For the generation of paths, it is considered x_0 following a lognormal distribution $\Lambda(0; 1)$. The values of the parameters in the simulation are $m = 1$, $\beta = 0.2$ and $c = 0.013$. Three different values for σ^2 have been considered, taking the values 10^{-5}, 10^{-4} and 10^{-3}. For each combination, 100 paths with 500 data each one have been simulated, from $t_0 = 1$ to $t_{500} = 100$, being $t_i - t_{i-1} = 0.2$.

Figures 1, 2 and 3 show the simulated paths with low, medium and high noise.

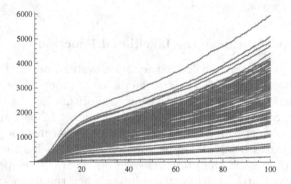

Fig. 1. Simulated paths for a Gompertz-lognormal process from $t_0 = 1$ to $t_{500} = 100$, with parameters $m = 1$, $\beta = 0.2$, $c = 0.013$ and $\sigma^2 = 10^{-5}$

For each set of paths the estimation of the parameters are done, using each method. For each one we calculated some error measurements [9]: mean squared error (MSE), mean absolute error (MAE), mean absolute percentage error (MAPE), symmetric mean absolute percentage error (SMAPE) and mean relative absolute error (MRAE). In the case of the MRAE, the error is calculated between the estimated mean function and the path that a simple model gives. In this case a *naive* model is used; the predicted value is equal to the value before it. For all error measurements the 5% trimmed mean is taken. The results are summarized in tables 1, 2 and 3.

Table 1 shows the estimation of the parameters m, β and c when the noise on the simulation are $\sigma^2 = 10^{-5}$, $\sigma^2 = 10^{-4}$ and $\sigma^2 = 10^{-3}$. In bold are the closest values with the ones used on the simulation, obtained with the recursive method for every value of σ^2. According to this table, all the methods considered give

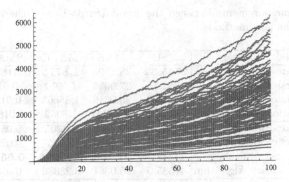

Fig. 2. Simulated paths for a Gompertz-lognormal process from $t_0 = 1$ to $t_{500} = 100$, with parameters $m = 1$, $\beta = 0.2$, $c = 0.013$ and $\sigma^2 = 10^{-4}$.

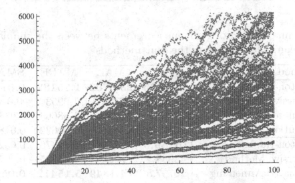

Fig. 3. Simulated paths for a Gompertz-lognormal process from $t_0 = 1$ to $t_{500} = 100$, with parameters $m = 1$, $\beta = 0.2$, $c = 0.013$ and $\sigma^2 = 10^{-3}$.

Table 1. Estimation of the parameters m, β and c and value of the function to minimize, by the four methods, for the paths simulated with $m = 1$, $\beta = 0.2$ and $c = 0.013$

Variability	Method	$\hat{m}$	$\hat{\beta}$	$\hat{c}$	Minimum obtained
$\sigma^2 = 10^{-5}$	Newton-Raphson	1.012898	0.202730	0.012986	**-256494.23**
	Recursive Method	**1.007560**	**0.200344**	**0.012986**	-205013.02
	Simulated Annealing	1.015183	0.203520	0.013261	-256409.80
	Evolutionary Algorithm	1.012941	0.202747	0.013196	-256494.22
$\sigma^2 = 10^{-4}$	Newton-Raphson	1.039485	0.208148	0.013541	**-199315.69**
	Recursive Method	**1.014367**	**0.198462**	**0.013375**	-194477.83
	Simulated Annealing	1.03675	0.20736	0.01343	-199311.55
	Evolutionary Algorithm	1.03948	0.20815	0.01354	-199315.69
$\sigma^2 = 10^{-3}$	Newton-Raphson	1.03292	0.18557	**0.02224**	-141733.84
	Recursive Method	**1.13657**	**0.22761**	0.01478	-88350.22
	Simulated Annealing	1.13572	0.22768	0.01500	-141799.63
	Evolutionary Algorithm	1.13659	0.22762	0.01478	**-141799.84**

Table 2. Error measurements between the simulated paths and the estimated mean functions using the four methods

Variability	Method	MSE	MAE	MAPE	SMAPE	MRAE
$\sigma^2 = 10^{-5}$	Newton-Raphson	**2785.32**	28.4796	**1.8715**	**0.0188087**	**32.1696**
	Recursive Method	2282.10	27.9635	1.9954	0.0197	15.4898
	Simulated Annealing	1825.22	25.9619	1.88663	0.01895	14.1732
	Evolutionary Algorithm	2611.59	**24.8847**	1.8962	0.018794	15.0744
$\sigma^2 = 10^{-4}$	Newton-Raphson	**25021.7**	87.1303	5.4305	0.05494	73.7287
	Recursive Method	51123.0	146.423	10.6957	0.09935	129.915
	Simulated Annealing	25348.5	**87.109**	**5.93996**	**0.05463**	**73.4791**
	Evolutionary Algorithm	47535.0	96.0361	8.28386	0.07800	103.418
$\sigma^2 = 10^{-3}$	Newton-Raphson	341394	267.023	**15.8838**	0.15965	**71.6209**
	Recursive Method	1.69×10^7	2306.49	148.913	0.75948	737.073
	Simulated Annealing	335844	264.757	15.9655	**0.15925**	71.9319
	Evolutionary Algorithm	**323337**	**252.174**	16.5020	0.15933	72.4040

Table 3. 5% trimmed mean of error measurements between the simulated paths and the estimated mean functions using the four methods

Variability	Method	MSE	MAE	MAPE	SMAPE	MRAE
$\sigma^2 = 10^{-5}$	Newton-Raphson	**1700.36**	**23.8702**	**1.75182**	**0.01756**	**13.5527**
	Recursive Method	2282.10	27.9635	1.99536	0.01977	15.4898
	Simulated Annealing	1825.22	25.9619	1.88663	0.018945	14.1732
	Evolutionary Algorithm	2611.59	24.8847	1.89622	0.018794	15.0744
$\sigma^2 = 10^{-4}$	Newton-Raphson	**16789.5**	74.3788	5.19373	0.052376	48.5443
	Recursive Method	43988.9	141.48	10.4825	0.097933	102.072
	Simulated Annealing	16797.8	**74.1349**	**5.15412**	**0.05202**	**48.349**
	Evolutionary Algorithm	40801.0	91.079	8.02253	0.076095	79.9726
$\sigma^2 = 10^{-3}$	Newton-Raphson	195856	227.489	**14.704**	0.150892	**56.5472**
	Recursive Method	1.63×10^7	2301.73	145.921	0.75987	595.135
	Simulated Annealing	195176	226.079	14.7542	0.150573	56.6839
	Evolutionary Algorithm	**182321**	**225.036**	15.0656	**0.150494**	57.9545

good results for the estimations of the parameters comparing with the values used for the simulation. This table also shows the values with these estimations for the function to minimize. Note that minimizing this function is equal to maximizing the likelihood. In bold are the minimum values of the function (corresponding to the maximum likelihood values).

Table 2 shows the error measurements MSE, MAE, MAPE, SMAPE and MRAE given by each method for the three sets of paths. These errors are calculated taking into account the estimated mean function given by the estimation of the parameters, comparing them with the simulated paths. In bold are the lower values for each error measurement.

Table 3 shows the 5% trimmed mean of the error measurements MSE, MAE, MAPE, SMAPE and MRAE. It avoids high values of the error measurements due to a few paths with a high error.

4   Conclusions

Table 1 shows the best results are given by the recursive method since the estimations are the closest to the values used in simulation. But it does not give the best approximation in terms of the value of the likelihood or the error measurements. These estimations are the ones that lead to the worst results in terms of error or evaluation of the likelihood function.

The results given in Table 2 and Table 3 show that for low variance ($\sigma^2 = 10^{-5}$) the Newton-Raphson method presents the lowest errors, and they are very close to those obtained with Evolutionary Algorithm when trimmed errors are observed. Moreover, the value of the optimization function is lower using this methodo but very close to those obtained using Evolutionary Algorithm approximation.

For a medium variability, $\sigma^2 = 10^{-4}$, the best results are provided by the Simulated Annealing method. All the errors and trimmed errors are the lower with this method, except for non-trimmed and trimmed SME, which are lower using the Evolutionary Algorithm. In this case, the value of the likelihood function is lower when Simulated Annealing is considered than when Newton-Raphson or Evolutionary Algorithm is considered. In the case of $\sigma^2 = 10^{-3}$, Simulated Annealing provides best results for MSE and MAE and trimmed ones. The Newton-Raphson method shows the best results in terms of non-trimmed and trimmed MAPE and MRAE. The SMAPE shows better results for the Simulated Annealing method (non-trimmed mean) and the Evolutionary Algorithm (trimmed mean). The value of the likelihood function is higher with the Newton-Raphson or the Evolutionary Algorithm estimate methods.

In short, the recursive method allows us to estimate the parameters close to the real set, although it does not mean the function estimated looks like the observed path. In terms of errors and likelihood value, when a low noise is present, the Newton-Raphson gives the best results. For high noise, optimization algorithms give better results than iterative or numerical methods do.

Acknowledgments. This research has been partially supported by FQM147 of the Andalucian Regional Government, and the project PYR-2012-14 of the CEI BioTIC GENIL CEB09-0010 program ot the University of Granada and by TIN2011-28627-C04-02 of the Spanish Ministry of Science and Innovation.

References

1. Gutiérrez, R., Rico, N., Román, P., Romero, D., Torres, F.: Un nuevo proceso de difusión para modelizar patrones de crecimiento mixto exponencial-Gompertz. In: XXX Congreso Nacional SEIO. Libro de Actas, pp. 1–15 (2007)
2. Gutiérrez, R., Román, P., Romero, D., Serrano, J.J., Torres, F.: A new Gompertz-type diffusion process with application to random growth. Math. Biosci. 208, 147–165 (2007)

3. Gutiérrez, R., Román, P., Romero, D., Torres, F.: Applications of the univariate lognormal diffusion process with exogenous factors in forecasting. Cybernet Syst. 34(8), 709–724 (2003)
4. Gutiérrez, R., Román, P., Torres, F.: Inference and first-passage-times for the lognormal diffusion process with exogenous factors: application to modelling in economics. Appl. Soch. Model. Bus. 15, 325–332 (1999)
5. Ingber, L.: Simulated annealing: Practice versus theory. Mathl. Comput. Modelling 18(11), 29–57 (1993)
6. Bäck, T.: Evolutionary algorithms in theory and practice. Oxford University Press (1996)
7. Kloeden, P.E., Platen, E., Schurz, H.: Numerical solution of SDE through computer experiments. Springer (1994)
8. Rao, N.J., Borwankar, J.D., Ramkrishna, D.: Numerical solution of Ito integral equations. SIAM Journal on Control and Optimization 12, 124–139 (1974)
9. De Gooijer, J.G., Hyndman, R.J.: 25 Years of IIF Time Series Forecasting: A Selective Review. Tinbergen Institute Discussion Papers No. TI 05-068/4 (2005)

Delta Analysis of
Role-Based Access Control Models

Maria Leitner

University of Vienna, Austria
Faculty of Computer Science
maria.leitner@univie.ac.at

Abstract. Role-based Access Control (RBAC) is de facto standard for
access control in Process-aware Information Systems (PAIS); it grants
authorization to users based on roles (i.e. sets of permissions). So far,
research has centered on the design and run time aspects of RBAC. An
evaluation and verification of a RBAC system (e.g., to evaluate ex post
which users acting in which roles were authorized to execute permissions)
is still missing. In this paper, we propose delta analysis of RBAC models
which compares a prescriptive RBAC model (i.e. how users are expected
to work) with a RBAC model (i.e. how users have actually worked) derived from event logs. To do that, we transform RBAC models to graphs
and analyze them for structural similarities and differences. Differences
can indicate security violations such as unauthorized access. For future
work, we plan to investigate semantic differences between RBAC models.

Keywords: Access Control, Delta Analysis, Organizational Mining,
RBAC, Security.

1 Introduction

Process-aware Information Systems (PAIS) support the automated execution
of tasks in business processes (cf. [23]). Authorization and access control are
key challenges when it comes to security in PAIS (cf. [4,14]). Role-based access
control (RBAC) models (e.g., [11]) are the de facto standard for access control
in PAIS. RBAC uses the concept of roles to restrict access; a role consists of
a set of permissions, i.e. authorizations to do certain actions such as executing
tasks in a business process. For example, only users having the role *Doctor* are
allowed to execute task *retrievePatientRecords* to get patient records.

Furthermore, process mining techniques extract and examine process-related
information from (process) event logs [1]. Process mining can be used for delta
analysis by comparing the discovered process model (i.e. the actual process represented by a process model obtained through process mining) with a prescriptive
process model [2] (i.e. how the process model is expected to work). Furthermore,
organizational mining techniques extract and derive organizational structures
with organizational models (e.g., [19]). These techniques can be suitable to derive RBAC models from event logs (further called *current-state* RBAC models)

R. Moreno-Díaz et al. (Eds.): EUROCAST 2013, Part I, LNCS 8111, pp. 507–514, 2013.

[15]. Current-state RBAC models reflect the operational reality; they provide information on which users acting in which roles have actually executed which tasks. Hence, these access snapshots can be used for analysis and evaluation.

This paper investigates delta analysis of RBAC models which compares a prescriptive RBAC model with a current-state RBAC model and analyzes and evaluates the models for structural similarities and differences. Therefore, we transform RBAC models into labeled graphs (cmp. [13]) and compare them with e.g., the graph edit distance (cf. [12,9]). With delta analysis, we hope to discover differences between the prescriptive and the current-state RBAC models. These deviations can indicate e.g., security and compliance violations or an outdated configuration of the RBAC model. Furthermore, a case study shows that the evaluation of a snapshot of RBAC models can be complex and can only be performed by domain experts.

The remainder of this paper is structured as follows. Section 2 outlines delta analysis of RBAC models by comparing the structure of RBAC models. Furthermore, structural differences of RBAC models are evaluated in a case study in Section 3. Section 4 reviews related work and Section 5 concludes the paper.

2   Delta Analysis of Role-Based Access Control Models

Delta analysis aims to discover differences between descriptive/prescriptive and discovered (current-state) RBAC models as shown in Figure 1. Current-state RBAC models contain which users in which roles have actually invoked which permissions i.e. reflect operational reality. Hence, these access snapshots can be used for an ex post analysis and evaluation of RBAC implementations. As shown in Figure 1, delta analysis uses this operational knowledge and compares the existing original, conceptual (prescriptive) models with reality to detect violations such as unauthorized access.

Delta analysis of RBAC models contains of three steps: (1) obtain prescriptive and discovered RBAC models, (2) compare RBAC models for e.g., structural similarities and differences and (3) analyze and evaluate differences to detect violations. In the following sections, we will define basic concepts and outline the structural matching of RBAC models.

2.1   Preliminaries

In this paper, we specify an RBAC model based on the NIST standard RBAC model defined in [11] and its administrative operations (further called edit operations). Specifically, our approach uses the following edit operations of [11]: addUser, deleteUser, addRole, deleteRole, addPermission, deletePermission, assignUser, deassignUser, grantPermission, revokePermission, addInheritance and deleteInheritance. A RBAC model contains a set users, roles and permissions ($PRMS$) and three relations exist: users can be assigned to roles (UA), permissions can be assigned to roles (PA) and roles can be associated with roles (RH) i.e. an inheritance relation exists between roles. To compare the structure

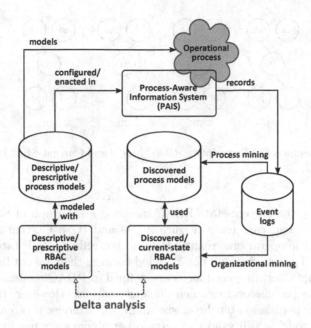

Fig. 1. Delta Analysis Overview (adapted from [2])

of RBAC models we transform RBAC models into labeled graphs. Therefore, we will give a definition of a directed acyclic graph (DAG) and describe the graph-transformed RBAC model.

An labeled DAG is denoted as $G = (N, E, \alpha, \beta)$ where N is a set of nodes, E ($E \subseteq N \times N$) is a set of edges, α is a node labeling function; $\alpha : N \to L_N$, and β is a labeling function for edges: $\beta : E \to L_E$. Let $(n, m) \in E$ be an edge, (n, m) is incident from node n and enters node m. The number of edges entering a node is called in-degree (id), and the out-degree (od) signifies the number of edges leaving a node. There exist no isolated nodes in G; $\forall n \in N : id(n) + od(n) > 0$. The label representation $\rho(G)$ of G is given by $\rho(G) = \{L, C, \lambda\}$ where $L = \{\alpha(n) | n \in N\}$ and $C = \{(\alpha(n), \alpha(m)) | (n, m) \in E\}$ and $\lambda : C \to L_E$ with $\lambda(\alpha(n), \alpha(m)) = \beta(n, m)$ for all $(n, m) \in E$.

Let a graph-transformed RBAC model be $G = (N, E, \alpha, \beta)$. Then, $N = \{USERS \cup ROLES \cup PRMS\}$ is a set of nodes and $E = \{UA \cup PA \cup RH\}$ is a set of edges. The labeling functions are identically defined as in the DAG.

2.2 Structural Matching of RBAC Models

We can identify three (use) cases of the comparison of RBAC models. In the first case, the current-state RBAC model equals the predictive RBAC model as shown in Figure 2 (A) and (B). This case is probably the rarest case. It seems likely that this case may only happen if a predictive model has been newly implemented or recently adapted. Delta analysis can be used to verify the latest RBAC implementation.

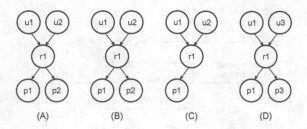

Fig. 2. Examples for a (A) Prescriptive RBAC Model and Current-State RBAC Models (B), (C) and (D)

Furthermore, the current-state RBAC model is a subgraph of the predictive model in the second case (cmp. Figure 2 (A) and (C)). Current-state RBAC models reflect the operational reality; they do not reflect a full state i.e. certain users, roles, and permissions are not included because they are not listed in event logs. For example, certain permissions are defined in RBAC models such as that a president has permission to launch nuclear weapons. However, the president might have the permission but he or she might not exercise it often. Hence, the current-state model is still valid and certain permissions are not included.

In the third case, the current-state RBAC model differs from the predictive RBAC model as shown in Figure 2 (A) and (D) e.g., new users, permissions or roles are included. For example, the role structure in RBAC depends on the applied technique such as role mining (e.g., finding a minimal descriptive set of roles [20]) or organizational mining (cmp., [15]). In order to minimize deviations in role structure, we recommend to use the same mining algorithm for the current-state RBAC model as the predictive model.

Based on these cases, we evaluated inexact graph matching techniques (e.g., [6,8]). We assume that RBAC models use unique labels i.e. users, roles and permissions have unique IDs. Given this structural requirement and based on an extensive literature review, graph matching techniques for graphs with unique node labels as specified in [9] are the most suitable for this domain. In fact, the problems graph isomorphism, subgraph isomorphism, the maximum common subgraph (cf. [7]) and the graph edit distance as specified in [9] can cover all three cases:

Let a graph-transformed RBAC model be $P = \{N_1, E_1, \alpha_1, \beta_1\}$, another graph-transformed RBAC model be $S = \{N_2, E_2, \alpha_2, \beta_2\}$ and their label representations be $\rho(P) = \{L_1, C_1, \lambda_1\}$ and $\rho(S) = \{L_2, C_2, \lambda_2\}$.

- Graph isomorphism between P and S is a bijective mapping $f : N_1 \rightarrow N_2$ such that $\alpha_1(n) = \alpha_2(f(n)), \forall n \in P$ and $\beta_1(n, m) = \beta_2(f(n), f(m)), \forall (n, m) \in E_1$. Graph S is isomorphic to graph P if $\rho(P) = \rho(S)$ i.e. $L_1 = L_2, C_1 = C_2$ and $\lambda_1 = \lambda_2$.
- Subgraph isomorphism between P and S is an injective mapping $f : N_1 \rightarrow N_2$ if there exists a subgraph $S \subseteq P$. Graph S is subgraph isomorphic to graph P if $L_2 \subseteq L_1, C_2 \subseteq C_1$ and $\lambda_2 \subseteq \lambda_1$.

– Let G be a graph with $\rho(G) = \{L, C, \lambda\}$ such that $L = L_1 \cap L_2$, $C = \{(n, m)|(n, m) \in C_1 \cap C_2\}$ and $\lambda_1(n, m) = \lambda_2(n, m)$ and $\lambda(n, m) = \lambda_1(n, m)$ for all $(n, m) \in C$. Then, the maximum common subgraph of P and S is G.

– The graph edit distance $d(P, S)$ measures the minimal number of graph edit operations necessary to transform one graph P into another graph S. Please note that we consider the RBAC edit operations outlined in Section 2.1 as graph edit operations. The graph edit distance between P and S is $d(P, S) = |L_1| + |L_2| - 2|L_1 \cap L_2| + |C_1| + |C_2| - 2|C_0| + |C_0'|$ where $C_0 = \{(n, m)|(n, m) \in C_1 \cap C_2\}$ where $\lambda_1(n, m) = \lambda_2(n, m)$ and $C_0' = \{(n, m)|(n, m) \in C_1 \cap C_2\}$ where $\lambda_1(n, m) \neq \lambda_2(n, m)$.

All problems are deployed and tested in a prototypical implementation. Using unique node labels, the computational complexity for all problems is $O(n^2)$.

3   Case Study

Figure 3 displays a graph representation of a (A) predictive and a (B) current-state RBAC model. As can be seen from the figures, the predictive RBAC model differs from the current-state model. The distance of both models is measured by the graph edit distance ($d(A, B) = 14$). The edit operations necessary to transform model (A) to (B) are shown in Figure 3.

Differences in the structure of the two RBAC models in Figure 3 can indicate violations. For example, user u7 is included in the predictive model (A) but is not shown in the current-state model (B). This could signify that u7 was not active during that time (e.g., on vacation) or that he or she is not a user any more (e.g., retired). However, it seems that u5 who was assigned to role r3 in (A) has r4 in (B). This could indicate that u5 changed roles (e.g., promotion) or that he or she violated permissions (e.g., acquired unauthorized access to access rights). In the case of u5, delegations of roles in RBAC or tasks in business processes can cause these deviations.

Furthermore, the models in Figure 3 differ in the role hierarchy. For example, role r6 is created in (B) and inherits permissions of r3 and r2. Interestingly, the inclusion of r6 adds only an additional role layer but does not change the semantics (e.g., user u6 can still perform the same set of permissions). In (A), u1 is assigned to the roles r1 and r3. These assignments are not included in (B) as r1 inherits permissions of r3 (e.g., reduced by the mining algorithm).

It can be seen from the case study that the evaluation of structural differences is complex. Deviations can be caused of the underlying mining technique (e.g., additional role r6), security violations (e.g., u5), inactivity or absence (e.g., u7) and misconfiguration (e.g., outdated assignments). Given these multifaceted causes, the evaluation has to be performed or monitored by experts with domain knowledge. Due to the large size of RBAC systems with thousands of roles (cf. [18]) an automated evaluation is preferred and can be cumbersome. By comparing a section of a RBAC model or by analyzing the RBAC model of a certain business process can reduce the size of the models.

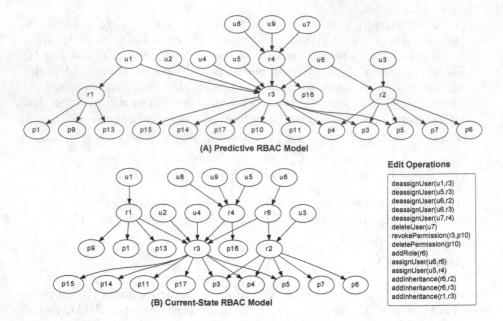

Fig. 3. Graph Representation of a Graph-based (A) Prescriptive RBAC Model and a (B) Current-State RBAC Model

4   Related Work

In recent years, many extensions of the NIST RBAC model [11] have been proposed to include aspects of PAIS. For example, the W-RBAC model [21] extends the NIST model for cases and organizational units. Further examples integrate process changes or structural and operational aspects in an RBAC model (e.g., [22,17,16]).

A graph-based formalism in [13] specifies static and dynamic consistency conditions in graphs. Moreover, graph optimization for role engineering is shown in (e.g., [24]). In this paper, we use graphs to compare the structure of RBAC models. A comparison of RBAC models proposed in [5] aims to migrate an existing RBAC model into a desired model (a designated state). The goal of delta analysis is to compare both RBAC models to analyze differences to detect security violations.

In business processes, current research provides similarity metrics for e.g., structural or label matching of processes (e.g., [10]). However, in this paper we center on RBAC models which have different structural requirements such as role hierarchies or unique node labels. The suitability of process mining for security audits such as evaluating authorization constraints is shown in [3]. In fact, the evaluation is performed manually and with respect to roles. As the event logs provide only user and task information, the analysis is cumbersome and an organizational model is needed. Delta analysis already considers the organizational model (e.g., roles) and enables an automated evaluation.

5   Conclusion

This paper described delta analysis of RBAC models which compares a prescriptive RBAC model with a current-state RBAC model. This approach aims to identify security violations such as unauthorized access. In this paper, we transform RBAC models into labeled graphs and analyze and compare the structure of RBAC models to identify differences which can indicate security violations. Furthermore, we show in a case study that the comparison of RBAC models can be complex and can only be performed by domain experts. For future work, we plan to include and examine semantic distance measures to compare RBAC models. As structure of RBAC models is an aspect, we want to examine semantic differences of RBAC models such as the impact on users having more or less access.

References

1. van der Aalst, W.M.P.: Process Mining: Discovery, Conformance and Enhancement of Business Processes. Springer (2011)
2. van der Aalst, W.M.P.: Business alignment: using process mining as a tool for delta analysis and conformance testing. Requirements Engineering 10(3), 198–211 (2005)
3. Accorsi, R., Stocker, T.: On the exploitation of process mining for security audits: the conformance checking case. In: Proceedings of the 27th Annual ACM Symposium on Applied Computing, SAC 2012, pp. 1709–1716. ACM, New York (2012)
4. Atluri, V., Warner, J.: Security for workflow systems. In: Handbook of Database Security, pp. 213–230 (2008)
5. Baumgrass, A., Strembeck, M.: An approach to bridge the gap between role mining and role engineering via migration guides. In: 2012 Seventh International Conference on Availability, Reliability and Security (ARES), pp. 113–122. IEEE (2012)
6. Bunke, H., Allermann, G.: Inexact graph matching for structural pattern recognition. Pattern Recognition Letters 1(4), 245–253 (1983)
7. Bunke, H., Shearer, K.: A graph distance metric based on the maximal common subgraph. Pattern Recognition Letters 19(3-4), 255–259 (1998)
8. Conte, D., Foggia, P., Sansone, C., Vento, M.: Thirty Years of Graph Matching in Pattern Recognition. International Journal of Pattern Recognition and Artificial Intelligence 18(03), 265–298 (2004)
9. Dickinson, P.J., Bunke, H., Dadej, A., Kraetzl, M.: Matching graphs with unique node labels. Pattern Analysis and Applications 7(3), 243–254 (2004)
10. Dijkman, R., Dumas, M., van Dongen, B., Käärik, R., Mendling, J.: Similarity of business process models: Metrics and evaluation. Information Systems 36(2), 498–516 (2011)
11. Ferraiolo, D.F., Sandhu, R., Gavrila, S., Kuhn, D.R., Chandramouli, R.: Proposed NIST standard for role-based access control. ACM Trans. Inf. Syst. Secur. 4(3), 224–274 (2001)
12. Gao, X., Xiao, B., Tao, D., Li, X.: A survey of graph edit distance. Pattern Analysis and Applications 13(1), 113–129 (2010)
13. Koch, M., Mancini, L., Parisi-Presicce, F.: A formal model for role-based access control using graph transformation. In: Cuppens, F., Deswarte, Y., Gollmann, D., Waidner, M. (eds.) ESORICS 2000. LNCS, vol. 1895, pp. 122–139. Springer, Heidelberg (2000)

14. Leitner, M.: Security policies in adaptive process-aware information systems: Existing approaches and challenges. In: 2011 Sixth International Conference on Availability, Reliability and Security (ARES), pp. 686–691. IEEE (2011)
15. Leitner, M., Baumgrass, A., Schefer-Wenzl, S., Rinderle-Ma, S., Strembeck, M.: A case study on the suitability of process mining to produce current-state RBAC models. In: La Rosa, M., Soffer, P. (eds.) BPM 2012 Workshops. LNBIP, vol. 132, pp. 719–724. Springer, Heidelberg (2013)
16. Leitner, M., Mangler, J., Rinderle-Ma, S.: SPRINT-Responsibilities: design and development of security policies in process-aware information systems. Journal of Wireless Mobile Networks, Ubiquitous Computing, and Dependable Applications (JoWUA) 2(4), 4–26 (2011)
17. Leitner, M., Rinderle-Ma, S., Mangler, J.: AW-RBAC: access control in adaptive workflow systems. In: 2011 Sixth International Conference on Availability, Reliability and Security (ARES), pp. 27–34. IEEE (2011)
18. Schaad, A., Moffett, J., Jacob, J.: The role-based access control system of a European bank: a case study and discussion. In: Proceedings of the Sixth ACM Symposium on Access Control Models and Technologies, SACMAT 2001, pp. 3–9. ACM, New York (2001)
19. Song, M., van der Aalst, W.M.P.: Towards comprehensive support for organizational mining. Decision Support Systems 46(1), 300–317 (2008)
20. Vaidya, J., Atluri, V., Guo, Q.: The role mining problem: finding a minimal descriptive set of roles. In: Proceedings of the 12th ACM Symposium on Access Control Models and Technologies, SACMAT 2007, pp. 175–184. ACM, New York (2007)
21. Wainer, J., Barthelmess, P., Kumar, A.: W-RBAC - a workflow security model incorporating controlled overriding of constraints. International Journal of Cooperative Information Systems 12(4), 455–485 (2003)
22. Weber, B., Reichert, M., Wild, W., Rinderle, S.: Balancing flexibility and security in adaptive process management systems. In: Meersman, R., Tari, Z. (eds.) CoopIS/DOA/ODBASE 2005. LNCS, vol. 3760, pp. 59–76. Springer, Heidelberg (2005)
23. Weske, M.: Business Process Management: Concepts, Languages, Architectures. Springer (2007)
24. Zhang, D., Ramamohanarao, K., Ebringer, T.: Role engineering using graph optimisation. In: Proceedings of the 12th ACM Symposium on Access Control Models and Technologies, SACMAT 2007, pp. 139–144. ACM, New York (2007)

Author Index